Deaf Mobility Studies

Deaf Mobility Studies

Exploring International Networks, Tourism, and Migration

Annelies Kusters
Erin Moriarty
Amandine le Maire
Sanchayeeta Iyer
Steven Emery

Gallaudet University Press
Washington, DC

Gallaudet University Press
gupress.gallaudet.edu

Gallaudet University Press is located on the
traditional territories of Nacotchtank and Piscataway.

© 2024 by Gallaudet University
All rights reserved. Published 2024
Printed in the United States of America

ISBN 978-1-954622-28-9 (casebound)
ISBN 978-1-954622-31-9 (paperback)
ISBN 978-1-954622-29-6 (ebook)

Library of Congress Cataloging-in-Publication Data

The Library of Congress's Cataloguing-in-Publication data for this title can be found online at https://www.loc.gov/.

∞ This paper meets the requirements of ANSI/NISO Z39.48–1992 (Permanence of Paper).

Cover description: Cover features a background with interspersed miniature human figures on top of interlocking grid lines and silhouettes of roadways. Each word in the book's title is centered on its own line in a different color. From top to bottom: Deaf (in blue); Mobility (in yellow); Studies (in red). Under the title the centered subtitle in black: Exploring International Networks, Tourism, and Migration. Under the subtitle the centered author names in a mauve tone: Annelies Kusters; Erin Moriarty. Below that are centered author names in a mauve tone: Amandine le Maire; Sanchayeeta Iyer; Steven Emery.

Cover design by Michel Vrana.

While the authors have made every effort to provide accurate internet addresses and other contact information at the time of publication, neither the publisher nor the authors assume any responsibility for errors or changes that occur after publication. Further, the publisher does not have any control over and does not assume any responsibility for third-party websites or their content.

Contents

Publisher's Note	vii
Part One Studying International Deaf Mobilities	
1 Deaf Mobility Studies *Annelies Kusters*	3
2 Doing Deaf Ethnography *Annelies Kusters, Steven Emery, Sanchayeeta Iyer,* *Amandine le Maire, and Erin Moriarty*	25
Part Two A Spectrum of International Deaf Mobilities	
3 Deaf in Kakuma Refugee Camp *Amandine le Maire*	67
4 Deaf Migrants in London *Steven Emery and Sanchayeeta Iyer*	91
5 Deaf Professional Mobility *Annelies Kusters*	118
6 Deaf Tourism in Bali *Erin Moriarty*	149
Part Three Patterns in International Deaf Mobilities	
7 Translocal Networks and Nodes *Erin Moriarty, Annelies Kusters, Steven Emery,* *Amandine le Maire, and Sanchayeeta Iyer*	177
8 Calibrating and Language Learning *Erin Moriarty, Annelies Kusters, Sanchayeeta Iyer,* *Amandine le Maire, and Steven Emery*	212

9 Spaces of Belonging   258
   Sanchayeeta Iyer, Annelies Kusters, Erin Moriarty,
   Amandine le Maire, and Steven Emery

10 Times of Immobility   293
   Amandine le Maire, Annelies Kusters, Sanchayeeta Iyer,
   Erin Moriarty, and Steven Emery

   Conclusion: The Deaf Mobility Shift   324
   Annelies Kusters

   References   331

   Index   353

Publisher's Note

Dear Reader,

We appreciate your interest in *Deaf Mobility Studies* by Annelies Kusters, Erin Moriarty, Amandine le Maire, Sanchayeeta Iyer, and Steven Emery.

In this book's print and ebook editions, you'll notice QR codes in the margins. The QR codes correspond with videos referenced in the text. In the print edition, you can scan the codes with a phone or tablet to be taken to the URL mentioned in the footnotes. In the ebook, click on the code to access the URL.

Funding

This project has received funding from the European Research Council (ERC) under the European Union's Horizon 2020 research and innovation program (grant agreement No. 714615). The views expressed in this publication are solely those of the authors and do not necessarily reflect the views of the ERC or the EU's Horizon program. Readers are encouraged to engage with the content and form their own opinions.

Open Access

We are pleased to announce that this book is available for open access on our Manifold site because of the ERC funding. Visit gallaudetupress.manifoldapp.org/projects/deaf-mobility-studies or scan the QR code to access the full text. We hope this accessibility facilitates wider dissemination and discussion of the ideas presented within.

The *Deaf Mobility Studies* Manifold page includes resources that will enhance your experience of the book. We encourage you to create a free Manifold account, which allows you to annotate the text, create highlights, and receive notifications if the authors update the book. By visiting our Manifold page, you can access these supplements:

- An enhanced version of the book that allows you to highlight and annotate the text for yourself and others and view the highlights and annotations of other readers
- Embedded videos in the text
- A link to purchase a physical copy of the book

We hope you enjoy reading *Deaf Mobility Studies* and exploring all the resources on our Manifold page. Be sure to check out the other open access titles.

Thank you!

Gallaudet University Press

Part One

Studying International Deaf Mobilities

1

Deaf Mobility Studies

Annelies Kusters

Deaf people meet deaf people from other countries in a wide range of contexts: visiting or hosting conferences, deaf sports events, and festivals; exploring a country as a tourist or guiding international tourists and visitors; migrating to a new country and interacting with local deaf people and/or with other migrants; relocating from a war-torn country to a refugee camp abroad and meeting other deaf refugees and deaf people from the host country. What unifies these deaf encounters is that they all happen in the context of *international mobility*. This book, which explores these encounters, is the result of Deaf Studies scholars venturing into Mobility Studies, an endeavor that I will call Deaf Mobility Studies. Both Deaf Studies and Mobility Studies are transdisciplinary fields in which a wide range of different theoretical and methodological approaches are drawn together around a common nexus: an interest in deaf lives and an interest in mobilities. In this book, the common foci of these two fields converge.

The research on which this book is based was undertaken as part of a 6.5-year project (2017–2023) funded by the European Research Council: *Deaf Mobilities Across International Borders*, shortened to MobileDeaf (mobiledeaf.org.uk). The project was undertaken by a team of five deaf researchers (four white, one brown; four women, one man) from three different countries; our positionality is discussed in depth in Chapter 2 and at various points throughout the book. Although affiliated with Heriot-Watt University in Edinburgh, the team conducted MobileDeaf fieldwork in sites across the world (outlined below); although most of this was concluded before the outbreak of the coronavirus pandemic in early 2020, some fieldwork was canceled or adapted in response to national and international lockdowns (see Chapter 2).

The MobileDeaf project considered deaf mobilities in a range of contexts: temporary and circular forms of mobility, short-term stays, and settlement over long periods of time. Within four subprojects, we focused on forms of professional, social, and personal mobility of diverse socioeconomic natures, which are differentially positioned on a continuum:

1. Forced migration (in Kakuma Refugee Camp, Kenya)
2. Labor and marriage migration (in London)
3. Professional mobility; that is, people who travel for conferences, conventions, and courses, such as activists, academics, students, athletes, artists, and their audiences (in a range of countries)
4. Tourist mobility (in Bali, Indonesia)

The first and fourth subprojects represent two extremes: They contrast forced and voluntary movement, precariousness and affluence, and survival and leisure. In between these two oppositional

4 CHAPTER ONE

Figure 1.1. The four MobileDeaf subprojects and their interweaving themes.

forms are two more ambiguous, in-between forms of migration and mobility. These combine social and personal mobility, socioeconomic need, and professional upscaling, in contrast to forced migration in pursuit of refuge and tourism in pursuit of leisure. By bringing together data from our various field sites, the research team was able to identify common patterns as well as contrasts, which are brought together around four themes (see Figure 1.1): how deaf people seek spaces of *belonging*, engage in *languaging*, expand their *networks*, and experience *immobility* (see Chapters 7–10).

In the next section, I explain what Mobility Studies is about, so as to link this field's focus with the impetus for the MobileDeaf project: the scholarly interest in deaf cosmopolitanism within Deaf Studies. I then give background to the conceptual coffer that is employed in this book and our methodological approaches.

Mobility Studies as an Inspiration

The MobileDeaf project, although firmly grounded in Deaf Studies scholarship, is inspired by Mobility Studies. Mobility Studies emerged in the early 2000s, challenging "the ways in which much social science research has been 'a-mobile'" (Sheller & Urry, 2006a, p. 208). It is a set of questions, theories, and methodologies in which *mobility* is positioned as central to the study of people, vehicles, things, and ideas. In these studies, "mobility" is an analytical category or a lens rather than an overarching descriptive term; it is "a certain way of seeing and ordering the world as well as social research" (Thimm & Chaudhuri, 2021, p. 277). Mobility Studies brings together the study of disparate forms of mobilities with different speeds, over different amounts of times, and over different distances—including migration, tourism, and everyday commutes. Because Mobility Studies involves a transdisciplinary focus on the study of these various forms of mobilities, it overlaps with fields such as Migration Studies and Tourism Studies (Sheller, 2021). Mobility Studies does not focus on movement only; it involves the study of how people "settle," wait to be settled, and make new homes (Boccagni, 2022). In brief, Mobility Studies "involves analyzing networks, relations, and flows and circulation, and not fixed places. Yet it also analyzes processes of mooring, grounding, dwelling, waiting and homing" (Sheller, 2021, p. 10).

Mobility is, of course, inherently political and infused with power dynamics (Cresswell, 2010). Mobilities are uneven: Various individual privileges, wider infrastructures, and political-economic systems impact who can travel where, when, and how—that is, who is mobile, and who is not. The study of mobility and immobility cannot be separated (Hannam et al., 2006). For example, mobility over a large distance (e.g., transcontinental migration) can be followed by experiences of immobility. Immobility is also experienced when confronted with other people's mobilities, such as by local guides facilitating the mobility of tourists, and it is brought into focus when attendees of international events are confronted by "who is not there" (Chapter 10). However, mobility and immobility are also "two dynamic sides of the same coin" (Salazar, 2021a, p. 3) because people often experience both mobility and immobility at the same time. People may feel immobile while having to stay in a refugee camp, for example, and being unable to move abroad, but they may be mobile *within* the camp and its immediate environment; other people may be internationally immobile but be hypermobile within the country in which they guide tourists (see Chapter 10).

The concept of motility has been used to indicate having *the potential or capacity to be mobile* (Høyer Leivestad, 2016). The previous examples indicate that motility does not correspond to mobility. People may be involved in a lot of movement or displacement (e.g., as refugees) but have low motility. Or, people may have a high degree of motility without actually being very mobile (e.g., people who spend their time locally, or even mostly at home, even though they have the means and ability to travel) (Sheller, 2021). Although immobility is often negatively valued and experienced as a restriction, it also can be a conscious choice or a privilege (Salazar, 2021a): not having to flee war or migrate to work abroad in underpaid jobs; being able to stay at home during the pandemic, whereas essential workers had to continue to be mobile in conditions that put their health at risk.

Mobility Studies is engaged with the larger political contexts of movement. As Toomey (2022) observes, "(im)mobilities are produced by settler colonialism, white supremacy and anti-blackness" (p. 3), and ingrained patterns of motility inequality in today's world are the result of imperialism and colonialism, the displacement of Indigenous populations, the slave trade, expulsions of large groups of people, and the migration of underpaid contract laborers. Indeed, because of this history, some people are positioned as "travelers" or "expats," and others as "illegal" or "economic migrants" who are "deportable" or "disposable," and these categories strongly intersect with race and ethnicity: "Black and nonwhite people's mobility is highly constrained by racial hierarchies and infrastructures that prioritize white mobility" (Toomey, 2022, p. 7). As Sheller (2021) writes:

> [T]he twenty-first century brought a growing splintering of mobility systems into hypermobile, friction-free, rich arrays of mobility choices for the kinetic elite who can afford to live in well-connected cities, versus the displacement, slow modes, and burdensome travel for the mobility-poor. (p. 49)

The mobility-poor are more heavily policed, their mobilities heavily regulated (e.g., through deportation, displacement, incarceration), and they are more likely to be subject to violence (Sheller, 2021).

Mobility Studies scholars juxtapose these different types of mobilities: those of the kinetic elite and of the mobility-poor; those of people who want to and can travel; and those of people who must travel but don't want to, or who want to travel but cannot (Salazar, 2021a). The aim of studying different types of mobilities (e.g., urban commutes, tourism, migration) all together is to "[think] about mobilities as complex interconnected systems" (Sheller, 2021, p. 54). Consequently, some scholars have brought together different forms of mobility in taxonomies, according to types of mobility or the profiles of those who are mobile. An often-cited example is Bauman's (1996) continuum between the emblematic figures of the "vagabond" and "tourist." These different "key figures of mobility" (Salazar, 2017) are found in the same spaces under vastly different conditions. Various key figures of (international) mobility—such as "migrant," "refugee," "diplomat," "businessperson," "nongovernmental organization (NGO) worker," "missionary," "athlete," "researcher," and "journalist"—each represent "an (ideal-type) person but also a lived experience of a particular kind" (Salazar, 2017, p. 8).

Different "key figures" may have commonalities in how they are mobile and interact with people. For example, in her study of the 2001 World Deaf Games (now the Deaflympics) in Rome, Haualand (2002) identified a number of profiles of spectators: the tourists (who tended to stop at the event as part of a longer trip, e.g., "Interrailing" through Europe), the cosmopolitans (who were well traveled and knew several sign languages), and the supporters (who brought flags and wore national colors and supporter outfits). Studying how different key figures of mobility interacted in the same space, she discussed the "invisible border" (p. 28) between the athletes and the tourists, because they differed in the demands placed on them and their respective goals. She considered these key figures to be interacting within "two different worlds at the games, with the athletes and official delegates in one, and the spectators and tourist [sic] in the other" (p. 28). In the same vein, key figures, their experiences, and the types of mobilities they represent are studied together in Mobility Studies. People engaged in various types of international mobility are all subject to regulations at national borders, including the various types of visas needed for "working holidays," students, tourists, partners of people who have already moved, and so on; these regulations make it very easy for some to enter a country and impossible for others (Sheller, 2021). Going back to the theme of taxonomies of mobilities, Toomey (2022) divides mobile subjects into three types:

> the hyper mobile (those who are allowed, and encouraged to, travel for work or leisure), the compelled mobile (those compelled, by design of the global economy, to move for work) and the forced mobile (those who move for survival but often end up contained, incarcerated or detained). (p. 1)

Hypermobile subjects possess citizenship, and they travel without threat of deportation; by virtue of their mobility, "all hyper mobile subjects come to participate in inequitable structures of mobility," including exploitation and exoticization (Toomey, 2022, p. 3). The tourism industry thrives on the labor of local people and on their dispossession when land is bought up for touristic purposes. Poverty is often itself seen as a tourist attraction, leaving colonial structures and racism in place; additionally, it is often assumed that tourists' visits are helpful for the visited communities through their acts of consumption or in the form of "voluntourism" (engaging in volunteering while traveling). In contrast to hypermobile subjects, *forced mobile subjects* face violence, life-or-death circumstances, and threats to subsistence, and they often face dependency and forced idleness. *Compelled mobile subjects* are typically migrant workers who are "coerced away from their homes," which are usually in "countries whose wealth has been drained by colonialism and the fiscal restructuring policies of Western financial institutions" (Toomey, 2022, p. 4), and the populations of which often rely on remittances. Compelled mobile subjects often do indispensable jobs that citizens do not want to do (e.g., farming, cleaning), for low pay. Many of these subjects have only temporary permission to work or are undocumented (Toomey, 2022).

Toomey's distinction roughly corresponds with the spectrum the MobileDeaf team worked with, with hypermobility covered in the tourism and professional mobility subprojects and, to some extent, in the labor migration subproject (which also came to cover marriage migration). Compelled mobility was also covered within the labor migration project, and forced mobility in the subproject on forced migration. As mobile deaf researchers, we were hypermobile ourselves, and we studied the process of doing international research as a form of mobility in itself (see Chapter 2). Importantly, although focusing on people who do (or have done) international border crossing, the project also focuses on people on the receiving end of international mobility. Internationally mobile people meet "locals"; for example, people who have migrated interact with people born in the host country. Locals may have different responses toward refugees, migrants, tourists, and visiting professionals and may be of very different socioeconomic backgrounds than their visitors.

Just as "figures of mobility" (e.g., "migrant" or "refugee") are essentialized constructs, the different categories of mobility are arbitrary to some extent. Mobilities can be temporary or permanent (legally, in terms of visa or residence permits; also in terms of personal decisions), but the boundaries between temporary and permanent migration are often blurred. For example, migration can happen in staggered ways, by living temporarily in a country (e.g., on a student visa) and then staying on, transitioning through visa categories (Robertson, 2019). Migration can be circular as well, with people moving through different countries or returning to a country in which they have lived before: "Movement and attachment is not linear or sequential but capable of rotating back and forth and changing direction over time" (Levitt & Glick Schiller, 2004, p. 1011). We capture examples of this in Chapter 9.

People can move between these categories of mobility in other ways as well. Formerly hypermobile people with high motility can be suddenly restricted in movement (e.g., due to the pandemic, in which "mobility has come under attack"; see Cresswell, 2021, p. 52), or they can be forced to move (e.g., due to a violent conflict); forced mobile people can become hypermobile at a different stage in their life (Toomey, 2022). Another example of links between different categories of mobility is a "local" marrying a "tourist" and then migrating to the tourist's country of residence (Simoni, 2015). Breivik (2005) noted links between types of deaf hypermobility, such as someone who attended the Deaflympics as a spectator becoming interested in meeting deaf people from other countries and then deciding to go to a high school in the United States for an exchange year. Several examples of these links are covered in this book, such as professional mobility and tourism being combined, tourism leading to (marriage) migration or repeated voluntourism, and forced migration leading to resettlement.

Thus, identifying key figures of mobility (e.g., "migrants" or "tourists"), and separating different forms of mobility (e.g., migration or tourism), exaggerates the distinctions between them (Feldman, 2017). This is a problem of the "mobilities" framework, but it also confirms the necessity of the framework—that is, of studying forms of mobility together. However, others have pointed out that, notwithstanding the benefits of studying different types of mobility within one overarching field, there are pitfalls to joining the study of different types of mobility (e.g., migration, tourism) under "Mobility Studies." Thimm and Chaudhuri (2021) argue that "adding migration just as another practice of mobility without any analytical explanations dilutes [...] migration research with its differentiated aspects of analysis like the causes of movements, the decision-making processes involved, and the regulation of movement" (p. 276).

In an attempt to combine a mobilities framework with more specific foci, the MobileDeaf project researchers utilized an overarching Mobility Studies framing to bring together data from the four subprojects (Chapters 7–10), but they also retained a specific focus on each distinct type of mobility under examination (Chapters 3–6). (Note that there are many types of mobilities that are not covered in depth in our study, some of which have been covered elsewhere; these include development work, volunteerism, academic internships, and the work of nongovernmental organizations—see the edited volume *It's a Small World* [Friedner & Kusters, 2015a] for examples.) Rather than studying all four types of mobilities in the United Kingdom alone, which undoubtedly would have led to more insights into the interrelations among them (as in the study by Simoni, 2015), we studied different types of mobility in vastly different research locations across the world.

The choice of specific locations for the subprojects (further explained in Chapter 2) was made with the aim of including *participants* from the Global North (subprojects 2, 3, and 4) and the Global South (all subprojects), in *locations* in both the Global North (subprojects 2 and 3) and the Global South (subprojects 1, 3, and 4), thus studying deaf Southerners' experiences in the Global North and vice versa. By "the Global South," I mean (typically postcolonial) countries in Africa, Asia, and Latin America with access to fewer resources than countries in the Global North—that is, countries in Europe, along with Canada, the United States, Australia, and other nations with access to and control over resources. I acknowledge that this distinction between Global North and South is overly general and sweeping, and it is problematic for "Global North" countries located in the Southern hemisphere, but for this project I also found it a useful one for studying the vast inequalities outlined by the authors in *It's a Small World* (Friedner & Kusters, 2015a) and by Hou and Ali (2024).

Deaf Studies Interrogating Deaf Cosmopolitanism

This book's primary focus is on *international* mobility. Mobility Studies' reach is broader, in that it also includes local mobilities, such as movement within cities or migration within national borders. In this book, the MobileDeaf team does focus on local and national mobility but always within the broader context of international deaf mobility (see the section on translocality). In terms of border regulations, people often have "free mobility" *within* nations but not *between* them, which means that focusing on international mobility is fundamentally different from focusing on national mobility. The MobileDeaf focus on international mobility was motivated by an interest by Deaf Studies scholars in what we have called "deaf cosmopolitanism."

In a genealogy of cosmopolitanism as it relates to mobility, Acharya (2016) begins with its origins in the Greek word *kosmopolitês*, a "citizen of the world" or "world citizen(ship)" (p. 33). Cosmopolitanism can be seen as a worldview or philosophy, a political project, an attitude or orientation, or a condition (Vertovec & Cohen, 2002, p. 4). Of the various uses and implications of the cosmopolitanism concept, Glick Schiller et al. (2011) direct attention to sociability, "in which a shared sense of common sensibilities does not override but coexists with ongoing diversity of perspective and practice" (p. 401). Cosmopolitan sociability consists of forms of competence and communication skills that are based on the human capacity to create social relations of inclusiveness and openness to the world (Nowicka & Rovisco, 2009).

The idea that there exists a "*deaf* cosmopolitanism" has circulated in various forms for centuries. Although the term itself has not always been used, the notion has appeared in European and American deaf magazines and literature since at least the late 18th century. For example, deaf Frenchman Pierre Desloges wrote in 1789 about international deaf networks in Paris that existed before the first public deaf school was established. Murray's (2007) dissertation on deaf transnationalism starts by quoting Amos Draper, a deaf American traveling with a group of approximately 20 Americans (likely to be predominantly—or exclusively—white men; see below) to the 1889 International Congress of the Deaf in Paris, describing the arrival of their steamship in Liverpool. Draper quotes Shakespeare in his narrative:

> When our ship reached Liverpool this morning and from her deck were seen several of your number conversing in the crowd that stood upon those wonderful docks, it recalled that line of your greatest poet which says "One touch of nature makes the whole world kin;" for though you dwell here upon an island and we upon a continent beyond the seas, yet in all essentials our experiences are probably the same. If you have troubles we can sympathize with you, for we have the same troubles; or if you have joys, those joys are ours, and we rejoice with you. (In Murray, 2007, p. iii)

Deaf cosmopolitanism is an attitude, orientation, and process that is embodied by deaf people who connect across national and linguistic borders (Moriarty & Kusters, 2021). The concept of deaf cosmopolitanism implies that because of these connections, deaf people are "world citizens"; indeed, the attendance of deaf people from Japan, Ecuador, the United States, Russia, and Mexico at the Paris World Fair in 1900 prompted a French deaf leader to say, "United as a community... we know no borders" (Congress, 1900, p. 258; as cited by Gulliver, 2015, p. 4). The ideology of deaf cosmopolitanism is undergirded by the assumption that deaf people have the same "joys" and "troubles" based on their shared deafness, even when they travel to the other side of the world. Deaf people, and Deaf Studies scholars, have argued that the "joys" of connecting internationally are motivated and facilitated by the shared experience of being deaf, and by the visuogestural linguistic skills that signing deaf people possess (e.g., Bauman & Murray, 2014; Ladd, 2015). Furthermore, the shared "troubles" are usually related to the majority society consisting of hearing and speaking people (Murray, 2007).

Deaf Studies authors studying deaf international encounters have often used the concept of *transnationalism* to describe the above, rather than cosmopolitanism (Haualand et al., 2016; Murray, 2007). The scholarship on transnationalism has focused on global interconnectedness, social networks, political links, and economic exchanges between people who are physically located in different nations. Initially, the transnationalism concept was used most often in the context of research on migrant diasporas (Vertovec, 2013), although it has also been used to talk about, for example, the transnational aspects of gay/queer identities (Boellstorff, 2005)—and, indeed, deaf identities. Yet transnationalism is "a necessary but insufficient condition for the growth of a successful cosmopolitanism" (Vertovec & Cohen, 2002, p. 20). Transnationalism "does not refer to qualitative feelings or attitudes of individuals, and it is not affected by what people think of it" (Roudometof, 2005, p. 118). Cosmopolitanism, on the other hand, explicitly involves affect, feelings, attitudes, and dispositions.

In Deaf Studies works where "transnationalism" has been used as a framework (e.g., Breivik, 2005; Murray, 2007), the authors have often discussed cosmopolitan practices without naming them as such. These authors adopted a view on cosmopolitanism supporting the notion that it "rests between universalisms and diversity constructed in mobile encounters between people" (Acharya, 2016, p. 43). This is the approach to cosmopolitanism advocated by Glick Schiller et al. (2011): Cosmopolitanism arises from "social relationships that do not *negate* cultural, religious or gendered differences but see people as capable of relationships of experiential commonalities *despite* differences [...] [moving] beyond the binaries of inclusion vs. exclusion, sameness vs. difference" (p. 403, my emphasis). As Moriarty and Kusters (2021) argue, "using 'deaf cosmopolitanism' as a concept emphasizes these moral orientations in ways that many scholars discussing deaf transnational connections, deaf universalism or deaf internationalism have done but not centralized in their analysis" (p. 9).

Scholars have made efforts to broaden cosmopolitanism beyond its Eurocentric values, applications, and claims to universalism (Vertovec & Cohen, 2002), moving away from its association with mobility and privilege (Amit, 2015; Hannerz, 2004). For example, people who do not travel outside the country where they were born can and do engage in cosmopolitan relationships, such as tour guides in tourist destinations (Salazar, 2015) and shop owners working in superdiverse neighborhoods (Wessendorf, 2014). Additionally, authors have criticized claims that cosmopolitanism can be gender neutral, racially neutral, or ethnically neutral (Glick Schiller et al., 2011, p. 404). The previously mentioned notion of sharing joy and trouble is, at root, a white, male, middle-to-upper class conception of being deaf and hypermobile—that is, with high motility (although white deaf men did face barriers at national borders in the 19th century; see Baynton, 2006). Amos Draper and his companions could access financial resources that enabled them to travel and to participate in transnational encounters—that is, to become "citizens of the world." To be sure, less well-represented groups, such as lower-class deaf people, Asian deaf people, black deaf people, and deaf women, were also internationally mobile through trade and art networks and as contract workers, teachers, employees, wives, and entrepreneurs—and, indeed, through violations of human rights such as enslavement and other forms of forced migration (Cleall, 2015; Mirzoeff, 1995; Murray, 2007). However, their connections, actions, experiences, and discourses are far less well documented, and they are less visible in historical literature on international deaf encounters.

Language is central to historical notions of deaf cosmopolitanism, and it has been foregrounded in celebrations of it. White deaf men in 18th- and 19th-century Paris convened at annual banquets with international scope (Gulliver, 2015; Murray, 2007), at which:

> Deaf mute foreigners, in their toasts, never missed a chance to emphasise the universal nature of signs, claiming that "it easily wins out over all the separate limiting languages of speaking humanity [...]. Our language encompasses all nations, the entire globe." (Mottez, 1993, p. 36)

As Moriarty and Kusters (2021) note, "this quote includes ideologies about deaf cosmopolitanism as well as language ideologies in relation to deaf cosmopolitanism" (p. 7). Deaf cosmopolitanism is grounded in early conceptions about the nature of sign language, which was seen (at the time) as being one sign language with multiple variants rather than as multiple sign languages.

Deaf people who engage in mobility may use and learn multiple languages, including local or national sign languages and spoken/written languages, and may make use of signed lingua franca, such as International Sign (IS) and American Sign Language (ASL). IS emerges when signers of different linguistic backgrounds come together; it typically incorporates signs from national sign languages (including ASL), and it often includes mouthings from English and other spoken languages. Its use is variable and dependent on the geographical, political, social, cultural, and linguistic contexts in which it occurs, and the backgrounds of the people who use it. There are conventionalized and less-conventionalized uses of IS (Rathmann & De Quadros, 2022; Zeshan, 2015), and they are typically used together in the same communicative contexts (e.g., at deaf international events). Traditionally, being able to use and understand the more conventional versions of IS was correlated to mobility, privilege, and the ability to make use of certain semiotic resources, including a range of literacies (Green, 2014, 2015). Today, an increasing number of people, of an increasing variety of backgrounds, learn IS online via YouTube and social media. Another sign language (or elements of it) that is very frequently used in international deaf spaces as a lingua franca is ASL, which has spread over the world in different contexts, such as through missionary work, development work, and higher education (Kusters, 2021). Instead of, or in addition to, using signed lingua franca, mobile deaf signers also may learn (the basics of) host country sign languages in a short time span (see Chapter 8 for examples).

In Chapter 8, the concept of calibration is used to show how linguistic differences are negotiated by deaf people who engage in language practices in ways that they think fit their interlocutors. They select features and strategies from "different languages" to communicate effectively, for example, by adapting their signing by slowing down; using pantomime; paraphrasing concepts; switching languages; or using signs, words, and fingerspelled alphabets associated with different languages (Byun et al., 2017). The MobileDeaf researchers were calibrating in communication throughout gathering the data for this book (see Chapter 2).

It remains an oft-repeated and essentializing refrain among deaf people that *being deaf signers* is the basis of an innate connection with deaf signers from other countries, and that this *forms the motivation for travel* (Breivik et al., 2002; Kusters & Friedner, 2015) and for being "citizens of the world." In some of the Deaf Studies literature, international connections between deaf people, and skills in international communication, have been described and celebrated as central to deaf identities, especially in the face of audist discourses and practices in which deaf signers are oppressed. It is even the case that, as Kusters and Friedner (2015) note, "in a number of deaf studies concepts, the international dimension of deaf experiences, networks, and signed languages has been explicitly included" (p. xvii), with definitions or examples of Deaf Gain and Deafhood often including the "special" or "typical deaf" ability to cross international borders (Bauman & Murray, 2014; Ladd, 2003, 2015). The consistency of these discourses in Deaf Studies theories has probably served as an extension and confirmation of the previously mentioned essentializing historical discourses, which have been passed on and amplified through the years, as well as experienced anew and repeatedly. Notably, works on deaf transnationalism have tended to emphasize—even exaggerate—"sameness" and connection between deaf people of different races, nationalities, cultures, ethnicities, religions, and languages, often uncritically (Kusters & Friedner, 2015).

Key to these overly emphasized notions of deaf cosmopolitanism in particular, and deaf mobility in general, is the fact that deaf people are scattered across wider society, are mostly born into hearing families, and most often tend to gather with other deaf people in spaces *outside* of the home. It is due to this experience of being scattered that national and international connectedness (in deaf schools, deaf clubs, deaf associations, and events—see Chapter 7) is so important, and it is so frequently (and often exclusively) described as being thoroughly enjoyable (Breivik, 2005). Deaf people's mobility is often made easier by free or discounted passes for travel within cities and nations (Chapter 4) and/or by government benefits (Chapter 6), which further make it possible for scattered people to connect and thrive. Dispersal, however, also means that many deaf people miss out on an education and a complex social life because they may go to a school that is solely tailored to hearing students (and they may potentially be the only deaf student there) or not have the opportunity to go to school at all; they also often miss out on participation in wider deaf networks.

Deaf cosmopolitanism on a global level, both in practice and in discourse, is thus somewhat the antithesis of the image of the immobile, lonely, locally stuck, isolated, language-deprived, and socially disconnected deaf person. This is an image that is also central to many deaf advocacy efforts, which may entail the connected deaf person "finding" and "helping" the lonely, disconnected (and possibly uneducated) deaf person "with no language" (Moriarty Harrelson, 2017c), typically in far-flung villages in the Global South, and "connecting them" by sending them to school or otherwise educating them, often in the context of missionary work or educational outreach (see Chapter 7). International mobility for deaf people, especially to places with a strong deaf presence and history, such as Gallaudet University, is often associated with empowerment, thriving, and flourishing (De Clerck, 2007), even when people on the receiving end of "empowerment" efforts may not be explicitly interested in meeting (or being "saved" by) foreign deaf people (Lee, 2012). The "scatteredness" is also contrasted with chance encounters with deaf people abroad. Many deaf people have stories about memorable times that they accidentally met (or were approached by) deaf people abroad, with some becoming their tour guides or entry points into local deaf networks (see Breivik, 2005, pp. 133, 173; see also Chapters 4 and 7).

Deaf international professional mobility, such as travel to conferences and sports events and for development and missionary work, has been better documented by researchers than other forms of deaf international mobility; the previously mentioned ideologies on transnationalism and cosmopolitanism thus mostly emerge from studies on professional mobility (mostly of white deaf people). One reason (both historical and contemporary) that these mobilities have been particularly studied is that they have been documented irrespective of researchers' interests, for example in magazines and reports, and also in a range of (self-)published books by (mostly white) authors who have documented (or criticized) the work of international deaf organizations, such as the World Federation of the Deaf (WFD) and the International Committee of Sports for the Deaf (Gannon, 2011; Harrison, 2014; Mesch & Mesch, 2018). In contrast, other forms of international mobility, such as forced migration and tourism, are much more individual, less documented, and often less privileged, so although researchers have been aware of such mobilities, they have been much more difficult to study.

The scholarship on forms of professional and tourist mobility was broadened in the book *It's a Small World*, in which the various authors were asked to critically engage with the universalizing DEAF-SAME concept (Friedner & Kusters, 2015). Reminiscent of Draper's quote cited in Murray (2007), "yet in all essentials our experiences are probably the same," DEAF-SAME implies that deep down, deaf people around the world are essentially the same; it is a belief in a "deep connection that is felt between deaf people around the globe, grounded in experiential ways of being in the world," and in deaf international communication (Kusters & Friedner, 2015, p. x). In the book, a wide range of different types of international mobilities in settings all over the world were covered, but it only focused on *short-term* mobilities, such as tourism, youth camps, courses, conferences, development work, and research trips, as well as on digital mobilities. The authors explored the aspirations and expectations of deaf people when reaching out to deaf people in other countries; motivations included the desire to make new friends, to have an "authentic" tourist experience, to guide tourists, to practice religion together, to profit financially, and to engage in study, research, development, or charitable works. They found that international deaf encounters are not only manifestations of (the discourse of) deaf universalism, but they are also often experienced as fraught, uneven, and ambivalent, thus challenging the notion of DEAF-SAME.

The MobileDeaf project broadens and deepens the study of deaf cosmopolitanism by not only taking a deep look at types of short-term mobility but also considering them alongside forms of migration. Our work complements the number of studies on deaf migration and deaf refugees that have proliferated in the past few years; see Chapters 3 and 4 for references. A key difference between these works and our study is that we study migration in connection with other types of international mobility. Earlier studies on deaf cosmopolitanism started from the observation that deaf people travel with the aim of connecting with other deaf people. In contrast, not all deaf people in the MobileDeaf study are internationally mobile with the *primary aim* of meeting deaf people in other countries or engaging in activities that involve deaf people from other countries. For example, some have moved to a new country to flee war or to join a new spouse, or some are in search of education and employment opportunities. In these contexts, they have worked to expand their networks with deaf people and they have explored various spaces where they could belong, including spaces in which they were the only deaf person among hearing people (Chapters 7 and 9).

The aim of this book is not to *validate* deaf cosmopolitanism. Rather, the discourse of deaf cosmopolitanism is taken as a starting point to critically *interrogate* whether and how it manifests in various field sites, over a spectrum of mobilities, and in a range of practices, including languaging. Appiah (2006) has argued that cosmopolitanism consists of two strands of values: "universal concern" for others, which is more ideological, and "respect for legitimate difference" between particular individuals, which is more practical (p. xv). In this context, he has said that "cosmopolitanism is the name not of the solution but of the challenge," asking, "A citizen of the world: how far can we take that idea?" (Appiah, 2006, p. xv). Cosmopolitanism is thus a *challenge* in relationships between specific human beings with specific backgrounds and specific beliefs, and who engage in specific practices. The MobileDeaf team critically interrogated the notion of deaf cosmopolitanism by exploring a spectrum of (im)mobilities, and not only privileged mobility.

Interrogating deaf cosmopolitanism, the MobileDeaf team here analyzes the enormous potential of—as well as the severe constraints to—the social and geographical international mobility of deaf signers. We show how these affordances and constraints have an impact both on the ability to travel physically and on participation within international deaf spaces. Within these spaces, we analyze experiences of connection and disconnection between deaf people of different (multi-) national backgrounds. On the one hand, international deaf encounters can indeed be manifestations of (a discourse of) deaf cosmopolitanism, where differences are put aside (or consumed) in favor of forming a connection based on being deaf. We have found examples of this, particularly in relation to language practices (Moriarty & Kusters, 2021; Chapter 8). On the other hand, discourses and practices that overly emphasize deaf cosmopolitanism risk sidelining differences, at the cost of downplaying racism, sexism, and ableism, meaning that deaf international encounters are made to conform to idealized "templates." We have found examples of how, in Canagarajah's (2021a) words, "racial segregation and nationalist exceptionalism rather than transnational cosmopolitanism are getting strengthened" (p. 570). Adopting an intersectional lens, we ask to what extent deaf cosmopolitanism is a Global North, white, hypermobile deaf signers' construct, and to what extent it resonates with deaf signers from a wider variety of backgrounds who are mobile in a wider range of contexts, for a wider range of reasons; additionally, we include the study of the ways in which deaf people in the host countries interact with deaf visitors. For this study to break away from perpetuated notions within Deaf Studies, we had to engage with a range of theories and concepts originating in other disciplines; these are outlined in the next section.

A Conceptual Coffer for Deaf Mobility Studies

Mobility Studies is by nature transdisciplinary, bringing together:

> some of the more purely "social" concerns of sociology (inequality, power, hierarchies) with the "spatial" concerns of geography (territory, borders, scale) and the "cultural" concerns of anthropology or communication research (discourses, representations, schemas), while inflecting each with a relational ontology of the co-constitution of subjects, spaces, and meanings. (Sheller, 2021, p. 12)

The necessity of engaging with social, spatial, and cultural concerns means that the MobileDeaf team needed concepts that could bring different fields together in a transdisciplinary approach. Because the work done by the team is grounded within Deaf Studies, we have worked with concepts that were already used within this field, such as "deaf space." However, we also looked "outward." The five of us have a combined training in philosophy, cultural studies, anthropology, geography, and international development, and we read widely across those areas while also exploring literature in relation to the specific types of mobilities each of us took as our focus. In addition, we familiarized ourselves with literature that we thought would be useful for developing a conceptual framework to be shared between us, such as texts on cosmopolitanism, translanguaging, transnationalism, translocality, and intersectionality. It is by way of regular meetings and reading groups (see Chapter 2) that we ultimately arrived at a shared "conceptual coffer."

Over the years of this project, there were several "keywords of mobility" (see Salazar, 2016) that came up repeatedly and to which we came to tie our data analysis. In the edited book *Keywords of Mobility* (Salazar & Jayaram, 2016), the authors each explored a keyword for thinking about mobility, such as "cosmopolitanism," "motility," "immobility," "capital"—all "big" concepts with broad meanings that shift as they accumulate over time, and shift in relation to each other. Many of the keywords that emerged within our study overlap with these keywords of mobility. Where a keyword is used to frame a single chapter in this book ("networks" in Chapter 7, "calibration" in Chapter 8, "belonging" in Chapter 9, and "immobility" in Chapter 10), they will be introduced *in the respective chapter*. There are, however, several keywords that are used *in multiple chapters*, whether as a framing device or even to structure the chapter; these are introduced in the next section.

Deaf Space

The concept of deaf space has been used a lot in Deaf Studies, mainly since the early 21st century. "Deaf geographies" literature has approached deaf spaces as embodied, visucentric, physical, or virtual spaces produced by deaf signers, directing a focus to the spatial forms and material environments of deaf gatherings (Gulliver & Fekete, 2017; Gulliver & Kitzel, 2016). Deaf space has also been used as an architectural concept describing the (re)design of buildings to suit deaf people (Bauman, 2014). In the deaf geographies tradition, however, deaf space has often been used to refer to *social* gatherings of *signing* deaf people (although O'Brien [2021a] has convincingly argued that a single deaf person also produces deaf space).

Institutional deaf spaces (which are called "place-nodes" in Chapter 7) include clubs, courses, organizations, and events, and these have traditionally been a focus of Deaf Studies (e.g., Van Cleve & Crouch, 1989). Some places have become nodes of different types of international mobilities: Documented examples include Adamorobe (Kusters, 2015), a village in Ghana with a high rate of hereditary deafness that has been frequented by deaf and hearing tourists, researchers, priests, NGOs, and so on. Gallaudet University is another such node of different types of mobilities, attracting students, researchers, tourists, and those on a journey of self-discovery.

Different from institutional deaf spaces are those that are produced *in public and semipublic spaces*, "rooms without walls" (Vertovec, 2015) that emerge in places such as parks, pubs, or restaurants or on public transport. These types of deaf spaces have been studied by O'Brien (2005) and myself (Kusters, 2017a, 2017b), among others who have demonstrated that these spaces operate under "deaf rules" yet can also "clash" with (people in) the wider surrounding space. Deaf spaces can also be produced in or around private homes, which become hubs for deaf people to meet each other (Heap, 2006; Kusters, 2015; see Chapter 3). Growing numbers of studies focus on virtual deaf spaces that are produced through the internet, which have allowed greater involvement and feelings of belonging in communities of shared interest and have permitted the sharing of information and resources across national borders (Ilkbasaran, 2015; Kurz & Cuculick, 2015).

Deaf spaces can operate as spaces of kinship, self-realization, and empowerment for deaf signers but also as places where deaf people are made to feel unwelcome, excluded, or challenged. One such example is deaf women in India in male-dominant deaf spaces, such as public transport (Kusters, 2019). In line with most previous studies on deaf space, the MobileDeaf team uses it as a descriptive concept rather than an analytical one. In Chapter 9, deaf belonging and lack of belonging are studied across different spaces, including experiences of belonging between or among queer deaf people, Indian deaf people, deafblind people, Czech hearing gay people, and deaf Muslims.

Scale

Deaf spaces are produced in relation to each other in networks, and these networks are layered in scale, such as local–national–regional–global (see Chapters 5 and 7). The deaf mobilities covered in this book range from local mobility to international mobility. Scale is also a central organizing mechanism for languages. Take, for example, the names of sign languages: *Adamorobe* Sign Language (a village sign language in Ghana), *British* Sign Language (a national sign language), and *International* Sign (an international lingua franca). Scale is also embedded in the name and/or the mission of many deaf organizations, such as the WFD or the Bali Deaf Community.

Scale has been one of the foundational concepts in geography, but it has also been engaged in depth within other disciplines, such as anthropology (Summerson Carr & Lempert, 2016). However, there are multiple problems with using scale as a key concept. Scale is "unwieldy" with a lot of conceptual baggage (Moore, 2008, p. 203) and is often conceptualized in static ways, similar to the way in which concepts such as identity (Brubaker & Cooper, 2000) and culture (Brumann, 1999) are used. Consequently, some authors have argued against the use of scale as a central concept in research.

Others, however, have urged against throwing out the baby (scale as a concept) with the bathwater (problematic uses of the concept). When using the concept, scales (e.g., local, village, national, international) should not be treated as fixed, as a priori givens, or as grounded in nature, in law, or in the divine. There is a need to study "*scalar dimensions of practices*, rather than *practices occurring at different scales*" (Mansfield, 2005, p. 468, emphasis in original). In other words, scale needs to be adopted as a *category of practice* rather than a *category of analysis*. The problem with treating scale as a category of analysis is that it reifies spaces as entities and treats scales (e.g., local, national) as objectively existing, preordained, hierarchical levels or platforms. However, "it is not necessary to retain a commitment to the *existence* of scales in order to analyze the *politics* of scale" (Moore, 2008, p. 213). Instead, scholars should study *scaling* as a political and ideological practice and process. The MobileDeaf team has found "scale" and "scaling" useful concepts to distinguish between types of (local, national, international) networks (Chapter 7), to theorize how these scales are constructed or produced (see Chapter 5 on the "national" scale and Chapter 6 on the "global deaf circuit"), and to theorize the *reach* of mobilities (Chapter 10). However, we acknowledge that we do at times write about scales as though they were fixed in place, as a necessary shorthand when exploring the nuances of scaling practices.

Translocality

Translocality is a term used to signify *connections* between different spaces across scales and within scales. This concept is useful because "[m]obility studies call attention to the myriad ways in which people become part, in highly unequal ways, of multiple translocal networks and linkages" (Salazar, 2016, p. 2). Translocality as a concept emerged in response to scholarship on *transnationalism*. Scholars who have used transnationalism as a framework have usefully highlighted some aspects of deaf international connections; the same is true of cosmopolitanism. In this book, the complementary use of the translocality concept highlights aspects of deaf international encounters that have been under-researched thus far. A problem with the scholarship on transnationalism (or cosmopolitanism) is that it has treated processes as dislocated, as not grounded or situated in particular *places*. In contrast, translocality is about "mobility and

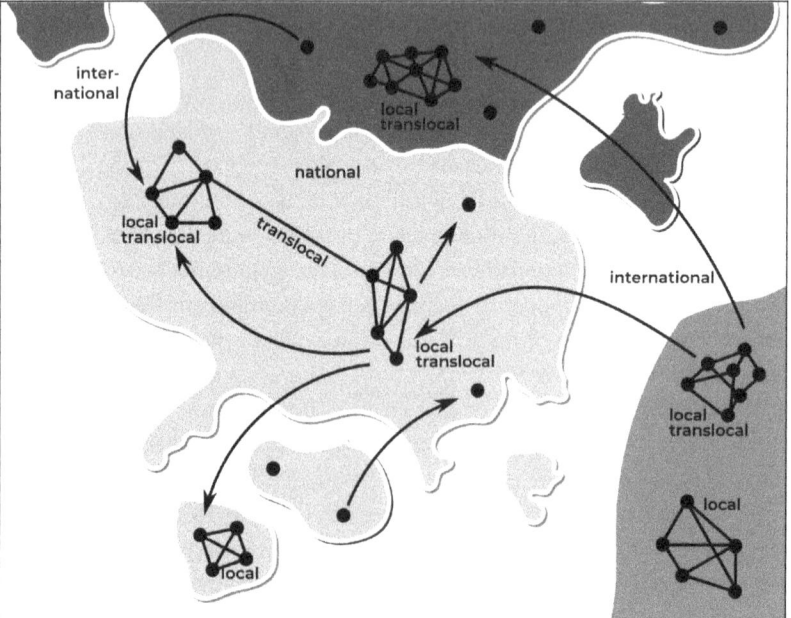

Figure 1.2. A fictional set of countries, showing local networks; translocal connections between the network clusters and between different places; the national scale; and the international scale.

emplacement as simultaneous processes" (Porst & Sakdapolrak, 2017, p. 114); see Figure 1.2 for an illustration.

Researchers working with a translocality framework have looked at local-to-local relations and have studied "situatedness during mobility" (Brickell & Datta, 2011, p. 3) in relation to specific *places* that are meeting points and reference points. Translocality is about these "[p]laces where mobility is actually grounded, where mobile actors meet, where connections converge, and towards which flows of resources are directed or from which they depart" (Porst & Sakdapolrak, 2017, p. 113). Translocal practices are *multi-scalar* (Brickell & Datta, 2011). Different scale-making processes (e.g., networks in specific neighborhoods, as well as global networks) are relevant to practices of mobility in and to these places. In *places,* distinctions between scales are blurred (Porst & Sakdapolrak, 2017). *Places* in our examples include a village in Bali, a house in Kakuma Refugee Camp, a pub in London, and a campus in Denmark. The translocality framework also implies a focus on connections *between* different places, including local–local connections and migration within the same country on different scales; for example, interregional, interurban, and intraurban. These local–local connections refer to the movement of people but also of ideas, of things, of money, and so on. Internal mobility (movement within national boundaries) often falls outside of the scope of studies of transnationalism and migration, but as mentioned previously, it forms part of the scope of Mobility Studies and of this book. For example, the local mobilities and networks (within a neighborhood, city, or country) of tour guides, deaf refugees, and deaf migrants are considered.

Local–local mobilities are highly relevant to the study of international mobilities: When international deaf events happen, for example, host locations are not merely *containers* for the events, but are *transformed* by them. Local "deaf places" (e.g., deaf clubs or deaf-owned businesses) are often visited by attendees of the event, members of local deaf communities are often involved in the event's organization, and the surrounding area often becomes "deafened" by the critical mass of deaf attendees (see Chapter 7). Additionally, by virtue of large events having happened there, such places are then put on deaf mental maps and included in ever more complex networks (see Chapter 7), and through this are shaped and/or transformed further, such as by the socioeconomic impact of an influx of deaf tourists (see Moriarty, 2020a). In Chapter 6, the notion of a translocal "global deaf circuit" is introduced, to flag how certain "deaf places"—such as schools, clubs, pubs, cafes, and "deaf villages"—are part of a deaf mental map that guides tourists. We join translocality scholars in drawing attention to this field of interconnected spaces across scales (Porst & Sakdapolrak, 2017).

Comparisons

"Comparisons" is not a keyword that I have often encountered in the Mobility Studies literature; however, the MobileDeaf team identified it as a key activity in international deaf mobility. We noted that deaf people who engage in international encounters seem to be very invested in making comparisons across scales, especially between nations (see Chapter 5): comparing problems and barriers encountered in relation to deaf educational policies, and the strategies to challenge them (Murray, 2007); comparing specific deaf landscapes (e.g., of schools and organizations) across countries (Friedner & Kusters, 2014); comparing legislation in relation to sign languages (De Meulder, 2015); comparing how deaf people in other countries live (this book); comparing the signs used in different sign languages (see Chapter 8); comparing how deaf people communicate with hearing people in various societies, and so on.

Comparing is scaling. In drawing comparisons, the facts, experiences, or stories that "do not fit" are frequently ignored, dismissed, or erased in favor of a few similarities that are identified as salient. Instances of similarity are taken as tokens of the same "type," and the produced ideological relation between types and tokens can be seen as a shift in scale, with "type" being of greater scale (Gal, 2016, p. 94). An example of this is the generalized notion of "sign language recognition," a term that is used in ways that sideline national differences between legislations (De Meulder, 2015). As mentioned already, the comparisons and generalizations produced in transnational encounters are very often made on the *national* level, such as the generalization of people from the Indian subcontinent as "Indians," and then comparing "India" and "Indians" with "the United Kingdom" and "British people" (see Chapter 9). Another example of national scaling involves rendering different nations commensurable: In international events, nations may be rendered "comparable" irrespective of their size or other characteristics, even if the activity of comparing identifies differences (Chapter 5).

In this context of rendering oneself, one's experiences, and one's nation as comparable in the deaf transnational sphere, deaf people may *behave more deaf*. Paradoxically, participating in "deafened spaces" (i.e., where the majority of participants are deaf) has led some deaf people to say that they feel "hearing" abroad because they no longer stand out (see Breivik, 2005, p. 169). Some deaf people have also had experiences in their home country of being seen as "oral," "deafened," "not from a deaf family," or "hard of hearing"; in contrast, they have been welcomed as "deaf" when abroad (see Stein, 2015). Again, the (more) "deaf way" in which people behave or feel is very specific. Haualand et al. (2015) noted that particular discourses on "the right way to be deaf" were circulating during the deaf mega-events they studied around the turn of the 21st century, including the WFD congresses and the Deaflympics. They observed that:

> The anticipated "right" way to be deaf is to take pride in and accept being deaf, use sign language, refrain from using hearing aids and/or cochlear implants at least during a deaf event and spend time on deaf culture and deaf politics. (p. 53)

"The right way to be deaf" differs among times and spaces. Taking a historical example, Murray (2007, p. 83) wrote that at the 1893 Chicago congress, deaf signers would interpret each other's signed presentations into spoken languages for the benefit of hearing people in the audience. Nowadays, however, a sharp distinction is drawn between speaking and signing: Although (increasing numbers of) deaf people may speak in their private lives, they are typically discouraged from doing so in deaf transnational spaces, where it is *hearing* interpreters who do the speaking if a voiceover is required. Signing, then, can be crucial to "the right way to be deaf," but which sign language or signed lingua franca is "right" can vary. For example, in Chapter 8, we show that ASL is seen as a good way to communicate internationally in some cases but is rejected in others.

As part of the process of comparing deaf lives, certain ways of being deaf are foregrounded over others, certain practices are seen as more appropriate than others, and the people who have relatively more power are able to institutionalize those expectations. In this context of comparing, differences of nationality and race (for example) are flagged but are also rendered irrelevant in favor of DEAF-SAME—and, in the process, racism, ableism, sexism, and other forms of ingrained systematic oppression go unacknowledged. This can lead to sharp contrasts and disconnects, as we show throughout this book, as people with relatively less power may have opposing perspectives and experiences in relation to being deaf in combination with their race, ethnicity, class, gender, and so on.

In summary, behaving "more deaf" or "deaf-first" makes comparisons possible, but is itself also the result of comparisons and a focus on differences. Indeed, "any conceptualization of cosmopolitanism starts from the premise of (radical) 'difference' which needs to be maintained (through boundaries) to allow would-be-cosmopolitans to overcome it in one way or the other" (Salazar, 2021b, pp. 4–5). The very act of "coming together as deaf signers with similar interests and behaviors" is a form of power-infused scale-making based on a history of comparing deaf lives between nations, with differences either temporarily put aside or made commensurable and consumable (see Chapter 5). But it is also through scaling and comparing that deaf cosmopolitanism is produced, which, as Appiah (2006) reminds us, is *the challenge* to interpersonal interactions, not the solution.

Bourdieu's "Theory of Practice"

How, then, do mobile deaf people navigate different spaces on different scales? A useful framework for this question is Bourdieu's "theory of practice," underpinned by a trio of interrelated "thinking tools"—field, habitus, and capital—which some Deaf Studies scholars (mostly based in U.K. universities) have been making use of over the last decade (O'Brien, 2021a, 2021b; O'Brien & Emery, 2014; Richardson, 2019; Sommer Lindsay, 2022). *Fields* are social spaces, or arenas, with their own rules, produced by the social actors who inhabit them (Bourdieu, 1992); they can be clearly defined places, or more abstract, such as "education," "the arts," "bureaucracy," and "religion." Societies consist of interwoven and interrelated fields. *Habitus* is the way that human behavior is characterized by regularities and tendencies, also called dispositions. Behavior is structured by past and present circumstances and by the rules of particular fields—that is, through internalizing social expectations and value systems (Bourdieu, 1992). By being immersed in a field, people develop habitus, which is inherently dialectic: It is individual (unique for each, based on personal experiences and agency), but also social (its structure can be shared with others in the same field, and/or of the same class, ethnicity, and so on). When field and habitus "match," people feel like a "fish in the water"; where habitus and field clash, they may feel like a "fish out of water."

To a considerable extent, *capital* is synonymous with "power." Bourdieu distinguishes between social capital (relationships with people that can be useful or important to proceed in life), economic capital (money, properties, skills that can be monetized), and cultural capital (cultural knowledge, educational qualifications, knowledge of one or more languages). Linguistic capital is often subsumed under cultural capital, but it is also discussed separately by Bourdieu (1992). In the Deaf Studies accounts that have used the Bourdieusian trio (or only the "capital" concept, as in De Meulder & Murray, 2021), the distinction of linguistic capital from other forms of capital has been crucial because of the minority status of, and oppression of, sign languages (O'Brien, 2021a). Forms of capital can be accumulated and "traded" and also have an impact on each other. For example, social capital and cultural capital (e.g., degrees) can lead to access to economic capital in the form of jobs, funding, or property.

Some authors have used other prefixes for capital than those of Bourdieu: For example, Sommer Lindsay (2022) used "deaf capital" for capital in deaf-specific and in hearing-led fields. Deaf capital is a summary term for deaf networks, sign language fluency, knowledge of deaf history, and deaf embodiment. Although pulling together these notions under the term *deaf capital* can be a useful approach, we do not use it as a catchall in this book; instead, we write about deaf people's social capital, economic capital, cultural capital, and linguistic capital separately because these distinctions were important for our analysis of the data.

Bourdieu's thinking tools have also been applied in studies of migration and mobility (e.g., Nowicka, 2015), showing that forms of capital are "valued, devalued, exchanged, and accumulated in the immigration experience" (Kelly & Lusis, 2006, p. 845). Forms of capital exist in relation to fields: The value of each form of capital depends on the field, and the prestige afforded by it (symbolic capital) can vary. Thus, forms of capital (e.g., degrees, currencies, savings, social networks, linguistic knowledge) acquired in a specific country (or another geographical entity) may be valued less elsewhere, impacting migrants' strategies in job seeking, for example (see Chapters 4 and 8). Additionally, some forms of capital are valued more in transnational fields (i.e., on the transnational scale) than in specific nations (Joy et al., 2020), such as knowledge of English or IS (see Chapter 8) or certain contacts in social networks (see Chapter 7).

The concepts of "capital" and "field" are easily applicable to the study of international mobility, arguably more so than "habitus." However, Kelly and Lusis (2006) have suggested that people who are internationally mobile also build up a repertoire of habitus in different fields (e.g., their habitus in nations of origin, in new nations, in transnational networks): "It seems quite possible that an individual could occupy multiple habiti simultaneously as different sets of taken-for-granted rules of practice, and evaluation of capital, are activated in different contexts" (p. 846). Indeed, people moving between different types of spaces on different scales (fields) are exposed to norms and rules in relation to those spaces, and in relation to the movements between them.

In this book, Chapters 3 and 4 make use of the *trio* of Bourdieu's thinking tools when dealing with contexts of migration; *capital* is the one notion used throughout the whole book. Isolating this term is consistent with other Mobility Studies scholarship, where "capital" (e.g., "social capital") is very often used without direct reference to Bourdieu's other concepts. However, this does not necessarily mean that capital is discussed in isolation of the wider context—rather that other terminology is used to talk about fields, such as "scales," "nations," or "networks." Indeed, we have found the catchall term "network capital," borrowed from Mobility Studies (Elliott & Urry, 2010; Sheller & Urry, 2006b), to be useful in our analysis of the ways in which mobile deaf people tap into different networks at different scales (see Chapter 7). The term covers the combination of skills, documents, qualifications, capacity for physical movement, contacts, and access to communication devices and travel infrastructure that facilitate networking; furthermore, Kaufmann et al. (2004) see motility as another form of capital, explaining that this encompasses "interdependent elements relating to *access* to different forms and degrees of mobility, *competence* to recognize and make use of access, and *appropriation* of a particular choice, including the option of non-action" (p. 750). *Access* refers to the transportation and communication devices available; *competence* includes skills, licenses, and abilities (e.g., physical ability, permits, degrees, planning skills); *appropriation* refers to how the access and skills are then mobilized. There is thus a certain overlap between "network capital" and "motility as capital," with the emphasis in the first concept being on the capacity to network, and the emphasis in the second concept being on the capacity to be mobile.

An Intersectional Lens in Deaf Ethnography

> Mobilities research is concerned first with the patterning, timing, and causation of face-to-face copresence. What brings person to person? When? How often? [...] Especially significant is the observation of how people effect a face-to-face relationship with places, with events and with people. (Sheller & Urry, 2006a, p. 217)

In the MobileDeaf study, face-to-face observation of deaf people who engaged in international mobility was undertaken: How do they move, where to, and how do they interact with other people? Although the team considered (and in some cases engaged with) widening the focus to include social media, the emphasis of our participant observation was on pre-pandemic face-to-face encounters between deaf people. We were *mobile with* our participants (see Bissell, 2009): accompanying them to the pubs and food joints in London where they met others, joining a tour group in Bali, moving around Kakuma refugee camp on the back of a motorcycle, traveling alongside hundreds of people to snowy towns in Italy for the Winter Deaflympics. In some of the field sites, we *waited with* people too: in line to meet officials in Kakuma Refugee Camp, in traffic in Bali, for sports competitions to start or end. In these and other sites where we moved and waited with people, observing and talking formed our key methods, as explained in Chapter 2.

To study the challenges of deaf cosmopolitanism, the lens of intersectionality was employed in an attempt to understand the importance and meaning of variables such as race, ethnicity, nationality, gender, religion, educational background, and class in the context of international deaf spaces. Crenshaw (1989) coined the intersectionality concept to draw attention to multiple inequalities experienced by working-class black women in the United States. Intersectionality scholars initially focused on a gender–race–class triumvirate, showing that working-class black women are doubly or triply oppressed by patriarchy, racism, and classism. More dimensions have been added in studies of intersectionality over time, such as sexuality, religion, age, and (dis)ability; the concept is thus "flexible in its applicability *and* tied to its history in Black feminist theorizing" (May, 2015, p. 91). Since its inception, the term has been used in multiple disciplines in multiple ways, including as methodology, as an action word (used in policy discourse), as a theoretical framework, as a descriptive tool, and as analytical tool (Lutz, 2015). In this book, intersectionality is not treated as a theoretical framework, nor as a mere descriptive term. Rather than "a study of intersectionality," the MobileDeaf team engaged in intersectional thinking throughout their methodology, in terms of both data gathering and analysis (see Lutz, 2015). We did so by avoiding "single-axis thinking," which is defined by May (2015) as follows:

> While intersectionality starts from the premise that our various identities and the many structures of power we live within and navigate should be understood as interconnected and enmeshed, conventional ways of conceptualizing identity or examining inequality tend to rely on either/or thinking and be "single-axis"—meaning that we are asked to examine (and address) race *or* class separately, or perhaps think about disability *and* sexuality, but insist that one factor be "primary" (they are still conceived of as separate, since one must be first or more significant). [...] When single-axis models are relied on, the experiences and knowledge of some are often (falsely) universalized as if they could adequately represent the experiences, needs, and claims of all group members: this obscures within-group differences, the relationality of power, and interactions among and permeability between

categories. Likewise, single-axis forms of redress adhere to, rather than challenge, the conceptual "building blocks" of domination—they leave the foundations of inequality intact and also reinforce them. (pp. 80–81)

One persistent form of single-axis thinking in Deaf Studies is talking about "deaf people" in general and subordinating all other identifications to that of "being deaf"; this is further explored in Chapter 9.

Using an intersectional lens, or using intersectionality as a theoretical framing, is both a trend and a necessity in Deaf Studies as a whole. Several Deaf Studies scholars have focused on intersectionality, whether or not they employed the term. Most of these studies have engaged in an intracategorical approach to intersectionality (McCall, 2005), which means looking at one specific social group that exists on a neglected point of intersection (e.g., black and deaf; queer and deaf; see Emery & Iyer, 2022, and Chapter 9 for references; see Ruiz-Williams et al., 2015, for an exception). The MobileDeaf team did not take an intracategorical approach to intersectionality, with the exception of the part of the London-based subproject that focused on deaf Indian female migrants. Additionally, most Deaf Studies authors studying intersectionality have used the intersectionality concept to focus on deaf racial, sexual, gender, and ethnic minorities *within a country* and not in the context of (international) mobilities (see Martens, 2020, for an exception). Patil (2013) has pointed out that most studies on intersectionality are based in one country and called this "domestic intersectionality"; this is in contrast to our approach.

There is a highly problematic tendency to use the intersectionality concept without reference to race. Yuval-Davis (2011) argues that "intersectional analysis should not be limited only to those who are on the multiple margins of society, but rather that the boundaries of intersectional analysis should encompass all members of society" (p. 8); that is, that intersectionality is produced in interactions and power relations between people, *all of whom* are characterized by race and/or ethnicity, gender, class, and so on. As May (2015) states, intersectionality's interest is in "dismantling oppressive structures" (p. 32). However, another problematic tendency in intersectionality research is that the study of *inequalities* has, over time, often been sidelined—a development that has been heavily criticized (Lutz, 2015). There is a tendency to interpret intersectionality as a synonym for "diversity," which is a reduction of the full meaning of the concept (May, 2015). The risk of using the term "identity" in the context of intersectionality is of falling into the trap of interpreting intersectionality as "multiple identities" (May, 2015). Therefore, by using intersectionality as a methodological lens and driver, rather than a theoretical framework, the MobileDeaf team intentionally avoided the language of identity, preferring the term "social locations" (Yuval-Davis, 2006), a concept that is akin to "positions" and understood as constellations that are time and context dependent rather than fixed characteristics possessed by individuals (further explained in Chapter 9).

Using intersectionality as a lens rather than as a theoretical framework, we adopted the definition of intersectionality as posited by Cho et al. (2013):

> [W]hat makes an analysis intersectional [...] is its adoption of an intersectional way of thinking about the problem of *sameness and difference and its relation to power*. This framing—conceiving of categories not as distinct but as always *permeated* by other categories, *fluid and changing*, always in the process of creating and being created by dynamics of power—emphasizes what intersectionality *does* rather than what intersectionality *is*. (p. 795, my emphasis)

This definition includes *both* the traditional focus on power, inequality, and oppression *and* the consideration of how intersections produce opportunities and/or empowerment. Throughout this book, we show (albeit without using the intersectionality concept as analytic) that people's social locations shape (and are shaped by) mobility in that they have an impact on motility, on where people go, on what strategies they employ when they are mobile (e.g., how they present themselves, how they communicate), on with whom they connect, on how they network, on what forms of capital they can draw upon, and on how people experience their mobilities.

In other words, and linking back to our conceptual coffer, translocality *needs* to be studied through an intersectional lens (Anthias, 2012). As Thimm and Chaudhuri (2021) point out in their study on intersectionality and migration, "any particular individual has to negotiate multiple intersectional social locations at multiple scales simultaneously"; they suggest "scaling intersectionality by examining intersectionalities across transnational scales" (p. 278). This is necessary because "intersectional constellations of a person's social locations can and typically will vary whether she is at home, at work or at a family gathering, for example, let alone if she is in her homeland or abroad" (p. 279). For example, gender values vary between contexts and countries within families, marriages, and work cultures (see Chapter 10 for examples).

Nevertheless, although we have used an intersectional lens, we have still privileged two social locations in our recruitment of participants and in our analysis: deafness and nationality. Our focus was on *deaf* people who were, for example, also queer, and/or Indian, and/or black, and/or a woman—but *deafness*, and being deaf *signers*, was the common factor. However, that does not mean that we treat "being deaf signers" as a totalizing status or axis of identification (see especially Chapter 9). May (2015) says that single-axis thinking—for example, thinking in terms of gender first or race first—is wrong, but she also argues that it is possible to focus on gender or race by taking an intersectional approach *to* gender or race. Our purpose was to do the same with regard to deafness. In Chapter 2, we explore the "double-edged sword" of doing deaf ethnography, pointing out that where deafness is a shared core identifier, deaf *differences* can come more sharply to the fore. At the same time, we acknowledge that we can only recognize, identify (with), or discuss intersections because of our own social locations and positionalities.

The second privileged social location in our study is nationality. We focus on international mobility, that is, deaf people of different nationalities who cross borders of nation-states. We are aware of the danger of methodological nationalism, such as "national" diversity coming first in our analysis at the cost of understanding ethnic and regional divisions. Our focus on "national" diversity also meant that other differences (e.g., race, ethnicity, gender, class) were often subsumed under "national" identities. In Chapters 2 and 5, the implications, as well as the role of "the national," are explored more in depth.

This Book

The way this book is structured reflects the way that the MobileDeaf project was structured. After Part One: Studying International Deaf Mobilities, consisting of this introduction and a methodology chapter, Part Two: A Spectrum of International Deaf Mobilities consists of four chapters. Each chapter contains a review of Deaf Studies literature relating to one type of deaf mobility (forced migration, labor/marriage migration, professional mobility, and tourist mobility), as well as an exploration of some themes and patterns that emerged during and from the case studies of the four subprojects. These chapters are primarily documentary for several reasons. We aimed to concentrate on each of these types of mobility in their own right, situating each subproject in relation to other studies of the same type of mobility (e.g., studies of deaf migrants, studies of deaf tourists) and demonstrating how it connects to and enhances this research area. We also use these chapters to provide background information about our field sites and the dynamics within them, allowing us to delve directly into specific examples in the chapters in Part Three: Patterns in International Deaf Mobilities. Although the chapters in Part Two are therefore more descriptive and less analytic than those in Part Three, we did engage with several of the analytics outlined within this chapter, particularly Bourdieu's framework and discussions on scale. In these chapters, we also work with materials that were too voluminous for, or did not fit well in, Chapters 7–10 but were nevertheless key to the types of mobility under study. In this way, we are able to shed light on themes that are specific to each type of mobility.

In Part Three (Chapters 7–10), we present the themes we have identified and explored *across* the four subprojects and throughout the different types of mobilities. It is by exploring our data together as a team that we made note of the patterns that emerged across mobilities: the experiences of (not) belonging, the various language practices and ideologies in play, the features of deaf spaces and networks, the confrontations with limits to mobility. We had started with a much larger conceptual coffer, which we reduced through this shared exploration of our data to four keywords: *networks*, *calibration*, *belonging*, and *immobility*. These structure Part Three and came to function as a nexus to which other keywords were linked. By engaging with theories and analyzing the data from each subproject individually and collectively, we underscore the potential of Deaf Mobility Studies—not merely as Mobility Studies conducted by Deaf Studies scholars, but also in "deafening" Mobility Studies. The implications of this I discuss in the Conclusion, in which I reflect on key facets of the MobileDeaf project, from the challenges of understanding deaf cosmopolitanism to the conceptual coffer that directed our exploration, and the invaluable teamwork underpinning this endeavor. Finally, I address the present and expected societal impacts of the MobileDeaf project.

2

Doing Deaf Ethnography

Annelies Kusters, Steven Emery, Sanchayeeta Iyer, Amandine le Maire, and Erin Moriarty

Anthropologists interested in deaf people have engaged in ethnography, typically creating broad accounts of deaf lives and deaf community life in a particular country, city, or village (for an overview, see Friedner & Kusters, 2020). Surprisingly, however, ethnography has been underused within Deaf Studies as a whole. By doing ethnography, we can capture aspects of deaf lives that can be captured with no other approach. Ethnographers participate in people's daily lives, observe what happens and what people say, engage in conversations, and ask questions informally. A continuum exists as to how the ethnographer is involved in the field, going from mostly observing to fully participating in the same activities as others. Field notes are taken to lay down details of observations, activities, and conversations (Atkinson & Hammersley, 2005; Blommaert & Dong, 2020; Emerson et al., 2011).

Ethnographers usually start from a set of broad questions, but they also let new themes and questions emerge within the research as they engage with people and learn about what keeps them occupied. Doing this, ethnographers identify recurring patterns in practices and discourses, and puzzle together a broad picture around a central set of themes. Ethnography can include scrutiny of language practices, studying closely how people communicate with each other and experience this—also called linguistic ethnography (Hou & Kusters, 2020). Participant observation is often complemented by ethnographic interviews, with the fieldworker's observations informing the conversation during the interview. New information is triangulated by observing the phenomena or discourses under study in a variety of contexts, and by discussing the same themes with a variety of participants. In other words, ethnographers' accounts are informed by the patterning and variability of the practices and discourses that they study.

In this chapter, we share, compare, and contrast the processes of doing ethnography in each of the four MobileDeaf subprojects: forced migration, labor and marriage migration, professional mobility, and tourist mobility. Although each subproject was undertaken independently, our research work was shaped by two overarching research questions. First, within the contexts of international deaf spaces, how does being deaf intersect with other social locations, particularly ethnicity, nationality, education, religion, and gender, and which meaningful connections or accumulated inequalities occur? Second, how do deaf signers in these contexts practice and experience international communication by calibrating, by learning and using multiple languages and language modalities, and by using International Sign (IS)? The questions were broad enough for us to keep an open gaze for salient themes within our respective research contexts, and specific enough to guide our research.

In ethnographies of deaf transnationalism, well-connected deaf people from Global North countries are disproportionately likely to be selected as participants (see studies in Friedner & Kusters, 2015a). For example, Haualand et al. (2015) admit that their study published in 2002 was focused on "a global deaf elite [who] had the money and resources to travel and a strong drive or interest in networking and connecting with deaf people from other countries" (p. 49). In the MobileDeaf project, we wanted to portray a wide variety of experiences of international mobility (leisurely, difficult, privileged, disprivileged) and of people with a wide range of backgrounds.

The prerequisite was that our participants had engaged in international deaf mobility, because the MobileDeaf project's focus was on *deaf people of different nationalities crossing national borders*. We focused on the deaf people who do the crossing but also on the deaf people who engage with people who do the crossing, such as deaf tourist guides, deaf hosts of events, and deaf teachers in the host countries. The focus on national affiliation as a core variable in our research was warranted by the fact that our focus was on international mobility (see Chapter 5). However, we had to constantly keep in mind that national affiliation is *one* variable in an intersectional analysis and not the overarching one. By using an intersectional lens (see Chapter 1), we were able to pay attention to some neglected points of intersection. However, we experienced limitations with regard to how much a single researcher could cover in a subproject, in combination with the limitations of our own positionalities. As a result, we applied an intersectional lens in different ways to the different subprojects. For example, experiences of sexual orientation and class were mostly studied within the subproject on labor migration, and disability was studied in the professional mobility subproject.

The MobileDeaf team consisted of five deaf researchers: the principal investigator, two postdoctoral researchers, and two doctoral students. Each of MobileDeaf's four subprojects was undertaken by one researcher, except for the project on migration to London, which was undertaken by two people. Even though MobileDeaf was not the first multisited team ethnography in Deaf Studies (see Breivik et al., 2002), what set the project apart was that the team of ethnographers comprised all deaf signers. This decision was both methodological and political. Methodologically, it increased the likelihood of successfully communicating and connecting with our deaf research participants (although this also depended on our positionalities, see below); studying our own experiences as mobile deaf people was also a core part of the methodology. Furthermore, it was political because Deaf Studies has been largely undertaken and led by hearing scholars, a pattern that would be unthinkable in, for example, Women's Studies and Black Studies, although it is also common in Maori Studies (O'Brien & Emery, 2014). Structural audism in all levels of education and workplaces (whether deaf-specific or mainstream) has had a huge impact on the position of deaf scholars in academia (Chua et al., 2022; Kusters et al., 2017b; O'Brien, 2020). Historically, most deaf researchers worked as research assistants under hearing project leaders. Research design and data analysis were thus generally initiated and concluded by hearing people. An increase in deaf-led studies has already brought about shifts in research foci, methodologies, theories, and writing styles (see chapters in Kusters et al., 2017a). We see our use of ethnography—and autoethnography—as part of this shift; we elaborate on this later.

The purpose of this chapter is two-fold: first, to explain how we built up the data shared in the following chapters, and second, to explore what it means to do ethnography with deaf research participants. Because ethnography has been underused in Deaf Studies, further exploration is needed into what it means to employ this approach in the study of deaf people's experiences, to build on the few accounts that have been published on this topic. By comparing our respective methodological journeys, taking into account our positionalities, we are able to shed light on a variety of strategies and procedures used in deaf ethnographies. Although we had a common set of overarching questions, our ethnographies were very different. The range of settings and temporalities of each subproject led us to engage in traditional long-term ethnography, multisited ethnography, and online ethnography. In this chapter, we discuss only the methods that *all of us* engaged in and that are key to ethnography: participant observation and interviewing. We have also made use of visual methods including mapping, drawings, photo/video elicitation, and language portraits in various subprojects; these are not discussed in this chapter but are mentioned elsewhere in the book where relevant.

Ethnography is predicated on making connections with others, and our shared deafness certainly facilitated these connections. Across each subproject, we engaged with deaf people from a wide variety of backgrounds; thus, we used and built up "calibration" skills communicating across different sign languages (see Chapter 8), a crucial facet of the research practice of deaf scholars researching internationally (Breivik et al., 2002; Dikyuva et al., 2012). Tapping into and expanding different types of networks was also necessary (see Chapter 7). Among us, we had access to a range of all-deaf or mostly deaf international spaces (e.g., workplaces, workshops, conferences, social gatherings, classrooms, domestic spaces), some of which would have been difficult or impossible for hearing researchers to access.

As other deaf researchers have reported previously, we experienced that deaf research participants said they were willing to share their experiences with us *because* we are deaf (see Kusters et al., 2017b, for a literature review of methodologies by deaf scholars). However, the question of how other characteristics—such as deaf researchers' race, ethnicity, gender, nationality, cultural background, language background, class, and so on—also have an impact on research has been understudied (for exceptions, see Kusters, 2012; Hou, 2017). Some of us worked with research assistants to complement our positionalities. Later in this chapter and book, we reflect on the complex ways that the positionality of the researchers and assistants, in combination with the positionality of participants, shaped the research.

A key method of the MobileDeaf project was video-recording observations. In observational filming, the camera is treated as if it is in the background, recording the ordinary details of everyday lives, and resulting in multilayered, "thick" data. These recordings allowed us to reexamine what people did and how they communicated (Kusters et al., 2016; Moriarty, 2020b). Video-recording data is crucial in linguistic ethnographies dealing with signed languages (Hou & Kusters, 2020): Through multiple viewings of a single filmed encounter, the data become thicker as more detail is noticed. Yet, our recordings of interactions were not merely for analysis: They were used to create ethnographic films, a type of documentary film based on research. The findings are not only gathered and analyzed, but also disseminated in their original (but edited) form. This is important in Deaf Studies because deaf signers are often studied and represented in ways that ultimately *obscure* the nature of sign languages, as well as the participants' expertise, subjective experiences, and participation in the process. The creation of the MobileDeaf films was a cooperative effort among the researchers, research assistants, and filmmakers. We discuss the process in our film *Birthing a Genre: Deaf Ethnographic Film*.[1] Again, that the process was participatory and deaf-led is important because many films on deaf people are made by hearing filmmakers and are

---

1. https://vimeo.com/857426224

often felt to not entirely correspond to lived deaf experiences. Indeed, in parallel to the need for deaf-led research, there is a need for deaf-led sign language media (Rijckaert, 2012).

Our collaborations gradually led to common insights, and in this chapter, we outline and analyze our processes. By considering four subprojects separately and together, we offer a broad and varied picture of the shapes that deaf ethnography can take.

Team Constitution

Our positionalities and privileges, which are related to our social locations (e.g., race, gender, language backgrounds, nationality, class, educational background, family background, previous mobility experiences), have had a profound impact on the type of data we have gathered. In this section, we outline our personal journeys into the MobileDeaf project. We show how we drew on the network capital we had built throughout our lives, and how we expanded them in our research (see Chapters 1 and 7 for a discussion of network capital). We thus see the biographies below as a *starting point* for considering our positionalities throughout the chapter and the book, rather than as the end of the discussion of positionality. Importantly, our journeys show how the growth of our personal and professional identities and networks was rooted in local, national, and international *deaf mobilities*, the key theme of this book. Different types of international mobility have shaped our own lives in profound ways. We thus not only research international deaf mobility, but also lead international, deaf, hypermobile lives; this formed the impetus for this study, as well as becoming part of our study.

Annelies Kusters

Annelies is the MobileDeaf team leader, whose focus was the subproject on professional mobility. She is a white, deaf, cisgendered woman in her late 30s, from Flanders, Belgium, who has been mobile to, and has lived in, several countries. She and one of her four siblings were born deaf, and Annelies grew up participating in Dutch-speaking mainstream education. Her hearing parents did not sign despite her father being a teacher of the deaf; her mother was a homemaker. Annelies could only communicate in spoken language one-to-one with certain people, and with difficulty; her best means of communication and learning was through reading and writing, and she completed her education through self-study. At university, Annelies studied anthropology; when selecting a topic for her master's dissertation at the KU Leuven (University of Leuven), one option was "deaf culture," supervised by a hearing, nonsigning professor specializing in the anthropology of disability. He recommended to her several books on deaf culture and deaf history; this marked the start of a new chapter in her life. Learning about the richness and diversity of deaf cultures, that plenty of deaf people "arrive late" in deaf communities, and that her personal history was part of a wider deaf history, led her to realize that she could "arrive late" too.

Annelies started to learn sign languages in rapid succession. She joined a deaf club in Flanders, where she learned Flemish Sign Language (VGT). She went to Suriname for her dissertation research in 2004 and there learned some Sign Language of the Netherlands (NGT), which was used in the local school. She volunteered in a deaf school in Ghana in 2006 and picked up some Ghanaian Sign Language (GSL). While working on her Master of Science and doctoral degrees in Deaf Studies at the University of Bristol, she learned British Sign Language (BSL); there, she was required to write in English rather than Dutch. Having met her husband at a deaf youth conference in India in 2006, she undertook research in India in 2007 for her Master of Science dissertation and started to learn Indian Sign Language (ISL). She learned Adamorobe Sign Language while conducting doctoral research in a village in Ghana in 2008–2009 (Kusters, 2015). She learned IS loosely in parallel with the sign languages listed previously, initially at the European Union of the Deaf Youth (EUDY) camp in Dublin in 2006, and she uses it in several domains of her personal and professional life. To make these mobilities possible, Annelies took employment while studying full time, vigorously applied for funding and scholarships, and made limited budgets stretch.

After marrying, Annelies lived in India (2010–2013), using mostly ISL with her husband, his deaf family, his friends, and their first son, who was born in Mumbai. Annelies finished her doctorate in India and worked as an independent researcher while applying for funding. The family experienced a period of financial insecurity until they moved to Germany in 2013, where Annelies obtained her first academic job. In Germany, she gave birth to her second child. When Annelies obtained funding from the European Research Council (ERC) for the MobileDeaf project in 2017, the family moved to Edinburgh. Annelies and her children have never experienced barriers to obtaining visas with their Belgian passports; they are also Overseas Citizens of India, permitted to travel to, live, and work in India visa-free. In contrast, her Indian husband has navigated a large number of bureaucratic hurdles for marriage and migration, and he has always been on a temporary visa or residence permit outside India.

As a deaf anthropologist, Annelies's first ethnography in Suriname investigated the meeting spaces and networks of Paramaribo's urban deaf community; in Ghana, she researched in Adamorobe village, where a locally emerged sign language is used by both deaf and hearing people due to the historically high incidence of hereditary deafness. In India, she focused on deaf spaces in suburban train compartments for people with disabilities, and on multimodal languaging (calibration) between deaf and hearing people in Mumbai's public spaces. The idea for the MobileDeaf project grew from this body of research and also from her observations and experiences during her own international mobilities.

Amandine le Maire

Within MobileDeaf, Amandine focuses on forced migration. She is a Belgian, white, cisgendered woman in her early 30s. She was born deaf to deaf parents, who used Langue des Signes Francophone de Belgique (LSFB) to communicate with her; she also learned some ASL from her father, who had studied at Gallaudet University, and from deaf American family friends. ASL was her father's first sign language because he had grown up using speech. Amandine's mother's family is from the north of Belgium, where the primary language used is Dutch. Through her mother's family, Amandine learned some Dutch.

After a few years in a deaf school where the main languages were French, LSFB, and cued speech,[2] Amandine was enrolled at age 7 in a mainstream school, supported by sign language interpreters using cued speech and LSFB. After high school, she stayed for 9 months in Denmark to take part in Frontrunners, an international deaf leadership program, where she learned IS

---

2. A manual system of eight handshapes in four positions near the mouth, which clarifies the lip-patterns of the speech.

through communicating with deaf peers from around the world. During Frontrunners, she undertook an internship in South America and worked as a volunteer in a youth camp organized by a Chilean deaf organization.

After returning to Belgium, she continued her bachelor of arts studies in anthropology at Université Libre de Bruxelles (ULB), inspired by her father's passion for deaf history and her mother's passion for deaf arts; she felt that anthropology would support a career in Deaf Studies research. Participation in the Erasmus exchange program enabled her to return to Denmark for 6 months of study, where she became interested in deaf migration. She wrote her bachelor's thesis on deaf families moving from Copenhagen to Malmö (Sweden) to access sign language medium education. Her master's thesis at Université Catholique de Louvain (UCL) covered the relocation of many deaf Belgian families to Namur, initially due to the presence of a bilingual deaf school there but, later, for various, more complex reasons.

During her studies, Amandine traveled to engage with deaf people around the world. She volunteered in deaf schools in Turkey and Bolivia and participated in the EUDY camp in Bulgaria (2014) and in the World Federation of the Deaf Youth Section (WFDYS) camp in South Africa (2011); she was Camp Director of the EUDY Junior camp in Belgium in 2014. She was also a board member and president of FFSB-Jeunes, a deaf youth association in Belgium, for several years, during which time she participated as a delegate in the General Assemblies of EUDY and WFDYS. Later, she was involved in Des Mains pour Dieu, a deaf Belgian Christian association, participating in a European Deaf Christian Youth (EDCY) conference in Germany, where she met her deaf husband, who is from Northern Ireland.

After graduating with her master's in anthropology, Amandine started an enterprise called MUSK in Namur with a deaf colleague, focusing on visual media and accessibility through sign language. She obtained certificates enabling her to interpret in legal settings and to act as a deaf museum guide. Amandine then moved to Edinburgh to start her doctorate with the MobileDeaf team, learning BSL—which she continues to use every day with her husband. Although her academic writing has previously been in French, she has now shifted to writing in English too.

Steven Emery

Steve focuses on the labor migration subproject. Steve is a British, white, cisgendered man who was in his mid to late 50s during the project. Steve comes from a family of laborers and grew up, sometimes in poverty, in working-class communities. He became deaf at the age of 4 from meningitis. His formative education was spent in mainstream schools, including, between ages 5 and 12, one of the earliest Partially Hearing Units (PHUs) in the United Kingdom, where he socialized with other deaf as well as hearing children. Between the ages of 12 and 16, he was the only deaf child in the school. On leaving secondary education at 16, he became a cleaner at a print factory and later became a typesetter. However, from ages 17 to 19, he experienced extreme isolation, with no friends outside of work.

He gradually gained class consciousness through the collective experiences of printworkers battling for fair wages and working conditions, and he took an active role in a trade union. His interest in migration stems from his engagement in far left-wing political activism in the 1980s, because the Left takes a strong stance against racism and border controls. In his late 20s, Steve started to socialize with deaf people, and he also began to learn BSL. He began a full-time degree in cultural studies at age 27. During this time, he learned about deaf history, deaf culture, and oppression of deaf people by society. After graduating in 1992, Steve worked in a variety of community development and counseling roles with local deaf people. Learning about deaf people's real-life experiences—and being involved in campaigning for BSL language rights—led him back to university in 2002 to undertake his doctoral degree in citizenship. Since graduating in 2007, his career has predominantly been in research and higher education. Although his doctorate and middle-class career has bestowed him with "status," Steve continues to identify strongly with international working-class struggles; a focus on class has thus pervaded his MobileDeaf research. Steve also identifies as disabled, particularly due to his experiences of mental health distress throughout his life; indeed, these experiences, along with his work as a counselor, adviser, and community development worker, have meant that he was profoundly aware of the adverse experiences of many migrant deaf people he was meeting.

Steve has been constantly mobile—a "lifelong sojourner"—since he finished formal education in 1979. Having grown up in Brighton, he was resident in London 1984–1991 (ages 22–29), during which he lived in seven different places across the city, saving up his wages, quitting his job, backpacking abroad, and returning to a new address and employment. He spent 3 months touring the United States, another 3 months crossing Europe, and 7 months on a round-the-world trip. Steve solely met hearing people while traveling; he was not then fully engaged with his identity as a deaf person.

Steve has lived in eight other cities and towns in the United Kingdom; in the Republic of Ireland for 18 months in 2001; and in Washington, DC, for 6 months in 2013 when working at Gallaudet University. He then moved to Colombia to be with his Colombian hearing girlfriend, whom he married the same year; however, he struggled to find work, moving back to the United Kingdom a year and a half later. Along the way, he picked up bits of ASL, Colombian Sign Language, Irish Sign Language, and IS.

Steve's life has thus featured frequent professional and leisure mobility, as well as international migration for relationships. He holds a British passport due to having been born in the country, which has brought with it travel privileges; he has been able to cross the world without facing many bureaucratic barriers. When living in Colombia, he was granted a cedula as the spouse of a Colombian citizen, which gave him rights to work there with few restrictions. In contrast, his then-wife had to meet stricter criteria to remain in the United Kingdom long term.

Sanchayeeta Iyer

Sanchayeeta focuses on marriage migration. She is a British, brown, cisgendered woman in her mid-40s, born in the northwest of London to hearing, immigrant parents. Her South Indian father immigrated to England in the late 1960s for employment, working as a civil servant until his retirement. Her Keralan mother came to London after an arranged marriage in the late 1970s and worked as a secretary in the Indian Embassy. Both parents were in full-time employment, and Sanchayeeta and her siblings were often in the care of an immigrant childcare worker. Sanchayeeta contracted meningitis and became deaf around age 2. Her parents had limited support, with no extended family in the city; nor were they active in local South Indian networks. Her mother left the embassy after the death of Sanchayeeta's youngest brother at age 3 (when Sanchayeeta was 8 years old), switching to "low-skilled" employment and subsequently returning to India for her mental health; she came back 3 years later. From age 8, Sanchayeeta looked after her younger siblings at home alone; following her mother's departure, she and her younger sister had to take up the household responsibilities and care for their baby brother. She and her family lived in a highly multicultural borough, and they experienced racism and xenophobia in both the borough and the city.

Sanchayeeta attended mainstream schools: a primary with a PHU and a secondary with a Sensory Support Unit. She used Sign Supported English (SSE). Her experience of schooling was negative due to racist and audist attitudes from hearing teachers and fellow students, as well as barriers to education. Only when studying for her GCSEs (the advanced stage of secondary education) did she receive full-time SSE provision. Sanchayeeta was not immersed in the deaf world or BSL until she was in her early 20s. She attended various mainstream colleges in London to study for A levels and a diploma, during which time she socialized with deaf ethnic people and deaf migrants, and she volunteered with the Catholic Agency for Overseas Development (CAFOD). There, she became interested in geography and international development. She participated in a youth development program with The Prince's Trust, Raleigh International, taking part in a 3-month expedition in Chile in 2000. She signed up for Voluntary Service Overseas (VSO), taking time off from her bachelor of arts degree to do a year-long placement with the Philippines Federation of the Deaf (2003–2004).

This year was a turning point: By immersing herself in the deaf Filipino community and using Filipino Sign Language with them, Sanchayeeta's deaf identity ignited. As a research assistant for Dr. Liza Martinez (director of the Philippine Deaf Resource Center), she conducted a study with deaf Filipino women in institutions in Manila and Cebu into awareness of sexual reproduction and sexually transmitted diseases. Returning to the United Kingdom, she completed her degree in Geography and Development Studies at the School of Oriental and African Studies (London). Her preferred language was now BSL, and in 2006 she joined the management committee of the Asian Deaf Women's Association, later the Deaf Ethnic Women's Association (DEWA). She was a trustee of Aurora Deaf Aid Africa (ADAA) during 2014–2019, visiting the deaf community in Kigali, Rwanda, in this capacity. Her first experience with participating in a large international deaf space was at the 2007 WFDY camp in Madrid, which was also her first encounter with IS.

For more than a decade following her bachelor of arts degree, Sanchayeeta worked with deaf children with additional needs. Disillusioned by the school system's failures, in 2013 she applied for a scholarship from the European Union of the Deaf (EUD) for a short course, Deaf Children, Youth, and International Development, hosted by the International Institute of Social Studies (ISS) and Royal Dutch Kentalis in Den Haag, The Netherlands (2014). This motivated her to take up a master's degree in Children, Youth, and International Development at Birkbeck, University of London. She also worked as a BSL teacher to migrant parents and guardians with young deaf children—an eye-opening experience because Sanchayeeta had not been exposed to the day-to-day struggles of migrant parents and guardians during her previous employment. After completing her master's degree, she returned to DEWA as a project coordinator until she was offered a position as a doctoral researcher with MobileDeaf.

Erin Moriarty

Erin is a deaf, white, cisgendered woman in her 40s from the northeastern United States. She was born in Syracuse, New York, to hearing, working-class parents; her father was a plumber and her mother worked in health administration. Realizing that Erin was deaf at 18 months old, they learned how to sign, using Signed Exact English (SEE) in accordance with the dominant deaf education philosophy in Syracuse at the time. In preschool and primary school, Erin attended a deaf program within a hearing school, and she had a small group of deaf SEE-signing peers.

Except for one year at the Model Secondary School for the Deaf (MSSD), Erin attended mainstream school with an ASL interpreter. She learned ASL from her peers at camp and MSSD, becoming immersed in the deaf community. After high school, Erin attended Smith College, an elite all-women's college in New England, where she discovered anthropology and museum studies. After Smith, she lived in Los Angeles briefly, hoping to break into the museum field. She then got a writing job at a dot.com news aggregation service in Washington, DC, through her Smith network. Unhappy working in a hearing environment with limited access provision, Erin moved to Sioux Falls, South Dakota, to work for the Communication Service for the Deaf (CSD), where she was given leadership roles and became part of a national network of deaf business and political leaders. She realized how empowering an all-deaf environment can be.

After 3 years at CSD, Erin moved back to the Northeast, working at Gallaudet University as a development officer and later as communications officer for then-President Robert Davila. Returning to an academic environment prompted Erin to enroll at American University for a doctoral degree in anthropology, during which she worked full-time at Gallaudet and later at the National Institutes of Health (NIH), a research-oriented environment. During her doctoral program, both employers gave Erin unpaid leave to travel to Cambodia for first 1 and then 3 months of research, during which Erin learned and used Cambodian Sign Language. For her third fieldwork period, she won a place in the first-ever cohort of the highly competitive Fulbright-National Geographic Storytelling Fellowship, which funded 10 months in Cambodia in 2014–2015.

Erin did not become fully immersed in Deaf Studies, or even consider herself a Deaf Studies scholar, until she moved to Edinburgh to work with the MobileDeaf team. During work on her doctoral program, she had felt pressure to distance herself from the canon of Deaf Studies in favor of mainstream anthropological theory and literature; she was concerned about being marginalized as a Deaf Studies scholar and was wary of the older canon's descriptive, white-deaf identity-based work. More innovative work in deaf anthropology started appearing around 2015, at which point Erin joined a cohort of deaf anthropologists.

How Did We Become a Team?

Our personal backgrounds contain considerable experience of various types of mobility. We have all spent long periods in other countries, whether researching, studying, working, volunteering, or traveling. At the time of the MobileDeaf project, three of us were in international marriages. We have all experienced privileged mobilities; some of us have also lived abroad unemployed and in challenging life circumstances. Most of us intensively interacted with disprivileged deaf people in the Global South before joining the MobileDeaf team. We have all accumulated knowledge of various sign languages. Thus, international deaf mobility was key to our personal lives before we started the project; this continued throughout the project, as three of us were migrants to the United Kingdom (where MobileDeaf is hosted), and three of us did MobileDeaf fieldwork abroad. We bring these experiences and networks to the project and into this book.

So, how was the MobileDeaf team assembled? When Annelies applied to the ERC for €1.5 million funding for the MobileDeaf project, she envisaged an international deaf team consisting of experienced and less experienced scholars with degrees in Anthropology and Cultural Studies. In particular, she wanted to combine the in-depth study of underresearched themes with capacity development and network building for deaf scholars. The starting point was the research interests of individual people whose profiles fit the project and whom she already knew were interested in the theme of international mobility; she wrote the proposal around her own and those people's interests and experiences. Steve had undertaken a postdoc at the University of Bristol, where Annelies did her doctoral work, and he had already (unsuccessfully) applied for funding to study deaf migration. As a fellow deaf anthropologist, Annelies knew of Erin's work in Cambodia and her continued interest in deaf tourism. Annelies knew Amandine from Belgium, where Amandine had completed her master's in anthropology focusing on migration; Annelies knew Amandine was interested in pursuing a doctoral degree in mobility. This is a classic example of how large research proposals are often the products of existing networks among people, in this case *deaf* networks (see Chapter 7).

Using networks to design a project can be empowering because it enables the creation of an all-deaf team. However, it also sustains patterns of exclusion. Very few deaf people had the necessary research profile for this project, and the initial team was entirely white, in effect perpetuating a problematic pattern whereby Deaf Studies remains predominantly *white* Deaf Studies (Dunn & Anderson, 2020; Emery & Iyer, 2022; Ruiz-Williams et al., 2015). Even when research happens with deaf black and Indigenous people of color (BIPOC) and with deaf people in the Global South, many of the researchers have themselves been white deaf and hearing people from the Global North. Later in the MobileDeaf project, a person from an ethnic minority joined the team. When Steve was seeking a research assistant for the London project, Sanchayeeta was recommended by a professional contact; while working together, Steve noted her interest in conducting more research and that she had the right skills and knowledge. Sanchayeeta then switched from research assistant to doctoral student within the project. This is another example of how networking leads to opportunities. Sanchayeeta joining the team had a profound impact on MobileDeaf in several ways. As an insider in the ethnic deaf community of London, she brought new insights and understandings. It was due to her that we could include stories from people to whom we would likely not have had access. This collaboration should not be taken for granted because it was not easy for Sanchayeeta to join a predominantly white team.

How Did We Work as a Team?

How did our team work together, and what did it mean for us to have deaf colleagues? Our language use was varied and typical for international deaf groups. The two British team members usually used BSL, and BSL was also the sign language that surrounded us in our department at Heriot-Watt University. However, this did not mean that the team always defaulted to using BSL. Calibration (see Chapter 8) was not merely something we studied but also something we ourselves did, and continue to do, both with each other and in other situations in our everyday lives. BSL, ASL, and IS were used to various extents, with some VGT, LSFB, and fingerspelled French. Gradually, the language use shifted toward more BSL, although we continued to mix sign languages. Amandine sometimes found the differences confusing between Northern Irish BSL and the BSL used in our university. Sanchayeeta sometimes got her signing mixed up with Filipino Sign Language. Annelies struggled to separate IS and BSL, and Erin kept incorporating Cambodian signs and ASL in her signing. This did not pose problems for us; we valued the flexible languaging environment.

The types of meetings we had included reading groups, writing meetings, documentary film discussions, and project meetings. Of these, only reading groups were held regularly throughout the project, initially in person and then online during the coronavirus pandemic. These presented an invaluable opportunity to critically discuss and digest articles or books relevant to our research interests, covering translanguaging, intersectionality, mobilities, language ideologies, globalization, ethnographic filmmaking, and visual methods. Some materials came from within Deaf Studies, whereas others were not about deaf people. Through our discussions, we built a common frame of reference; we were also able to practice discussing these English concepts and English texts in sign languages. Sometimes, we coined ad hoc signs for concepts we used frequently, such as "cosmopolitanism" or "translocality." Sometimes, these signs stuck; other times, they didn't.

The reading groups grew into a space to discuss all matters relating to being a deaf academic. We talked about our research positionality, our findings, our lives and research experiences (sometimes from many years ago), and being a deaf academic in a hearing-dominated system. Team members with more extensive research experience offered advice to the doctoral students on the team, but we all mentored each other as peers. In years 4–6 of the project, the reading groups enabled us to identify common patterns across the four subprojects because we drew on examples from our field sites when discussing texts. The reading group was thus key to forging and maintaining ties within the MobileDeaf team; we also believe that reading groups are productive for growing and sharing knowledge even when researchers are not working within an overarching project.

Tapping Into Networks and Identifying Locations

Ethnographers allocate time to specific places, closely observing and engaging with people within those contexts. The accessibility of these places and the willingness of people to participate as research subjects are greatly influenced by the researcher's positionality. What determines the choice of these places and participants? *Places* are usually selected with the aim of observing people's practices in relation to the specific research questions. As for *participants*, there are typically one or more key participants with whom the ethnographer builds rapport and interacts most. In unfamiliar places, researchers often are guided by gatekeepers and leaders, who introduce them to participants. Relatedly, a popular method to expand networks is *snowball sampling*, in which participants point the researcher toward other potential participants (Bryman, 2012). Deaf researchers have made use of their own deaf networks to locate potential deaf participants in other countries (Boland et al., 2015; Dikyuva et al., 2012), and, in our biographies above, we discussed the personal mobilities through which we have built up networks. Making use of and expanding these networks was key to our ethnographies; "networks" even became a keyword in our data analysis (see Chapter 7).

Within the different subprojects, we did not all draw on our networks to the same extent. Although Amandine and Erin explored a country new to them, Annelies did fieldwork in a mixture of familiar contexts and new settings, and Steve and Sanchayeeta carried out research in the city where they live. Below, we discuss our strategies in each of these contexts, beginning with the labor migration project.

When commencing this project, initially without Sanchayeeta, Steve had to actively look for places where deaf migrants gather. There were no noticeable or identifiable places, spaces, or organizations that *specifically* drew deaf migrants in London, so Steve attended as many London deaf events as possible to get an idea of which ones were attracting deaf migrants. Steve also contacted two deaf British Asian people whom he already knew; they advised him where to go, and he then made regular visits to, for example, Beckton Deaf Club and a "Deaf Café" evening in Redbridge, which were cited as two places where deaf migrants frequented. This is how he started to expand his existing network to specifically study the experiences of deaf migrants.

In all the spaces where he was observing, Steve initially approached the event's contact person to introduce himself and explain his research aims. He often would then start communicating with different deaf people and in that way learn who were migrants and who were born in the United Kingdom. This was not difficult to do because the events tended to be small and, as a new face at many of them, people would ask him about himself and what he was doing there. Thereafter, whenever Steve attended, he would be known. Deaf people were keen to support the research and would often point out deaf migrants or introduce them to Steve.

During his visits, Steve learned about other events taking place elsewhere, and he found participants via snowball sampling. This process enabled Steve to access some aspects of London deaf life that were less visible, or even deliberately hidden, and that migrants attended (e.g., a Hare Krishna event, cryptocurrency events). Steve thus acquired a broad overview of where deaf migrants gathered, and he realized how dispersed, irregular, and precarious many of these spaces were (see Chapters 4 and 7). It gradually became evident that City Lit (City Literary Institute, an adult education college in Holborn, London, popular for deaf education and BSL tuition) was a key place where many migrants studied and/or congregated with British deaf people, and where migrants' networks converged. Most of the fieldwork became focused there.

Although Steve was able to meet and observe deaf migrants in a wide variety of settings across the capital, he ultimately struggled to recruit people to engage with the research project via formal or informal interviews. Some migrants told Steve they were supportive of the research aims but did not feel they were the right people to become involved, suggesting that they were "not intelligent enough" for the research. An alternative explanation for the reluctance of deaf City Lit students in particular is that they may have become fatigued with being repeatedly asked to be filmed for college-based work, such as BSL portfolios. However, it is equally likely that they were uncertain of Steve's motives, and Steve suspected his various forms of privilege—his whiteness, Britishness (i.e., nonmigrant status), and class status (as an academic)—were factors. Although he was a deaf London resident, Steve was an outsider in terms of the migrant networks with whom he was aiming to engage. The political climate is also worth mentioning: The research was taking place just after the 2016 vote by U.K. citizens to leave the European Union, and this could well have been a factor in migrants' reluctance to be involved in research touching on their status.

As his fieldwork continued, Steve became increasingly conscious of his privilege as a citizen with a U.K. passport and thus with more freedom to travel and work than the deaf people he was seeking to interview. Many were in precarious positions: He met one person who was due to be immediately deported, another who had been threatened by other (hearing) migrants, and one who was undocumented and at risk of deportation at any moment. Trying to build trust with people across a vast urban sprawl was a new experience for Steve, too, whose previous research meetings and events had generally relied on his existing networks within the British deaf community.

This is the context in which Steve sought a female research assistant from a minority ethnic or migrant background to work with him in interviews, ethnographic filming, and other research activities, including observations at City Lit. Sanchayeeta was able to tap into the personal and professional networks she had built up in schools and organizations, including her contacts in the ethnic deaf community in London. Within a year, Sanchayeeta was promoted to doctoral researcher and developed her own research focus within the London subproject, researching the experiences of several deaf Indian women who had arrived in London around the same time as newlyweds. Some of these participants she met through her interviews with Steve, and others were identified through snowball sampling. Sanchayeeta's doctoral focus thus emerged from, and was embedded within, the larger subproject on migration.

Even after Sanchayeeta became involved in the project, there were varying rates of success in recruiting participants at City Lit, particularly for the ethnographic film *Finding Spaces to Belong*,[3] suggesting that Steve's race and gender were not the only factors in play. When people did state why they did not wish to participate, they gave many reasons. Some feared for their lives if they were seen on film, others feared a negative impact on their immigration status, and others did not want to participate for religious reasons (e.g., having converted to a different religion and not wanting to make this public). Some migrants were not confident that they had valuable information to offer. In other cases, students opened up after a few weeks, and visiting City Lit regularly was thus important for building relationships with participants (although it caused confusion for some in an English class who assumed the researchers were there to learn English). It is crucial to find a sensitive balance between taking the time to build up trust and convince people their stories are worth sharing, and respecting people's decision not to participate.

As well as observing classes at City Lit, Steve and Sanchayeeta became involved in events that deaf migrants attended, and the two researchers set up and ran events themselves. They organized a screening of *Double Discrimination*,[4] deaf filmmaker Rinkoo Barpaga's documentary about racism in the British deaf community, at the Stratford Picturehouse's monthly "888 Club" for deaf people, at which Steve had previously met many deaf migrants. The film was shown to stimulate discussion on racism in relation to migrant experiences. Steve and Sanchayeeta also presented their research at events attended by migrants, such as "Deaf Day" at City Lit and a Black History Month event. These were valuable spaces for research because they helped to identify potential interviewees and to collect evidence on deaf migrant experiences.

Whereas Steve and Sanchayeeta were able to tap into existing contacts within the city in which they lived and to use their existing networks to identify places where deaf migrants met, Erin had to navigate a country new to her. In her subproject on deaf tourism in Asia, Erin aimed to include deaf tourists, deaf people who cater to tourists, and deaf people who experience the effects of deaf tourism (e.g., in schools and organizations). Erin had initially planned to return to Cambodia, where she had studied deaf tourism (Moriarty Harrelson, 2015). However, following the closure of the deaf-owned hostel where she had planned to stay and observe, she changed her field site to Bali. This was becoming an epicenter of deaf tourism, partly due to interest in Bengkala (a village with a high percentage of deaf residents and where a local sign language, Kata Kolok, is used) and because of the popularity of a deaf tourist guide, Wahyu Cahyadi ("Bali Deaf Guide"), who had been featured in the social media posts of American deaf travel influencers Joel Barish and Calvin Young. Erin found out during her fieldwork that there was another deaf guide working

---

3. https://vimeo.com/854367099
4. https://www.bslzone.co.uk/watch/zoom-focus-2014-double-discrimination

in Indonesia: Giovanni Mansilla, a deaf man originally from France who supplies tours for deaf tourists for Travass, a travel business run by a hearing Indonesian friend, Adelia Kiranmala.

Whereas London had key locations where deaf migrants met, in Bali there was a lack of central physical places, such as cafés or hotels, where deaf tourists gathered. Given this context, it was challenging for Erin to decide where to be based. First, she stayed in Ubud because most deaf tourists seemed to go there; later, she realized that many seemed to be in the south, so she moved to Canggu. However, it ended up being more practical for Erin to meet Wahyu at the hotels where tourists were staying. Because deaf tourist activity in Bali is decentralized, Wahyu became a nexus for this subproject.

An initial challenge with recruiting participants was that, unlike the subprojects on migration in London and Kenya, time spent by tourists in Bali is limited. Most people visit Bali for 10 days to 2 weeks, giving fewer opportunities to spend time with individual tourists. It was also difficult for Erin to predict who would be traveling in Bali while she was there. Realizing the need to be proactive in finding participants, Erin posted a 2-minute video on Facebook explaining who she was, describing the project and its objectives, and asking people to contact her if they were interested in being involved. More than 50 people reposted this video on their news feeds, with hundreds of referrals through the tagging of people's names in the comments section and by personal messages via WhatsApp. The sheer density and strength of the deaf network made it possible for Erin to interview more than 40 deaf tourists from a range of countries and to observe, over 7 months, an average of one (single- or multiday) group or individual tour every week. Like Steve and Sanchayeeta, Erin also made use of snowball sampling, with participants introducing her to acquaintances who were traveling to Bali at a later date. People in deaf networks in Australia and the United Kingdom were particularly helpful with this because most of the deaf tourists in Bali were from Australia and many were part of an interconnected network of BSL and Australian Sign Language (Auslan) signers stretching between the two countries.

While the use of existing contacts and attendance at deaf events in London helped Sanchayeeta and Steve locate places and participants, and Erin relied on Wahyu's schedule and social media, Amandine had to use yet another strategy to identify key participants and places in her subproject on Kakuma Refugee Camp. She started with a single contact: Evans Burichani, a Kenyan deaf researcher, to whom she was introduced via email by Shane Gilchrist, a deaf man from Northern Ireland who had frequently visited Kenya. Evans introduced Amandine, also via email, to Anthony, a Kenyan deaf teacher in Kakuma Refugee Camp. Amandine and Anthony exchanged WhatsApp video messages before her arrival, and in Kakuma, Anthony became one of the key people who introduced Amandine to hearing contacts at, for example, the Lutheran World Federation (LWF), which runs the deaf units in primary schools. As a teacher for LWF, Anthony had built up a large network in the camp; with his support, Amandine visited various nongovernmental organizations (NGOs) and institutes to identify places where deaf refugees gathered. Those she met led her to other deaf people. The introductions by Anthony thus enabled her to engage in snowball sampling. Atem, another deaf teacher who was a refugee from South Sudan, became one of Amandine's key informants. A leader among deaf people in the camp, he had good connections with deaf refugees and understood what she was looking for as a researcher.

One NGO, Handicap International, directed Amandine to certain deaf households in the camp, but otherwise she found it challenging to identify additional places where deaf people met. After about a month, she identified small groups of deaf people meeting each other on a regular basis in a shop owned by Halimo, a deaf Sudanese woman. This became a central location for her fieldwork.

Amandine repeatedly asked deaf camp inhabitants if there were larger gatherings of deaf people, such as at football [soccer] sessions, because she had read that deaf footballers gathered in Dadaab, another refugee complex in Kenya (Youngs, 2010). One day, she learned from Atem that LWF was organizing a football event for deaf people, so she went with Anthony and Atem to the football pitch. Nobody came and when Amandine asked Atem to show her the message from LWF, she learned that Anthony had himself organized this football event to please Amandine. Amandine's quest to "find deaf spaces" thus potentially influenced patterns of gathering in the camp.

A recurring pattern in these three subprojects is that it took considerable time and effort to identify suitable sites of research in places where deaf spaces or events are not publicly advertised, take the shape of smaller informal gatherings, or occur sporadically. This was not a challenge in the professional mobility subproject conducted by Annelies. This multisited ethnography partly focused on events organized by international organizations and partly on places where deaf people study or work in international groups. The aim was to study IS in a variety of professional contexts established for sports, culture, education, religious outreach, advocacy, and research in both the Global North and Global South, and covering North–North, North–South, and South–South interactions. The main challenge in this subproject was to select a feasible yet diverse number of events and locations for the study. Mostly accompanied by a camera team and sometimes a research assistant, Annelies attended the following:

- Four conferences with a variety of language policies: the 8th Deaf Academics conference in Copenhagen (2017), the SIGN8 conference in Florianopolis (2018), the XVIII WFD Congress in Paris (2019), and the World Association of Sign Language Interpreters (WASLI) conference in Paris (2019)
- One course: Frontrunners, an annual 9-month course for international deaf youth in Denmark (2017–2018)
- One workplace: DOOR International in Nairobi, the headquarters of an international organization, where deaf people from primarily African countries translate the Bible into their sign languages (2019)
- Two sports events: the 18th Deaf Chess Olympiad in Manchester (2018) and the 19th Winter Deaflympics in Italy (2019)
- One cultural festival: Clin d'Oeil in Reims, France (2019)

Annelies thus did fieldwork in two "permanent" settings (DOOR International, Frontrunners), whereas the others emerged as deaf transnational spaces for a few days, connected to more permanent institutions (e.g., WFD). Whereas it was straightforward to select global events like the Deaflympics and the WFD congress, it was more difficult to find suitable spaces in the Global South. Annelies had heard about DOOR International in Nairobi from two American white deaf academic colleagues who had spent time there who informed her that international interactions in this venue were predominantly among deaf Africans. Plans to go to an Asian deaf youth camp and to an Asian deaf sports event both fell through at the last minute: The youth camp board in the Philippines did not give permission for filming, and the sports event was canceled due to political unrest in Hong Kong.

The need to build long-term enduring relationships with a few key participants was less acute for Annelies than for the other subprojects' researchers. The nature of the settings meant that

Annelies never engaged with the same participants for more than a few days in total. Instead, the pressure lay in making the best use of time during these brief visits and in ensuring that a nuanced picture of experiences with IS could emerge.

Annelies had various strategies for locating interviewees at the events she attended. At the Chess Olympiad, she was an entirely new face and did not bring a camera team, relying instead on introductions by Ian Carmichael, a Scottish deaf man and father of a colleague at Heriot-Watt University, who had recommended that she attend. At the other events, however, there were always several people she already knew. She knew the Frontrunners teachers from having given guest lectures there, and she had also worked with them on a book chapter (Kusters et al., 2015). Of the Brazilian organizers of SIGN8, one had studied with Annelies's husband at Frontrunners in 2007 (and had come to their wedding), and others were those she had met before at conferences. At Clin d'Oeil, she recognized performers and audience members she had met at conferences, at Frontrunners, and in various contexts when living in Belgium, India, Germany, and the United Kingdom. At DOOR, Annelies recognized deaf people from India and Burundi whom she had met before. In each of the settings, Annelies took care to also talk with many people she did not know or to whom she had not been introduced, by observing them (e.g., when they gave presentations) and then approaching them, following the conventions for new introductions in these settings.

The ways that places and people in the different subprojects were identified demonstrate how central the concept of networks is for understanding deaf sociality (see Chapter 7). Some of us have been able to tap into our personal deaf networks, but all of us have also expanded our networks and tapped into other deaf people's networks—on Facebook, through assistants, and by snowball sampling. Deaf ethnographers are reliant on successfully building contact with key participants, as there is typically a small range of places and people to choose from. There being only two deaf tourist guides in Bali, it was crucial for Erin that they agreed to participate in the project; the same was true for Amandine in Kakuma, where Anthony and Atem were among very few deaf leaders. These key informants, and in some instances also research assistants, directed us to situations, events, or people likely to be helpful in ethnographic fieldwork.

Informal and Formal Consent

In the first instance, potential participants typically give informal consent to the research in conversation with the researcher, by agreeing to interact with the researcher and/or to be interviewed. The next step is to gain "informed consent," which is a formal agreement between researcher and participant. MobileDeaf had a common template for procuring informed consent; however, the process necessarily differed between settings.[5]

A participant information sheet and informed consent form was created for all MobileDeaf subprojects. These forms were templates created as part of the ethics procedure agreed upon with

---

5. In some locations, a first step is obtaining a research permit. Amandine had to apply for two different research permits before being allowed to undertake fieldwork in the camp; for these, she had to wait in Nairobi for weeks. Erin had to obtain a permit in Indonesia as well, a process that can take 6 months or more and that requires sponsorship from an Indonesian counterpart—a challenging relationship to develop for a deaf researcher because of communication access barriers.

the funder (the ERC) and could be edited to fit the methodologies used in the subprojects. On the forms, it was specified what types of data were to be gathered (e.g., interview data, video recordings, photographs) and how they would be used for dissemination of research findings (e.g., presentations, publications, ethnographic film). There were different levels of consent, ranging from full use to selected use of data and from full anonymization to nonmasking. Over the years of the project, the templates had to be revised several times when ethical regulations or fieldwork circumstances changed—for example, during the coronavirus pandemic, when Sanchayeeta took her ethnography online.

The language and the register of the consent forms conformed to strict ERC guidelines, making them inaccessible for many participants. We had to ensure that the consent procedures were appropriate for deaf people; this was informed by our previous experience and by other researchers who have considered informed consent with deaf participants (Dikyuva et al., 2012; Singleton et al., 2014; Young & Temple, 2014). Gaining informed consent for ethnographic fieldwork is particularly complicated and consists of more steps than gaining informed consent for an interview study (see Kusters, 2012). We prepared several solutions: having the form translated into a local language (Portuguese, for Annelies's fieldwork in Brazil), creating a signed video translation (BSL, for Sanchayeeta's fieldwork in London), and translating the form live to the participant while recording this process (all subprojects). Gaining informed consent was most challenging (and sometimes problematic) when working with people for whom participating in research was entirely new. It was difficult for some participants to understand the purpose of ethnography; for example, they assumed we were conducting research in order to improve services for migrants in London or to help refugees in Kenya be resettled.

It is not possible to ask consent of each individual person who is observed, interacted with, or captured on camera. As a rule, we asked for formal informed consent from people who participated in planned research activities, such as interviews and focus groups. The act of signing the form was often preceded by informal announcements and/or obtaining informal informed consent. For example, Amandine first participated informally in Kakuma Refugee Camp by meeting people and explaining about her research in conversation. During these interactions, Amandine was able to learn the basics of Kenyan Sign Language (KSL), a crucial component for ensuring consent, and to engage with deaf leaders Anthony and Atem, who gradually came to understand well what she wanted to do and could assist in explaining the project to others. Of the 80–100 deaf refugees Amandine met, she identified several people as potential key participants, and she organized a formal consent procedure as a public event. No filmed interviews took place before this.

Because most of Amandine's participants had limited English literacy, the written English consent forms were not treated as standalone. Amandine explained her research objectives and the consent forms in KSL, and Anthony assisted by re-signing the forms' contents in KSL, using signs, examples, and explanations that would be better understood by participants. After this, the forms were filled in, during which the participants were individually assisted by Amandine and by the deaf leaders in the camp who acted as gatekeepers. The whole process of asking consent was video recorded to evidence the procedure. Amandine suspected that some people did not fully understand the consent forms, even after explanations by Anthony and Atem, but they seemed to trust Amandine because of this mediation and they signed the forms.

In some subprojects, participants signed consent forms *after* interviews. Knowing what they had just shared with the researcher, they could specify on the consent form if the researcher could use "all" or "selections" of the interview content. In the latter case, the researcher was required to contact the participant to ask whether particular parts of their narrative could be used in writing or films.

We knew it was especially important to clarify issues of anonymity and how photos and video-recorded images were to be used. Could only the researcher see the footage? Could parts be shown in presentations? Could interview quotations be posted on the MobileDeaf website? Could video images be used for our films? Would we have to check each image with the participant before using it, or could we use anything? In Annelies's research, only two of 145 video-recorded people did not want the interview recording to be used for the ethnographic films. However, quite a few people wanted Annelies to check with them before quoting them in the film or in writing, and a few specified which parts of the interview should not be used—for example, asking Annelies to leave out where they had talked negatively about ASL or Americans. In London, full anonymization was important for several participants, and many were reluctant to be filmed due to their vulnerable migration status; conversely, some Kakuma participants believed that being interviewed on film would help their resettlement process.

Researchers often have a better understanding of what happens to publications than their participants. Most participants understood that not anonymizing them would mean that they could be visible online and in print. However, not all participants used the internet extensively, especially Amandine's refugee participants and some of Erin's Balinese participants. It can be difficult to predict what impact naming someone will have. Even when a person is comfortable being named or visible at the point of the research, later they may regret having their personal stories, faces, and opinions being exposed in an ethnographic account or film. For example, several participants for the film *Finding Spaces to Belong* withdrew their consent after being interviewed. Also, deaf people who have been named in an ethnographic account of an exotified place can be easily looked up by journalists, researchers, or tourists in the future (see Chapter 6; Braithwaite, 2020). Pseudonymizing or anonymizing is not necessarily an easy solution because the identity of "a deaf migrant from country X living in city Y" can easily be surmised by an informed reader. This can be mitigated by leaving out details, but in doing so we also lose insights into context and intersectionality. Furthermore, many of our participants wanted their names to be used *because* they wanted their stories to be shared: Anonymizing people's stories and roles in history means removing a key element of deaf emancipation processes (De Clerck & Lutalo-Kiingi, 2018). As a result, most personal names in this book are real names, but these are interspersed with pseudonyms. The ethnographer has to carefully consider when to name people and which aspects of their identities and stories to obscure, and we made our decisions about what to share and how on a case-by-case basis.

Participant Observation

In the field, the ethnographer aims to learn about settings and from people by conducting "participant observation"—that is, by participating in the setting and observing what happens around them. One moment, ethnographers may be in the background (e.g., at the back of a classroom); the next, they may participate more actively by chatting with people, asking questions, responding to their questions, and doing things with or alongside them. In our settings, "doing things with" or being "mobile with" (see Bissell, 2009) included eating and drinking together, taking a guided tour together, walking to school or work together, watching a sports competition together, and attending a conference together. Most of these were things that participants were already doing rather than activities planned by the ethnographer. However, participants also do things differently *because* of the ethnographer's presence, such as guiding the ethnographer to various places, observing the ethnographer, and organizing gatherings for the ethnographer. Observing and participating teach an ethnographer about the field, its rules, and the people; the participants also learn about the researcher, including what they are seeking and how they work (Blommaert & Dong, 2020). At times, we blended in (e.g., as a tourist, conference attendee, or pub goer), whereas in other situations we stuck out by virtue of our positionality or the nature of our activities as researchers.

Shifts between the extent of our observation versus participation enabled us to experience settings from various "outsider" and "insider" and "observer" and "participant" positions in the field. An ethnographer works systematically toward understanding certain themes within the setting. If the setting is *new to them*, they start by aiming to notice and observe "everything" to develop as broad and thorough an impression as possible. By systematically observing a broad range of situations or themes repeatedly and exploring them on different scales, from different angles, and from different people's perspectives, a layered understanding of these phenomena will emerge. Small events are seen in larger contexts. Ethnography allows us "to see, in microscopic events, effects of macroscopic structures, phenomena and processes" (Blommaert & Dong, 2020, p. 18). Patterns in behavior will appear, and the ethnographer will increasingly zoom in on specific themes emerging from the setting. When conducting participant observation in a site that is *already familiar*, the researcher will aim to notice or discover aspects of the setting or theme of which they were previously unaware, and they will explore familiar phenomena from new angles and in more depth.

This learning process, laid down in extensive field notes, ultimately results in theoretical statements by way of an inductive analysis. Writing field notes is challenging: The researcher does not know in advance exactly what will be relevant later or which themes will emerge as crucial (Emerson et al., 2011). Field notes tell us "a story about an *epistemic process*," which Blommaert and Dong (2020, p. 37; emphasis in original) explain as the way in which ethnographers process new information, interpret this information, and make connections between events happening at different times and in different places. The field notes are a record of the learning process and of how the fieldworkers' gaze and understanding shift over time.

We recorded our observations, whether jottings (quick notes on the go) or extended field notes, on various platforms. Amandine always carried in her trouser pocket a small notebook to jot down ideas wherever they occurred or to note observations during conversations with deaf refugees. Steve would usually draw a visual map of the outline of the Deaf Club, pub, or event he visited and note the ethnicity of the people present (if known), as well as their gender and estimation of their age. Erin and Annelies found their smartphones useful for making quick notes on the move, both for writing and for adding photographs and video clips. When observing in a classroom or conference hall, a laptop or iPad was also used for jottings. Making jottings openly was a reminder for participants that we were conducting research. Where making notes was not possible or appropriate, we memorized details to later type up in extended field notes. We usually wrote our extended field notes in our first written language: English for Erin, Sanchayeeta, and Steve; French for Amandine; and Dutch for Annelies. In these field notes, we would detail our observations as well as what we could remember about each conversation, and we made decisions about what or whom to follow up with. We also included methodological notes and reflections on our positions in the field.

Participant observation often involves language learning, although the process of language learning, as well as researcher language proficiency, is often obscured in ethnographic accounts (Gibb et al., 2020). The amount of language learning required differed between our sites, ranging from learning a new sign language to a degree of fluency to learning "bits" of other sign languages. Generally, it is easier for deaf people to learn new sign languages than for hearing people to learn new spoken languages within a short time period. For us, sign language learning during research typically happened by way of interacting with people and picking up signs from them. When we were not yet fluent in a sign language, we included elements from other sign language(s) and relied on features such as fingerspelling in English and mouthings based on different spoken languages; we also relied on calibration strategies such as using a larger signing space, using highly transparent signs, and engaging in enactments (see Chapter 8 for a fuller exploration of such processes). This does not mean that communication in sign language always goes smoothly. Communicating can be challenging if the linguistic and cultural distance is very large. We will give examples of this below.

Our approaches to participant observation differed considerably between settings. Erin started her research by performing online data collection, following on social media several deaf travel influencers who were on months-long tours of different parts of the world. Observing these people's content, the topics they chose to write or sign about, and the hashtags they used led to insights into what was important to deaf travelers and what differentiated deaf tourism from "regular" tourism. For example, as well as posting photos of the places they visited, many also posted about the deaf people they encountered, their experiences with languaging, and their views of the barriers faced by deaf people outside of Europe and North America.

At the beginning of the project, Erin hired Wahyu to guide her around Bali and offered him the role of a research assistant. He declined, preferring to focus on guiding, but he did allow Erin to accompany him on different tours for deaf tourists; she initially participated as a tourist but increasingly took on the role of observer, making jottings or short videos for expansion into field notes later. Erin often sat in the front seat of Wahyu's car and asked him questions as he drove. Wahyu would then talk to Erin at length about different topics, such as his feelings about his relationship with his hearing wife's family, who had helped him set up his business, and stories about his earlier life and employment.

In her first month of fieldwork, Erin took classes in BISINDO (Indonesian Sign Language) at the deaf school in Denpasar, partly to meet deaf leaders and researchers, but also because it was a way of acclimating to Bali. However, she did not use BISINDO very much during her fieldwork because most deaf people in Bali knew some ASL or IS. Erin also learned some Kata Kolok when she was in Bengkala, the "deaf village." The tourists that Erin interviewed were mostly ASL or Auslan signers; Erin could understand Auslan because of similarities with BSL, which she had learned at Heriot-Watt University, where MobileDeaf was based. She used IS with tourists from Europe.

During the drive between sites, Erin would actively ask tourists questions about how they communicated with other people of different nationalities and why they chose to visit less "touristy" sites such as deaf schools. Erin found it easier to connect with deaf people from India, the United States, and Australia, whom she knew personally or through friends of friends. She found it harder to connect with Wahyu on a personal level, perhaps because of their classed, gendered, and racialized positionalities, but most likely because he was very busy with his work. Erin's status as a white, deaf, female researcher from the United States certainly had an impact on the ways in which she was perceived, and there were some limitations on her ability to connect with Indonesian men. In the late 20th century, Bali emerged as a site of sex tourism for women; young Balinese male sex workers continue to be sought by Japanese, European, and Australian female tourists, and this may have influenced how Erin was perceived by some men in Bali.

In general, deaf tourists understood Erin's role as a researcher; however, Wahyu did not seem to fully understand why Erin wanted to follow him around for several weeks. This type of confusion is typical in ethnography because people can understand the purpose of interviews more easily than participant observation. When Erin asked to join Wahyu on a tour of the Monkey Forest with a group of young men from Germany, he responded, "Again? Really? I have already taken you two times before. Are you okay with seeing the same place again and again?" Erin visited the same tourist spots in Bali many times with different tourist groups, and she spent a lot of time on the road in gridlock traffic. As a result, Erin often wrote her field notes in the car.

Erin also traveled without Wahyu. She visited Yogyakarta with deaf tourists to observe the phenomenon of "informal" guiding of deaf tourists by deaf people who live in the area (see Chapter 7). She also visited the "deaf village" Bengkala several times, observing on two occasions camera crews from Japan and Singapore who were there creating documentaries about the deaf villagers (Moriarty, in press; see also Chapter 6). The days Erin spent in Bengkala were an opportunity to observe the impact of tourism and research on dynamics within the village. In all these settings, Erin took notes on what she observed, including particular words or phrases that were used often and recurring themes such as concerns about sign language imperialism and "the deaf economy."

After 5 months in the field, two white deaf cameramen from Belgium in their early 30s (Jorn) and late 20s (Jente) arrived for 6 weeks of filming for the MobileDeaf project's ethnographic film. They went on tours with Wahyu and also joined a 10-day tour with a group of multiethnic deaf people in their 20s and 30s from Europe, the United Kingdom, and the United States. This was organized by the company Travass, led by the other deaf guide working in Bali, Giovanni Mansilla. Erin and the cameramen constantly sought a balance between blending in as part of a tourist group and being a group apart (i.e., a team). They were also always looking for a balance between "insider" and "outsider" positions. As they were making an ethnographic film in which they did not participate themselves, they could not fully participate in the tourist groups they interacted with (this topic is also explored in *Birthing a Genre*). At the same time, they *were* part of the various tourist groups and the Travass trip, and paid the full fee for participating. The team spent time with the other tourists *as tourists*, without doing any filming; however, they also distanced themselves from the groups when filming, planning, and conducting interviews. Tourists took lots of group photos and sometimes took two group photos on the same occasion: one with the team included and one without.

Over time, Jorn's role shifted. Erin felt that he had an ethnographer's disposition and found that some tourists, particularly younger women, responded better to him. She asked him to take the lead in some fieldwork, using their positionalities strategically to ensure productive interviews. At first, Jorn was reluctant, saying that he was "just a cameraman" and jokingly using the Kata Kolok sign for "boss" when referring to Erin; over time, however, he began to see himself as a co-researcher.

Although Erin was able to blend in as a tourist at times, Amandine always stood out as an "outsider" in Kakuma Refugee Camp. For one thing, she was not allowed to stay with deaf refugees or live in the camp for safety reasons. Due to recurrent armed robberies, thefts, rapes, and killings, the Kenyan government stations policemen in the camp between 6 in the morning and 6 in the evening; after sunset, the camp is not guarded, and violence often recurs. Thus, every evening, Amandine had to return to the compound where she lived, a few minutes' walk from Kakuma Refugee Camp. Transportation inside the camp was often difficult: The hot weather and distances of up to 15 kilometers made it arduous to navigate on foot, so Amandine traveled with teachers or staff from the NGOs in cars or by the popular taxi motorbike, called a *bodaboda*.

When Amandine visited places frequented by deaf people, such as the deaf units in primary schools, she would mostly observe without interrupting; when accompanying deaf camp inhabitants to various destinations or waiting in line with them, she would ask questions about their everyday activities, where deaf people lived in the area, and their communication strategies with deaf and hearing people in the camp. Amandine arrived at the camp with some knowledge of KSL because she had started picking it up in Nairobi during the few weeks spent waiting for her research permit. Her previous knowledge of ASL helped her to understand KSL because KSL has absorbed some ASL signs. ASL was also used in the camp. When Amandine and camp residents did not understand each other, they would fingerspell words in English, use gestures, or use ASL. Amandine found communication with educated deaf refugees easier because deaf people who had not been to school signed in a different way, using what they called "village signs" (see Chapters 3 and 8). Atem or Anthony would then translate into KSL for her.

Once Amandine had located Halimo's shop, a place where deaf people gathered, she began to start her day there. Halimo would update Amandine on news regarding other deaf refugees, and Amandine would chat with the people who visited. Conversations varied in theme: courses taken by deaf refugees; questions of resettlement; and everyday news about fights, arguments, new relationships, and family problems. On evenings and weekends, Amandine would eat with Anthony at his compound in the camp, and deaf refugees would often join them. This is an example of how the presence of researchers themselves also creates or expands deaf spaces (see Kusters, 2012, for other examples). Indeed, it is impossible to study a place or event as if you are not there yourself (Blommaert & Dong, 2020).

Responses to deaf researchers' race have been noted by white deaf people who do research in situations where the majority demographic is not white (Boland et al., 2015; Kusters, 2012) and where the researcher's race was associated with a geographical location in which the researchers had not grown up (e.g., China in the case of Hou, 2017; America in the case of Kusters, 2012). The presence of a deaf white person was a curiosity in the camp, and deaf refugees were initially shocked to discover that Amandine was deaf because many of them expressed surprise that a white person could be disabled. When Amandine went to crowded places, such as the United Nations High Commissioner for Refugees (UNHCR) Protection Delivery Unit or a dancing session on the street with hearing Sudanese people, she was stared at for a long time. Amandine felt she could not observe deaf refugees' everyday lives without having an obvious impact on the settings she was in because she could not blend in. Frequently, when visiting deaf people in the camp, hearing camp inhabitants would also come to watch her chat with deaf people. Sometimes, it became crowded and Amandine left. This was different from Erin's experience in Bali, where tourism is a major industry and white visitors are not unusual; indeed, most (although not all) of Erin's tourist participants were white.

Later in the fieldwork period, Amandine's husband Adam, a deaf white man, came for a 3-week visit and accompanied her around the camp in all her interactions, visiting houses, the Protection Delivery Unit, the deaf units, and church. Adam could communicate with deaf refugees using IS mixed with ASL. Amandine observed that some male refugees (including some of her key participants) interacted with him differently than with her. During visits to their houses, the men shared more personal stories when Adam was present, showing childhood pictures, dancing outfits, and tribal flags. Some deaf men discussed marriage and dowry with Adam and talked with him privately (see Kusters, 2012, for a similar situation in Ghana). Amandine had similarly gendered conversations with deaf female refugees but rarely with deaf men. Anthony, the deaf Kenyan teacher, had often invited Amandine to his house alone; during Adam's visit, he made more frequent invitations to both of them and also invited other deaf male refugees to join them. Back in the compound, Adam shared his observations and conversations with Amandine, enabling her to learn more about what kept male deaf refugees occupied.

There were additional implications regarding Amandine's position as a white person. Kakuma Refugee Camp is managed by UNHCR, which has responsibility for providing legal protection and meeting people's basic needs, such as shelter, food, water, sanitation, and medical care; it is also responsible for repatriation to people's homelands or their resettlement outside the camp. Because UNHCR is managed mostly by white people, refugees tend to associate any white people they meet in the camp with UNHCR. Because Amandine is white, some refugees made strategic use of her white privilege, noticing that her presence gave them quicker access to certain spaces and that UNHCR agents were cooperative with her (see Chapter 10). Additionally, several deaf refugees retained the expectation that she could assist them, despite her reiterating that she had come to learn about their stories and could not directly influence resettlement processes. Presumably due to their assumptions about Amandine's power to make changes in their lives, deaf refugees approached her to make complaints about their living conditions in the camp, including to report domestic abuse and conflicts with neighbors and regarding problems or confusion about registration with UNHCR. These issues are common in the camp but are exacerbated for deaf people (see Chapter 10), and the lack of access to bureaucratic processes, questions of immobility, and refugees' hopes for the future became central themes in Amandine's research.

Amandine also gathered data from organizations. When she first arrived, she was introduced to representatives from the Refugee Affairs Secretariat, various humanitarian nonprofits, NGOs, and key compounds and institutions around the camp. This was with the support of a BSL interpreter, who was with her during her first 2 weeks in Kakuma. Later, through informal conversations in written English with hearing staff working in the LWF office, Amandine gathered data about the management of deaf educational programs. In this way, Amandine puzzled together pieces of the everyday lives of deaf refugees in the camp and the role that different (deaf and nondeaf) institutions played in their lives.

Whereas Erin's research featured institutions (deaf schools) as (volun)tourist destinations, in Amandine's research, deaf units in schools and deaf vocational courses were havens for deaf refugees, in stark contrast with other institutions in the camp where they experienced a lack of access. Additionally, homes were important places for research in the camp, in particular Halimo's home. This was different in the London-based subproject, where most people were not comfortable receiving researchers in their homes. This limited the opportunities for participant observation within domestic spaces; instead, as outlined previously, institutions and public deaf spaces were central research sites in this subproject.

For Steve, communication with deaf migrants generally took place in BSL, but there also were instances of BSL being mixed with IS or the interviewee's sign language (e.g., from Bulgaria, Lithuania, Romania). There were some occasions where Steve found it very difficult to communicate, especially with migrants who used a lot of signs from their country of origin. Sanchayeeta used BSL and ISL with her participants, and her knowledge of Filipino Sign Language helped her to communicate with migrants who used ASL. Sanchayeeta noted that mouthing in English helped to bridge different language backgrounds.

Many times, Steve and Sanchayeeta were asked if they wanted to get involved in the activities of those they observed: to participate in religious settings, to play games, and to contribute to monetary investment schemes. As with Amandine, it was also common for Steve and Sanchayeeta to be asked for help, often with immigration advice or advocacy support, but also for emotional support (sometimes, in times of acute crisis). This indicates that the deaf spaces visited by Steve and Sanchayeeta remain vital places of deaf support, where knowledge and assistance of all kinds are exchanged (see Chapters 4 and 7).

In the early stages of her involvement, Sanchayeeta's participant observation was mostly conducted alongside Steve, and sometimes Jorn. On some occasions, she had her son with her (age around 10 during that time), and sometimes her 2-year-old daughter in the later stages. Participants saw Sanchayeeta as a mother, and she felt that they were particularly open with her because of this. However, with hindsight, some may also have been cautious about what they said or did because Sanchayeeta's son could understand some signs. In her solo research into the experience of female deaf marriage migrants, she had fewer opportunities to do participant observation, due in part to the pandemic and also to her own pregnancy and those of two of her five participants; this, and their subsequent maternity periods, limited their mobilities within the city. Sanchayeeta's methodology consisted mostly of interviews conducted online, and each participant was interviewed multiple times (see next section).

Sanchayeeta felt able to connect with her participants through her positionality as a brown deaf woman who is part of a minority community in London with similar foodways and other cultural markers (e.g., Indian gestures), and who has visited India and met Indian deaf people known to some of the participants. However, she also experienced being an outsider due to not having grown up in India and not being part of the extensive Indian networks of deaf people. Unlike her participants, Sanchayeeta is a born Londoner (not an immigrant herself) and is not constrained by her family's cultural values (she is not required to get married or expected to follow Indian cultural norms). Her researcher positionality was further complicated by friendships—those between participants and those developing between herself and participants. As participants kept aspects of their lives hidden from each other, Sanchayeeta, who had detailed knowledge of their lives through the interviews, had to be careful about what she revealed to whom socially. Due to their long-term involvement in the project and the personal information they shared, participants expected to learn personal details about Sanchayeeta in return. They also asked advice on pregnancy, postbirth, and breastfeeding issues, as well as for BSL-to-English translations of documents (see Chapter 8 for an example) and support with job applications and studying. At times, Sanchayeeta experienced these requests as an invasion of her personal space and time, and she chose not to respond to nonurgent text messages and to decline some invitations. One participant came to rely on her as her main source of study support, so Sanchayeeta encouraged her to ask her teachers and classmates as well.

Because Sanchayeeta went on maternity leave in the middle of her doctoral research, the study extended over 4 years. Maintaining a years long relationship with a very small number of participants led to long-term perspectives on migration and on the impacts of changes in the women's lives (see Chapter 10). Yet, it was challenging to maintain the relationships. When some of Sanchayeeta's participants started to show reluctance to undertake further interviews, she realized that more informal in-person interactions were needed. However, in the middle of her research, she had moved 1.5 hours from London, which limited her opportunities to attend events in the city. When the country started to open up after the pandemic lockdowns, Sanchayeeta met with her five participants individually for coffee or in their homes; she also complemented her interview-based study by engaging in a limited amount of participant observation by attending meals and parties with them and other Indian deaf migrants and British South Asian deaf people.

Like Sanchayeeta, Annelies made heavy use of interviews; she also employed various ratios of observation to participation in her different field sites. In most of the conference settings, Annelies was attending as presenter. In this regard, Annelies was, like Steve and Sanchayeeta, doing "ethnography at home," because her research took place at events that were already familiar to her. In some field sites where Annelies participated with a camera team, she did an especially high number of interviews, and there were fewer opportunities to observe without cameras and to have informal chats with attendees. In contrast, at the Chess Olympiad in Manchester, she took the position of observer and had solely informal conversations with others about their experiences. Her attendance at this event, during which she did not do any interviews or filming, was beneficial when approaching the delegations of chess players for interviews at the Deaflympics 1.5 years later because she recognized several people and they recognized her. People, themes, and sites being linked in circuitous ways is typical for multisited ethnography (Wulff, 2002).

In the different sites, Annelies mostly knew in advance what she wanted to cover; this was necessary given the short duration of the events. At the 2019 WFD congress, she focused on the institution of IS interpreting as experienced by interpreters and participants; at the DOOR institution in Kenya, she studied the ideologies attached to deaf multilingual interactions outside of Europe. Research in some settings informed others; the settings were nodes in translocal networks (see Chapter 7), which were connected via institutional histories. In advance of the 2019 Winter Deaflympics, for example, Annelies had done interviews at the WFD congress and SIGN8 conference with people also immersed in the sports world, who compared dynamics in the sports and other international deaf networks. This helped to anticipate some of the issues that would come up at the Winter Deaflympics.

In certain settings, working with a research assistant was crucial. The 2019 Winter Deaflympics in north Italy took place over 12 days in five different locations, with more than a thousand attendees. Annelies was not familiar with the sports context and sports networks, and therefore preemptively employed a research assistant: Dawn Jani Birley, a former Deaflympics athlete with a wide network in the deaf sports world and who was an expert in IS. Dawn provided Annelies with context and helped her identify and approach participants. At the WFD congress, a 4-day event attended by thousands of people, Annelies worked with her husband Sujit (with whom she had worked on ethnographic projects before). While she spent most of her time interviewing, he carried out observations, video recording field notes several times a day with a focus on participants' experiences of accessing (or not accessing) the conference. The four different deaf camera operators with whom Annelies worked over 2.5 years of filming also shared their observations with her, which she fed into her field notes. Additionally, participant observation happened *within* the research team. Both the deaf cameramen at the Winter Deaflympics and the research assistant Dawn were (former) top sportspeople who talked about their own experiences in the deaf sports world. This led to additional insights for Annelies. (Note: see *Birthing a Genre* for brief interviews with assistants and cameramen.)

In terms of positionality and connecting with research participants, Annelies experienced this study as profoundly different from her previous research in Suriname, Ghana, and India. Professional mobility is an activity in which she has often engaged, and she could blend in at many of the spaces she visited. Sometimes, however, her positionality as researcher (rather than journalist, supporter, or tourist) had to be clarified. At WFD and Clin d'Oeil, a press badge helped her to access some spaces as observer (e.g., backstage) and to approach unfamiliar people, but it also created some confusion about her role. Annelies did participant observation in unfamiliar spaces, too, such as at DOOR International in Kenya and the Winter Deaflympics, where the learning curve for understanding what was going on was steep. However, at the Deaflympics, she had both a press badge and Dawn's support, and those at the DOOR translation center were welcoming, highly skilled in communicating internationally, and happy to talk about their experiences. Annelies's knowledge of BSL, ISL, VGT, and basic ASL helped when communicating, especially in situations where not everyone communicated in IS. Although Annelies did not have the time to build up lasting research relationships with her participants, she found that people were almost always cooperative when she approached them for conversations or interviews, which is probably typical behavior in the context of professional mobility. Many of the deaf people she encountered were already used to being interviewed, although occasionally Annelies could not successfully engage with people who had very different linguistic backgrounds from hers and with whom she had little knowledge in common, such as with some athletes at the Deaflympics and some performers at Clin d'Oeil.

We have noted our respective positionalities in various sections previously, including our race, nationality, and citizenship; previous experience of living and working; language knowledges; and age and stage of life. We have also noted that, whether planned or unplanned, working together with a person of the opposite gender led to the emergence of additional and different data: Erin with Jorn the cameraman, Steve with Sanchayeeta as his research assistant, and Amandine with Adam when he visited her. We want to explicitly comment on race again. For Erin, Annelies, Steve, and Amandine (as well as Jorn and Adam), our whiteness had an obvious impact on the type of data and people to which we had access. No one has said to our faces "I can't talk about this with a white person," but it would be disingenuous to take this to mean that our whiteness had no influence. This was explicit for Amandine, who was openly seen as a representative of UNHCR; it was unquestionably also in play when Annelies, Erin, and Steve were working with people of color and people from ethnic minorities, who tended to give no or minimal details about their experiences of racism, microaggressions, and white fragility (see Eddo-Lodge, 2017). This was a weakness in the initial project design and something that we will reflect on in the design of future projects. Sanchayeeta and Sujit were much more successful in discussing these themes with participants and contributed crucial insights; additionally, the screening of *Double Discrimination*, at which Rinkoo Barpaga gave a presentation, successfully prompted discussions of racism. Sanchayeeta and Sujit also experienced some barriers of their own. In the London subproject, Sanchayeeta found it easier to connect with deaf people from ethnic minorities than with white deaf Eastern European migrant women. Sujit connected with a large number of participants from the Global South at the WFD congress but, as a man, sometimes found that Muslim women were reluctant to speak to him. Religion also played a role in Amandine's study because most of her participants were religious, and Amandine did not want her own Christianity to be a barrier to engagement with Muslim deaf people. She avoided talking about religion with most participants; however, their shared Christianity helped her connect with some of the key participants. In these latter examples, race, gender, and religion all impacted how we connected (or not) with our participants, demonstrating the benefits of a team approach for studies of this nature.

There are also less-discussed elements of our positionalities that impacted how we approached research. For example, all of us identify as queer; although we all had straight-passing privileges at the time of research due to being in relationships with a person of the opposite sex, our sexual orientations and past experiences helped us empathize with some of our participants' testimony. Experiences of ill health and disability also inform our experiences of doing participant observation (and, indeed, the writing process). Challenges in relation to states of the bodymind are often omitted from discussions of participant observation; it seems more common to consider factors such as gender and race. However, participant observation is a difficult, demanding, intensive, and immersive research approach. Like many other (deaf) researchers, each of us has dealt with the impact of various experiences of, and changes to, our states of bodymind, including "invisible" disabilities, neurodivergence, and health challenges such as depression, pregnancy and lactation, and advanced cancer, resulting in overstimulation, exhaustion, insomnia, anxiety, high stress levels, and difficult emotions. To give some examples, Steve has had to be absent from the MobileDeaf project for stretches of time to manage a chronic and complex mental health diagnosis. Erin, an introvert, found participant observation over multiple-day group tours, including room-sharing, to be highly draining. During her fieldwork, Amandine had to deal with symptoms of her undiagnosed cancer, which made fieldwork particularly challenging. Amandine was only able to complete the planned first stage of her fieldwork because her diagnosis and treatment (and later, the pandemic and her subsequent pregnancy and maternity leave) meant she was unable to return to the field. Annelies juggled short but intensive periods of fieldwork, managing the team, and other high-stress professional demands with having young children, one of whom was still breastfeeding during the first year of fieldwork. Additionally, conducting long-term fieldwork alone, far from home (or at home during a pandemic), can be isolating. Amandine slept and ate in a compound with only hearing people, where she felt excluded. Sanchayeeta started her fieldwork while pregnant, behind a computer screen at her parents' home in the midst of a pandemic; following maternity leave, she continued to work at home with a baby and minimal support, affecting her mental well-being.

Often, these experiences had to be suppressed in the field, and we typically did not disclose our states of bodymind to participants. "Hiding" mental ill health, masking neurodivergence, and repressing emotions takes a toll on the researcher, the impact extending beyond the field. Amandine experienced vicarious trauma from the stories of abuses, rapes, and deaths that deaf people in the camp told her in vivid visual detail. Atem, one of her key participants, passed away during the writing of this book, and Yanto, one of Erin's key participants in Bali, died just after she completed her film. These deaths were deeply upsetting and made it difficult to engage with certain data sets. During the coronavirus lockdowns, Erin also received many desperate messages from people in Bali, a country almost completely dependent on tourism, asking for funds because they were on the brink of starvation. Although we saw the "problems" caused by states of our bodyminds as being "to overcome" or "to circumvent," and we tried to minimize the impact on our work, several of us have had to pull out of planned research activities, and three of us have dealt with months-long disruptions.

Interviewing

Participant observation is the core of ethnography; however, there is a common misconception that ethnographic research *is* interviewing. Even though conducting interviews does not make research ethnographic, many ethnographies do include interviews of various types (Blommaert & Dong, 2020), and this was the case in each of the MobileDeaf subprojects. *Ethnographic interviews* do not take the form of interrogations but are conversations intended to explore topics; in these, the researcher tries to avoid behaving like an interviewer because participants will then behave like interviewees (Blommaert & Dong, 2020). In contrast, *semistructured interviews* are based on a pre-created list of questions but are responsive to the interviewee: The questions may be reordered or omitted entirely, allowing the interviewer the flexibility to follow up on points made by the interviewee (Bryman, 2012). Although we shared common research questions, we did not create a shared list of interview questions; all of us constructed our own, and the way we conducted ethnographic and semistructured interviews was specific to the subprojects' settings. We interviewed people where it suited them, often within or close to the settings where we did participant observation. This resulted in an interesting range of interview locations, including a plane, a football pitch, a hospital, auditoriums, mosques and churches, cafés and restaurants, cars, classrooms, the beach, conference rooms, a UN office, a boat, and participants' homes. Some of our interviews were with people who were our friends or colleagues prior to the research, especially in the projects on professional mobility and labor and marriage migration. The prior familiarity in "acquaintance interviews" (Roiha & Iikkanen, 2022) can lead to more honest and in-depth responses as researchers build on existing rapport and shared prior knowledge. Some of us also made use of other interview formats, such as focus groups and the use of visual data (e.g., drawings, language portraits) to elicit narratives (see, e.g., Kusters & De Meulder, 2019); we do not discuss these here.

Each subproject had a different ratio of interviews to participant observation. Annelies's multisited study was heavily based on interviews and focus groups, whereas Amandine's study was more heavily based on participant observation, although she interviewed six deaf people toward the end of her fieldwork. Erin did interviews with people whom she had traveled alongside and observed, but she also interviewed tourists whom she had not observed at all; conversely, some tourists she observed did not have time to be interviewed. Steve mostly interviewed people he had met during participant observation, some of them with Sanchayeeta. Due to the pandemic, Sanchayeeta's individual study was based primarily on interviewing. Below, we explore the implications of these different balances and how different interviewing styles were used in different contexts.

In the London-based migration subproject, Steve interviewed 12 people by himself; Steve and Sanchayeeta interviewed nine together; Sanchayeeta interviewed five by herself, and eight with Jorn for an ethnographic film on migration to London. The interviewees came from a wide range of countries, including Brazil, Ghana, Burundi, Romania, Somalia, Italy, Pakistan, Afghanistan, India, Lebanon, Canada, Czech Republic, Guatemala, and Norway. The interviewed people's backgrounds varied regarding race and ethnicity, class, disability, employment status, gender, religion, and sexual orientation. Although the initial focus of the project was on labor migration, the focus broadened over time. Some participants had initially arrived in the United Kingdom as refugees, others as a child with their parents, others after marrying a person in and/or from the United Kingdom, and yet others for work or study opportunities.

The main challenge in relation to interviewing, as highlighted in the participant observation section, was finding research participants who agreed to be interviewed on camera. Several people agreed initially and then did not respond to messages to arrange the interview; conversely, some people who were not deaf migrants wanted to be interviewed. These challenges are typical when arranging semistructured interviews with people who are otherwise unknown or new to the researcher. Of the 12 interviews done by Steve, the majority (seven) came about through contacts of Sanchayeeta or Annelies, reiterating the importance of networks. Five interviews were done with people met at City Lit. Seven were female, five were male, and all but one (a white female from North America) were from an ethnic or minority background. Steve and Sanchayeeta continued to meet, see, or communicate with the majority of interviewees after the interviews, whether socially, formally, or via social media and text messaging.

Steve's semistructured interviews were fairly formal, beginning with the informed consent procedure and then drawing on the same pool of questions for each interviewee (e.g., "When you first arrived in the United Kingdom, how did you communicate with deaf and hearing people?"). They lasted approximately 1 hour, with all except one recorded on video camera. All interviews were held one-to-one, with the exception of two interviews involving two participants. Steve found it easier to build rapport with interviewees from a similar ex-mainstream background to his own and who had knowledge of BSL. Although communication was mostly through BSL, in several cases a mixture of BSL and IS was used. Communication in interviews leaned more toward BSL than the communication observed during participant observation, which was more varied depending on the backgrounds of those conversing.

In the interviews that Steve and Sanchayeeta did together, Steve was strongly focused on class and labor issues, whereas Sanchayeeta was more concerned with gender and feminism; she would ask additional questions after Steve. Sanchayeeta knew some of the interviewees' backgrounds well and was able to use this knowledge to invite them to share experiences. In the interviews that Sanchayeeta and Jorn did together for the ethnographic film *Finding Spaces to Belong*, Sanchayeeta led, and Jorn added questions in relation to themes emerging from his work on the other ethnographic films.

Interviews for *Finding Spaces to Belong* took place in 2019, with recruitment of participants beginning 2 months after Sanchayeeta had begun her doctorate. Of her participants, two were contacts from previous employments, two she had met at the "888 Club" film screening, two were recommendations from other contacts, and one was from City Lit. The film had to be put on hold until 2023 due to the coronavirus pandemic; resuming it allowed for the documentation of shifts in participants' reflections on their sense of belonging and also their signing styles over the intervening years, which was particularly acute for those who had only recently arrived in London in 2019. The film illustrates that belonging is an ongoing and dynamic process, shifting over time through ongoing experiences, social interactions, and language acquisition; the enforced interruption of the pandemic, therefore, not only changed the framing of the film but also gave greater insights into the subject. To accommodate the new framing, and to ensure that the film did not exceed 1 hour in length, it was decided to reduce the number of participants to four.

For Sanchayeeta's one-to-one interviews with her five Indian female newlywed participants, she used a rather different interview process: a collaborative (re)construction of the participants' reflective narratives of their life trajectories and journeys. Each person was interviewed three times, and each interview was between 45 minutes and 2 hours long. The first interview for each participant was semistructured, with questions such as "How has married life changed you?";

the following interviews were conversations built around material the participants provided on Sanchayeeta's request—photos of their everyday lives, video diaries, and self-portraits (collages and drawings about their lives in India and the United Kingdom). Sanchayeeta began these interviews with a recap narrative, reconstructing key moments of the participant's life using these different materials and also drawing on the semistructured interview and the participant's social media accounts. Seeing their narrative summarized by Sanchayeeta helped the participants to reflect on how they had presented themselves. Follow-up questions expanded these narratives. When a participant struggled to answer specific questions about their experience, Sanchayeeta prompted interviewees to respond to previously gathered data. For example, one participant was struggling with Sanchayeeta's question about factors that led her to marry and move to the United Kingdom, focusing only on her compatibility with her husband. Sanchayeeta shared what she knew about the participant's life at the time, which reminded the participant that her mother had also encouraged her to marry, due to being singularly responsible for her daughter. Although this approach risks spoon-feeding responses to participants, Sanchayeeta found that it gave participants space to reflect when they struggled with telling some parts of their life story. Sanchayeeta also shared clips of the early interviews with them, prompting reflections on changes—both in their signing and in their outlook on life.

This interview process also prompted Sanchayeeta to reflect on her own experience of growing up with Indian immigrant parents, and her own Indian heritage. The research gave her a sense of connection to her ancestral homeland, which is the lens through which she understands and presents the data. Sometimes, Sanchayeeta shared these aspects of her own experience with the participants, although mostly during informal interactions rather than the interview itself.

Whereas Steve and Sanchayeeta's interviews were exploratory and provide the bulk of their subproject's data included in this book, Amandine's interviews were undertaken with the aim of recording the stories that she had already been told during her everyday conversations with deaf refugees. Amandine interviewed seven Sudanese and Somali deaf people between ages 20 and 40, three men and four women, with whom she had already had many informal interactions. Having already built rapport extensively with her participants before asking to interview them, Amandine did not face the same challenges that Steve had in London with recruiting participants and building trust.

Amandine interviewed most people in their houses, and the interviews lasted between 30 and 60 minutes. She generally started the interview by asking deaf people about their journey to Kakuma Refugee Camp, moving on to their daily lives and how they communicated with other deaf and hearing people. This question-and-answer format is recognizably similar to that employed in classrooms and official interviews, and the perceived authority of the person conducting the interview, in addition to factors such as race and ethnicity, may have a profound impact on the interviewees (Blommaert & Dong, 2020). On reflection, Amandine realized that some of her questions resembled those asked by UNHCR upon the refugees' arrival at the camp to determine their need for support, leading her to wonder whether this reinforced the misconceptions of deaf people as to her role in the camp.

In general, deaf refugees said they felt honored to be interviewed and that they had a desire for their stories to be recorded—although this may have been in hope of resettlement. In some interviews, other people were present (this was unplanned) and observed the interview, which influenced the responses in terms of depth given and the themes highlighted. Despite their apparent keenness to be interviewed, some responses were very short, and Amandine felt the same need as Sanchayeeta to expand on questions by giving examples. However, the response then frequently contained the example she had just provided: When Amandine asked which sign languages they used in the camp, the interviewee responded with examples she had given (KSL and ASL). Additionally, some of the responses to interview questions contradicted what Amandine had seen during her fieldwork, for example, deaf people stating in the interview that they distrusted hearing people and had no hearing friends, whereas Amandine had observed them communicating and laughing with hearing inhabitants of the camp (see Chapter 9). Through these interviews, she received new insights into how deaf refugees preferred to *represent* their lives. Ultimately, however, she found the interviews of limited use compared to what she had learned through participant observation. As she was unable to return to the field to do additional, more in-depth interviews, most of the data on Kakuma Refugee Camp in this book are based on participant observation.

In Erin's study, interviews and participant observation were balanced in terms of importance. To collect data on tourist perspectives, Erin interviewed more than 50 people from a wide range of backgrounds (e.g., Asian Americans, black Americans, white Australians, Muslims, Hindus, Christians, queer people, nonsigning deaf people, signing deaf people) who identified as solo travelers, "voluntourists" (tourists doing volunteer work), backpackers, honeymooners, or long-term travelers. She conducted group interviews with people who were traveling together—for example, a couple from Australia and a group of friends from France. Erin also interviewed some experienced deaf travelers who were active on social media, such as those in the Facebook group Solo Deaf Travel. She interviewed some people together with the filmmakers, these interviews being potential material for the film *#deaftravel*. Some people made repeated visits to Bali, and Erin was able to interview them twice: once on her own, early in the project, and then again with Jorn for the film.

After the initial struggle to locate potential interviewees, Erin did not experience much reluctance to be interviewed, possibly because tourists are typically in positions of privilege and a context of leisure compared to, for example, the more precarious situation of migrants on temporary visas in the United Kingdom. She asked questions about whether they sought out deaf people when traveling, about their motivations for travel, and about how they communicated with different people. She also explored local perspectives on tourism, with local interviewees including the two deaf tourist guides working in Bali, deaf people in Bengkala, deaf people working in schools, and deaf community members; additionally, she interviewed some hearing people about the history of tourism in Bengkala.

In Bengkala, some of the deaf interviewees did not want their data used because it was sensitive information about power dynamics in the village. She conducted some interviews with the assistance of a person who knew Kata Kolok because she was not fluent enough then to ask detailed questions; later, she had picked up enough Kata Kolok to conduct interviews unaided. She also drew on interviewees' family photos to help with communication.

In each of the field sites in the professional mobility project, Annelies focused her interviews on a few key themes in relation to participation and use of IS. There were more than 2 years between the first and last case study, and during that period Annelies's research foci gradually shifted away from gathering perspectives on the nature of IS and toward the specific dynamics and ideologies of using IS in various contexts. Each of Annelies's previous ethnographies had been based in one city or one village, very different from conducting interviews in a multisited project due both to the type of setting and the themes; in many ways, it was easier because most of the interviewees already had metalinguistic and/or professional knowledge that helped them engage with the questions and give precise answers. This was in contrast to Amandine's and Sanchayeeta's experiences; they had to work harder to build rapport during interviews. Similarly, Erin found it easier to interview tourists than to interview deaf people in Bengkala due to shared frames of reference.

Not everyone understood the aim of Annelies's interviews, however. At the Winter Deaflympics, interviewing athletes proved more difficult than interviewing coaches or technical directors. Athletes often said they didn't know IS or deferred to their coaches or captains, who acted as gatekeepers and spokespersons. This is reminiscent of Steve's experience in London with deaf people who felt they were not the "right" person to be interviewed. Some individuals approached by Annelies did not want to be interviewed but were happy to have an informal conversation instead—and, as in Amandine's case, sometimes these informal interactions (laid down in field notes) worked better than interviews.

In some settings, interviewees reacted with surprise when Annelies asked questions about language use. Interviewees at the Winter Deaflympics expected to be interviewed about sports competitions, and deaf performers at Clin d'Oeil expected to be interviewed about themes in their creative work. This expectation was probably exacerbated by the team wearing press badges. There is a parallel here with Amandine's interviewees' expectations about the nature of the interviews she was conducting, based on their previous experiences and their perception of the interviewer.

In total, Annelies undertook 145 interviews over a period of 2.5 years. This may seem a very large number, but the duration of the interviews was wildly variable, ranging from 2 to 90 minutes. Some interviews explored only one theme—for example, a conference presenter's experience of giving a presentation in IS. Other, longer interviews went deeper and explored several themes with the same person over time. Annelies interviewed Frontrunners students and teachers twice, at the beginning and then at the end of the year. In the second interview, the interviewees rewatched their first interviews and ethnographic recordings, which led to reflections on how their signing and their positions in international deaf spaces had changed (see Chapter 5). As in Sanchayeeta's follow-up interviews with her participants (both in her doctoral study and in the ethnographic film), these second interviews led to an understanding of processes of language learning over several months (see Chapter 8). At some of the professional events, it was challenging to plan interviews around people's participation in the program, a challenge also experienced by Erin with participants who were on holiday; this contrasts with the projects on migration, where people were interviewed within their everyday routines. About a third of Annelies's interviews (approximately 50) were with people she had met through her previous mobilities and her migration trajectory, which helped to plan a large number of interviews during brief fieldwork stints. She did not, however, wish to fully rely on previously established networks because there is a danger of solely engaging with and reinforcing "echo chambers."

Annelies wanted to include a wide range of different experiences of international deaf communication and professional mobility, and she explicitly sought out (and asked assistants to seek out) people whose experiences are underrepresented or for whom IS was new or challenging. Interviewees from underrepresented minorities (e.g., deaf people with additional disabilities, female leaders in deaf sports) did not always mention being underrepresented, perhaps considering it irrelevant to the interview or unsafe to talk about with Annelies and/or on camera. Although deafblind interviewees generally would reference being deafblind at some point during the interview, neurodivergence, chronic illness, or sexual orientation were rarely mentioned.

Almost all Annelies's interviews were conducted in IS. Although several people declared that their IS was not good enough (despite having already had conversations in IS with Annelies), Annelies assured them that she understood their signing. There were a few cases in which the interviewee did not use IS; for example, in Kenya, most would sign a mixture of KSL and ASL. In many of the interviews, Annelies was not the only person asking questions; as such, the interviews became a team effort, similar to those in the labor migration project and in the tourism filmmaking process. For example, Jorn would typically add one or more questions at the end, keeping in mind the film as a whole. Research assistants interviewed participants together with Annelies, sometimes asking questions before Annelies but mostly afterward—and, on a few occasions, instead of Annelies (with Annelies observing). The benefit of this was that, when one fieldworker was asking questions, the other(s) had time to think of additional questions. Additionally, on approximately five occasions, a deaf interpreter or broker supported the interview in an impromptu way, typically when interviewing deafblind people, deafdisabled people, and deaf people who did not know IS.

In sum, we employed a range of interviewing styles and approaches. We interviewed people we knew from outside the research setting or whom we had met through participant observation; we also conducted interviews with people with whom this was our first meaningful interaction. Interviews lead to highly quotable data, and this book is thus interspersed with quotations in which deaf people narrate their experiences. A key issue with using interview data is how it is presented: In this book, it is inserted in translated form.

Translations

Translation of sign language content into written languages is a challenging process due to the differences between linguistic structures and the modality shift (Young & Temple, 2014). Signers make frequent use of simultaneous structures, whereas written languages are largely linear; decisions regarding the ordering of some narratives are, therefore, complicated. Additionally, the crucial and often subtle use of nonmanual features in sign languages can be difficult to lay down in words. In any translation, underlying cultural meanings can get lost; signed idioms and the underlying cultural meanings of particular ways of signing are particularly hard to convert into written languages (Ladd, 2003). A lot of information is thus lost in translation. It can be argued that using written translations of video-recorded signed interviews as the basis for analysis is too problematic to continue as standard practice in Deaf Studies research, and there is an increasing number of ways of annotating signed interviews, such as adding tags to video fragments in ELAN (a video data annotation program). Qualitative data analysis programs that have traditionally worked with text are also increasingly allowing smoother working with video.

Analyzing video data directly rather than analyzing written translations allows the researcher to stay close to the primary data. However, all of us have found it quicker to recall and skim written data, especially when in large volumes. For that reason, we have opted to work with translations of interviews in our analysis. Some translations were done by us; others were outsourced to research assistants and translators. We treated translations as *complementary* to, rather than for use *instead of*, the video data, and we developed strategies for staying close to the original footage, such as coding (annotating) the transcript immediately after viewing the video while the signing was still fresh in our minds, noting sign choices that were relevant or interesting to our study. Sometimes, when we were uncertain about a translated quotation, we would get in touch with our interviewees to cross-check the meaning. We have made direct, video-recorded quotations available on blogs, in presentations, and in our ethnographic films. In many places in this book, we have therefore linked directly to time codes in the ethnographic films where (parts of) original quotations can be viewed. (Note that the subtitles are often shortened versions of the original translations and therefore do not exactly match the quotations in this book.) We also include photographs in our work when discussing particular signs (e.g., in Chapter 8). Thus, even when working with written translations, there are multiple ways to avoid losing touch with the original signing in the analysis and dissemination processes.

Where translations were done by members of the MobileDeaf team, we have struggled with our fluency in English in comparison to other languages. In addition, we are not trained as translators ourselves, and the interviews were the result of intercultural exchanges. Sanchayeeta felt uneasy about her use of informal British English to translate Indian informal gestural phrases. Some types of signing were especially difficult to translate, including some uses of IS, home sign, translanguaging, signing without mouthings, and idioms. Larger cultural distance between interviewees and researchers also leads to challenges with translation. In Amandine's case, she had only been immersed for a few months in the specific sign languages used by the people she interviewed in Kakuma Refugee Camp. The interviews conducted at the end of the fieldwork consisted mostly of questions that she had already asked in informal conversations, and she drew on that background knowledge when working on the translations. Still, it was sometimes hard to translate when deaf refugees used very little mouthing to accompany their signs. Amandine also struggled to get in touch with her participants online, so opportunities to check translations were limited. Conversely, Sanchayeeta was able to contact the participants for clarifications; in that process, the participants reflected on their responses, and Sanchayeeta could ask further informal questions to bring in extra dimensions to their narratives.

Where translations were outsourced, translators received context. When Annelies sent in the batch of interviews done in Kenya, she made a video of KSL signs that frequently occurred in the interviews, gave context about the setting, created a spreadsheet with background information about the interviewees, and sent a set of notes on recurring themes. Naturally, mistakes in translations were common because translators were not present at the interviews themselves. It was imperative for the translations of outsourced interviews to be checked and fine-tuned by the interviewer.

Conflicts of interest can arise when outsourcing translations. Annelies's study was about IS, and the company to which she outsourced most translations was the main company providing IS interpreting and translation. The company did not want to tell Annelies who did each translation, and different data sets went to different translators. This was deeply uncomfortable, due to the very specific (and sometimes sensitive) content of her data. Most of the data were *about* IS politics and thus close to home for translators working from IS. Although translators are subject to confidentiality agreements, they cannot "un-know" what they have translated and can benefit from it. Annelies was even approached by one of the translators for a film they wanted to make, inspired by the interviews.

Analysis and Writing

We analyzed our data in different ways. Steve and Sanchayeeta started by going through the full interview transcripts multiple times, and then wrote summaries and noted recurrent themes alongside each transcript. Most of us, but not all, used computer-assisted qualitative data analysis software (Atlas.ti and Nvivo, depending on individual preference) to annotate the data with codes that we created as needed (see right side of Figure 2.1). Coding gives names or labels to components that seem to have a potential theoretical significance or that are salient within the social world of those being studied (Bryman, 2012). Often, data excerpts (such as single sentences or a paragraph) were coded with multiple codes.

When coding, we knew roughly what types of themes would come up in the data because these had emerged through our fieldwork. Erin's codes were often words or descriptions that the participants used themselves, such as the recurring phrase "see how they live"—frequently uttered by tourists when asked why they were interested in visiting deaf schools or the deaf village. These codes serve as the basis for the generation and development of theory. When coding and closely observing data, new insights occur, new details are spotted, and new categories are created.

In the writing process, data excerpts connected to codes were retrieved and reviewed to identify patterns and exceptions to these patterns. This inductive method, following the principles of Grounded Theory (Glaser & Strauss, 1967), enabled us to analyze patterns from the bottom up to build theory, both within our individual chapters in this book and in the shared chapters. Within and between each subproject, we identified overlaps between these key themes and parallels and divergences in our findings. An important setting for identifying these overlaps was our regular reading groups in which we discussed our shared theoretical framework and considered illustrative examples and anecdotes from fieldwork. We also undertook other activities to find connections between our data sets, including creating a shared set of hashtags in an online application for which we each had an account. Whereas the codes used in our individual analysis were specific to our subprojects (e.g., for Amandine: "village signs," "Sudan signs," "Somali signs"), the hashtags were intended to be broad ("networks," "class," "aspirations," "time") to engender connections as we shared data. There did tend to be an overemphasis on sharing excerpts from interviews, as

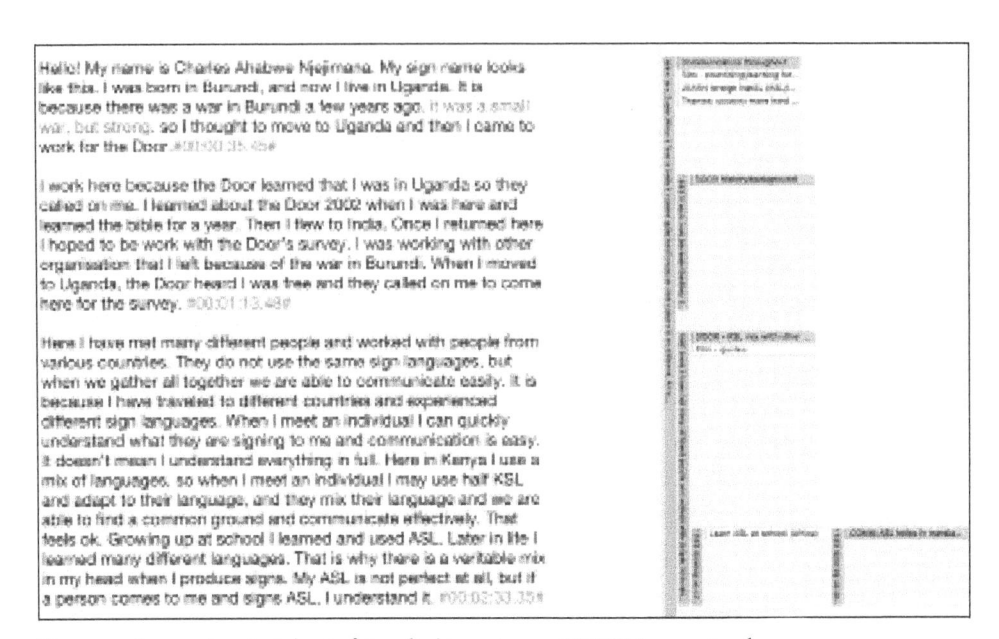

Figure 2.1. Annotations in Atlas.ti of Annelies' interviews at DOOR International.

opposed to sharing field notes, because quotations are more immediately accessible. However, they can also be decontextualized, whereas our notes from participant observation made it possible to write in more general and summarizing terms and to give specific examples of what we had observed. We have thus taken care to ensure that the presentation of observation data is not drowned out by interview data. The shared themes informed the structure of this book, which has been further simplified and streamlined during the writing process. We held regular online writing sessions and three in-person writing weeks to maintain cohesion.

The differences in our respective methodologies are reflected in our writing. The different types of interviewing we employed and the different balances between interviews and observations have enabled us to compile a rich combination of in-depth, multilayered portraits of a few deaf individuals across multiple chapters, alongside examples from people who are mentioned only once or twice in the book. We share very specific situation descriptions, as well as broad generalizations, based on our repeated observations in a range of settings. Our approach extends beyond the boundaries of traditional ethnography, incorporating elements of autoethnography. Autoethnography allows researchers to explore their own experiences through self-reflection, connecting these personal narratives to broader social, cultural, and political contexts. Autoethnography essentially bypasses one of the interpretative stages that research data usually undergo. It emphasizes the researchers' understanding of their personal experiences instead of their interpretations of others' experiences. Recognizing its importance, a growing number of deaf scholars have begun incorporating autoethnographic elements into their work, intending to amplify more deaf "voices" within academia (see Kusters, 2022, for references).

Our utilization of autoethnography serves three central functions. First, as mentioned previously, our initial research questions have been partly shaped by our prior experiences, some documented in field notes, others drawn from memory. Second, autoethnography forms an essential component of our ethnographic process as part of our research within our field sites. Third, during the duration of the MobileDeaf project, we have applied autoethnography to different aspects of our internationally mobile lives (outside of research practice), leading to the inclusion of personal anecdotes in this book.

The narratives that we present are thus derived from a diverse array of sources. Some details stem from our planned research, whereas others have sprung from unexpected experiences. The various elements are all integral to our research and to isolate planned from unplanned fieldwork and formally observed data from the impressions formed over the courses of our lives would be somewhat arbitrary given our own involvement in deaf international networks and our positionalities as mobile deaf people. As such, we do not too rigorously differentiate in the following chapters between data gathered as part of planned ethnographic fieldwork and incidental data drawn from our lived experiences. Instead, each chapter should be understood as an illustrative mosaic of different international mobilities assembled from multiple methodological and experiential approaches, which we feel captures the nuanced dynamics of living mobile deaf lives.

Our states of bodymind have also impacted our writing processes, often slowing it down. We gradually came to the insight that "crip time," the use and experience of time as a disabled person (Samuels, 2017), has impacted us in productive ways. Sanchayeeta collected data before and then after her 9-month maternity leave, and through this was able to take a longer-term perspective on her participants' lives. The disruption to the production of her planned ethnographic film due to the pandemic gave space and time for the story to "mature" and different perspectives to come to the fore. Steve returned to the MobileDeaf project to work on the book reenergized from having spent a year working part time for a small local deaf organization. Amandine's interruption of study due to advanced stage cancer gave her the distance needed to process her vicarious trauma. We all noted that letting data, drafts for this book, and film scripts sit for months—even years—led to additional and new insights when we returned to them. These are examples of what is known as slow scholarship, or slow science. Crip time can, intentionally or unintentionally, permit slow scholarship, which we see as a strength of the MobileDeaf project. We are fortunate that the project duration (5 years) and the deadline extension we received (18 months) made it possible for us to stretch the process over 6.5 years, during which the project—and we ourselves—matured.

Labels in Writing

A challenge for this book is how to inform the reader about the backgrounds of the various participants, many of whom are only mentioned once. Space limits us from including lengthy introductions for each person. We are conscious that the visibility of diverse people, especially minoritized groups, and the affirmation of their perspectives, is crucial to providing a full picture. Yet, this is not a straightforward process: There is a fine line between visibility and representation on the one hand and tokenism and essentialism on the other. In addition, in writing, the categories to describe people are "frozen"; in film, explicit labels can be more easily avoided, but although certain features such as skin color are inescapably visible (and subject to the interpretation of the viewer), other positionalities are entirely invisible unless explicitly commented on.

A key identifier in our project on *international* mobility was participants' nationalities. Nationality can give some clues as to race and ethnicity when considering majority demographics in countries, but solely mentioning nationality also *erases* race in, for example, the case of black Americans or Turkish Belgians. We considered informing readers of each participants' *race or ethnicity, nationality, and gender* throughout, for example, by writing "X, a black woman from the United Kingdom, said..." but there are problems with this approach. Regarding *gender*, there is a danger of misgendering people. *Racial* markers such as "black" or "Black" are cultural constructs and have different meanings and connotations in different national contexts (Bonnett, 2022). A complication with *national labeling* is the use of combined labels of national and cultural heritage (e.g., Iranian German), the use of which varies widely and is not limited to those who have moved in their own lifetime.

In an *international* project focusing on *mobility*, it is crucial to note that labels for race, ethnicity, and nationality are highly relative and dependent on the settings in which the labeling happens. Certain frameworks for labeling race (such as labeling all nonwhite people as BIPOC) do not necessarily resonate broadly or translate well across national and cultural contexts. Similarly, one's skin color and tone can be labeled differently in different places. Examples include a person who identified as a "light-skinned" person in Ghana but as "black" in the United Kingdom, and a person from Portugal who was labeled as "white" in Europe but seen as a "person of color" in the United States. Skin color is not always the key identifier: The type of hair or the shape of the eyes or nose are often referred to when marking racial and ethnic differences, as when people in Indonesia call white tourists "big-nosed people" (see #deaftravel). We also note that people from many countries in the Global South identify by the *ethnic group* they are part of within that country; in contrast, at the WFD congress or after having moved to London, people who look similar in the eyes of "outsiders" are often grouped together as "Indians," "Africans," or "Arabs." However, these terms are profound overgeneralizations: To take just one example, members of the Indian diaspora may come from various parts of the Indian subcontinent, practice various religions, have different caste backgrounds, and so on. In the context of international mobility, there is a tendency for "Indian" or "British Indian" to be used by non-Indians as generalizing categories, whereas people *from* India make more fine-grained distinctions.

There are other labels that can be crucial to people's identity, such as religion and sexual identity. People may choose not to foreground crucial aspects of their identities where they feel that it is not safe or relevant to do so, especially on film. Although our interviewees have a wide variety of backgrounds and claim various identities, these identities were not always disclosed in the interviews. The foregrounded labels varied between contexts. People may see religion (e.g., Muslim, Christian) as a key identifier in some contexts but not in others. Some deaf queer professionals traveling to Muslim-majority countries refrained from mentioning their queer identity; in contrast, a deaf queer person who had moved to the United Kingdom, and had come out there, openly asserted this new label.

Another set of labels that we grappled with was whether to label our participants as "migrants," "refugees," "tourists," and so on. In labeling people by the type of mobility they were engaged in, we were trying to explore patterns in distinct *types* of mobilities (see Chapter 1). However, the people themselves may not have necessarily identified with these labels. Some "tourists," for example, prefer to be called "travelers" (see Chapter 6). Labels were especially challenging in the labor and marriage migration subproject because many participants did not identify as a "migrant." For example, when Sanchayeeta approached one participant from Sierra Leone to inquire whether he was interested in participating in the study, he contended that he was not a migrant because he had obtained British citizenship and had been living in London for a long while. In other examples, European migrants typically did not use that term for themselves. However, because we wanted to highlight patterns in sociality in relation to types of mobility, we found it necessary to use these labels in this study.

For most participants, we did not know what labels each of them would use for themselves in the context of this book, including their gender pronouns. This led to conundrums during the writing process over how to ethically make diversity—and thus intersectionality—visible without knowing which labels people would use themselves, especially when these identities were not explicitly discussed during interviews. Another pitfall is that labeling people may (inadvertently) give the impression of essentialism (see Chapter 5). Consequently, we decided to mention participants' nations of origin as a minimum because in most cases it was clear which national labels participants used for themselves, and we have often added gender and race or ethnicity as well. We ask the reader to take into account the above-mentioned pitfalls with these identifiers. Other labels were added where the participant had explicitly identified them or made them relevant.

Conclusion

In this chapter, we have explored the different strategies we used to do ethnography, both individually and as a team of deaf researchers. We have shown that even in a project with overarching research questions and a broadly shared methodology, our approaches were necessarily different. By outlining our solutions in this chapter, we hope to inspire future ethnographers looking for strategies for their research settings. A feature that all the projects had in common is that we often participated in deaf-only international spaces, going from groups of deaf tourists to deaf-only courses, to deaf gatherings in homes. Our being mobile deaf signers was thus a prerequisite for accessing many of these spaces. Other aspects of our positionalities shaped our research as profoundly as our being deaf, however. In some contexts, factors such as our race, gender, and education stood out especially sharply, but in each of the contexts, these factors shaped how we engaged with our participants.

Doing deaf ethnography around the core theme of international *deaf* mobilities meant making use of deaf networks, asking questions that are grounded in deaf experiences letting themes emerge from settings where "being a deaf signer" was always one of the shared features or shared interests. The implications of this approach are that other meaningful axes of identification were, inevitably, positioned as "additional to deaf" (e.g., deaf and queer, deaf and black), both in our positionalities and in the positionalities of our participants. This approach can give the impression that "deafness" is the first or most important axis of identification for participants in our study, which is a common problem in Deaf Studies research and one that we were not able to circumvent. Doing deaf ethnography was thus a double-edged sword. Through having deafness in common with our participants and as core identifier in the project we were able to put deaf–hearing differences to the side, and deaf–deaf differences could come much more sharply to the fore.

Part Two

A Spectrum of International Deaf Mobilities

3

Deaf in Kakuma Refugee Camp

Amandine le Maire

Forced migration is the involuntary movement of people away from their home country or region for reasons related to violent conflict, famine, persecution, or natural disasters. The number of refugees has increased rapidly over the past decade, and most of these displaced people remain in their home country or neighboring countries. According to the United Nations High Commissioner for Refugees (UNHCR) Global Trends reports, 82.4 million people had forcibly migrated worldwide by the end of 2020 (UNHCR, 2022). Among them were nearly 26.4 million refugees (UNHCR, 2022). In Syria, where a brutal civil war has raged since 2011, millions of Syrian refugees have fled their homes. More recently, the escalation of conflict in Ukraine has caused civilian casualties and destruction of civilian infrastructure, forcing people to flee to neighboring countries. Refugee crises are thus a current and salient issue, debated in science, politics, and journalism. However, there are few existing data or statistical research carried out on deaf refugees worldwide (Sivunen, 2019).

Refugee camps are established to respond to the needs of people seeking asylum following their escape from their home countries. In refugee camps across the world, deaf refugees live alongside other refugees. To investigate the lived experiences of deaf refugees in one such camp, I went to Kenya for a total of 4 months (1 month in Nairobi and 3 months in Kakuma Refugee Camp), from January until May 2018. I undertook participant observation, including daily conversations with deaf refugees, in several places within Kakuma Refugee Camp, as well as semistructured interviews with selected key participants. My methodology and my positionality as a white, deaf, female, Christian ethnographer are detailed in Chapter 2.

In this chapter, I embed my study of Kakuma Refugee Camp within the nascent but growing field of Deaf Refugee Studies. I examine and offer a critical review of the current (limited) body of research about deaf refugees. I first give an overview of what little scholarship there is on deaf refugees' lived experience of education, the challenges they face with interpreting services, and deaf refugees' introduction to deaf networks in the host society. I then turn to Kakuma Refugee Camp, providing a brief overview of the historical and geographical background of the camp and then outlining the findings of my research. I consider both the journeys made by deaf refugees into the camp and the structure of their lives within it. The chapter concludes with a discussion regarding the contribution made by my research to Deaf Refugee Studies.

Throughout, I make use of Bourdieu's conceptual tools of habitus, field, and capital to construct my data analysis and to explore the dynamics of mobility among deaf refugees. As seen in Chapter 1, these concepts help to explain how social structures and power relations are maintained and reproduced. Within a particular *field*, each actor's *habitus* shapes their perceptions and actions, and their assemblage of skills, knowledge, resources, and advantages—their *capital*—determines their power, influence, social positioning, and opportunities when navigating social structures. In Kakuma Refugee Camp, although few refugees possess substantial *economic capital*, they often rely on their *social capital*, comprising networks, relationships, and obligations (Bourdieu & Wacquant, 1992). Additionally, the value of *cultural capital*, such as educational credentials and work experience (Bourdieu, cited in Joy et al., 2020), is essential. Bourdieu stated that social capital differs from cultural capital in the sense that the possession of resources is attached to one person, individually, whereas the resources of social capital are acquired via a form of relationship of "mutual acquaintance and recognition" that comes from "membership in a group" (Bourdieu, 1986, p. 249). *Linguistic capital*—the form of cultural capital covering language proficiency, eloquence, and mastery of linguistic codes that enable individuals to assert themselves in specific social contexts—is built up in the camp by deaf refugees, who may acquire a national sign language there for the first time. *Physical capital*—the embodiment of resources, such as physical appearance, health, and physical abilities (including strength and endurance), that can also influence social positioning (Bourdieu, 1978)—is particularly salient given the physical implications of forced migration and life in a camp. Bourdieu's framework is thus a helpful lens through which to understand the deaf refugees' everyday experiences of moving to and living in a refugee camp.

Deaf Refugee Studies

Previous work in Deaf Refugee Studies, which lies at the intersection of Refugee Studies and Deaf Studies, has mostly focused on deaf refugees' education. These studies have focused on deaf refugees from Lebanon, China, Turkey, Syria, Afghanistan, Iraq, Egypt, Sudan, Somalia, Ethiopia, Kenya, Eritrea, Cambodia, Vietnam, Sri Lanka, India, the Philippines, Myanmar, and Nepal who have arrived in host countries in the Global North—for example, in Canada (Akamatsu & Cole, 2000), the Netherlands (Prawiro-Atmodjo et al., 2020), Sweden (Duggan & Holmström, 2022), Finland (Sivunen, 2019), the United States (Fishbeck, 2018; Moers, 2017; Reimers, 2011), and Australia (Willoughby, 2015). An exception is Youngs' (2010) work, which is a small study based on deaf refugees' lived experiences of education in Dadaab Refugee Complex in Kenya.

Several authors have noted that many deaf refugee children from the Middle East and Africa have "a lack of language" upon their arrival in the host country, which has caused them to be isolated from the surrounding hearing world of the host country (Akamatsu & Cole, 2000; Prawiro-Atmodjo et al., 2020; Reimers, 2011). Many of these children have not had access to (deaf) education in their home countries and are from hearing, nonsigning families. For example, Akamatsu and Cole (2000) note that "Many newly arrived deaf students lack not only English, but any form of language (spoken or signed), as well as appropriate study skills for North American Schools" (p. 1). The terms used in these studies—such as "lack of access to spoken or signed language" (Akamatsu & Cole, 2000, p. 1), "no language," and "lack of any form of spoken or signed language"—indicate a negative view of refugees' language (Duggan & Holmström, 2022). A crucial problem with this negative discourse on deaf refugees' language is that these terms could imply a problem arising from the child, rather than looking at problems arising from the environment (Fishbeck, 2018). In contrast, others have highlighted that this discourse underplays the fact that many deaf refugees do have some oral or literacy skills in the languages of their country of origin and use home signs or have fluency in a sign language (Duggan & Holmström, 2022; Sivunen, 2019; Sivunen & Tapio, 2020; Youngs, 2010).

Several studies have thus investigated the context of educational systems, and authors suggest using a holistic approach involving a team of teachers, interpreters, and other personnel, alongside families, to provide support to deaf refugee students, as well as using assessments to determine which instructional techniques and materials are appropriate (Akamatsu & Cole, 2000; Prawiro-Atmodjo et al., 2020; Reimers, 2011). Willoughby (2015) uncovered several issues faced by deaf refugees from the Middle East and Africa, and by their families in Australia, in terms of learning a new language, navigating the educational system, and integrating into the new country. She recommends the provision of more Australian Sign Language (Auslan) and English classes for deaf refugees outside of the educational system. Several authors also reported that engagement and cooperation with deaf refugee children's parents is difficult due to cultural or language barriers (Akamatsu & Cole, 2000; Prawiro-Atmodjo et al., 2020). The studies mentioned previously have been limited to the perspectives of the professionals working in educational settings, such as teachers, interpreters (Olsen, 2019), and personnel with a variety of specialities, and the focus has been on children, not on adults. Although this approach is interesting for educational purposes, it fails to take into account the perspectives of deaf refugees themselves. There are a few, but not many, exceptions to this approach; some of these are outlined below.

Holmström et al. (2021) are part of the Multilingual Situation of Deaf Refugees in Sweden (Mulder) project, which aims to investigate through an ethnographic approach the linguistic situation of deaf adults who are new arrivals in Sweden. Holmström (2019) points out that deaf migrants, who are mostly from West Asia (46%) and Europe (26%), often arrive in Sweden with limited educational background, which complicates the Swedish Migration Agency's interview process. Deaf migrants (including refugees) are offered the opportunity to learn Swedish Sign Language (SSL), the Swedish language, and aspects of Swedish society in adult nonformal education classes so as to be able to undergo the interview process with the Migration Agency. Teachers at some adult folk high schools believe that they must start by teaching deaf migrants SSL before they are able to teach Swedish, because migrants need to first learn the more accessible language. Other schools in Sweden prefer to teach both languages, SSL and Swedish, to deaf adults in parallel (Holmström, 2019). In addition, adult folk high schools meet difficulties in teaching deaf migrants because of the variable linguistic and educational background of each student within the same group (Holmström, 2019).

The presence of interpreters—and, specifically, deaf interpreters—is significant in overcoming some of the communication barriers faced by deaf refugees when encountering the hearing professionals who work with them, for example in education, health care systems, and reception centers. Sivunen (2019) undertook an ethnographic study of 10 adult Middle Eastern asylum seekers with an Arabic background in different reception centers in Finland. She draws our attention to the communication challenges faced by individuals during the asylum process. Deaf refugees reported that "there had been misunderstandings and that their way of explaining and communicating was often not understood correctly" (Sivunen, 2019, p. 10). During the asylum process in Finland, the hearing interpreters who had been hired were not aware of the deaf refugees' sign language of origin, nor were they familiar with any sign language from Arab countries (Sivunen, 2019). According to Sivunen (2019), communication improved between the authorities and deaf refugees during the second interview of the asylum process due to the improvement in deaf refugees' Finnish Sign Language (FSL) skills. Some deaf refugees believed that their disability, deafness, and limited language proficiency were reasons for not being granted asylum in the host country (Sivunen, 2019).

A review of this area of interpreting in Norway (Olsen, 2019) notes that it is difficult to find an interpreter skilled in a refugee's native sign language, and that interpreters do not feel qualified to interpret for deaf refugees due to their inability to understand the sign languages used by them or to produce signing that can be understood by them. Regarding this challenge, Ataman and Karar (2017), based in Germany, propose a variety of interpreting strategies to maximize understanding across sign languages, including allowing time for consecutive rather than simultaneous interpreting, using more visually transparent vocabulary, and reducing the amount of mouthing and fingerspelling used.

Several studies have found that deaf interpreters can connect with deaf refugees more effectively than can hearing interpreters, using several modalities of communication (Ataman & Karar, 2017; Balachandra et al., 2009; Olsen, 2018, 2019). Most deaf interpreters have more skill than hearing interpreters in understanding (some of) the language used by deaf refugees and are better understood by the refugees because of their own native use of sign language and high levels of visual-spatial ability. These skills have been called "Deaf Extra Linguistic Knowledge" (DELK) (Adam et al., 2014). Ataman and Karar (2017) argue that one of the challenges of multicultural community interpreting settings is the absence of deaf interpreters. Other challenges involve administrative difficulties in organizing interpreters and their payment, confidentiality issues within double-minority communities, and competing preference for simultaneous interpreting rather than consecutive interpreting (Ataman & Karar, 2017).

Balachandra et al. (2009) are similarly convinced of the importance of deaf interpreters' presence in health care contexts to mitigate complex cultural and linguistic barriers. In a case study of a Vietnamese deaf couple, Balachandra et al. (2009) explained the process of interpretation, in which a deaf interpreter with the skills to communicate with the couple would translate into ASL for a hearing interpreter, who would then interpret into English. For some members of the couple's family, a Vietnamese/English interpreter had been provided as well (Balachandra et al., 2009). Due to the need for deaf interpreters in such settings, and for deaf/hearing interpreting teams, Ataman and Karar (2017) argue that it is imperative to develop specific training for both deaf and hearing interpreters working with deaf migrants and refugees.

Many studies have reported on the significant role played by networks of deaf locals from the host country, which provide opportunities for deaf refugees' social participation (Elder, 2015; Emery & Iyer, 2022; Olsen, 2018; Sivunen, 2019). In Finland, deaf refugees have been found to be isolated and lonely in reception centers due to communication barriers; deaf volunteers supporting their introduction to society have had a positive impact on their well-being. Deaf volunteers can be role models to deaf refugees, whether as deaf teachers or as guides to navigating Finnish society (Sivunen, 2019). Olsen (2018) argues that in the nearby country of Norway, the Norwegian deaf community is vital in the process of deaf refugees' learning of new languages, both through socialization and during training programs teaching Norwegian language and society. Reimers's (2011) study reports the case of a deaf refugee student from Somalia, traumatized from his time at a refugee camp and suffering vicious assaults from other hearing children, being resettled in the United States, learning ASL, and integrating into the deaf community through schooling. The role of various welcoming deaf networks is thus crucial for deaf refugees building a life in a new country. Some authors, however, have stated that inclusion in the local deaf community is not systemically positive, because deaf refugees may face exclusion and discrimination (Olsen, 2018); this is not well documented.

None of the above studies has focused on refugee camps or on the reception of deaf refugees in Global South settings. As I will show in my study of one such setting, there are comparable issues in relation to education and community support as those detailed previously, but there are also large differences in how deaf refugees go about their lives and how they are supported.

To date, I have identified only one study of deaf refugees that was undertaken in a refugee camp in the Global South: that of Megan Youngs (2010), a deaf researcher who undertook 6 weeks of fieldwork in the Dadaab Refugee Complex in Kenya. Her aim was to understand the role of deaf units (i.e., where deaf students are enrolled together in a class) in the refugee camp's schools, in terms of opportunities and obstacles for deaf refugees. According to Youngs, the deaf units play an important role in empowering deaf refugees through a flexible approach to communication (including Kenyan Sign Language [KSL], fingerspelling, lip-reading, Signed English, and Signed Exact English) and in strengthening their identities and self-determination (Youngs, 2010). Youngs notes that deaf people of different national and ethnic backgrounds meet at intracamp deaf football tournaments between the three parts of the Dadaab Refugee Complex. These events provide a space for deaf youths to encounter other deaf people from other sections of the camp, both to socialize and to strengthen their signing skills in KSL, which has "gained uniformity and popularity" compared to deaf refugees' home signs, such as Somali signs (Youngs, 2010, p. 62). My study is based on a longer period of fieldwork in a different refugee camp in the same country, and it confirms some of Youngs' findings; it also uncovers differences between the two camps and covers wider and more diverse aspects of deaf lives in the camp.

Journeys Into Kakuma Refugee Camp

Kakuma Refugee Camp is located in the semi-arid Turkana district of the northwestern part of Kenya, about 1,000 kilometers from the capital of Nairobi. Kakuma, meaning "nowhere" in Swahili, is a remote area with temperatures reaching 104 degrees Fahrenheit in most months of the year. It is located very close to the neighboring country of South Sudan, at about 60 miles distance. At the beginning of 1992, armed conflicts emerged in Kenya's neighboring countries, particularly in South Sudan and Somalia, as well as in East and Central Africa. People fleeing from these regions arrived en masse, and Kakuma Refugee Camp was established as an urgent response to those seeking refuge, including those who had been expelled from Ethiopian refugee camps (Ohta, 2005).

The origins of forced migration from Sudan can be traced to its colonization by Britain between 1899 and 1956, when the country was administered separately in the south and the north (Hyndman, 1999). The British government had made several attempts to reunite the northern Sudanese and the southern communities of rural Nuer and Dinka, but it was not successful (Sarwar, 2012). Following decolonization, the rapid acquisition of power by the people of the (majority Muslim) north caused discontent among the (majority Christian) southern population, resulting in civil wars (Sarwar, 2012). The first lasted from 1955 to 1972, and the second lasted from 1983 to 2005; following the establishment of the Autonomous Government of South Sudan, the Republic of South Sudan was recognized as independent from the Republic of the Sudan in 2011. During the 22 years of the second civil war, a total of 4 million southerners were displaced both internally and across international borders (Newhouse, 2015); Ethiopia by the early 1990s was the key destination because large numbers of displaced southern Sudanese had heard of the existence of camps with education, food, and safety (Jansen, 2011). In 1991, Ethiopia's Mengistu regime made the decision to expel Sudanese refugees, fearful that the camps were becoming sites of recruitment for the rebel army (Jansen, 2011; Ohta, 2005). Expelled from Ethiopia, southern Sudanese people started to arrive at Lokichoggio, a town in northern Kenya not far from Kakuma (Hecht, 2005). To control the massive influx of refugees, the Kenyan government made the decision to craft tougher laws stating that refugees were no longer allowed to settle wherever they wished (Newhouse, 2015). Instead, the government decided to set up a more permanent camp in the small settlement of Kakuma and to move refugees into that place.

The second country from which many refugees in Kakuma Refugee Camp originate is Somalia. Unlike Sudan—which contains nearly 200 ethnic groups with many languages and religious traditions, including Christianity, Islam, and religions originating in Africa (Sarwar, 2012)—most of the Somali population is part of a single Muslim ethnic group and shares the same language. However, the country has experienced one of the most terrible civil wars in Africa (Elmi & Barise, 2006); the war has multiple and complex political, economic, and cultural causes. To give a brief summary, Somalia and Ethiopia signed a peace accord in 1964 after years of conflict; however, this led to an intensification of civil unrest in the northwest of Somalia. Siyad Barre, president of the Somali Democratic Republic between 1969 and 1991, instituted policies that armed the Somali Armed Forces with equipment supplied by certain countries in the Global North in an aggressive bid to suppress his enemies: the various armed rebel groups in the northwest, northeast, and south of Somalia. Resistance to Siyad Barre's military junta led to general militarization and the disintegration of the Somali state (Lewis, 2008). Siyad Barre's rule became increasingly dictatorial, using indiscriminate killings, burning villages, and torture as instruments of control (Elmi & Barise, 2006); 50,000 people of the Isaaq clan fled to Ethiopia to escape government repression (Lindley & Hammond, 2014). After months of civil war, Siyad Barre was overthrown by guerrillas in 1991.

Following the fall of the Siyad Barre regime, the various armed rebel groups began competing to influence the central government, particularly in the south of Somalia. The civil conflict had a direct consequence for the general population of Somalia, in the form of a severe famine (Hyndman, 1999). The images of malnourished Somalians were relayed worldwide by the media, and this prompted a large number of donations from foreign governments, and the public, to fund humanitarian actions (Hyndman, 1999). As the violence and instability continued, the presence of humanitarian agencies in the country increased, attempting to relieve the spreading famine in the southern Somali war zone. Some clans, such as the Daarood clan, were being persecuted by the Hawiye clan, which was prominent under Barre's regime. This "clan cleansing" campaign of 1991–1992 caused the displacement of the Daarood people to Kenya (Horst, 2006). The Somali Civil War remains ongoing.

Kakuma Refugee Camp, which has received many refugees from South Sudan and Somalia, is administered by the UNHCR, working in cooperation with a variety of services established within the camp. These include schools, hospitals, and humanitarian services with different responsibilities: the World Food Program (WFP); the International Organization for Migration (IOM); the International Rescue Committee (IRC); the Jesuit Refugee Services (JRS); the National Council of Churches of Kenya (NCCK); the Windle Trust Kenya (WTK); FilmAid International; the Norwegian Refugee Council Organization (NRC), which is responsible for the provision of food and subsistence to refugees; and the Lutheran World Federation (LWF), which runs the schools in the camp.

Since its creation in 1992, the Kakuma Refugee Camp has grown significantly; by 2017, the number of refugees had increased to 168,224 (UNHCR, 2017a). Based on these numbers, Kakuma

Refugee Camp is one of the two largest camps in Kenya; the other, and bigger, is Dadaab, where Youngs (2010) did her study. The camp is divided into four main zones—Kakuma 1, 2, 3, and 4—and a newly developed area called Kalobeyei. During my fieldwork at Kakuma Refugee Camp, I had six key participants; details from their stories are included in this chapter. Figure 3.1 shows each participant's duration of their stay in Kakuma Refugee Camp and other refugee complexes.

The six deaf refugees all shared one common factor in being forced to move to Kakuma Refugee Camp: the political conflict, war, and violence arising in their home and neighboring countries. They sought recognized refugee status from UNHCR because of their forced displacement. Many had had to walk for several months to reach the refugee camp. Their ability to endure the physical demands of such a journey, often at very young ages, is a resource that allowed them to survive and potentially thrive in a new environment:

Ken:	I was born in Sudan, but when I was 3 years old, I went to Ethiopia. I was very small and walked a lot and it was tough. There was a soldier who helped me because I was deaf; he brought me to Ethiopia. And since then, I missed my mum and lost her.
Amandine:	You walked a lot in Ethiopia.
Ken:	Yes, I walked a lot in Ethiopia.
Amandine:	How long? One week, 2 weeks?
Ken:	Three months, 3 months.
Amandine:	How did you eat?
Ken:	I asked people to help me, to give, lend me food. They helped me because I was deaf. When I had enough food, I walked, but it was painful in my knees, so people helped me to carry me on their back.

Ken was born in 1981 in what is now South Sudan and, at just 3 years old, was forced to flee to Ethiopia. He believes his mother died while they were fleeing Sudan; being so young at the time, he cannot remember what his mother looked like. Due to unsolved interethnic clashes and political instability in Ethiopia, Ken had to flee once again in 1992, this time to Kenya. He journeyed on foot with friends and relatives for 3 months, relying on others for food and water, and even to carry him.

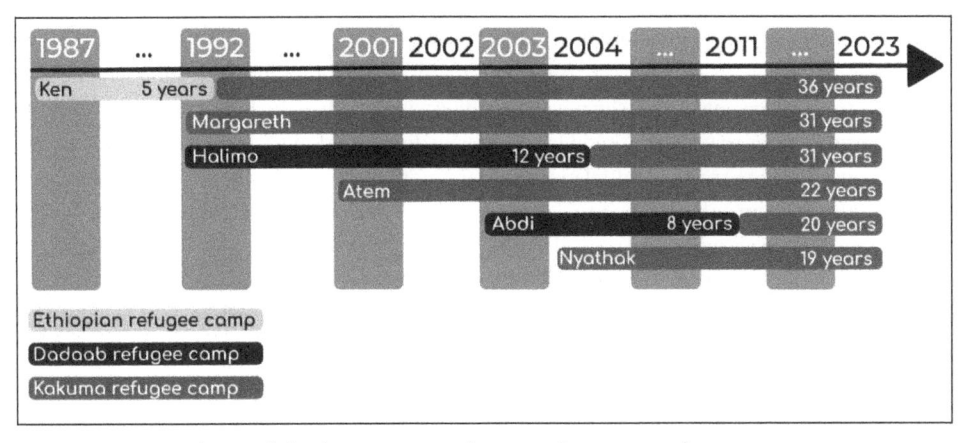

Figure 3.1. Duration (in years) that key participants have stayed in various refugee camps.

In this context, Ken's social capital is reflected in his ability to rely on friends and relatives for support during his journey. The relationships and network that he built over time provided him with access to essential resources such as food and water, which were critical for his survival during the journey. This example also highlights the importance of embodied resources, such as physical capital, as discussed previously. The pain in Ken's knees was a physical limitation that affected his ability to complete the journey on his own; however, through his social capital, he was able to access the support he needed to complete the journey. He attributed the kindness of those who helped him to their sympathy for his being deaf. At the border between Ethiopia and Sudan, he was collected by car and brought to a village in Kenya called Loki; from there, a UNHCR driver brought him to Kakuma Refugee Camp. He was 11 years old at this stage. Bourdieu's theory of capital is helpful to understand how social networks and relationships can provide individuals with access to essential resources, including physical support and care, that enable them to navigate difficult situations and to overcome barriers and physical limitations.

Ken's story is similar to that of the famous "lost boys and girls of Sudan": a group of more than 20,000 children from the Nuer and Dinka ethnic groups who embarked on a journey by foot to refugee camps in Ethiopia and Kenya and were forced to rely on the charity of inhabitants in villages as they traveled (Eggers, 2006). After arriving in Kakuma Refugee Camp, most of the children had to live on their own; they had difficulties finding adequate food, education, and medical care. In addition, they struggled with the uncertainty of finding their missing parents and siblings (Hecht, 2005; Luster et al., 2008). Children still frequently arrive at Kakuma Refugee Camp with no parents or adult relatives.

Others do arrive with an adult relative. Margaret, for example, was brought to Kakuma in 1992 by her uncle. She was born in 1990 in southern Sudan into the Didinga tribe, and her journey to the camp took 4 days by car. She explained her disorientation at being left at the camp and that she did not understand why her parents remained living in their home village without her. She told me she had not seen her parents since she moved to Kakuma.

Halimo was born in 1980 in Somalia, and she grew up there until she was 11 years old. Due to the start of the Somali Civil War in 1991 and the subsequent violence and insecurity in her home country, she had to flee. She traveled by foot, but her family was able to support her as they journeyed, reiterating the significance of family networks as sources of social capital. By providing social, economic, and emotional support to their members, families can help individuals achieve their goals and navigate difficult situations. In this case, Halimo could turn to her family for assistance to access resources that she might not otherwise have had, including financial support. Bourdieu emphasizes that social capital is not equally distributed in society and that individuals with stronger social networks and relationships are more likely to have access to resources and opportunities that can enhance their social mobility. In this sense, social capital can play a significant role in shaping an individual's social status.

Halimo and her family initially went to the Dadaab Refugee Complex, a UNHCR site based in Kenya. Halimo has many painful memories of the Somali Civil War, and she told me how she saw her brother, sister, and father being killed by soldiers. She had to walk for 15 days with water in her bag, and the distance she walked every day made her feet ache. Similar to Ken's story, she too relied on others to give her food and water. After 15 days of walking, Halimo arrived at a hospital to be treated and there realized she had been deafened by the loud gunshots; they were so loud, they caused her ears to bleed. Because she had been born hearing and became deaf when she was older, she was still able to speak well in Somali and Arabic, the languages used by her ethnic group, Dhulbahante, and her clan, Daarood.

Halimo arrived at the Dadaab Refugee Complex in 1992. The complex contains three refugee camps: Dagahaley, Hagadera, and Ifo; Halimo met her husband in a hospital in Ifo, the oldest of the three camps in Dadaab. They married and had 10 children. In Ifo, Halimo owned and ran a tiny general store with her husband, but they had problems with Somali terrorists who attacked and robbed her:

[There are] a lot of problems in Ifo. I had a business there. Somali terrorists asked for money from us. We were afraid. We gave a lot of money to them. Tomorrow, again! I didn't feel good. The business didn't go well. My mum was mad, a Somali kicked her head. Her husband as well, kicked on his heart. My sister, 6 years old, was raped. We were mad, we waited for 5 months in 2001, [...] 2002 actually, again raped. My mum wanted to go to Kakuma. We asked [the] UN to help us.

Having asked UNHCR to help them move away from their terrorizers in Ifo, in 2004 they took everything from their home and moved via a UNHCR car to Kakuma Refugee Camp, traveling for 2 days. Similarly, Abdi traveled from Dadaab Refugee Complex to Kakuma Refugee Camp in a car provided by UNHCR. The overcrowding in Dadaab Refugee Complex is a significant push factor that induces many refugees to seek refuge elsewhere; many felt that they were forced to move from Dadaab Refugee Complex to Kakuma Refugee Camp (Betts et al., 2020). In 2008, around 13,000 Somali refugees were relocated from Dadaab Refugee Complex to Kakuma Refugee Camp due to overcrowding.

Refugees may also mobilize for other reasons than war and political conflict: that is, to access education and health care. Margaret narrated:

I was sleeping, [and] my mother woke me up and told me to go with my father to go to Kakuma. I don't understand it, my father took my hand and I don't know, I don't understand what they said, I asked where [do] we go? I don't know where I go. They said I was to go to Kakuma to go to school. I went there in Kakuma, I don't know all the people in Kakuma.

Atem was born into the Dinka tribe in southern Sudan; he arrived at Kakuma Refugee Camp in 2002 when he was 10 years old, in a bid to escape the civil war and to receive an education. After saving money for some time, his mother was able to go to Kakuma Refugee Camp:

I arrived in Kakuma in 2002. I came here because I want to learn in school, I want to have a good education because if I learn a lot I can become clever later, and live better than to be lazy and to be not clever. That's why I wanted to go to Kakuma to learn more. So I can help, support deaf people in the world. To help them to grow up for the future and to have a better life.

Atem's journey to the Kakuma Refugee Camp can be seen as an effort to build his cultural and linguistic capital. By escaping the civil war and seeking refuge in the camp, he gained access to educational opportunities that he might not have had otherwise. Through education, he was able to acquire knowledge and skills, a form of cultural capital that could then be used to enhance his social capital. Furthermore, being in a refugee camp like Kakuma can also provide opportunities to develop linguistic capital through learning new languages. Atem had the opportunity to develop his sign language skills through education in the deaf units. Atem's educational journey enabled him to become a teacher, sharing his expertise and knowledge with deaf refugees in deaf units. His investment in education and acquisition of cultural knowledge augmented his social status while simultaneously increasing his economic capital.

The provision of education in the camp was also given as one of the reasons for Nyathak's family's decision to move there. Nyathak is the youngest of the six deaf refugees whom I interviewed; she was just 18 years old when I first met her at Nassibunda Primary School in Kakuma 3. She arrived in the Kakuma Refugee Camp in 2004 with her family members, who were motivated by the desire to provide her with educational opportunities—that is, to acquire cultural and linguistic capital. By receiving an education, Nyathak would be able to acquire knowledge, skills, and credentials that could enhance her opportunities; her acquisition of sign language would also enhance her linguistic capital. Her family stayed until 2007, returned to southern Sudan until 2013, and then came back to Kakuma Refugee Camp.

Another factor for going to Kakuma Refugee Camp, shared by all of the deaf refugees and their families, is access to health care. There are various health care institutions within the camp. Abdi's family decided to move to access the health services provided by UNHCR so that his sister, who had cancer, and his brother, who had sustained leg injuries, could both receive the appropriate treatment. His family's decision to move to Kakuma Refugee Camp was motivated by the need to access health care services in the camp. By accessing health care services, Abdi's family was able to access resources that could improve their health outcomes and potentially enhance their social and economic opportunities.

Deaf Lives in Kakuma Refugee Camp: A Bourdieusian Lens

Having described some of the ways that deaf people have arrived in Kakuma Refugee Camp, I move to a description of some aspects of their lives within the camp. Following a brief description of the camp to provide context, I examine the networks that deaf refugees have developed when navigating this field. I then look at how embodied knowledge (habitus) shapes processes of socialization in the camp and consider the various forms of capital that deaf refugees may accrue, develop, and transfer over the course of their daily lives.

Kakuma Refugee Camp is a massive camp of 5.62 square miles (UN-Habitat, 2021), constructed in largely arid terrain and characterized by dirt roads with huge potholes and many rocks; it contains numerous houses built with mud-brick walls and roofs of corrugated iron or plastic sheeting (see Figure 3.2). Houses are grouped in ethnic neighborhoods, such as a Somali area, an Ethiopian area, and a South Sudanese area. The camp is full of life, with people walking through the streets carrying firewood sticks on their heads, and with the UNHCR cars and *bodaboda* (motorbike taxis) trying to pass through the crowds while avoiding the streets' potholes. Camp inhabitants are busily buying and carrying goods from the sites of their numerous economic activities, such as food markets, shops, restaurants, and bars. These economic activities are complemented by services provided by the inhabitants

Figure 3.2. A dirt path and buildings in Kakuma Refugee Camp.

themselves, such as internet and telephone services, hairdressing salons, and tailoring. Overall, the camp gives the impression of an urban-like form of living in a dense and informal settlement.

Network Nodes for Deaf Refugees

The field of Kakuma Refugee Camp also contains deaf spaces produced by deaf refugees, and the network formed among them. The nodes of this network (see Chapter 7) are the different spaces where deaf refugees gather to perform their everyday activities and to socialize with other deaf people. Some spaces are where deaf people often meet, such as in deaf units and adult learning courses; these are regular deaf spaces. Other deaf spaces include the shop and house of Halimo, a deaf Somali woman, where deaf people informally gather (discussed below). The concept of "deaf spaces," and the networks formed among them, illustrates the role of social capital in the lives of deaf refugees. These networks can be drawn upon to access resources and support, such as information about job opportunities, advice on navigating the refugee system, and emotional support during difficult times.

To explore these networks, I engaged in participatory mapping with participants. In her fieldwork on deaf people in Tanzania, Lee (2012) stated that "participatory mapping utilizes participants' knowledge of legal boundaries, important spaces, and their own representations of their geographic and social maps" (p. 60). In order to find out where deaf refugees could be found in the camp, I asked Atem to show me where people lived on a map that I had drawn based on the official map provided by UNHCR (2017b) and to tell me their names and ages. From the drawings we made, I created a map of Kakuma Refugee Camp showing Kakuma 1–4 (see Figure 3.3) with the details of meaningful places for deaf refugees and, by extension, the research project: the houses of the refugees that I went on to interview; the deaf schools; the food distribution center; places where deaf people work; institutions with courses attended by deaf people; and the UNHCR Protection Delivery Unit, which deaf refugees had cause to visit on several occasions during my fieldwork. Because most deaf refugees' houses are concentrated in Kakuma 1, more activity and meaningful places for deaf people are focused in that area. There are fewer deaf refugees' houses in other parts of the camp, and these are scattered far from each other. One important place for deaf people in Kakuma 2–4 is the Nassibunda Primary School's deaf unit, which is situated in Kakuma 3.

The most obvious place for frequent gatherings of deaf people in the camp are the three deaf units in the primary schools, similar to the ones that exist in Dadaab Refugee Complex (see Youngs, 2010). In Kakuma Refugee Camp, a deaf unit was created in 1997 in MPC1 Primary School, funded by the IRC. In 2005, the LWF took over responsibility for supporting the education of deaf people within their Special Needs Education program and displaced the deaf unit in MPC1 Primary School to Fashoda Primary School, also in Kakuma 1. In 2014, two deaf units were created in addition to the one in Fashoda Primary School, in Tarach Primary School (Kakuma 1) and in Nassibunda Primary School (Kakuma 3). The units have a broader remit than providing education for primary-age children; many deaf refugees attend primary school as adults because

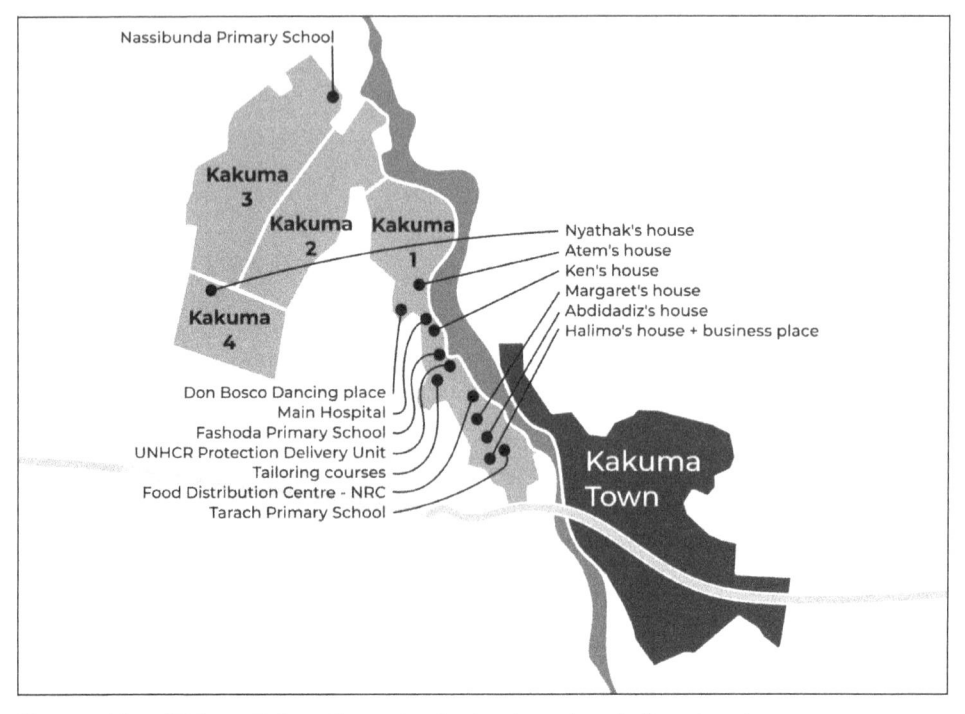

Figure 3.3. Map of Kakuma Refugee Camp, showing locations where deaf people gather.

they arrive in Kakuma Refugee Camp later in life and may not have had the chance to be schooled or to complete primary school in their home countries.

Most of my key participants had studied in one of these deaf units when they were growing up. Here, they were able to develop cultural capital, including linguistic capital, because these units offer a space where deaf people can meet their peers and communicate in sign languages. Margaret, who moved to Kakuma Refugee Camp when she was 2 years old, went to MPC1 Primary School, where she learned sign language alongside Ken and Atem. Their teacher was a hearing Chinese man who taught them ASL, and a deaf Burundian teacher, Chris, also stayed in the refugee camp to teach deaf children in the school.

Abdi, a deaf Somali man, had been to primary school in Ifo, Dadaab, in the 2010s, but he had to repeat this schooling in Kakuma due to administrative problems regarding his diploma. In contrast, Halimo, who also had been in Dadaab first, explained that when she was young, she had not had the opportunity to go to school or learn to read and write because in 1992 there was not yet a school for deaf refugees in Dadaab. Halimo learned how to sign by watching other deaf people, which she did every day to help her learning. Halimo's experience highlights the way in which social capital can facilitate the accumulation of linguistic capital. In this case, the social network of deaf individuals provided a resource for Halimo to learn a new language, and this resource was made available through the relationships she formed with others. Nyathak initially lived with her family in Kakuma 3 and studied in the deaf unit in Tarach Primary School (Kakuma 1). The family home sustained terrible damage in a storm, and the family was forced to move to Kakuma 4. This move meant that Nyathak was obliged to change schools and joined the deaf unit in the Nassibunda Primary School (Kakuma 3).

A Kenyan deaf teacher, John, works with the LWF as a special needs education teacher in deaf units. He supports deaf refugees through teaching new deaf students, and he is involved in social encounters with other deaf refugees. Some deaf refugees also work as deaf teachers; one of these was Atem, who was South Sudanese. After attending primary school in the camp, they each graduated from a Kenyan high school outside the camp and were employed by LWF as teachers. Their accumulation of linguistic and social capital by gaining education credentials provided them with a source of income, converting to economic capital. In addition, being employed as teachers by LWF not only provided them with a wage but also allowed them to use their linguistic skills to support and empower other refugees. Being personally aware of the details of life in the camp, the deaf teachers tended to use a lot of everyday examples specific to deaf refugees in their teaching.

These schools also function as meeting places. On numerous occasions during my fieldwork, I noticed deaf refugees gathering near one of the deaf units, where they would meet to socialize. Deaf people living near the deaf units also tended to congregate nearby. Some deaf refugees have even intentionally moved their homes (having asked permission from UNHCR) to enable them to meet other deaf refugees; often, their new habitation will be near deaf units and/or other deaf households. By coming together in these meeting places and forming relationships with one another, deaf refugees are able to build social capital through connections and support systems that can help them navigate the challenges in their situation, providing resources and support that they would not be able to access on their own. The decision to move closer to deaf units echoes the findings of my previous study in Belgium (le Maire, 2015), where several families had made the decision to move to Namur, a city in the south, due to educational opportunities provided by the city as well as sociocultural factors. However, despite deaf refugees moving closer to one another, they nonetheless continue to reside in the area associated with others of the same ethnicity because habitations inside the camp are typically grouped according to ethnic identity.

Aside from deaf units in schools, other educational spaces were identified as places of gathering for deaf refugees. Refugees often attend adult learning courses on a weekly basis, such as cookery courses at the Saint Clare of Assisi Training Institute. Margaret and Ken were apprentices who improved their sewing skills in a tailoring class running in the afternoon at the same institute. The institute is situated in Kakuma town, about 2 hours' walk from the refugee camp. Thus, the deaf refugees who attend the courses have to journey considerable distances by foot to get to the institute in time for their morning class. Journeying long hours by foot to attend classes is a labor-intensive process and requires physical capital. It thus requires significant physical effort to have access to social and cultural resources, including education.

There are also religious spaces where deaf people gather in groups. Depending on their beliefs and religion, deaf refugees attend Christian churches or mosques in Kakuma town or inside the refugee camp. The Full Gospel Church of Kenya (FGCK) is located in Kakuma Town, near the Saint Clare Institute, and is attended by some deaf refugees along with a KSL interpreter. One participant, Ken, had previously attended a church in Kakuma, but he left because they did not provide a sign language interpreter, leaving him to sit passively, unaware of what was being said. Instead of accepting this situation, he decided to move to the same church that Atem attended. Only one to three deaf refugees typically attended the FGCK every Sunday. Atem was one:

> Yes, I always go to the same church. Before, there were no churches there [in Kakuma town], then first there was a church known as WORLDWIDE. There were deaf people at the church but, with time, the deaf people felt bad because there should have been money for them, but the church would only give a pot of maize and rice. It is not enough food, so deaf people stopped going to church and waited, and then another church appeared [FGCK] and asked deaf people to come, and deaf people asked other deaf people to come. And now, still, deaf people go to that church.

This excerpt tells us two things: that, in addition to the presence of a KSL interpreter, the presence of other deaf people affects attendance, as does the receipt of food and other resources. In the case of Ken, the lack of a sign language interpreter at his previous church meant that he was unable to fully participate and engage with the community there. This likely limited his ability to build social and cultural capital within that community and may have contributed to his decision to seek out a church that was more accessible to his needs. Similarly, Kusters (2015) observed that deaf inhabitants of Adamorobe, Ghana, were more eager to attend deaf-led church services in the village if they were offered resources and donations, such as rice. Several Deaf Studies scholars have pointed to the importance of deaf churches, or of churches where sign language interpretation is provided, as meeting places for deaf people and/or as places of learning (Friedner, 2015; Heap, 2003). As deaf inhabitants already practiced deaf sociality in various deaf spaces in Adamorobe village, they perceived that there was little or no need to go to a deaf church that brought them few benefits (Kusters, 2015). Similarly, deaf refugees in Kakuma did not go to church once they found out that it did not provide enough food for them; instead, they waited for another church to provide what they needed.

Some of the deaf spaces mentioned previously consist of a reasonably large number of deaf people (10–15), typically from a mix of countries, ethnicities, and religions; other spaces consisted of only two deaf people. Indeed, it is likely that I had some influence on the size of some deaf spaces, because the number of attendees appeared to grow when I visited them, probably due to curiosity about me as a white deaf newcomer (see Chapter 2). On only one occasion did I witness a larger deaf space, with 50 to 60 deaf people in attendance; this was when the Starkey Hearing Foundation, a charity distributing free hearing aids (le Maire, 2020), visited Kakuma Refugee Camp (see Chapter 10).

Deaf refugees' mobility is not restricted to the camp; as outlined previously, they are able to go out of the camp to visit, for example, Kakuma town on foot (see also Chapter 10). Some venture farther into the country in order to access high school education in one of several different deaf boarding schools in western Kenya, located in the cities of Webuye, Kericho, Mumias, and Kisii. Attending a boarding school for deaf students in a different region of the country serves as a strategic approach for accumulating both cultural and language capital while also highlighting the importance of the physical capital that facilitates travel. This educational journey enables students to expand their social networks beyond the confines of their immediate surroundings, transcending local scales (see Chapter 7). By connecting with peers who share similar experiences and perspectives and by interacting with individuals from different regions and backgrounds, students have the opportunity to develop a deeper understanding of sign language and to build stronger social and cultural connections. Through these expanded networks, they enhance their overall cultural and linguistic capital, transcending the limitations of their initial social contexts.

Having moved into Kakuma Refugee Camp, both Atem and Nyathak later returned to their home countries and stayed for extended periods before returning. Atem, who died as we were completing this book, continued to have a strong desire to return to South Sudan when it became safe to do so and once he had adequate resources to make the journey. Because some deaf refugees grew up in the camp from a very young age, they do not have contact with deaf people in their home countries and cannot compare their interactions with deaf refugees in the camp with those elsewhere. Conversely, Atem had stayed for extended periods in his home country, and he explained to me that he had found a contrast between his deaf friends in South Sudan and the deaf refugees in Kakuma Refugee Camp. He saw himself as the only one to know a "proper" sign language, whereas others in his home country used what he called "village signs" (see Chapter 8 for more on this).

Although there are several regular meeting places for deaf people, some of which are specifically designed for deaf people or have been made accessible to deaf people, there is no deaf-led institution in the camp, such as a deaf association or deaf-led nongovernmental organization (NGO). The Kenyan deaf organizations that I visited in Nairobi while I was waiting for a research permit are not involved in the camp, perhaps partially due to the camp's distance from the city. Some deaf Kenyans (e.g., deaf teachers) have visited the camp but have never stayed long term. Anthony, the Kenyan deaf teacher who lives next to the camp, was planning to create an association of Kakuma's deaf refugees, with the aim of giving opportunities for them to socialize, to work together, to find jobs within the camp, to find solutions to problems at work, and to improve their living conditions inside the camp. At the moment of writing, Anthony is trying to create this association, but he is finding it very challenging due to financial constraints.

Embodied Knowledge and the Socialization Process

When people move, be it from the countryside to the city or across national boundaries, it involves a shift in their habitus, which may result in what Bourdieu called a "split habitus" (*Habitus clivé*)

(Reed-Danahay, 2019). In the case of the refugee camp, the refugees have all experienced a shift in habitus from leaving their home country, arriving in and living in a different country, and acquiring a new identity or primary label—that is, as a refugee (Mijić, 2022; Zetter, 1991). In doing so, they have internalized a very different way of looking at and understanding the world. Additionally, deaf refugees are confronted with a second "split habitus" due to their being a minority with a different physical and sensory experience of their environment compared to that of their hearing peers. When deaf refugees enter the Kakuma Refugee Camp—many of them as children or young people—they have to learn a new language, a new rhythm of life, and a new sense of time, and they must internalize a new worldview. In addition, they are now refugees in a field governed by UNHCR and are thus subjected to a very different set of rules from their home countries and communities.

Bourdieu's research provides a framework of theories that relates to his perspective on the social space of Algerian resettlement. In a collaborative study with Sayad, Bourdieu discusses how Kabyle peasants were forced to leave their villages and move to resettlement camps. These camps were created during the Algerian war, and the "quasi urban camps brought people together who had previously been distant in both social and physical space" (Reed-Danahay, 2019, p. 51). Bourdieu also stated that ethnic or national divisions may manifest more clearly when people move closer geographically (Reed-Danahay, 2019).

In the field of Kakuma Refugee Camp, deaf people who come from different countries, follow different religions, and have had different educational journeys all gather in common spaces. This means that deaf people who had previously been distant in social space and geographical space (in terms of coming from different countries) are now in physical proximity. There is a marked disparity between Kakuma Refugee Camp and the places where they grew up—usually villages in Somalia or Sudan—in terms of access to deaf education, the sign languages used, and the people with whom they socialize. Many of their new relationships allow deaf refugees to form a very different networking group than they had before arriving at the camp.

The deaf camp inhabitants are from different ethnic tribes, a term that is difficult to define. In anthropology, "tribe" has historically been used to define *in a negative way* the small ethnic groups that live in an "underdeveloped" ("primitive" or "savage") manner (Glatzer, 2002). However, in some parts of the world, the term is used with pride, and people are honored to be part of one (Glatzer, 2002). Although some tribes are small, the term can also be applied to highly developed human social groups containing groups of "clans," which are hierarchically smaller and less populous groups. The deaf refugees I interviewed explained to me that they came from various tribes, including Dinka (which is a similar ethnic group to Bor), Didinga, and Aweil; from different religions, such as Islam and Christianity; and from different countries, such as Somalia, South Sudan, and even Kenya. In deaf social gatherings, the space was mixed gender, but deaf refugees tended to remain close to those of the same gender when they were in private spaces. This tendency can be seen as a manifestation of their habitus, which is shaped by their experiences as deaf refugees and their internalized cultural norms around gender. Examples included Atem with Ken, and Halimo and her two female Muslim friends from the same home country who live near her.

I did not observe gatherings between deaf LGBTQIA+ people in Kakuma Refugee Camp,[1] likely because deaf refugees would not usually disclose these identities due to safety concerns; it

---

1. LGBTQIA+ stands for Lesbian, Gay, Bisexual, Transgender, Queer or Questioning, Intersex, Asexual, and more.

is highly likely that they would assume straight identities when in the camp. Nor did I observe gatherings of deaf people with disabilities such as deafblindness, which could also be attributed to individuals preferring not to disclose hidden disabilities. Physical capital plays a crucial role in facilitating connections and networks within refugee camps, and it is important to consider that some deaf refugees with additional disabilities may not be effectively networked with other deaf refugees in the camp. One exception is Ken. Ken often explained to me that he had issues with his sight, but he did not use the term "deafblind" to identify himself; it is possible that he was unaware of this term or concept. To overcome barriers relating to his disability, such as there being no light available in Kakuma Refugee Camp at night, he employed the social capital strategy of asking his friend Atem to sleep in his house.

Deaf refugees often explained to me that they do not consider ethnicity as something that is important in their relationships with other deaf refugees. Rather, they place value on their mutual deafness, language modalities (e.g., signing, writing), and life experiences as deaf people, which would typically trump the value placed on religion, ethnicity, or country of origin:

Ken: I know a Somali man and he is my friend. I have friends from Sudan and Somalia who are deaf; we are united and friends, and it is good. But there are bad [hearing] Sudanese people, it's better to keep them away from us. In the countries of Somalia, Sudan, and other countries of the world, with refugees from Kenya, Somalia, Sudan, Congo, Burundi, all of them are friends if they're deaf and we are united.

Amandine: And for hearing people?

Ken: Hearing people are hard, they talk together without us. But deaf people with sign language, refugees from Somalia, Sudan, Congo, Ethiopia, Burundi, and different countries, all of them are united and the same. Deaf people use only sign language, but hearing people do not. Hearing families talk alone together [without deaf people] and, separately, there are deaf people communicating with only sign language.[2]

Deaf refugees may have developed a habitus that emphasizes the importance of their shared life experience and language modalities, which can create a strong sense of solidarity that transcends ethnicity or religion.

Narratives collected from deaf refugees contain a lot of apparent contradictions and ambivalences in the distinctions made between "good" and "bad" people. For example, a Somali may say that the Sudanese are "friends" or "bad," depending on where they are from. In my observations, I found that if a deaf refugee is from a Somali tribe, he would tend to label a group of Sudanese people as "bad" people. Despite the fact that deaf refugees from a mix of different ethnicities and/or countries of origin gather together and are friendly with each other, they would often talk to me about their differences and disagreements with people from other ethnicities and countries and would negatively portray them as being violent or oppressive, mapping the incidences of violence in the camp onto particular ethnicities (see Chapter 9). Negative portrayals of individuals from different ethnicities and countries of origin can be seen as a reflection of deaf refugees' habitus,

---

2. In this excerpt, Ken refers to deaf refugees from Congo and Burundi. However, there were very few deaf refugees of these nationalities at the time of my fieldwork because most had resettled or moved back to their home countries.

which is shaped by their experiences and socialization in different social fields. For example, deaf refugees may have experienced discrimination or marginalization based on their ethnicity or country of origin, which could lead to negative perceptions and attitudes toward individuals from other ethnicities or countries. Yet, although ethnic, national, and religious differences among deaf people are identified, a greater distinction is made between deaf versus *hearing* people. Hearing people are often designated as the "bad" people irrespective of their ethnicity; for example, a deaf Sudanese person would tell me that a hearing Sudanese person is "bad," whereas deaf Somali people are their friends. At the same time, many deaf people socialize with hearing people within their households, so it is not the case that hearing people are avoided.

Another aspect of habitus in the refugee camp is linguistic habitus. Due to the diversity of its inhabitants in terms of country of origin, language practices in the camp are also very diverse. Hearing inhabitants use multiple spoken languages depending on the ethnic and linguistic groups they are in and the context of the communication. Swahili and English are the languages mostly used in the camp because those are the main languages used in Kenya. These languages are used for intergroup discussions, such as at markets, water collection points, and schools. The Sudanese people use a lot of Juba-Arabic, a pidgin lingua franca spoken mainly in Equatoria province of South Sudan for communicating among the different linguistic groups. When there are only Somalis in the group, they may use the Somali language except for discussions of religious topics, wherein the Arabic language is used.

Deaf people's habitus is profoundly infused by their being deaf. Using Bourdieu's concept, O'Brien (2021a) explains that deaf people using a visual-spatial sign language have a different physical and sensory experience of their environment compared to their hearing peers. Regarding the language situation for deaf people living in Kakuma Refugee Camp, KSL is predominantly used. Most deaf refugees learned KSL in the previously mentioned deaf units in the primary schools around Kakuma Refugee Camp, and they continue to use it if they go on to study in Kenyan high schools outside of the camp. As mentioned previously, ASL has been used within the deaf units as well, by foreign deaf and hearing teachers from different countries, including the United States and China. Education services provided by Kakuma Refugee Camp and the Kenyan government are not the only way to learn sign language, however; deaf refugees also learn and develop their sign language in informal settings and everyday encounters with other deaf refugees, such as in churches, houses, and adult learning vocational courses within the Kakuma Refugee Camp. Deaf refugees can accumulate linguistic capital through their social networks with other deaf refugees, which is also a form of physical labor relying on the physical capital to walk to meet people, to network, and to converse with others. Physical capital can thus contribute to the accumulation of linguistic capital through social capital.

KSL and ASL are not the only sign languages used by deaf refugees because there is some use of the signing of their home countries, such as signs from Sudan and Somalia. Deaf refugees conceptualize some of the signing from their home countries as "village signs," which are, for them, different from the sign language they use in the camp. The sign VILLAGE is signed with one finger on the head (see Figure 3.4), and it is the sign that is used by deaf refugees to refer to the deaf inhabitants of their home village and also to refer to the deaf refugees living in the camp who do not have knowledge of the official sign languages of KSL or ASL. Some deaf refugees would claim that there was "no sign language" in their home countries. There are two possible interpretations of this: They had not seen other signs than "village signs" in their countries of origin (having, e.g., never been to a deaf school) or that the sign language in their home country was not as established as other sign languages. They often perceived their home countries' sign languages as being of lesser value, along with other sign languages that do not hold any official

Figure 3.4. Atem signs VILLAGE.

status in schools, associations, or statutory bodies (see Chapter 8 for a longer discussion of this). As mentioned in Chapter 1, the concept of *comparison* applies in the case of deaf refugees: They make comparisons between different languages and between countries, and they give more value to some sign languages compared to others.

The deaf inhabitants of the camp communicate with hearing refugees and hearing employees working in the camp in a variety of ways. As mentioned previously, in the evenings they return to their (mostly hearing) families to eat and sleep. Deaf people communicate with hearing people from their own tribe or ethnic group by using gestures, lipreading, speaking, or writing. Deaf refugees who are part of a particular tribe or ethnic group may have been exposed to that group's language from an early age through interactions with their family or community members, which can contribute to their overall linguistic capital and provide them with additional resources for communicating with hearing people who share their background. The communication that I observed being used within the family and with neighbors was often informal and repetitive, usually focused on daily life practices (e.g., what to eat, when to sleep).

Signing marks deaf people as different from the surrounding hearing majority. Similar to their childhood experiences of being the only deaf person (or part of a small number of deaf people) in their home village, in the camp the refugees again encounter a mostly auditive environment, where deaf refugees are met with barriers causing problems and difficulties with communication. Deaf refugees face issues of communication during their initial interview with officials following their arrival at the camp, as well as in discussions with healthcare workers in hospitals, because mostly English or Swahili is used. Deaf refugees face these communication barriers in their everyday lives and are therefore often marginalized. They remain ignorant of the discourse and information that exists within the camp that could be obtained from other refugees and NGO volunteers. Facing these situations, deaf refugees draw on a large resource of strategies for communication, using their linguistic and social capital to obtain what they need to achieve their aspirations (see Chapter 10).

One of these strategies is working with sign language interpreters. I met four sign language interpreters during my fieldwork, all of whom are Kenyans using KSL. Interpreters are used during the Refugee Status Determination (RSD) interviews, when deaf refugees have first arrived at the camp. I did not have the opportunity to observe any of these processes and, therefore, did not witness these interactions firsthand. However, during the fieldwork, I had many opportunities to observe how KSL interpreters work with deaf refugees, specifically during meetings between NGOs and Anthony, a Kenyan deaf teacher, and during classes held in the adult learning center.

My impression was that some interpreters did not faithfully interpret the information. Their interpretation tended to be very concise, not matching the length of the utterance. They were thus making decisions about what information to deliver to deaf refugees, and how, leaving deaf refugees without access to much of what was being said. I also witnessed deaf refugees attempting to ask a question but being completely ignored by the interpreters, who refused to voice their questions. There are notable power differences between Kenyan interpreters and foreign deaf refugees. Being both hearing and from Kenya, interpreters are in a position from which they can easily oppress deaf refugees in this context. Some interpreters are unreliable and arrive late or not at all; they are difficult to coordinate and schedule, and, according to Anthony, they are afraid to interpret in any public domain. These issues frequently come up in daily interactions.

The interpreters in Kakuma Refugee Camp work as volunteers. Most of the interpreters are teachers working for the LWF, and this NGO sometimes asks hearing teachers with knowledge of KSL to interpret for deaf refugees. In other cases, for example, in adult cooking classes, an interpreter may be interested in working for deaf refugees because it is expected that they will offer the interpreter the food they cooked during the class; put in Bourdieusian terms, the interpreter anticipates receiving a form of economic capital (food) in payment for the service.

Due to these problems and the general lack of interpreters, in some situations deaf refugees decide not to use interpreters at all—for example, when going to hospitals or meeting with UNHCR officials. Instead, they use other strategies to communicate with hearing people. Some draw on family members for interpreting, but this is not always possible for deaf refugees because their families may not be present, perhaps because they were deceased or still living in their home countries.

Exploring the Various Forms of Capital

We have seen that deaf refugees develop social capital through networking; thus, social capital is based on the relationships and proximity to each other in physical and social space, where they can get and share advice and support. Cultural capital in the camp comes in many forms and is developed through many channels, such as studying in deaf units and graduating from primary and secondary school. As mentioned in the section on deaf refugees' journeys to Kakuma, the educational opportunities for deaf people that exist in the Kakuma Refugee Camp are a strong motivating factor for families of deaf refugees to move into the camp. These schools allow the refugees to develop cultural capital, not only through formal education but also through informal encounters with their peers with whom they learn and practice their new sign language skills.

Some deaf refugees have opportunities to develop their economic capital through their work with NGOs, including deaf teachers in deaf units (such as Atem and John), shop owners, or workers for the Norwegian Refugee Council (NRC), which provides food and subsistence to refugees via food distribution centers. One deaf refugee, Ken, worked in a food distribution center, but this job was not as consistent as other forms of employment because the system at the NRC operates such that refugees who work there are only provided with food and subsistence for 1 week per month and thus only work there for that period. Usually, refugees can collect their resources in the first week of the month.

Deaf refugees who lack economic and other forms of capital usually come to rely more on their social capital as their main source of agency. For example, they may draw on support from their families to be able to communicate with UNHCR officers and collect information from their social contacts. Sharing information (e.g., about the process of resettlement) helps them to be competitive in the refugee camp. In my fieldwork, I identified Halimo's house as a key site where deaf refugees gathered to share information with other deaf refugees. Halimo owns and runs a business with her hearing husband, a tiny general store providing basic goods such as powdered juice, sweets, shortcake biscuits, and single cigarettes. Previously, Halimo's hearing sister ran the business, and she owned a house provided by UNHCR. She decided to move to Nairobi and allowed Halimo and her husband to take over the business and to use her home. Halimo, therefore, is economically in a better situation than other deaf refugees due to the economic capital of her family. The business is successful because of its excellent location, and Halimo and her husband employ other, hearing refugees to cook and clean for them.

Halimo's house was a key site for my research because every time I visited, I met about 5–10 deaf refugees from different tribes, ethnicities, countries, and religions who gathered to eat and socialize there (see Figure 3.5). Halimo is a very hospitable person and often told me how she loved to host other deaf refugees in her house and give them food for free. She enjoyed sharing what she had and talking with them:

> We share stories, we eat together. Deaf people come to visit me and we talk a lot, sometimes I feel that I had better help them and I give food to them. Then, we talk and they are not hungry, and they say thanks and talk and then go home. Deaf people from Sudan come to my home to talk. Me, Halimo, I am happy and ask, "Do you want to eat?" I give them pasta and then they are full and go home. Later, they come again to talk with Halimo.

Halimo's house has grown into a key deaf space for several deaf refugees in the camp, alongside other key places such as the deaf units in the schools, and the courses and church in Kakuma town. Socialization at her place involves the exchange of gossip, information, and advice, and deaf refugees regularly come to her house to ask her for assistance. Some ask to be accompanied by Halimo to the hospital or to the UNHCR Protection Delivery Unit because many deaf refugees know that Halimo is skilled at navigating these spaces and, due to her experience and social capital, specifically knows what is required for deaf people to have successful interactions in these places. Halimo is able to speak to hearing people using Somali and Arabic, the languages

Figure 3.5. Halimo with other deaf refugees in her house.

used by her ethnic group, Dhulbahante, and her clan, Daarood, and she is also very skilled in communicating with gestures; this linguistic capital has given her knowledge of the dynamics in the camp. Linking back to the Bourdieusian concept of field, Halimo's knowledge of the "rules of the field" means she is a source of information for others. Even hearing refugees who have deaf relatives will visit her to ask for advice about deaf education or sign language, asking Halimo's opinion on which school to enroll their child in, and gathering social networks from Halimo's knowledge of people working for the NGOs who are responsible for deaf education in the camp.

According to Bourdieu, different forms of capital can "change into one another" (Bourdieu, 1986). In the situation with Halimo, she is building relationships and networks with deaf refugees by providing free food and hosting them in her home; in other words, she is transforming her economic capital into social capital. By facilitating deaf and hearing refugees to gather in her space to share information and advice with her and each other, she not only allows her own social capital to develop but also the social and cultural capital of other refugees. Through the networking that takes place in her space, and through Halimo's own guidance of people into spaces of education, they can build up even more cultural capital. Therefore, although deaf refugees may struggle to expand on their economic capital inside the camp, they may be able to capitalize on other areas using the social, cultural, and linguistic capital that they bring into and develop while staying in the camp. Refugees thus try to compensate for barriers and the lack of resources with various other forms of capital.

As a result of Halimo's social, cultural, and economic capital, she is seen as a leading figure and a central source of information when she moves through other places in the camp:

> We go to the kitchen for the cooking class. It is only Ken and Halimo who are there, the other deaf people are not there. The refugees ask Halimo directly where the deaf refugees are, and she says precisely what the deaf refugees are doing: Someone is now at the UNHCR Protection Delivery Unit to complain because her ex-husband does not pay her at all for her baby; someone else has a new baby and needs to rest. I ask Halimo how she knows this, and she tells me that she goes to every deaf house near her in the morning to find out who is going to do what. (Fieldnotes, March 9, 2018)

This example shows that houses are central meeting places. Deaf people making the rounds to deaf houses is described in Kusters' (2015) ethnographic study in Adamorobe, where about 40 deaf people live in the same village due to local hereditary deafness. Kusters (2015) noticed that deaf people in Adamorobe tend to gather in the houses of deaf people who are taking informal leadership positions in relation to deaf people living in the village; she observed that these deaf people would make "greeting" rounds in the morning, going to houses of hearing relatives and of deaf people. Similar to this phenomenon in Adamorobe, Halimo's mobilities in various hearing-run places (e.g., the hospitals, the NGOs, the houses of other refugees), as well as deaf people's houses and other deaf spaces in the camp, play an important role in her leadership alongside the forms of capital she employs and expands in and through these mobilities. Halimo's mobility as a central person thus coincides with her house being a key destination for other deaf and hearing refugees' mobilities within the camp. The accumulation of capital, particularly social capital, is often a labor-intensive process that involves a significant amount of effort and investment. In the case of Halimo, her mobility and interactions with others play a key role in her accumulation of social capital, but the labor (physical capital) involved in this process is not always explicitly acknowledged. This labor may take various forms, including the physical labor of walking around to meet people, the emotional labor of networking and conversing with others, and the intellectual labor of strategizing and building relationships. Bourdieu's ideas highlight the importance of recognizing and valuing this labor, even in situations where traditional notions of work may not apply. Despite the immobility and "stuckness" of the people living in the refugee camp (see Chapter 10), there is an immense amount of mobility and labor involved in building and maintaining social capital.

Discussion and Conclusion

In Deaf Refugee Studies, few scholars have considered deaf refugees' views; instead, most studies have focused on the perspectives of teachers, interpreters, and other professionals working with deaf refugees. Additionally, most studies are focused on deaf refugees, particularly children, who are being resettled in and hosted by countries in the Global North. There has been very little focus on deaf refugees living in refugee camps and/or in the Global South. This study contributes to the field of Deaf Refugee Studies in taking an approach centered on the deaf refugees' own experiences and perspectives, and in being situated in a refugee camp in the Global South.

Several earlier studies (Elder, 2015; Olsen, 2018; Sivunen, 2019) have argued that deaf locals from the host country play a crucial role in providing opportunities for deaf refugees to access networks in the host country. In Kakuma Refugee Camp, few deaf nonrefugees socialize or work in the camp; one exception is Anthony, the Kenyan deaf teacher working in the Nassibunda school's deaf unit. He would sometimes be involved in interpreting for deaf refugees, for example, when he was volunteering at the event organized by the Starkey Hearing Foundation. In addition, some students go to school outside the camp, attending high schools in Kenya (see Chapter 10). This is an indicator of networking with deaf people in the host country.

Deaf refugees often learn one or more new sign languages in their host country. For some of them, it is the first time that they are formally taught in a signed language (Duggan & Holmström, 2022). Returning to Holmström's earlier study (2019), deaf migrants or refugees in Sweden must learn both Swedish and SSL; in contrast, Sivunen (2019) states that deaf migrants or refugees in Finland have no access to FSL classes and only have access to interpreters using International Sign (IS), which means that refugees quickly learn some signs in IS (Sivunen, 2019). As in the Swedish case, deaf refugees in Kakuma Refugee Camp learn the national sign language (KSL) in classes where all the students—and even some of the teachers—are refugees living in the camp. Because there are so many refugees from the same countries (e.g., Sudan, Somalia), they also use signs from their own countries among themselves.

Earlier studies on deaf refugees in new host countries have also explored the role of interpreters in providing access for deaf refugees. For example, as Sivunen (2019) reports, deaf migrants often have difficulties understanding and communicating with interpreters during asylum processes because the interpreters are not aware of the deaf refugees' sign language of origin. In Kakuma Refugee Camp, on the other hand, interpreters are more aware of the signing used by deaf refugees because they are interacting with them frequently. However, problems can arise in the lack of professionalization and training, as well as interpreters' lack of understanding of their role. There are some deaf interpreters, such as Anthony, who volunteer to translate KSL into village signs. However, deaf refugees do not always work with interpreters because they can themselves employ a large resource of communication strategies, including writing or gesturing.

The Bourdieusian framework of field, habitus, and capital has been helpful in uncovering more details of deaf refugees' daily practices than previous studies, which focused only on educational spaces or interpreted situations. The field of networks between deaf refugees emerges in different spaces in the Kakuma Refugee Camp. Deaf refugees' habitus includes characteristics specific to being deaf, such as the use of sign languages, which confers access to deaf spaces, including schools and other educational spaces, workplaces, and more intimate spaces like households. These spaces play an important role in deaf refugees' growth of their linguistic, cultural, social, and physical capital. The settings invite and encompass a diverse and changing group of refugees in terms of ethnicity, gender, and religion, with some spaces being gendered and religion- or ethnicity-specific. Some forms of economic capital are also transformed into various other forms of capital, such as into the social capital derived through networking with deaf people to gather relevant information about how to improve their living conditions in the camp or how to be selected by UNHCR for resettlement. People who do not have the chance to obtain cultural capital through education, or who have limited economic capital, rely on their social capital.

4

Deaf Migrants in London

Steven Emery and Sanchayeeta Iyer

According to the United Nations (UN), there is no consensus on a single definition of the term "migrant" (Anderson & Blinder, 2019). It is used in this chapter in a broad sense because the research includes people who may not have settled status in the United Kingdom: For example, those on a spouse visa or people who hold temporary residency, asylum, or refugee status and are seeking settlement; hold long-term residency or British citizenship; or are studying with a view to staying long term. The project we report on initially focused on labor migration, but its scope was later broadened to include participants who had moved as children with their families, as students, as resettled refugees—and, in particular, those who had migrated for marriage. Marriage migration, studied in depth by Sanchayeeta, refers to those who marry with the aim to migrate, or who migrate to join their partner. The categories of labor and marriage migration can, of course, overlap; some marriage migrants also look for work in the new host country. Our data on labor migration cover the experiences of a large number of deaf people from a wide range of nationalities, whereas our data on marriage migration focuses on five Indian women. Because our study was ethnographic (see Chapter 2), we were focusing on participant observation and migrant narratives. We appreciate that we come from positions of privilege, working at academic institutions and not being migrants ourselves; however, whereas one researcher, Steve, is from a white British ethnic background, Sanchayeeta is from an ethnically British-Indian background. We consciously brought our respective "lenses" to the fieldwork (see Chapter 2).

The chapter starts with a review of the literature, which includes a brief outline of the mainstream literature on migration to the United Kingdom. This is admittedly a very broad sweep, but the literature is vast. There follows a longer critique of the deaf migration literature. The latter remains sparse in spite of increasing amounts of scholarship being published since 2015. We then move on to the key themes that make up deaf migrant narratives: the social context; the journey, arrival, and first impressions of London; how migrants navigate connections in the capital; and their experiences of employment and class. Whereas the thematic sections are largely focused on migrants' individual journeys, the final two sections widen the focus, mapping and exploring deaf migrants' experiences in deaf spaces more generally. Even though deaf spaces are not migrant-specific spaces and thus have an impact on the wider community, the range of events we discuss provides us with a snapshot of deaf spaces that are vibrant and active. We found it useful to devise a visual map of these deaf spaces and places, which we will introduce by explaining how we designed it and what it means in practice. This map highlights how deaf migrants become part of the fabric of these spaces over a period of time. We conclude with a section on xenophobia and racism within these deaf spaces.

We use a Bourdieusian lens in this chapter (see Chapter 1 and Grenfell, 2012, for an overview). We visualize deaf migrants navigating deaf "fields" across London, their "habitus" (where relevant), and the "capital" they bring or acquire in the process. To summarize these key terms, a field refers to any particular space or place—a deaf center, a sports field, a doctor's surgery, a refugee camp in Kenya (see Chapter 3), or deaf networks in London (as in this chapter)—but it is important to stress that each field interlocks with habitus (unconscious dispositions internalized from learned behaviors in a particular field) and capital (the resources acquired in or brought to a field that help navigate it). Some of our participants were able to move in some fields differently to others, depending on which learned behaviors they had already internalized—for example, the discourse used within a field (particular words/signs and terms, which may be familiar or not), and its conventions (e.g., the use of sign language in a deaf club).

A Brief History of Migration to the United Kingdom

London is a super-diverse city featuring intense migration (Vertovec, 2007). At least one-third of its citizens were born abroad, with the most recent statistics showing the figure at 40.6% (ONS, 2022). A number of researchers have investigated how diverse people live together in London and the "axes of belonging" along which people tend to associate (Ehrkamp & Leitner, 2006)—for example, associating primarily with people from a specific ethnic group and/or within a specific neighborhood (Wessendorf, 2014).

Migration is not a new or recent phenomenon in the United Kingdom. As Fryer (1984, p. 1) illustrates in his scholarly research, black people have been resident in the British Isles as far back as the time of the Roman Empire, having settled in various parts since then. A similar pattern can be found in various other historical periods regarding people of various ethnicities. For example, there is a long history of Jewish people migrating to the British Isles to escape European expulsion, particularly since the 17th century (Endelman, 2002), and of Huguenots (French Protestants) escaping persecution in France in the 16th century (Cottret, 2009). Fryer (1984) also illustrates historical periods where the settlement of black people was far from voluntary (e.g., during the slave trade of the 17th and 18th centuries) and also when it was encouraged (e.g., after the Second World War with the "Windrush generation"). This term refers to the black and South Asian people and their families who arrived in the United Kingdom from Caribbean countries such as Jamaica and Trinidad and Tobago, traveling on the ship HMT *Empire Windrush*. It should be noted that Asian people had been migrating for work to the British Isles as far back as the 16th century, and although this migration was quite small compared to migration in the aftermath of the Second World War, it does nevertheless show that migration (be it for work or enforced) has a very long history and involves far wider ethnicities than we are able to include here.

Returning to the Windrush generation, it was the British Nationality Act of 1948 that granted the rights of subjects of the British Empire to settle in the United Kingdom, whether to live or to work, ostensibly due to an increased demand for a workforce to assist in rebuilding Britain in the aftermath of the Second World War. This act led directly to the Windrush generation moving to and settling in the United Kingdom, but it also gave rights to people from other Commonwealth countries such as India and Pakistan. In fact, it is people from India who make up the largest group of non-British residents in London, as of 2022 (Vargas-Silva & Rienzo, 2022). Britain's relationship with India goes back to the 1600s, when the East India Company, an English (later, British) company, was formed to trade across East Asia; this predates the era of British colonization of India and the rise of the British Empire in the 18th and 19th centuries. Communities from South Asia were dispersed as a result of this colonization; for example, people from India who were working for British companies in Africa settled in several African countries, including Nigeria, Uganda, and South Africa—all of which had been subject to brutal British rule. This dispersal left the minority Indian communities vulnerable once British colonial rule had been overthrown across African countries in the 1960s and 1970s, leading, for example, to the expulsion of Indian communities from Uganda in the early 1970s under President Idi Amin. The following years saw the growth of the Indian diaspora in London and elsewhere in the United Kingdom (for further details, see Hussein, 2005). The Indian diaspora is made up of various regional, religious, cultural, and ethnic groups from different parts of the Indian subcontinent. However, these groups are lumped together as "Indian" as a single category; Indian as a nationality label is also used as an ethnic category (see Anitha & Pearson, 2013; del Pilar Kaladeen, 2018a, 2018b; and Chapter 5 for a discussion of national stereotypes).

Two factors led to the expansion of migration to the United Kingdom in the 2000s. The first was the election of three New Labour governments in 1997, 2001, and 2005, whose neoliberal outlook and policies favored globalization and free trade; the second was the increased number of countries admitted to the European Union (EU). The EU's principle of free movement across its nations led to an increased number of European nationals moving to and settling in the United Kingdom, until the United Kingdom formally departed from the EU in 2020 following a U.K.-wide referendum called by the Conservative government in June 2016. Our research took place in the context of both "Brexit" and the ongoing, officially mandated "really hostile environment" (to quote then–Home Secretary Theresa May in 2012) for migrants in the United Kingdom. Of course, hostility to migrants did not begin then; institutionalized racism has long been recognized as being in place in the United Kingdom (Goodfellow, 2019; SSAHE, 2020). However, the adoption of the "hostile environment" as official government policy in the United Kingdom in the early 2010s was a deliberate means to provoke hostility toward people deemed to be "illegal migrants"—that is, "undocumented" (Tyler, 2018). This had the knock-on effect of increasing institutionalized racism and discrimination against migrants in the United Kingdom. Additionally, despite the closeness of the Brexit referendum (with 52% voting in favor and 48% objecting) and strong opposition to it both inside and outside the U.K. Parliament, the vote emboldened right-wing anti-migration political factions, leading to an intensification of the hostile environment policy. A key example was the "Windrush scandal," which first came to light in 2017. The people of the Windrush generation were, as outlined previously, legally entitled to live and work in the United Kingdom, but they had not been provided with legal documents by the British State at the time; additionally, in some cases, existing documents had been deliberately destroyed by the state. As a consequence of this, and in line with hostile environment policies, people who had lived in the United Kingdom since the 1940s were being deported through force to their country of origin in the Caribbean.

Studies on Deaf Migration

Research and literature on deaf migration is sparse; also, with very few exceptions (e.g., Vasishta, 2011; Wang et al., 2016), it has not been written by those who have experienced the migration journey themselves. We are careful to offer respectful critique to studies on migration, given that much of the literature is aimed at informing social policymakers of the (often adverse, even life-threatening) experiences that migrants go through to arrive at their destination. As there is no strict distinction between labor migration and other forms of migration (see Chapter 1), including that of refugees and asylum seekers, we also discuss some resources on refugees. Some of the data in our own study are heartbreaking, as we will show, with asylum seekers and migrants experiencing a range of struggles in their attempts to seek safety and settlement.

Since 2015, there has been an increase in studies looking at deaf migration beyond the United Kingdom, and thus in this context there have been far more sources to draw upon. The authors Holmström and Sivunen (2022) have done much to critically highlight the growing literature, and they cite Crawley et al.'s 2018 assertion that "there has been increasing interest in scientific research into deaf migrants, particularly in connection to the so-called migration crisis in Europe 2015" (in Holmström & Sivunen, 2022, p. 409). A significant working paper undertaken recently by McAuliff (2021) demonstrates this fact. McAuliff critically reviewed all the literature about deaf refugees up to 2021, which is a welcome resource for scholars who are researching this field. We share the author's conclusion that many studies focus on refugees as victims and hence obscure their agency—indeed, if we have one criticism of McAuliff's review, it is that the use of the term "refugee" risks placing in the reader's mind a range of experiences limited to refugees, whereas many people who first migrated as refugees will now be long settled (see Chapter 10 for an example). However, we are also mindful of the second critique that McAuliff raises, namely that there are huge gaps in the literature from the perspective of refugees or migrants from the Global South, a concern also raised by Holmström and Sivunen (2022). We add our voices to these concerns, conscious that our research has been undertaken by scholars from the privileged Global North.

There has been very little research on deaf ethnic/racial minorities in the United Kingdom, with a few notable exceptions (i.e., Ahmad et al., 1998; Atkin et al., 2002; Emery, 2008; James & Woll, 2004). Although it is possible that some of the participants in these studies were not only part of an ethnic minority group or groups but *also* migrants, migration is not mentioned in these studies; this is a typical pattern within Deaf Studies (see Emery & Iyer, 2022, for more references).

When we set out our analysis of the U.K.-based literature prior to the start of the project, we identified that the central aim of research studies of deaf migrants has been largely positivist in nature, seeking to find out how deaf "immigrants" "integrate" into the United Kingdom. The majority of this literature focuses on deaf refugees or asylum seekers. Emphasis is placed on the problems deaf migrants face; the struggles they experience to integrate; and what role, if any, organizations play in assisting or supporting them. The research literature is further complicated by the way in which deaf migrants tend to be positioned alongside disabled migrants (Patel & Kelley, 2006; Roberts & Harris, 2002; Ward et al., 2008), which means that their similarities to other linguistic minorities have been overlooked, as has their position in the wider deaf community in London. For example, Ward et al. (2008) interviewed representatives of community and voluntary charitable agencies, who suggest that deaf asylum seekers and refugees have no access to refugee community organizations due to the latter's lack of deaf awareness or provision of sign language interpreters.

There is evidence, however, that once contact is made with local deaf people in the United Kingdom, the social situation of deaf migrants improves (Ward et al., 2008, p. 62). We wanted to explore this further because another prominent and unique research study of "deaf third country nationals" (carried out between 2007 and 2009) confirmed that migrant lives become networked through contact with deaf communities (Parr et al., 2010). The studies also identified an array of multiple intersections that migrants face, in addition to the challenges of communicating in and learning new languages. Whereas these were identified as *background* issues in previous studies, in our subproject the aim was to *foreground* such themes, in line with the overall research focus of the MobileDeaf project (see Chapter 1). Whereas the project undertaken by Parr et al. (2010) focused on deaf migrants from non-EU member states who had been in the United Kingdom for 5 years, our project included both non-EU participants (including from the Global South) and EU participants. Our project's key focus was to seek deaf migrants from all backgrounds who had moved to London, be they laborers, students, professionals, entrepreneurs, job-seekers, or spouses.

Deaf Migrants' Pathways Into London

Deaf migrants shared with us stories of the journeys they had undertaken to reach London, and their experiences on arrival were also widely discussed. As we will demonstrate, the "field" in which migrants arrived was often one that felt completely outside what they were accustomed to. Often, their journey to London was not linear; they had arrived having *passed through several other countries*. For example, one East African deaf man had come via Kakuma Refugee Camp in Kenya (see Chapter 10); others had moved to countries such as Germany, Denmark, or the United States before moving to the United Kingdom. This illustrates that migration cannot be put down as a one-time occurrence in deaf migrants' lives, and at each stage of their journey, they are likely to encounter different fields that may each require different capital. Habitus is a far more complex concept; deaf migrants may feel familiar in some cultural settings more than in others, depending on their background and upbringing. For example, migrants whose first language is a sign language (i.e., native signers) and who come from another large European city may feel familiarity in London deaf spaces where a large proportion of people are native users of a sign language; this is because of shared aspects of habitus or habiti (i.e., several types of habitus, see Joy et al., 2020).

There were several reasons for and circumstances in which deaf migrants initially moved from their home country. These include arriving in the United Kingdom with their parents when very young; moving to seek work; moving to be united with their partner or family; moving to study, having achieved a scholarship to do so; and having come from a refugee camp after initially fleeing from war in their country. Although the circumstances of, and motivations for, migration are very similar to those of hearing migrants, and although the fields navigated are the same (e.g., the bureaucratic and authoritarian fields of the border force and the Home Office), there are a few "deaf elements" to the stories we collected. To give one example of a "deaf element," a deaf tutor from City Lit college said in our interview:

> The asylum seekers looked to stay here because it was safe, because they had so many stories about the abuse they suffered in their home countries, being thrown in prison for religious reasons or for refusing to wear head or face coverings—there were all sorts of reasons and stories for wanting to stay here. [...] *One deaf person from a Gypsy* [sic] *family had no language* [...] He didn't even understand the concept of an "alphabet" or question forms or gestures. [our emphasis]

Observations and ideologies regarding deaf refugees "having no language" are common and are critically discussed in Chapter 8.

A few deaf migrants we met during our fieldwork were a child or young person when they came to the United Kingdom. For example, Samba's parents specifically moved from Sierra Leone so he could obtain a better education in a deaf school in London (see Chapter 9 and the film *Finding Spaces to Belong* for Samba's story);[1] this example also highlights how there may be a "deaf element" to a story. First impressions could be quite powerful, especially for young deaf people arriving from Africa or Asia who had never seen a white person before and who were in awe of the buildings and transport networks in comparison to those of their native countries. On arrival, migrants may feel like a "fish out of water" (to quote Bourdieu, in Maton, 2012, p. 56) in their new environment; indeed, our participants reported a general wonderment about infrastructure, race, language, and the way that people in London looked, dressed, and behaved. This was particularly true for *young* deaf migrants who arrived in the United Kingdom with their parents or family; in our study, all their families were hearing, and many were highly educated. Lena's father, from Russia, was a university professor, for example. Rohel, originally from Bangladesh, had come to the United Kingdom as a 9-year-old child and vividly expressed his reaction on seeing white people for the first time:

> When I was 9, my mother told me that we were going "up," but communication with my mother was very difficult and we really didn't understand each other [...] The plane arrived at Heathrow; I will never forget it. Honestly, when I tell you when the doors opened my eyes were on stalks! I could not believe it. [...] The whole experience is branded on my memory, but one picture sticks in my mind and I cannot forget it: I saw this really large white woman with high heels [she looked so huge] and I was so confused! I thought that everyone had the same skin color—I had never seen a white woman like this before! Then I saw a man in a smart suit, walking confidently—remember, I hadn't had an education, and seeing white people, Chinese people—all these different people! [...] I was so confused [...] especially [by] that large woman in her heels.

This example shows that the first impressions of this young deaf migrant are strongly remembered as visual impressions, which is partially due to the lack of information received before his arrival because of communication difficulties within the family.

Some stories of migrants were quite harrowing. Hawa, who arrived from Somalia in her mid-teens with her sister, was placed straight into a mainstream school without communication support (see Emery & Iyer, 2022). Her narrative represents an example of *institutional racism and discrimination*, in which being a child, female, black, and deaf intersect. The following quote is Hawa's narrative of when she was attempting to obtain Home Office approval for her application to stay in the United Kingdom, another example that demonstrates the "deaf elements" in the stories told by deaf migrants. In Hawa's meeting with the Home Office, a sign language interpreter was provided; however, he was evidently not very experienced:

> We moved here and my family took me to the Home Office, but it was a really long process without access. I felt like the family dog, being dragged along and not knowing what was happening. There were these big meetings with lots of people, and I had no idea what they were talking about. My sister

---

1. https://vimeo.com/854367099#t=10m41s

tried to explain to me what was going on, but the Home Office blocked her. Instead, they brought in a male interpreter; he said he signed but he didn't really. I remember he brought a book with him, and tried to talk to me but I was really put off and didn't know what was happening. I tried to talk to the man who leads the meetings, but he told my sister to stop so I had to pull back and put up with it. They made another appointment and again it was full of people, and my sister and I had to sit there passively while they discussed my case. I really don't know what they said, but I think [bearing in mind I couldn't access any of the information] that the Home Office were objecting to my application a bit? I'm not sure. They seemed to be saying "why are you here?" and not accepting me.

Other migrants moved to the United Kingdom as adults, on their own, which meant they had more agency than deaf child migrants. They often moved for work; we cover this in detail in the section on employment. On arrival, and with a lack of social capital, they needed to navigate all kinds of mainstream fields (e.g., colleges, workplaces, community and neighborhood centers) in a language (i.e., English) that they may have had little or no knowledge of, which could leave them feeling immobile, stuck, or in limbo; we cover these issues in Chapters 7 and 10. Others moved to be with their partner and were able to make use of the partner's social capital. For example, Laura moved from Latvia to be with her Latvian husband, who had moved to the United Kingdom to find work.

In Sanchayeeta's study on marriage migration, two of the Indian women had come to the United Kingdom in their early 20s and had lived in London for nearly 20 years, whereas the other three came in their early 30s. These five women had moved to the United Kingdom from Mumbai and Kolkata to start a new chapter of life with their newlywed husbands, most of whom were men of Indian heritage holding British citizenship. One woman, from Kolkata, had married a man from a Hindu family of Indian heritage, who had originally moved to the United Kingdom from Uganda during the aforementioned period of expulsion. Another was from a Muslim family of Indian origin who had moved from Kenya under similar circumstances. Both women's husbands had been born in the United Kingdom. Another woman's husband was a migrant from the Middle East, having arrived in London in the 2000s. Two women were of the Islamic faith and three were Hindu. All five women accepted the condition of migration upon their acceptance of the marriage proposal. Among their motivations were sociocultural expectations, personal desires, aspirations to have a certain lifestyle, and the desire to acquire a British passport for further mobility. Beyond the "getting married and settling down" purpose of their migration, they had their own dreams, desires, and aspirations, including to advance their career path in a foreign country or to travel to new places. These aspirations colored their decision to accept marriage proposals from the men with British citizenship with whom they had interacted for varying lengths of time. Mobility based on education, work, and life experiences is becoming a normative part of imaginary middle-class life trajectories (Robertson, 2021). This shows the complexity of the reasons behind the decision to migrate.

Many migrants were eager to stress that they had a *successful or positive journey* and were in a good place personally and professionally. This indicates they had learned to navigate the fields in which they had arrived, both by acquiring the necessary capital (e.g., by learning British Sign Language) and, to some extent, by internalizing the habitus or habiti. They ended their narrative or interview with a positive comment, such as "thank you to Britain" (Laura, Latvia), "now I am happy" (Maria, Romania), "I appreciate the opportunity to live here and develop here"

(Paul, Tanzania)—potentially to ensure that their narrative was framed as positive, because they thought that was what the researchers wanted to hear. Our positions of privilege in academia, particularly deaf academia, may have left participants feeling they had to emphasize that there was a positive side even though they might have had some negative experiences. They reported that things were easier and more relaxed now that they were more settled and that this was due to a number of factors: They had worked hard to get to where they were, their families had been supportive, and they felt a real sense of passion and pride at having become part of a deaf community by participating in deaf spaces (see later in the chapter).

Being a deaf signer was central to our participants' narratives, both in terms of barriers to information (see Chapter 10) and in terms of socialization within deaf spaces. Stories of first impressions upon arriving in the United Kingdom often involved comments on British Sign Language (BSL). Samba was from Sierra Leone, where ASL is familiar, and was shocked to find that ASL is not a universal language, that ASL is not used in the United Kingdom, and that BSL uses a two-handed fingerspelling alphabet. Abdikal, from Somalia, shared his shock at BSL, too. He had migrated to Denmark when young and learned Danish Sign Language, and then he came to the United Kingdom in his teens: "I started in a new deaf school. But I didn't understand anything! I couldn't sign BSL, and they didn't understand Danish Sign Language." Learning BSL was an integral part of their journey; we share many examples where deaf migrants have needed to build up their linguistic capital and have stressed the *importance of learning BSL* (see Chapter 8). By learning BSL, they could begin to feel at ease in deaf spaces. Indeed, most migrants shared their experiences with us *by signing in BSL*, which they had acquired in the United Kingdom.

However, some migrants also shared their experiences of criticism from British deaf people over the uneven pace of their signing, their slowness in learning BSL, their accents in BSL, and their use of ASL to facilitate communication. Some had responded to this criticism by preserving their own mode of signing, as they felt they could manage to communicate with BSL interpreters and in different sectors of the British deaf community without needing to sign fluently in BSL (see Chapter 8). It is possible that this experience—that is, of continuing to use (an)other sign language(s) in the United Kingdom—is evidence that some migrants find deaf fields in the United Kingdom tricky to navigate; they may only acquire enough BSL to "get by" without reaching a "fully fluent" level, and otherwise they retain their own sign language. This may depend on the field or fields through which they navigate: Some fields are particularly welcoming to migrants, such as City Lit college; the deaf group that gathers at the East London Mosque; or, as Steve observed, at the weekly deaf gathering at the Slug and Lettuce pub in Leicester Square. Alternatively, it is possible that their habitus allowed them to feel familiar across borders and that they felt they possessed enough knowledge and experience to get by in London's deaf fields.

There were a remarkable number of instances in which migrants *"found" their deaf identity* in London. Previously, they had either known no sign language or had been getting by largely in mainstream, hearing communities. Francesca, for example, who had started to lose her hearing in her early 20s, moved to London after losing her job and struggling to build a life as an independent woman in her native Italy. She went through various jobs as she struggled both in a hearing environment and in understanding English, especially spoken by people with different accents. She had progressive hearing loss, often felt tired, and felt that her speech had deteriorated. Initially, when she first started to lose her hearing, Francesca did not view herself as a deaf person but as a (hearing) person with a "problem," and in London she came to see herself as "a deaf woman."[2] She first encountered signing deaf people during a lipreading course in London, which led her to take BSL courses and actively go to meet deaf people in various deaf events around London:

> The BSL courses taught me a great deal, and from there I went to deaf clubs, met more deaf people, and I asked where there were deaf clubs in central London, and when I went there for the first time I was quite overwhelmed—I was still on the Level 1 course back then so I struggled a bit initially. But I felt welcomed, and I went along every week, and I still go to that club every week. From there I found other deaf pub nights and meetings and I felt from there more fully involved in the deaf community. Also, I wanted to know more about the deaf world, so I did two courses in deaf history, so really [...] I've worked hard to become a member of the deaf community—I know a lot of people, and really learning BSL has changed my life.

Her narrative shows she had to "work hard" to become an active member of the deaf community and that gaining linguistic capital in the form of BSL is required in order to move across fields in deaf communities. This involves language adaptation, attending and actively participating in deaf events, and learning BSL in courses; later, she also started working with deaf people. For Francesca, "being deaf" comes with being independent, feeling rooted, and feeling "at home" among "the community." She expressed feeling more "at home" with the British deaf community than the Italian deaf community, because her "deaf identity was born here." This placed her in the position of knowing BSL but not the sign language of her native country.

Another female migrant, Rosa, originally from Russia, had moved due to her father's professional occupation. Although she had attended a deaf school in her country of origin, it was only in the United Kingdom that she began to learn sign language and search for her deaf identity. This theme is more common than might at first be imagined: The 30-minute documentary *Found in the UK* (Swinbourne, 2018b)[3] showcases the stories of three deaf migrants who discovered sign language and deaf culture in the United Kingdom. It may be that this phenomenon is facilitated by the existence of an established network of deaf communities across London and the United Kingdom. There are longstanding LGBTQIA+ deaf groups,[4] for example, and a variety of well-established meeting places such as deaf clubs and particular "deaf cafés" that deaf people can choose from.

We also note in our participants' stories that some people are prevented from participating in deaf community spaces. In the case of marriage migration from India, the women moved into their new husband's natal household and encountered various shifts of power—often in relation to their new mother-in-law. For example, Meera explained that her position as deaf, and as a migrant from India with high school qualifications as her highest educational attainment, placed

---

2. See https://vimeo.com/447619481
3. https://www.bslzone.co.uk/watch/found-uk
4. Lesbian, Gay, Bisexual, Transgender, Queer or Questioning, Intersex, Asexual, and +. The "+" refers to other sexual identities, including pansexual, asexual, and omnisexual people, who are recognized as not identifying as straight and/or cisgender. Our definition is the result of consulting multiple references, but it is largely drawn from the definition in use at the United Kingdom's *Pink News* (Bloodworth, 2019).

her in a position where she had to take on the household responsibilities (see Chapter 10 for more details). This prevented her from participating in deaf spaces and from building up social and linguistic capital.

While making a new home in London, many migrants retained *active links to their home nation and to other countries where they had lived*. This could take many forms. The most common (although not during the coronavirus pandemic) was simply regularly returning to visit their family or partner; indeed, several participants had aspirations to return regularly, whether to buy property in their homeland, to undertake advocacy work with their deaf compatriots, or to consult family members for help with running or setting up a business in London. One woman from India had previously lived in the United States, and she often returned there for personal or business matters. That the importance of maintaining links to their country of origin was such a central theme highlights the way in which deaf people's lives can often be seen through a translocal lens (see Chapter 9).

In studies of mainstream migration, a common feature is the tendency of some migrants to try to find various spaces of national, ethnic, and religious belonging within London, such as through attending a church or mosque (see Chapter 9), and to try to maintain linkages across transnational borders—for example, in the form of remittances (Joy et al., 2020; Kelly & Lusis, 2006). However, this was rarely evident in our fieldwork. The focus of the migrant narratives in our study was on what they experience *in the host nation*. Rosa, for example, had arrived in London from Russia not knowing anyone, and she decided to attend a mainstream church event relevant to her religious faith; however, communication barriers made this difficult. Kwame, a student in his 20s from West Africa, told us that he believed that it was his duty to attend church with people of a West African ethnicity, and this was the place he went to form connections with other deaf and hearing people when he first arrived in the United Kingdom to undertake a postgraduate course. However, he encountered what he referred to as jealousy from his peers: He believed them to be jealous that he had been able to obtain a scholarship to study in the United Kingdom and to move to London as a result. He found it hard to maintain friendships, and he encountered suspicion from deaf people at the church who believed that he had moved to the United Kingdom for marriage rather than to obtain a qualification and advance his career. As a result, he found it easier to make hearing friends at the church. Similarly, Meera had experienced a sense of jealousy from some British Indian women due to her marriage partnership with a desirable British Indian bachelor ("taken their man") and her attainment of a desirable lifestyle. She found it more preferable to interact with hearing British Indian people in her residential area with whom she shared similar backgrounds, including class and ethnicity. This shows that people, including other migrants, may doubt others' reasons for migrating and also that some forms of migration may be more prestigious than others.

Finally, there was some evidence of what was called "modern-day slavery" (used here, in line with the U.K.'s Modern Slavery Act of 2015, to mean "the recruitment, movement, harboring or receiving of children, women or men through the use of force, coercion, abuse of vulnerability, deception or other means for the purpose of exploitation," as per Such & Salway, 2017) in relation to deaf migrants. This was highlighted by Samba and Lenka N. (from Sierra Leone and the Czech Republic, respectively; their stories feature in *Finding Spaces to Belong*) in an open webinar event, *Deaf Migration London*, run by the MobileDeaf team via Zoom in 2020.[5] Both Samba and Lenka

---

5. https://mobiledeaf.org.uk/presentations/deaf-migration-london

have come across modern-day slavery in their respective work fields of the church and mental health services. They highlighted a form of migration that renders deaf people very vulnerable: deaf people being brought into the country (e.g., by relatives) and being forced to work for no pay. Samba knew of at least three cases, including one in which the deaf migrant had been claiming the benefits to which they were legally entitled, but they had not been receiving the money themselves; instead, it was being controlled by family or someone else close to them. Lenka shared another example:

> A deaf young woman who is in her early 20s, who moved to the United Kingdom to be with her auntie and uncle because she was told that she would have better quality of education here. She attended school and then went to college. But she told the staff there that when she's in the home she was actually sleeping in a cupboard under the stairs and she was being forced to work all hours. She had these really cramped quarters. She was deprived of food and because she was being hosted by her aunt and uncle, she thought it was normal. She had no idea that she was being abused in this way, so it was only when she mentioned this to college staff that they were able to intervene.

Lenka suggested that this issue requires more exposure and stated that it is something the deaf mental health support organization SignHealth is aware of and are working with the Home Office to address. Harrowing examples similar to those Lenka shared have been reported in the national media (Addley, 2012). Crucially, it is not only at an official level that this matter is being recognized. As Samba suggests, community also plays a role, because migrants may not find it easy to report the matter to the police and may be wary of going through official channels:

> They don't have any power and it makes you wonder what's happening. They are really invisible. These are very difficult situations that they find themselves in [...] But of course we can hopefully identify people through persistent communication, asking them out to the park or taking them to deaf events or football [soccer] and encouraging them to take part in life, and piecing together the information to work out what is going on in their lives.

This is another example of the crucial role of deaf spaces for supporting deaf migrants, and it also shows the need for people to advocate for vulnerable deaf migrants.

Employment and Class

Class is about power relations in society, and given that the initial focus of this project was on labor migration, and that the majority of deaf migrants we met had moved to the United Kingdom for work, had searched for work there, or were currently seeking work, class was hugely relevant to how they searched for or found employment. The deaf migrants in our study were seeking economic capital; however, as many examples have already illustrated, they were conscious of the need to acquire symbolic capital in its various forms too. Linguistic capital in the form of BSL was particularly marked. This is a language that can be learned over time, but not all deaf migrants will necessarily become fluent in BSL, which may limit the extent to which they can engage in and move within deaf fields.

When discussing employment, deaf migrants narrated a range of strategies and issues that were specifically related to their being deaf *and* a migrant. Lenka from the Czech Republic was anxious when applying for jobs in regard to her combined status as a foreign deaf person:

> Sometimes, when I've applied for a job, I'm anxious about it as my name isn't English and then to add that I'm deaf would be too much. So, I don't put on the application form that I'm deaf. If I get on a shortlist, then offered an interview and asked if I have any special requirements, then I'll tell them I need an interpreter. They may get a bit flustered but, by that stage, they can't do anything. Well, they can actually, and it's happened a lot. So, that's problematic...

Deaf migrants, in common with deaf nonmigrants, sometimes deemphasize their status as a deaf person in job applications. This can be a difficult decision to make; sometimes *emphasizing* the status of being deaf can help one gain access to services, get employment in deaf-related jobs, or speed up the bureaucracy process. For example, deaf people are legally entitled to an interpreter at a job interview through the British government's Access to Work scheme, but to obtain it, they must state that they are deaf on the application form. Additionally, some employers have "positive discrimination" policies in place, which guarantee an interview to a deaf person who meets the requirements in the job description. These and other employers may, unbeknown to the applicant, already have an interpreter or speech-to-text technology reserved for job interviews, particularly if the job is with a large company or one with a policy of ensuring provisions are already in place for deaf applicants and employees (see Napier et al., 2020, for recent research on deaf people's experiences of employment in Britain).

Although deaf migrants have these experiences in common with British deaf people, they also discussed experiences that struck them *as a migrant*. Aisha, a deaf Indian woman who is a marriage migrant, shared her experience of frustration with the job application process in the United Kingdom, comparing it to applying for a job in India:

> When applying for a job, you can't physically go somewhere to apply—I was always being told to apply online and to make an appointment at a specific time on a specific date. You have to get permission for this by email, but in India you don't need the email exchange, you can simply go somewhere and write notes, quickly getting to the point. The long waiting time in the electronic process here was difficult for me.

In India, Aisha could physically meet with an agent who would help her to find a job; she appreciated that this enabled her to get the face-to-face communication with which she feels comfortable. A direct approach suited her better because she could directly explain her situation as a deaf person, and the agent could adapt to her. The United Kingdom's application system, in contrast, seemed cold and impersonal, with the obligation to apply online and the insistence on making appointments and receiving permission through email exchanges. In other words, job-seeking is a bureaucratic and labor-intensive process with long waiting times. Following the British approach, Aisha could be rejected for a job in a cursory manner without knowing the reasons behind the refusal. There is the added stress of having to write in English on a job application form or in an email to the prospective employer, whom she would never get to meet beforehand and to whom she would have no opportunity to showcase her initiative and flexibility. Hence, there are different cultural expectations with regard to the temporal aspects of migration (see Chapter 10) that deaf migrants in London have to negotiate or get used to, including in the process of applying for jobs.

We met many deaf migrants working in deaf fields. Francesca, from Italy, was employed as a deaf support worker at a mainstream college, having initially worked in many different occupations when she first arrived in London. Samba, from Sierra Leone, was well respected by his local church (where BSL events were organized) and worked there as a caretaker (see Chapter 9). Chris, from Burundi, was employed as a social worker working with deaf people, having migrated to London from Kakuma Refugee Camp, Kenya, 20 years previously. Hawa, from Somalia, worked in the deaf care sector. Charlotte, a young woman from Canada in her 20s, had moved to the United Kingdom to teach an American deaf parents' child ASL, and she eventually found employment working in the arts. These, and many more examples, give credence to the assertion that deaf migrants *become part of the fabric of deaf spaces to the extent that they are employed in these spaces*. We regularly met migrants who had moved to the United Kingdom years ago and who were now working in occupations with other deaf people as tutors, social workers, or artists, or in business. There have been well-known deaf migrants who became vibrant "movers and shakers" within deaf spaces and beyond: Examples include Heroda and Hermon, deaf female twins in their 30s who are originally from Eritrea-Ethiopia, who are now renowned fashion bloggers.

Deaf migrants who worked with deaf people in their country of origin also experienced barriers getting employment in a similar field in the United Kingdom. Aisha's attempt to enter the labor market was met with obstacles. Her bachelor of arts degree and experience working with deaf children had been discredited because they were not recognized by the British qualification system. She resorted to low-skilled employment while returning to education to acquire the essential qualifications (in Bourdieusian terms, to acquire cultural capital in the form of a recognized qualification) with which to get her foot in the door of the deaf education sector in the United Kingdom (see Chapter 8).

Cultural capital in the form of education was a key theme in the stories of other migrants, with emphasis on gaining qualifications that opened up job opportunities, whether with deaf people or generally, and for which they were grateful to the United Kingdom. Laura (Latvian), whose words were cited earlier, shared her experience:

> I have qualifications, but could not find work because people only saw my deafness as a barrier and wouldn't take me on. I found this very frustrating. When we moved here, I thought maybe I could try to find work here as the attitude might be better. I could see that here there are many deaf people who set up their own businesses, and these were very positive role models for me. I tried to find work with my qualifications, but found that they were not recognized here as they are European qualifications, not British ones. I was not deterred; I was patient and went back to study again. I now have my qualifications and can work in the United Kingdom, and am much happier [. . .] Oh yes, last February I was invited to go to a prestigious fashion and sewing show in [Royal Castle], as I work in tailoring and dressmaking. I work in Savile Row. Thank you to Britain.

A central aspect in relation to employment is class as it relates to economic capital. The term *class* arose from the Enlightenment period of the late 17th and early 18th centuries, and its nature and meaning have subsequently been strongly influenced by Marxists. Even though the concept may not be as well studied in the 21st century as it was in the 20th, it still attracts scholarly attention

(Carter & Brook, 2021; Mattos, 2022) and remains influential among scholars like David Harvey and Noam Chomsky. Yet, class as an identity category is one that has been largely subsumed (or left out entirely) in Deaf Studies, notable exceptions being Ladd (2003), Robinson (2016), and Sommer Lindsay (2022). With very few exceptions (e.g., Ladd, 2003), the nuances of the term *class* have received no deep analysis in Deaf Studies, and indeed, it is rarely clarified at all (see Emery & Iyer, 2022). Although class did occasionally come up explicitly in our interviews and observations, this was extremely rare. One instance was the following extract taken from an interview with the tutor at City Lit who told us about a deaf man from Kuwait who had said to him that:

> There are two different groups of people in Kuwait: the rich people, and those segregated living in a fenced-off compound full of housing. People in this lower class are really dismissed and don't even have passports. I couldn't believe his story. He said they didn't have enough food, they can't work and they are bottom of the heap. This man who came here escaped from that life with his brother, traveling through Turkey. They didn't have a passport but had a special identity document.

Deaf migrants did not generally refer explicitly to themselves as coming from a particular class background. However, as we show below, it is still possible to categorize people by class, even if we only do so tentatively or strategically.

It is worth remembering *why* this categorization is taking place. Despite having been largely omitted from Deaf Studies scholarship, class continues to be commented on and researched in U.K. academia, and it is featured in considerations of intersectionality—that is, it is accepted that class relations and class positions are a significant intersection of people's lives. Table 4.1 shows the working copy of a spreadsheet used by Steve during his observations, in which we have attempted to categorize those we met through our fieldwork, placing each into a respective "class" in relation to their job description. This is because a "class" of people is defined not by their salaries, or what or how much they own, but their relationship to production and ownership of capital, inherited or possessed.[6] In line with the methodology used by the United Kingdom's Social Mobility Commission (2021), we use three broad class categories: laborers (working class), professionals (middle class), and those forming an upper class. Our categorization is necessarily simplistic and observational, and it is illustrative of the *whole* field; it includes class categorizations for some hearing people who were present—whose data are not otherwise used in this subproject. We offer the caveat that our categorization is temporary and strategic, used to illustrate what is meant when we refer to "class" in the context of our study. We recognize the limitations of our study; our sample is far too small to be deemed empirical; our approach temporarily defers deeper analysis of issues such as the tensions that exist *between* classes; and, in our avoidance of treating class as *the* central, overarching power structuring wider society, our analysis is not strictly Marxist. Furthermore, we acknowledge that dividing our sample into more class categories—for example, lower and upper middle class, precariat, elite—could yield further sociological insights. However, we find the three provisional and strategic class categories sufficiently useful for this study because a deeper analysis of the meaning of class is beyond its scope.

---

6. Britannica online, "social class." https://www.britannica.com/topic/social-class

Table 4.1. Copy of spreadsheet used by Steve during observations, to simplistically denote the class background of participants he met.

Pure Class composition - crude - simplistic orthodox Marxist		
Labour (skilled or semi-skilled) and Capital - deaf migrants unless otherwise stated; H denotes hearing	Professionals	Capitalists
Bakery	Teachers/Tutors	Cryptocurrency investors
McDonalds	Development workers	Owners of business (self or employ labor)
Waitrose	Artists	
Post Office	Film and Fashion	
Electrician	Dance	
Cafe worker		
Voluntary shop worker (UK)	Students	
Cleaners		
Second Generation: (Road Work laborer / Nurse)		
Tailor/Dressmaking		
Multiple (cleaning, caring, tutoring) H		
Firefighter H		
Care worker		
Unemployed (skilled labor)		
Labourer		
Domestic work		

The first category, deaf laborers, contains those who use their labor purely to work for a wage. Good examples of this are Adrian, from Romania, and Fareed, from the Middle East, who both worked in the hospitality services sector. Adrian had arrived from Romania with no fixed guarantee of a place to stay. A hearing compatriot had provided him with the name of a hotel, and he traveled there to work and stay; he took this risk without any guarantees of employment. Fareed had become stranded in the United Kingdom on a longer migration journey (see Chapter 10), and he had been obliged to find work. They were both "selling their labor" in the traditional sense, in that they worked for an employer who paid them a regular wage at the end of the week or month. Adrian and Fareed had clear similarities to traditional working-class people who need to sell their labor to earn a living, with all the struggles that can often entail, but being migrants and of non-British ethnicity, they were at a disadvantage in the labor market and more liable to discrimination, especially in a contemporary neoliberalist labor market where precarious work situations are increasing, including zero-hours contracts. One deaf man in his 30s, originally from Albania, had been working undocumented for several years, and the threat of deportation by the U.K. state was ever-present for him. There are many *common class experiences* associated with this category, including feeling let down by the local job center, being bullied at work, and holding down several jobs, as well as a lack of insurance preventing the capacity to work at all; several of these were experienced by our participants.

The second category, deaf professionals and managers, overlaps with the first. As workers, professionals sell their labor too, but they have some degree of control over how they organize their work, or they have some supervisory duties and therefore have some privileges (in the labor sense) in comparison to the first category. For example, Lena, from Russia, worked in the information technology sector and had some supervisory responsibilities. Similarly, Katerina, also from Russia, whom we met tutoring at City Lit college, organizes her own workload and supervises deaf students; she may have a paid job, but she can be flexible in terms of the materials and activities she brings to the classroom. In fact, the majority of those interviewed could be deemed to be part of this class; for example, Luis (Guatemala), Emily (Canada), and Pedro (Brazil) were or had been students or travelers, studying or aiming to work in the arts or education sectors. Samba (Sierra Leone), Amar (Burundi), Francesca (Italy), and many more also had some leeway to organize and structure their work. A key point of concern common to this group of workers was whether they could obtain BSL interpreting provision to help them in their job, and whether Access to Work payments could be used to cover these costs.

The third category is the rarest and includes those who use and own capital, and/or employ people, to make profit. Shahina, a mobile woman from India (see Chapters 7–10 for her story), was one example because she ran her own business along with her family. She had more mobility and was at less risk of poverty than other participants. However, she also experienced barriers due to her deafness, gender, and ethnicity, and she was not able to make use of Access to Work provision due to her status as self-employed in a business based abroad. Another example of those we met in this category is of deaf people working in the cryptocurrency field. Care is needed in categorizing deaf people in this class, because those we interviewed or observed cannot, arguably, be placed in the same category as, say, an Elon Musk or a Bill Gates—that is, highly wealthy and powerful individuals. Yet, this category tends to include small business owners (or the *petit bourgeoisie*) who, in hearing society, are mainly men and overwhelmingly white, and whose mobility means they can jet with ease from one country to another. When Steve attended a large event encouraging people to invest in cryptocurrencies, one of the striking features was that it showcased successful investors, deaf and hearing, who had fallen on hard times in some way or who had experienced lifetime struggles with their mental health. This point is stressed to highlight how disability can be an intersection in class and employment.

We are treading carefully, mindful that class is an unexplored area in Deaf Studies, and further research, critiques, and discussions are welcome. Breaking down migrant experiences by class carries with it disadvantages. Migrant experiences are intersectional, for example, and factors such as ethnicity, gender, and disability play a crucial role; thus, any categorizing around class is intended to be temporary in the context of this study. Migrants, regardless of their class background, need to navigate a new environment that entails a different level of mobility. Also, how a deaf migrant navigates various deaf spaces and places in the field is not as simplistic as depending entirely on gaining capital in the form of, for example, knowledge of a language or a qualification.

Seema, for example, held an established position in the fashion and design industry in her native India. Since arriving in the United Kingdom for marriage, however, she has had to start over in her skilled trade: making new contacts, advertising her abilities, and enrolling in a course at a further education institution. She needed to gain cultural capital in the form of qualifications and skills, but she also needed to network and learn to navigate the new fields in the United Kingdom that are related to her expertise. Shahina experienced a higher class status when traveling to India or the United States compared to when she was in London. This points to the complexity of the experience of class in relation to mobility. As they moved to London, the Indian marriage migrants entered a "middling" stage where they experienced uncertainty and precarity in their position—first, as they attempted to access resources and maintain their lifestyles, and second, as they moved through multiple social locations, social milieus, and economic situations (Robertson & Roberts, 2022).

We recognize that although there may not be evidence of class consciousness among deaf migrants, there may be a cultural consciousness. This is why a Bourdieusian framework is valuable when we think about class, albeit one that is not entirely without critique; we will address this later in the chapter.

Mapping Migrants' Involvement in Deaf Spaces

We have mentioned how deaf migrants become part of the fabric of London deaf spaces in terms of employment. Becoming part of the deaf community can often be a long process. Many deaf migrants arrive with no idea of where they can find deaf spaces in the fields that constitute London, and they have minimal social, cultural, or even linguistic capital to navigate these fields. At the time of our research (2018–2022), there was no organization or group in the United Kingdom that specifically supports deaf migrants, asylum seekers, and refugees. London was thus lacking in having no obvious central place where deaf migrants can congregate, and deaf spaces (not specifically for migrants) are geographically dispersed across the capital. Despite this, many deaf migrants have been successful in connecting with deaf networks in London. In 2023, Steve and Sanchu were invited to present their research at a workshop event hosted by the University College London in which 10 migrants from different countries took part (Woolfe et al., 2023). Following the event, the migrants present were invited to be part of the London Assembly "Migrant Londoners Hub" to support future planning and developments.

Migrant deaf people found deaf spaces in a number of different ways. Hawa (Somalia), for example, was visited by a deaf male teacher from her day college who taught her some BSL signs and encouraged her to visit the deaf center in Harrow; she did this, and from that point she became more involved. When Chris arrived in the United Kingdom from Kakuma Refugee Camp, he was supported by the UN's Red Cross. He asked his hearing contact for information about where he could go to meet deaf people, and he was told about City Lit college (see Chapters 7 and 8). He went there to learn BSL and found that he had to start completely from scratch because his language was ASL; by continuing to learn BSL at City Lit, and also at another mainstream college, he met deaf people in London from then on. However, it was the internet that was, perhaps unsurprisingly, the most prominent place through which to find information and knowledge on where to go and what to do. Luis, a young man from Guatemala/Portugal (and a participant in *Finding Spaces to Belong*), cited his use of social media as a means to find out where deaf people met. Adrian, from Romania, had used Facebook to make friendships and find out information about London before he arrived, and Lena, from Russia, tried to set up a Facebook group in an attempt to make friends. There were numerous other examples.

In order to study how and where deaf migrants take part in deaf spaces, we engaged in a mapping exercise, noting where we encountered deaf migrants. The spaces we visited were mainly generic rather than migrant related. Each service was for British deaf people too, and each event was managed mainly by deaf, but sometimes hearing, volunteers and/or development workers—some of whom were migrants themselves. The activities taking place included viewing films; playing sports or other games, including bingo; betting on horse races; and artistic performances, including music. Two were places intended for the activity of learning: one for learning English and the other for learning BSL (albeit aimed at hearing people, but these places were also attended by deaf migrants). By far, the most significant activity was attending a presentation of some sort, whether about dementia, Access to Work funding, Brexit, the MobileDeaf project, racism, Islam, or the Somalia and Somaliland communities in London and abroad. These became spaces where information could be shared and passed on, and where people learned about other countries and cultures through discussing their experiences (see Chapter 7).

Most of these spaces provided a bar; some were held where café drinks and food could be purchased, and at others, soft drinks and snacks were provided for sale or for free by the organizers. For the larger events, free Indian vegetarian food was on offer. The wide range of activities and the provision of food and drink reflects the "everyday" nature of these events, in that these were proactive and vibrant spaces offering a variety of activities to attract deaf people, including deaf migrants. For migrants, these were places where the habitus will feel somewhat familiar because (nearly) everyone is deaf and is using sign language; these were also spaces, particularly for new migrants, where they had the opportunity to build on their social and cultural capital and to learn how to navigate fields in the United Kingdom. These spaces were thus vital *knowledge exchange hubs* for deaf people, a trope that is familiar in Deaf Studies (see Chapter 7). In other words, they catered to people who were hungry for information as well as for fun, friendships, and relationships. Examples of conversations observed during these events included deaf migrants asking where they could learn BSL, how they could obtain U.K. residency status, how to pass their driving test, where to go out—and, of course, how to find work.

The map of deaf spaces participated in by deaf migrants (Figure 4.1) was created as the result of 44 observations at 23 locations, making a "snapshot" of the year 2018. The majority of locations were meeting places for deaf people, with the exception of two events for deaf and disabled people (the "Brexit and You" and Somaliland events); one was a nation-themed event (Somalia), and one was a business-themed event (cryptocurrency). Two took place in spiritual or religious spaces, one being a Hare Krishna event and the other at a mosque. Most of these occasions were attended by a large number of deaf people. We categorize the 23 locations as follows:

- Two are *traditionally rooted deaf spaces*, permanent buildings for the use of deaf people (Saint John's Deaf Club; the Jewish Deaf Association)
- Thirteen are *mainstream deaf spaces*, permanent established buildings that deaf people frequent (e.g., City Lit college, the Shakespeare's Head pub in Holborn, the "deaf cafés" at Redbridge or Starbucks in central London; several observations shared in this book took place in these locations)
- Eight are *temporal deaf spaces*, for example, a one-off event, or the same event being held at a different place in the city (e.g., Beckton Deaf Club and Deaf Rave)

'Mainstream' deaf spaces

1. Redbridge Deaf Centre
2. Enfield Deaf Club
3. 888 Club
4. Clapham Deaf Club
5. Harrow and Brent Deaf Centre/Diwali
6. Slug & Lettuce
7. Shakespeare's Head
8. Conduit Street
9. Deaf Church events
10. Saint Marks Church & Community Centre
11. City Lit
12. Deaf Day
13. BSL (Cafe) Social
14. The Rooted Forum & Al Isharah Deaf Club
15. Bromley Deaf Pub
16. The East London Mosque & London Muslim Centre
17. British Deaf Association
18. Deaf Unity Cafe
19. Deaf Social Event Victoria
20. Holy Trinity Church
21. BSL Social (Cafe) Meet up

Traditionally-rooted deaf spaces

22. St John's Deaf Community Centre
23. Jewish Deaf Association
24. DeafPlus

'Temporal' deaf spaces

25. Deaf Rave
26. Deaf Street Party
27. Somaliland Event
28. Hare Krishna event
29. Cryptocurrency Investment Opportunity event
30. Somalia Event

Researchers' homes

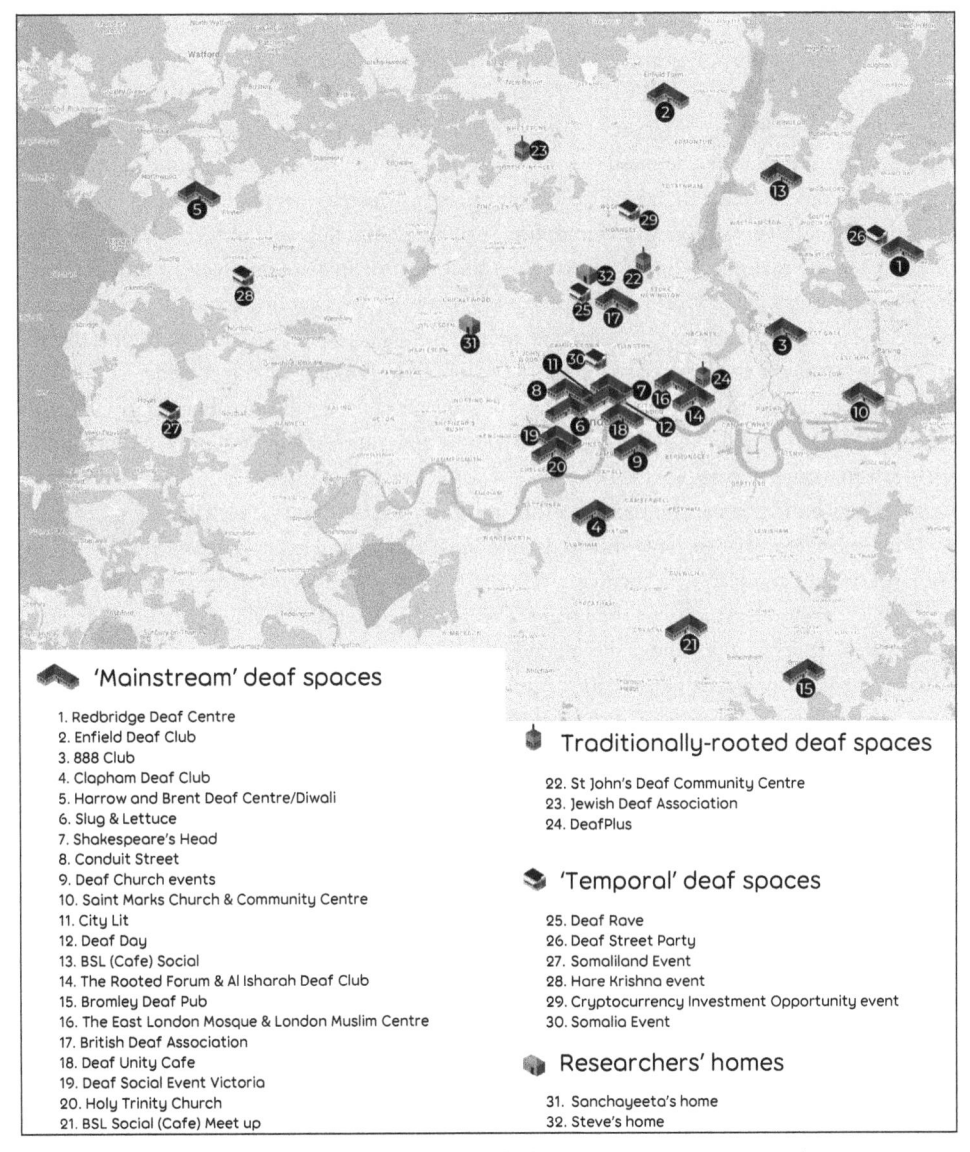

31. Sanchayeeta's home
32. Steve's home

Figure 4.1. The map we used to mark places visited for fieldwork. Map data @2022 Google.

We estimate that we met deaf people of 44 nationalities in this mapping exercise; however, this figure should be taken as a minimum. Migrants were present in the spaces but were generally in a minority. Between January and April 2018, Steve estimates that a total of 360 people were present across all the observed places, of whom 32 were migrants; this means that for every 23 people observed, at least two were migrants. This summarizes just 4 months of observations across the vast metropolis of London, and it highlights the mobility of migrants across the capital city. The migrant figure is a minimum because it pertains to those we *knew* were migrants in these spaces—because, for example, the contact person we had communicated with pointed them out to us. Participants who were interviewed were often witnessed at these locations, and sometimes we recruited individuals to take part in the interviews during the observation stages of the project.

Of the 23 locations, we suggest (based on our observations and discussions with those present) that only seven (roughly one-third) could be considered truly local spaces—that is, places that are mainly attended by people who live locally. This observation is crucial because it provides compelling evidence that, for deaf migrants, their place of community belonging, or "home," in London is *geographically variable* rather than *geographically rooted*. With regard to the nature of the mobility of deaf people, it is rare that they live their lives almost entirely within a localized geographical boundary. Researchers studying deaf migrants' experience of living only in the London borough of Hackney, for example, would be limited because deaf people's social lives beyond Hackney are likely to be extensive. Deaf people receive a free travel pass, enabling travel all over London, whereas hearing residents may be restricted from traveling across the city due to high transport costs. The fact that two-thirds of the spaces we recorded in London are not considered "local" in a geographically bounded sense reflects how the concept of "scale" (as highlighted in Chapter 1 of this book) is crucial for visualizing the lives of deaf migrants—that is, as highly mobile, almost diasporic in nature (Emery, 2015). Note, however, that deaf migrants also *do* socialize in localized ways, such as Indian female migrants meeting in Indian neighborhoods (see Chapter 9).

We suggest that what we have observed can best be understood as an *encapsulation* of migrant lives in London. The places on the map we have drawn may not always remain deaf spaces, host deaf spaces, or even exist at all in the future. The deaf spaces within the field that we frequented tended to be precarious or under threat, and this issue is explored in more detail in Chapter 7, where we look more closely at networks. Additionally, there are many more places we *could* have visited than those we observed, as is apparent from the Facebook page "Deaf UK Socials." We did not visit spaces frequented by deaf LGBTQIA+ people, although we did meet migrant deaf people who identified with this community and were aware that these spaces existed (see Chapter 9). There are many other examples of fields that are an important part of the landscape of deaf lives but that are not included in this study: deafblind groups, friendship groups that migrants may become part of, places where migrants of a particular nationality meet (a migrant from Nepal and another from Somalia told Steve that deaf people from these nations meet regularly socially), migrants working within mental health services, and sport events such as football (soccer) matches.

London deaf schools (e.g., Frank Barnes, Oak Lodge) are not mapped, specifically because we could not ethically include anyone younger than age 18 in the research project. However, we know that there are deaf migrant young people at these places (see Oktar, 2019). Sanchayeeta had worked at Oak Lodge School for more than 6 years; during that time, the majority of the students were from migrant families (mostly from Africa and Bangladesh), and most of the deaf students were migrants themselves. Some of these students had not attended school prior to joining this secondary school, and they were first exposed to sign language there. This is a common pattern in relation to migration and deaf children (Oktar, 2019). Deaf schools, along with deaf clubs, have long been in decline, but we recognize their ongoing value and importance as vital, traditionally rooted places for the nurturing of sign language and deaf culture.

Migrants Experiencing Discrimination in Deaf Spaces

Despite their presence in deaf spaces across the city, many deaf migrants experienced difficulties "integrating" in the deaf community (especially during the pandemic; see Chapter 10). Several female migrants felt unsafe at deaf spaces due to the behavior of men, and female migrants avoided spaces where alcohol was served. We were also struck by the *isolation* that many reported feeling, including feeling culturally less respected in the United Kingdom and living on the outskirts of London with little opportunity to meet other deaf people or go to deaf events. We discuss some of the experiences regarding (lack of) belonging in deaf spaces in Chapter 9. In this section, we focus on xenophobia and racism, demonstrating that these—especially racism—were consistent themes not only in institutional contexts and in relation to hearing people, but also at the grassroots level and among deaf people.

In terms of xenophobia, from our observations, the migrants we communicated with were generally not fully aware of the discourse around the "hostile environment" in the United Kingdom. This is probably partially due to not having full access to media coverage of this issue—that is, because of their limited English. Thus, they may not be aware that they are being discriminated against due to their migrant status. Also, deaf migrants from outside the EU might not necessarily have seen Brexit and the "hostile environment" (at the time, directed primarily toward EU workers) as affecting their lives, as compared to hearing migrants who would be able to hear negative remarks being made around them and would receive abuse based on their accented English.

A notable example of experiencing xenophobia comes from Lenka, a white European woman, who *was* able to overhear what people around her were saying in a way that many deaf people would not. She challenged the xenophobia she heard expressed when she was on a train one day:

> A family was sitting opposite me, eating burgers. I was looking at my phone, as deaf people usually do. I didn't know the people opposite me. My friend was sitting next to me and we were chatting in Czech. It was time for my friend to get off the train, so I said goodbye to them, and they left. The next thing that happened was I noticed one of the people opposite saying "Bloody foreigners. They come here and take over." I wasn't sure if they were referring to me. Anyway, I said nothing, ignored it and continued looking at my phone. They continued their discussion until I felt I had had enough. So, I stood up and I asked them "Can you tell me how many languages you all speak?" and I also asked them what school qualifications they had. When I found out they claimed benefits, I told them that since the time I arrived in the country, I have never claimed benefits and worked hard to pay off university fees and my mortgage. I work and pay my bills. I've never even had a loan. I contribute to this society, so how could they tell me that I was a "bloody foreigner." I advised them to think twice before speaking because what they said was very offensive. They were so shocked that one of them dropped their burger. I told them that I was proud to be a foreigner, then I walked off.

Additionally, some deaf migrants may also feel sheltered from xenophobia by the deaf community. For example, Francesca, from Italy, did not feel affected by xenophobia because she felt she had a strong attachment to the deaf community in London. She had seen some of her friends experiencing xenophobic abuse, and she felt lucky to be sheltered by the community (and, at the time of the interview, her British hearing white partner).

Until 2015, racism was not a subject that had had much exposure, discussion, or debate within Deaf Studies in the United Kingdom. James and Woll (2004) highlighted empirical evidence of racism in deaf spaces in the United Kingdom in the early 2000s, although interestingly, they state the study was "outside London" (p. 198), within deaf clubs, and the racist views were expressed by older generations. James and Woll (2004) stated that Asian and Jewish deaf groups "also slighted Black people" (p. 199), an issue that is beyond the scope of this study but which the authors conclude is evidence of "Deaf apartheid" (p. 199) and requires deep, wide-ranging further research. Studies on the subject of racism go back much further in the United States, with the first U.S.-born black deaf person to receive a doctorate, Glenn B. Anderson, coauthoring *Racism Within the Deaf Community* (Anderson & Bowe, 1972). Although a large number of publications on the experience of black deaf Americans followed, these do not seem to have included the experiences of black migrants. Similarly, discrimination and racism toward migrants more generally have been documented (Fernández-Reino, 2020; Quinn, 2013; Rzepnikowska, 2019), but the extent to which it pervades deaf spaces is less researched. It is for these reasons that, as part of the research process, we collaborated with the 888 Club (a monthly cinema club for deaf people held at the Stratford Picturehouse in East London) to publicly show Rinkoo Barpaga's documentary *Double Discrimination* (Barpaga, 2014).[7] The film explores the subject of racism in the British deaf community, examining whether it existed and, if so, to what extent. We invited Barpaga to give a presentation about his film and run a question-and-answer discussion after the film showing. Before showing Barpaga's film, we held a short presentation about the MobileDeaf project in the lobby of the cinema and invited people present to share their experiences of migration. We filmed this discussion, and it has formed part of our research findings. One of the most vivid accounts of racial discrimination was given by Sarla, a woman of Indian heritage in her early 50s, and her deaf brothers. Their parents had come to the United Kingdom when she was still a baby:

> [My two brothers went to] Oak Lodge School, which in 1966 had a lot of racism. My brothers had their hair pulled and were told they smelled, and the teachers wrote home to tell my father to cut their hair; they had no idea what was happening or why. They were constantly teased and bullied [...] I went to a deaf school in Fulham [...] but the teacher there said I didn't suit a deaf school and sent me to a mainstream school. The mainstream school was even worse! I was targeted because I was Asian, deaf, and used sign language! I had to lipread there. I didn't understand why they called me "Paki"—my family are from India, not Pakistan! They told me I smelled of curry. The worst thing was this duplication of discrimination: being deaf as well as Asian. They used to say, what have you come here for? Are you an illegal immigrant? But they didn't know about the history of the British Empire welcoming Indians to come here.

Sarla's story highlights the intersectional nature of her experiences as an Asian British deaf woman, in addition to the racism experienced at a deaf school and the combined experience of micro- and macroaggressions. In *Double Discrimination*, deaf people from ethnic minorities share similar experiences of racism, although it is important to note that *migrant* deaf people did not feature in the film—symptomatic of the pattern we noticed in the literature on deaf people from ethnic minorities.

At the event, Barpaga stated: "I wanted to get to grips with what I was finding in the deaf community, and when I started doing this, many people in the deaf community did not believe that there was racism in the deaf community." The film discussion took place in 2018, prior to the explosion of activities around the Black Lives Matter (BLM) movement in the United Kingdom, and it should be understood in that context. BLM as a movement had been well established in the United States since 2013, and the first formal U.K. BLM movement emerged in 2016 following police racism and the Brexit referendum; however, it was only with the worldwide protests

---

7. https://www.bslzone.co.uk/watch/zoom-focus-2014-double-discrimination

against the killing of George Floyd in the United States in 2020 that BLM reached wider recognition. At the film discussion, Barpaga stated that although *Double Discrimination* had stimulated much open debate in Chile, Italy, and Spain since its release in 2014, the MobileDeaf/888 Club screening—which took place in 2018—was the first time there had been a public discussion of it in the United Kingdom.

We want to stress that we are aware that there have been discussions and debates in the United Kingdom by activists within deaf black and ethnic minority communities since well before the BLM movement began, and much of which will not have been documented in academia. Since we finished our fieldwork, Black Deaf UK (https://www.blackdeaf.co.uk/) was established (in 2020), and this organization may well include and involve deaf migrants. However, this material is beyond the scope of the book. As we highlighted previously, post–Second World War discussions of racism started to be included in Deaf Studies academic discourse in the United States as far back as the 1970s (Anderson & Bowe, 1972); the United Kingdom has lagged behind. Barpaga stated that the initial reaction to the film in Britain was a reluctance to admit racism even existed in the United Kingdom but that gradually there was some acceptance that it did. The event included a discussion around what signs should be used for the term *black*. Barpaga, a working-class man born to Punjabi parents and who grew up in Birmingham, stressed that racism took place on different levels and that there could be linguistic racism and/or attitudinal racism at play. He also referred to the historical roots of British colonization and how previous generations of his family had been forcibly moved out of Africa. Note that he addressed migration within the larger time frame of colonialism, situating the migration found in the family histories of people who have been born in the United Kingdom:

> My family was from a part of the world colonized by the British Empire, in my case forcibly removed from Africa. We were supporting the British, helping them in war, and we had a huge involvement in British history, and then I thought to myself, "right, now that I know this history, I can challenge and fight back against these comments." So I think that immigrants have to find a way to respond and maybe they are in too weak a position to do so.

In response to a question from an audience member as to whether racism was being "swept under the carpet," Barpaga suggested that in the making of his film, "deaf people weren't ready to talk about racism. A lot of deaf people who had experienced racism were really uncomfortable, saying 'we're fine' [. . .] [or] 'latterly it has got better.'" Similarly, in our research, there appeared to be a reluctance to elaborate on experiences of racism, especially to Steve—probably influenced by his status as a white British man (see Chapter 2). Often, the question was answered quickly—again, likely due to the participant feeling the need to provide positive representations of life in the United Kingdom. For example, when Hawa, who had migrated from East Africa with her family when she was a teenager, was asked if she had experienced racism, she stated that "I have experienced plenty of what you have described" before quickly stressing that she enjoys meeting people "and the attitudes are good." There was a similar refrain in other interviews. A typical pattern was that interviewees stressed that any racism and prejudice was more the result of ignorance than, say, deliberate actions intended to flame racial tensions within deaf communities.

Nonetheless, racism was a theme that arose consistently throughout our study. There were the experiences of migrants who had faced violence. These instances and experiences were shared with us very briefly and sensitively, so it was difficult to follow up on them without potentially causing distress; however, due to the fact that we were coming across many such narratives, we concluded that they are clearly happening regularly and require addressing by deaf communities in the United Kingdom. Some examples are given here. We learned of the suicide of a deaf migrant. Another deaf migrant had left the country because of being fed up with "being picked on." Another migrant, an African man, had been threatened with a knife by a white deaf person when he was a young man. At the time of research, there was also a Facebook group called "UK Deaf Britannia" that posted highly inflammatory Islamophobic comments, ostensibly under the guise of being supportive of Brexit. Despite many complaints to Facebook, this group remained active, although at the time of writing (2023) it appears to have been deactivated. The views expressed by the group were constantly and persistently challenged, with deaf people regularly being expelled from the group for challenging the racism that the moderators did nothing to curtail.

Racism (and, indeed, xenophobia and Islamophobia) can exist in the form of microaggressions. Amare, a woman in her 30s from India who had also spent many years in the United States, stated that "some people when they found out I had not long arrived in the United Kingdom, they would just walk off and not try to communicate with me." She elaborated:

> When first meeting someone, they might not engage with me because they would see me as different. I would have to reassure them; others would be very direct with me, but I always had to respond with patience and stay calm. Yes, there is racism in the United Kingdom; for example, they would ask me "where are you from?" […] Sometimes they were very direct about it, and would ask why I came here […] So yes, there was a lot of that definitely.

These are examples of "racial microaggressions," a term first coined by Pierce in 1970 and which has been further developed through empirical research by Sue et al. (2007) and others. This racism is mainly hidden and covert, but the daily experience of this form of racism accumulates and impacts on the feeling of black and ethnic minority people that they are marginalized by a majority white society. Additionally, racism and xenophobia were often combined, such as in comments like "Where are you from?" being targeted at black and brown people, and are often difficult to disentangle. This is a newer manifestation of racism in society, as Delanty et al. (2008) write:

> The "new" racism differs from the older kinds in that it is not expressed in overtly racist terms or in the terms of neo-fascist discourse, for instance by some notion of biological or racial superiority, white supremacism or skin colour. Instead, the repertoires of justification that are typically employed use social characteristics (for example, protecting jobs, concern about welfare benefits) or cultural incompatibilities or differences (migrants lack "cultural competences," "they do not want to integrate," they are not "tolerant"). The new racism exploits established xenophobic frames (fear of the other), ethnocentrism, masculinities and "ordinary" prejudices in subtle ways and often, too, in ways that are unconscious or routinized. (p. 2)

Xenophobia and racism often overlap, and also intersect with Islamophobia. Islamophobia, or anti-Muslim sentiment, is one form of discrimination, exclusion, and oppression that Muslim communities, including deaf Muslim migrants, are subjected to in the United Kingdom. Since the attack on the World Trade Center's Twin Towers in New York (9/11), hate crimes toward Muslim communities have multiplied, especially toward Muslim women (Allen et al., 2013).

Muslim women serve as a visual identifier of Islam due to Islamic attire such as hijab and niqab; for oppressors, these symbols represent "Muslimness" (or perceived Muslimness) and Muslim identity in a way that is viewed as "other" and thus as synonymous with anti-Britishness (Allen et al., 2013). All Muslims have arguably been branded an extremist group, with differentiation between Muslims ignored. Discourse has arisen over the definition of Islamophobia and whether it should be seen as a form of racism. Yet, Islamophobia is rooted in racism. The function and processes of racism and Islamophobia are similar, with Muslim women being targeted due to their visibility (Allen et al., 2013; also, see Bonnett, 2022, for further information on different forms of racism linked with modernity).

At the time of writing, there has been a growing public awareness of racism due to the BLM movement. Black and ethnic minority deaf people have come to the fore to challenge white privilege and power within deaf communities, including within Deaf Studies academia. It is in this historical moment that the black deaf community has been able to find the platform to share its experiences of exclusion and marginalization at the hands of the dominant deaf community, something that Barpaga's film could not impact to the same extent. Following the arrival of the BLM era, deaf organizations and institutions (often led by white people) invited well-known black deaf figures within the United Kingdom's deaf communities (including those who had migrated there as a child) to participate in discussions about racism in British deaf communities, which took place online during the pandemic (and which the black deaf community felt were long overdue). One of the main issues identified by Black Deaf UK is that there is a lack of awareness of black history, culture, and identity, and thus there is a need for education to fill this gap in order for the community to be active in challenging systemic racism in the United Kingdom. However, little had been discussed about experiences of discrimination related to how race and ethnicity intersect with migration status. As mentioned previously, some of the well-known black deaf figures who had migrated to the United Kingdom as children had not mentioned or shared their experiences of discrimination as a black *migrant*. We find this intriguing, and we put forward the suggestion that prioritizing blackness as political identity within black deaf communities could be due to concerns that a recognition of the very diversity of race would be of advantage to white supremacy, and in the process dilute black deaf people's efforts toward equality and dignity.

Conclusion and Discussion

Our focus in this chapter has been to bring to life the experiences of deaf migrants living in London and to highlight the most common themes we encountered, all the while recognizing the impacts of our positionality as researchers. We have, in our analysis, attempted to cover a wide range of experiences from deaf migrants from all over the world. We were particularly focused on factors of class, race, and gender, and we recognize that there are many intersectional dimensions missing from this chapter, such as the experiences of deafdisabled, deafblind, deaf transgender, and deaf queer migrants (see Chapter 9 for a few examples of some intersectional experiences).

However, given that ethnographical, anthropological, and sociological approaches to deaf migration are newly emerging, our research provides a base from which to explore the subject further. There are also implications here for social policy. In our study and data collection, that is, through exploring the narratives that deaf migrants shared with us, we confirmed that migrant deaf people do experience adverse social exclusion, and we have expanded this narrative by addressing wider issues such as racism and xenophobia. However, an overemphasis on adverse experiences risks missing or neglecting the informal networks that exist, and hence underplaying the way migrants often demonstrate, or negotiate, agency. Recognizing *how* deaf migrants become part of the fabric of deaf communities throughout the United Kingdom is crucial, not only for the purposes of epistemology but also for social policy. Deaf migrants often have to face and confront racism and xenophobia from within deaf communities, but, as Barparga has been instrumental in highlighting, this subject has not been addressed. The formation of Black Deaf UK (2020) will surely go some way to addressing the issues facing deaf black and brown people in the United Kingdom. The implication of this analysis for social policy, therefore, is a question of how (overwhelmingly white) deaf organizations address and challenge racism from within their ranks. Similarly, regarding deaf women from South Asia who are excluded from deaf spaces due to the assumptions and expectations placed on them after their marriage and arrival in the country, the question must be: What can deaf groups or organizations do to raise awareness of these issues and support the empowerment of deaf migrant women in the United Kingdom?

What deaf organizations emphatically should not do is fall into the practice of misusing funds. We became aware of implicit discussions circulating within various deaf groups in London about the use of deaf migrants for financial gain by certain deaf organizations. This was elaborated on by Shahina, who had worked with a deaf organization where Access to Work funding was used to provide her with an interpreter for certain aspects of her role. Having previously lived and worked in the United States, Shahina had the social and cultural capital to know how an interpreter should be used both effectively and appropriately. At this organization, however, she was surprised to find that the "interpreter" they had employed was not qualified and was treated as though assigned to the organization *as a whole* rather than to Shahina as an individual. Shahina tapped into her new network of British deaf people (which she had developed through her previous volunteer work with another deaf organization), seeking information about how Access to Work should be used correctly; the information she obtained led her to realize that the organization was misusing the funds. Deaf migrants who are new to the United Kingdom and unfamiliar with the benefits system for deaf and disabled people can be easily manipulated by such organizations, which take advantage of their ignorance to deprive them of the qualified professional support they are entitled to, essentially using the Access to Work funding in lieu of paying the salary of an additional member of office staff. As a result, the deaf migrant is unwittingly implicated in benefit fraud. Shahina used the social and cultural capital at her disposal to assess the situation at work and to advocate for herself and her Access to Work entitlement as a deaf or disabled employee, reporting the misuse of funds to ensure that she was protected.

Shahina's social and cultural capital gave her agency in a potentially disempowering situation; her experience highlights that the converse is also true and that another migrant in the same position but without her prior knowledge and networks might not have been in a position to exhibit similar agency. Those we interviewed and observed throughout the subproject included deaf migrants who were teachers, social workers, and church leaders, and we know of others who are a vital part of mental health support networks—that is to say, migrants who have demonstrated agency to arrive at their position in society and who also come face to face with migrants who do *not* experience agency. The majority of literature and research surrounding deaf migration is heavy on the latter but not so much on the former, and in this study, expanding the narrative highlights how agency might be acquired: through support and provision *for* deaf spaces (the lack of deaf-led and owned deaf centers in the capital is a particular worry); through accessibility and awareness *in* deaf spaces (challenging racism and Islamophobia); through flexibility in employment recruitment practices (e.g., deaf migrants should be able to apply for jobs through an informal application process); through robust and ongoing support through education (City Lit classes, for example); and through mental health support services and in churches and secular spaces.

Where we have approached our subject with a theoretical lens, we have chiefly used Bourdieu's capital-field-habitus framework. This framework has proved highly useful and relevant, although we have barely skimmed the surface of what this frame can offer. We were able to identify the various forms of capital that migrants possess or come to acquire, and we could label the fields through which they navigated, but identifying habitus and showing how it works in relation to the field and capital proved more complex. The indications for using a Bourdieusian framework are, however, positive. We also attempted to analyze the data by categorizing migrant people by class, albeit tentatively. Although we found it was possible to do so, we saw that we could do so only temporarily, not least due to the fact that we found migrant narratives rarely covered class and are dominated by issues relating to deaf experience, gender, ethnicity, and, to a lesser extent, sexuality. Nevertheless, because we researchers wore a class lens at times, it was important for us to elaborate and clarify what we meant by class, and we trust this has been achieved to some extent.

Deaf studies *academia* has, we believe, badly underperformed in studying how racism and discrimination are being tackled in deaf communities and, even though discrimination is not only migrant-specific, there were some overlaps in our research when we asked people about it. As discussed in Chapter 2, there is also evidence that people were more open to sharing experiences with a person from the same or similar background (Sanchayeeta), in comparison to being asked by a white male researcher (Steve). However, Deaf Studies academia in the United Kingdom remains highly dominated by white people; it should therefore come as no surprise that it has lately been called "White Deaf Studies" by those seeking to call out this reality. We were heartened to learn that Gallaudet University has established the first Black Deaf Studies conference, and we have high hopes that this study contributes to opening up academia to deaf people of color and highlights the value of the visibility of migrant deaf people.

Finally, although we see a growing focus on intersectionality in Deaf Studies, the topic of migration is almost absent from these discussions. We also needed to distinguish between people from ethnic minority backgrounds. There are differences between, for example, British deaf people from ethnic minorities, and deaf migrants from ethnic minorities. The experiences of deaf migrants from ethnic minorities are often made invisible within studies of the experiences of deaf ethnic minorities. We hope to have addressed this imbalance to an extent and, in this conclusion, demonstrated the importance and relevance of this study to social policy as well as epistemology. It is, therefore, particularly useful research for deaf communities in London and the United Kingdom, where organizations, policymakers, activists, and academics are striving to support deaf migrants, be they asylum seekers, refugees, or those who have moved to seek employment, a better life, marriage, or to study.

5

Deaf Professional Mobility

Annelies Kusters

International deaf professional mobility takes a wide range of forms. Deaf athletes go to deaf international sports events such as the Deaflympics to compete against each other. Deaf youth from all over the world take part in the 9-month Frontrunners program, part of which entails living in Denmark for education about Deaf Studies, media, and sign language work. Deaf advocacy workers, educators, and researchers give presentations at a range of international conferences, such as the SIGN conference series, and World Federation of the Deaf (WFD) congresses and conferences. Deaf translators from various African countries (and beyond) gather in Kenya to translate Bible stories into their sign languages, staying from a few months to a few years.

Although these examples are varied, they have something in common: Deaf people engage in days, months, or even years of international mobility for knowledge exchange, competition, performing, creating materials, or skills development. They do this within the context of specific events, international workplaces, and educational centers. In such places and events, deaf people's paths converge across nations on the basis of a *shared* profession, orientation, interest, mission, or passion. As discussed in Chapter 1, there are obviously links and overlaps between professional mobility and the other forms of mobility covered in this book; for example, many deaf professionals *migrate* to one or more other countries for several years, or they combine conference travel with *tourism*. The grouping together of these forms of mobility under the catchall term "professional mobility" is contingent on my primary research focus: the use of International Sign (IS) and other multilingual signing practices in these settings. Because of this focus, I wanted to include contexts of learning and, with them, student mobility; other definitions of *professional mobility* do not include these contexts. There are forms of deaf professional mobility that are not covered in this chapter, such as the mobility of deaf business owners or development workers.

My focus is not only on "the professionals" themselves but on the broader context of the international gatherings built around these professional activities. Local hosts and organizers make the events happen, often in collaboration with international committees and a team of (local) volunteers. Enthusiastic spectators travel to the Deaflympics to cheer on the athletes and to mingle with other deaf people. Delegates attend WFD congresses to gather new information. Presenters, performers, audiences, hosts, volunteers, and tourists have in common that they interact within this larger context of professional mobility.

By grouping an admittedly broad range of activities together under the term *professional mobility*, I was able to note patterns that cut across different settings. A key example of this, on which I focus in this chapter, is the production of *scales*. By this, I mean that terms such as *international, global, regional, nation(al),* and *local (host)* function as dominant frames of reference in discourse about these networks, events, and places, and the language practices within them. Labels of scale are often included in the structure, mission, or name of deaf organizations (e.g., *World* Federation of the Deaf; Ghanaian *National* Deaf Association; DOOR *International*), as well as in the names of sign languages and signing practices (*International* Sign, *Kenyan* Sign Language, *village* signs).

However, scales are not just categories that refer to the focus and reach of organizations or languages. I am interested in scaling as a process: Scales are produced through discourses and practices. In this regard, I am greatly influenced by Lefebvre's (1991) paradigm-shifting perspective that social space, akin to scales, is not merely a given but is continuously produced and reproduced through social practices and relations. Similarly, the concept of scale can be understood not as a fixed hierarchy or a neutral framework, but as produced by social, political, and economic processes. For instance, the notion of a "local" scale is continually produced in relation to other scales that are also (re)produced in the process of defining a locale's embeddedness in regions, nations, or global contexts. Similarly, a "transnational" scale is produced through transnational flows of people, goods, ideas, and capital, but also in contrast to and in relation to nations. So, in line with Lefebvre's theory on space, scales are not just passive backgrounds for processes but are actively shaped by, and contribute to, those processes. As such, we should not study scales as preexisting hierarchical levels. Instead, we should understand them as changeable and contextual products of the processes of scaling, and focus not only on the products but also on these processes (Mansfield, 2005; Moore, 2008).

In this chapter, I explore the production of scales through deaf professional mobility. Scales materialize when deaf professionals, their entourages, and their audiences get together at events and/or establish organizations catering to their interests. Here, scaling (as in getting together "nationally" or "internationally") shapes and influences the professional interactions that take place, and, produced by these interactions, scale-based organizations and workplaces are products of scaling. Thus, my focus encompasses these readily identifiable scales-as-products—that is, those implied by and in the names of various sign languages and organizations. But I am also fascinated by the reasons and mechanisms behind the process of producing scales. In pursuit of these, I make references to historical literature.

There are many useful examples to be found in deaf history showing how scales are produced and that they are not preexisting. By way of illustration, the WFD (the world's oldest and largest international disability organization) was established in 1951, but Murray (2007) has shown how a deaf transnational scale (which he calls "sphere") was produced long before international deaf organizations were established, through the actions of white deaf American and European men in the late 19th and early 20th centuries. This transnational scale was produced through individual travel, the exchange of national periodicals, and a series of ad hoc conferences held on both sides of the Atlantic (see also Gulliver, 2015; Mottez, 1993). In these spaces, the white deaf men in attendance commemorated their history (e.g., the anniversaries of the establishment of influential deaf schools), celebrated signing and deaf networks, and shared experiences of, and strategies for, living as a deaf minority among a hearing majority. Participants returned from these conferences feeling recharged and with "energy and optimism for further battles back home" (Murray, 2007, p. 66).

"Back home" was often framed in terms of "the nation," Murray (2007) writes. The events were often attended by the same (or an overlapping) group of white deaf middle-class males from Europe and the United States who were teachers, missionaries, or in other prestigious occupations, and who specialized in international deaf travel. These individuals formed a connection, or mediating position, between their respective *national* communities. Murray (2007) notes that the deaf Americans he studied "claimed the economic and social privileges of whiteness, using it as a baseline for their construction of a *national* identity that positioned sign language-using Deaf people as fully a part of the *nation*" (p. 39; my emphasis). In their quest to be part of the nation, white deaf men were able to center deafness *because* of their race and gender. African American deaf people in the American South went to segregated deaf schools, were often consigned to manual labor, and were not in a position to publicly contribute to these white-led *national* networks. This then led to black deaf people's underrepresentation in *international* events. For example, at the 1893 World's Fair in Chicago, white deaf people organized a world congress, but African Americans were nearly completely excluded from the event. Additionally, where white deaf women attended similar congresses, they were typically not official delegates or presenters, and they did not always have voting rights: "If Deaf men dominated Deaf political life in a *national* setting, it would be Deaf men who would be chosen as *international* delegates" (Murray, 2007, p. 87; my emphasis). White women were involved in social events and humanitarian efforts, however: One example is their fundraising for deaf refugees of the First World War. National norms as to who participates in organized deaf activism are thus reflected on the transnational level.

From this, we see that the *transnational* scale was produced before most *national* deaf associations existed. In the 19th century, information about deaf education traveled more quickly between metropolitan cities, such as Paris, Edinburgh, London, and New York, than to other parts of each respective country (Cleall, 2015). It was often during *international* events that deaf people became inspired to establish new *urban* and *national* associations. For example, it was after a congress in Paris in 1889 that British delegates established what is now the British Deaf Association. Many national deaf associations were set up in response to the threat of oralism in deaf schools, which had also spurred an increase in transnational interaction due to the many issues in common for deaf people from different nations (Murray, 2007). National themes were thus central in the production of the transnational scale, and transnational discourse flowed back into nations. In the aftermath of the historical conferences documented by Murray, the deliberations were made accessible to women and working-class people through public lectures given by men who had attended them, and through accounts in periodicals. Where international travel was funded by local deaf clubs or associations, there was the expectation that knowledge would flow back to them at the local level. However, although information was distributed locally and nationally, and therefore (supposedly) made more broadly available, it is important to keep in mind that the themes discussed on the transnational scale were those identified as priorities by the people who *represented* the nations—that is, the white male leadership. This means that the issues of marginalized and underrepresented groups of deaf people were deemed of low priority. Transnational discourse at these congresses would undoubtedly have looked very different were, for example, more people of color, women, and working-class deaf people given the opportunity to push their agendas.

A second example of the interrelated production of local, national, and transnational scales are national and international sports associations. Traditionally, being strongly involved in deaf sports on a local scale (in schools or clubs), and then on a national scale, were the typical first steps toward international participation. This pathway was later formalized through organizations. For example, the Canadian Deaf Sports Association was established so that Canadian athletes could compete in the then World Games for the Deaf because participation was only permitted to athletes representing a national deaf sports organization (Stewart, 1991). In the book *The Deaf Sport Movement in Europe* (Mesch & Mesch, 2018), many more examples are included of the requirement for a hierarchical institutional structure to be established before participation in international deaf sports can take place. For instance, without a national deaf sports organization, a nation cannot be affiliated with the European Deaf Sports Organisation. Therefore, the production of a national scale is solidified through the formation of a national organization due to the perceived need for a hierarchical relationship between a national and a European organization. Another scale-related problem is that the statutes of the International Committee of Sports for the Deaf require federations to be deaf led, whereas in some instances (e.g., in the United Arab Emirates and France), deaf sports is classified under disability sports and is thus hearing led (Ammons & Eickman 2011).

In a third example of the interrelationship of scales, we see the tensions and shifts between nationalism and deaf transnationalism in deaf sports. In a study of the 19th Summer Deaflympics in 2001, Haualand (2007) notes that throughout the 2 weeks of the Deaflympics, there was a gradual orientational shift from nationalism to transnationalism across the event as a whole. Nationalism was visible during the opening ceremony as athletes filed behind their country's flag and grouped accordingly; however, during the closing ceremony, they walked as one crowd. In the evenings, spectators and athletes from various nationalities mixed with the audience that had gathered beyond the national banners. Breivik (2002) reported an incident where deaf football (soccer) supporters of opposing national teams wanted to be able to mix across nationalities rather than sitting in separate areas in the stands; this led to a rebellion against the security guards in the stadium. Thus, the transnational scale (in the sense of transcending the national scale) was produced with increasing strength through the event, even while markers of nationality (flags, supporters' outfits) remained omnipresent. Haualand (2002) reports a reordering of the hierarchy of belonging: "What had opened as an international event, in order to celebrate both outstanding sportsmanship and the spirit of brotherhood, had been fused into a transnational family" (p. 30). Fians (2021b) points out a similar process at the Universal Congress of Esperanto: "Esperantists draw lines distinguishing nationalities so that they can later cross these lines" (p. 118), and "elements—such as flags [...]—that have been historically used to justify the existence of nations, nationalities and nation-states are mobilized here to ground an *international* community" (p. 97, my emphasis).

In summary, scholars focusing on deaf transnationalism (Murray, 2007; see also authors in Breivik et al., 2002, and in Friedner & Kusters, 2015a) have studied how deaf people cross national borders, "know no borders," "are one family," and are "citizens of the world." This book's focus on interrogating cosmopolitanism, inspired by these and other works, often backgrounds "the nation" in its analysis. Indeed, in my contributions to Chapters 7–10 of this book, I focus on *international* interactions, on experiences of *crossing* national borders. Yet, it is also clear from the previous examples that "the nation" is prominent in practices and discourses on deaf transnationalism and cosmopolitanism. Noting a similar prominence of "the nation" in the data I collected on deaf professional mobility, in this chapter I have been inspired to pay special attention to meanings given to "the nation," "national identity," and "national sign language." I engage in this with an awareness of the danger of methodological nationalism (Wimmer & Glick Schiller, 2002)—that is, nationalist thinking in research. Wimmer and Glick Schiller (2002) caution against "describing processes within nation-state boundaries as contrasted with those outside" (p. 307), because assuming that nation states are the "adequate entities for studying the *international* world" is problematic and reductionist (p. 304; original emphasis). Yet, they also acknowledge that it is just as important to remember the continued potency of nationalism, because "nationalism is a powerful signifier that continues to make sense for different actors with different purposes and political implications" (pp. 326–327).

Thus, I asked the following questions when looking at my data: How are nations made visible or relevant in international deaf professional settings? Do national organizations act as gatekeepers to "the transnational scale"? In international settings, what does it mean for deaf people to be identified as being from a particular nation? What does it mean that politics in different nations are rendered commensurable or comparable in international events? What does it mean for national sign languages to be used alongside each other, and alongside IS? I focus on a series of events and workplaces where deaf people identified with a number of different nations have gathered in a professional setting. The main themes of my project were the practices and ideologies of IS in these contexts of professional mobility, but the focus of this chapter is wider. I have chosen five settings on which to focus, each of which also corresponds with a film in the series *This Is IS*. The settings are as follows: Frontrunners, a 9-month international deaf education and leadership course with IS as the language of tuition and communication (held in Hedensted, Denmark, with fieldwork conducted 2017–2018); DOOR International Africa, a campus where teams from different countries work on Bible translations (Nairobi, Kenya; 2019); SIGN8, a conference on sign language research (Florianopolis, Brazil; 2018); the XVIII WFD congress (Paris, France; 2019); and the 19th Winter Deaflympics (northern Italy; 2019). I also occasionally mention other settings in which I have done fieldwork for this study.

The chapter is structured in sections following the various ways that the concept of "nations" was prominent in my data: international mobility channeled through nations or limited by national identity; deaf people representing their nation abroad; deaf people using national sign languages in international professional gatherings where IS was the norm; deaf people trading in national stereotypes and essentialisms; the expectation that deaf professionals bring knowledge and materials back to enable national development; nations as hosts for international events; and the use of national sign languages in the context of hosting. In line with the rest of the book, I use the term "transnational" to describe contexts where national borders are "transcended"; "international" to talk about situations where national borders are crossed but kept intact (e.g., making comparisons between countries); and "multinational" to talk about contexts where deaf people from a number of nations gather. I use both of the partially overlapping terms "nation" and "country" in this chapter. "Nation" as a term tends to be associated more with a national community and culture than "country," and "national sign language" is the usual term to talk about sign languages used within a country. However, when talking about nations in IS, deaf people often sign COUNTRY (Figure 5.1) or FLAG (Figure 5.2) with the mouthing "country" rather than "nation." In my analysis of scale that follows, I more often use the term "nations" and "national" to juxtapose with "international," "regional," and "local."

Figure 5.1. COUNTRY

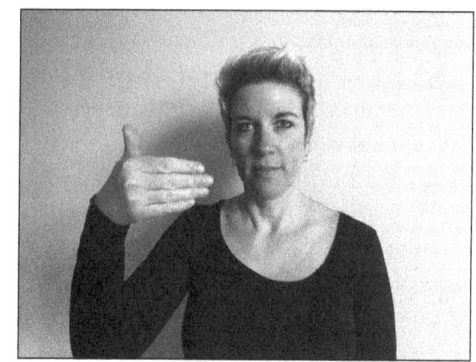

Figure 5.2. FLAG

Nations as Channels or Containers

National organizations sometimes have the power to determine who is internationally mobile. When deaf people "go international" in the context of professional events and gatherings, there often are regulations in place as to who can access them, or statements about for whom the events are organized. For example, to participate in the Deaflympics, athletes must be able to demonstrate a minimum of 55dB hearing loss, but they are not expected to know how to sign (see Chapter 9). At the SIGN8 conference (discussed later), presenters were expected to use IS or Brazilian Sign Language (Libras). In the Frontrunners program, participants are age restricted (18–35) and must be motivated to use IS.

There are other rules, however, that specifically relate to the national affiliation of an attendee. For example, only one national association can join the WFD as an Ordinary Member (OM). Up to two delegates from each OM can attend the General Assembly held before the WFD congresses. Individual delegates at such events thus represent national organizations, but only one organization on the national level has this link to the international level (although the WFD can make exceptions and extend this to more than one national organization). It also means that those participating at the international level in this space are almost certainly already in a leadership position at the national level. A similar structure is also in place for the camps organized by the World Federation of the Deaf Youth Section (WFDYS) and the European Union of the Deaf Youth (EUDY). Young people are usually selected through their national deaf (youth) organizations and thus benefit from having already been networked within their countries. There is a cap on the number of participants from the same country to ensure that no nationality is in the majority, irrespective of the size of the country. Thus, a small country like Belgium is rendered commensurable to much larger countries, such as India—effectively ensuring that deaf youth from India will statistically be much less likely to have the opportunity to participate in the camps. In the Frontrunners program, anyone can apply in the sense that there is no national go-between organization, but there is a similar cap on how many people from a single nation can participate (typically no more than two or three, although exceptions have been made).

In the sports world, the nations that are represented on the international level strongly vary depending on the sport. For example, at the 2019 Winter Deaflympics, for ice hockey there were only (exclusively male) teams from Finland, the United States, Canada, Russia, and Kazakhstan—all countries with a strong tradition of playing ice hockey. In the case of team sports, there need to be enough athletes to create a national team for the Deaflympics, which is a problem particularly in the case of some women's sports teams (see Chapter 10). In individual sports, people compete as individuals and more nations tend to be represented. In the chess competitions, there were many chess players from Russia, Eastern European countries (i.e., post-Soviet states), and India. The relative popularity of particular sports in given countries, their availability in deaf schools, and the costs associated with playing all factor into which nations are represented in which sports competitions. Strong leadership on the national level is crucial as well, as Pavel, the Russian chess captain, told me in an interview:

> I think what's important is that you have charismatic leaders that others will flock to and follow. [...] When you see a growth of interest in a country and investigate why, you will often find that this is the reason. For example, in America, there was nothing going on [in relation to deaf chess], there wasn't

anybody for the youth to follow but as soon as there was, you saw participation increase. The youth responded to this leader, and you can see similar examples of this all around the globe.

When one person from a country leads the way, others may follow and place a nation on the map for this sport, becoming agentive in the production of the transnational scale of deaf chess. This pattern is visible in the Frontrunners program as well: Several countries, such as Belgium, South Korea, and India, have "supplied" Frontrunners students over a number of years. Prospective students learn from previous Frontrunners about their experience, learn about the program, learn about ways to fundraise in their countries so as to attend the international program, and may even learn some IS. Hyemi, from Korea, described her experience of this:

> [When I was growing up,] I thought that there were deaf people in Korea and nowhere else. I thought the rest of the world was hearing. Later, I met a [Korean] woman from Frontrunners 5. She signed in IS. I was so surprised when I learned that people in the world use IS. I gained information from her and that got me interested. After that I started to learn IS in Korea for 7 years. When I came here, I was surprised that it was not as easy to communicate in IS with people from other countries as when I used IS in Korea. [...] So, I am trying to learn more IS here. (*This Is IS*: Episode 1, 00:13:02)[1]

Even though Hyemi felt that the IS used in Europe was very different, her meeting with several former Korean Frontrunners over the years had exposed her to knowledge about the program and about the concept of IS, which helped her to prepare for the experience.

In other contexts, people go to international events as individuals, through a "flat" rather than hierarchical structure—that is, they can join without "passing through other scales" first *and* without there being a cap on the number of participants per nation. Examples include presenters and audience members at the SIGN8 conference and the WFD congress. Structural barriers—such as having caring duties, lack of access to funding, disabling environments (see Chapter 10), and struggles to belong (see Chapter 9)—may deter people from participating, as may events' or organizations' explicit or implied language policies, for example, the requirement to use IS (see Kusters, forthcoming). What is most relevant in the context of this chapter, though, is that national organizations are *not* the primary gatekeeper or main identifier for participation in these international events. The affiliated nation of each participant plays a lesser role in their access to the event. The existence of these events means that deaf people can socialize internationally even if they are not well connected in their home country or involved in national organizations. Given the large number of people who "arrive late" in deaf communities, some start to travel to international events at much the same time as their introduction to their local and national deaf communities, and they may learn to use their national sign language and IS (almost) simultaneously. Some people even participate *more* in international networks. In these contexts, deaf people do not necessarily "pass through scales" to participate in and (re)produce the international scale, and these forms of individual mobility are therefore less hierarchical than those mediated through national and international scale-based organizations.

---

1. https://vimeo.com/686852215#t=13m02s

Representing a Nation Internationally

In the previous section, I established that national organizations, and a person's nationality, can play a larger or lesser role in their ability to access an international professional gathering as a delegate, presenter, athlete, or student. However, when I did participant observation at these gatherings, it was immediately obvious that national identities invariably played a central role *as an identifier*. Often, one of the first questions attendees were asked was "Where you are from?" in the sense of which nation or country; this was a key part of people's introductions. For example, when Ian, a deaf acquaintance from Scotland, introduced me to people at the International Chess Olympiad in Manchester in 2018, he would point to chess players and tell me the country they were from, rather than their name. This is perhaps to be expected in deaf sports, where athletes are usually representing their nation, but this pattern was also observed in situations where people were *not* national delegates. For example, at the World Association of Sign Language Interpreters (WASLI) conference in Paris, some people who came to the stage to comment during a panel only introduced themselves using their nation: "I am from Iran," "I am from Uganda" (*This Is IS: Episode 5*, 00:20:21).[2] Similarly, in the film series *This Is IS*, people are introduced in the captions by name, nation, and sometimes their function (e.g., as "director," "interpreter").

In another example, when the new Frontrunners arrived in Castberggaard, the building complex in Hedensted where the program takes place, they typically introduced themselves to those they did not yet know with their name and their nation (or, in some instances, two nations), using both fingerspelling and sign names (*This Is IS: Episode 1*, 00:14:14).[3] Some other important identifiers (e.g., race or ethnicity, approximate age, coming from a deaf or hearing family, class, sexual orientation) were observed or suspected on first meeting, whereas others were learned later. In the subsequent days, I observed how people remembered which country the others came from before they remembered personal sign names and the spelling of each other's names. On the morning of day 4, one of the Frontrunners asked who had the key to the shared accommodation; someone responded, "Spain." Esther, from Catalonia in Spain, saw this and responded, "I have a name!" It was clear that she felt it was time that they knew each other's names, instead of just using a (potentially contested) national label. This will be discussed later.

The Frontrunners group of 2017–2018 consisted of 17 students, of whom there was no more than one student per nation for all except Belgium (which had three) and France (two). This diversity probably contributed to the inclination to remember a person's nationality rather than their personal name. In larger events like the Deaflympics, there were typically more people present from each nation. The opening of the 2019 Winter Deaflympics was in Sondrio, a city in northern Italy (Figures 5.3–5.8). After the opening ceremony, the athletes were split over three different, smaller towns, each of which had specific facilities for hosting the various sports competitions: Chiavenna for chess and ice hockey; Madesimo for curling; and Santa Caterina di Valfurva, high in the mountains, for skiing (alpine and cross-country) and snowboarding. However, during the opening ceremony, the national teams for the different sports had not yet dispersed, and thus gathered as one crowd behind their national flag, together with the support staff for each nation. Before the opening ceremony, delegations had arrived in Sondrio on buses

---

2. https://vimeo.com/783318465#t=20m21s
3. https://vimeo.com/686852215#t=14m14s

126 CHAPTER FIVE

Figure 5.3. Nations lining up for the opening parade, starting with France and then alphabetically.

Figure 5.4. Some Russians in the opening parade, part of a very large crowd of Russians.

and stood in groups, wearing jackets (and sometimes hats) that displayed the name, and often also the flag, of their nation.

The opening ceremony started with a parade of the various countries' delegations through the streets of snowy Sondrio. France was in the lead (see Figure 5.3), as the country that had hosted the first Deaflympics in 1924; other delegations followed in alphabetical order. Arriving under a big tent that blocked the snow, attendees sat in national delegations during the opening ceremony (Figure 5.7). Some delegations, such as those from Russia (Figure 5.4) and the United States, which had brought teams to compete in several sports, were huge and took up a lot of space in the parade and under the shelter. Other nations were represented by only a few people, such as the Brazilian delegation of chess players (Figure 5.5). The size of the delegation was largely considered irrelevant,

Figure 5.5. The whole Brazilian delegation (chess players).

Figure 5.6. Supporters waving flags in the audience of the opening parade.

Figure 5.7. The opening ceremony of the 2019 Deaflympics where groups of people were sat in national groups. The Canadian team can be seen from the back.

Figure 5.8. Some flags of participating countries in the square in Santa Caterina.

however; a single delegate meant that the nation was represented and thus "included" at the event. The nations' flags were displayed at the central square in Santa Caterina, where the medals for the ski and snowboard competitions were announced every day (Figure 5.8). "The nation" thus became visible (and countable) in terms of flags, and, whereas some nations became more visible at the event because of the size of their delegation, small delegations were also made visible and relevant. This was the rhetoric adopted in discourse on the (Winter) Deaflympics, as evidenced in the following interview with Urban Mesch, a Swedish deaf sports historian:

> Four years ago, in Russia [the 18th Winter Deaflympics in Khanty-Mansiysk], that was huge, but here in Italy, it's the biggest yet. Thirty-four countries are represented here and it's inspiring to see all those nations' flags flying together, including flags from countries we have never seen at these games before, including Pakistan and Brazil, and yet they are here at these games. To see all those new flags makes me feel good about the growing future of deaf sports. The Summer Deaflympics are even larger! They've grown to an enormous scale to the point where they had 116 participating countries at their most recent edition. So, the Deaflympics has grown and grown throughout all the years that I've been involved, and that's terrific. [...] In the past, we didn't get competitors from countries that used to be in the Soviet bloc, in the east of Europe, or from China. The sports world was smaller, traditionally being confined to Europe and the United States with not much happening in South America. Australia and Japan were involved, but other parts of the world weren't, such as Africa. There has been some work in this area, and we've seen athletes from South America and Africa who take part a lot more in the summer games, but not so much in the winter games. Countries like Australia and New Zealand, and the Asian countries, however, have become much more involved. At these games you can see competitors from China and Korea, even though it is winter sports here. Previously they never used to attend, so it's good to see the world opening up, less exclusion and more inclusion, allowing athletes from across the globe to compete with one another. (*This Is IS*: Episode 6, 00:01:03)[4]

4. https://vimeo.com/809000011#t=1m3s

Growth and inclusion in the Deaflympics are measured in terms of the number of nations competing. Urban emphasized that this has been a process over many years, and that the representation of nations at the Deaflympics is highly dependent on deaf leadership and on government funding. He gave the example of Russia and Ukraine (see Chapter 10), both of which got strong government support in 2019. His narrative above zooms in and out of geographical scales, going from individual countries' flags to whole continents, which illustrates the ways in which scales are (re)produced in discourse depending on the points people want to make. Urban pointed out the leadership of individuals in getting nations and regions to become more involved in sport. He also discussed the financial side and pointed out that African nations had been unable to send delegates to the 2019 International Committee of Sports for the Deaf (ICSD) Congress, as opposed to the 2019 WFD congress (at which many African nations were represented): "For sports," he said, "there is no money."

Nations were also made visible in other contexts and settings. At the 47th ICSD Congress (which was held just before the 2019 Winter Deaflympics, in the same area; see Figures 5.9–5.11), national delegates sat together behind a sign with their country name and flag. Also at the ICSD congress, a row of flags flanked the room. A common practice at international deaf conferences is that the participants' respective nations are introduced one by one from the stage, with people in the audience raising their arms or cheering when their country is announced; this is another example of the nation being made visible. At the opening of the 2019 WFD congress in Paris, a video clip was shown where the names of nations (I assume the nations of the Ordinary Members) were listed in English along with their sign names (sometimes a sign name for the country that was internationally used, otherwise in French Sign Language [LSF]), which were signed by people wearing stereotypically "French" attire (see Figure 5.11).

Figure 5.9. The room where the ICSD's 2019 congress was held, taken during a break. The room is lined with flags.

Figure 5.10. An example of a national marker at the ICSD congress.

Figure 5.11. Announcing Belgium at the WFD congress.

The previous examples show how nations can become literally visible at international conferences, although in a different way than during the Deaflympics parade. The presence of others from the same nation can lead to expressions of pride and self-confidence, and a sense of pride did appear to be in the air during the opening parade of the 2019 Winter Deaflympics and also at the 2019 WFD congress. Johanna Balaguera, a presenter from Colombia, said to me, "A friend from Columbia, a deaf person, told me welcome! I assumed no one from Columbia would be here, only international people. When I saw a deaf Columbian, they gave me confidence."

Grouping people by nation as the foremost identifier does have certain implications and brings some challenges. In sports, national teams often recruit players, trainers, or coaches from other nations, and there are Deaflympic athletes and coaches who have represented more than one nation throughout their career. More broadly, using nation as identifier in transnational events disregards the fact that deaf people may have moved between countries and/or may have multiple nationalities. Indeed, many deaf people do not live or work in the country in which they were born. This can lead to conundrums as to which of these nations they should affiliate themselves. At the 2019 Winter Deaflympics, people regularly asked Dawn Jani Birley, who worked as my research assistant at the events (see Chapter 2), whether she supported the Finnish or Canadian ice hockey team; Dawn had grown up in Canada but had been living in Finland for 20 years. Their interest in her affiliation reflected the fact that, for many, ice hockey was "the" sport of the Winter Deaflympics. It is an exciting, fast-paced team sport, with the ice hockey final traditionally marking the end of the tournament. Dawn responded that she supported the Finnish team because they were strong signers, whereas there were too many people in the Canadian team who could not sign. The sense that there was an overpresence of nonsigning athletes was often discussed at the Deaflympics, and it overlapped with the question of nation. In the context of an international deaf multisport event, certain nations tend to be associated with a higher presence of nonsigning deaf and hard of hearing people, who are observed using speech with each other (see Breivik et al., 2002; see also Chapter 9). Dawn's self-affiliation with Finland should be understood within this context.

As these examples show, a particularly interesting issue encountered at international gatherings is the apparent need to affiliate to one country *exclusively*. A potent symbol of this, in some gatherings, is the use of name tags. At the 2019 WFD congress, I observed that people's eyes constantly went to other people's badges, to "place" them. The WFD badge showed the congress' logo, the delegate's name, their country affiliation, a barcode, and the label "participant" or "press." A person's country of residence and country of origin were often conflated and/or presumed to correspond to their nationality (Fians, 2021b). Thus, although many people were personally affiliated to more than one country, the congress name tags usually listed only one. It is typically the organizers of the congress who arrange the badges, and it is usually the case that only one country can be listed by the delegate during the registration process. If someone goes to an event representing an institution (as is commonly the case at conferences), the country in which that institution is located is likely to be listed, which may not correspond with the nationality *or* the country of residence of the delegate. For example, a British-born and British-resident deaf man had "Kosovo" on his WFD badge (I believe that he was employed as a freelancer by a Kosovar company at the time of the congress). There were, unsurprisingly, many brief conversations about national affiliations. Danny, from Belgium, had "Finland" on his badge because he worked and lived there; he said that people he encountered had remarked that his name did not sound Finnish. My own participant badge said "U.K." because I had registered through my workplace; when people looked at my badge to check which country I was from, I was quick to say, "I am from Belgium." Sujit worked with me as a research assistant at the WFD congress; his badge said "India," based on his nationality. He told me that he had thought it necessary to clarify to people that he did not live there at the moment. That people (myself included) feel the impulse, often preemptively, to correct (mis)conceptions about affiliation(s) to place (whether of birth, residence, heritage, and so on) indicates the importance placed on these affiliations. Yet, examples such as Dawn's, above, show that these affiliations are not fixed but can be deliberately and strategically shifted according to context. It is in these practices and discourses that the national scale is reinforced by using the nation as a central frame of reference.

Conference badges, in their rigidity and fixity, clash with this fluidity of affiliation; so, too, do group photos where "nation" is made visible. A popular activity at deaf international events is to take group photos. At the WFD congress, people who had attended the same WFDYS camp 25 years ago or who had participated in one of the Frontrunners programs assembled to take group photos together. At the Deaf Academics conference in Iceland, we took a group photo with people who had, at some point in the past 20 years, studied at the Center for Deaf Studies at the

University of Bristol. Additionally, people take group photos with others from the same nation, and it can be interesting to observe who is included or not. When photos of Belgians were being taken, for example, sometimes people from Flanders (the northern part of Belgium) would take a "Flanders photo" rather than a "Belgian photo," and I also noted hesitation about whether to include people who had only recently migrated to the country. With some exceptions, these people were generally not included, whereas some people who had moved out of Belgium 20 years ago were still included in the group photos. On one occasion, I noted the inclusion of people who had a Belgian passport or parent, but who had never lived there themselves. The concept of international events as a "family of nations" is here deployed by participants "to legitimate their own versions of national identity and to exclude or problematize others who are out-of-category" (Malkki, 1994, p. 61). Using "the nation" as the basis for inclusion or exclusion in ad hoc groupings appears, on the surface, to be a straightforward framework, but it is ambiguous at best, as these examples show.

Another issue with "representing the nation" is that people may not identify strongly with *any* given nation, but with a family of nations (e.g., the Gulf area) or with a region hoping to break away from a nation (e.g., Catalonia). People may identify particularly strongly with (minority) ethnic, cultural, or identity groups, or with regions rather than a nationality. Stein (2015) gives the example of Chile, where deaf individuals "pledge allegiance first to their local (urban) deaf association and then to the Chilean deaf community as a whole" (p. 177), and explains that attempts to create a national confederation of associations were in vain. In other words, the solidification of the national scale in the form of a nation-based organization failed. This leads us to a different problem than the ambiguity of national affiliations. The *diversity* of an audience is typically measured in terms of the number of *nations* represented and not in terms of gender, or race/ethnicity, or other variables. Nations can be important categories of identification, but people may also (and more strongly) identify with region, religion, class, ethnicity, gender, or language (Holliday, 2010). At the 2019 WFD congress, one could see racial and ethnic diversity, and also cultural diversity: People wearing traditional attire associated with particular cultures gave the event a visual appearance of diversity. However, "forms of diversity [are] subsumed under the label 'national'" (Fians, 2021b, p. 98). This can obfuscate who is present from each specific nation and who is *not*. For example, people from minoritized and underrepresented groups, such as Indigenous people, people of color, and deafdisabled people, may face systemic barriers to attending international events. Learning that 50 people from the United Kingdom attended the event does not tell us anything about the *backgrounds* of these 50 people. Furthermore, the people who came to WFD may have been very diverse, but representation *on the stage* was not always seen as diverse. During the closing ceremony, people in the audience complained that most people on the stage were white men, who were giving prizes to other white men, and then handing over the organization of the XIX congress to the next organizational committee, fronted by three South Korean men. If participation on the international scale is, in the first instance, measured in terms of the *number of nations* that attend, then other forms of diversity can be overlooked, as well as diversity within leadership. The act of counting nations allows it to be made visible how whole regions are included or left behind, as in Urban's example above, but also can render invisible that whole groups of deaf people are underrepresented in events or on the stage.

National Sign Languages in International Settings

The nation is not merely an identifier or category. It also can be the main basis of socialization and communication during an international event. In the other chapters of this book, we have mostly focused on socialization between and across nations; in this section, I wish to show that people also stay in national groups when in international settings. At some events, such as camps, people from different nations and regions (i.e., groups of neighboring countries) may be explicitly instructed to mingle, by way of the design of the activities. At the WFDY camp in Durban in 2011, for example, Merricks (2015) reports that mixed activities challenged (to some extent) the tendency of participants to bond and group with others from the same continent, especially at the beginning. At other events, however, the opposite is true. The activities do not preclude sticking together within national groups, and separation by nation can even be systematic. To give some examples of national clustering at international events, at the Clin d'Oeil deaf cultural festival in 2019, I observed a group of deaf people from an East Asian country being directed to a designated place by someone walking in front holding a paper in the air to lead the group. At the 2019 WFD congress, people from one nation were often observed sticking together for the whole or parts of the event and using their national sign language with each other. Groups of people from the same nation (e.g., groups of friends, colleagues, or family members) often stayed in the same accommodation, with this arrangement extending beyond that space into experiencing some, or all, of the event program together.

Some of the reasons for staying mostly with people from the same nation include not knowing other people at the international event, and/or not knowing IS. Sticking with the nation group during a conference, for example, and using a national sign language during lunch breaks and the evening social events can also function as a way to recharge from the exhaustion of meeting new people and using IS. Conferences are also places where people from the same nation, but who do not see each other often, can reconnect. At the 2019 WFD congress, there were regular pub and restaurant gatherings of a group of deaf people from India that mostly comprised those living in India and those who had moved out of India in their own lifetime.

Sometimes, certain people from a nation stick together because there are hearing people in the group, such as hearing parents who have come to a sports event to support their children. These hearing people may be signers and know the national sign language, but they may not be confident in IS. Another example is the hearing colleagues of deaf people. At the SIGN8 conference in Brazil, I met two deaf academics from European countries, each with a hearing colleague under their wing. Another attendee, the previously mentioned Danny from Belgium (who had also been at the WFD congress), observed them and remarked to me: "If my hearing colleague from Finland was also here, I'd spend more time with him, which would mean I'd spend less time with deaf international people." In international deaf gatherings, hearing people can (often inadvertently) prevent deaf people from their nation from socializing more internationally, and this can increase the use of national sign languages in the wider environment of the event.

Sometimes, a national group attends an international event with interpreters; typically, these groups stick together more than groups from other nations who come without interpreters. For example, at the 2019 WFD congress, a group of deaf Norwegians and their seven (hearing) interpreters moved through the event and ate together. Hilde, another deaf Norwegian woman, told me she felt uncomfortable being expected to socialize with them as well: "In Norway, I can meet Norwegian deaf people; at international events, I want to meet international people." She commented that she preferred to experience the international event through IS rather than through the lens of Norwegian Sign Language (NTS), via interpreters, and by socializing predominantly with Norwegian people.

National sign languages are thus used socially and by national sign language interpreters in the context of interpreting. With regard to the organization of the 2019 WFD congress, there were tensions surrounding its language policy (see *This Is IS*: Episode 5). The congress had two official sign languages, IS and LSF, the latter because France was the host country. Presentations at this congress could only be delivered in LSF, IS, English (the official working language of the WFD), or French. There were about 40 national sign language interpreters, including from Nigeria, Malawi, Oman, Jordan, Sweden, Norway, Denmark, the Netherlands, and Germany. The WFD bolsters support for education and services in national sign languages *within* nations; however, at the 2019 congress in Paris, IS was positioned as the global signed lingua franca to be used on an international stage, even though many deaf people struggled to use and/or understand it. What is more, presenting in one's own national sign language was discouraged at the Paris congress, even if presenters brought national sign language interpreter(s) with them. This is not uniformly the case for WFD congresses: notably, the policy of the XIX congress in 2023, held in Jeju, South Korea, was that presenters could use national sign languages other than Korean Sign Language on stage if they were to arrange for interpreters themselves. However, the larger context here is that IS is *increasingly* being used on the WFD stage by deaf professionals, and the increased quality, provision, and professionalization of IS interpreting services runs in parallel with a noticeable *decrease* of national sign language interpreting services at the WFD congresses (Nilsson, 2020). To illustrate this, compare my observations of the XV WFD congress in Madrid in 2007 with the XVIII congress in Paris in 2019. In Madrid, I noted that deaf people from the same country sat together in an area marked by the flag of that country, with the size of the area calculated based on the size of the country's delegation, from which they could view their national sign language interpreter(s). The situation at the 2019 congress was very different, with no designated areas, and deaf people from different nations being spread throughout the audience, and with most national sign language interpreters being positioned *within* the audience (Figure 5.12) or in the aisles.

Figure 5.12. National sign language interpreter (standing) positioned within the audience.

In an ethnographic study of the 102nd Universal Congress of Esperanto, Fians (2021b) noted that:

> as Esperantists from across the world are regarded as carriers of differences perceived through the scope of nationality, Esperanto becomes the mediator that forges stereotyped perceptions of alterity to, then, overcome them and partially turn congress participants from national Others into fellow Esperantists. (p. 90)

Although Esperanto and IS have very different histories and characteristics, there are similarities in the ways in which their uses in international conferences are described. Fians (2021b) shows that, in the context of the Universal Congress of Esperanto, "a specific grammar of national diversity is highlighted and addressed, examining how this community emerges in constant tension via an internationalism that simultaneously embraces nationalities and rejects nationalisms" (p. 90). Similarly, whereas national sign languages were represented and used at the 2019 WFD congress, both within the audience and in the larger event setting, their use was *discouraged* on the WFD stage itself, even while the number of distinct nations present was emphasized and celebrated on the very same stage.

National Stereotypes and Essentialisms

In the previous sections, I have explored the ways in which people are perceived as representing nations at international events and how they may also socialize within nation groups, using their national sign languages to do so. In this section, I briefly expand on this issue of "representation" in international contexts by exploring how visitors to events may be seen as a *sample of a national variety* (Malkki, 1994). International communities can be imagined as a "family of nations," where "globality is understood to be constituted by interrelations among discrete 'nations'" (Malkki, 1994, p. 41). In this context, "nationness" is reinforced, legitimated, and naturalized—and produced as a scale—in the pursuit of the "international"; there cannot be "internationalism" without *nations*. I came across myriad examples of this in my study, finding that people were not only seen as "tokens" of (national) "types" but also that these "types" were *stereotypes*.

As an example, international deaf events often organize a "national" evening, in which national attire or colors are worn, flags are displayed, national snacks and treats are put out for sampling, and national dances are shown. Sometimes, the organization or delegation representing the host country does this as part of the opening ceremony and/or reception, and at youth camps a row of tables may be put next to each other, with each national delegation showing what they have brought, such as Belgian *speculaas* or Indian *laddoos*. In this way, nations can be "sampled" next to each other, through a form of essentialized cultural consumption. Nations are expected to each have a distinctive culture, spirit, and even contribution to humanity. In other words, culture is likened to nation and to identity, and boundaries between cultures are seen as boundaries between nations (Brubaker, 2010). National diversity is foregrounded (and the national scale (re)produced), as "the proxy of difference to be valued and celebrated by particular forms of cosmopolitan openness" (Fians, 2021b, p. 90). However, it is demonstrably true that dietary cultures and folklore are often *not* easily ascribed to a single nation, and that nations often have a very wide variability within them (consider the diversity contained within the vast nation of India, for example). Furthermore, this does not even consider further cultural diversity resulting from migration. In these events, deaf people are trading in widely circulating nationalist essentialisms by bringing things from their preferred region or culture to deaf events where people can savor them as "samples" of their nation.

In this type of activity, people not only engage in essentialized representations of "national" cultures, but also these nations are rendered commensurable. Malkki (1994) compares this to the Disneyland ride "It's a Small World," in which visitors are drawn along past displays of more than a hundred nations—and where inequalities are erased and differences between nations are rendered superficial and uniform. In the same vein, Friedner and Kusters (2015b) discuss a well-known video clip created by Joel Barish in 2010, called "We Are Deaf,"[5] which shows deaf people in national attire standing in front of iconic architecture or nature, signing "I am deaf" and "no barriers" with subtitles in the national languages of each country. Here, differences between national units are not only rendered equidistant, but also dehistoricized, depoliticized, and homogenized. In Malkki's (1994) words:

> [R]elationships between countries like Belgium and Burundi, say, or the United States and the Dominican Republic are represented not as continuing neocolonial relations conceived in radical political inequality, but as relations between separate, equal entities of the same type—such that the differences between these nationalities appear homologous with quaint taxonomic differences between their national flags and costumes. (pp. 57–58)

Indeed, the expectation is one of "discrete peoples whose relations are ideally ones of diplomacy, complementarity, and cooperation, and who from time to time come together to celebrate their common humanity" (Malkki, 1994, p. 61). The themes of several previous and upcoming WFD congresses underscore these aims: "Securing Human Rights in Times of Crisis" (2023), "Sign Language Rights for All" (2019), "Strengthening Human Diversity (2015), "Human Rights through Sign Languages" (2007), and "Towards Human Rights" (1995).

Although deaf individuals and organizations do draw on "generalized" national essentialisms that circulate widely (i.e., in "hearing" spaces), there is also a repertoire of stereotypes based on observations of how groups from various countries behave at international deaf events. For example, I was often told that British and American deaf people are—in general terms—less experienced at (and less interested in) interacting internationally; reasons given included an island mentality (in the case of the United Kingdom), an imperialist history (both), and a proud history of using ASL/BSL. Some other nations were known for sticking together at sports events more than others, leading to stereotypes. At the 2019 Winter Deaflympics, the Indian delegation was mentioned to me several times as being "stuck together" and communicating minimally with people from other countries, instead using Indian Sign Language (ISL) with each other; I observed this as well. Similarly, at the curling competition where I tried (in vain) to interview Chinese deaf people, I was told by non-Chinese athletes that "communicating with people from China is difficult because they only focus on their country." Furthermore, as mentioned previously, some country groups at the Deaflympics (such as the Canadian ice hockey players) had more deaf nonsigners, or nonfluent signers, which also contributed to the people in the group sticking

---

5. https://www.youtube.com/watch?v=qymfHrKdLLw

together. Sticking with the nation group "too much" was often commented on in a disapproving way. Staying in a group associated with a national sign language, and using that national sign language in the group, thus leads to generalized national stereotypes.

Given the existence of various types of comparisons, essentialisms, and stereotypes, it is not surprising that people may feel the pressure of representing their nation, especially if they are the only person from their country present in a given space. This was the case for several students in the Frontrunners course. I did fieldwork and made recordings with a camera team for *This Is IS:* Episode 1 with the 2017–2018 Frontrunners group twice: in their first week and during a week toward the end of the 9-month program. During the second visit, I showed a montage of recordings from their first week, including their interactions with each other, as well as interview quotes and excerpts of class discussions. After showing this recording in the group, a discussion ensued, and the theme of "representing the nation" emerged. Several of the students stated that they felt they had to represent their nation in a certain way; Hyemi, for example, had felt reluctant to ask for clarification of unfamiliar IS signs at the beginning of the program because she thought it would reflect badly on all Korean people (see Chapter 8). She became more confident to ask questions when she saw other Frontrunners do the same.

Another student, David, remarked he did not want his personality to be seen as representative of deaf people across the whole of the United States: "Right, if I sign what I am doing, people would respond 'Ah . . . American.' I wonder why, because I am not representing all of America, it is only my personality." Hyemi explained that she felt the same regarding her country: "All the responsibility is on my shoulders. I have to show myself as nice and charismatic." Fie, from Norway, added that people were also expected to be experts about their countries. A guest lecturer had directed her: "Norwegian, explain about the political system there!" Such questions made her feel uncomfortable: "I don't have a degree in it. I felt pressure then, I am not an expert, I am only Fie." Lara, from Flanders (North Belgium), had felt that she needed to defend her region when mocked by a Frontrunner from Wallonia (South Belgium). Esther, from Spain, said, "When people look at me, they see the south [of Europe]. It has happened many times, if I come in late they say: 'Ah Southerners.' Why is that? That is only me. *I* came back late." In summary, these Frontrunners felt that they were expected to represent their nation through their behavior and assumed expertise on their country's political systems and histories. Although this expectation usually went along national lines, there was also focus on regions within a country (Wallonia) and on multinational regions (Southern Europe).

Such stereotypes are mobilized when people are *outside* their nation (Kelly & Lusis, 2006). Through these stereotypical expectations, nationality becomes the main salient feature of the person, at the expense of their other characteristics; only through getting to know each other are these stereotypes overcome (Fians, 2021b). At the same time, the desire to be known by name (as shown in the earlier example of Esther's response to being called "Spain"), and as an individual, was in constant tension with *wanting* to represent their country. The Frontrunners wanted to see their country represented well and for it to be clear which country they came from—especially if their origins were often confused or contested. At Frontrunners, although Esther did sometimes describe herself as being from Spain, she also repeatedly pointed out that she is from Catalonia, a contested region. Hyemi emphasized that she is from Korea, and not from Japan: "Everyone always thinks of Japan first, not Korea. I want to change that." People also resisted being labeled "the wrong country" because they were sensitive to stereotypes relating to that country or did not want to be associated with it due to a relationship of conflict, competition, or mockery between neighboring countries or regions (e.g., between Flanders and Wallonia, Flanders and the Netherlands, and Wallonia and France).

I noted similar examples of people challenging national stereotypes at DOOR International Africa, in Kenya, a setting which I discuss further in subsequent sections. During an after-dinner conversation with Charles (from Burundi), Rahul (India), and Eric (Kenya) about cultural differences and differences between sign languages, Charles (who had studied in New Delhi) said that many people there had thought he was Nigerian and that, as a result, vendors often tried to overcharge him. The stereotype about Nigerians in New Delhi is that they are cocaine traders who "throw money around." In the same conversation, I explained that many white Europeans see it as an insult if they are mistaken for Americans in international settings—for example, when deaf people in African countries equate "white" with "American." Eric's reaction to this was one of surprise, but Rahul said he had observed this, adding that hating Americans is typical of Europeans, and it is also related to hating ASL (see Chapter 8, and also *This Is IS:* Episode 2, 00:43:01).[6] Rahul had even encountered a European who had raised their middle finger at him when Rahul mistook them for American. From his perspective (as neither a European nor an American), Rahul found this "European hate" for Americans odd and exaggerated.

Conversations about national and regional stereotypes, and challenging such stereotypes, frequently occur in international deaf encounters on the transnational scale. By talking about differences between nations, people engage in scaling; people are "tokens" of national "types," entailing a shift from the individual to the national scale (Gal, 2016). By engaging in practices of scaling, deaf interlocutors may challenge the idea that individuals are simply tokens of (national or regional) types, but they also maintain and redefine the "types" by engaging in comparisons and by replacing national stereotypes with other generalizations.

Bringing Resources Back to the Nation

As "specimens of nations," mobile people are often (implicitly or explicitly) expected to "bring back" things to their nation, be it information, new knowledge, leadership skills, or materials. Doing this, they are engaging in processes of scaling, transposing models from other nations or international organizations to their own national and local contexts. Many international deaf events bring together deaf leaders and may educate these leaders—both through the exchange and refinement of discourse around deaf participation in wider society and by building and strengthening the transnational bonds between deaf leaders, who may be each other's peers, mentors, and/or role models. By visiting transnational events, or deaf places of work and study that are "more advanced" or "more strong," deaf people may have a "wake up" experience, as De Clerck (2007) called it. De Clerck studied the experiences of a cohort of (mostly white male) Flemish deaf leaders and professionals, such as people working in the Flemish deaf association, and found that such international visits had been turning points for them. They learned about so-called "barrier-free" environments in all-signing settings, such as Gallaudet University and the Center for Deaf Studies at the University of Bristol, and also about "strong" deaf associations, such as those in the Nordic countries. In other words, they were inspired by making evidence-based comparisons with countries or institutions that they perceived to be "more advanced." They were also offered what

---

6. https://vimeo.com/728777656#t=43m1s

De Clerck called "a rhetoric of equal opportunities, rights, participation, oppression, deaf culture, emancipation, integration" (p. 9)—new conceptual tools with which to advocate for change. The people who had "woken up" then applied what they had learned to their own country—installing an all-deaf board in the deaf association, for example. The visits abroad thus offered a combination of comparisons with examples of "best practice" and the empowering rhetoric to support it, which could then be applied in order to achieve what was (now) aspired to.

Other examples of activities and events designed to "empower" are the regular WFDYS camps, which offer a mix of educational and fun activities. For example, the educational activities at the 2011 WFDYS camp program in Durban (South Africa) consisted of presentations about the WFD and WFDYS; presentations by inspiring deaf leaders who had done community work and advocacy; workshops about themes that resonate internationally, such as the closure of deaf schools; national delegations sharing "country reports" about their youth organizations; and a culture-themed night, where participants brought their national flags and "introduced" their country through food, clothes, dances, and so forth (Merricks, 2015). In such programs, there is a strong emphasis on inspiring and promoting leadership in local and national communities, coupled with intercultural learning through drawing on generalizations and stereotypes, doing team-building activities, and the processes of international communication.

Although not always the explicit goal, "comparing" nations is an undercurrent in many such activities. Comparing as an activity is prevalent in international deaf spaces (see Murray, 2007, for historical examples, and also Chapter 1), whether in formal settings, such as conference presentations and work meetings, or in international conversations (Breivik, 2005; De Meulder, 2015; Kusters et al., 2015). Information gathered through comparison is then often generalized (upscaled) to a "national" level (or memorized as belonging to a "nation"), even when it may relate only to a particular institution, city, or region. As explored in Chapter 8, comparing the signs of different *national* sign languages is also a central activity in deaf transnational encounters, even if national sign languages may themselves show considerable internal variation. Using the nation as a comparative framework can lead to disregarding inequalities and differences *within* nations, such as regional signing variants, urban–rural divides, and complexity of national histories. Another consequence is that, through the repeated comparison of ideas, practices, policies and signs, certain perspectives on or approaches regarding "the right way to be deaf" become ingrained in international deaf discourse (Haualand et al., 2015; see Chapter 1). The perspectives of the people who initiate or dominate the comparing and scaling activities in transnational encounters get foregrounded, and their priorities gain traction. For example, Friedner and Kusters (2014) discuss a brief "exchange" program in which deaf people from the United States went to India to "empower" deaf Indians. During the program, deaf Americans replicated widespread beliefs about the United States being "more advanced" regarding deaf rights. Without having much knowledge about India, they painted India as a "deaf hell" in comparison to the United States—for example, by highlighting that sign language interpreting services are not well established in India. The interventions of people from the United States, who saw themselves as trying to "wake up" (De Clerck, 2007) the deaf Indians, were justified by predetermined ideas of what constitutes "good ways" of living deaf lives, based on international comparisons made in the contexts described previously, and against which deaf lives in other locations were compared and measured. Such comparisons often happen on national levels, and they may disregard or be unaware of contexts in which deaf people thrive or urgent problems that are not discussed openly (such as sexual education).

Returning to the youth camps and Frontrunners programs, the expectation is that participants would bring the knowledge acquired back to apply in their home countries afterward, perhaps in the form of presentations to home audiences, a written article in a deaf magazine, or through activism, entrepreneurship, and advocacy. In countries without national deaf youth associations, WFDYS camp participants are encouraged to establish them (Merricks, 2015); similarly, it was former Frontrunners who established a national youth deaf association in India. During a class discussion recorded during my second visit to Frontrunners, Majdi (from Jordan) stated that he was inspired to set up a youth organization for the Arab area: "I will focus on Jordan first and then think about the Arab countries. I want a strong Arabic network, like the one in Europe" (*This Is IS*: Episode 1, 1:07:34).[7] In so doing, he underscores his commitment to his region and nation, aiming to facilitate the production of a regional scale ("Arab countries") by strengthening networks and building a robust organization.

However inspiring participants such as Majdi may have found such programs, it must be acknowledged that the flow of "knowledge" about "how to develop" is most often contained within the Global North, or unilinear from the Global North to the Global South—in the latter cases, offered in the form of "crash courses," as in the U.S.–Indian "exchange" program mentioned previously. This has implications for the participants. In the film, Majdi is shown in a brainstorming session with Frontrunners from the Czech Republic, Italy, France, and Belgium; we see him looking back and forth between the others, and sinking down in his seat when he does not understand (*This Is IS*: Episode 1, 1:04:27).[8]

Such experiences of exclusion set Majdi and the three other students from the Global South apart from the European and American Frontrunners. When I interviewed him in the first week of the Frontrunners program, Majdi explained that he fell behind in group conversations because of the huge cultural distance between them. He felt the Europeans and the American were able to understand each other more quickly using IS; they had had more opportunities to network internationally before joining the Frontrunners program, and the themes of discussion and frames of reference were Europe dominated. Even when Majdi understood the signs people were using, he often did not understand the specifics of what they were referring to. He seemed hopeful that it would improve over time. During my second fieldwork visit toward the end of the course, Majdi was clearly more active in similar group interactions. When he was shown the images of the brainstorm session and his interview from the first week, and was asked to reflect on how his experience had changed, he said:

> I still don't understand everything, just half of what is signed. I was wondering why I didn't understand everything. All I learned in Jordan was about rights. Deafhood, Deaf Gain, sign language, linguistics, etc., I did not learn that there. Here at Frontrunners, I learned many new things, but I lack the basis for these issues. Frontrunners doesn't give me a foundation to build up these different topics, they rather select themes, assuming a basis is in place. That's why I only half understood the whole thing. I did not learn such topics in Jordan.

---

7. https://vimeo.com/686852215#t=1h7m34s
8. https://vimeo.com/686852215#t=1h4m27s

In the Frontrunners program, Modules 1 and 3 take place on campus in Denmark, whereas Module 2 consists of an internship. During Module 2, most Frontrunners visited deaf professionals and organizations in countries other than their own. Majdi went back to Jordan for his internship, during which time he experienced contrasts between what he knew, as opposed to what others in Jordan knew:

> I did build up skills here that I can bring to Jordan. During Module 1, I felt that I didn't catch anything or learn much, but during Module 2, I returned to Jordan [for my internship]. There I realized that I actually had learned a lot in Module 1. I was really happy. I've built up my knowledge. I was able to explain a lot to the people there. [...] I gave lectures. I met people there and explained to them. I also met important, senior people there, and was able to keep up with them. Before, it was not possible, but now I can talk to them and discuss or explain. Through this, I have realized I can do it. (*This Is IS*: Episode 1, 01:07:10)[9]

Majdi thus reported feeling split: He felt that he still could not keep up with the Europeans, but at the same time, through his participation in Frontrunners, he had gained new knowledge, which he said helped him in his country. By comparing himself with other Jordanians, rather than with his Frontrunners peers, he saw what he could offer. What is learned, and what is brought back to the nation, is very much dependent on how much the person can relate to the dominant frames of reference in international settings and whether they feel they can apply this knowledge in their country.

A second example of an international activity that aims for participants to bring resources back to the nation is the missionary work done by DOOR International. At the DOOR campus in Nairobi, Kenya, teams from different countries work on Chronological Bible Storytelling (a type of Bible translation) into their national sign languages. KSL, as the host national sign language, serves as a bridge to other national sign languages. When I was at DOOR, teams from Mozambique, South Sudan, Kenya, and Russia were working there. John, from South Sudan, explained how he had been recruited within his country:

> Paul [the director of DOOR International Africa] came to our town, and I met with him at deaf church. He chose some people, including myself, to come here to Kenya. I learned KSL for the first time. Deaf people were signing the Bible. In South Sudan we do not have the Bible translated into sign language. I am learning to do it for the first time. Once I am finished and bring it back to them, deaf people will be happy to see it in sign language. That is what I think.

John explained that he had grown up using village signs (see Chapter 8) because he never went to school; later, he acquired the signs used in a town in South Sudan, and then KSL in Kenya (*This Is IS*: Episode 2, 00:10:37).[10] His task while in Kenya was not just to translate the KSL Bible into South Sudanese Sign Language, but to then *bring it back* to South Sudan. Translators worked in offices with others from their nation (see Figure 5.13, the South Sudanese translation team in

---

9. https://vimeo.com/686852215#t=1h7m10s
10. https://vimeo.com/728777656#t=10m37s

Figure 5.13. South Sudanese translators.

their office), in contrast to the Frontrunners group who were treated as one international group. The national teams were not only allowed to, but also *supposed to*, carry on communicating in their national sign language in order "not to forget it"; they needed to use it for their translations. Note the contrast with the IS settings of the Frontrunners course and the WFD congress, where people were supposed to represent their nation, but not necessarily their national sign language.

In this context, it becomes clear that national sign languages are strategic essentialisms, most clearly evidenced by the work that the South Sudanese team is doing. George, from Kenya, was a consultant for the South Sudanese team and explained that, having worked in six other African countries, he found the South Sudanese team the hardest to work with "because they have no original sign language" (see Chapter 8, and *This Is IS*: Episode 2, 00:15:53).[11] He explained that they were documenting South Sudanese Sign Language, which consisted of local signs as well as numerous foreign influences, *through* the translation work. This shows that the expectation is for a nation to have its own sign language, or to work toward having a national sign language.

Through the work at DOOR, translators were engaging in *producing* the national scale in the form of national sign language materials. The translators used national sign language translations as templates for other national sign language translations, rendering the different translations commensurable, even for countries where there "is no original sign language." This was with the aim to create materials *for the nation*, in the national sign language but by following an internationalized template; they were working from a similar source text, and they had the shared aim of disseminating the target texts far and beyond. Although the work done at DOOR was very much along national lines, this is not dissimilar from the Frontrunners example, where terms such as "linguicism" (see Chapter 8), or the value of the establishment of youth associations, can be learned and then be "brought back" to the country.

---

11. https://vimeo.com/728777656#t=15m53s

Nations as Hosts for International Events

Deaf international physical events happen in geographical places, which are, of course, within nations. The hosts of deaf international events are disproportionately nations in the Global North. There are often a lot of barriers to organizing events in the Global South, including political instability, insufficient networks, lack of access to local or government funding, and, in the case of sports events, the correct facilities for a very wide range of sports. Where events are held does matter, however. International events are often seen as occurrences that will make an impression on local or national organizations and even governments (see Gulliver, 2015, and Murray, 2007, for historical examples). They enhance the visibility and status of the local and international deaf community, and they are often attended by sponsors, press, and officials. Host governments can work with deaf organizations to raise the host location's international profile, as well as to support, develop, and diversify local businesses and services (Harrison, 2014). In addition, international events are typically more accessible to locals—not only the events themselves, but also the side events open to non-attendees, which can be attended by local deaf people. For example, some of the Deaf Academics conferences have involved events in local deaf clubs. Side events also include informal gatherings in hospitality venues such as pubs, cafés, and food joints, and there is often a general "deafening" of the space around the event, attracting further attendees and tourists (see Chapter 7). An event branded as national can also be experienced as transnational if it is attended by many foreigners. For example, many of the earliest deaf congresses were not branded "international," yet the "All-German Deaf-Mute Congresses" were attended by people from outside Germany and the Austro-Hungarian empire, and deaf people from other countries were invited to attend the 1897 London congress (Murray, 2007).

A congress branded as, or promoted as, an international congress can also feel "too local" or "too national." This can be because of its chosen themes or because of its mostly local or national attendance. Murray (2007) gives the examples of the 1911 Rome congress, which mostly focused on controversies between Italian deaf people and Italian teachers of the deaf, and the 1910 *World Congress of the Deaf*, which was held in Colorado and attended by only two non-U.S. participants. Branding a national event as "international" can be a strategy employed to attract more international participants, but "a name does not an international congress make" (Murray, 2007, p. 62). To this day, there are international conferences and international deaf expos with only a few delegates from other countries than the host country. One example of this was the SIGN8 conference in 2018, which was held in Brazil and at which the majority of the 300 attendees were Brazilians. Although the small number of international visitors did appear to interact with Brazilians during breaks, presentations, poster sessions, meals, and so on, because the majority of people present were Brazilians using Libras with each other, some of the international participants (including me) gravitated toward each other. Several of the international participants knew each other already, whereas they did not know many Brazilians. I observed a similar pattern among international attendees during the SIGN6 conference in India, where the majority of attendees were Indians.

The SIGN conference series attracts an audience from a larger number of nations when organized in Europe, but then it attracts mostly national audiences when organized outside of Europe, leading to a more "host nation-flavored" conference experience for the international visitors. This can result in a deeper learning experience about the host nation because of the number of presentations given by people from that country, the presence of the host country's national sign language, and the immersive experience of meeting many locals and potentially picking up bits of the hosts' sign language (see *This Is IS*: Episode 3). Yet, it can also mean that there is less contact between host country participants and internationals, and that internationals feel "drowned out." A conference can also be experienced as (or expected to be) "too local" for people from other countries who attend primarily *for* the international aspect of the event, and only secondarily to encounter a local deaf community different from the ones they know (i.e., to "see how they live"; see Chapter 6). I illustrate this with another example.

In Europe, international parties are popular among the youth, including New Year celebrations, Oktoberfest, and the evening parties at Clin d'Oeil. Parties are "low-threshold" social events and are sometimes organized in combination with workshops. I observed Frontrunners planning a "Frontrunners party" in the Czech Republic, in cooperation with the Czech deaf youth association. They discussed concerns about the low number of registrations and thought that it was probably because people expected that the party would be attended by only a small number of international participants, and would consist of mostly Czech deaf people using Czech Sign Language with each other. One of the Frontrunners, Esther, from Spain, made a comparison with an event in France that was "sold" as an international event, but almost everyone there was from France and used LSF in conversations with each other. France is a big country, she explained, and it is understandable that people who do not see each other regularly would use an "international" event in their country to catch up with French people from other regions. If information about an event is presented in a bilingual way (e.g., in Czech Sign Language and IS), Esther reasoned, it can give the impression that it is, in the first place, a national event, even if it is presented as an international one. She emphasizes that an international scale can be produced by properly *branding* an event as international—for example, by disseminating information *only* in IS. An example of this can be seen in the Deaf Academics conferences, which make exclusive use of IS and do not necessarily attract a high number of attendees from the host country.

There can, therefore, be a precarious balance to maintain. Where more people from local deaf communities attend, the transnational scale becomes more accessible to them. People who may not be able to travel abroad to meet deaf internationals can meet them in their own country (see Chapter 10). Locals may benefit from reduced participation rates, and even if they do not participate in the conference itself, locals may dip into the side events. Local audiences can experience impact for many years through the networks built up during an international event. The SIGN6 conference held in India, for example, has led to several international marriages between deaf Indians and non-Indians who met each other at the conference, and the event was even referred to several times during my fieldwork at DOOR in Kenya, because both Rahul (from India) and Charles (from Burundi) had attended the conference. For many Indians, including Rahul, SIGN6 provided them with major exposure both to IS and to foreign deaf people, and it was an important part of the collective memory of deaf sign language professionals in India, where I lived at the time the conference was organized.

However, hosting international events, such as the 2027 WFD congress, can involve significant controversy, exemplified by the discussions about the United Arab Emirates' bid to host. In light of the nation's anti-LGBTQIA+ laws, concerns have been raised about LGBTQIA+ rights and safety, especially regarding conference discussions on related topics. This presents a conflict between the WFD's international mission to champion deaf rights, including deaf LGBTQIA+ rights, and the prospective host nation's laws. These concerns were chiefly raised by individuals and organizations from Western countries where LGBTQIA+ rights are generally acknowledged.

This opposition, vital for advocating LGBTQIA+ rights, has unfortunately collided with the goal of enhancing participation in the WFD congresses by deaf communities from different (underrepresented) regions. The selection of the host nation can drastically boost national and regional event inclusion, as the predominantly Asian attendance at the 2023 congress in South Korea clearly showed. The ensuing debate has regrettably ignited expressions of homophobia and Islamophobia, both at the 2023 congress and via social media. Organizations like the WFD are confronted with the delicate task of accommodating various group needs without creating marginalization, while also addressing intersectional issues and redressing historical imbalances in global representation.

National Sign Languages in Host Countries

A theme that is often raised in relation to host countries is the presence of the national sign language at international events. Its presence can be limited, as at the Deaf Academics conferences and at Frontrunners, where IS is used and no interpretation into the host country's national sign language is provided. In contrast, it was made very clear at DOOR that KSL was the language to be used because it was the language of the host country. Learned through immersion and socialization, basic KSL was seen as the campus lingua franca, with the KSL translation of the Bible often used as a model for other translations. Most international employees stayed on campus, interacting socially during meals and in the evenings; KSL was used alongside other sign languages, which were often mixed with each other. People working as consultants for the Bible translations took responsibility for using or learning both KSL *and* the sign language of the translators (see Chapter 8). It became clear to me that the expectation that people who work together will learn each other's *national* sign language is strongly present at DOOR, and this further confirms their focus on the nation(al sign language) as the basis of socialization, translation, and evangelism. In short, at DOOR, the *international* scale serves to create resources for *national* use, in order to spread *global* messages that respect the uniqueness of each nation's sign language.

Another example where the role of the host's sign language was discussed was at the 2019 WFD congress in Paris. As mentioned previously, presentations in (nonhost) national sign languages were not allowed, even if the presenters brought their own interpreters to voice into English or French. French people could present in their national sign language, however. Emi, from France, decided to present her doctoral research in LSF. Episode 5 of *This Is IS* (00:40:50)[12] shows how Emi afterward was approached by a few friends, who challenged her about her language choice. In an interview afterward, she explained her reasoning:

> I decided on LSF because I can express myself better and deliver all that I want to say. I can sign smoother in LSF, and my topic is very political and academic. I can express all my points that way. In IS, I can deliver less information because IS is not an official language. It has poor vocabulary—I mean limited. I think I made the wrong choice. LSF was good for the French LSF users as it gave them full access, but it was not so great for those using IS. Those people received the information through IS interpretation. In order to get to IS, it had to go through a chain of interpretation in three languages. I was signing in LSF, then it went into spoken French, then spoken English, and lastly IS.

---

12. https://vimeo.com/783318465#t=40m50s

> I was told that the IS interpretation was delayed and not exactly equivalent to what I was saying. [...] It was off track from the intended meaning. [...] This has been a powerful experience. [...] I thought that it was important to represent France and to show I come from here rather than another country. When an international event happens, all deaf people are equal, so IS should be signed regardless of where an individual [is from] so that all feel welcome. Also, other speakers didn't have an opportunity to present in their national sign language. It is not fair that I could sign in my language. I was more privileged being in my own country of France. I have decided from now on to always use IS!

Emi chose the national sign language over IS because she wanted to benefit from her fluency and to *represent* her country (which was also the host country). She realized that by doing so, she had an advantage over many other presenters who were presenting in a second language, and that this also meant that she could only really *reach* people from her own nation. Additionally, the way the interpretation process was organized disprivileged the host country's sign language, despite LSF being one of the two official sign languages of the conference. She lost her international audience.

The converse can also occur: it can feel jarring, or even "wrong," to use IS in one's own country. At SIGN8 in Brazil, some Brazilians struggled with using IS. Libras and IS were listed as conference languages in parallel, which led to the interesting situation in which people could choose a conference language but no interpretation was organized *between* the languages. Separate preconference workshops were organized in Libras and IS, lasting a few hours each. Flaviane, who was part of the organizing committee, explained that initially they had received a lot of questions about the language policy:

> I've worked three days at this congress, organizing. I've had so many requests from people saying "Please, please, I need an interpreter." And I've had to say, "sorry, we're not providing one. I understand your right to have 100% access. Just be patient and keep pushing through over one or two days, and that way you will take it in." In this way I try to encourage them, and the deaf people reluctantly accept. And then, a few days later, they came back again and say, "Thank you so much, I'm learning so much IS," and I'm really pleased. It's better to give them guidance in this way, and steer them into understanding over a few days, and they'll get better. (*This Is IS*: Episode 3, 00:50:17)[13]

Many presenters adapted their signing by using Libras in their IS or moving their Libras toward IS, combining the two languages of the conference. *This Is IS*: Episode 3 shows how international guest presenters learned Libras signs, being aware that the audience was mostly Brazilian, and incorporated some of these signs in their presentations, such as MOTHER, FATHER, and THANK YOU. This did not occur without resistance. Flaviane told me that some internationals complained about not understanding presentations that were heavily Libras dominant. Additionally, some of the Brazilians I talked with felt torn about using IS in their own country. One of these was Leticia, who gave a workshop in IS:

> It's hard, because I am Brazilian myself and there are other Brazilian deaf people. I do understand that for the global deaf community, IS is necessary. I do try and use IS, I feel I'm making a good effort. I can see that some deaf Brazilians don't really understand. After my workshop finished, they came

---

13. https://vimeo.com/744266936#t=50m17s

up to me and said "I don't understand. You're using IS. You are Brazilian yourself and I am Brazilian. Why do you do this?" And I found that really hard to answer. I was lost for words. But I also knew that in the workshop, there were also Germans and I'm mindful of that. That's why I use IS, but yes, it's hard. It's hard to use IS in a direct conversation with a fellow Brazilian. Libras is much smoother. (*This Is IS*: Episode 3, 00:27:53)[14]

Yet, as was clear from Flaviane's quote, in the end the conference was a positive learning experience for many participants. This conference was a powerful example of how the national scale (i.e., "the nation") can be assertively produced within an international event, both in terms of the size of the host country delegation and the use of the national sign language, and how this can lead to tensions for both internationals and nationals.

Conclusion

There has been a turning away from "the nation" in much of the scholarship of transnationalism, "re-scaling" attention to address the subnational (local, urban, regional) and supranational (continental, global) scales. However, "the nation" is still a central frame of reference (Mansfield, 2005). Studies of transnationalism or internationalism need to include the national, albeit not as a "container" or a fixed unitary entity. Mansfield (2005) acknowledges that the national needs to be "decentered," but "in such a way that helps us understand its ongoing importance" (p. 460). This chapter has uncovered many ways in which the national scale is produced in deaf international professional gatherings, counterbalancing the ways in which "the nation" has been decentered in other parts of this book.

In this chapter, I have shown how nations, national organizations, and/or national identities can be made prominent in international settings. Nations serve as identifiers and are subject to essentializations and stereotypes, with national identities tokenized, projected, or contested according to context. National organizations function as mediators of access to the transnational or international, are "targets" for resources, serve as hosts for international gatherings, and function as the basis of "nationalized" comparisons; they, and nation-as-identifier, also serve as the basis of socialization (which can further feed national stereotypes). Mobility to international deaf professional events can be channeled by national organizations, and/or nations are seen as "containers" limiting the size of "delegations." When people arrive at the international gathering, nation is often a primary identifier—a phenomenon that is very visible in the Deaflympics (in terms of flags and uniforms) but is also relevant in other settings. People in international settings may experience tensions about representing a nation (and thus reproducing "the nation"), because they may identify with several nations or not strongly identify with "nation" in contrast to the other bases on which they construct belonging (see Chapter 9). They may also feel under pressure to represent their nation, rather than being present as an individual.

Although the range of nations represented at international deaf events is often overtly celebrated by the organizers and attendees, the position of national sign languages at these events can be more ambivalent. In some contexts, people may wish to use their national sign language at international events (such as through national sign language interpreters), but they may be

---

14. https://vimeo.com/744266936#t=27m53s

discouraged or prevented from doing so, with IS elevated by a "no barriers" rhetoric. Yet, the use of IS favors those who have been previously exposed to it; language practices may vary among attendees, with spaces of *national* socialization carved out within the *international* event. Attendees may also combine the use of their own national sign language with what they have learned of the host country sign language, with other sign languages or with IS. Indeed, the development of resources in national sign languages may even be the explicit target of international gatherings, as in the example of DOOR; in this context, those present must balance maintaining fluency in their national sign language with international languaging practices.

This account of deaf professional mobility into multinational settings shows how the national, and the nation, is always implicated in other scaled activities, that "it is in multiscaled interactions that the national gains its significance and gives significance to other scales" (Mansfield, 2005, p. 460). In addition to being cosmopolitan (explored in other chapters in this book), deaf professionals are seen as, or present themselves as, products of their nations, producers of their nations, the faces of their nations, and the producers and receivers of national sign languages.

6

Deaf Tourism in Bali

Erin Moriarty

Tourism is a truly global, far-reaching industry (Thurlow & Jaworski, 2011); according to the anthropologist Edward Bruner, it is "one of the greatest population movements of all time" (2005, p. 10). Tourism involves rituals in various forms, including the ritual of preparation and the ritual of entry and exit—which can be symbolic and/or physical, as in the experience of crossing national or regional borders. Travel in the form of tourism involves relationships with people and places, as well as certain practices, such as "the tourist gaze" (Urry & Larsen, 2011)—the desire for, and imaginary of, certain places and people. According to Urry and Larsen (2011):

> Tourism is a leisure activity which presupposes its opposite, namely regulated and organised work; tourism relationships arise from a movement of people to, and their stay in, various destinations [...] which are outside the normal places of residence and work; [and] [...] places are chosen to be gazed upon because there is an anticipation, especially through day-dreaming and fantasy of intense pleasures [...] constructed and sustained through a variety of non-tourist practices, such as film, television, literature, magazines, records and videos, which construct and reinforce the gaze; an array of tourist professionals develop who attempt to reproduce ever-new objects for the tourist gaze. (p. 4)

As the authors note, tourism is a leisure activity that involves and operates on multiple scales. As such, there are several interrelated forms of mobility in tourism, including physical movement through space and time and social mobility through consumption and cultural capital. Tourism includes the mobility of people, as well as ideas, semiotic resources, bits and pieces of languages, and so on. Tourism is a significant form of mobility with an oversized role in the circulation of people and ideas (Sheller & Urry, 2006a; Urry, 2000).

During my fieldwork observations, I noted that many deaf tourists tended to refer to themselves as "travelers" and almost never as "tourists." The term *tourist* tends to be seen as implying a superficial understanding of, and relationship to, the people and places being visited. Conversely, being a *traveler* has a special significance for many people, both deaf and hearing, because there is a deeply ingrained belief that travel leads to greater empathy and a global consciousness—in other words, a cosmopolitan outlook (Lew, 2018; Moriarty & Kusters, 2021). Travel has long been believed to be a form of cosmopolitan engagement with "the other" that leads to the expansion of knowledge of other people, places, and ways of life because travel involves learning about other groups of people and places through experiencing them (Falk et al., 2012; Lew, 2018). This worldview has a considerable history. The Grand Tour in the mid-1600s to late-1800s was explicitly devised as a way for young Europeans from the upper classes to acquire gravitas and worldliness by traveling through Europe, visiting artists, learning languages, and acquiring cultural artifacts

(Towner, 1985). The ideal of travel as a way of becoming worldly and informed holds true for deaf tourists, especially because travel is linked with cultural capital and the ideals of deaf cosmopolitanism (Moriarty & Kusters, 2021).

As we observed in Chapter 1, deaf people have always traveled; however, it is the "elite" mobilities of white men of certain nationalities with greater access to capital that have historically been better documented and studied than those of nonwhite people, women, queer people, and so forth (Moriarty & Kusters, 2021; Murray, 2007; see also Chapter 10). As leisure travel has become increasingly easy for those with sufficient material resources—including, for example, a powerful passport that allows tourists of certain nationalities to cross borders easily, often without an advance visa (Henley & Partners, 2022)—a wider range of deaf mobilities can now be observed, including the visible proliferation of deaf travel influencers on social media, of whom some are people of color. It should be noted that, as with any other identity group, it is difficult to categorize deaf tourists except by using "deaf": Deaf tourists are not easily categorized as backpackers, spiritual tourists, dark tourists, cruisers, and so forth. Deaf people engage in all kinds of travel—they travel solo, in groups, in chartered tour groups, with friends, and with strangers. Deaf tourists may stay in upscale hotels, do homestays with deaf "locals" (see Chapter 7), and use social networking accommodation services such as Airbnb, Couchsurfing.com, and so forth. However, the majority of deaf people in the world do not necessarily participate in tourism, whether due to a lack of interest or to limited access to material and/or social capital (see Chapter 10).

In this book, we focus on deaf tourisms that involve encounters between deaf people of different nationalities, disparate socioeconomic backgrounds, and various language backgrounds. Just as deaf tourism itself has expanded, so too has recent scholarship expanded to increasingly focus on differences in the expectations of tourists and local deaf people (Cooper, 2015, 2017; Friedner & Kusters, 2014; Haualand, 2007; Kusters, 2015; Moriarty, 2020a; Moriarty & Kusters, 2021; Moriarty Harrelson, 2015, 2017). Different kinds of deaf tourism operate on different scales: Some are tied to major international deaf events (see Chapter 7), others involve solo deaf backpacking around a region, yet others entail a small group of friends going on holiday together. In many of these cases, deaf tourists will seek out "the deaf stranger" (Breivik, 2005, p. 9) so as to find a sense of belonging (see Chapter 9). These deaf strangers are sought in places such as the Bakery Cafes in Kathmandu, Nepal, which are staffed by deaf Nepalis and have become deaf tourist attractions (Hoffmann-Dilloway, 2016), as well as other "deaf" spaces on what I have referred to elsewhere as the "global deaf circuit" (Moriarty Harrelson, 2015). In this book, we refer to the global deaf circuit as *translocal*, which I use in this chapter to highlight the connections and interrelationships between different places and people at different scales (see Porst & Sakdapolrak, 2017, and Chapter 1).

I report in this chapter on my research on deaf tourism in Bali, but I first became interested in the field of deaf tourism while conducting fieldwork for my doctoral dissertation in Cambodia. There, I met many tourists, which led me to think more about language ideologies in international encounters and to consider deaf values in relation to sign languages and "appropriate" ways of socializing. I began to consider deaf tourists and expatriates as a vector for ideologies about deaf empowerment, identity, and sign languages. The sheer volume of foreign visitors circulating through Phnom Penh, the capital of Cambodia, was striking; many of these visitors, if they were deaf themselves or affiliated with deaf people, had an interest in other deaf people. They found their way to schools for deaf children in Phnom Penh and Siem Reap, as well as to relevant nongovernmental organizations (NGOs), usually through having researched online and through social media. Through my observations, I began to recognize that there was a significant number of deaf tourists following the same travel paths, and that many of these tourists did not realize that their visit was not unique. As a postgenocide country, Cambodia is often imagined to be a challenging place in which to travel, and these tourists frequently assumed that they were among very few people from the Global North to visit. As such, they underestimated their cumulative impact on "local" deaf people. I continued to observe this phenomenon elsewhere in Southeast Asia, conducting fieldwork with deaf tour guides and deaf tourists on the global deaf circuit and finding that small businesses, shops, cafés, deaf schools, and NGOs have become important destinations throughout the world for deaf tourists intentionally seeking out other deaf people and deaf spaces (Moriarty Harrelson, 2015, 2017). These sites are "stops" on the "global deaf circuit," which should be understood as a form of tourism that involves "seeing how they live," learning and communicating in new sign languages, and meeting "local" deaf people (Moriarty Harrelson, 2015). The global deaf circuit is an inherently translocal deaf space because "local" deaf people encounter tourists; this is discussed further below.

Deaf tourism has its own moral landscape characterized by deaf social values and expectations. For many deaf people, travel is conceptually linked with emancipation (or the potential for such); through mobility, deaf people become cosmopolitans via the breaking down of boundaries between nations, localities, and languages. There is also a somewhat controversial element involved in deaf tourism, regarding employment. Some deaf people are underemployed and/or, if they are located in the Global North, receive government benefits; many use these benefits to travel the world. Most likely, this is because, in the short term, it takes a similar degree of material resources to travel through the Global South as it does to live at home in the Global North, and there is increased cachet in being known as a deaf world traveler and in earning money through social media platforms and sponsorships. Ironically, being on benefits or receiving government assistance leads to *increased* mobility for some deaf tourists. This is not without controversy: There are also many deaf tourists who work full time and/or do not receive benefits, who then become angry about perceived "freeloaders" who travel for months on end using their government benefits.

In my research in Cambodia, I focused particularly on the deaf Cambodians who worked as informal guides, and the transition from a *moral economy* of informal guiding to a more commodified relationship between deaf "locals" and tourists. As tourism became more of an economic activity, deaf "locals" recognized that tourism offered an opportunity for "professional" employment, leading to conflicting expectations between deaf tourists and "locals." Another element of morality involved in deaf tourism is the ethics of deaf hospitality, which I observed in Cambodia, Laos, and Indonesia; this theme also emerged during interviews. In Indonesia (and in many other places), "local" deaf people will gladly guide foreigners through their city or area without expectation of compensation; however, this is changing because an increasing number of deaf people have started for-profit businesses catering to tourists (see Moriarty Harrelson, 2015). The ethics of deaf hospitality involves inviting solo deaf backpackers or small groups of deaf backpackers into the home, allowing them to sleep there for free; however, this is not necessarily reciprocal.

In a different example of "deaf" moral values in tourism, Cooper (2015) describes a conflict that occurred during her fieldwork in Vietnam, when a deaf-led tour company, owned and staffed by people from the United States, scheduled a tour to Vietnam but did not include local deaf people in the planning or hire them as guides. She also describes a situation where deaf Vietnamese people were disappointed by the service they received when they visited Cambodia with a deaf tour company. They had believed that they would have a deaf guide and became angry when they realized their tour guide was hearing despite his ability to sign.

Tourism scholars have noted that tourists seek out new, yet familiar, experiences that are driven by tourist imaginaries, which are "socially transmitted representational assemblages that interact with people's personal imaginings and that are used as meaning-making and world-shaping devices" (Salazar, 2012, p. 864). Without stories, images, and desires, there would be no tourism (Salazar, 2010). Salazar and Graburn (2014) note that tourist imaginaries are structured by binary essentialized dichotomies, such as nature–culture, here–there, inside–outside, and global–local. In the case of deaf tourists, their imaginaries are sometimes based on extremes of comparison (see Chapter 1)—the idea of there being deaf "heavens and hells" (Friedner & Kusters, 2014), with the deaf experience in the Global South typically imagined as "hellish" because of lack of education, legal protections, and services. However, deaf tourists also seek out the familiar in the deaf people and deaf spaces where they visit, as well as the different sign languages they are exposed to (Breivik, 2005). Deaf people with diverse backgrounds and nationalities travel in search of other deaf people, motivated by the commonalities they believe that deaf people throughout the world share, as well as by the desire to see some form of difference (Moriarty Harrelson, 2015). Deaf tourists may yearn to experience local deaf lives firsthand, and meeting other deaf people in the context of tourism is a way of doing this. A common refrain among many deaf tourists expresses the desire to "see how they really live"; in doing this, deaf tourists are searching for a deaf home abroad—that is, a sense of belonging (see Chapter 9).

The desire to "see how they live" compels tourists to seek out deaf people for home stays. In Cambodia, I observed and talked to two deaf tourists from France, who told me that they canceled their hotel room, losing their deposit in the process, to stay with a deaf Cambodian woman because they "wanted to see what a Cambodian home looks like and how they really live." It could be argued that the desire to "see how they really live" indicates the embodied, sensory nature of deaf tourism; deaf tourists desire to bodily experience other deaf lives so that they can truly feel that they are members of a common "deaf world." There is a personal, affective element to deaf tourism—it often includes making connections with other deaf people, as well as experiencing *otherness*. To experience otherness in the form of encounters with people and languages, deaf tourists have posted vlogs asking where to find local deaf people in the countries they will visit or asking for the "right" sign for a specific country or place (Moriarty, 2020a). These acts signal a moral stance in regard to being aware of, and showing respect for, local signs and sign languages.

As a part of the deaf experience, many deaf tourists and the people they meet (such as other tourists, deaf guides, and/or the people who live in the places they visit) engage in *comparisons* (also see Chapter 5 for comparisons in deaf professional mobility). These comparisons include comparing different signs for the same thing or concept, such as comparing signs meaning "toilet" in Indian Sign Language (ISL) and Indonesian Sign Language (BISINDO) (see 00:45:30 in *#deaftravel*),[1] comparing deaf rights and accessibility in their respective countries, and/or comparing lived experiences (e.g., getting a cochlear implant, learning sign language for the first time) (see 00:41:00 in *#deaftravel*).[2] There are also comparisons to be made between different deaf lives

---

1. https://vimeo.com/588352737#t=45m30s
2. https://vimeo.com/588352737#t=41m0s

and life circumstances—that is, "seeing how they live." Visiting deaf schools is an important element within this kind of deaf sociality, because it seems that deaf education settings and methodologies (such as oralism) are treated as a kind of litmus test for the level of deaf rights and empowerment the country is perceived to have (see Friedner & Kusters, 2014).

Deaf cosmopolitan aspirations (for tourists) are entwined with the desire to meet deaf people, contribute to local deaf businesses, and "help" deaf local people; this is done by moving through a glocal deaf circuit, in which can be found localized place-nodes such as deaf schools, deaf organizations, and so on (Moriarty Harrelson, 2015; see also Chapter 7). However, these aspirations are different for tour guides, about which I explain more below. As deaf people navigate different networks, they might also be participating in "the deaf ecosystem," a term for the circulation of capital (e.g., money, knowledge) among deaf people, with the aim of deaf self-reliance. The term "deaf ecosystem" was first coined by a deaf lawyer in the United States, Kelby Brick, as a social media campaign to promote deaf patronage of deaf-owned businesses and service providers. In the deaf ecosystem, deaf people hire deaf guides (or, on the flip side, deaf guides provide services to deaf clients); they go to deaf-owned breweries and restaurants; and they establish mutual support networks where knowledge, goods, food, and money are exchanged between deaf people. In this chapter, I expand on the term to include the circulation of other forms of deaf capital and the moral imperative to support deaf businesses. In addition to its use in popular deaf discourse, #DeafEcosystem is also a popular hashtag on social media, connecting various aspects of deaf mobility, including the circulation of deaf moral imperatives, such as the patronage of deaf businesses (hostels, restaurants, and tour guides) by tourists, and also these businesses being tourist destinations in their own right.

Social media platforms, especially Facebook, are spaces where deaf people interested in travel can share experiences, photos, and videos in groups such as "Solo Deaf Travelers" and "Deaf Travel Group." Individuals' social media identities, used to share their travels, often flag their identification as deaf people. Some of these content creators include Marlene Valle, a deaf Mexican American travel content creator in her late 20s, who is known on social media as Deafinitely Wanderlust; the Deaf Wanderer (a deaf white man from the United States, who is no longer creating content); and pages such as "Seek the World," managed by Calvin Young, a white man in his 30s from the United States whose sponsorship by Sorenson (a U.S.-based video relay interpreting provider) enables him to travel and make films of fellow deaf people and deaf-related things and businesses in different parts of the world. Another American deaf tourist who travels with sponsorships is Joel Barish, a white man in his late 40s or early 50s, who is one of the most well-known deaf influencers on social media. His website states that he has

> visited 92+ nations around the world in an effort to live as much of the Deaf experience as possible. Joel has discovered Deaf individuals in every corner and has shared thousands of unique stories with others with sign language videos and social media. (Barish, 2021)

One example of his work is the film of deaf Rohingya refugees living in Kutupanlong Refugee Camp, Bangladesh (see Barish, 2020).[3] Deaf travelers from Europe have also established a website,

---

3. https://www.joelbarish.com/videos/nb-asia/nb-bangladesh/deaf-refugees-at-kutupanlong-refugee-camp/

Blank Canvas Voyage. The combination of corporate sponsorships and social media promotion can thus be used as a way of financing travel for some deaf tourists and, through this, showing their audiences "how they live."

Many deaf tourists who are not sponsored influencers also engage in making short videos of their travels to post on social media, filming sign languages, deaf businesses and craftspeople, and deaf people in different circumstances. Social media plays an important role for deaf tourists in sharing these experiences and also in seeking deaf contacts and places to enrich their travels. Hashtags such as #DeafWorld and #DeafTravel are used by deaf tourists on social media to promote their photos and travel blogs, to find other deaf tourists, to ask for recommendations, to find out the "correct" signs for specific cities or countries (Moriarty, 2020a; see Chapter 8), and to spotlight deaf businesses and deaf spaces.

In this chapter, I focus on the translocal nature of deaf tourism within the global deaf circuit. The concept of translocal readily illustrates the dynamic interrelationship between the global and the local, and it fits with the translocal framework used throughout this book. I then present the findings of my research on deaf tourism in Bali—in particular, two deaf tour guides working there. The "deaf village" of Bengkala receives particular attention as a popular deaf tourist destination tying in with deaf utopian imaginaries. Chapters 7–10 of this book include data on the deaf tourists I encountered in Bali, as well as their ideologies and practices.

The Global Deaf Circuit

Traveling on the global deaf circuit involves many interrelated but potentially contradictory elements. There is the desire to meet other deaf people or to help them by volunteering, as well as a sense of nostalgia and a quest for authenticity that leads to the commodification of deaf people and sign languages. Deaf tourists often begin their search for other deaf people at established places, such as deaf schools, deaf organizations, "deaf cafés," and similar places where deaf people gather (see Chapter 7). Deaf schools throughout the world are popular destinations for deaf tourists; many deaf tourists to France make the "pilgrimage" to the Institut National de Jeunes Sourds de Paris, the first public school for deaf children, which was established in 1760.

The purposeful quest for spaces where deaf people live and work—whether deaf clubs (Cooper, 2015), cafés staffed by deaf people (Moriarty Harrelson, 2017b), coffee shops operated by deaf associations (Hoffmann-Dilloway, 2016), "deaf villages" (Kusters, 2015), and NGOs working with deaf people (Moriarty Harrelson, 2015)—can be understood in terms of a global deaf circuit that deaf tourists traverse. However, the global deaf circuit is very much a translocal phenomenon. The term *translocal* refers to the interconnectedness of the global and local, highlighting the fact that local deaf spaces and identities involve (and have always involved) global contacts in some form; indeed, *translocal* is useful across the board for understanding the process and impact of globalization, because globalization also happens at the *local* level and its impacts are embedded in localized spaces and experiences. The translocal framework explicitly highlights the global–local dynamic of globalization: It is fundamentally shaped and transformed by the *connections* between people, things, and spaces, both across and within different scales. "Local" deaf spaces are never quite local because of the density of interconnectivity between deaf people in various locations throughout the world (see Chapter 7), especially since the advent of social media and more affordable technology. However, the glocal deaf circuit is not a recent phenomenon because there have been many deaf tourists throughout history who have sought out other deaf people and deaf spaces.

Earlier deaf travelers on the global deaf circuit documented their experiences in travelogs. Breivik (2005) notes that many of these travelogs refer to "the ease of communication" with deaf "native" signers abroad and to the experience of feeling at home with other deaf strangers, as well as the purposeful seeking out of other deaf people (e.g., Nieminen, 1990; Parsons & Chitwood, 1988). These deaf travelers include Henri Gaillard, a deaf French activist who traveled to the United States in the early 1900s, and Frances Parsons, a prolific deaf traveler from the United States who traveled in Africa, Latin America, and Asia in the 1980s–1990s. Gaillard first traveled from France to the United States for an event to honor the founders of the American School for the Deaf (ASD), and he wrote about deaf spaces and organizations such as the National Fraternal Society of the Deaf, Saint Ann's Church for the Deaf, the New York Institution (the world's first military college for the deaf), the Goodyear Tire and Rubber Company (a large employer of the deaf), and what was then Gallaudet College, now University (Gaillard, 1917/2002). Frances Parsons spent her childhood in California and Tahiti, and then attended Gallaudet College in the 1940s and 1960s (Parsons, 2005). Because of her privileged access to influential decision-makers, Parsons was able to influence ideas about education and language in the countries she visited and, as such, had an outsized impact on the trajectories of deaf education across the Global South—an example of how ideas and values from the United States circulate on a global level and travel in the form of language ideologies and beliefs about deaf education (see Chapter 7 for parallels with Andrew Foster).

Across the world, there are now many businesses that cater to deaf tourists on the global deaf circuit, and they comprise a part of the deaf ecosystem. These businesses often started out as an informal economy of expatriates, many from the United States, hosting other deaf people in their homes or by "showing them around" in exchange for a meal and/or similar small forms of compensation (Moriarty Harrelson, 2015). The question of compensation has sometimes led to conflict, when tourists have misunderstood this and believed that they were being shown around because of the DEAF-SAME affinity, as in the case of a group of older, white, deaf French tourists who had invited a few deaf Cambodians to join them for a meal at a restaurant in Phnom Penh but did not pay the deaf Cambodians for their time or the meal. The meal was at a restaurant that catered to tourists and expatriates, and it was beyond the means of the deaf Cambodians. After this meal, a deaf Cambodian woman cried because she was so angry; she felt that she had been taken advantage of, and she could not afford the meal. Some of these conflicting expectations have also resulted in friction between deaf tourists and guides, because some deaf tourists may have personal relationships with the guides or be connected to them somehow through national or regional deaf networks (see Chapter 7), and tourists have come to expect that guiding will be provided for free based on that friendship or on personal connections.

Deaf people from the United States have also established tourism businesses in Cambodia, Italy, and Japan. One expatriate from the United States established Cambodia Deaf Tours after a number of people contacted her, wanting to visit Cambodia at a time when deaf tourism was only just emerging. The steady stream of deaf visitors led her to recognize a business opportunity, and she started training a hearing Cambodian former tuk-tuk driver who had learned ASL and Cambodian Sign Language (CSL), as well as deaf Cambodian guides (see Moriarty Harrelson, 2017b). Cambodia Deaf Tours started as a small-scale, informal guiding service for friends of friends; as the number of visitors to Cambodia increased, it became an established business with a website and a list of offerings. The business eventually merged with another major player in the deaf tourism industry, Hands On Tours, an international tourism business based in Italy but owned and operated by deaf people from the United States. The idea for Hands On Tours was seeded in 1999 when a deaf graduate of Gallaudet University, Terry Giansanti, traveled to Italy to work for the Italian Deaflympics committee in Rome. In 2002, Giansanti founded Hands On Italia with the support of Roberto Wirth (now deceased), the deaf owner of the five-star Hotel Hassler, located at the top of the Spanish Steps. The company became Hands On Tours (henceforth HOT) in 2005.

According to its website, HOT was founded in response to negative comments made by deaf tourists about the chaos of Rome and how badly organized the 2001 Deaflympics had been. Since then, the demand for deaf-centric tourism has grown, and HOT has steadily expanded its offerings beyond Italy to include tours of diverse parts of the world. It now offer tours in more than 60 countries worldwide, in the form of small group tours with deaf guides and deaf-centric itineraries. It focuses on providing "exceptional travel experiences" with sign language guides, and what it has termed "uniquely deaf experiences," such as visits to historic deaf sites in, for example, Paris. More recently, due to the standstill of travel during the coronavirus pandemic of 2020–2022, HOT has started to offer sign language classes in French Sign Language (LSF), Mexican Sign Language (LSM), and Italian Sign Language (LIS). These classes take place online and seem to be a marketing strategy to generate excitement about HOT's tours.

As noted previously with the example of Frances Parsons, deaf travelers often have a "development agenda" (Baptista, 2012). In this sense, *development* refers to the practice of international development and also personal development. For about a decade in the 2000s, there was a proliferation of North Atlantic–based organizations (e.g., Discovering Deaf Worlds, Global Reach Out, Global Deaf Connection) with the mission of facilitating "empowerment" exchanges, which are intended to empower deaf people in developing countries through informal social interactions, as well as through the formal programming of team-building activities, leadership enrichment, and workshops (Friedner & Kusters, 2014; Kusters et al., 2015; Moriarty Harrelson, 2015). Many of these "voluntourist" experiences are focused on "uplifting" other deaf people who are perceived as having less access to resources such as formal educational opportunities, and on circulating discourses on "deaf empowerment."

Friedner argues that "morality, or acting as an appropriate deaf person, is a key component of deaf sociality" (2015, p. 159). Deaf sociality includes engaging in what Friedner (2015) calls "sameness work," which is when deaf people negotiate class, caste, geographic, educational, religious, and gender differences. However, anthropologists studying encounters among deaf people in tourism in the Global South have noted that sameness work is a fraught endeavor, and it is not necessarily seamless (Friedner, 2015; Friedner & Kusters, 2014; Kusters, 2015; Moriarty Harrelson, 2015). Deaf people who are less mobile and, as such, are perceived as having a lack of access to robust educational and professional employment opportunities, have been (Murray, 2007) and still are referred to as deaf people "with no language" (Moriarty Harrelson, 2017b) and are perceived as the deaf Other, living in "deaf hells" (Friedner & Kusters, 2014). For this reason, many deaf tourists feel a moral obligation to "do something" for the deaf Other; however, the above-mentioned scholars have shown that the tourists have often taken away more from the encounter than the "local" people they met.

A different kind of tourism involves humanitarian work or volunteer tourism: that is, "the *conscious*, seamlessly integrated combination of voluntary service to a destination and the best, traditional elements of travel—arts, culture, geography, history *and recreation*—in that destination" (Clemmons from Voluntourism.org, quoted, in Wearing & McGehee, 2013, p. 121). Some people travel as a part of a humanitarian mission as in the case of Off the Grid, an organization based in the United States that provides light sources and water to deaf people living in areas where disasters have occurred (e.g., Puerto Rico, Haiti, Indonesia, Ukraine). In Indonesia, some of the volunteers who worked with Off the Grid then traveled through the archipelago on their own, visiting other islands after their mission was completed. Other examples of mobilities that overlap with tourism include academic travel and exchange programs with a "service learning" component, such as those formerly offered by Frontrunners, Gallaudet University, and the National Technical Institute for the Deaf. Study abroad programs such as these were advertised as opportunities for participants to become "global citizens" and as an experience that would enhance the students' marketability as they earn a certificate, or credits toward their degree, by immersing themselves in a new culture, learning a new language, expanding their cultural awareness, and increasing their confidence. Gallaudet University offered the First Year Study Tour for the first time in 2009 following a decline in enrollment; the idea was that offering a free study tour to Costa Rica for 100 students and faculty in their second semester would help to recruit and retain students.

During these "exchanges," students were expected to interact with "local" deaf people; these tours are translocal because attending deaf events and spaces is considered an important part of the experience. Gallaudet's First Year Study Tour had the aim of introducing students to international travel and the concept of global citizenship, claiming that students who experience other languages and cultures become "citizens of the world"—or, in other words, deaf cosmopolitans (Moriarty & Kusters, 2021). To fulfill the service learning component, students collected used teletypewriters (TTYs), BlackBerry pagers, and laptops for distribution to the Costa Rican deaf community. The faculty member involved in organizing this explained to me that they would travel to Costa Rica with TTYs in their suitcases, to distribute to deaf people; however, it is not clear how "local" deaf people benefited from this, nor how they were "exchanges" in the true sense, given that they did not have the same level of mobility as the students involved and that it was not necessarily reciprocal.

Kusters et al. (2015) noted that the encounters outlined previously are not sustainable and that, as the people interviewed in Ghana said of the various tourists they had met over the years, "People just keep coming and going" (p. 258). It is important to note that all of the programs discussed in this chapter are now defunct for various reasons. Gallaudet no longer offers the First Year Study Tour program because the university's retention rates did not improve as hoped, and the Frontrunners teachers decided not to continue the "exchange" program in Ghana because of the lack of sustainability, a disconnect in expectations, and growing awareness of the unequal power dynamics involved in these "exchanges" (Kusters et al., 2015).

In this section, I have introduced the notion of the global deaf circuit as a translocal phenomenon as a way of understanding deaf tourism, especially the strong affective experiences and expectations that drive specific deaf tourist practices. In particular, this includes seeking out other deaf people to experience both sameness and difference. I expanded the literature on deaf tourism to include motivations and rationales for tourist mobilities, as well as the specific experiences that deaf tourists seek out and how deaf tourism ties into the deaf ecosystem. In the next section, I discuss tourism in Bali, as well as my data from fieldwork undertaken in Indonesia in 2018.

Tourism in Bali

Tourism in Bali, a tropical island in Indonesia known as "the island of gods," dates from the Netherlands' colonization of the island in the early 20th century (Vickers, 1989). In the 1920s, the Dutch company KPM (Koninklijke Paketvaart-Maatschappij) promoted the island and attracted

European visitors. During this initial stage of tourism development in Bali, a number of highly circulated magazines, such as *National Geographic*, published stories and images representing Bali as a magical place, the last tropical paradise, the island of temples and dances, and so forth (Vickers, 1989). The tourist imaginary of Bali that emerged in the 1920s and 1930s has become an enduring representation of the island, evolving to include more contemporary spiritual elements such as yoga and self-actualization, which were depicted in films such as the 2010 movie *Eat Pray Love* (Murphy, 2010; see also Picard, 1996; Vickers, 1989). The legacy of Bali's representation can be observed in contemporary tourists to Bali; on my flight to Bali from Doha, Qatar, in 2018, I noted in my field notes the number of white middle-class women with yoga mats, as well as young white women and couples in expensive-looking yoga or gym clothing, and many people with Russian passports. I had previously observed on Instagram that many of the posts from Bali were in Russian, typically featuring thin, white women in bikinis, posing in front of beautiful natural scenes or by hotel pools; this indicates that Bali is seen as a place to engage in conspicuous consumption on social media.

Since the construction of the Ngurah Rai International Airport in 1969, the numbers of foreign tourists visiting Bali have dramatically increased, and, as such, mass tourism has become a central part of Balinese socioeconomic life. The centrality of tourism to the economy has led to less agricultural production and the expansion of sectors providing products and services to tourists (Fagertun, 2017). Tourism development has had unintended consequences in Bali, including a transformation in social relations and "traditional" livelihoods, such as the loss of irrigated rice fields to tourism development and conflict over access to resources such as water (Fagertun, 2017; Pickel-Chevalier & Budarma, 2016). Additionally, Balinese temples are still active sites for religious ceremonies and worship, and tourists are often actually intruding on religious ceremonies when they visit. However, many Balinese say nothing about this because of the economy's reliance on tourism, and temples increasingly are divided into public areas and private areas that are off-limits for tourists.

Bali's local economy has steadily grown as the number of visitors to the island has increased. Deaf tourists visit Bali from all over the world. There is not an accurate way to track their originating countries; although the Indonesian government does track tourist demographics in general, it does not drill down into subcategories of tourists with regard to disability and so forth. The literature on tourism development has shown the ways in which it can generate revenue but also have negative impacts on social cohesion and relationships within a local community in terms of new class relations and dependence on tourism-based income (Baker & Coulter, 2007; Fagertun, 2017). Some analyses of the impact of tourism in Bali claim that it leads to the total destruction of "culture" and "traditional" ways of life, with the commodification of social practices and sacred rituals, such as dancing and making temple offerings; however, this is a somewhat simplistic way of understanding the complexities of tourism (Howe, 2006).

Deaf tourists to Bali stay in different places depending on their interests and budget. The most popular locations for tourists to stay are Ubud, known for its yoga scene, and Kuta, the party area. However, the deaf tourists who participated in this project have tended to circulate through various parts of Bali, moving from town to town, depending on the kind of activity they want to do. I made the following field notes in Ubud:

> I asked [my guide] where deaf tourists tend to stay, and he said that they tend to stay in Kuta, which would be a difficult place for me to situate myself for fieldwork [and find participants]. [...] There

was a continuous traffic jam from the moment we entered the vicinity that lasted until we passed Kuta. The area is very commercial, built up like a strip mall type area in the United States. [...] It is interesting how people paint Bali as a paradise but, in reality, Kuta is really unattractive with many cheap hotels, [and] angry white people on motorbikes, zooming in and out of traffic jams. It seems to be an incredibly stressful place, not Zen or relaxing at all.

Kuta seems to attract a certain kind of tourist, mostly white men who want to have a good time, drinking and partying, although some of the deaf tourists I met stayed there because it is cheap. Others stayed elsewhere, because Bali is a large island with diverse "scenes," depending on the person's age, physical fitness, discretionary income, values, and preferred activities. Bali also specifically attracts tourists who identify as gay, lesbian, and/or queer, because they believe that it is safer to be openly gay in Bali as opposed to many of the other islands in the Indonesian archipelago.

Languages are an important part of the touristic experience (see Heller et al., 2014; Pietikainen & Kelly-Holmes, 2011). The deaf guides I met in Bali were skilled communicators, drawing on wide repertoires; as they interacted with deaf tourists, both parties engaged in learning and using new signs, as well as the strategic use of foreign sign languages such as Australian Sign Language (Auslan), International Sign (IS), and ASL, and local sign languages such as BISINDO and Kata Kolok, plus spoken languages—specifically, Indonesian and English (Moriarty, 2020a; see Chapter 8). During fieldwork with deaf tourists, I observed many examples of flexible multimodal and multilingual languaging practices and the creation of translanguaging spaces—that is, "a space for the act of translanguaging as well as a space created through translanguaging" (Li, 2011, p. 1223). This led to the realization that languages and languaging practices are central to deaf cosmopolitanism.

Deaf Tour Guides in Bali

My fieldwork largely focused on two tour guides in Bali, each with different backgrounds, approaches, and target audiences. The first, Wahyu Cayhadi, is a deaf Indonesian man, originally from another island, operating as a private tour guide in Bali, the "Bali Deaf Guide"; he has become a tourist destination in his own right on the glocal deaf circuit, because many deaf tourists who visit Bali have him on their checklist as a "must-see." In this way, Wahyu is both a node on the glocal deaf circuit (see Chapter 7) and also part of the deaf ecosystem, in the sense that he is a deaf entrepreneur. Wahyu, by his own estimate, has given tours of Bali to more than 1,200 deaf tourists over about 10 years. Interestingly, Wahyu often calls himself a "driver" and refers to his work as "driving" as opposed to guiding. Bali itself does not have a robust public transportation system; tourists are ferried around the island by an intricate network of private drivers who have divided the island into territories based on *banjar*, or local community, boundaries. Drivers adhere to strict banjar boundaries, and respecting these traditions means that drivers can travel across the island to drop off tourists outside of their territorial line, but they are not typically allowed to pick up tourists outside of their own zone. I have had situations where hearing drivers that I worked with in Ubud have refused to pick me up in other towns because it was dangerous for them; hearing drivers who violate banjar boundaries are subject to beatings and harassment. However, Wahyu seems to be an exception to this rule because he is a deaf driver working with deaf customers; this may be an example of "deaf gain," in the sense that "whereas popular constructions of deafness are defined exclusively by the negative effects," there are also "a number of social [...] benefits" to being deaf (Bauman & Murray, 2014, p. xxiv).

Most of the time, Wahyu works with individual tourists or with a group of friends who book him for a day tour or sometimes for a few days at a time. Wahyu takes deaf tourists to deaf schools and to the deaf village, Bangkala, working with a set list of destinations that people can negotiate with him to visit; sites on the global deaf circuit can be blended with popular "hearing" tourism sites. He tends to divide tourist sites into clusters based on geography, proximity, and time, to avoid driving randomly all over the island, especially because the roads of Bali are so congested with tourists driving motorcycles with surfboards attached to the side and Balinese men driving SUVs (driving tourists in Bali seems to be an exclusively male occupation). It is typical for people to spend hours traveling short distances. Wahyu has given thought to optimizing both his business and the tourists' experience by reducing time spent in the car and seeing more sites located in the same area (e.g., the Monkey Forest and the rice terraces of Tellangang, both in Ubud, and a coffee plantation nearby). It is more effective for Wahyu to drive to different tourist attractions in the same area within a half-day or full-day block. Due to the time and distance involved, Wahyu does not offer bespoke tours that do not include the items on his laminated "menu," which lists 15 different tours covering various sites (he also uses a generic "menu" with photographs of Bali's main tourist sites). Wahyu also accepts bookings for multiday tours, such as a tour of the Ubud area with another day spent in the south.

Wahyu does not make hotel reservations for his guests or any other kind of arrangement for lodgings; instead, he focuses exclusively on day or multiday tours. He explained to me that he does not make accommodation arrangements because when he previously did so, he had a bad experience. The people that Wahyu had made the arrangements for were not satisfied with his choice of accommodation and complained that it was "not nice enough." From that point forward, Wahyu decided to not make hotel arrangements.

Before becoming the Bali Deaf Guide, Wahyu worked as a cleaner in a hotel in Kuta. During one of our first conversations in the car at the beginning of my fieldwork, Wahyu explained:

> I was working cleaning at [...] a hotel, but [...] the hotel owners warned the employees that layoffs were coming because business was so bad after the Kuta bombing [in 2002]. [...] One day a list of names was posted on the wall; 200 people lost their jobs, including me. I saw my name on the list and went to the owner, said, I am deaf, would you change your mind? Please keep me, I am deaf. But he said no. [...] I was unemployed for a year. I searched for a job at other hotels, but they would not hire me because I am deaf. I went to see my old teacher, who told me that I should volunteer at the deaf school as an IT teacher. I volunteered at the school for a while, then went back to school for a diploma in IT. After I graduated, I started looking for jobs again. I couldn't get a job because I am deaf. With my free time, I started showing foreigners around Bali.

Wahyu told me that, one day, he met a deaf Australian woman who was crying because a hearing driver had just dropped her off at the school for the deaf without any explanation or information (see *#deaftravel* 00:20:10,[4] where Wahyu repeated this story in an interview). She told Wahyu that the "hearing driver" stole from her, asserting, "Hearing people are bad!" Wahyu continued, the "deaf [Australian] told me, 'you would be a good guide,' so I thought about it and asked other hearing Indonesians for advice on how to start as a tour guide. They told me I needed a website, Instagram,

---

4. https://vimeo.com/588352737#t=20m10s

and Facebook." Wahyu used his IT skills to build his website (https://www.balideafguide.com/) but then realized the website was not working because he needed a server to host it, so he borrowed some money from a deaf friend to pay for a server. For a while, there was no profit. Wahyu had been renting a car, and he made no money because all his earnings went toward paying for the rental. Then, someone told him that he needed to add a little overhead on top of what he was charging people so as to make some money for himself. He started working for the hearing man who owned the car that he was renting. Wahyu said, "I felt wrong. It all felt wrong."

Wahyu explained that, one time, he was giving a tour to a deaf person who wanted to pay him directly. Wahyu explained that all of the money went to the man with the car business, who paid him a small salary. The deaf person was shocked and said, "No, this money is yours!" Wahyu had been working for the hearing man for many years and earning very little, while the man was profiting handsomely from deaf tourists. Wahyu went to his family and asked for a loan to buy his own car so that he could break away from his hearing boss; his father-in-law sold land to help him. At the time we had this conversation, he had owned this car for 7 months.

Throughout Wahyu's narrative, he continually identified the various protagonists as either "deaf" or "hearing." As I typed up my field notes, I had the insight that many of the hearing people in Wahyu's narratives were framed as obstacles to his independence. I wrote, "Wahyu seems really proud to be able to support his family (wife and baby) with his own money. He is successful because of this. He didn't come out and say so, but I can see he is proud of what he has accomplished as a *deaf* person."

Wahyu's old employer continued to contact Wahyu, asking him to come back and work for him and harassing him for his list of deaf clients, to the extent that Wahyu had moved away from where he used to live. Most of his clients are from Australia, and some are from Europe; he told me that he didn't have as many clients from the United States and made sweeping comparisons of the destination preferences of different nationalities: "America is too far. Australia is closer. Americans love Hawaii. Europeans love Thailand. Australians love Bali" (see Chapter 5 for more on deaf comparisons and national stereotyping). Wahyu told me that he keeps a record of his clients by photographing himself with them and then posting it on Facebook, partly to remind himself of who he has met over the years, and partly as a form of marketing (see #*deaftravel* 00:15:13).[5] When I had first landed in Bali, Wahyu met me and immediately asked to take my photo, and then again when he dropped me off at my lodging in Ubud. This is an interesting example of how it is not only the tourists who take photos, but also the guides and other local deaf people (see Chapter 10).

I asked Wahyu if there were any other deaf guides in Bali. He said that there were three Indonesian deaf guides, but that two had been giving tours without a license and were now "blacklisted." Wahyu used the signs BLACK NAME, as if their names were "black" with the police, the implication being that they can never work again as tour guides. Tour guiding is a licensed profession across Indonesia, and provinces have the legislative power to pass regional regulations; tourist guides in Bali are regulated according to the Bali Province Regional Regulation Number 5 (2016), or "Bali Regulation No. 5" (Pratiwi, 2019), which defines a tourist guide as "an Indonesian national having a duty to provide assistance, guidance and advice regarding tourism and all matters needed by tourists." Tourist guides are required to obtain a *Kartu Tanda Pengenal*

---

5. https://vimeo.com/588352737#t=15m13s

Pramuwisata, or Tour Guide Identity Card (KTPP); foreigners are not eligible to apply for a KTPP under this regulation. In addition, Bali Regulation No. 5 requires a tourist guide to wear Balinese traditional clothing, unless they are assisting tourists who are doing trekking, camping, or water sport activities. Wahyu will sometimes wear traditional clothing when guiding tourists through a temple, but most days he wears shorts and a polo with "Bali Deaf Guide" on the front (see Figure 6.1), probably for the reason that his tours are diverse and often include a range of activities, such as a coffee tasting in the morning and a hike to a waterfall in the afternoon.

Cosmopolitan encounters happen between tourists and between tourists and their guides; sometimes these guides are themselves not only guiding people through Bali but also brokering these international encounters (see the example in Chapter 8 where Wahyu acts as a language broker, using signs from Auslan, LIS [Italian Sign Language], and IS to make clarifications in an interaction between Heena and an Italian woman). Moral considerations in deaf tourism often involve giving in some form (Kusters, 2015; Moriarty Harrelson, 2015), and this "giving" extends to the exchange of signs from different languages.

I have already highlighted that deaf tourists have cosmopolitan aspirations that are entwined with the desire to meet deaf people and to contribute to the local deaf ecosystem while moving through the glocal deaf circuit. However, "local" deaf tourist guides must also be recognized as cosmopolitans in their own right, especially those like Wahyu who have an extensive repertoire of many different sign languages and access to knowledge of the way that other people live. Wahyu will often engage in the sharing of knowledge, not only about Bali but also about the wide roads in Australia, the "ways" of people from certain nationalities, and so on. One day, Wahyu shared

Figure 6.1. Wahyu wearing his polo shirt.

with me his observation that "Australians don't smile. They don't look happy. They have a good life in Australia, but don't smile and are not happy." He appeared to feel a responsibility to share his own philosophy of life, noting that privileged people are not happy because they don't appreciate what they have.

Wahyu also made distinctions about certain spaces and things being "Indonesian" as opposed to "tourist." Most tourist sites (both deaf and hearing) are attractions for in-country and foreign tourists, and the sites have different prices for the different groups; this extends into ordinary purchases too. When I first arrived in Indonesia, Wahyu drove me around as I ran several errands (e.g., purchasing a new SIM card for my iPhone, searching for a place to live), and it became clear that he was very conscious of the differences between "local" and "tourist," especially when it concerned the cost of things. He delineated certain brands of consumer products as being more appropriate for Indonesia than others: Apple phones were too expensive, whereas Samsung and Oppa (made in China) were popular; the cell service 3 had less good signal, whereas Telek was better for signing on video calls. When I was looking for somewhere to stay, Wahyu told me that Denpasar was a good area to find an affordable place with AC, but he cautioned me that "it is all Indonesian." I said I was fine with this, and he continued to drive me there. The following excerpt is from my field notes:

> We continued our drive through Denpasar. Wahyu pointed out the area we were driving through and said, "This is not a good tourist area, this is an Indonesian area. Indonesian people come here and walk around, sightseeing and shopping in the evenings." He then said, "See, no white people, only you" (with a smile).

Through the months that I followed Wahyu around on his tours, I noticed that he continually made a distinction between what was "foreign" and what was Indonesian. When it was just the two of us, without any tourists, Wahyu would take me to small Indonesian restaurants (*warung*); the first time we ate at a *warung* in Kuta, Wahyu said to me with a concerned expression, "Can you eat Indonesian food? [i.e., Do you like it?] It is cheaper."

Wahyu has a clear cosmopolitan disposition and rich cultural and linguistic capital that he draws on to better understand and entertain the people he guides. He shapes his narratives and observations to the people with whom he interacts—in other words, he *calibrates*. He also has a strong desire to "help" people—including me, by explaining which SIM cards work best in Indonesia and where I should stay or eat in accordance with my budget and fieldwork requirements.

Giovanni Mansilla is the other deaf tour guide who operates in Bali and other Indonesian islands. He is originally from France, but Gio has made a home in Indonesia, and his love for the country is also permanently etched on his body in the form of a tattoo of the Indonesian archipelago. He is based in Labuan Bajo, a fishing town located at the western end of the large island of Flores in the Nusa Tenggara region of east Indonesia. From this village, Adelia Kiranmala operates her business, Travass Life, a bespoke travel agency with two boats that they sail through the islands of Flores and Komodo. The Travass Life website describes it as specializing in trips "to authentic tropical islands in Indonesia," where travelers will be exposed to "local experiences, cultures, exotic islands, wildlife, and new inspiring people" (Travass Life, 2022). One of Travass Life's offerings is a bespoke tour called "Deaf Trip by Travass Life: The Sound of Smile." These "well-curated deaf trips by sign language" claim to provide "unforgettable journeys for our deaf friends"; the website states, "we believe everyone can travel, there's no limit. We want to hear you smile" (Travass Life,

2022). The first Sound of Smile tour, which I joined in 2018, was a special tour with Calvin Young of Seek the World (described previously) as one of the guests, tasked with taking photographs and making videos with his drone as part of Travass Life's marketing strategy.

Gio leads the Sound of Smile tours, but he also works with Adelia on her tours for hearing people. Gio explained to me that he prefers to work with deaf groups because it is more accessible in terms of communication and because he feels more at home with deaf clients; however, the connections made with deaf tourists have not always been smooth. Gio explained that he has had awkward encounters with tourists from Russia and his native France who expected him to guide them around Bali as a favor; he turned them down, saying that he was "trying to run a business" (see *#deaftravel* 01:39:00).[6] Like Wahyu (who uses multiple sign languages, as well as IS, English, and Indonesian), Gio is multilingual: He can speak Indonesian and will speak it with hearing Indonesians, and he also signs in BISINDO, ASL, and LSF. Gio has also learned English because of its role as a lingua franca in tourism. Gio said in an interview that he had not placed much value on English, being French himself, but that when he started traveling so much, he realized how important English was for tourism; he thus learned English as a part of his tourism experience. Gio's translingual skills were especially evident during the 10-day Sound of Smile tour that he led with a multinational, multilingual deaf tour group.

I participated in the Sound of Smile tour in July–August 2018, with a group consisting of mostly white people in their 20s and 30s from Europe, the United Kingdom, and the United States (see *#deaftravel* for footage and analysis of this tour). The 10-day group tour included 3 days on a boat, a flight to another island, and movement through Bali in a minibus, as well as moving between hotels every 2 days. The tour comprised 12- to 14-hour days and required quite a bit of physical fitness and ability. This tour group was thus a different demographic from the tourist clients who usually engaged Wahyu's services. Wahyu has a wide variety of clients of different ages and physical abilities, with many being older, less fit, and more car dependent; as a consequence, his network is composed primarily of older white people from Australia and elsewhere, with his linguistic influences and translanguaging practices being shaped accordingly. Wahyu's wide variety of clients can be attributed to his reputation as a "must-see" among deaf tourists of different backgrounds; conversely, the focus of Gio's tour is more niche, prioritizing sailing around the islands of Flores and Komodo (see Figure 6.2) over visiting more well-trodden destinations. Gio's demographic is, like Wahyu's, mostly white, but it is more youthful, social media focused, physically fit, and aesthetic oriented. Professional photography and video services are an important part of Gio's tour package; Travass Life offers to "capture all your travel memories that you'll cherish forever" (Travass Life, 2022), and during the Sound of Smile tour, he and two others (including Calvin) were dedicated to taking photographs and making videos for the tour group. Indeed, the Travass tour had to skip some sites because some group members were so focused on getting the right photo for their Instagram that it took hours to visit a particular site; this upset other group members.

Some tourists on the Travass trip did appear to find the pace set by Gio challenging. Many activities required a level of physical stamina, such as hiking up Mount Agung, jumping off boats, and scubadiving. One of the participants had a challenging time on the mountain during the group hike because of issues with her balance. Kate successfully made it to the top of the mountain with the group but had to be taken back down by motorcycle because she had fallen a few

---

6. https://vimeo.com/588352737#t=1h39m0s

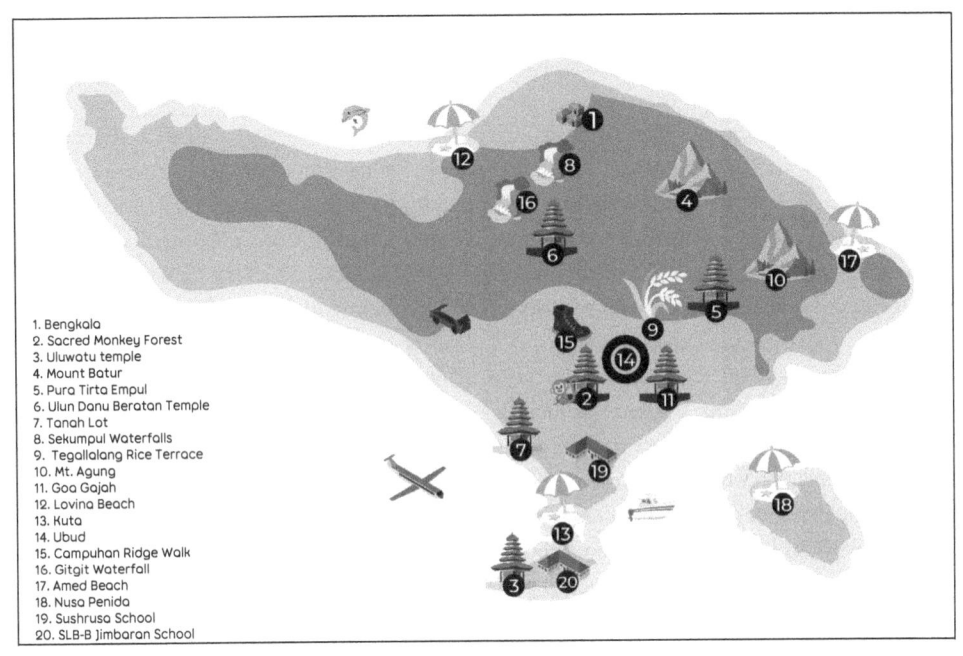

Figure 6.2. Map showing tourist sites in Bali.

1. Bengkala
2. Sacred Monkey Forest
3. Uluwatu temple
4. Mount Batur
5. Pura Tirta Empul
6. Ulun Danu Beratan Temple
7. Tanah Lot
8. Sekumpul Waterfalls
9. Tegallalang Rice Terrace
10. Mt. Agung
11. Goa Gajah
12. Lovina Beach
13. Kuta
14. Ubud
15. Campuhan Ridge Walk
16. Gitgit Waterfall
17. Amed Beach
18. Nusa Penida
19. Sushrusa School
20. SLB-B Jimbaran School

times. Later, another participant in the group commented that he felt bad for Kate because some of the other group members had walked on, leaving Kate behind with Gio and Jente, one of the MobileDeaf cameramen. Due to the physical and social demands placed on them, people with disabilities can be excluded from tour groups on multiple levels; for some neurodivergent people, being around people all the time in enclosed spaces (e.g., sharing bunkrooms, riding in a minivan) and constantly processing new impressions can be overwhelming, especially because the tour schedule may change on short notice. The ability to be flexible with food was also important in the context of Travass tours: the food served on the boats was Indonesian, and the group ate at Indonesian restaurants most of the time, in part because Gio believed in providing an "authentic" experience but also because Indonesian food was more readily available and cheaper (meals were included in the tour price). Wahyu was able to be more flexible regarding individual needs and preferences, accommodating people with mobility disabilities and food preferences, because he works with individuals, couples, and small groups of close friends.

Gio and Wahyu appear to have different approaches to tourism. Gio is openly social media influencer oriented, focused on finding "Instagram-worthy" locations; he has stated that he enjoys sharing beautiful places with deaf tourists. Gio goes off the beaten track and invests time in visiting potential locations on reconnaissance trips. His positionality overlaps with his clients in many ways: He is savvy regarding photography and editing, he values social media as a marketing tool and works with social media influencers, is of a similar age, has similar language use, and so on. Yet, interestingly, Gio emphasized that he is a "local" because he lives in Indonesia and speaks and writes Indonesian (see *#deaftravel* 00:36:08).[7] Gio's emphasis on being a local is likely to be down

---

7. https://vimeo.com/588352737#t=36m08s

to the influence of certain deaf politics and expectations regarding economic opportunities for other deaf people—for example, the emphasis on supporting the local deaf ecosystem by working with local deaf guides.

In general, there appear to be certain expectations in deaf tourism, especially related to notions of authenticity and to supporting "local" deaf people. When I first arrived in Bali, a deaf person from the United States with whom I was acquainted sent me a message on Twitter asking if I would intervene with Gio about working in Indonesia, and this was only the first in a series of people contacting me to personally intervene with Gio about his "taking work away from locals." In a different example, deaf tourists visiting Vietnam and Cambodia through a foreign tour agency were assigned guides who used ASL, leading to anger on the part of deaf Vietnamese people, who described the situation in terms of "colonialism" (Cooper, 2015). Similarly, an Australian tourist told me about an acquaintance (also a deaf Australian) who complained that he was "just" a driver for the foreign tour group touring Australia and the tour guides leading the tour were "outsiders" from the United States. A deaf man originally from Ecuador, now living in the United States, told me that he was angry with a foreign tour company for leading tours in Ecuador without his involvement, even though he is no longer living there. As a result of widespread criticism of tour groups not engaging with the local deaf ecosystem, HOT started working more with local deaf guides; this is emphasized in their marketing materials, with the repeated use of the word "local" when describing their offerings, and this aligns with Cooper's observation that a strong value is placed by many deaf people on deaf connections as being "authentic," both culturally and linguistically (p. 106).

For reasons related to the above, Gio has been challenged by some deaf tourists who have visited Indonesia for not explicitly including deaf Indonesians in his business; he has, however, established an ongoing relationship with a local deaf organization, Bali Deaf Community, with which he has organized tourist-focused events (see Chapter 7 for an example). Yet, some deaf tourists who adhere to the morality of the deaf ecosystem to the extent of only supporting *local* deaf businesses will only work with Wahyu, and some have contacted Gio and confronted him about his work in Indonesia, which Gio found hurtful and bewildering (see *#deaftravel* 01:35:45).[8] Gio explained that his business has a different focus and demographic than Wahyu, and for this reason, there is no real competition. Based on my fieldwork data, Wahyu sees a greater volume of clients than Gio, especially because he is so well known and has been in business for much longer. Wahyu also offers a form of authenticity by being Indonesian himself (therefore, a bona fide "local" deaf guide), so his popularity seems to be about his reputation, visibility, and authenticity, as well as deaf morality (e.g., the insistence on support for "locals").

In contrast to Gio's emphasis on visually beautiful scenery and "Instagram-worthy" sites, Wahyu's approach is to take on the role of "translating" Balinese culture for tourists and showing them "how they live." As a guide, Wahyu "translates" Balinese culture and traditions while making connections to what visitors already know or what is familiar to them (Salazar, 2015). Wahyu finds common ground with tourists, and he uses this as a point of departure from which to calibrate (see Chapter 8), as well as working hard to interpret for and guide people in international encounters. Indeed, some scholars do not consider tourists to be cosmopolitans because of their limited role in interpreting difference, in contrast to the tour guides who translate between

---

8. https://vimeo.com/588352737#t=01h35m45s

cultures but who may never have left their home country (Salazar, 2015). Indeed, the same can be said of many Balinese deaf people who engage in international deaf encounters even when they do not travel much (or at all) outside of Bali, simply by interacting with tourists. Although deaf tourists and deaf hosts and guides connect with each other, there are marked inequalities in financial capital and the ability to travel internationally (see Chapter 10). For example, although Wahyu is hypermobile *within* Bali, he does not have the same international mobility as a deaf person with a European or United States passport; furthermore, however cosmopolitan he and other deaf Balinese people are, tourists continue to *perceive* tour guides as "local" and themselves as cosmopolitan (Salazar, 2015, p. 62).

Wahyu has only traveled abroad once: to Australia, at the behest of the various Australian tourists he met in Bali, who worked together to raise funds for him to visit them and to sponsor his visa (see Chapter 7). Wahyu was proud of the number of sponsors he gained for this trip; he told me, "I went to the visa office and they asked me, who is your sponsor? I said, I have over 1,200! They were shocked." This trip was Wahyu's first time abroad: first time inside an airport, past security, and on an airplane. He explained, a little shyly, that he had asked someone at the airport for help because he didn't know where to go and needed guidance. This was a reversal of roles, because Wahyu is usually the one who is guiding the tourist through the unfamiliar, having waited *outside* of the airport hundreds of times. This demonstrates that cosmopolitanism is not necessarily dependent on international mobility. In the next section, I discuss a popular tourist destination on the glocal deaf circuit in Bali.

Bengkala in the Tourist Imaginary

Bengkala, known as "Desa Kolok" ("deaf village" in Balinese), is a village in north Bali with a high degree of hereditary deafness. It is increasingly popular with tourists, both hearing and deaf, domestic and foreign, because of Kata Kolok, a shared sign language that is believed to be used by more than half of the 3,031 hearing villagers to communicate with the 44 deaf villagers who live there. The residents of Bengkala are carriers of a recessive gene, and due to its concentration in the area through endogamous marriages, there have been several successive generations of deaf people, resulting in Bengkala becoming a "shared signing community" (Kisch, 2008). Other examples of shared signing communities include the Al-Sayyid Bedouin, Ban Khor in Thailand, and Adamorobe in Ghana (Kusters, 2014; Zeshan & de Vos, 2012). Tourists arrive in Bengkala in different ways: Some deaf tourists arrive with a hearing driver, but many take a day tour with Wahyu, who drives them there and introduces them to a deaf family with whom he is acquainted, sharing his knowledge about Bengkala as a way of supporting the deaf villagers.

International tourism to Bengkala has been strongly influenced by its position as a site of research, attracting (predominantly hearing and mostly nonsigning) researchers from universities in Australia, the United States, and the Netherlands, as well as domestic researchers from Indonesia. Over the past 30 years, researchers in genetics (Friedman et al., 2000; Wang et al., 1998; Winata et al., 1995), linguistics (de Vos, 2012, 2016; Marsaja, 2008; Perniss & Zeshan, 2008; Schwager & Zeshan, 2008), and sociolinguistics (Branson et al., 1999; Hinnant, 2000; Marsaja, 2008) have all worked in Bengkala at different times, continuing to the present day. During my own fieldwork period in 2018, there was a team of two hearing, nonsigning researchers, one from the University of Kansas and the other from an Indonesian university, eliciting data from the deaf villagers on the Balinese geocentric directional system.

Early sociolinguistics researchers in Bengkala chose not to name the village in their publications, referring instead to "Desa Kolok," the local designation (Branson et al., 1996, 1999; Marsaja, 2008). This seems to have been an effort to conceal the location and identity of the village. Other sign language linguists have adopted a similar approach when dealing with "deaf villages": Kisch (2008) did not refer to her research locations by name in her early publications, and Johnson (1991) referred to his as "a Yucatec Maya village," later identified as Chican by other researchers working there (e.g., Escobedo Delgado, 2012). These attempts to protect the anonymity of the people living there, and to prevent these sites from becoming the target of tourist and media interest, ultimately failed. Bengkala has had a steady stream of touristic visitors for several years now, many of whom are deaf foreigners; as of 2019, the volume of visitors has since intensified.

In an interview with one of the hearing villagers, I asked how Bengkala came to be a popular tourist destination. He explained that a researcher in the village made a video to raise money for the village primary school as a way of supporting the community. After this video was made and uploaded to the internet, increasing numbers of people started visiting Bengkala. De Vos (2012) dates the increase in international visitors in Bengkala to 2009, when two volunteers from the Netherlands began working at the village elementary school, the construction of which was funded by Vrienden van Effatha, a Dutch foundation; this connection led to an uptick of Dutch tourists. She also attributes the increase in media attention to a publication supported by the World Bank (de Vos, 2012). However, there seems to have been various "moments" when Bengkala became famous, such as during the second Cross-Linguistic Sign Language Research (CLSLR, now SIGN) conference in Nijmegen in 2007, which included two presentations by researchers on the village. One person whom I interviewed explained that he learned about Bengkala from a paper presented at an academic conference.

The continuing media interest in Bengkala was evidenced by the number of television and film crews that I observed during my stay in the village; they came from Singapore, Japan, and France. Intensified media attention has also brought corporate endorsements from Pertamina (an Indonesian state-owned oil and natural gas company based in Jakarta) and Wells Fargo (an American multinational financial services company headquartered in San Francisco, California); in 2018, the latter sponsored the making of a 3-minute film with Great Big Story, "an award-winning global media company owned by CNN Worldwide dedicated to inspiring wonder and curiosity," showcasing the "uniqueness" of Bengkala and Kata Kolok.[9] In response to the increased publicity and visitors, the Deaf Alliance, a local group of deaf and hearing community members advocating for the rights of deaf villagers and their hearing relatives, has begun a process in which they evaluate and approve requests for media coverage and research projects (de Vos, 2012). My research was endorsed in this way by the leader of the Deaf Alliance at the time.

Tourists from the United States and Europe who have visited Bengkala have described it on social media and in interviews as "isolated" and "remote"; however, this is somewhat inaccurate. Bengkala is far from the areas where most of Bali's tourism is concentrated, but it is easily accessible by car, being located just off of one of the main north-south routes running through Bali, and a 3-hour (approximately 44 miles) drive from Ngurah Rai airport. Furthermore, Bengkala is connected to neighboring villages and towns through kinship links (Branson et al., 1999), and

---

9. Great Big Story is now defunct, but the video can be seen in *#deaftravel*: 01:03:52. https://vimeo.com/588352737#t=1h3m52s

there are several villages in the region whose residents have similar signing practices as in Bengkala (Branson et al., 1999). Despite this, some researchers have used the representation of Bengkala as geographically and socially isolated to explain the emergence of a local sign language (Marsaja, 2008). This overlooks the likelihood that Bengkala is considerably more touristed and publicized than other "deaf villages" with similar characteristics in other countries *because* it is located in Bali, a popular tourist destination, and easily reachable from the south of Bali, where most tourists circulate.

The village has developed public spaces specifically to accommodate the increased tourism, such as a small open-air "cultural center," where tourist-facing activities such as dance performances take place. This was built using donations from Pertamina and support from the local government, and the blue, green, and red Pertamina corporate logo decorates the sign at the entrance to this area; inside, there is a glass display case with stacks of woven cloth for sale to tourists, as well as a visitors' logbook (see Figure 6.3). In a building behind the pavilion, four weaving looms stand, emblazoned with stickers with the Pertamina logo. The weaving hut is part of a development project to provide livelihoods for deaf women in Bengkala; however, at the time of writing, only one woman works there. The pavilion has a television set; sometimes, when they know to expect visitors, deaf men go there to watch television as they wait to perform *Janger Kolok*, or "deaf dance," for tourists. This dance, accompanied by hearing men beating on drums, is similar to a Balinese performance called *janger*, which emerged in the 1930s and involves loud gamelan (a traditional orchestra). Janger kolok incorporates elements of Balinese traditional dance with

Figure 6.3. Erin and two people from Bengkala in the "cultural center."

innovations developed by the Bengkala community, such as an imitation of the gamelan via vocalizing from one of the deaf men (de Vos, 2012; Marsaja, 2008).

The touristic experience of Bengkala involves interactions in sign language with deaf villagers at their homes. These encounters, and quickly learning a few signs in Kata Kolok, have become exchangeable objects as part of a broader trend toward the commodification of sign languages and deaf experiences. During fieldwork, it became clear that Bengkala is a popular destination for deaf tourists because, in the deaf tourist imagination, it is a "deaf utopia": a place where "everyone can sign" and where deaf people are fully accepted. "Deaf utopias" hold special significance for many deaf people because they are imagined to be sites where large numbers of deaf people congregate and where the use of sign language is prevalent and unmarked; small-scale shared signing communities are thought of as deaf utopias because the ability to interact with everyone in everyday contexts, such as on the street, in the store, and/or in the fields, can be taken for granted (Kusters, 2010). Deaf utopias are believed to be fully accessible in terms of life opportunities, experiences, and language ecology.

Deaf tourists to Bengkala are frequently fascinated by examples of unique deaf-related cultural forms and practices, such as the presence of a deaf god in the village cosmology (see Marsaja, 2008), which some interpret as an indicator of the positive social construction of deaf people. This itself then becomes a draw for deaf visitors. Other forms of exceptionalism attributed to deaf people in Bengkala include the assignment of special roles to deaf men because of their reputed strength and fearlessness; these include fitting and repairing water pipes and acting as security during village festivals. Some villagers claim that deaf people are invulnerable to the evil spirits that haunt the graveyard because they cannot hear them. Many of the hearing villagers say that deaf people are strong and are therefore better suited to manual labor and security. Deaf people are also responsible for the catching and butchering of animals for feasts and celebrations, and carrying the *wadah*, a tall pyramidal wooden structure full of ornamental decorations in which a dead person's body is placed for cremation, to the cemetery (Marsaja, 2008). The most unique role of all is grave digging, exclusively assigned to deaf men. This is not common in other villages in the area because this is usually the task of close family members of the deceased (Marsaja, 2008). These details have filtered through the media and are known to some deaf tourists, who tend to see this exceptionalism as positive and affirming of the special role deaf people have in the village. However, this interpretation may obscure or downplay the caste-based stigma often associated with these jobs across South Asia.

In becoming a tourist landscape, Bengkala has thus acquired a place-based, utopian heritage, including the assumption of full communication access for deaf people in all aspects of life, and equal access to education and employment opportunities. In other words, in the tourist imaginary, Bengkala is a place where there are many deaf people, and they have opportunities equal to hearing people. Yet, in the process of touristifying a place, tourist imaginaries can flatten particular locations and sites into one-dimensional places, erasing the experiences of the people living there, their histories, social relations, and global connections (Devine, 2017; Salazar, 2010). Deaf tourist imaginaries of Bengkala as an isolated deaf utopia erase the complexity of social relations in the village, such as inequalities between deaf and hearing people, as well as its historical and geographical networks with not only nearby villages but also with the south of Bali, the Netherlands, and Australia, where some villagers have migrated for work or marriage.

Additionally, although many deaf tourists imagine that Bengkala has a vital signing ecosystem and that everyday conversations with other (hearing) villagers are effortless because "everyone can sign," the reality is that Kata Kolok is not "everywhere" in Bengkala, and there is a varying degree of fluency among the hearing villagers. In the following excerpt (quoted at length), James, a deaf tourist from Australia, explains how he came to learn about Bengkala and his experience there:

> [On Wahyu's website] there are different locations listed you can visit, and I saw a blurb about a deaf village so I clicked on it. [...] I intended to book Wahyu himself to guide me, but that day there were a lot of people in the group who went off somewhere else, so I had to book a hearing driver for that day, and we went to the deaf village. Honestly, for me it was an anticlimax. I had anticipated something exciting with lots of sign language and had glorified the idea of a "deaf village" with everyone signing and mingling with shops and streets, and so on. What it was in reality was some small houses with a few deaf people sitting around signing a bit. That was all. I felt a bit... deflated. How to say this? It's not what I thought it would be. [...] [Would I give] a referral [...] from my visit, would I encourage others to go? Probably not. I felt that for the deaf people living there, having to continuously put up with tourist groups coming and endlessly photographing them was intrusive and interfering with their way of life. And really... well, they wouldn't like me saying this, but it felt like there just isn't that much to see there really. Just some houses and a few deaf people, which could be anywhere. We can go and create our own deaf space somewhere. I feel like it is over visited there—there are other places to see. [...] Before I saw it in reality, I envisioned an empowered, exciting, lively deaf environment. From my perspective, it was just completely subdued and was not what I had imagined. Maybe that is just my experience and others have more positive experiences. Not for me. (Also see #*deaftravel* 01:11:56)[10]

James was not the only tourist to express these sentiments. Nathalie, a young white deaf tourist from the Netherlands, was also disappointed by her experience in the village, saying that she had hoped to see a strong deaf identity there, but she did not see it (see #*deaftravel* 01:11:06,[11] and see Chapter 9). For this reason, Gio does not take clients to the deaf village because he feels it is like "going to the zoo." The deaf village is a popular offering for Wahyu, however, and his willingness to take tourists to Bengkala often results in donations being made to the deaf families there, as well as to the deaf schools. Wahyu strongly encourages the tourists he guides to make a donation, highlighting the poverty of the families they visit in Bengkala.

In this section, I expanded on Bengkala, a major destination on the glocal deaf circuit in Bali, noting the reasons why people visit and their experiences there. Bengkala is seen as a deaf utopia in the deaf tourist imaginary, and hearing tourists are equally fascinated by the shared sign language, as well as by deaf dancing. However, deaf visitors to Bengkala are sometimes disappointed because the village does not meet their expectations of a deaf utopia. Deaf Balinese people living in the south, and also some researchers, have expressed concern about the potential impact on Kata Kolok of so many deaf visitors to Bengkala. A deaf teacher at the school for the deaf in Denpasar, the capital of Bali, spoke at some length about language "contamination," the "spread" of "foreign" sign languages in the village, and sign language endangerment—as did Wahyu

---

10. https://vimeo.com/588352737#t=01h11m56s
11. https://vimeo.com/588352737#t=01h11m06s

(see Chapter 8). Socioeconomic changes in Bengkala have led to increased contact with more dominant urban or national sign languages, which often endangers village sign languages. However, this may be mitigated in Bengkala because of hearing Kata Kolok users who are less exposed to other sign languages (see Kusters' findings about hearing signers in Adamorobe, a "deaf village" in Ghana, 2015).

Conclusion

There are a few general themes that I identified after data collection, many of which I have already discussed in this chapter and elsewhere in this book. The primary theme is a fascination with *difference* between deaf people from various national backgrounds, and—both complementing and contrasting with this—how a belief in deaf *similitude* is a way of bonding across cultural, linguistic, and national differences (see Chapters 7 and 9). Deaf tourism also involves the deaf tourist gaze, which tends to focus on "seeing how they live," as well as the imaginary of certain places and people as *deaf*. The desire to "see how they live" is a part of the practice of *comparisons*, often between nations and cultures (see Chapter 5), and especially where languages are concerned (see Chapter 8), in order to establish deaf similitude across differences.

The global deaf circuit and deaf ecosystem are often entwined. In this chapter, I focused on the two deaf tour guides working in Bali and on the deaf village as a way of understanding different approaches to deaf tourism, the translocal nature of the global deaf circuit, as well as the languaging practices and morality of the deaf ecosystem. The data in this chapter illuminate the importance of experiencing sameness and difference, as well as "authenticity." There are different ways that authenticity is experienced in deaf tourism in Indonesia, which is illustrated by the differences in the ways that Wahyu and Gio position themselves. Gio, who is a white deaf man from France, positions himself as a "local" by speaking and writing in Indonesian and by emphasizing that he lives in Indonesia, introducing tourists to the Bali Deaf Community, and making use of hearing Indonesian drivers. Gio explained that he sees himself as sharing with people the beautiful places that he has discovered during his travels through Indonesia, and thus sharing his love for Indonesia, which he also shows with his tattoo of the archipelago.

On the other hand, Wahyu, who is an Indonesian-born person, is perceived by some tourists to be more "authentic" because of how well known he is and his "localness." He is "local" in a different way from Gio. Wahyu advertises himself as Bali Deaf Guide, has lived in Bali with his family for more than 2 decades, and is perceived by tourists as being Balinese; however, he was actually born on another island in Indonesia. Wahyu is also a multilingual cosmopolitan who uses IS and several other languages, but sometimes he is not recognized as such because his customers are focused on his *localness* in their search for authenticity.

Both Gio and Wahyu's tours are shaped by their individual positionalities and by the clients they service. These differences (and similarities) shape how they move geographically, as well as their narratives about the places they take deaf tourists to—such as Gio's desire to avoid the "deaf village" and deaf schools because of the perceived voyeurism, in contrast to Wahyu's recognition of the desire of many deaf tourists to experience an imagined deaf utopia and the necessity of giving his customers what they want.

In this project, we are interrogating the notion of cosmopolitanism as an overarching framework to understand deaf tourism. Although some of the material covered in this chapter seems to provide examples of the *ideal* of cosmopolitanism (such as the desire to connect across national and language boundaries, to support local deaf ecosystems, and to establish authentic relationships with "the other"—all desirable forms of cultural capital), the reality of deaf tourism is more complicated and infused with other dynamics and motivations, including a personal desire to experience travel and the potentially voyeuristic impulse to "see how they live" and "consume" commodified cultural tokens. As Salazar (2015) noted, transnational travel is often discursively linked to a greater understanding of and appreciation for difference (i.e., a cosmopolitan outlook); however, deaf tourists often seek out deaf similitude by traversing the glocal deaf circuit, where they sometimes face *limits* to their cosmopolitan outlook. This can be seen in the case of James and Nathalie, among others, who were disappointed by their experience in Bengkala, which was not the so-called deaf utopia they sought. Deaf cosmopolitanism is imbued with a dynamic interplay of ideals, expectations, and moralities, all of which shape and complicate the mobility and the gaze of deaf tourists on the glocal deaf circuit. The question of who is eligible to "see how [other deaf people] live," who is permitted to expect hospitality and guiding, and who gets to make judgments about whether other deaf people "count" as "local," or whether their languaging, actions, and/or the very way they live meet the criteria of the viewer's preconceived imaginary, demonstrates that sameness work is fraught with power differentials and ambivalences. Our findings with regard to deaf cosmopolitan ideals, expectations, and moralities qualify the idealized notion of deaf cosmopolitanism. In other words, the idealized view of travel as an expansion of knowledge of other people, places, and ways of life through experiencing (indeed, consuming) them has its limitations, because tourists' experiences are filtered through their guides, and also because the imaginary often does not—maybe cannot—match reality.

Part Three

Patterns in International Deaf Mobilities

7

Translocal Networks and Nodes

Erin Moriarty, Annelies Kusters, Steven Emery, Amandine le Maire, and Sanchayeeta Iyer

International deaf mobilities shape and are shaped by networks. Deaf networks are complex interconnected webs that expand and contract as deaf people move through physical and virtual spaces. Indeed, we cannot talk about deaf mobilities by only using static and exclusive concepts like "the deaf community," *community* being a term that is associated with stability, coherence, long-lasting ties, and common histories (Wittel, 2001). Deaf people rarely live as spatially coherent, closed social groups: Deaf communities are multiple, overlapping, and shifting (see Chapter 9). The notion of interlocking networks offers us a more fluid and process-oriented framework for understanding the ways in which diverse deaf people and spaces are dynamically interconnected (Heap, 2003).

Networks are typically thought of as a set of nodes and the ties between them (see Figure 7.1). "Nodes" can be either persons or places; in this chapter, we focus on both. "Ties" between nodes are formal or informal, horizontal or hierarchical relationships, existing between people, between places, and between people and places. Ties between people in networks can be strong or weak; people may be known to others only by name and/or face, or they may have more intimate relationships (Glick Schiller & Fouron, 1999; Lubbers et al., 2018). Weak ties often function as bridges between clusters of nodes (areas of networks with a higher density of nodes), enabling people to reach different network clusters and expand their networks (Granovetter, 1983). People are thus not stationary nodes; furthermore, a person can be a point of convergence for various networks as they make introductions or connect other people. Deaf networks alter in composition as people engage in networking and as network clusters link up with other network clusters.

Places can also be nodes: locations "where the mobility flows of passengers, goods, materials, information and so on intersect" (Adey, 2006, pp. 75–76). Deaf clubs, deaf-owned businesses, and deaf schools are examples of places that are nodes in deaf networks—that is, places where connections are made. Nodes can also be smaller and more private. For example, some deaf people's houses are "hubs of sociality" (see Heap, 2006), such as the house of Halimo, a deaf Somalian woman in Kakuma Refugee Camp. Her home was frequented by deaf camp inhabitants from various countries. Halimo provided her guests with food and was a contact point for information and support (see Chapter 3).

Some place-nodes are mostly frequented by deaf people who live in the vicinity; international visitors may then enter these local networks and spaces, such as Amandine participating in the deaf space of Halimo's house. Other nodes can exist as "bubbles," disconnected from local spaces and people, such as a deaf tour group in Bali that included no local participants and was guided

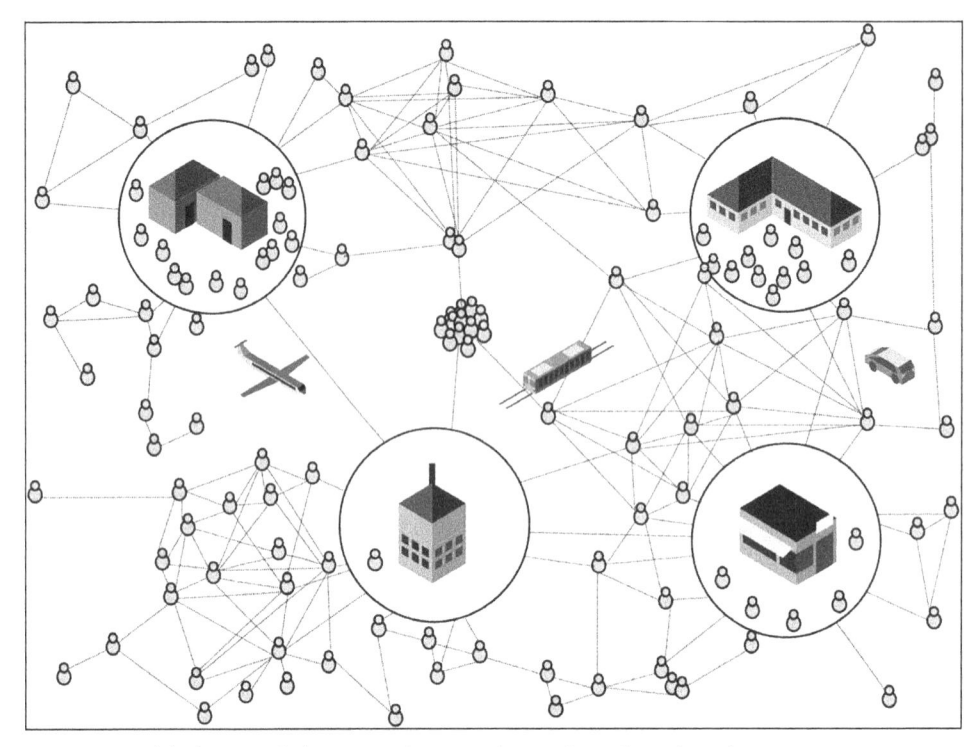

Figure 7.1. Model of a network showing ties between place-nodes and people-nodes.

by a tour guide from another area. Yet others are a confluence, such as the World Federation of the Deaf (WFD) congress, which is organized in cooperation with a local organizing committee (see Chapter 5 for more on host countries).

Deaf networks *facilitate* international deaf mobilities. As we show in this chapter, deaf networks are used for gathering information, finding accommodation, asking for support, gaining sponsorship, and finding guides, other tourists, or potential clients—and for acquiring various forms of capital. When deaf people (e.g., tourists, researchers, migrants) go to a new country, they often seek out deaf schools, deaf clubs, deaf organizations, or other landmarks on the deaf landscape as a way of meeting other deaf people with similar backgrounds or interests and tapping into local community knowledge. Some of these place-nodes resonate as "known" places where other deaf people can be found. For migrants in London, nodes in deaf networks are sources of information and language learning. However, many deaf place-nodes are also precarious and at risk of closing down, or they exist in temporary, ephemeral ways. As we show in this chapter, this affects where deaf newcomers can go to meet other deaf people in the host country.

The reverse is true, too. Some place-nodes have become part of widespread deaf tourist imaginaries, and thus they receive high numbers of visitors. For example, Bengkala, a "deaf village" in Bali (see Chapter 6), and Adamorobe, a "deaf village" in Ghana (Kusters, 2015), are often visited by deaf and hearing tourists, researchers, missionaries, nongovernmental organization (NGO) workers, and so on. Gallaudet University is another well-known node where different types of mobilities intersect: It attracts faculty and students, as well as researchers, identity-seekers, and tourists (De Clerck, 2007). We call the mental map consisting of these nodes the "glocal deaf circuit" (Moriarty Harrelson, 2015; see Chapter 6).

International deaf mobilities can also be planned to *expand* deaf networks and thus facilitate exchanges of knowledge and other resources. For example, deaf club leaders in Indonesia, such as members of Deaf Art Community (Dacjogja) in Yogyakarta, and the Bali Deaf Community, Bali, participated in an American/Indonesian Deaf Youth Leadership Exchange, for which they traveled to the United States and networked with a deaf lawyer, doctor, professional athlete, and White House staff member (U.S. Embassy Jakarta, 2016).

Networks are thus not static entities consisting of sustained ties, but they are *changeable*. The strength of these ties also can change over time, becoming stronger or weaker. Networks are changeable not only in the sense of expansion but also in the sense of lost and severed ties. Crucially, the continuation and/or expansion of networks relies on relational efforts: "One agent always relies on the other agent to maintain the network connection" (Schapendonk, 2015, p. 811). Social ties in networks are thus *interdependent*. In other words, social capital in the Bourdieusian sense (see Chapter 1) resides in networks (or *fields*) that are actively maintained, rather than in individuals. In other words, a network only functions if it is "intermittently 'activated' through occasioned co-presence" (Larsen & Urry, 2008, p. 93). Schapendonk (2015) therefore emphasizes that people engage in networking (as a verb), referring to the work people do to create and maintain networks. A person's "networking capacity" depends on their individual skills, as well as on the power dynamics between individuals and on the efforts of other individuals with whom they connect (Schapendonk, 2015). To network effectively, individuals need access to relevant documents (e.g., visas, qualifications), communication technology, accommodation, transport, movement capacities, and the spaces where people meet, as well as technical, cognitive, and social skills; that is, network capital. Network capital is "the capacity to engender and sustain social relations with individuals who are not necessarily proximate, which generates emotional, financial and practical benefit" (Larsen & Urry, 2008, p. 93); it enables people to produce social capital, and social capital can stretch across long geographical distances if there is also network capital. In Kakuma Refugee Camp, for example, deaf residents of the camp meet with aid workers in the hope of growing their networks so that they can "fly away"; however, because deaf refugees are in a vulnerable position, many of these networking efforts will be in vain.

Different types of mobilities necessitate different types of network capital. For example, a tourist traveling on a budget may rely on social media networks to find accommodation, whereas a professional who travels to an event may have been funded by their employer or the organizer. Network capital has a spiraling character: As Elliott and Urry (2010) put it, "[t]he greater the scale of network capital, and, hence, the greater the networking that is made possible, the more that access to such capital is necessary in order to participate within such a 'networked society'" (p. 61).

Complementing Deaf Studies approaches that use a "community" lens, the networks perspective directs focus on the active and maintained ties between people, and it acknowledges that ties can be weak or strong. By using the "networks" lens, it also becomes obvious that ties between deaf people can span different borders and scales. Network clusters can be national when they stay within national boundaries, but there typically are not neat divisions between local, national, transnational, or global networks. A person may participate in networks that connect them to people in other regions or countries without being mobile across international borders themselves

(Levitt & Glick Schiller, 2004). For example, some deaf inhabitants of the "deaf village" of Bengkala (see Chapter 6) continue to sustain connections with deaf and hearing people overseas who have taken an interest in the village and its sign language, even if these villagers never travel outside Bali themselves.

Marxist geographer David Harvey developed the concept of time–space compression to describe the ways in which contemporary forms of economic organization (e.g., late capitalism) have sped up the circulation of capital (Harvey, 1991). This concept can be applied to the expansion of networks over short amounts of time. In deaf networks, the concept of time–space compression is expressed by the common deaf refrain upon meeting another deaf person and discovering connections in the form of shared acquaintances: "It is a small world!" The "small world" phenomenon refers to the experience of discovering that two individuals anywhere in the world may be connected by a limited number of links (Watts, 1999). The refrain is so prevalent that it became the title of an edited volume of Deaf Studies scholarship relating to international deaf spaces and encounters (see Friedner & Kusters, 2015a). In this chapter, we show that not only people *but also places* are connected in this "small world" phenomenon. However, it must also be remembered that time–space compression is an ethnocentric concept, and that it is "a western, colonizer's view" that time–space compression has happened in equal ways across diverse places (Massey, 1994, p. 147). In Chapters 9 and 10, we show that certain places and individuals are better networked (and more mobile) than others.

Places are where ties between nodes are established, where (mega-)events happen, and where people meet. Therefore, people moving through deaf networks often have shared *mental maps*. Mental maps are maps that reside in individuals' or groups' minds, which correlate to the physical world and lay down perceptions of the geographical world (Götz & Holmén, 2018). Mental maps contain shared geographical knowledge linked to physical places. They are grids of place-nodes embedded in the mind. Often, a known deaf space becomes a marker for spatializing people and relationships: that is, people and the relationships between them are imagined in spatial ways and are associated with specific places—for example, a particular deaf person's house (Heap, 2006; Kusters, 2015). These maps can exist on the most local level, such as deaf people in Kakuma Refugee Camp locating some other deaf people's homes (Chapter 3), or researchers mapping London deaf spaces (Chapter 4). On a global scale, many people involved in deaf sports have a shared knowledge of the locations where the previous few editions of the Deaflympics have been organized. Caxias do Sul, Samsun, Sofia, and Tapei are connected in this way, having hosted the 24th, 23rd, 22nd, and 21st editions of the quadrennial Summer Deaflympics, respectively; many people who have some knowledge of the Deaflympics have automatically memorialized the sign names of these cities (which are otherwise less well-known internationally), and use them as short-hands to evoke collective memories of each specific time, place, and context.

These mental maps are thus a means of organizing collective experiences, community memories, and stories. Sometimes, events and networks are memorialized in new signs that emerge *within* a specific context. One such example is the sign ROME that emerged during the 19th Summer Deaflympics in Italy in 2001; it means "chaos" (Figure 7.2), which is how the event was experienced by many deaf attendees and participants (see also Breivik et al., 2002). This sign thus captures and evokes the collective memory of a chaotic and disorganized experience. Places can also be associated with individual people, such as in the case of Thiruvananthapuram, a city in

Figure 7.2. ROME.

Figure 7.3. THIRUVANANTHAPURAM.

south India; one sign for the city, a three-fingered sign on the neck (Figure 7.3), is based on the sign name of a deaf leader who lived there. Signs thus come to act as relics of collective knowledge or memories. Deaf knowledges and histories, implicit and explicit, travel and/or are anchored in the form of signs for places as they relate to people and experiences. Knowing the "right" sign for a specific place or event is a way of demonstrating "deaf knowledge" and/or social and economic capital (Moriarty, 2020a).

To emphasize these *connections between places*, we foreground the fact that networks are *translocal*, connecting people and places across borders, and that mobilities depend on, and create, translocal networks (Greiner, 2011) (see Figure 1.2, in Chapter 1). The translocality concept is used to describe "phenomena involving mobility, migration, circulation and spatial interconnectedness not necessarily limited to national boundaries" (Greiner & Sakdapolrak 2013, p. 373). By talking about "translocal networks," we approach networks as multiscalar, that is, as existing on various scales and in various places *simultaneously*. Translocality focuses on both mobility and place, building on previous work done by scholars of transnationalism to focus more on the importance of *local dynamics* in specific locations such as homes, neighborhoods, refugee camps, and international conferences. Networks are "the overlapping and contested material, cultural and political flows and circuits that bind different places together through differentiated relations of power" (Featherstone et al., 2007, p. 386). In other words, the translocality concept is used to emphasize ties *between place-nodes* across the world and to investigate transnationalism as *place-based*. What happens in one place has an impact on other places when ties between places and people solidify, such as the streams of visitors from Australia and the Netherlands to the previously mentioned village in Bali. Networks are *embedded* within places; interactions within networks occur in situ and therefore are influenced by, and may influence, places' histories, cultures, laws, political frameworks, and so on. The contextualization of networks in the places where they manifest is thus crucial to their study (Lubbers et al., 2018).

Attending to the specific histories and contexts of various mobilities allows us to understand the dynamics that shape people's individual mobilities and life trajectories, as well as the nature of the networks they build and engage in as shaped by race and ethnicity, gender, ability, class, and so on. Below, we use the life story of Andrew J. Foster as an illustration of the ways in which networks unspool across time and space, at different scales, and with enduring effects. The example of Foster also demonstrates the importance of understanding the specific contexts of the places in which networks and nodes are formed—in this case, the mid-20th century, in both the United States (with its established educational routes for deaf people, but concurrent institutional racism) and the African continent (with its then-limited number of deaf schools and its designation as a key destination for missionary and charity work from the Global North; see Figure 7.4).

Andrew Foster was a late-deafened black person, born in the Deep South of the United States during the Great Depression and the segregation era. He attended the Alabama School for Colored Deaf, where he received an education up to the sixth grade, the maximum level allowed to African Americans under the Jim Crow laws. In common with many other African Americans of this era, he moved north seeking better educational opportunities; this trend was known as the Second Great Migration (Agboola, 2014), and it shows how mobility can be related to barriers caused by racial discrimination. Foster continued to face institutional racism in the North, and he was rejected from Gallaudet University several times due to being black. Eventually admitted in 1951, in 1954 he became the first black deaf person to graduate with a bachelor of arts degree (in education) from Gallaudet, and he went on to complete two master's degrees, one in special education and one in Christian missions (Moore & Panara, 1996).

Having learned that there were very few deaf schools in Africa, Foster was inspired to bring education to—and to evangelize—deaf people in Africa (Moore & Panara, 1996). He moved to Ghana in 1957, and from there, he started his migratory journey through Africa (Amoako, 2019; Runnels, 2017), establishing a total of 32 schools for deaf students across 13 African countries between 1957 and 1987. Foster engaged in outreach to locate students for the new schools, personally seeking out deaf children who could be sent to school (Oteng, 1988). During Annelies's fieldwork in Adamorobe village, Ghana, older deaf people shared stories about Foster's missionary activities in the village and his collecting deaf village children to go to school—not without resistance from their families and the village chief (Kusters, 2015). Foster also established numerous deaf churches, and he founded the Christian Mission of the Deaf to use as a base for fundraising for this work, spending a lot of time on fundraising tours throughout the United States (Ndurumo, 2003).

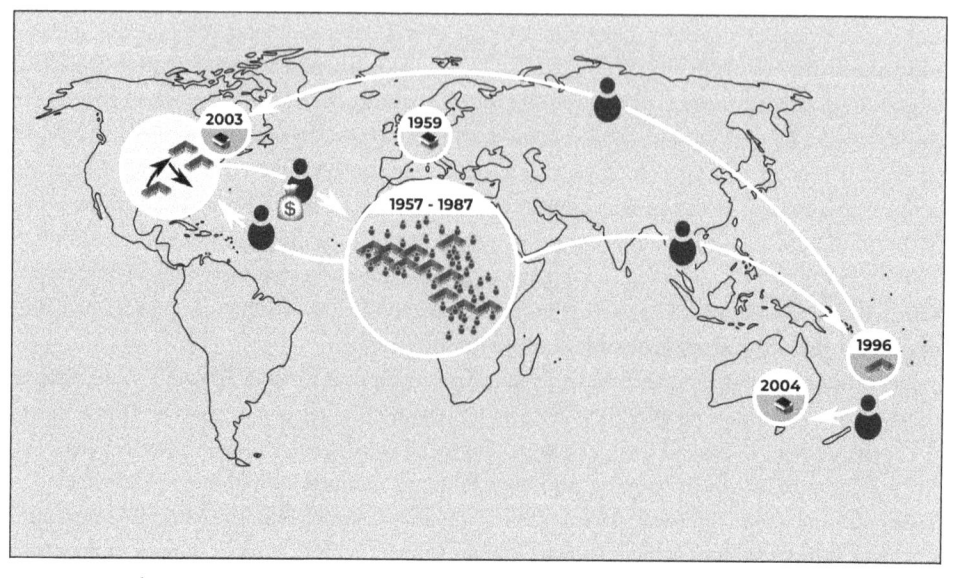

Figure 7.4. Andrew Foster's network.

Foster, then, is an example of a node that then went on to establish place-nodes—and, indeed, other people as nodes—by personally training and mentoring deaf teachers and leaders in many African countries (Moore & Panara, 1996). Seth Tetteh-Ocloo, a deaf Ghanaian, came to Gallaudet from the Ghana Mission School for the Deaf, established by Andrew Foster (Aina, 2015); he went on to earn a master's degree in education and doctorates in both educational psychology and rehabilitation. Having returned to Ghana to work for the Ministry of Social Welfare, Tetteh-Ocloo founded Ghana's second school for the deaf, another deaf place-node. Another illustration of the impact and expansion of Foster's network is Ezekiel Sambo, from Nigeria, who met Foster during elementary school and returned to Ghana after graduating from Gallaudet in 1970 to set up the Plateau State School for the Deaf in Nigeria, which has since sent more students to Gallaudet to continue their education (Aina, 2015).

Foster's network was evidently translocal: his mobility within the United States, his international mobility, his local mobility within African countries (between schools, churches, and villages), and the reverberations of his activities found in the actions of other deaf leading figures have thus *connected places* in various ways. His mobility led, directly or indirectly, to new ties between people, to the international mobility of other people, and to the flow of money between countries. The networks he built through his deaf education and missionary projects and his fundraising efforts exemplify how ideas and resources travel between places: *ideas* (about missionary work and deaf development through education) and *resources* (such as funding from donors who supported Foster's missionary work) traveled from Gallaudet to Nigeria and then onward to Fiji in Oceania through the new deaf development projects undertaken by the leaders whom Foster trained. In this case, Matthew Adedeji traveled from Nigeria to Fiji in 1996 to do volunteer work and "give something back to the Deaf community there" (Aina, 2015, p. 134). In an example of the reproduction of ideas and deaf development approaches, Aina (2015) describes the ways in which Foster's faith-based work inspired similar approaches in Fiji, including using personal networks to find deaf children in rural areas and to encourage their parents to send them to school (these strategies have also been used by NGOs in Cambodia; see Moriarty Harrelson, 2017a). On a larger scale, South–South cooperation between deaf people and organizations also led to the identification of future deaf leaders in Fiji by the Nigerian deaf volunteers, resulting in Fiji's participation in the 20th Summer Deaflympics in Australia in 2005 (Aina, 2015).

Andrew Foster's life story and legacy is thus an illustration of how networks operate at different scales, creating new nodes and connecting people, places, and events across multiple countries and continents. It also illustrates the role that *international deaf events* play in deaf networks. For example, Foster met his deaf German wife, Berta, at the III World Congress of the Deaf (which became the WFD congress) in Wiesbaden, Germany, in 1959; as two nodes, they were "tied," and their transcontinental networks became linked. Furthermore, it was at the XIV WFD congress in Canada in 2003 that Matthew Adedeji and Wale Alade (a man from England who Adedeji met through their shared efforts to establish deaf education in Fiji) approached deaf sports leadership to advocate for the inclusion of Fiji in the 2005 Deaflympics (Aina, 2015). It is at these large-scale events that many deaf people become a part of international networks, make new connections, enable others to connect, and direct the trajectories of resources such as funding and expertise.

The examples we have given in connection with Foster's life story exemplify how deaf networks involve affective entanglements, the deep feelings of connection and/or fracture that both drive and emerge from encounters between people, languages, and spaces. Just as affective entanglements shape the formations of deaf networks, they also sustain the circulation of ideas, resources, and knowledge among deaf people. They are found in the sentiments expressed by deaf missionaries or tourists when prompted to explain why they choose to visit deaf schools or sponsor deaf children in other countries: "I want to see how they live," for example, and "I am not a wealthy man, but I have knowledge and expertise that I can offer at the school" (see #*deaftravel: Deaf tourism in Bali*). Many of these sentiments are tied with ideas and moral values that flow through networks, such as the idea that deaf people with privileges have a "responsibility" to engage in deaf development. Ideologies and resources travel—here, to locations in the Global South through the travel of "experts" (e.g., sign language linguists, deaf activists, deaf professionals, deaf consultants), as exemplified in the example of Foster and his former students (see Cooper, 2015; Friedner & Kusters, 2014; Moriarty Harrelson, 2015).

Lastly, although this chapter mostly focuses on in-person networking, we acknowledge that networking is profoundly entangled with and affected by *social media*. Mobile deaf people have developed different networking strategies to meet people within a country, including but not limited to the use of hashtags on Instagram, like #DeafTravel and #DeafWorld; crowdsourcing contacts in Facebook groups; turning up at a particular pub on publicized "deaf nights"; and gravitating toward a café or coffee shop that has developed online recognition as a business where deaf spaces have the potential to be produced between local deaf workers and tourists, such as the signing Starbucks in Kuala Lumpur, Malaysia, or The Bakery Cafe in Kathmandu, Nepal, with its deaf waitstaff (Hoffmann-Dilloway, 2016). In our research methodology, we used the same strategies to identify deaf spaces (see Chapter 2). People also use social media to locate and connect with other deaf travelers and hosts with similar interests and similar backgrounds (see Chapter 10).

In this chapter, we unpack the previously mentioned ideas in relation to deaf networks. We start with a focus on place-nodes: traditional nodes such as deaf schools and clubs, but also pubs and organizations, and how they do or do not function as central place-nodes within international deaf mobilities. We make a case for moving on from discussions about the "death" of permanent deaf place-nodes, and instead we focus on the vibrancy of the networks, and the flexible spaces that have taken the place of permanent deaf place-nodes. We then move to egocentric networks—that is, networks of individuals that span several countries—and explore how individuals tie into network clusters on various scales. The last part of the chapter focuses on international deaf events as confluences of deaf networks.

Institutions as Nodes

Place-nodes like deaf schools and deaf clubs—and to some extent also deaf churches and workplaces—are the traditional backbone of deaf communities. These nodes have long been destinations for internationally mobile deaf people, whether teachers, tourists, migrants, or refugees. For example, within and beyond the British Empire, schools in the United Kingdom, Australia, and Canada existed within a web of interconnections along which deaf professionals have traveled as teachers, job-seekers, and school founders (Cleall, 2015). The travels of deaf white men from the United States and Europe who had the social and economic capital to move internationally have been documented and circulated. Some of them published their travel notes (e.g., Gaillard, 1917/2002), which were then analyzed by historians (e.g., Cleall, 2015; Murray, 2007).

The deaf white male international travelers whose journeys were documented were often literate, sometimes in several languages, and able to access information about the location of deaf schools and clubs in print. For example, Murray (2007, p. 101) mentions a "directory for deaf-mutes" published in Germany in 1898, containing an overview of deaf clubs in Germany, Austria, and the United States, as well as deaf schools in Germany. This deaf "mental map"—a precursor of the Internet and hashtags on social media—became a way for deaf people to tie into local network clusters (as in Figure 7.4). Through their visits to deaf clubs and schools in Europe, deaf travelers made contact with "local" deaf people who then acted as "guides," socializing with them, passing on information, and helping them to find employment. Networks were thus expanded in a snowballing effect, by which connections were made through mutual acquaintances. By way of their specific and privileged positionalities and their high network capital, these people "could navigate a preexisting web of interconnectedness across transnational space" (Murray 2007, p. 102).

It is significant that deaf schools and deaf clubs were internationally known to be deaf nodes and thus functioned as anchors for travelers. This is still the case: These places continue to function as tourist destinations—and even as local tourist offices—for deaf travelers, with deaf teachers and/or leaders sometimes asked to guide visitors. For deaf people who arrive in Kakuma Refugee Camp, deaf educational spaces have become havens; they are spaces where deaf people gather for education and socialization—assuming that they successfully find their way to these spaces (which is not always the case for deaf people born in rural areas; see Chapter 3). As mentioned previously, deaf people may be brought to school by other deaf people, such as Andrew Foster bringing deaf children from Adamorobe to the school he had established in Mampong, Ghana (Kusters, 2015). One day, in Kakuma Refugee Camp, Amandine and Abdi, a late-deafened refugee from Somalia, went to see a family with a young deaf girl. Adbi told Amandine that he had seen the girl on the street by chance. He had asked her where her family was, and he was able to meet her family—who are Somalis as well. Because Abdi could speak Somali, he was able to explain to the family about sign language. He taught the girl the fingerspelling alphabet that is used in Kenyan Sign Language. Thereafter, the child went to school in one of the deaf units. Similarly, Deng, the teacher at Fashoda Primary School, told Amandine that sometimes he went into the camp to seek out deaf children who were not yet in school.

Historically, deaf clubs and residential schools have been acknowledged as sites of identity formation, language learning, and transmission of deaf cultural practices, especially in the Global North and especially for white deaf people (Ladd, 2003; O'Brien et al., 2019; Padden & Humphries, 1988, 2005; Van Cleve & Crouch, 1989). As an illustration of this in the United Kingdom, the British Sign Language Broadcasting Trust (BSLBT) documentary film *Found at the Deaf Club* (Swinbourne, 2018a)[1] features three deaf people's stories of how their discovery of the local deaf club changed their lives, because they "found" a new identity, learned a new language, and became a part of a community. Many deaf people, including migrants (see Chapter 4), have found their way into deaf communities "late," and the existence of deaf clubs as more or less permanent spaces has facilitated this. Deaf clubs have not provided a haven indiscriminately, though; they have also been sites of racism to various degrees in different clubs. Some deaf clubs have also been attended mostly by deaf people from ethnic minorities (see Rinkoo Barpaga's 2014 film, *Double Discrimination*).[2] Today, however, deaf clubs and schools are no longer havens and nodes to the same extent as in the past, with many of these "traditional" deaf nodes

---

1. https://www.bslzone.co.uk/watch/found-deaf-club
2. https://www.bslzone.co.uk/watch/zoom-focus-2014-double-discrimination

having been closed down in many parts of the world. Because institutions have been in decline for decades, it is now more difficult for mobile deaf people to find other deaf people by going to traditional deaf place-nodes. To put it baldly, the deaf club as we know it is dead—or, at least, it is dead in the United Kingdom, the location of the subproject on migration and the country where the MobileDeaf project is based. A shift in deaf educational policy in the 1970s and 1980s toward mainstreaming has led to the disappearance of permanent deaf spaces from British cities and towns from the 1990s to the present day (Jamieson et al., 2021). The abrupt closure of the Glasgow Deaf Club in 2019 after more than 200 years of existence reinforces the point that the deaf club as the central pillar of deaf sociality has been dying a slow death in the United Kingdom for the past 30 years and more—clinging on but showing little sign of renaissance.

In light of the growing trend of deaf club closures in the United Kingdom, United States, and Europe, Padden and Humphries (2005) argue for the need to move away from the centrality of deaf clubs as the "core" of "deaf culture." However, emotional discussions about the demise of deaf clubs and the closure of residential schools continue to resonate in the British deaf media—including on the BBC's *See Hear* (a program aimed at deaf viewers), in the *British Deaf News* magazine, and on the popular *The Limping Chicken* blog—as if it is a new or recent phenomenon. The impact of and responses to the closure of Bristol Deaf Club (which is in what was once Steve's and Annelies's home city, and where Steve briefly served on the management committee), and the University of Bristol's Center for Deaf Studies were documented on film in David Ellington's *Lost Community* (2014)[3] and *Lost Spaces* (2016).[4] Ellington captured the profound effect that the closures of permanent deaf spaces—despite intense protests and activism—had on deaf people living in Bristol, which was indicative of the emotional attachment that local deaf people feel toward their clubs (O'Brien et al., 2019). Our statement about the death of the deaf club is thus not intended to be flippant.

Even though we suggest that the deaf club as we know it is dead, this does not mean that we believe that networks are drying up or that deaf communities are disappearing; nor does it mean that we believe that deaf clubs should be given up or that they have been completely wiped out. On the contrary, the continued existence of deaf clubs is evidence of the resilience that deaf people all over the world have repeatedly shown in keeping their culture and language alive, just as they continued to do when signing was prohibited in deaf schools (Ladd, 2003). Deaf clubs are precious, and they require preserving and protecting. There is a case for the still-existing ones diversifying into "hubs" or cultural centers, as, for example, in the cases of Edinburgh, Birmingham, Cardiff, and Manchester.

However, the dwindling of these traditional spaces has closed off some of the typical avenues for becoming a part of deaf networks and finding spaces to belong (see Chapter 9). It is time to look back on the clubs as relics of an era where they were central to deaf experiences, while recognizing that they play a small or minor role in modern deaf experiences. In other words, to focus only on the deaf club as a central deaf space for deaf locals—and thus also for deaf international visitors and migrants—no longer holds. Although local and national deaf communities mourn their deaf clubs and their histories, the demise of deaf clubs also affects deaf international

---

3. https://www.bslzone.co.uk/watch/lost-community
4. https://www.bslzone.co.uk/watch/lost-spaces

visitors and migrants, changing (and perhaps reducing) the places in which they can "tie in" to deaf communities.

In the London-based subproject, Steve and Sanchayeeta examined how new migrants to the United Kingdom find their way within London's deaf landscape. In the map they created of the 22 different spaces visited (see Chapter 4), only two were deaf club buildings. One of the two deaf clubs was modern and thriving this being the Jewish Deaf Association—a lively place, with enthusiastic workers and supporters, and a café that not only serves the public but offers work experience for deaf people. The other, Saint John's Deaf Club in north London, was typical of the deaf clubs with which Steve is more familiar: a jaded-looking building in need of repair. On an evening when Steve visited, it was sparsely attended; nevertheless, at other times it was a vibrant, central meeting point for events such as games (e.g., men's and women's poker and bingo), festivals, and special occasions, such as to celebrate national events related to the British monarchy or to watch football [soccer] matches on screen.

The map exercise also visualized how contemporary deaf spaces are increasingly ephemeral, temporary, and/or borrowed spaces, such as the deaf pub evenings that take place in mainstream bars in the United Kingdom. When creating the map, Steve and Sanchayeeta documented a multiplicity of spaces other than deaf clubs where deaf people meet, including "deaf cafés," so-called because they are frequented by deaf people. These deaf spaces are created by the people who coordinate these events, as well as by the people who attend them (O'Brien, 2005). These organized events and affinity groups are examples of how deaf(blind) people capitalize on existing infrastructures to create their own (minoritized) spaces (see Edwards, 2018; Kusters, 2017a). For example, Kusters (2017a) has shown how daily gatherings of deaf people in train compartments are hubs (i.e., place-nodes) in Mumbai deaf networks, where deaf spaces flourish. Deaf people adapt (to) material, social, and virtual environments, developing strategies to build and maintain social networks. Deaf migrants often attended the events documented by Steve and Sanchayeeta, but not always and not on a regular basis. Yet, participation in one space often leads to further participation—including in other, connected spaces. The fact that some deaf migrants were observed at several different events shows that the places identified and documented by Steve and Sanchayeeta were interconnected nodes.

Tying into these networks was not automatic for many migrants: Entry points were needed. Deaf migrants found the patterns of gathering of British deaf people different from what they were used to: For example, British deaf people tend to form into "closed groups" that are hidden but thriving across the capital. Hence, Shahina, from India, longed to meet more deaf Londoners to discuss broader political and social issues, but she struggled to find any that matched her interests. However, Emily (Canada) met regularly with British deaf Londoners to enjoy meals out, the theater, and other social events, and Lena (Russia) socialized at a "deaf café" with people who felt that they fell "in between" deaf and hearing groups. Often, being brought into a certain place-node was a turning point. Adrian, from Romania, spent at least 2 years working in the capital before he was introduced to City Lit college, a key place where deaf migrants from all over London congregate. When Chris arrived in London from Kakuma Refugee Camp, a support worker from a mainstream charitable organization took him along to City Lit. Significantly, it was not a deaf organization that provided this link, even though deaf organizations were far more visible and active when he arrived in the early 2000s compared to the time of this writing.

City Lit has had connections with deaf people going back several decades, having run courses in British Sign Language (BSL) and English. It has a service dedicated to providing other courses for deaf people, such as classes in math or computing, and it also provides access to mainstream courses with communication support (e.g., interpreting, note-taking). City Lit is a remarkably international deaf place-node in terms of the numbers and variety of deaf migrants who attend. Just a sample of those taking City Lit courses include people from Latvia, Romania, Venezuela, Iran, Kuwait, Mongolia, Sierra Leone, Poland, Pakistan, Ireland, Australia, and many more. The English courses delivered in BSL that Steve and Sanchayeeta observed (see Chapter 8) are not exclusively for migrants, but they were, nevertheless, mainly made up of deaf people who have migrated. On visiting, it became quickly apparent that, in addition to being a place where deaf people could improve their English and gain other skills, City Lit was highly recognized as a "hub of sociality" (see Heap, 2006) for meeting other (British and international) deaf people and for getting a variety of information. People were not only learning BSL and/or English, but they were also learning about "British culture"—vital for acquiring the social and cultural capital to navigate the United Kingdom. In other words, it was a node where deaf migrants had the opportunity to socialize with each other before and after courses, and so to learn from one another informally.

One of the tutors explained to Steve that "often students arrive early, and stay on afterward; it's the only social time they have meeting with other deaf, otherwise they would be stuck at home doing nothing."

The precarity of deaf spaces is a reality of deaf people's lives in London, including those of deaf migrants when they arrive in, or pass through, the capital. Although it may not seem like it on first consideration, City Lit college is a good example of a precarious deaf space: Despite having provided BSL courses for several decades, and despite the courses typically having long waiting lists, budget cuts and restructuring have led to them being reduced in recent years, and they remain somewhat at risk. Additionally, the precarity of London's deaf spaces may manifest itself in other ways. For example, a deaf migrant might discover and attend the Victoria Wetherspoons pub social and meet many people there, but arrive the following month to find that, unbeknown to them, the social had had to move location or had ceased to exist. Or they might visit Beckton Deaf Club, as Steve did on several occasions—a large hall in a modern community center, which is hired by the voluntary association. On one occasion, they would find several migrants present mixing with other deaf Londoners; on another, just one or two; at other times, no migrants at all. The number of deaf club attendees would fluctuate week to week, so visiting on a poorly attended evening, with just a few people in a large hall, would likely be intimidating for a newcomer.

The erratic level of attendance prompts the question: How long will these spaces continue to operate? The Redbridge Deaf Cafe and Enfield Deaf Club, for example, had already moved location once and were, during the fieldwork period, either moving again or at risk of closing down entirely, victim to cuts in funding and service provision. The Slug and Lettuce pub gathering, held at the Leicester Square branch, is one space that has enjoyed long-term success, and its attendees were planning for its 10th anniversary while the research project was under way. Even so, this too had a precarious feel to it, being wholly reliant on volunteers and the permission of the pub management to keep it in place; indeed, there were occasions when the management moved the gathering to different areas in the pub or allocated inappropriately confined or too-public spaces that affected the "deaf space" feel of the event.

These experiences of deaf place-nodes as frequently shifting may be shared by any Londoner and by any British deaf person moving to the capital for the first time; however, the latter are likely to have deaf networks already in place in the United Kingdom to tap into and use to find alternative deaf nodes. For example, as a British deaf person who had recently moved back to

London from another city in the United Kingdom, Steve already knew some deaf Londoners and could meet them at the Stratford Picturehouse's "888 Club" and the Shakespeare's Head pub in Holborn. At these and other places, Steve would encounter people he had not seen for many years, or he would be introduced to other deaf people via those he already knew. A newly arrived migrant, on the other hand, would not necessarily know a single person when they attend a deaf event, nor would they have any known connections with people in deaf spaces. Another observation about precarious deaf spaces is that deaf migrants do not automatically feel at home in the spaces that they do find and access (see Chapter 9). It may take a lot more effort and searching to find spaces where they feel they belong, and being well-networked would make it considerably easier to access these.

In the excerpt below from the London project, we can see how crucial networks are for finding information within this context of precariousness. Although many deaf migrants were able to establish some social contacts within the spaces covered by Steve and Sanchayeeta, many others were not just in search of signing spaces but also of information, and they were not immediately able to locate the right institutional spaces where they could find support. For example, Fareed, a migrant from Lebanon, was trying to resolve issues with his and his deaf brother's visas. Due to communication barriers, the brothers struggled to access information from the Home Office. They attempted to find local deaf networks by identifying physical locations where they hoped to get help from local deaf people, but for a while they could not find anyone who could help:

> As deaf people, we had problems accessing any advice, we were very disheartened and struggled to find anyone or anywhere to help us. We didn't know anyone either. We found a pub, and asked if any deaf people were local, but the answer was no. There were three deaf men who would come to the pub in the evening after work, but when we met with them, they really weren't sure how they could help. I only had ASL, and didn't understand much BSL, and they were British and not sure how the system worked with the passports and so on. My brother and I didn't know where to go; these men didn't know who could help us, and they [...] did give us the name of a pub where deaf people met. I think it was in Clapham Junction. There's a get-together every Wednesday there, and they gave us the address. We were able to find this pub, but the people there didn't know how to help us either. They had no knowledge of immigration or the Home Office or local services and so on. We gave up. It took a very long time to find anyone who could help; eventually we found a deaf person [...] who finally helped us, and we could tell them everything that had happened.

In the absence of a central information point for deaf migrants, an individual willing to help the brothers needed to be identified, and being unable to make use of previous connections, the two had to start networking (Schapendonk, 2015) from scratch. In this process, temporary deaf place-nodes were not sufficient, and institutional deaf place-nodes could not be found. The deaf brothers' reliance on networking was successful in the end, but it was an arduous process made more difficult by their own lack of BSL and social capital, and by the lack of relevant knowledge held by the deaf people they managed to locate. It is not unimaginable that there was also an undercurrent of xenophobia and Islamophobia at work: The deaf locals did not know the new deaf arrivals and may have been reluctant to help them.

These examples show that translocal networks manifest *in* places and *through connections* between places and people, that these places are often precarious, and that these connections may be fragile, dependent on social capital, unevenly distributed, and subject to gatekeeping.

In 1 week, 1 month, or 1 year, the place-node could be gone—either shut down without being replaced, or having been moved to a different location or venue. This is a far cry from the situation in the mid- to late-20th century, when the deaf club or deaf center was a vital deaf node in every city and most towns; the majority were far from precarious, at least in the United Kingdom.

Returning to the topic of deaf schools, formerly hubs for international visitors, those remaining in the Global North have become increasingly inaccessible for deaf visitors for reasons including safeguarding and security. In the United States and Europe, it is no longer usually considered appropriate for tourists to show up unannounced at deaf schools, and they are not always allowed in. Conversely, visitors often show up unannounced at schools in the Global South expecting access (see Moriarty Harrelson, 2015). Deaf schools and clubs are still considered important places for tourists to the Global South to visit because of the emotional resonance, sense of novelty, and invocation of nostalgia due to the demise of equivalent institutions in much of the Global North; it also feeds the desire to "see how they live" (see *#deaftravel*), and the relative accessibility of these deaf schools to tourists is considered problematic by some (see Moriarty Harrelson, 2015, and Chapter 6; also *#deaftravel: Deaf tourism in Bali*).

The question of visits to deaf schools usefully illustrates that, in addition to differences in levels of *access* to certain nodes, there are also different *ideas* about which locales are appropriate, or not appropriate, to visit as a tourist. Deaf tour guides Gio and Wahyu had different philosophies on tourist visits to deaf schools in Bali: Gio, the French guide living in Indonesia, who compared tourist visits to deaf schools and to Bengkala with going to the zoo, remarked on the cumulative disruptive effect of so many visitors on the children's education, explicitly commenting on the local impact of international deaf mobility. On the other hand, Wahyu, who is Indonesian, frequently brings deaf tourists to schools in Bengkala despite the arduous drive, because it is "what they want to see."

The differences in Gio's and Wahyu's philosophies also reflect their networks in Bali. Gio has access to the sociopolitical organization Bali Deaf Community (which he has previously sponsored) and draws on this for tourist activities. He was able to organize a dinner to introduce members of Bali Deaf Community to members of the Travass tour group; this was built into his tour schedule, and it involved hiring hearing Balinese drivers to bring the group to the *warung* (a small restaurant serving Indonesian food). In contrast, Wahyu's guiding is smaller scale, typically limited to the number of people who can sit comfortably in his car; for larger groups, he hires a small van. Different place-nodes are thus linked together and marked up on the deaf mental map of Bali by virtue of the differential practices of the two guides. Indeed, as well as shaping *which* place-nodes are tied into (and *to what extent*), influential individuals may themselves become "destinations" on the deaf mental map. In the following section, we explore the various roles played by person-nodes within a network.

Individuals as Nodes

Individuals are nodes that connect other individuals in the network to each other; these connections can result in international mobility. For example, for South Asian communities, networks are vital for meeting a potential bride or groom. All five Indian women in Sanchayeeta's study had moved to London in the context of marriage, and they had been introduced to their husbands through family or friends' networks. Aisha met her deaf husband through his deaf aunt on his mother's side. In the United Kingdom, the husband's deaf mother had been seeking a suitable bride (preferably a Muslim Asian) for her oldest son, but the deaf women he had met and interacted with in Britain all had "histories" known to their social groups (reflecting the previously mentioned "it's a small world" feeling). In common with many men in this community, he had a tacit preference for someone with "a clean slate." Because the mother and son could not find anyone who met their expectations, his mother turned to her deaf sister, who lives in India, to find someone suitable. This deaf aunt attended various deaf events and deaf clubs in Mumbai with her sister's request on her mind. When she encountered Aisha at a deaf wedding in Mumbai, she enquired if she was single and whether she was interested in meeting her nephew as a possible future partner. Because Aisha's mother was pressuring her to get married, she agreed to be introduced to the man online. After 4 years of interacting with him online, they got married. Seema's husband had also been unable to find a suitable bride in his U.K. network and was introduced to Seema by Meera, another of Sanchayeeta's participants. Meera had already taken up the role of matchmaker for Indian deaf people, and she used her network in India to connect with Seema in Mumbai. The two women first met in person after Seema's migration to London.

Individuals themselves are not stationary nodes, but they are points of convergence for networks. This is exemplified by Shahina, whose individual network operates on multiple scales, from London-based networks, India-based networks, and U.S.-based networks to global networks of deaf people encompassing a wide geographical area—from Korea, to London, to San Francisco. Shahina is a woman originally from India who resided in London at the time of interview but who had spent many years in the United States for study at Gallaudet University and other institutions. In Shahina's early interviews (which took place during the coronavirus pandemic), she explained to Sanchayeeta that she felt more connected to the deaf friends that she had made in the United States, where she used to live and study. She also had a close friend from South Africa whom she had met at Gallaudet University, who was living in London, and she met up with her from time to time. Her deaf best friend, who she met while traveling around Korea, is originally from the Philippines, and their friendship deepened after Shahina's friend visited her in India and then in London. Shahina's network also includes another layer of connections through her husband (a deaf Londoner, originally from Lebanon), whose deaf brother also knew her Filipino friend. It was during a visit to London from San Francisco that she met her future husband's deaf brother through a video-chat application, Camfrog, that deaf people used to connect with each other in the early 2000s. Shahina later arranged for a group of deaf people from India to visit the Philippines, and her Filipino friend asked if a Lebanese man living in London (now Shahina's husband) could join them. They connected first on Facebook and WhatsApp, he joined the tour group, and they became a couple. After a long-distance relationship, Shahina moved to London to marry him.

This brief example showcases the various scales and formations of deaf networks. It shows the complex, multilayered, deeply tangled interconnectedness of globally mobile deaf people. The key people involved originate from multiple countries in the Global South, and some of them, including Shahina, who has high network capital, are financially privileged and hypermobile for professional and personal reasons. They engage in different types of mobilities, some of which are covered in this book: Shahina *migrated for study* from India to San Francisco, traveled to Korea for *tourism*, and then hosted her best friend from the Philippines in both places that she considers to be "home"—that is, India and London. As a result of Shahina and her friends' tourist mobilities, she met her future husband, first via social media and then in the Philippines, and then she *migrated for marriage* to be with him in London. This is an example of the necessity of studying different types of mobility *together*, because mobilities manifest as interconnected (see Chapter 1).

Shahina's mobility trajectory also shows that Gallaudet is a key node where international connections are made, and these networks can be reactivated after international students return home (also see Breivik, 2005). Another illustration of this comes from Erin's fieldwork in Bali. When she mentioned to one group of tourists that she lived in Washington, DC, three of them (one from Mumbai, India, and a couple from Australia) asked her whether she knew Gallaudet. Erin explained that she had worked at Gallaudet for several years before finishing her doctorate and moving on to Heriot-Watt University. The white couple from Australia mentioned the name of a person who was originally from Australia but had moved to the United States and then worked at Gallaudet. Erin said that she knew that person. This led to sharing the names of other people who had connections with Australia and Gallaudet, as well as people with similar connections from India, to try to identify overlaps in their respective networks. This name-sharing is a means of placing people within a constellation of overlapping networks.

In the excerpt below, a tourist that Erin interviewed in Bali, who is from the United States and of East Asian descent, told her about her use of a different kind of deaf network of individuals when traveling through Europe, through the social networking service Couchsurfing. Through this network, travelers can connect with people who are happy to host them in their home for free (i.e., on their couch or elsewhere). She met her deaf husband, a white Italian citizen, through the deaf network on Couchsurfing:

> After university, I went backpacking for 1 year on my own. I went to Belgium for a deaf academic conference, and I thought to use that time to travel around Europe. I saw Belgium, Germany, Switzerland, Italy—which is where I met him. It was while I was traveling. I found him on the internet, through the website Couchsurfing. There is a deaf, signing group on Couchsurfing where the names of countries are posted, and he volunteered for me to stay at his place. After that I was considering how I could move to Italy, to have the experience of living in another country since I grew up in America. I found a [study] grant and it was easy for me to do that for 2 and a half years. Now, I live there because I married him.

This is another example of how different mobilities and movements through different networks flow into each other: *professional mobility* in the form of a conference, then *tourism* in the form of backpacking (and meeting the future partner in that process), and then *migration for study* and *marriage migration*. These two examples show how networking—that is, individuals actively maintaining their own networks and/or expanding these networks—affects decisions about where to be mobile to, and where to migrate or travel to.

In the previous Couchsurfing example, a deaf tourist used an existing network to access different kinds of resources, including the social capital associated with meeting and/or staying with local deaf people in their homes. Through this, she could experience (or "consume") aspects of local lives, receive free local guidance, and experience a kind of authenticity. Other approaches can be used to learn about destinations without a strong internet presence, as explained in an interview Erin conducted with a group of frequent travelers from the United States. A deaf man who identified as an Asian American and who had traveled extensively, stated:

> When I went to Brazil, I knew people that had been there before and used that information to my advantage. It's the same thing with deaf clubs. There are some unknown places, or places without any information that I have seen. For example, in the Galapagos, I asked if anyone knew any deaf people

who were living there, and I didn't get any details or contacts. There weren't even any deaf schools. It seems it is different on the mainland, but it just depends on where you go. It depends on what kind of information is already there online and what people are already there in that particular place. [...] The key is to find people who are already there. There is a person from Chile who I asked if they knew anyone [in Easter Island], and they sent me the name of someone and I made the effort to get in touch with them.

This example further exemplifies that traditional deaf places like clubs and schools are still automatically thought of as destinations or network hubs by internationally mobile deaf people; it also shows that it is a common practice among deaf tourists to locate individuals in their networks who can then either facilitate their travel or can introduce them to others. These often are weak ties that then serve as bridges between clusters of nodes—that is, introducing deaf newcomers into local networks. Individuals who connect clusters of nodes are thus gateways into networks in other countries.

In another example, when Annelies lived in Mumbai with her husband Sujit, they were often contacted by Frontrunners students who wanted to do their internship in Mumbai, and by former students traveling in India. Sujit had himself participated in Frontrunners in 2007, and the Frontrunners of previous and subsequent years knew of him. They often asked to stay in Sujit's deaf parents' flat (so as to "see how they live") or in the nearby flat where Annelies and Sujit were living, or they asked to be introduced to other deaf contacts in India with whom they could stay. Sujit and Annelies's place also was a "hub of sociality" for deaf people (Indian as well as international) to gather in groups because, unlike most local deaf people, they did not live with extended family. It was therefore a translocal place-node, where deaf mobilities (local and international) of different scales converged.

The use of the internet in general (e.g., email), and social media in particular, is often central to contemporary connections of this type. Many deaf people collect the social media accounts (e.g., Facebook, Instagram) of deaf people from other countries, including people they have met online or face to face in international encounters (e.g., in the context of tourism or sports events) and whose contact details they save for possible future use (including for information, guiding, or hosting). They may have met this person only once and only briefly, but even this type of weak tie can be mobilized. Facebook also can be used to create links with deaf locals. This is the strategy used, for example, by Ambrose Murangira, from Uganda, who Annelies interviewed at the XVIII WFD congress in 2019. Ambrose is a well-traveled deaf person and disability activist who has worked in several deaf organizations, including as president. He has visited the United States, the United Kingdom, several European countries, China, several Arab countries, and many countries in Africa. He was working for a disability organization at the time of the interview, and he said:

> When I fly somewhere, and it is not related to deafness but for a general program, I research on Facebook if there are local deaf people there. There must be some. I contact them and then I meet with one or two local deaf people for a chat and beer. Beer, yes—and we chat. I feel comfortable meeting deaf people. [...] They are always happy to show me around and tell me stories about some things. [...] Hearing people tell me they don't have time for me. If I am going somewhere—let's say on a train—[and] I ask a hearing person for help, they say it with spoken words and leave. If I show another person where I want to go, they just leave as well. That is a challenge, but when a deaf person realizes we are both deaf, they get excited and they explain everything to me. That is soothing and feels like home.

Ambrose taps into local deaf networks via social media. It is likely that Ambrose's positionality as a man, a good communicator who is fluent in International Sign (IS), and a well-respected deaf professional, has helped him to tie into local networks in the countries he has visited. Ambrose mentioned that he bonds over a beer. Alcohol often functions as a social lubricant in deaf spaces. He refers to international deaf networks as "home," using a metaphor that is very common in deaf communities (Breivik, 2005; see Chapter 9). It is noteworthy, however, that Ambrose, a black African, did not talk about racism or other negative experiences in this interview; other deaf people of color have shared stories of racism when trying to connect to white people in the Global North (see Chapters 4 and 9).

Familiar with this networking practice of connecting to (often well-connected) deaf individuals, deaf tourists also have posted vlogs on social media asking their social networks and affinity groups (e.g., the people in the *Solo Deaf Traveler* Facebook group) where to find local deaf people in the countries they will visit. Hashtags are often used with great success to find other deaf travelers with similar interests, which is why the MobileDeaf film on deaf tourism is called *#deaftravel*. It highlights the various scales and functions of deaf networks, such as the deaf networks on social media, which sometimes become real-life networks. Many deaf travelers (and entertainers and social media influencers) use the #DeafTravel hashtag to find other accounts to follow, and as part of her fieldwork methodology, Erin also used it to find and contact people who were traveling in Bali to see if they would be interested in participating in her research project (see Chapter 2).

Hospitality, in the form of guiding or hosting in homes, here emerges as a mechanism based on networks and used to expand networks. The mobilization of weak ties between hosts and guests does not necessarily carry the expectation that long-term relationships (i.e., strong ties) will be established (although some hosts may have such expectations). Instead, the expectation is that people who have been hosted will also host others at another time. That is, there appears to be a type of "generalized reciprocity" between deaf people that is similar to the reciprocal, intercultural rationales of both the Couchsurfing community and the Esperanto movement, both of which are emerging as cosmopolitan practices (Fians, 2021a).[5]

By hosting, deaf people perform deaf cosmopolitanism: hosts by interacting with the "stranger," and guests by "seeing how they live" (see Chapter 6). Typically, deaf guests will reciprocate by handing over a small souvenir from their own country; cooking a meal from their country; telling the host more about their country; sharing travel stories; paying for drinks, food, or meals; featuring in photos; spending time with the host and their family; and demonstrating signs from one or more foreign sign languages (see Chapter 8). In Bengkala, Erin observed that tourists reciprocated by buying a birthday cake for one of their hosts, paying for some of the deaf villagers to join them on a boat trip in Lovina, and other similar acts. Hosting thus involves "scale shifts" from "individuals to representatives of entire collectivities" (Fians, 2021a, p. 13). The host and the hosted represent their home nations, often in stereotypical ways (see Chapter 5), exchanging food, stories, signs, and souvenirs. In the process, memories are created, which function as gifts in

---

5. A planned language intended to be used as an international second language, Esperanto is used for the express purpose of crossing linguistic borders without using "national" languages. Thus, the act of using Esperanto is inherently cosmopolitan, because its stated function and aim is to enable international and intercultural exchange. In this, it has obvious parallels with IS, despite the latter having emerged spontaneously (see Chapter 8).

themselves. In this way, individual people (i.e., nodes) can be as much a destination as the country one visits (see Fians, 2021a). In one key example, Erin has observed the ways that people on social media (and in real life) talk about the Balinese guide Wahyu as if he himself is a deaf tourist attraction. It can be challenging to schedule a tour with Wahyu because he is so popular, and people rearrange their schedules to work with him. It is almost as though he himself is a "not to be missed" tourist destination, or an item on the Deaf Bali itinerary to be checked off along with a visit to Bengkala. In this sense, Wahyu himself is a node in the glocal deaf circuit.

Hosting can also happen with the (indefinite) expectation of being able to tap into financial or material support in the future (see below). However, although an ethics of deaf hospitality involves inviting solo deaf backpackers or small groups of deaf backpackers into the home and allowing them to sleep there for free, this is not necessarily reciprocal because many deaf hosts (especially in the Global South) do not have the means to travel abroad. This is true of most, if not all, of the deaf villagers in Bengkala who welcome deaf tourists into their homes; as such, it is not an equitable ethos of exchange as idealized by the deaf ecosystem (see Chapter 6). One participant explained to Erin that when he traveled through Indonesia, he was wholeheartedly welcomed into strangers' homes based on their signing deaf connection; however, when Erin asked him if the same thing would happen in his home country in Europe, he said, "No, my mother would not allow this, even though she is deaf herself."

Deaf people from affluent countries who have lived for a long time in a country in the Global South, but have returned to the Global North, are often the point of contact for people from the Southern country looking for a home stay, especially as costs in affluent countries are typically steep. People do, of course, differ in terms of how far they are prepared to go in hosting: They may only host friends from that country, for example, or maybe friends of friends, but not people who are merely acquaintances. Similarly, although groups of deaf people visit the Global South to participate in, for example, empowerment camps (e.g., the Frontrunners trip to Ghana), reverse trips rarely happen (Kusters et al., 2015). Mobile deaf professionals generally have an easier time finding hosts (or are found hosts for) if they travel for an official visit (such as Ambrose) through their "official" position.

These examples show that internationally mobile deaf people who have privileged positionalities and high network capital, live in affluent countries, and/or have already expansive networks have more chances to tap into local networks—often in nonreciprocal ways. This does not mean that tourism (or indeed professional trips abroad) is an activity in which it is only, or even mostly, the *tourists* who are active in mobilizing networks. Deaf local people also show agency in creating connections with foreign deaf tourists. For example, as a part of a tour of the Yogyakarta area by "informal" deaf guides (i.e., nonprofessional, often uncompensated guides), a few tourists and Erin visited a site known as the "chicken church," a building ostensibly shaped like a dove (see Figure 7.5a). To Erin, the most interesting thing about this site was not the oddity of the building itself, but the deaf man who materialized at its entrance. He was one of two deaf brothers from a family living nearby (see Figure 7.5b). They told the deaf tourists they helped build the church, and they pointed out younger versions of themselves in the photographs displayed in the small exhibition area. At first, Erin thought it was a coincidence that the deaf tourist group had run into them. Later, she realized that there was a network of deaf people living in this part of Java who were communicating via WhatsApp video calls about the group of foreigners who had shown up. Erin realized this after observing these men on a WhatsApp video with their friends, one who lived next to a small temple, which then became the next

Figure 7.5a. "Chicken church" in Yogyakarta.

Figure 7.5b. The two deaf men Erin met at the "chicken church" in Yogyakarta.

destination on the tour. In this example, interconnected deaf individuals facilitate deaf tourism by positioning themselves in opportune places and by combining local networking with networking with deaf people from abroad. Often, this is done without financial compensation for their informal guiding services; tourists will typically pay for gas, meals, and entrance fees, but they will not necessarily pay the guide a fee. This is an example of translocality that shows how mobilities exist on different scales (local/international) simultaneously, and it demonstrates the role of links between people and places on the local level. It is also an example of how the visual languaging of deaf people makes them easy to spot in public spaces; it is therefore easy for spontaneous international meetings to be instigated between tourists and locals, some of whom come to offer their services as guides (also see Breivik, 2005, pp. 132–133).

The previous example also illustrates the relationship between networks and material resources. Deaf networks are channels through which money, gifts, and patronage travel—that is, through which social capital is converted into economic capital, and network capital can be relied on as well as expanded. In other examples, deaf people from the Global North—as well as hearing people with a connection with deaf people, such as hearing heritage signers or hearing sign language interpreters—have met local deaf people while traversing the "glocal deaf circuit" (see Chapter 6) who have made a significant impression on them. These personal encounters may then inspire them to fundraise for these specific individuals. For example, Sujit (Annelies's husband) worked as a sign language teacher and was active in various deaf associations in Mumbai. When a well-connected hearing man with deaf parents from the Netherlands learned that Sujit wanted to attend Frontrunners, he ensured that Sujit received funding from a Dutch deaf association. This shows how access to economic capital (i.e., funding) travels through deaf and other networks. Similarly, some deaf Indian filmmakers whose films were scheduled to be shown at the Clin d'Oeil festival in France were able to attend the festival themselves as a result of fundraising by Dutch people they had met in India who had been impressed with their films. These are examples of successful networking with people whose wealth or connections can enable others to travel internationally, sometimes upon the visitor's initiative and at other times after explicit requests (see Chapter 10 for more on sponsorship and funding).

In other situations, "deaf villages" have attracted visitors and, therefore, material support; as nodes, some of these villages have been the focus of benefactors over a period of decades (Kusters, 2015). In Bengkala, some families have benefited from tourist benevolence. When she first arrived in the village, Erin was frequently asked, "Where do you sleep?"; sometimes, rival families would pressure her to stay with them. She was puzzled by this at the time, but after staying in the village for a few weeks, she realized that the villagers had a vested interest in where she stayed, because hosting tourists could result in material benefits (typically money, but occasionally appliances such as a new refrigerator or a television) and/or less tangible ones, including expanding their international networks, "collecting" contacts, and learning about life outside the village.

Although the previous examples show successful transactions and interactions, there are many stories where deaf people, especially from the Global South, have been unable to gain support. For example, deaf refugees in Kakuma Refugee Camp also try to make use of networks, many of them in vain. When Abdi and Amandine would walk together through the streets of Kakuma Refugee Camp, he would often show her the former homes of those who had been resettled outside the camp. These homes had become deaf place-nodes on the deaf mental map, where memories of now-absent people would linger and be shared. Abdi would tell Amandine about the resettled deaf people's lives, their friendships, and how he had lost contact with them after they were resettled:

Abdi: My neighbor was a very good one. Do you remember I introduced you to him before? We were good together; we chatted a lot and respected each other.
Amandine: Where has he gone?
Abdi: The United States helped him, he stayed here for a long time and now his life is changing, he wanted to change his life and he is now in Minnesota.
Amandine: Do you still have contact with him?
Abdi: I asked him to help me, he doesn't have work and I asked him to help me a bit with money, such as a phone for example. He can't help me, so I left him alone. I asked him for money to help deaf children in Kakuma. Money for books, pens, clothes, water. He doesn't give me money. I left him alone.

After his deaf neighbor's relocation, Abdi tried to maintain the relationship, seeing the potential for economic and social support for himself and other deaf people in the camp. This did not materialize, and the contact came to an end. Atem also reported how he had lost contact with deaf refugees who left Kakuma Refugee Camp:

Amandine: At the RAJAF school [in Kakuma 1], there were a lot of deaf people?
Atem: Yes, a lot. Some went to fly to America, some disappeared to go to Somalia, some disappeared to go to Sudan, some to go to Uganda. Some stayed here, but few of them.
Amandine: Deaf people [who] disappear, do you contact them?
Atem: No, I don't know why. Before I didn't have a phone, I was small, I didn't know about phones, how to use it as well. I don't know how to meet deaf people who disappeared from Kakuma again.

This is an example of how deaf people may wish to access forms of capital via international deaf networks, but, having low network capital, meet with no success. It also shows how networks consist of *interdependent* contacts: If networks are not maintained, ties are broken (Schapendonk, 2015). Similarly, after her fieldwork in Kakuma Refugee Camp, Amandine found it difficult to contact deaf refugees online during the pandemic because of the low quality of internet connectivity in the camp. Indeed, the success of networking depends on timing, the means of contacting others, and the (potential) mutual benefits.

A person's capacity to mobilize international networks is thus to some extent dependent on the degree to which they can access the resources necessary for maintaining their contacts. The unequal distribution of these resources, and the privilege of those with access to them (including ourselves), was a constant thread throughout each subproject. Through our respective research processes, we each became part of more and different networks (see Chapter 2), in which we were often asked for financial support—sometimes by people who employed the DEAF-SAME argument to undergird their requests (see, e.g., Kusters, 2015). Erin received many requests for financial help from her contacts in Bali, especially during the COVID-19 pandemic lockdowns (see Chapter 10), and deaf refugees often asked Amandine to buy bikes, phones, and other valued items as gifts. It is likely that many deaf people in the Global South know stories about foreign deaf and hearing people who have helped others in their communities, or simply know that, through networks, they may gain access to financial resources; in other ways, they may be able to rely on, and expand, their network capital. These dynamics demonstrate the importance of recognizing the *translocal context* of relationships within international networks—that is, that they may be imbued with (implicit) hopes, assumptions, and/or expectations informed by geopolitical power imbalances and unequal distribution of resources.

Events as Nodes

In the previous sections, we have shown that deaf people tie into local networks and locate place- and person-nodes when navigating a country as newcomers, whether as tourists or migrants. We now focus on deaf professional networks that, by design, span multiple countries (often described as "transnational"; see Murray, 2007), and on the places where these networks manifest in in-person events. Scholars have theorized these connections and spaces in various ways. For example, writing about international deaf arts events and festivals in Europe and the United States, Schmitt (2015, p. 16) conceptualizes deaf interconnections as moving networks of physical and digital relations, with people themselves as knots and their connections as rubber strings. These networks are dynamic and constantly changing as people attend arts events and festivals in different places at different times. Schmitt imagines specific festivals as "a mess of entangled knots, as many related people are present in a single place at a single time [...] [T]hen until the next festival, a net spreads, still with visible knots" (2015, p. 16). The rubber strings constantly contract and expand, and people are progressively entangled or disentangled in a form of compression

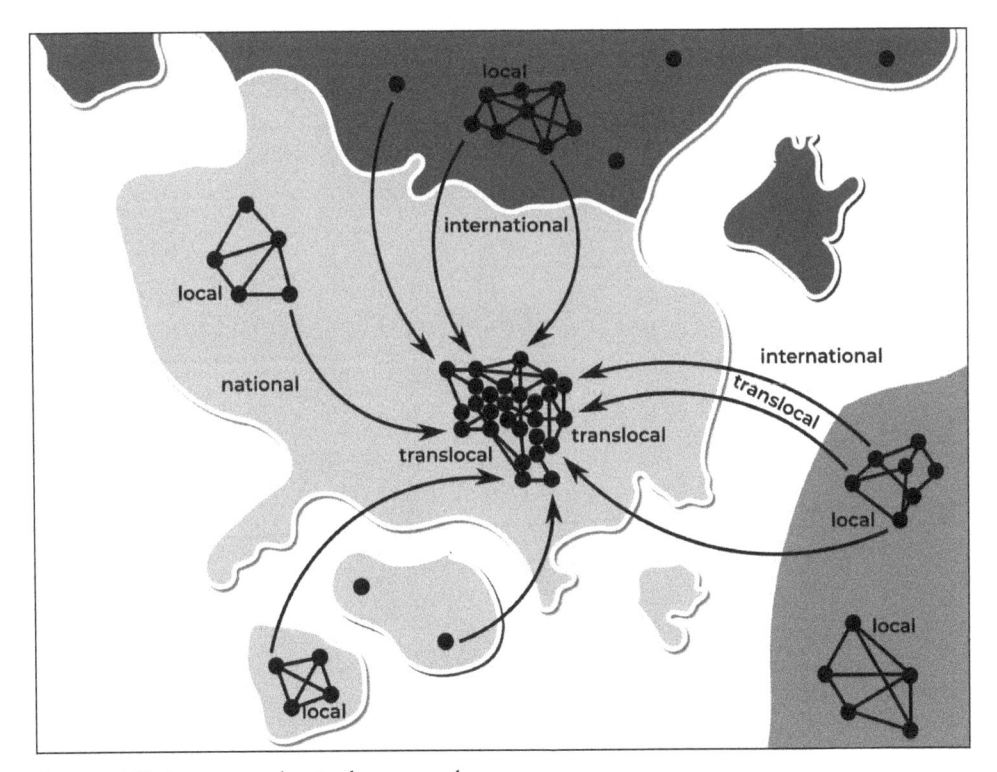

Figure 7.6. Fictionary map showing how networks converge at events.

and expansion of time and space. This visualization (see the center of Figure 7.6) is useful when thinking about how professional networks converge in places during events. In the discussion that follows, we focus mostly on Europe.

In contrast to Schmitt's dynamic conceptualization of international deaf networks, deaf transnationalism in early 19th century central Europe was imagined as a wheel. Alumni of the deaf school in Paris formed the hub, and spokes connected white deaf men to other white deaf men of a similar social status in the United States and other European cities (Gulliver, 2015). Paris was thus seen as the central *place* for deaf transnationalism. At the 1889 International Congress of the Deaf, held in Paris, the demographic had become less Eurocentric and male, with more white women and non-European (primarily American) visitors joining. As more delegates from the United States participated in "global" deaf social and political activities, Paris was displaced as the center of deaf sociopolitical activity (Gulliver, 2015), and the connections became more net-like, spreading throughout Europe and the world.

Historically, the two primary spheres of deaf international engagement in Europe were sociopolitical network events and, from the early 20th century, deaf sports events (elsewhere, networks have been constructed along different parameters, such as focused on religion and/or education, as the example of Foster's network demonstrates). Although international deaf professional networks have diversified today (see below), this history is still visible in some deaf Europeans' discourse about networks. Within the sports world, the space of the World Federation of the Deaf (WFD) and the European Union of the Deaf (EUD) events is often called SOCIAL (or SOZIAL)—the sign used is often produced with the mouthing "social" or "sozial," and it is the same as the DGS (German) sign SOZIAL (see Figure 7.7). This sign roughly translates as "society" and is used in IS to refer to the sphere of deaf political leadership and language rights advocacy. Similarly, in the SOCIAL sphere (i.e., at WFD and EUD), SPORTS is often cited as an example where international deaf social norms and sign language use are *different* from those used in SOCIAL (and academic) "worlds."

Many people participate in both types of spaces, sometimes at different points in their lives, with many deaf SOCIAL leaders having started out in SPORTS networks. People also can, and do, *shift* the space (and thus network) in which they primarily participate. For example, Danny

Figure 7.7. SOZIAL.

de Weerdt, a white deaf male academic from Belgium who lives and works in Finland, started meeting people through international deaf sports events when he was 16 or 17, playing football [soccer], futsal, volleyball, and beach volleyball. A few years later, Danny began to attend EUD and WFD events, and later yet, he attended academic conferences, such as the Deaf Academics and SIGN conferences. His deaf father played an important role in his introductions to the sports and political worlds, as he described in an interview at the SIGN8 conference in Brazil:

> My father was a leader of a sports delegation [where we mix with different people], and he's also involved in EUD as he works with the Flemish Federation of the Deaf. They asked me to get involved, so I agreed to give it a try. I wasn't sure about being involved in SOCIAL, as it's a bit political for my liking. But I was encouraged to give it a try, so I went to have a look for myself and met various people: social workers, campaigners, EUD speakers. [...] My dad insisted I meet Markku Jokinen, so I went and talked with him, then a while later I studied in Finland, so this is how I started getting involved in SOCIAL and academic spheres, and my involvement in SPORTS decreased.

Markku Jokinen, who Danny met through his father, is himself a sports leader who became involved in the SOCIAL world as president of the WFD and EUD; he formed an individual entry point for Danny into other networks. Later, Danny interacted with Markku at the University of Jyväskylä, Finland, while he was studying and Markku was working there. This example shows how certain connections—and privileges—lead to further ones: Danny, his father, and Markku Jokinen are all white men who are well connected in their countries. Other privileges also play a role, such as access to finances for travel and being part of a deaf family, which potentially bring access to, and status in, deaf networks. This shows how network capital works as an upward spiral.

As the examples of Danny and Markku indicate, deaf people may not limit their international activities to one network. They are involved in deaf SOCIAL, academic, *and* sports networks and may shift participation at various points in their lives. Today, there are myriad opportunities to build networks through participation in events that are not located in either the SPORTS or SOCIAL sphere, such as theater festivals, international parties, youth camps, academic exchanges, or other activities. There is an increasing number of smaller-scale events in more diverse sites which are targeted at different demographics; examples include the party that Frontrunners held in the Czech Republic for #FRWeekend with Czech Deaf Youth (see Chapter 5) and deaf yoga retreats in Bali organized by deaf Australian yoga teachers.

Danny explained how, in the past, deaf people traveling to participate in deaf sports in Europe (e.g., to sports competitions) would travel by buses to neighboring countries; today, it is easier to reach a broad range of places by plane. "Back then you met more of the same crowd in the same places, the same meeting places...," said Danny. Nowadays, network clusters are connected in more disparate ways, as person-nodes travel between them. In an example of this, the first time that Mark, a teacher in the Frontrunners program, met Hyemi, a South Korean student, was at a World Federation of the Deaf Regional Secretariat for Asia camp in Singapore, in his role as a facilitator; he later met her again at Frontrunners in Denmark, in his role as a teacher. We met Hyemi at Frontrunners and then 2 years later at the 2019 Deaflympics in Italy, where she worked as a deaf interpreter with the South Korean snowboard team (see *This Is IS*: Episodes 1 and 6). Hyemi went from camp participant to student to interpreter, and she moved between networks to end up working at a SPORTS event.

Participation in international deaf professional networks can start at a young age, especially for white deaf Europeans. Some have the opportunity to attend children's or youth camps organized by the European Union of Deaf Youth and the World Federation of the Deaf Youth Section (WFDYS). Some deaf children and youth with internationally mobile deaf parents may be taken by them to events, or they may meet international deaf visitors who visit their parents at home. Undoubtedly, the international scale is far more expansive for adults older than age 18, many of whom travel independently and either have the money to do so or can access other sources of funding. Frontrunners, for example, is a significant networking opportunity for deaf youth with the means to attend, but it is notable that it is attended mostly by Europeans who are already well networked, with quite a few of them coming from deaf families. In *This Is IS*: Episode 1, we learn that several of the European attendees had already attended various international deaf camps and sports events where they had used IS (the language of Frontrunners), whereas participants from the Global South tended to be newer to international networking and to IS. There also is evidence that networking leads to participation in Frontrunners: Different participants from the same country (e.g., India, South Korea) have attended in subsequent years, having learned about Frontrunners from former attendees (see Chapter 5).

In contrast, some people only "go international" in one particular or specific context. Some people from India, Lithuania, and other countries whom Annelies met at the 18th Deaf Chess Olympiad in Manchester, United Kingdom, in July 2018 told her they only traveled to international deaf events in the context of chess competitions. These events were thus contractions of nodes in chess-based deaf networks. However, the inclusion of chess in the 19th Winter Deaflympics in 2019 meant that deaf chess players who usually only traveled for chess competitions could now play chess within the context of a larger event, during which they would watch a wider array of sports and meet people with other interests. The Deaflympics was thus an event where different deaf (SPORTS) networks converged.

Sometimes, individuals traveling to events such as camps or the Deaflympics become friends with other attendees and then stick with them through the event or gathering (also see Breivik, 2005, p. 134). Additionally, deaf people who engage in international interactions often try to find out which international deaf networks they have in common. During an IS preconference workshop at the 2019 Deaf Academics Conference (DAC) in Iceland, participants were practicing IS and, at a given moment, the theme of sports came up. People were asking each other who had attended the Deaflympics, and being a (former) Deaflympics athlete was portrayed as being part of a "family." The SPORTS world in general was often described as one big, egalitarian, "warm" family and contrasted with the more formal, "high-level," "cold," political, SOCIAL world. Similarly, people who had been to Frontrunners at one point since its establishment in 2005 were described as part of the Frontrunners "family." People thus try to find out who "belongs" in which international deaf "family" (see Breivik et al., 2002).

In these conversations, people would also often discuss which events they had been to (e.g., which editions of the Deaflympics or DAC), marking locations on the deaf mental map of these networks. This is significant because it further marks these networks as translocal, connected to specific *places* where sets of nodes have converged in specific years. Many of these contractions of nodes take place in temporary host locations: The Deaflympics, for example, is held at a different location every time. However, they also can be based in the same place every time, such as the Clin d'Oeil festival in Reims, France. As this is a regular event occurring in the same city, it has become part of the glocal deaf circuit, a destination around which deaf people may plan a longer trip. Clin d'Oeil thus differs from events like the Deaflympics, WFD congresses, or DACs, as the latter examples become affixed not to one single location but to a series of locations on the deaf mental map. Whether fixed in one place or held in various places, official transnational deaf events are often entwined with deaf tourism (Solvang & Haualand, 2014), with visitors combining holidays with attendance at congresses and sports competitions. Indeed, in the summer of 2019, many deaf people from the United States planned several weeks of travel in Europe, beginning and ending in France: Clin d'Oeil took place from July 5 to 7, and the XVIII WFD congress in Paris from July 23 to 27 (see Chapter 7). The summer of 2019 thus functioned as a microcosm of deaf tourisms on various scales, oscillating around official international deaf events.

As noted previously, certain events function more than others as places where multiple networks and nodes converge, and people (e.g., new acquaintances) often find out many years later that they were at the same event in a certain year. Essentially, large events such as Clin d'Oeil, the WFD congress, and the Deaflympics are places where different deaf networks converge. Attendees at these events come from a range of different backgrounds, are different types of travelers, and approach the event in different ways; this is reflected in the wide range of accommodation typically used, including five-star hotels, bunk beds in youth hostels, Airbnbs, staying with local friends, Couchsurfing, and staying at campsites. At mega-events, people from disparate networks are suddenly part of the same large deaf space (or a series of deaf spaces) consisting of hundreds or thousands of deaf people spread over a venue or city (Breivik et al., 2002). Enjoying a temporary majority status by "taking over" a neighborhood or city was an especially powerful experience for many mobile deaf people (Haualand, 2007).

The "deafening" of public spaces can happen on different scales and levels of organization. It can entail the deafening of a particular bar or pub on the first Friday of every month, as at the monthly Deaf Night Out event in Washington, DC, or of a small-scale public space like the steps of a now-defunct nightclub on the river in Kampot, Cambodia, where deaf people meet daily after work to chat and informally circulate knowledge (Moriarty Harrelson, 2015). In the case of international deaf mega-events, the deafening of public spaces can be at the scale of the "takeover" of a street or part of a city. As public spaces become deafened, the linguistic landscape (Shohamy & Gorter, 2008) of the city becomes marked by the event itself. Examples of this visibility include banners in the towns where the 2019 Winter Deaflympics were organized (see *This Is IS*: Episode 6), posters directing people to specific lecture halls or venues, and clusters of people signing to each other. The deafening of public space includes large numbers of deaf people eating, drinking, and partying in public restaurants, bars, and so forth. In hospitality venues around the conference location, deaf people become very visible and expect service to be on their terms—that gesturing and writing will be used, for example (Haualand, 2002). Several participants stated that the deafening of public spaces that accompanies participating in huge events allows deaf people to feel like hearing people typically feel, because they are in the majority and sign language use is assumed (see also Breivik, 2005, and De Clerck, 2007). Transnational events may have reverberations beyond the conference or festival site, transforming the broader locality; this transformation of place indicates that these events are not only transnational but also translocal. The deafening of public space is a powerful magnet, putting a mark on the international deaf mental map.

At large events, there are often one or more large pubs and/or other public venues that become central places for attendees to meet (Breivik et al., 2002). At the 2019 WFD congress, this was The Canadian Embassy Pub (or the "Canada Pub," as it was known to delegates), the "official" WFD pub whose staff had learned some relevant signs. Other venues around the conference center also served the purpose, with pubs and restaurants surrounding the venue used for ad hoc gatherings of international groups of people who knew each other or who had met each other at the event.

Examples include "rainbow evenings" for LGBTQIA+ attendees, meetings of deafblind people using Protactile and hands-on signing, and a group of people from the Indian delegation and Indian migrants. The temporary reversal of deaf-as-minority to deaf-as-majority often involves more people than those with a ticket to the event itself. Many people travel only to participate in the convergence of networks—and the resulting intensive socializing at parties and pub evenings—and not to attend the event itself, due to the high cost of participating. Others only purchase a day ticket for an event that lasts several days, combining this with a city trip and meeting friends in pubs and restaurants outside of the event location. They thus enjoy the deafened city landscape and can participate in deaf-friendly tours of the city and in museums; the WFD congress is especially known for this.

When Annelies and Erin did fieldwork at Clin d'Oeil, large numbers of signers were visible everywhere in Reims, sitting in cafés and chatting or walking in groups. During these events, attendees often recognized each other as "fellow travelers" at the festival. Sometimes this appeared to happen on an intuitive level, because deaf people are often able to spot other deaf people by picking up on cues such as their way of looking around them (see Bahan, 2008); additionally, attendees were easily identifiable by their Clin d'Oeil lanyards. Annelies noted that when she and the cameramen she worked with (Sujit and Jorn) were slightly lost on the first evening, they were able to simply ask a deaf person, who was easy to identify by their public signing, lanyard, or hearing aids; similarly, they themselves were identified by their conference lanyards and approached by a pair of lost Australians looking for WINK (the sign name of Clin d'Oeil). The Australians were walking in the wrong direction and had identified the team by their lanyard rather than by signing (because they were not signing when they were approached, but eating croissants). Within a deafened space, deaf people thus act like compasses or guides.

While at Clin d'Oeil, Erin struck up a conversation in a busy café with a group of three white people in their 60s or 70s. Two of them were a couple from Cyprus; the other was a woman from Italy who explained that they had met through a mutual friend while on vacation in England. They had been friends ever since and had decided to come on vacation to Clin d'Oeil together. This is another example of how different forms and scales of deaf mobility can flow into each other: Tourism within Europe led to an international friendship, which was then maintained at a deaf mega-event at another European location.

At these place-nodes where different networks converge, people may move to varying degrees between the different groups that emerge within the event. Some move through the entire event alone or with the same friend or the same group of people, whereas others "hop" between people and groups. The latter may sit with one person to watch a presentation or performance, have lunch together with others, have meetings with yet others, and so on, networking with people with similar interests or from the same country and catching up with people who went to the same camp or event many years ago (see Chapter 5). People who maintain networks at conferences may not only do so in person but also via WhatsApp, in groups established before or during the conference. These WhatsApp groups may be used for practical arrangements (e.g., liaising with people from the same country and their national sign language interpreters, keeping in touch with people sharing the same Airbnb) or for networking and sociality (e.g., groups of like-minded people interacting during the event).

All these opportunities for and ways of grouping serve similar purposes: Within a large, homogenizing conference, people reach out to each other and maintain and/or expand networks based on common backgrounds, interests, or experiences. When people identify as being part of more than one minority, they may move between different networks that have formed based on various minority identities—and may also experience conflicts. Annelies noted the example of a queer deaf person of color, who told her they had been "called out" by another deaf person of color for their interactions with white queer deaf people.

Large events also often have "satellite events": events that are organized either at the event venue or in the environment of the event venue, but that are not officially part of the event program. At the 2019 WFD congress, these included a Viking Party (an invitation-only party in an adjoining hotel, hosted by the Nordic Council of the Deaf) and an open evening for women and nonbinary people in the congress venue, for discussing issues regarding gender and feminism. Some of these events were well planned in advance (e.g., the Viking Party); others were arranged during the congress itself. For an example of the latter, it was observed that at the congress, deaf people from East Africa grouped together for meetings at lunch and in the evenings, usually standing in one of the large halls of the venue; West Africans and Central Africans did the same, as one group. Deaf people from the 22 Gulf countries also had a meeting. At these meetings, many of which were attended by Sujit (who was working with Annelies as a research assistant), they discussed local and regional politics, including language politics. For example, the Gulf group discussed whether there should be a pan–Arab Sign Language interpreter at the next WFD congress, the XIX Congress to be held in South Korea, because many of them did not understand the IS used at the event in Paris.[6] Indeed, these smaller satellite events and groups also provided spaces where the main event could be vehemently criticized for the way it had been organized, and where the lack of access to IS could be discussed (see Kusters, forthcoming), as well as issues connected to ableism, white privilege, and racism.

Festivals such as Clin d'Oeil are spaces where deaf people of all ages and of different (mostly European) networks converge, more so than at the WFD congresses. This is probably because they are associated with leisure and have a festive vibe, with the focus being on performances and screenings. Thomas Kold, a white deaf man from Denmark who was attending as a spectator, told Annelies in an interview that he considered Clin d'Oeil, which has been organized biennially since 2003, a "new Mecca":

> We need one important place where you can charge yourself up. In the past, people would go to the Deaflympics, but I'm sorry to say that the Deaflympics are being managed by more hearing people using interpreters. It's become less of a sign language space, which is why the Deaf community have looked elsewhere for a sign language space and found Clin D'Oeil. It's Deaf-managed, Deaf-led, and it's an international space. You have culture here, children here, partying here, everything you could possibly want. It's become our new Mecca where we can reflect on our Deafhood process and really examine who we are. You can meet new friends, new partners. You can meet all people from the Deaf community, watch diverse people perform, and even perform yourself.

---

6. The term "pan–Arab Sign Language" is used by Al-Fityani and Padden (2009) to describe the "newly devised sign language which uses vocabulary drawn from different Arab sign languages, including Egyptian Sign Language and Saudi Sign Language" and which is "heavily influenced by LIU [Jordanian Sign Language]" (p. 1).

The festival featured a variety of performance styles: theater, film, stand-up comedy, Visual Vernacular, poetry, street performers, and music. In comparison to the WFD congress, the atmosphere was informal, boozy, and often flirtatious, with some single deaf people attending the festival in hopes of meeting a new romantic partner. Many people did not seem focused on meeting new people for serious conversations; rather, most of the attendees enjoyed the performances, chatted, and partied with people they already knew or whom they met through their network connections or by socializing, often under the influence of alcohol. Clin d'Oeil is a place where networks converge in a celebratory way and are reinvigorated.

At leisure-focused or celebratory events such as these, different networks converge—a function that Thomas suggested was formerly fulfilled by the Deaflympics before it became "more hearing" (see *This Is IS*: Episode 6, and also Chapter 9). This latter comment reflects an underlying concern that these mega-events are, in essence, precarious spaces, despite the increasing number of different countries taking part in them. This sentiment was shared by many of the participants in Annelies's fieldwork at the 2019 Winter Deaflympics, who told her that there are not as many "truly deaf" athletes as before (see Chapter 9). Clin d'Oeil is seen as an example of a "truly deaf" event; certainly, it was an event where a very broad diversity of networks converged—probably more than at the Deaflympics and the WFD congresses. However, it must be noted that these networks were much less international: People from African countries were virtually absent from the Clin d'Oeil scene (see *This Is IS*: Episode 3).

As an example of the convergence of networks at the 2019 Clin d'Oeil festival, Annelies, Sujit, and Erin were struck by the range of people they met and re-met during their fieldwork there. Annelies, who has lived in several countries, re-met people she had previously encountered from all over Europe, the United States, Canada, Brazil, and several Asian countries. Some of these she had met as a student in Bristol (2006–2010)—at the time, a node for other international students and visitors. Others had visited India as volunteers or tourists when she lived there between 2010 and 2013, and there were also people she'd met while living in Germany and (now) Scotland. She re-met people from the 2019 DAC in Iceland, a few months before Clin d'Oeil; at Frontrunners she had taught as a guest teacher; and she re-met participants from earlier MobileDeaf fieldwork at the SIGN8 conference in Brazil. She knew these people from different times, places, and networks, and different types of mobilities (labor and marriage migration; professional mobility as a researcher and lecturer; student mobility; tourism). Many other faces were vaguely familiar to her, but she could not immediately place them within her mental map, given how many different sets of networks had converged at the festival.

Annelies learned that many people at the festival had had the same experience of meeting people they knew from disparate places and networks in one place. Walking around the event with Sujit, people from India and from the "Frontrunners family" would sometimes recognize him first. Erin re-met at least 10 people from Australia and Europe whom she had previously interviewed in Bali. Another attendee, Adam, a white man originally from the United States who lived in Edinburgh at the time, said: "I saw so many faces I forgot I had forgotten about!" His experience of meeting people again after a very long time, people who were not part of his usual network—or even social media feeds—confirmed our impression of the extent of the convergence of networks at Clin d'Oeil. All four of us were at the festival for the first time, so the people we recognized were not as a result of previous attendance. This indexes Clin d'Oeil as a locale where (mostly European and majority white) networks converge, and as an event where people are embedded within a web of intersecting networks. Its location in the center of Europe, and the fact that Clin d'Oeil is organized every 2 years in the same venue on the same weekend, has helped to "fix" it as a node, as people can easily plan for it.

Some people found the densely networked social aspect of Clin d'Oeil overwhelming. A Flemish white deaf couple, Tom and Sophie, who were both very active in youth work, remarked to Annelies that they were tired of having to greet people every few seconds: "There are too many people we know here," said Tom. Sophie was surprised at how many people she knew from different contexts—from deaf camps, from the WFDYS, from DAC, and so on—and found the frequent greetings exhausting. Tom did not enjoy the superficial nature of the contact, saying: "People ask you how you came here, when you arrived, where you are staying. I would prefer to exchange information about which shows are worth visiting." Phatic conversation (e.g., "small talk") on such a frequent basis negatively affected his enjoyment of the event. Sophie added: "Now I know what it must be like in a deaf village; it's not for me." This is an interesting contrast with the people who actively *seek out* the experience of belonging that comes with immersion in a fully deaf space—or, in other words, the experience of being in a "deaf village" where everyday conversations with other deaf and hearing villagers in sign language is an imagined possibility (see Chapter 6).

The "village" metaphor is explicitly used at Clin d'Oeil: There is a particular space called "The Village" with food stalls, performances by street performers and dancers, and exhibitions where people can hang out in beanbag chairs to drink beer (or champagne!) and chat. Sophie's comparison of Clin d'Oeil with "deaf villages" (which are in themselves diverse with regard to the amount of signing used therein; see Kusters, 2010) is symptomatic of the recognized search by deaf people for "deaf utopias" in the form of deafened spaces. People's imaginings of such utopias render all spaces where signing is omnipresent as commensurable or comparable. However, living in a "deaf village" such as Bengkala is, evidently, very different from attending the Clin d'Oeil festival.

Examples such as these confirm the extent of networks for people who have the capacity to travel regularly over a long period of their lives (i.e., have privileged positionalities as well as high network capital) and who move through different networks on different scales. A person who only participates in one international event in their life, and who does not participate in online deaf spaces, would find it challenging to build on the networks developed there at other events and in other networks. It is often the repetition and perpetuation of international mobility that leads to this privileged experience of knowing people in different networks, and growing network capital in an upward spiral. Something that is not apparent in the previous stories are incidents based on categories of difference, such as racism and ableism, that take place at these international events, often in the form of microaggressions (e.g., pretending not to recognize people, not greeting them, or being unwilling to interact with them; see also Chapter 9). For example, while working as a cameraman at Clin d'Oeil (for *This Is IS*: Episode 3), Sujit noted that responses toward him, an Indian man with a camera, were very different from the responses to Jorn, the other, white cameraman. People tended to be reluctant to be filmed by Sujit, while being accepting of Jorn.

In another example, the black deaf organization Saved By The Sign released a "public service announcement" video on social media at the 2022 edition of Clin d'Oeil, requesting white people not to touch black people's hair (Saved By The Sign, 2022).[7] After the event, they released another

---

7. https://twitter.com/SavedByTheSign/status/1543500357736824832

video, in which Romel (a black Swedish man, one of the founders of Saved By The Sign) reported that he had especially appreciated meeting black deaf people at Clin d'Oeil, some of whom he had only met online before, and expressed his dream for a future festival for black deaf people of all ages from all over the world to celebrate, share, recharge, and provide role models for each other (Saved By The Sign & Belcher, 2022).[8] His video articulates the need for a place-node where networks of black deaf people can converge.

The networking experience at Clin d'Oeil starkly contrasted with Annelies's fieldwork at the 2019 Winter Deaflympics 5 months later. At the International Committee of Sports for the Deaf (ICSD) congress and in the various sports events, she did not recognize more than a dozen people because she was very new to the sports world. It also contrasted with her experience at the DOOR International campus at Kenya (see Chapter 5). Many people she met at DOOR did not know the organizations and events she mentioned to them (e.g., Clin D'Oeil, Frontrunners), and Annelies did not know some of the Christian deaf international organizations and events the people at DOOR mentioned to her. Conversely, although many people in Europe did not know about DOOR when Annelies mentioned it, many deaf Indians *did* know of it as a multilingual and international deaf place. While at DOOR, Annelies happened to meet two people she knew from India: Rahul, a former student of Sujit, and Charles, who was from Burundi and had, with Rahul, taken an international degree course in Applied Sign Linguistics in North India. Rahul and Charles are part of networks of applied linguists seeking South–South collaboration (see *This Is IS*: Episodes 2 and 3), as well as Christian networks; this is reminiscent of Foster's network mentioned in the introduction to this chapter. These examples show how, whereas some network clusters frequently come together, others have minimal overlap but may still be linked via weak ties.

It can be very challenging to start networking "from scratch" at such large events. Some participants at the WFD said that they had experienced racism within this larger space. While working as Annelies's research assistant at the WFD congress, Sujit talked with a deaf person from Kenya on the evening of the closing gala. Attendees were transported to the gala in buses; the black deaf Kenyan was the last person to get on a bus. As he walked to the last seat, he smiled at the people he passed (who were almost exclusively white) and tried to make eye contact, but they ignored him. He sat down next to Sujit (one of the few other nonwhite passengers) at the back of the bus, and they started a conversation. The Kenyan man said that he had felt like he didn't exist at the congress. He felt that other (white) attendees didn't see him, and there was no eye contact. He asked Sujit: "What's wrong with me?" He thought that they saw him as being stupid or "a monkey." He said that white people had made no effort to acknowledge his presence, and that he had experienced barriers when he tried to approach people. This man experienced a combination of being minoritized and having less social capital at the event (in the sense of having insufficient previous connections), which affected his networking experience. Being embedded in a smaller group from the outset can help in the process of networking (as in the tour groups we mentioned previously), although it is no guarantee. The Frontrunners course in Denmark is an example of one of these smaller groups, but students from the Global South still felt they were "behind" the Europeans (see Chapter 5). However, they were also able to become well networked

---

8. https://www.instagram.com/tv/CgLP7tOonu1/?igshid=MDJmNzVkMjY=

internationally through interactions with deaf guest lecturers and during their study visits and internships.

We noticed that people who have met each other at multiple international deaf events over the years often reminisce about *when and where* they have met. Doing so, they engage in a mental mapping activity, the creation of a corresponding timeline, and the (re-)production of collective memories. During the writing of this chapter, Annelies and colleague Maartje (also from Belgium) were teaching a 5-day "Dr. Deaf" research methods workshop to 22 deaf academics at Aal folk high school for deaf people in Norway. In the evenings, the group got together to chat, and some people who were previously acquainted would figure out where and when they had met each other for the first time. Sometimes, it was easy to establish this quickly; at other times, people *challenged each other's recollections*. Annelies thought she had met Liona, from Germany, when Liona was working on her doctorate in the German town where Annelies worked for a few years. Liona reminded her that they had met years earlier, in India, at Annelies's wedding: Liona was there with a Brazilian group of friends who were traveling through India, accompanying one who had taken part in Frontrunners 3 with Sujit and had thus been invited to the wedding. Different types of mobility to deaf place-nodes and/or in deaf groups (here: study in a deaf folk high school, a deaf youth camp, visiting a deaf couple's wedding, tourism as part of a deaf group, staying at a deaf person's home while going to a deaf-related conference) thus connect deaf people across networks.

In other examples, people *realized that they had been at the same event* but had not remembered each other, or they remembered (or discovered) other people whose paths had co-converged in various place-nodes. At Aal, Arjun from Nepal and Annelies realized they had taken part in the same youth camp in Dehradun, India, 14 years earlier; they did not remember talking to each other there, but they shared memories of the camp and used the sign names of other attendees to discover shared acquaintances. Indeed, by reminiscing about events (and thus engaging in the exploration of collective memories), people may remember who else was there and mobilize dormant ties. This occurred in Aal when Annelies and Maartje were reminiscing with Marta, a Portuguese woman now living in the Netherlands (where Maartje works), whom they had first met in Vancouver during the 2010 International Congress on the Education of the Deaf (ICED). The three women had been staying at the house of Nigel, a Canadian deaf person who had been Maartje's classmate at the Centre for Deaf Studies in Bristol; it had been a full house, and Marta remembered that the two other guests had been a British and a Norwegian young deaf man. She then realized that, serendipitously, this Norwegian person happened to be taking a different (noninternational) workshop at Aal folk high school at the same time as Dr. Deaf. When she approached him in the cafeteria, he was not sure that he remembered Maartje and Annelies, but on his phone, he found group photos from that time featuring all of them. Taking and sharing photos is a common activity when people reestablish connections: Annelies, Maartje, and Marta also took a group photo of themselves at Aal to send to Nigel, to show their reunion and to remind him of the time they stayed in his house 12 years before.

It is significant that this activity of reconnecting and reminiscing often happens at, or alongside, place-nodes such as deaf folk high schools, workplaces, or events where the paths of loosely acquainted people can converge. The activity of remembering, digging up photos, reexperiencing and consolidating memories, and making new photos is typical of the process deaf people undergo when developing closer working relationships or friendships over time. People who meet each other only briefly or vaguely may incidentally develop their acquaintances further at some later point, and they may look back to pinpoint a specific event when they became better acquainted or even friends. Shared memories, including recreated memories, are put on a mental map showing where place-nodes and people-nodes have converged.

Conclusion

Recent scholarship in Deaf Studies has considered the ways that social, physical, and virtual infrastructures interact with, shape, and are shaped by deaf people's communicative and social practices. This work has contributed to conceptual shifts, such as an increased focus on scale and networks, as opposed to a dominant focus on the "deaf community" concept and (the disappearance of) "permanent" deaf spaces like metropolitan deaf clubs and schools. By using the "networks" lens to look at deaf sociality, we rethink the ways in which deaf people connect, make connections, and are interconnected—especially as permanent deaf spaces increasingly give way to, or are complemented by, more ephemeral deaf spaces.

Networks consist of clusters of nodes that get connected via (often weak) ties that act as bridges. Internationally mobile deaf people are nodes that converge in places as people and ideas traverse networks through different routes on different scales. The examples we shared in this chapter show how deaf people build up networks through different types of international mobilities (e.g., education, marriage migration, tourism, work). These mobilities can lead to each other, can overlap, and can flow into each other, especially in the case of hypermobile individuals. At different stages of their lives, deaf people may circulate in different networks, encompassing different places and spaces; through this, networks expand. Social bonds are continually produced, reproduced, and consumed during events and activities, at specific places, and at points in time. Deaf mega-events manifest as a performance of networking, exemplifying intensified networking during certain times and in certain places. The concept of networks, we believe, allows us to think of people being involved in multiple (deaf and other) collectivities, with different rates of overlap.

Networks are scaled: For example, some network clusters are connected to a place (e.g., Gallaudet University, Kakuma Refugee Camp) but also have connections around the globe (e.g., with international alumni and colleagues, with deaf people in refugees' countries of origin, or with resettled refugees). We have also shown how international mobilities get linked to local mobilities, as within local deaf networks in Bali. Indeed, although networks can exist among people in a village, a nation, or on an international scale, these networks are always connected and overlapping with other networks, in the sense of there being bridges between clusters of nodes. There are networks that seem to overlap with others less, however. Some deaf networks may exist mostly, or exclusively, in online spaces, but in this book, we focus on how networks are also *spatially bounded* and *emplaced*, focusing on *physical places* that function as nodes. Still, we have touched on links between offline and online networking in a couple of places in this chapter: the use of hashtags, social media, Couchsurfing websites, and WhatsApp.

Information travels through networks and nodes, as do material resources. We showed that different forms of capital are exchanged in networks (e.g., social and economic; see Chapter 8 for linguistic capital), how people rely on network capital as well as expand it, and that effective use of network capital produces a further increase in network capital. Our emphasis is on networks as existing and maintained ties, and we acknowledge that this risks neglecting (or being less sensitive to) ties that fail, are absent, are negative, or break down (Schapendonk, 2015). The networks approach has been criticized for saying little about the nature or quality of ties between people and places, and therefore obliterating power differences (Vertovec, 2003). Networks are not always experienced as connection; they can be associated with disconnection and barriers (Cleall, 2015). We focus on these power differences and the search for spaces of belonging across networks in more depth in Chapters 9 and 10—for example showing that, when a person's network is limited to a particular area, is not yet built, or is based on acquaintances, this can become a barrier to mobility.

Not only is it the case that networking practices can be unsuccessful, but many deaf place-nodes are also precarious. Local and often long-established nodes are often felt to be crumbling, in the sense of the closure of deaf schools and the breakdown of the deaf club landscape. Precariousness also manifests in the fact that hubs of sociality are transient or movable. This reality often necessitates active networking by mobile deaf people in new countries. Also, because networks and ties need to be actively maintained and be to some extent reciprocal, networking is not always successful. Networking can be hard work, and it can be performed in vain. There is not always reciprocity in initiating contact, hosting, financial support, or flows of information, to give some examples.

Finally, real places and contexts, linked with each other through time–space compression, are key to translocality as a concept (Low, 2017). Place-nodes like Clin d'Oeil "can be imagined as articulated moments in networks of social relations and understandings [...] where a large proportion of those relations, experiences and understandings are constructed *on a far larger scale* than what we happen to define for that moment as the place itself" (Massey, 1994, p. 154; our emphasis). At the same time, when talking about networks, it is important to think about how nodes are *localized*. Local places matter, even if deaf spaces are temporary and ephemeral. Deaf spaces and people are embedded in the deaf mental map, as are temporal events and collective knowledge, and place-nodes within networks create contact zones where new translocal relationships are formed. When these specific sites are imbued with meaning in deaf networks, they are shaped and/or transformed by their relationships with other sites or spaces. By approaching networks as translocal, we have shown how places become markers for stories and collective memories, and places can be immortalized in certain signs and memories tied to people and events.

8

Calibrating and Language Learning

Erin Moriarty, Annelies Kusters, Sanchayeeta Iyer, Amandine le Maire, and Steven Emery

Calibrating (see Figure 8.1) is an English translation of a sign used in British Sign Language (BSL) and other sign languages that depicts a person spinning one or two dials on the body (Hodge & Goswell, 2021; Moriarty & Kusters, 2021). This sign (here displayed in two variants) is used to describe how people align to their interlocutors by communicating in ways that they hope the other will understand. It is often used to describe a person adapting while signing with someone who has a different sign language background from their own, such as someone from a different region in the country (Palfreyman, 2019), from a different country (Zeshan, 2015), or who is a new signer (De Meulder, 2019). It can involve using different signs for the same concept, enactments and examples, repetitions and changes of speed, more or fewer mouthings, more or less fingerspelling, and so on.

In the literature on spoken languages, a word that has a similar meaning as "calibrating" is "languaging": "a cover term for activities involving language" (Love, 2017, p. 115). This includes signing, speaking, writing, reading; in other words, it means "doing language." "Languaging" as a practice precedes languages as bounded entities (e.g., "British Sign Language"), as "[t]here must be languaging before there can be languages" (Love, 2017, p. 117). Put simply, labels for languages (e.g., "British Sign Language" or "English") are the result of commonplace understandings that a particular set of language practices can be categorized as a single language, and that a range of linguistic variation can be grouped together. The consensus that there is a British Sign Language means an agreement to group (regional) variation under a single nomer (Palfreyman & Schembri, 2022). In this chapter, our aim is to explore calibration as a deaf-authored practice and ideology—hence, our use of a term that is a translation of a sign emic to deaf communities rather than using the term "languaging."

Calibration can involve "translanguaging," which is a term often used to describe the languaging practices of bilinguals and multilinguals in which elements of different languages are combined (Garcia & Li, 2014). For example, deaf people may mix two or more different sign languages when communicating (Zeshan & Webster, 2020). They may also use mouthings of different spoken languages in their signing or point at written English to connect their signed narrative with specific English terms. The meaning of the term "calibration" is different from translanguaging because it is broader: Calibration does not necessarily entail multilingual language use, which is what translanguaging researchers typically focus on. Also, at the core of (the sign) CALIBRATION is the practice of signing: Even when people make use of nonsigned resources such as text, calibration is about using signing (in alternation) with these other

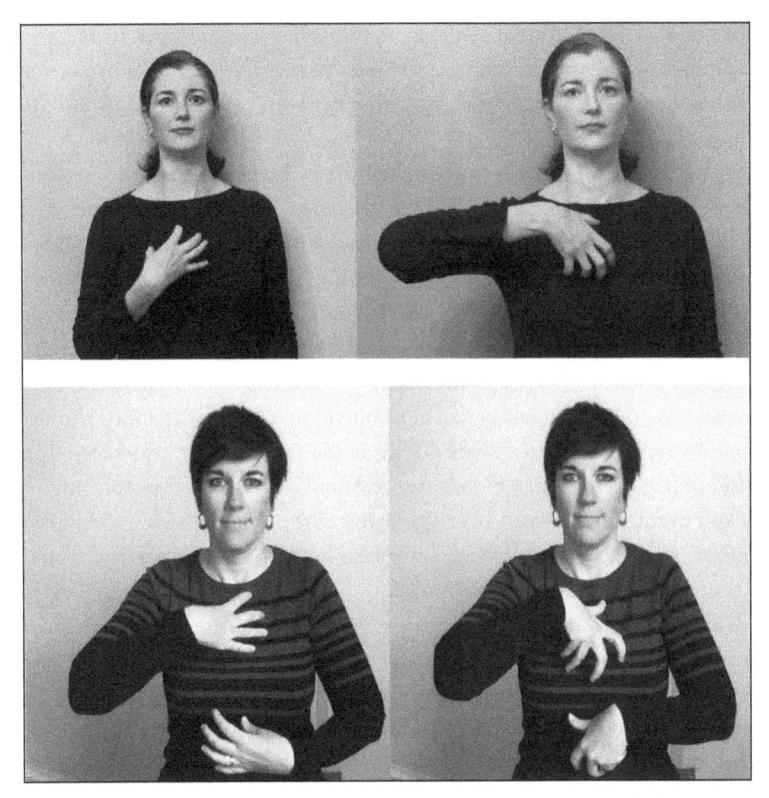

Figure 8.1. CALIBRATING (two variants).

resources. Many of the examples in this chapter involve International Sign (IS). Conversations in IS make use of a variety of calibrating practices. When people use IS, they may slow down, unmark signs (i.e., simplify handshapes), and engage in enactments and other visualizations (e.g., mapping) to explain things. IS also can be (and often is) a translanguaging practice that makes use of resources from different named languages. Interlocutors may use signs from different national sign languages (often, European sign languages and American Sign Language [ASL]), which they regard as relatively transparent and/or widely known, and often, two or more semantically equivalent signs (e.g., from different sign languages) are offered or exchanged. IS often includes mouthings and fingerspelled words from spoken languages (usually English). The process of calibration in IS could be said to be specific to it because certain resources and strategies are preferred over others, as we explore in this chapter.

Over the years, repeated interactions at international deaf events, like the Deaflympics and the World Federation of the Deaf (WFD) Congress, have led to the emergence of common repertoires of signs, primarily derived from various European national sign languages and ASL. Although the lexicon used can differ based on the event type, there is overlap. In this chapter, when we use expressions such as "know IS," "learn IS," and "exposed to IS," we mean conventional IS as used in conferences. IS takes a wide range of forms in different contexts and between different interlocutors, being both the process of calibrating between people who have little shared language in common (Zeshan, 2015) and the product of it: the use of a more conventionalized lexicon at, for example, international conferences (see *This Is IS*: Episodes 3 and 5). In such contexts, both adept users and novices calibrate to better connect with their audiences or interlocutors, which shows that there is no strict demarcation between conventional IS and the process of calibration in these contexts.

In this chapter, we show that deaf cosmopolitanism—the possibility of connecting with deaf people across national and linguistic borders—is based on this ability to calibrate. When calibrating, deaf people deploy a variety of semiotic resources, which are used to understand or be understood in communication, such as gestures, signs, spoken words, mouthings, and various forms of writing (Kusters et al., 2017c). Deaf people who are mobile constantly add to their semiotic repertoires by learning words, signs, and concepts from different national and local sign languages, as well as spoken and written languages (Moriarty & Kusters, 2021). We will mostly write about repertoires as residing in individuals as sets of resources that can be expanded through learning. However, semiotic repertoires also include objects in the environment, which people may or may not use or refer to (e.g., pens, paper, mobile devices), and locations that people point at, both on their bodies and in the environment (Canagarajah, 2021b). The semiotic repertoires of interactions are not only specific to the individuals involved but also incorporate and span the broader environments in which these interactions occur.

Mobilities are intimately tied to a person's life trajectory. This trajectory may include moving between places and shifting between languages, in what Busch (2012, 2017) calls the "language trajectory." The languages that people use in their everyday lives move with them when they travel or migrate to a new place. People may also learn new (bits of) languages. Language learning may take place in formal educational settings, or informally. When people are mobile, they encounter other people from different languaging backgrounds and learn new words or signs. Language learning practices are also intimately tied to mobility on different scales; a person's language use in a local context is likely to change as they move into regional, national, international, or transnational domains. For example, a deaf person in the Global South who moves from a rural village to a city for work, training, or educational opportunities is likely to encounter and/or have the opportunity to learn the national sign language for the first time (Moriarty Harrelson, 2017b). Additionally, people may expand their repertoire in advance of moving, by joining language courses or asking someone to practice with them. Sometimes, a person's accumulated repertoire may not fit the place they are in (Blommaert et al., 2005; Busch, 2017). As people move through places, they learn what types of languaging are appropriate in which locations or on which scale. For example, the flexible use of IS that takes place in an intimate gathering of friends would not be appropriate on the stage at a World Federation of the Deaf congress, where conventionalized IS lexicon is used.

In this chapter, we describe contexts and encounters where deaf practices of calibrating and language learning take place. We connect these practices to "language ideologies," the attitudes, thoughts, and beliefs that shape them. As deaf people travel and circulate languages, so do their ideas about languages. For example, some sign languages may be valued more than others, for reasons including their earlier emergence, comparative prestige, and/or their more widespread use (Kusters et al., 2020). Language ideologies serve social interests and, as such, they are always multiple and contested (Piller, 2015). Ideologies about languages also shape (and are shaped by) how people think about themselves, other people, and their languages (Irvine & Gal, 2000).

Language and ideology influence each other, and this is a moral process. Differences in language practices can lead to value judgments about people who communicate differently. The ideologically laden nature of languages and languaging thus sometimes leads to conflicts, tensions, and grievances between people in transnational settings. Often, these value judgments lead to people telling others what they are doing "wrong" with language (Straaijer, 2016); this includes statements about people using "too much ASL in IS" (Kusters, 2020) or that someone is using the wrong language in the wrong place (e.g., migrants in the United Kingdom who use ASL).

ASL (or parts of its lexicon) has been introduced in various forms by missionaries, educators, and development workers in a significant number of countries in Africa, Asia, and South America (see Kusters, 2021, for an overview). Deaf people from all over the world have attended universities in the United States (such as Gallaudet University) and often brought ASL signs to their home countries (Parks, 2014). ASL is abundant on the internet in the form of vlogs, stories, performances, and news broadcasts. Therefore, in deaf communities outside of the United States, ASL is often seen as a language with more status, depth, breadth, visibility, and/or complexity than other sign languages (McKee & McKee, 2020). ASL has also been associated with linguistic imperialism and the loss of linguistic diversity in sign languages outside the United States (Moriarty, 2020a). The ideology of ASL being a "super spreader" or "killer" language may or may not shape languaging practices. In some contexts, its use is minimized because of its negative connotations; in others, ASL is seen as a useful bridging language in international deaf communication.

In another example of morality, people choose to use certain forms of signing to align with others and show respect to people from the country they visit, such as deaf tourists picking up "bits" of Indonesian and Balinese sign languages (Moriarty & Kusters, 2021). Everyday sense-making involves words and signs tied to distinct bounded languages, especially among people of different national or local language backgrounds. However, our research shows that mobile deaf people, through their everyday experiences of languaging practices, also challenge language boundaries. Our own meetings demonstrate this, because the MobileDeaf team used combinations of BSL, English, and ASL to communicate effectively. Sign languages are in contact in various forms, ranging from sign-sign contact to the incorporation of mouthings and fingerspelling (Adam & Braithwaite, 2022). Due to historical contact between deaf signers and the iconic motivations of some signs, it is often not possible to determine the origins of a sign (McKee & McKee, 2020; Zeshan & Panda, 2019), and we agree with Pennycook's (2010) argument that the idea of having discrete, countable languages is an ideological project. Classification of languages and languaging practices is a colonial idea that reduces complex situations of languaging and language mixing into easily understandable categories (for the colonizers). In practice, there is no such thing as a delineated, "pure" language bound to a territorial area such as a nation-state. We view language as emergent from contexts of interaction (Pennycook, 2010, p. 85), hence our emphasis on calibrating as a social activity.

Although we believe that language boundaries are ideological (i.e., are themselves language ideologies), we also believe that sign languages are "real" languages, and we acknowledge that boundaries between languages may be important, productive, empowering, or disempowering (Kusters et al., 2020). Within this context, our data not only focus on languaging as a practice, but also on how mobile deaf people are expected to learn bounded languages—not just a few "bits," but attaining fluency. Examples include deaf migrants to the United Kingdom being expected to learn both BSL and (written) English, and deaf refugees in Kakuma Refugee Camp being expected to learn Kenyan Sign Language (KSL) and (written) English. Perceptions of skilled calibrating practices *and* linguistic competency in bounded languages are often tied to opportunities for advancement. However, the system often does not work to people's advantage: Long waiting lists for BSL classes are a barrier to formal language learning for deaf migrants in London.

Many mobile deaf people have complicated feelings about their own language practices and learning processes. It is common for deaf people to have some form of language trauma or to experience the stigma of language deprivation, having faced barriers to informal and formal language learning within the family or in the larger community/village/city (Glickman & Hall, 2019). Many deaf refugees and migrants arriving in new host countries had not formally learned a sign language in the country they left. For these deaf people, learning a new language in their new host country may be paired with an ideological "devaluing" of their previous language practices, which may then be labeled "not language," "village signs," "home sign," or "gesture." For example, many deaf people in Kakuma Refugee Camp claimed that their country of origin does not have a sign language despite evidence to the contrary.

In our analysis, we draw on data collected across the four subprojects to show examples of the ways in which mobile deaf people engage in calibrating and language learning, and how they understand and talk about what they are doing. We draw heavily on linguistic ethnography and on film materials recorded in the field (Moriarty, 2020b), especially our ethnographic films *#deaftravel: Deaf Tourism in Bali, Finding Spaces to Belong,* and the *This Is IS* series. We show how meaning-making is a morally laden, mutually constructed activity that draws on the semiotic resources afforded or constrained by specific life trajectories, ideologies, and communicative settings.

Calibrating

We start with a number of examples showing how deaf people calibrate in international encounters.

- Example A (*#deaftravel*, 01:14:49):[1] Wahyu, the Balinese Deaf Guide, brought a group of deaf tourists from the Netherlands to Bengkala, the "deaf village" in north Bali (see Chapter 6), and introduced them to one of the deaf families living there. The group sat chatting on the porch in front of the house. Using Kata Kolok (the village sign language), one of the deaf villagers asked if two women from the Netherlands were sisters (Figure 8.2a). They did not understand, so another deaf villager (her sister) repeated the question (Figure 8.2b). The latter then turned to Wahyu, who explained to the tourists that the Kata Kolok sign just shown means "sister," using the ASL sign SISTER and mouthing in English (Figure 8.2c). He then added fingerspelling in the ASL/IS alphabet, S-I-S-T-E-R (Figure 8.2d). During this interaction, Wahyu also explained that Kata Kolok is "very different" from BISINDO (Indonesian Sign Language) and gave the example of signs for "age." He fingerspelled A-G-E in ASL/IS alphabet and mouthed in English, and then showed the signs used in the south (of Bali) (Figure 8.2e) and in the village (Figure 8.2f), and a widely used IS sign (Figure 8.2g). Wahyu connected each of these signs to geographical locations, saying that a particular sign is used "here," "over there," and "in the south."
- Example B: Abdi, a refugee from Somalia, was talking about experiencing war in his country in an interview with Amandine in Kakuma Refugee Camp, Kenya. He used a KSL sign that Amandine did not understand (Figure 8.3a). She asked for clarification. Abdi spelled T-R-O-O-P-S using ASL fingerspelling (Figure 8.3b). To check that she had understood

---

1. https://vimeo.com/588352737#t=1h14m49s

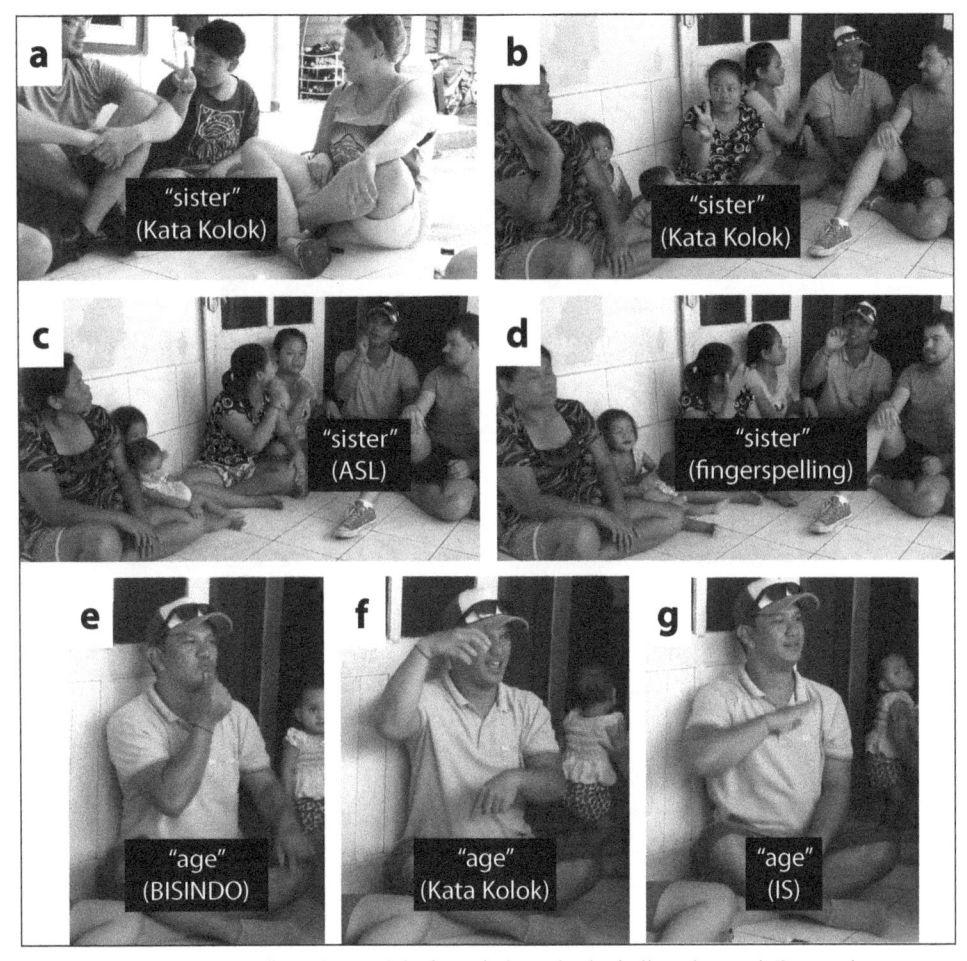

Figure 8.2. Balinese tour guide Wahyu and deaf people from the deaf village discuss differences between Kata Kolok and BISINDO signs.

- him correctly, Amandine replied with the sign in ASL meaning "army" (Figure 8.3c). Abdi seemed to recognize or understand the sign, and he copied Amandine's sign with a slightly different hand orientation (Figure 8.3d).
- Example C (*This Is IS*: Episode 1, 00:12:10):[2] Hyemi from Korea and Lenka S. from the Czech Republic were among a group of youths arriving in Denmark to take part in the Frontrunners course. They first met each other at the train station. After exchanging their sign names, Lenka signed: FROM CZECH-REPUBLIC. Hyemi looked questioningly at Lenka and repeated Lenka's sign. Lenka responded with the sign PRAGUE (Figure 8.4a). Hyemi continued to repeat CZECH-REPUBLIC in a puzzled way (Figure 8.4b), to which Lenka responded by fingerspelling C-Z-E-C-H-R-E-P-U-B using the IS/ASL alphabet (Figures 8.4b–c), while Hyemi simultaneously used her finger to write out the word in Roman script on her palm (Figure 8.4c). Hyemi, who uses a different fingerspelling

2. https://vimeo.com/686852215#t=12m10s

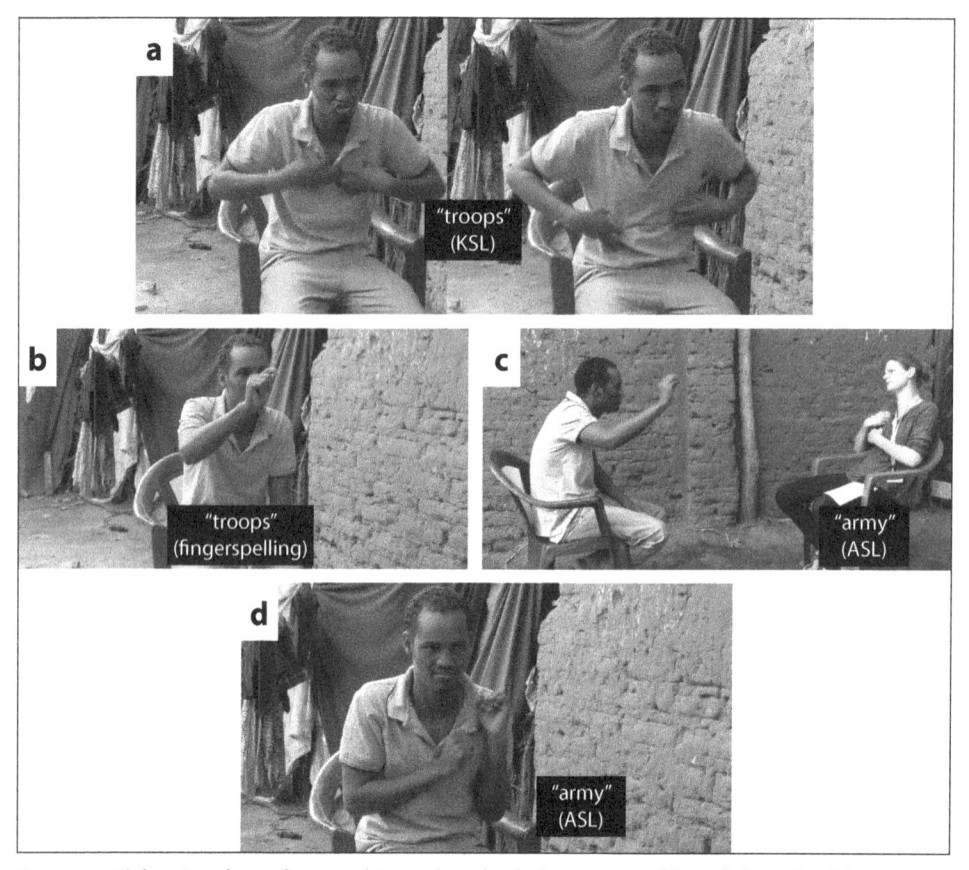

Figure 8.3. Abdi, a Somalian refugee, and Amandine clarify the meaning of "army" through calibration.

alphabet and a different written script in Korea, later explained that this transition from fingerspelling to the Roman script helps her understand it. At the letter "B," Hyemi shook her head to indicate that she gave up, and Lenka switched tactics, signing CLOSE GERMANY with a questioning expression to check whether Hyemi understood. Hyemi responded quickly: GERMANY KNOW. Lenka then visualized where the Czech Republic is situated in relation to Germany (Figure 8.4d) and outlined the shape of the Czech Republic (Figure 8.4e). She then also showed the location of Poland and Austria (in a similar way to Figure 8.4d), along with internationally used sign names for these countries. Hyemi kept repeating the sign CZECH-REPUBLIC. She understood that Lenka was showing where the Czech Republic is located, but she struggled to visualize the map in her head. Lenka ended the interaction by telling Hyemi that she would show it to her on a physical map later, recognizing that the map she had conjured through signs relied on a frame of reference they did not share. Hyemi understood and nodded, signing THANK YOU and NICE TO MEET YOU. The two embraced.

- Example D: Aisha, an Indian woman who had recently migrated to London, asked Sanchayeeta to aid her in advancing her English skills. She sent occasional text messages via WhatsApp, asking Sanchayeeta to explain English text. Aisha sometimes sent screenshots of text, underlining or circling words and sentences she did not understand. In Figure 8.5a,

a	b
"Prague" (sign name)	"Czech Republic" (fingerspelling)
c	d
"Czech Republic" (<= fingerwriting)	"Czech Republic" (location)
e	
"Czech Republic" (shape)	

Figure 8.4. Lenka S. and Hyemi use various calibration strategies to communicate the name and location of the Czech Republic.

Aisha asked Sanchayeeta for the meaning of the word "whether." Sanchayeeta responded at first by explaining the meaning in an English sentence. When Aisha responded that she did not understand, Sanchayeeta sent a BSL video of herself giving a definition. Aisha responded with a BSL video to check whether she had understood the explanation correctly (Figure 8.5b), and a screenshot of the word used in a textbook (Figure 8.5c). Later in the research project, Sanchayeeta changed the strategy in her explanations, using more gifs and emoticons. In Figures 8.5d–g, Aisha asked for the meaning of *nappy* and *tantrums*. Sanchayeeta first thought that Aisha was asking the meaning of the sentences "(nappies) *may still be needed*" and "(tantrums) *may still be a thing*," and explained these in English (Figures 8.5d and 8.5e). However, Aisha clarified that it was the words "nappy" and "tantrum" that she did not understand, and Sanchayeeta explained these using text and gifs (Figures 8.5f and 8.5g).

Across the different subprojects, we found that many of our participants engaged in a collective process of calibrating and language learning, sometimes involving us as researchers (as in Examples B and D). As people engaged in calibrating, they would slow down the speed of their signing or use more visual and gestural styles (e.g., Lenka S. outlining a map in Example C). In the deaf mental map (see Chapter 7), the body can become a geographical entity, which is a widely used method of demonstrating specific places in relation to each other. For example, a hand may

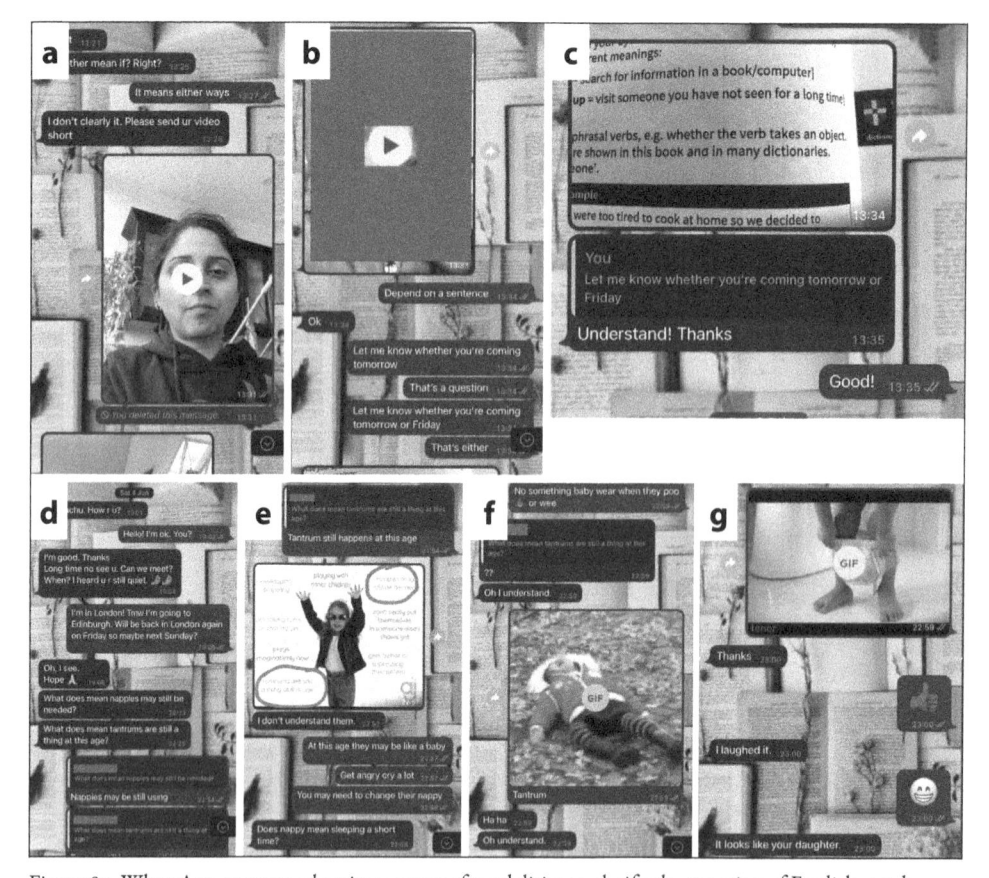

Figure 8.5. WhatsApp messages showing a range of modalities to clarify the meaning of English words.

be used as a map by pointing to the location on the hand corresponding to the approximate geographical location of a specific place (see *#deaftravel*, 00:38:25):[3] Ubud, a town in Bali, is described with a tap of an index finger in the middle of the back of the hand, whereas Bengkala is at the top of the back of the hand, further north than Ubud.

In Examples A and B, previously, people made use of fingerspelling, which helped to identify the term and acted as a bridge for exchanging signs when people knew corresponding English terms for the signs *and* knew the alphabet used in ASL and/or IS (both are similar and widely used). In other situations, this did not work, as the example of "Czech Republic" (Example C) shows. Different communication strategies are used in different spaces and through different media, as shown in Example D where communication via WhatsApp is more text-based than the other interactions and is stretched out over a longer time. Visual elements are inserted by way of emoticons and GIFs, and by using images on which lines and circles are added to point to key terms; sign language videos can also be sent. Example D

---

3. https://vimeo.com/588352737#t=38m25s

illustrates how the semiotic repertoire spans between people *and* objects, text, and images external to people's bodies.

In these and other examples of calibrating, people are oriented toward understanding each other, and they often learn language, such as signs from other languages and the meaning of English words, as part of the process. The use of smartphones can be a mediator, too: We observed the use of phones in face-to-face interactions to pull up a picture or to translate a word or phrase into another written language (see, e.g., 00:25:47 in *This Is IS*: Episode 1).[4] The diversity of people's bodies and their use (or not) of parts of their bodies were reflected in the ways that they calibrated in international space. Examples Annelies observed in her study on IS (Kusters, forthcoming) include deafblind people using Protactile, or touch-based, signing (see Chapter 9 for more on deafblind people's experiences), and writing numbers with a finger on the hand palm rather than holding up a number of fingers. Deaf people whose mouths were covered—for example, those wearing a niqab or a face mask—adapted their signing by using more fingerspelling and adjusting their pace. A deaf person who used a wheelchair used their leg in the role of the nondominant hand. Deaf people at the 19th Winter Deaflympics were observed writing with their finger in the snow or on their snowboards, or simplifying signs when signing with thick gloves.

The people in these interactions were motivated to communicate, to make each other understand. We interpret these examples using the deaf cosmopolitanism concept as defined by Moriarty and Kusters (2021). Deaf cosmopolitanism is an (idealistic) orientation of openness to sameness and difference among deaf people of various backgrounds (see Chapter 1). A common refrain among deaf people is that shared deafness and signing skills lead to potential connection with other deaf people and allow them to communicate across national and linguistic borders (Green, 2014). IS could be said to be a manifestation of deaf cosmopolitanism. A particular scene in the film *#deaftravel: Deaf Tourism in Bali* shows several examples of calibrating during a dinner with members of the local deaf community (00:35:46).[5] The scene concerns Ronja, a woman from Germany who is a new signer of German Sign Language (DGS). New signers are those who have learned how to sign later in life rather than as a child, often outside home or school, and often after acquiring a spoken language first (De Meulder, 2019). Ronja, who was new to IS, had a travel "buddy" from her country, Sabrina, who took responsibility for Ronja's learning of IS and ASL and provided brokering support (see *#deaftravel*, 00:40:47–onward).[6] Sign language brokering is a form of informal interpreting used to mediate expected or experienced communication difficulties (Napier, 2020), and having this support is a form of social capital and an indicator of privilege. On the 10-day multinational and multilingual Travass tour, Sabrina explained that she felt like Ronja was her child and that she felt "responsible" for her enjoyment of the "deaf travel" experience, in which language learning and brokering are central to engaging in deaf sociality. Sabrina was morally oriented toward supporting Ronja's communication with other tourists in the group and with deaf Balinese people, and she used familial and affective terms to describe this orientation (see Chapter 9 for further discussion of family terms). The clip illustrates how calibrating and language learning is a shared task.

---

4. https://vimeo.com/686852215#t=25m47s
5. https://vimeo.com/588352737#t=35m46s
6. https://vimeo.com/588352737#t=40m47s

However, although IS is *international* in that it is used for international communication and incorporates signs from different sign languages, this incorporation is not necessarily evenly distributed. Many signs that are used in conventional versions of IS are from European sign languages or are used in European gestural cultures. The term "International Sign" (or alternatives such as "International Sign Language") is widely understood in Europe, and deaf white Europeans dominate much of the discourse around IS. An example of this also concerns Sabrina. In an interview, she explained that it was important to meet the other person in the middle, and she talked about a young Balinese man she met during the previously mentioned deaf community dinner:

> I was explaining things to him, and he felt lost. [...] I noticed [Balinese deaf people] didn't know English. They only signed without any mouthing, which was hard to follow. They signed their own way [BISINDO]. It was a bit hard, not very gestural with pointing. I said that we do not need examples in signing, we need gestures. For them, the alphabet was hard because they use a two-handed alphabet. I can understand it is hard, but the world uses it [i.e., a one-handed alphabet]. [...] Since I am from Germany and they were from Bali, we should meet in the middle and sign IS. They need to learn IS. IS must be gestural. I learned some of their signs while I was watching carefully. I signed IS gesturally. (*#deaftravel*, 00:40:01)[7]

Calibration is integral to the deaf cosmopolitanism ethos, and both examples concerning Sabrina illustrate "ethical" language practices and the ways in which language ideologies are shaped by moral orientations. However, as the above quotation suggests, not all parties in the communicative encounter calibrate in the same ways, because semiotic resources are unevenly distributed and tied to scales of (im)mobility. Sabrina understood that there were differences and inequalities tied to language and mobility, and she found the Balinese person's calibration strategies unsuitable to international communication.

However, this Balinese person calibrated in different ways, with different semiotic resources and strategies that Sabrina did not necessarily recognize. Palfreyman (2019) found that BISINDO has a high degree of regional variation and that Indonesian signers are constantly calibrating to other signers from elsewhere in the archipelago. In contrast to Ronja, the Balinese deaf person did not have a more experienced "buddy" to share metalinguistic information with them and to support the process of international communication. Instead, the Balinese people worked together as a group to clarify meanings through chaining. Chaining means that different modalities are sequentially employed to highlight equivalents—for example, by fingerspelling the (English) word for a concept and then signing it in the relevant sign language(s), as described in Example A. Other chaining processes include pointing at a written word and then signing/saying it, simultaneously mouthing and signing, or mouthing and fingerspelling (see also Bagga-Gupta, 2000; Tapio, 2019). These various processes contribute to learning different, often overlapping aspects of new languages. An example of this is shown in *#deaftravel*: when Sabrina asked to see the sign for *rice*, one Balinese deaf man demonstrated the BISINDO sign RICE, and the other Balinese man repeated the sign in a validation of its correctness (*#deaftravel*, 00:39:40).[8]

The previous quotation also shows that there are language ideologies about how IS communication should happen: that interlocutors should use "universal" (ASL/IS) fingerspelling (which

---

7. https://vimeo.com/588352737#t=40m01s
8. https://vimeo.com/588352737#t=39m40s

is harder for deaf people who use very different alphabets in their everyday life, such as Hyemi in Example C, previously) and should avoid using too many signs from their own sign languages (such as BISINDO). Instead, what people call "gesturing" or "signing more visually" is valued as a border-crossing visual phenomenon that is not influenced by national sign languages. However, as mentioned before, "gesturing" practices that are commonly used in IS are not necessarily familiar to everyone in the interaction. Finally, the quotation shows that there are language ideologies circulating that define IS as the "golden middle way" (see Moriarty & Kusters, 2021). However, we met many deaf people who did not see IS as "meeting in the middle" but as a "European thing." We return to this later.

As a tourist-facing professional of several years' standing (see Chapter 6), Wahyu has a wealth of experience of calibrating to tourists of different nationalities because his ability to adjust to foreigners from a range of countries is key to his business:

> When I work as a deaf guide, I use IS and Auslan mainly. When I meet deaf people from Bali, I switch to BISINDO, but during work I generally use IS because most people come from America, Belgium, the Netherlands, Germany, and so on. When Australians come, I need to switch the way I sign, and that is a bit more difficult because of their two-handed alphabet. [...] When they slow down it is fine. [...] When a Chinese person comes, I sign differently compared to when a German or a Dutch person comes—I use a different IS. [...] I have to adjust, yes. When deaf people come here and don't understand my IS, I have to adjust. I use some German signs if a German person comes, but only a bit. For example, I will mouth "Willkommen" while signing WELCOME, it is only a bit and we understand each other better after that. But I mostly use IS. [...] I learn while communicating. When I meet a deaf person, I use the signs I learned before, which helps us to communicate.

Wahyu reported that he learns and adopts from other languages, incorporating a range of signs, mouthings, and fingerspelling alphabets into his languaging to various degrees. He also indicated that IS takes different forms, or "looks different," depending on whom he is interacting with. His language learning is connected with tourist mobility, and he uses "bits" from the semiotic repertoire he has accumulated from previous encounters with tourists. Sometimes he has had to adjust to tourists from different countries at once: Erin observed Wahyu changing his fingerspelling system in response to his interlocutors, using BSL/Auslan fingerspelling with tourists from Australia and immediately switching to IS/ASL fingerspelling with deaf Indian and Italian tourists in the same tour group (#deaftravel, 00:47:18).[9] Wahyu also adapted topics and frames of reference to the nationality of the person or group he was guiding at the time. For example, Erin observed that Wahyu talked openly about the Dutch colonization of Indonesia with a tourist from the United States, but he avoided an overly negative framing when he was with tourists from the Netherlands.

Tourist encounters are short-term encounters, ranging from a few hours to a few days in duration. Conversely, Annelies observed a group in which IS was learned and used over a longer time: the Frontrunners course in Denmark. The language of the course is IS, which students acquire through immersion; some already have considerable experience of IS when they arrive, whereas others are still new to it. Over their 9 months in the program, the Frontrunners learn to calibrate in various ways, including by changing their signing speed, being "more visual" or "using gestures," avoiding

---

9. https://vimeo.com/588352737#t=47m18s

ASL signs, and signing some concepts in different ways. Some of this calibrating is learned from their teachers, but much is picked up through trial and error. It appears that deeply rooted in the practice of IS is the cosmopolitan ideology that all participants in the interaction should make an active effort to bridge linguistic differences. Many people value the exchange of national signs, viewing it as a form of communicative creativity and cooperation. Relatedly, many of Annelies's Frontrunners interviewees said that they found IS more difficult to understand if a lot of ASL signs were used because ASL-dominated IS tended to be signed more quickly and is seen as less adaptive, "less visual," and thus less cooperative (Kusters, 2020). Ideologically, using IS is supposed to be "meeting in the middle," to use Sabrina's words; however, we noted that this process tends to be skewed toward ways of calibration and uses of (IS) lexicon that are more particular to Europe.

After 8 months in the Frontrunners program, the students said that they had internalized IS sufficiently, both IS as calibration and conventionalized IS lexicon. Their signing was faster, and they asked for fewer clarifications. Many frequently used signs were understood by all; ASL signs, IS signs, and signs from the students' national sign languages had circulated. However, whereas they recognized that their communication had sped up, they also said that they had become better at slowing down when required and had learned strategies to make themselves more understandable. When signing for outside audiences, on video, or with people in the group who did not understand their signing, students had learned to sign "more visually"—for example, using a large signing space or enacting scenarios. They had learned to use forms of IS with more or less ASL in it, depending on the audience. In other words, they had not only expanded their semiotic repertoires by learning new lexicon but had also learned a variety of calibration strategies to adapt to a variety of audiences.

In this process of calibrating and learning, there were inequalities within the group. Repetition is an important strategy in calibration, but not everyone was equally comfortable asking for repetition. People who understood less had more need for repetition, but they worried about how requesting it would reflect on them. Hyemi, the South Korean woman mentioned in Example C, explained:

> In Korea, it is culturally different—if I don't understand, I can't ask for someone to repeat themselves over and over again. People who ask for repetition because they continually don't understand are seen as inferior. In Asia, we are always polite and calm. I can't always say everything, so instead I stay still [i.e., passive]. Later, I understand [having absorbed and processed new signs]—that is how I learn. It is not easy. I really have to try and ask others. That is important. I don't want to ask the same person over and over again, so instead I ask everyone. Through that approach I can learn. (*This Is IS*: Episode 1, 00:25:59)[10]

Due to her cultural background, Hyemi hesitated to ask for repetition too often. She also expressed concern about national stereotyping, that is, that people will think that "all Koreans are the same and do not understand" (see Chapter 5). "Not understanding" is not purely a question of not knowing particular signs but also not knowing about underlying concepts and cultural mores. In addition to having had less exposure to "European" IS lexicon before arriving at the Frontrunners course, students from the Global South explained that they felt removed from European cultures (*This Is IS*: Episode 1, 01:05:28 onward).[11] Majdi, a student from Jordan, explained:

---

10. https://vimeo.com/686852215#t=25m59s
11. https://vimeo.com/686852215#t=1h5m28s

I come from an Arab country. When they [the other students] refer to something, I can understand the sign, but I don't understand the context or culture. They know many films that I don't know of. We will see how it progresses.

Although Hyemi and Majdi gradually became more comfortable asking questions, Majdi reflected at the end of the course that he still understood "half of what is signed." With less background knowledge about Deaf Studies and Sign Language Studies, Majdi felt it was not possible to "catch up" with the Europeans and the person from the United States in the group. Majdi and Hyemi both felt that they had to work harder to learn IS lexicon as well as English (the language used in mouthings and fingerspelling and on PowerPoint slides), *and* to learn about the other attendees' underlying cultures, in addition to "cultural deaf" concepts. They had a bigger linguistic and cultural distance to bridge. Thus, even as the Frontrunners expanded their semiotic repertoires by learning to calibrate to people with various backgrounds, those with shared frames of references and prior knowledge of IS lexicon were privileged over others. Some students in the group were aware of this and actively brokered communication with students who struggled. Others admitted that they were "lazy" in this regard because they wanted to communicate quickly.

We observed that well-traveled Europeans and people from the United States who are fluent signers tend to say "I am calibrating" to signal a cosmopolitan attitude. In practice, however, it was often new signers and Global Southerners who did most of the calibrating. They experienced the steepest learning curve and worked the hardest to understand certain cultural references (such as the sign for *Einstein*; *This Is IS*: Episode 1, 01:06:04).[12] This labor seemed largely invisible to their (often white) interlocutors, who would announce their own "openness" to cultural differences and willingness to "adapt" their signing. Calibrating and language learning are branded as cosmopolitan, but they are uneven processes that do not happen on a level playing field.

Deaf cosmopolitanism is not limited to people who travel widely to different countries and continents. Amandine met deaf refugees in Kakuma Refugee Camp who come from different countries on the African continent and have broad semiotic repertoires, including signing in different national or local sign languages and writing and/or speaking one or more spoken language(s). Deaf inhabitants of the camp were seen to communicate with each other using different national sign languages, such as ASL and/or KSL, and also using so-called "village signs," also known in the literature as "rural sign language," "rural homesign," "local sign(s)," and "natural sign(s)" (Green, 2022; Nyst et al., 2012). These are forms of signing that have emerged in local communities and that include gestures from the local gesture substrate. Despite using village signs, many deaf refugees considered themselves only to have become good signers when they learned KSL or ASL. In the camp's schools, deaf signers tended to shift toward more "formal" signing, using Signing Exact English (SEE) (which they called "ASL," as discussed later in this chapter) and KSL. Historically, KSL has been strongly influenced by ASL, and this influence was evident in the signing taking place in schools; however, when people were informally communicating outside of school, they shifted toward informal KSL, using signs specific to Kenya and Kakuma Refugee Camp and incorporating signs they had picked up in their home countries. People thus calibrated according to the interlocutors and contexts, and village signs remained part of their repertoires. Abdi, from Example

---

12. https://vimeo.com/686852215#t=1h6m4s

B, explained that he used village signs from Somalia to converse with his deaf Somali friend who was also living in the camp.

In this process of calibration, certain resources are privileged over others. On the structural level, KSL is seen as the main sign language used in the camp, whereas ASL has been imported into the schools (see Chapter 3). Historically, ASL was dispersed throughout Africa through the establishment of deaf schools, often crowding out local sign languages and tending to be considered of higher status (Nyst, 2010). ASL has influenced KSL through missionary workshops, American sponsorship of some deaf schools via the provision of ASL teaching materials, deaf Kenyans who have lived or studied in the United States, and volunteers who visit Kenya from different countries (Morgan et al., 2015). When communicating with Amandine, deaf refugees in Kakuma Refugee Camp used ASL and English fingerspelling (in the ASL alphabet) as bridging languages when Amandine did not know particular signs in KSL. In Example B, we saw that ASL functioned as a lingua franca.

Amandine noted that in informal conversations or interviews she had with deaf inhabitants of the camp, they tended to use the same signs that Amandine used—that is, from ASL or from IS, instead of KSL. As we explain in the following section on language learning in migration contexts, newcomers to the United Kingdom are often expected to learn the host country's sign language (i.e., BSL); however, in the context of Kakuma Refugee Camp, deaf refugees calibrated toward *Amandine's* language use, despite her being the newcomer in Kenya and in the process of acquiring KSL. Deaf refugees using non-KSL signs with Amandine could be interpreted as calibrating toward someone perceived to be of higher status and/or whose language is given higher status. However, another interpretation is that it was an intuitive attempt to share the burden of communication with someone learning a new sign language, because refugees in the camp were also observed calibrating toward each other in similar ways.

Annelies did field work in a very different site in Kenya: the DOOR International campus in Nairobi, where various teams were working to translate the Bible into their national sign languages. As mentioned in Chapter 5, KSL was seen as the lingua franca of the campus, and teams who spent time (often months or years) there were expected to learn KSL through immersion and socialization (similar to the Frontrunners' acquisition of IS). Indian Sign Language (ISL) also made its way into the semiotic repertoire at DOOR because of interactions between deaf Indians and Kenyans in both Kenya and India. Each translation team had several consultants who were expected to learn their team's sign language, so deaf consultants from Costa Rica and Kenya learned Mozambican Sign Language to work with a team of translators from Mozambique. Kenyans were also aware that they were in a privileged position due to being from the host country, and they tried to mitigate this. Zablon, one of the Kenyan translators, said: "They learn KSL, but it doesn't mean they must know KSL in its entirety. I also learn their language. If I don't understand something, they explain in their language, which means I learn too" (*This Is IS*: Episode 2, 00:06:22).[13] Paul, the director of DOOR International Africa, had worked with teams in Ethiopia, Tanzania, Uganda, and Nigeria, and he explained his communication with deaf people from different African countries as follows:

> I think the best way is for me to sign KSL, and for them to express themselves in their sign language. We meet in the middle and connect, because it helps them to see the bigger picture. [...] Most of the time it is a 50/50 split between their signing and my own. I would not know their sign language in

---

13. https://vimeo.com/728777656#t=6m22s

its entirety, and the same would go for them. It is a sharing form of communication which is called C-O-D-E M-I-X-I-N-G. It is my signing and their signing integrated together, and we would be able to understand each other clearly that way. (*This Is IS*: Episode 2, 00:03:21)[14]

There are obvious parallels here with strategies used in IS: Language socialization and calibration are two sides of the same coin, and an open orientation is key. However, whereas IS use is often seen as the golden middle way, there are signing communities of practice where other international communication norms have emerged from calibrating (see Part II in Zeshan & Webster, 2020). At the DOOR campus, signs from the employees' national sign languages were used alongside ASL and ISL when people mixed during meals and sports. At the same time, people were working on translations *between* sign languages, meaning there was a strong emphasis on learning each other's sign languages and keeping bounded sign languages separate during translation work. There were spaces of calibration (e.g., dinners, sports) and spaces of separation (the translation labs).

Exchanging and Bestowing Signs

Not only are sign languages the key to deaf sociality itself, but they are also a frequent topic of discussion. Deaf people in multilingual groups often compare their respective signs for concepts, which has developed into a "deaf meme" video template that circulates on social media. Often, these videos are created by deaf tourists or deaf project workers who have traveled to another country and encountered deaf "locals." They usually involve two people in the frame of the video signing at the same time, so as to compare the lexicon of different sign languages. These videos are made by multiple people in different locations—for example, a man from Bengkala has posted a video on Instagram of himself signing the alphabet in BISINDO alongside a woman from Germany signing the alphabet in DGS. In her online ethnography, Erin found multiple videos produced by deaf people of different nationalities with different sign language backgrounds, demonstrating how their sign languages differ from each other; this may be seen as an example of the commodification of languages in tourism. The social media videos are the result of, or elicited version of, a common practice in international deaf encounters: exchanging signs. Our observations of conversations between deaf people of different nationalities led to the insight that deaf people in transnational encounters often engage in metalinguistic conversations, comparing certain signs from their native sign languages, speculating about the origins of certain signs, and/or discussing the influence of hegemonic sign languages, especially ASL and BSL, on IS and on less widely used sign languages.

The videos produced for social media compare signs in the manner of a dictionary, whereas the MobileDeaf ethnographic films feature naturalistic metalinguistic discussions. For example, in the beginning of *This Is IS*: Episode 1, a scene at a coffee machine shows three Frontrunners from Brazil, the United States, and Togo exchanging their signs for "sugar," the meaning reinforced by pointing at the sugar and fingerspelling S-U-G-A-R; they then note both similarities and differences in their respective signs, going into more depth than the social media videos (00:07:26).[15]

---

14. https://vimeo.com/728777656#t=3m21s
15. https://vimeo.com/686852215#t=7m26s

In *This Is IS*: Episode 2, three deaf men from Mozambique, South Sudan, and Kenya compare their signs for numbers by signing them simultaneously (00:07:23; Figure 8.6).[16]

In *#deaftravel*, tourists from India and Italy and their Indonesian guide, exchange signs for "belief." When visiting a Balinese temple, Wahyu, the guide, talked about belief using the Auslan sign and English mouthings. Heena, from India, copied the Auslan sign that Wahyu used and asked whether she was reproducing it accurately; Wahyu repeated the sign twice, modeling it for Heena and confirming she had it right. An Italian man standing behind Wahyu then also copied the sign. Heena then asked an Italian woman for the Italian sign for "belief." In response, Wahyu produced the LIS (Italian Sign Language) sign, while the woman (who had not seen Wahyu nor understood Heena) copied the sign that Heena had produced. The Italian woman then turned to Wahyu, who repeated the LIS sign to her; she and then Heena copied it. In this short interaction, lasting only a few seconds, Heena learned and embodied two new signs for "belief," and people copied each other multiple times (*#deaftravel*, 00:46:11).[17] Copying new signs is a key strategy for learning: The learner takes in the new sign and then demonstrates through reproducing it whether or not they have mastered it and understood it (Hoffmann-Dilloway, 2021). Wahyu played a key role here because he knew several signs signifying "belief," and from there engaged in chaining (see Tapio, 2019).

It is through the comparison of signs, in which copying and chaining are key practices, that the differences between signs are embodied, indexed, and marked, rather than the similarities. It is effectively a way of noting that DEAF-SAME (see Chapter 1) does not mean SIGN-SAME. However, the people in the MobileDeaf films do engage in comparing signs as a form of sameness work, by which we mean the ways in which deaf people of different national backgrounds

Figure 8.6. Deaf men from Mozambique, South Sudan and Kenya signing "6."

---

16. https://vimeo.com/728777656#t=7m23s
17. https://vimeo.com/588352737#t=46m11s

connect to one another and establish DEAF-SAME through metalinguistic discussions about sign languages. We therefore see the act of comparing and copying signs as an example of deaf cosmopolitanism. Being able to pinpoint and compare specific signs allows people to align, understand, and exchange with each other. By showing openness toward each other's signs, they take a moral stance toward cosmopolitanism.

Sometimes, signs learned in this way come to function as souvenirs. Souvenirs have a long association with travel and the memory of travel; they are material objects of tourism, and they travel home with the people who acquire or purchase them. Souvenirs are incarnations of memory; they can be a thing, a place, an occasion, an event, or even a person that recreates memories of travel (Morgan & Pritchard, 2005). In international deaf mobilities, sign names may function as souvenirs. Sign names may be based on striking physical or personal characteristics of the person, their history, their name (including loan translations or initializations), a memory associated with them, or even the enrollment number by which they were known at their deaf school (Day & Sutton-Spence, 2010). While they were working in Bali, Erin had a conversation with Jorn (the cameraman with whom she worked on *#deaftravel*) about his sign name, which led to the insight that sign names sometimes served as a reminder of a person's mobility. Jorn was given his sign name, which looks like a figure diving into the water, during his participation as a swimmer for Belgium in the 20th Summer Deaflympics in Australia in 2005. Jorn kept this sign name as a reminder of his experience of participating in the Deaflympics.

Having sign names that originated abroad is a recurring theme in the data. Kareer, a man from London who was a part of the Travass tour group in Bali, explained that he was given his sign name by young deaf students when he worked as a Voluntary Service Overseas (VSO) volunteer in the Philippines. His sign name is an iconic sign that denotes "beard"; the students gave it to him because he had a beard at the time. Kareer no longer has a beard, but he kept the sign name as a memento of his experience in the Philippines. Ronja, from Germany, who was part of the same tour group, did not have a sign name yet, and one of the ongoing themes of the 10-day tour was the process of assigning her a sign name. On the island of Lombok, as they waited for their boat to arrive, Erin observed the group discussing their sign names and debating what Ronja's sign name should be. This became a humorous exchange because different members of the group used their observations of Ronja to create signs based on her characteristics and behavior.

Like souvenirs, language also plays a significant role in tourism as a marker of "authenticity" (Heller, 2003). In their study of the linguistic landscape of Chinatown in Washington, DC, Leeman and Modan (2009) write:

> Souvenirs with writing in another language signal that one has been somewhere foreign, exciting or exotic, and thus serve as commodified markers of distinction as well as keepsakes of the experience. (p. 340)

Encountering a "foreign" or minority language in the linguistic landscape can give visitors to a country the sense of having visited an authentic place rather than going to a "tourist trap" (Leeman & Modan, 2009). In the "deaf village" in Bali (see Chapter 6), deaf tourists tended to learn a few signs that are used in the village, such as the sign DEAF, mediated through Wahyu (see Figure 8.7a, and *#deaftravel*, 01:09:16).[18] They were thus exposed not only to BISINDO (through interactions with Wahyu and other Indonesian deaf people) but also to Kata Kolok, the sign language used in the village. Tourists tended to learn a few specific signs through Wahyu's demonstrations while brokering conversations between the tourists and villagers, as shown in Example A (see Figure 8.2).

An Indian deaf tourist, Harish, who was on honeymoon to Bali with his wife Heena, talked about "taking signs home" in the same way as taking a souvenir home:

> It's fun; when we come back from traveling, we feel the need to meet up with friends and discuss new signs and what we've learned. I think that's the deaf way. To be fascinated by signs and report back what you've learned, and that way you pass on knowledge. If they go there one day, they will already know some of the signs. [. . .] So, by telling our friends back in India, when they visit the same places [as us], they can reference us and the locals remember and that's an essential part of the deaf community, the close bonds that we form. For example, one of our friends might ask us what the Indonesian sign LIKE is [uses the ISL sign, then gives both the ASL and BISINDO signs]. If one of our friends asks us, we would show them and that's how we exchange information. Also, we will be taking back their sign DEAF [Figure 8.7b], as people will no doubt find that fascinating. In that way, we learn from each other in our network where we can import and export signs. That's the deaf way of doing this. (*#deaftravel*,00:46:44)[19]

Heena and Harish both talked about sharing new signs and new knowledge with their friends after they returned home from their travels. This is a form of deaf development (Friedner, 2015b), where deaf people pool resources and knowledge with their own deaf networks (see Chapter 7). As Harish put it, to be fascinated by new signs and to pool semiotic resources and social capital "is the deaf way." Sharing signs is a form of networking, anchoring connections that can be drawn on in the future. By showing his friends in India the BISINDO sign DEAF, Harish introduces a point of reference for possible future encounters between his friends and the people in Indonesia. The sign itself is a mnemonic device for both Harish and his network; as the BISINDO signs DEAF and LIKE travel from Bali to India, a potential future encounter between Heena and Harish's friends and the deaf people they met in Bali is established. As BISINDO signs become part of their repertoires, they may act as a talisman for future networking, as Harish and Heena's friends could, on a visit to Bali, use these signs *and* explain who taught the BISINDO signs to them, thereby potentially plugging into Heena and Harish's network.

People using signs they had picked up from others is something we also observed in the Frontrunners course. As students interacted with each other and with their teachers over a period of months, they naturally adopted signs from each other. In *This Is IS*: Episode 1, we see the teachers in positions of authority and influence, often standing in front of the classroom. Students picked up signs from them, such as a widely used IS sign, ATTITUDE (00:28:56, Figure 8.8a),[20] and a Finnish sign, IDENTITY (01:15:19, Figure 8.8b).[21] Students also picked up signs from each other:

---

18. https://vimeo.com/588352737#t=1h9m16s
19. https://vimeo.com/588352737#t=46m44s
20. https://vimeo.com/686852215#t=28m56s
21. https://vimeo.com/686852215#t=1h15m19s

Figure 8.7. Demonstrating the signs for "deaf" in Kata Kolok (a) and BISINDO (b).

Figure 8.8. Teachers at Frontrunners demonstrating the IS sign ATTITUDE (a) and the Finnish sign IDENTITY (b).

For example, the Catalan signs AGREE (Figure 8.9a) and DISAGREE (Figure 8.9b) and the Libras (Brazilian) sign FINISHED (Figure 8.9c, with Portuguese mouthing, 01:15:59).[22]

The Frontrunners lived in small groups in cottages on the campus, where the atmosphere was more informal than the classroom and often playful. Here, they picked up many more signs from each other's sign languages. In *This Is IS*: Episode 1, students are shown laughing and teasing each other by using signs from Denmark, Italy, and Jordan (01:20:38).[23] The students joked about using Danish signs, and then they exchanged their respective signs for "proud." Majdi, from Jordan, mixed the Italian and Arabic signs into one composite sign, made possible by the two signs being located in different places on the body (Figure 8.10). Majdi showed amusement at the Italian sign PROUD, because it reminded him of shampoo. Esther, from Spain, teased him that this is an example of "linguicism" (language oppression), a term they had just learned in class.

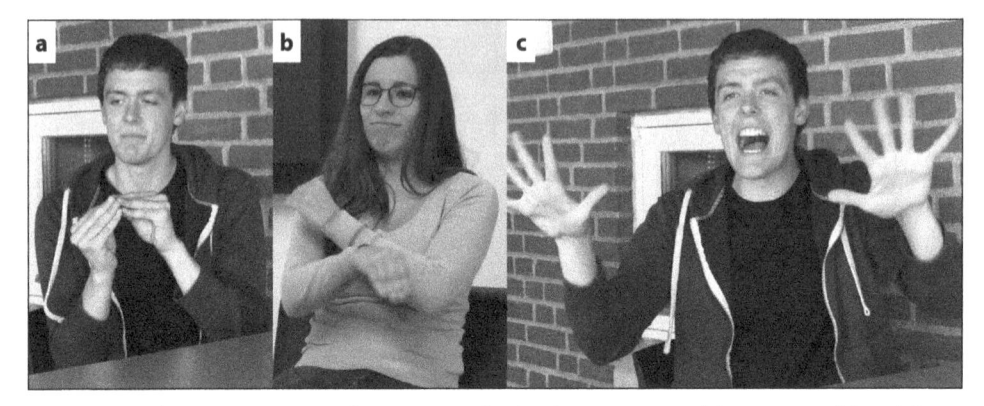

Figure 8.9. Students at Frontrunners demonstrating the Catalan signs AGREE (a), DISAGREE (b), and the Libras sign FINISHED (c).

Figure 8.10. Frontrunner Majdi simultaneously produces Arabic and Italian signs for PROUD.

---

22. https://vimeo.com/686852215#t=1h15m59s
23. https://vimeo.com/686852215#t=1h20m38s

In the same scene, we see the other students showing amusement with Arabic signs and mouthings that they have learned from Majdi. Majdi appeared to enjoy that the other students were so entertained by his signs, which, as Esther explained to Annelies in an interview, are "completely not visual" and "very different." Here, we see how language play may have embedded within it a tendency to signal othering of sign languages and, by implication, the people who use them. It seemed that Arabic signs were primarily seen as a source of humor and entertainment.

In contrast to Majdi, Hyemi seemed to have experienced people laughing at her signs as discriminatory. She mentioned an example of people making fun of a sign she used and wondered if it was racism:

> One day, one of them made fun of me, and I was offended. I was wondering if they did it because of racism. [...] The signs for "hearing" here [in Europe] and in Asia are different [see Figure 8.11]. They laughed at the Asian sign HEARING [Figure 8.11b]. I argued back why the European sign HEARING [Figure 8.11a] is not great, and how it can be confused for DEAF since it might seem the person does not speak. We discussed it and pranked each other until we all accepted our differences. Now we use both signs for "hearing" flexibly. (*This Is IS*: Episode 1, 01:12:12)[24]

Linguistic humor can be a form of language shaming, and in some cases, it is based on linguistic racism, as Hyemi suggested in the previous example. Language shaming (Piller, 2017) refers to interactions that deride, disparage, or demean particular ways of using language, and practices and ideologies that produce or perpetuate unequal linguistic power. It frames certain ways of using language as "backward" or "stupid," and this framing is often directed toward language users who are migrants or people whose languages are less dominant or less widely known outside their territorialized contexts, including the sign languages used by deaf signers in the Global South. This is a reflection of the power dynamics involved in interactions between people of different positionalities. Linguistic racism can be explicit, including abusive and racially charged attacks targeting people's language use, but it can also be more implicit and subtle (Dovchin, 2020). In the case of humor, it can be hard to identify.

Figure 8.11. Frontrunner Hyemi demonstrates the sign HEARING as used in Europe (a) and Asia (b).

---

24. https://vimeo.com/686852215#t=1h12m12s

Laughing about or critiquing signs can, however, also be the result of cosmopolitan wonder at variety in language use, rooted in genuine curiosity about difference, and can lead people to converse happily about language differences. People can find each other's pronunciation or word choice cute, funny, or sexy, and they can discuss these at length on, for example, social media (Rymes, 2020). The line between wonderment and curiosity at each other's signs (e.g., Harish's wonderment about the BISINDO sign for "deaf") on the one hand, and linguistic racism or language shaming on the other, can be thin, especially when the involved people are friends. In the Frontrunners group, we found that friendships between students made it difficult for them to determine whether or not these occurrences were examples of racism. In the following example from Erin's research in Bali, the interaction described did not happen between friends, and it resulted in an altercation. Ferdy Yanto, a deaf teacher at the school for deaf children in Denpasar, explained an experience that he had had with two women from Croatia, where they disparaged the way that the letter "A" is signed in BISINDO:

> The only person I had a bad experience with was with two dirty-minded lesbians from Croatia. We have similar alphabets, but we sign the letter A differently from them [see Figure 8.12; the Croatian letter A uses the middle finger]. She [signed A in Croatian Sign Language, then] flipped me the middle fingers, which is negative in our culture. I was not angry, I only said that she needs to show some respect. [...] That is forbidden—what that person from Croatia did is forbidden. (see *#deaftravel*, 01:00:00)[25]

The Croatian tourists appeared to want Yanto to change his signing to conform to their own norms, which he found distasteful:

> BISINDO is beautiful, there is no need to sign the same as it is done in Croatia. I showed them respect since they are tourists in Bali. I said that showing a middle finger is not appropriate in Balinese culture, and that first they need to learn our language. These people didn't know anything. That is the reason: They had no education, and that is why they tried to influence our sign language. I told them to show respect to our culture. The people just left without even saying thank you. Fine—no problem—go away.

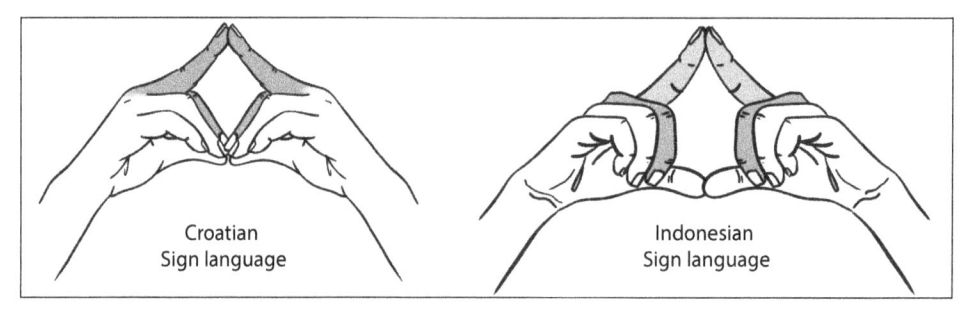

Figure 8.12. The distinction between the fingerspelled letter A in Croatian Sign Language (left) and BISINDO (right).

---

25. https://vimeo.com/588352737#t=1h0m0s

These excerpts give an example of the ways that tourists engage in language shaming. According to Yanto, these women did not like the way that the letter "A" is signed in BISINDO, and they tried to force their perspective—and their sign—on him, "flipping the middle finger" at him in the process. Yanto pushed back by telling them that they needed to respect Bali or leave; however, he also claimed that he was not angry and was respectful toward them because they were tourists in Bali. Bali's economy is heavily dependent on tourism, and it should be noted that hearing Indonesian people shared similar ambivalent sentiments with Erin, telling her that they were both appreciative of tourism-based income and also angry because of the ways in which tourists violated their religious beliefs. For example, menstruating women are explicitly forbidden from visiting temples; Erin's interviewees attributed the increased frequency of volcanic eruptions on the island to disrespectful tourist behavior and flouting these religious rules.

Deaf cosmopolitanism is related to the mobility of language ideologies, semiotic resources, concepts, and people at different scales. This is illustrated by Yanto's observation that the two tourists from Croatia "didn't know anything [...] and that is why they tried to influence our sign language." Yanto's observation is a commentary on the Croatian tourists' lack of cosmopolitanism because they did not calibrate in a way that he saw as appropriate, in contrast to his own openness to and respect for difference.

As Yanto narrated his interaction with the Croatian tourists to Erin, he dismissed them with negative facial expressions and described them as "dirty-minded lesbians from Croatia." Because Erin did not meet these tourists, we do not know whether they were actually lesbians, but this example shows how language ideologies can be used to position people and the ways in which this can occur at multiple levels and from different directions—for example, that Yanto's characterization of these women as "dirty-minded lesbians from Croatia" followed them criticizing BISINDO and making offensive gestures toward him. It also suggests that when people do not mutually respect each other in terms of culture, education, sexual orientation, and so on, they may be less generous in their interpretation and acceptance of each other's signs, showing a "failure" of deaf cosmopolitanism.

Learning a New National Sign Language

The examples in the previous section feature the informal learning of bits of national sign languages in short-term contexts of mobility: through tourism, on residential courses, and while undertaking fieldwork. In the context of long-term mobility (migration), expectations of language learning are often more explicit and have higher stakes attached. Deaf migrants are often expected to know or learn two or more new languages upon arrival in a host country: the (written version of) the main spoken language and a/the national sign language. Some of these expectations are official—for example, migrants may have to demonstrate sufficient written language proficiency to obtain residence permits. However, the expectation to learn is usually more implicit. The ability to use the host country's national sign language(s) is typically linked to feelings of belonging (see Chapter 9), access to certain social spaces, and access to educational spaces.

As has been shown, there are different processes involved in language learning, and several routes toward it, both formal and informal. Whereas formal education is often perceived as the most appropriate way to learn a new language, we have seen that informal language learning is an important feature of deaf sociality: Mobile deaf people typically pick up new signs from those they meet, even briefly. Learning a new language (signed, spoken, or written) is likely to involve the strategy of "copying," discussed in the previous section, as well as translating new vocabulary via a lingua franca (e.g., English, IS, ASL), often through the process of chaining. For example, some mobile deaf people learn the national sign language of the new country first, and then they apply their knowledge of the accompanying mouthings when learning the written version of the national spoken language. This was the experience of Sujit, Annelies's husband, who learned VGT (Flemish Sign Language) and in so doing became able to recognize written Dutch words from their similarity to VGT mouthings.

There are structural differences in who can or cannot easily learn a new national sign language. The examples that follow show that the learning of a new national sign language upon migration is a multilayered racialized, classed, and gendered process. It is also an emotional process that results in different feelings for different people, including pleasure, surprise, disappointment, and frustration.

We start with examples from the United Kingdom, both as a research site (London) and as the site of our research team's base (Edinburgh). In the United Kingdom, deaf spaces are typically dominated by the use of BSL, Sign Supported English (SSE; a mix of BSL and English), and English in various modalities. Many migrants are not necessarily familiar with BSL, because the linguistic distance between BSL and the sign language(s) they already know varies. BSL is linguistically close to sign languages such as Auslan and New Zealand Sign Language (NZSL), but it is considerably distant from others, such as ASL. Some deaf migrants to the United Kingdom learn BSL online in advance of moving, whether via webcam conversations and/or through watching videos, but most are socialized into BSL *after* arrival, such as the Indian female migrants whom Sanchayeeta interviewed; they learned BSL from their new husbands in the United Kingdom.

Not knowing BSL does not mean that deaf signers will be completely unable to engage in British deaf spaces, however. As we have seen, many deaf people (new migrants and deaf people in the host country alike) are skilled at calibrating and are able and willing to communicate flexibly. Additionally, many deaf people who live in the United Kingdom are knowledgeable in sign languages other than BSL (such as ASL), having traveled or lived abroad. This previous language knowledge can help when communicating with new migrants. However, within institutional fields, including service provision to deaf people (e.g., nongovernmental organizations [NGOs], social services, education programs), BSL is dominant; hence, migrants require a degree of mastery of BSL to access these fields. Many migrants have reported finding it easier to communicate with other deaf people than with hearing people, including hearing BSL interpreters; however, it is hearing BSL interpreters who provide the bulk of sign language access to services. The desire to learn "proper" and "pure" BSL can be related to the wish to access these services.

Our first example of language learning in the context of migration concerns three of the authors of this chapter, who migrated to Scotland from Belgium, Germany, and the United States at the beginning of the MobileDeaf project. Deaf professional academic mobility is highly privileged mobility: We came to the United Kingdom upon securing employment or a funded doctoral position (see Chapter 2). In order to enroll as a doctoral student at Heriot-Watt University, Amandine was required to demonstrate her knowledge of written English through an IELTS test; for BSL, however, there was no requirement to demonstrate fluency or enroll in a formal course. Instead, in common with the tendency for internationally mobile deaf professionals to learn new sign languages informally, we acquired BSL by socialization.

The priority for the MobileDeaf team was to understand and to be understood, without necessarily adhering to language boundaries. Annelies had picked up BSL in Bristol (England) years earlier, and she mixed her southern English signs with IS. Erin and Amandine were both new

BSL learners, and Amandine's emerging BSL incorporated Northern Irish signs learned from her (then new) partner. She had previously learned ASL, so she and Erin used ASL to fill in the gaps in their knowledge of BSL. Steve and Sanchayeeta, the British people in the group, were familiar with both ASL and IS as well.

The team's mixed language practices (BSL variations, ASL, and IS) initially limited our ability to work efficiently with some BSL interpreters, and it also produced tension with some hearing BSL learners at the university. The department offers degree courses for training BSL interpreters, and there is a group of deaf and hearing signers (research assistants, master's/doctoral researchers, postdoctoral researchers, and other staff) researching various topics related to deaf people and sign languages. Within this larger group, some deaf and hearing people knew IS and/or ASL and were comfortable mixing sign languages, but within wider departmental activities, there was the expectation that we should use BSL as much as possible. One hearing new signer of BSL expressed frustration about their own acquisition of BSL because of the lack of "pure" or "correct" BSL used in meetings and workshops. Other hearing staff members and doctoral students expressed (to us or to others) that they could not understand our signing. These hearing people had English-speaking privilege and used this within the university. The complex mosaic of language privileges and language choices foregrounded the MobileDeaf team's work.

Over time, as our BSL improved, our repertoires changed to fit particular spaces. We made more effort to learn and use "correct" BSL at the university, retaining our more flexible use of ASL and IS in informal settings—such as when socializing at Annelies's home, where ISL and VGT were also used. An example of how blurred language boundaries were in our practices, and how context dependent, is that for several months, Erin assumed that the sign she had learned at Annelies's home for *wine* (a topic more common in informal spaces than in academic workshops) was a VGT sign, and not a BSL sign.

In common with the teams of translators at DOOR International in Kenya, the MobileDeaf team alternated between spaces where sign languages are mixed (*spaces of calibration*) and spaces in which we were expected to adhere to (sign) language boundaries (*spaces of separation*). Our personal experience of this brought to the fore the ways in which signed communication can be very flexible in practice, but it can also be a source of anxiety due to the expectation of "correct" language in some contexts. "Correct" BSL was challenging to pick up informally because we frequently translanguaged with people inside and outside of the MobileDeaf team. Language learning, language practices, and language ideologies had always been at the forefront of our research agenda, but they also became personal to us as a team of deaf researchers, of whom half were migrants to the United Kingdom and new language learners. The situation of having to rapidly learn and use one or more new sign languages in a range of different registers is the reality for many deaf academic professionals (Byun, 2020).

Other examples of language learning in the context of migration are given next. These examples relate to people who had already mastered a sign language and then added BSL to their repertoire; the experience of learning a sign language for the first time after moving to the United Kingdom, and the resulting shift in identity, was discussed in Chapter 4. Starting with the subproject on migration to London, many of Sanchayeeta and Steve's research participants undertook informal processes of language learning similar to those of the MobileDeaf team; some also attended formal BSL courses. Pedros, a man from Brazil in his 20s, talked about his aspiration to learn BSL, and he worked to improve his fluency by attending courses. Having first visited the United Kingdom on holiday, Pedros decided to move there because he believed there to be better opportunities for deaf people—one of many examples in this book of how different types of mobilities (e.g., tourism and migration) are linked. Pedros stated that he aspires to be able to communicate fluently in BSL with deaf and hearing BSL signers, and he described his experience of language learning:

> When I met people, they would sign in BSL so fast, and I couldn't understand the two-handed fingerspelling. Even the signs went over my head. I had to practice little by little with my friend. He taught me and I enjoyed making progress with this different sign language. It was interesting. My signing improved, as did my communication. I surprised myself with my own BSL skills. Then I went to City Lit [college], where I did [a Regulated Qualification Framework test] Level 1 [in] BSL and I enjoyed signing away. My BSL got better and better, and I was able to communicate within the deaf community. I was determined to keep improving.

Pedros experienced pleasure and surprise at his own improving skills. Importantly, practicing BSL with his friend allowed him to establish a base level of fluency upon which he could build by taking a formal class. He found that as his communication improved, so did his feeling of belonging within the British deaf community.

Not every migrant has both the opportunity and the tenacity to learn BSL, however. Some people with learning disabilities, language deprivation, and some forms of neurodivergence may have difficulties learning BSL, whether in a (neuro)typical classroom setting or by informal interactions with (neurotypical/able-bodied) people. Furthermore, life circumstances can create barriers. Meera, who moved to the United Kingdom from India, is a working woman and her children's primary caregiver, and has limited time to immerse herself in BSL. Her experience demonstrates the classed and gendered nature of access to language learning. She noted that she had been in the United Kingdom for nearly two decades, but she felt that she still did not know BSL well:

> Now it has been 17 years, and I still haven't mastered BSL skills. I am disappointed. No time to go to deaf events, pubs and other social gatherings. No time to learn to sign. I [am responsible for] two children, cooking and the house. I used to work from Monday to Saturday. I used to work in central London and had no time to learn sign. I just gave up, and now I prefer to use SSE. It suits me, because I use lip patterns and have hearing friends in my area. It is full of hearing mums and there are no deaf ones. You understand? It is hard work [to learn BSL]. There are some British people who know ASL. I use ASL with them like [with other Indian deaf migrants], they know ASL.

Meera undertook traditionally gendered work, which limited her ability to engage in informal BSL learning. She labeled her language use as SSE and noted that this enabled her to socialize with other (hearing) mothers who communicated in spoken English. She grew up with an oral approach in school and was able to speak; she had also learned ASL because some deaf schools in India teach using ASL rather than ISL (also the case in Kenya, where ASL is present in deaf education alongside KSL), and she used ASL to communicate with some deaf people.

In a different scenario, Shahina, another of Sanchayeeta's participants in the London study, explained how time constraints, work, and networks shaped her language learning. Shahina was first exposed to ASL at her school in India, and she had been educated at Gallaudet University and two other universities in the United States, living there for a number of years prior to moving to the United Kingdom. She owns a business in the United Arab Emirates and, prior to the coronavirus lockdowns, frequently visited her family in India. As a result, she was hypermobile between countries, and she felt she had not fully settled in the United Kingdom. There, she used ASL with her new husband. Her hypermobility resulted in her feeling unmotivated to become fluent in BSL:

> I don't have the motivation to learn BSL because the timing is wrong. I fly regularly to Dubai and other places. I haven't settled in this country yet; I have no stability yet. I fly to Dubai for work and to America to see my friends, to India to attend my cousins' weddings, so I fly a lot and I don't stay here constantly. So, I don't try BSL with people. If I'm here constantly, I will use BSL with people. When I see an NHS doctor, I don't have a problem with [communicating with] a BSL interpreter. My access via an interpreter seems fine, they seemed to understand me so it's fine, I'm confident.

In the few settings where she needed to, Shahina felt confident working with BSL interpreters, and she felt that English mouthing facilitated her communication with BSL users; she thus did not feel the urgency to learn more BSL lexicon. In this example, we can see how aspiration, class, and mobility can lead to *not* engaging in language learning. Shahina not only referenced her own hypermobility, and the resulting language switches, but also how the mobility of others had an impact on language use in London. She referred to the Shakespeare's Head pub, a London pub where international deaf people gather regularly (see Chapter 9), and she noted that BSL was not exclusively used there but was featured alongside IS and other sign languages. She thus did not see this pub and other spaces where sign languages were mixed as optimal spaces to learn BSL. This is reminiscent of the situation encountered by the MobileDeaf team at Heriot-Watt University: Participating in a mixed international space can slow down national sign language learning.

However, in an interview a year later, Sanchayeeta remarked that Shahina's use of ASL had decreased and that she was using BSL signs for terms she had previously expressed in ASL (e.g., UNIVERSITY). When Sanchayeeta pointed this out to Shahina, she confirmed that she had been signing more in BSL. The context for this shift was that her attachment to London had strengthened. Shahina had, through necessity, spent more time in the United Kingdom during the lockdown periods, and she had started to envision London as a place where she wanted to raise her children and make her home, so she became more open to learning BSL.

The extent to which deaf signers pick up BSL after moving to the United Kingdom is, thus, hugely variable. Some deaf migrants gradually shift to full BSL; others do not—because of barriers, because it is not their priority, or because it is not necessary for them. Similarly, while Frontrunners students in Denmark picked up a few Danish Sign Language (DTS) signs, they did not feel obliged to learn more DTS because IS was used in their course. In another example, during the years Annelies worked in Germany in an all-hearing, English-using workplace, she worked with BSL interpreters rather than DGS interpreters, and she did not learn or use much DGS during that time; this was because she was there temporarily, in a small town with few deaf people, and pregnant or on maternity leave for a large proportion of her stay. These examples show complex combinations of priorities and opportunities, or the lack thereof.

As the example from our own university department shows, migrants not knowing the/a national sign language of the host country can lead to tensions. Shahina experienced criticism from a woman who had moved to the United Kingdom from Belarus:

> The Belarusian woman, she is white, told me that my BSL was not good, it was rubbish. It knocked my confidence. [...] She said I was signing like a hearing person who is learning the language.

Shahina contrasted this comment with her experiences with BSL interpreters:

> I went to an NHS hospital and an interpreter came. I explained to her that I am an ASL user and my BSL is not strong, but I can understand BSL. The interpreter was fantastic, [...] she was able to interpret for me with the doctor. Afterwards, I asked her if she understood my BSL: "Is my BSL ok?" She told me that it is good and it's improving. I was like, really? I felt [...] this [Belarusian] person was negative, and the interpreter was positive, you know what I mean? Again, I was at my next hospital appointment and had a different interpreter, she said the same thing, that my signing has improved. This was a different interpreter, so I got suspicious of that Belarusian woman's comment over my signing skills.

Both the white Belarusian deaf woman and Shahina were migrants, although the Belarusian woman had been living in the United Kingdom for longer. Notably, Shahina positioned hearing BSL/English interpreters as language experts over her fellow deaf migrant. Yet, hearing people are not only positioned as experts but also as novices; being accused of signing "like a hearing new signer" is something that several deaf migrants have experienced. Lenka N., a migrant to London, left what was then Czechoslovakia with her deaf identity suppressed. Her first employment in the United Kingdom was as an au pair for a hearing family, and she hid her deafness from her employer out of fear of losing her job; she was able to do this because she could speak English. When she became aware of the deaf community in the United Kingdom, questions of deaf culture and sign language became central to her experience:

> I grew up in Czechoslovakia, and growing up I never questioned how to sign—it was just my way. I made sure I matched whichever deaf person I was talking to, whether that meant a slower pace, more facial expressions, or professional conversations with more lip patterns. However, when I arrived here, I was criticized a lot by other deaf people. That discrimination toward a deaf person by other deaf people really struck me. I'd never experienced anything like that before. It happened a lot here, and it forced me to think of that distinction between small d and large D deaf. [...] They would tell me that I didn't look like a natural signer. I didn't even know what that meant! [...] They would also criticize my lip patterns as foreign and not British. I don't know what they expected me to say to them—that's just me. I can't change who I am. I can't adopt full English lip patterns. My handshapes are just that—mine. It's the same with foreign hearing people who speak with an accent. You should never judge how other people sign. (*Finding Spaces to Belong*, 00:48:47)[26]

Lenka N. experienced language shaming in the United Kingdom. She had been used to calibrating flexibly in her native country, but she was criticized for signing differently from the average British deaf person, for using accented mouthings, and for signing in a way that people did not find "natural." "Natural signing" refers to a natural flow within sign language use, and the signing of "new signers," or of signers who use a lot of English in their signing, is often seen as inauthentic or "unnatural" (Kusters & Fenlon, 2021). Signing can be accented, too: Migrants may use handshapes, facial expressions, or body movements that are different from those used by deaf people who have grown up in the United Kingdom. Learning a new national sign language is also an unequal process of acculturation. The pressures that Erin and Amandine felt, as white women in a university setting

---

26. https://vimeo.com/854367099#t=48m47s

in Edinburgh, were very different from the pressures that people of color may experience in migration to the United Kingdom. In *Finding Spaces to Belong*, Sana, from India, commented that it had taken her a long time to embody the "stiffer" style of British signing (00:45:40),[27] and Sanchayeeta's Indian newlywed participants also felt they had to work to reduce their Indian body language (such as wobbling the head to indicate "yes" or "no") in favor of more British norms.

Whereas the majority of migrants to the United Kingdom move voluntarily (Kierans, 2020), the migrants in Kakuma Refugee Camp had all experienced forced migration. Refugee camps are initially set up in times of emergency as temporary housing, but many people end up staying for years, even decades, and thus their situation is one of long-term migration. There are well-established institutions in the camp in which the host country's national sign language (e.g., KSL) is used, including deaf units in schools—indeed, some deaf refugees were brought by relatives into Kakuma Refugee Camp specifically to access education (see Chapter 4). At the same time, the camp has a temporary feel as people prepare for resettlement. This also has an impact on their language learning aspirations: Some deaf camp inhabitants expect that becoming fluent in ASL may increase their chance of being resettled in the United States.

Different generations of deaf refugees in the camp have had different exposure to ASL and KSL within the schools' deaf units. Initially, more ASL was used in the deaf units, due to teachers coming from several countries; by the time of Amandine's research, KSL was also used. Atem, a deaf South Sudanese man, explained that he had used "village signs" during his childhood, then progressed to learning ASL at a deaf unit in Kakuma Refugee Camp, and then learned KSL in a residential deaf high school in the west of Kenya. The younger generation learned KSL in Kakuma: Nyathak, a woman from Sudan who was 18 years old at the time of interview, had been taught by Kenyan teachers using KSL. However, deaf refugees also expand their repertoire outside of formal education, picking up bits of KSL, ASL, and other sign languages in everyday encounters with other deaf refugees in churches, in private homes, and on vocational courses. Halimo, a Somali woman, came as an adult to Kakuma Refugee Camp from Dadaab Refugee Camp; at the time of her arrival in Dadaab, there were no schools there, and thus she had never had the opportunity to attend a deaf unit. She learned to sign by watching deaf refugees play football:

> I have never been to school. I stayed at home in Dadaab Refugee Camp with my husband and I became pregnant. I noticed [deaf] people playing football and signing. I watched them every day and I learned through that [i.e., watching their interactions]. I learned signing fast. [...] I stood and watched from morning to lunch time, and I went home to sleep and came back the next day. I learned fast.

Halimo took the opportunity to learn sign language in informal contexts, by watching natural interactions.

For many deaf refugees, the camp is the first context in which they have the opportunity to learn a conventional sign language (e.g., KSL, ASL), whether formally in deaf units or through informal interactions. When certain deaf people migrate to a new place—typically those from the Global South moving into the Global North or from rural to urban districts—they are frequently said to have "no language"—that is, to have language deprivation (Moriarty Harrelson, 2017b). The trope of "language deprivation" (Humphries et al., 2012) is considered crucial by those advocating against

---

27. https://vimeo.com/854367099#t=00h45m40s

deaf children receiving inadequate or no access to sign language; the term emphasizes that deaf children *need* full access to language, and they experience cognitive and social delays without it. The label of language deprivation, however, can obscure the fact that deaf refugees with "no language" *do* communicate: They calibrate by using gestures and pointing, and they use physical objects as part of everyday languaging (Sivunen & Tapio, 2020). Indeed, in communities where the "village signs" draw on local gesturing conventions, the line between gesturing and signing can be so blurred that people may not agree on whether somebody "can sign" or not (Hou, 2020). Henner and Robinson (2021) use the term "crip linguistics" in a call to validate forms of languaging that are seen as "broken language" or "no language," rather than "full language" or "proper language" (and to reject such labels). Duggan and Holmström (2022) also flag that the terms "language deprivation" and "no language" are used too liberally because some of the people defined as having no language had been to deaf schools where signing was used in their home countries. The ideology of "no language" can display a language hierarchy between "real"/"better" languages (i.e., the languages used in the host country) and "nonlanguages" (the signs migrants bring with them). This ideology is often related to race, ethnicity, and country of origin. One legacy of colonialism is that black people have frequently been framed as having no language both historically and also in the present (Oostendorp, 2021). Deaf people from the Global South are most vulnerable to being labeled as "having no language," both within the Global North (as Duggan & Holmström [2022] show) and also within the Global South, as the following example shows.

When Amandine asked refugees in Kakuma Refugee Camp about whether there were deaf schools or sign language in their home countries, the reactions were always the same: "No, there is no deaf school! No sign language!" This was despite the fact that many deaf refugees used "village signs" that they had brought from their home villages in Sudan, Somalia, Ethiopia, and Congo. On one occasion when Amandine visited with a group of deaf refugees socializing at Halimo's house, the conversation turned to various sign languages and forms of language use. The group was talking about different sign languages and engaging in the common deaf sociality practice of comparing signs. They signed variants of PREGNANT, saying, "this is in KSL" and "that is in ASL." Amandine took the opportunity to ask Halimo how PREGNANT would be signed in Somalia, and she reacted strongly, adamantly stating, "No! There are no signs in Somali, there are no Somali signs." The common assertion made by deaf refugees that there was an absolute lack of native sign languages in their homelands is at odds with research showing the existence of sign languages in both Somalia and Sudan (Morgan et al., 2015; Woodford, 2006). One reason for this discrepancy might relate to refugees' fear of the prospect of going back to these countries; the absence of sign language and/or deaf education there validates their need and desire to be resettled in a Western country. Another potential reason is the early age that many of the refugees moved to the camp, having had little or no exposure to Somalian or Sudanese signs or to the education system there, because deaf schools do indeed exist in both countries. Certainly, there is a strong association between formal sign language learning and national sign languages. Atem, when explaining his desire to ultimately return to his home country of what is now South Sudan, described a sense of responsibility toward improving the educational system there:

> When I went back [...], I was the only one who knew sign language, the only one to understand well. All the other deaf people are not like me, they are village people. I want to teach sign language. I want

in the future to write a paper to ask our government in Sudan to support us to build a school for many deaf people. But now, deaf people don't have schools [there].

The establishment of schools was seen as central to the development of sign language learning in their home countries, and Atem expressed the intent to return and educate the village people with formal sign language. He may have meant that there are no deaf schools *in many areas of Sudan*, rather than no deaf schools there at all, but in either case he saw a responsibility to "bring sign language" there. This is an issue of language hierarchies: Deaf refugees who state that there is "no sign language" in their home country are likely responding to the sign language in their home country being less well-established and formally recognized than other sign languages. In other words, if there is signing taking place, it is not a "formal" sign language and is therefore discounted.

There is an interesting link between the above example and Annelies's data gathered in another part of Kenya: at the DOOR campus, where South Sudanese deaf translators were translating the Bible. The existence of this translation project seems to indicate that there *is* a sign language in place to some extent in South Sudan. Cesar, one of the translators, explained to Annelies that the sign language in South Sudan consisted of "village signs" combined with influences from other sign languages:

> In South Sudan, there is still no sign language or sign language dictionary. There is nothing official. It's because of the war, and it caused a lot of mayhem. The capital, Juba, was the only place where there was signing. At that time, it was Arabic-based signing that then was spread throughout the country and remembered for years. Once the separation [from the Republic of Sudan] happened, they had to learn English-based signing from Uganda and so on. They learned different sign languages, mixing them. I remember seeing and using some village signs, so these different signs were inserted into the translation videos too. (*This Is IS*: Episode 2, 00:12:43).[28]

This is not an unusual situation: Many countries in the Global South have a complicated linguistic history, with their own indigenous signs existing alongside signs that have been imported—often from several different sign languages—in the context of colonialism or postcolonial development (see Moges, 2015; Parks, 2014). Furthermore, countries in which deaf education is more established, such as Kenya and Uganda, also play a role in the export of signs. Deaf people from surrounding countries often go to school there and then bring Kenyan and Ugandan signs back to their home country (Morgan et al., 2015). This history of a truncated and layered import of signs, often combined with the devaluation of local, "village" signs, may give the impression that there is "no sign language" or "no own sign language" in a country. In other words, "no sign language" can mean the use of village signs, and/or it can mean the use of signs from *different* sign languages (e.g., from ASL and/or from the sign languages used in adjoining countries); it means there is no "own *national* sign language."

Learning and Using English

As a global language, English is widely believed to be important for achieving social inclusion and material success. It is not surprising, therefore, that knowledge of English was a much-discussed

---

28. https://vimeo.com/728777656#t=12m43s

theme in each of the four MobileDeaf subprojects. Because English is a worldwide lingua franca, knowledge of English is often tied to capital, mobility, and opportunities for hearing and deaf people alike (Kellett Bidoli & Ochse, 2008). When traveling internationally, knowing how to read and write English is helpful for accessing information from the environment in many parts of the world, and it is often a crucial tool when navigating communication with hearing people. English is also often used in interactions between deaf people, especially in the context of deaf professional mobility, whether through fingerspelling, mouthings, written documents, PowerPoint slides, and so on. There have been several projects for the online teaching of English through national sign languages and IS (e.g., Hilzensauer & Skant, 2008), so as to enable deaf people to use written English as a lingua franca. Many mobile deaf people have complicated feelings about English. In countries where English is not an official language, many deaf people do not have access to English at school. Access to and the ability to use English, as well as people's thoughts and feelings about English, reflect broader social inequalities.

As described previously, Wahyu, the deaf tour guide in Indonesia, is an expert when it comes to calibrating. Wahyu had a diverse repertoire, including English, that he drew on as a part of his work. He writes in English when necessary, but he only learned a small amount in school. To develop his fluency, he took the initiative to teach himself more English:

> I write in English. From junior school onward, we had to write in English; however, we learned only a bit from the teacher. When I started working, I realized I had to learn English because people from across the world come here and I need it for communication. I learned it on my own. I don't know it 100%, because I have to use five different languages and adjust all the time. I write less than I sign.

Wahyu had to learn English out of necessity, and he expanded his knowledge of it on the job. For example, he explained that he first came across the English term "deaf village" when someone messaged him requesting to book a tour there, and he needed someone to explain it to him in BISINDO. Despite not considering himself fully fluent, Wahyu uses written English to communicate with tourists via Facebook and Facebook Messenger, and he also uses English in his signing, fingerspelling English terms for concepts. He often uses English to bridge when a miscommunication happens between himself and a tourist. He has a knowledge of English vocabulary that is relevant to his work, like "deaf village" and "ceremony," which he fingerspells (*#deaftravel*, 00:47:12).[29] This is a way that many deaf people use English: in the form of words inserted in signed discourse.

Although English is used in many international settings, it is often not an official language of the country where the gatherings happen. For example, the Frontrunners course used English and IS rather than Danish and DTS. Prior knowledge of English is somewhat presupposed in the Frontrunners course, where it is used in PowerPoints and in the form of fingerspelling and mouthing. Some students made heavy use of Google Translate to translate English to other written languages, looking up single words by typing them in or taking photographs of slides which are then automatically translated. Making use of this strategy requires knowledge of another written language. Majdi, the student from Jordan, did not consider this an option because he did not know Arabic well enough to benefit from English-to-Arabic translations.

---

29. https://vimeo.com/588352737#t=47m12s

Another student, Aline, experienced a transition in her feelings toward English during the Frontrunners course. She had learned a little bit of written English at school in Brazil, but she was not interested in learning English further. Despite this, her mother kept encouraging her to learn English, connecting English with international mobility. When Aline met other deaf people from throughout the world, she became motivated to learn more English on her own, but her learning process was challenging:

> When I got older and I had a chance to see Frontrunners, Europeans, Americans, and others from around the world, I realized my mum was right. I started reading, watching movies, but it was not going very well. When I was chosen to join Frontrunners 13, I was so excited and motivated to learn English, but it wasn't easy. I was dealing with time constraints because of work. I learned a bit. Then I came here, and I was ready to learn—not nervous, but confident. On the plane I was given a note [by a flight attendant]—something written in English. I could only understand one word out of the entire note—it was the word "HELP." I told them: "Yes, help me [by pointing to the word] [smiles]." Then they wrote "Thank you" on the other side. I said thank you. When I meet deaf people, I sign in IS. When I encounter hearing people, I would like to be able to write something in English—like at the airports, in a restaurant, and so on.

Even a minimal knowledge of English can be useful while communicating with hearing people during short interactions. Aline understood one word on a written note and was able to infer that the attendant was offering her help; making informed guesses based on minimal information is a common deaf practice. Aline was motivated to learn more English during Frontrunners. However, 8 months later when she was reinterviewed by Annelies, she felt that she had made only limited progress despite making huge efforts to learn the language. She had ultimately put the importance of knowing English into perspective after experiencing getting by without advanced English during her internships in Module 2 of the Frontrunners course:

> I do not have to learn English. It can be good to know it; however, I can live without it. For example, during Module 1, I had been trying to learn English. I could see only small improvements. In contrast, my IS improved a lot. During Module 2, when I had to go out and do internships on my own [in England, France, and Italy], I was taking the initiative. For example, I can use a phone to translate words from Portuguese to English, or I can use more gestures. A basis [in English] is good, but a large amount is not necessary. Basic words can help me when I travel, for going to restaurants for example.

Aline still feels that English is useful but has also learned that she can communicate in more diverse ways. This change of perspective is reminiscent of the repertoire expansion the Frontrunners students went through.

Both Wahyu and Aline were using English in the context of international interactions. They learned English later in life, after learning other written languages in school, and they learned the bits of English that were particularly useful to them in their work and travels. The context of migration to an English-majority country is different: English may then be needed in more domains of life. Deaf migrants to the United Kingdom (and to other countries where English is the/an official language) may know some English upon arrival. However, the degree of knowledge and understanding of English varies between migrants. Kwame is from Ghana, where English is the official language inherited from the colonial era;

he had come to the United Kingdom to do a postgraduate degree, and his knowledge of English enabled him to access captions during lectures. Other participants, such as Adrian, from Romania, had only basic knowledge of how to write short English sentences; he could not make use of these same resources. There are fields in which deaf migrants will have some degree of linguistic capital (i.e., knowledge of a language deemed of value) that may be of use when reading signs or purchasing food; however, they may not be able to get a job or enter a course where greater fluency in English is required.

Many deaf migrants seek to improve their English in the United Kingdom. To complicate matters, English is often learned at the same time as BSL and other language learning—for example, picking up signs from other sign languages as part of the cosmopolitan practice of exchanging signs. At City Lit adult education college in London, Sanchayeeta and Steve observed classes for migrants who were learning English and English classes that were mainly made up of deaf migrants but that deaf U.K. nationals could attend, too. The class, which Steve observed, taught by a tutor who had themselves migrated from Russia more than 20 years before, was for beginners (the next level would be "English entry 1") and consisted of deaf people from Kuwait, Mongolia, Romania, Iran, Ireland, and Ukraine. The class was very lively; the students were signing with and teasing each other. The key method through which students were asked to demonstrate their grasp of English was fingerspelling, in combination with learning (a) BSL sign(s) for the same concept. Throughout the class, two brothers from Kuwait helped each other by explaining terms in their native language. Although they were reminded to sign in BSL, students often used non-BSL signs, especially during breaks. They found it fascinating to learn the different signs of each country, and they engaged in the act of comparing signs, which we also observed in the other subprojects. The second class (a more advanced English class) was taught by a white hearing British man, and it consisted of nationals from Sierra Leone, Latvia, Estonia, Sudan, Venezuela, Australia, Pakistan, and the United Kingdom. Most of the class were migrants who had been in the United Kingdom for many years and therefore mainly used BSL in the class; here, English competency was demonstrated through both fingerspelling and writing (Aldersson, 2023).

The desire to improve in English is not necessarily enough for successful language learning due to barriers to accessing education services. The City Lit classes are free, but they are heavily subscribed and subject to cutbacks. Adrian, for example, had to be put on a waiting list to learn English, and he was frustrated by this:

> I had a look around [City Lit], liked what I saw, and they asked if I wanted to study. I really wanted to get good English. Then I met [...] the teacher here, but the course was full, so I had to go to the bottom of the waiting list. They said they would let me know by email, but I had to wait 2 years to start.

Adrian was in the country and eager to improve, but his desire to learn a new language was thwarted by the unavailability of services, and obtaining access to classes was a slow process. There are systematic barriers in place that make it challenging for deaf migrants to the United Kingdom to learn English.

Some deaf migrants have used English extensively in their country of origin, but they experience barriers in relation to English upon arriving in the United Kingdom. Adult literacy courses for deaf people in the Global South very often focus on English literacy (e.g., Webster & Zeshan, 2021), yet English literacy skills that are sufficient to get by in one country may not "transfer" well to other countries. In India, English courses for deaf adults are manifold, offered by different nongovernmental organizations, universities, and charities, and many Indian deaf people in cities have subscribed to multiple (typically entry-level) English courses in succession (Friedner, 2015b). Aisha had attended, and even taught, such courses before she moved from India to the United Kingdom for marriage. In India, she had established a career as a teacher in a deaf school in Mumbai, with stability and a good pay scale. To gain this role, her skills had been assessed through classroom observation. Her limited English literacy skills were not an obstacle to this and had not been an obstacle to her obtaining a bachelor of arts degree. However, in the United Kingdom, she found that her limited English became a barrier to her transitioning into the deaf education sector. Aisha was disheartened when she did not get a job interview for a learning assistant role at a deaf school, with the feedback stating that an interview could only be offered to candidates with a minimum of Level 2 English (a government-accredited English qualification equivalent to a General Certificate of Secondary Education grade C/grade 4). She had obtained an entry-level course (pre-Level 1) at City Lit and was seeking access to English Level 1, which City Lit college did not offer at the time due to a shortage of BSL-using English teachers.

Aisha expressed her frustration with the United Kingdom's employment system, feeling that her employment pathway in India had been more advantageous. She felt that in the United Kingdom, her English was not considered good enough, whereas in India she could get by. She was committed to improving her English skills, as shown in Example D at the beginning of this chapter: She read and practiced her English daily, and she often texted Sanchayeeta to ask for explanations of vocabulary. She was also involved in the previously mentioned English courses from India, which were offered online during the pandemic. Having progressed to Level 6 in BSL, she subsequently experienced barriers in her efforts to join a higher level BSL course due to the requirement for written English in assignments. BSL courses are almost exclusively modeled for hearing BSL learners who already have foundational skills in English; deaf learners with limited English are disadvantaged (also see Barnes & Atherton, 2015).

Deaf migrants who have moved to the United Kingdom also face obstacles because of the assumption that they do not know English, based on their status as "foreign." Lenka N., from the Czech Republic, explained that her aspirations for self-development through higher education were almost derailed by systemic barriers and ignorance. Lenka had previously obtained a bachelor of arts degree in the United Kingdom, but when she tried to enroll for a master's degree, she was told that she needed to take a test to "prove" her ability in English. Despite having passed the entrance interview, her enrollment was blocked until she passed a specific language test—one that was inaccessible:

> I didn't understand what [the test was] for, as I already had a [BA] degree, which I'd achieved 3 or 4 years prior. Nobody had ever asked me about my English. [...] The female administrator blocked my enrollment, saying it was impossible without going for an academic English fluency test. [...] [I]t was an online assessment that would require me to wear headphones and select the right answers on a computer screen. But I can't do that [...] I explained this, but they still said I couldn't do it. So, I asked them to put this in writing and they sent it to me. When I had that evidence, I knew I had a strong case in relation to my rights and how I'd been treated. I sent this to my boss, copying some important people, so that they could understand that any future deaf professionals should be treated with respect and not have to face barriers over their spoken English. I got a flurry of apologetic replies and I was allowed into the degree program.

Despite Lenka N.'s high levels of written English, she experienced barriers because the testing system was designed for hearing people. This is reminiscent of Aisha's experience of barriers to a BSL course designed for hearing learners. Lenka already had a university degree, fluency in English, and valuable contacts; she thus had the linguistic and social capital to make a case for her discrimination. Other deaf migrants without the same level of fluency, or the same support system, may have felt shame for their perceived lack of fluency in English.

Language Out of Place

In general, people tend to subscribe to the ideology that languages are territorially bound—for example, that ASL belongs to the United States, and BSL belongs to the United Kingdom. In other words, people often see the use of specific semiotic resources or calibration practices as being appropriate only in certain spaces or within certain boundaries. As mentioned previously in the chapter, there are ideological spaces of calibration and spaces of separation. In various subprojects, occasions arose where participants felt that there was too much ASL being used in spaces where its use was contested, which they said was disrespectful, oppressive, and/or simply out of place. Conversely, Meera, the Indian woman who felt she had not become fluent in BSL despite living in the United Kingdom for 17 years, explained that she felt that BSL users were not willing to calibrate and that she had experienced prejudice and anti-migration rhetoric as an ASL user of Asian descent:

> When I first moved here . . . British deaf people are so different—they use BSL and I use ASL. They signed faster with blank expressions, and I didn't understand what they were saying. [. . .] It was stressful for me to understand them and to process what they were saying. Secondly, some deaf complained to me, "Why would you move here if you are still using ASL?" They were annoyed that I was using ASL and they couldn't understand me. They were also making negative comments to me. I was patient. I couldn't help learning slowly. [They asked] why was I proud to use ASL? I grew up using an oral approach and one-handed alphabets. My behavior was different from British deaf people; they were more fluent and freer with their signs and with their facial expressions. They asked my husband what he married me for. [They said that] since I moved here, I have to respect [the community] by using BSL. I had told them that I had just moved, and it takes time for me to learn the new language, but they misunderstood. I had to remain calm when I continued to receive negative comments, and I'd distance myself from them.

This excerpt shows how language ideologies intersect with xenophobia and antimigrant ideologies. Meera was subjected to language shaming by way of comments about being a "proud" (i.e., arrogant) ASL user, and she and her British Indian husband (whose parents, of Indian heritage, were from Uganda) were subjected to questioning about their decision to marry. Meera saw learning BSL as "respectful" of the community and was trying to improve, but she was taken aback by the blank facial expressions and pace of signing, which did not signal a cosmopolitan attitude of calibration. She felt this slowed down her learning process. Having a history of communicating orally further set her apart as "different." Meera, as a migrant, was positioned as "out of place," as was her "inappropriate" language use.

In the United Kingdom, ASL may be unwelcome and considered "out of place," but this is not necessarily related to acute endangerment of BSL. Conversely, in many developing countries,

ASL is seen as threatening the "own" (e.g., local, national) sign language. When Erin accompanied various tour groups in Bali, she observed conversations and languaging practices that revealed ambivalent attitudes about sign language contact in tourism, in relation to other sign languages (e.g., BSL, French Sign Language) as well as ASL. In one example, a deaf teacher at a Balinese deaf school told tourists to sign only to him so as not to "confuse" the children or "contaminate" their BISINDO (Moriarty, 2020a). It was not only ASL and other Global North sign languages that were perceived as contaminators. The opinion of Wahyu and the deaf teachers at the deaf school was that the BISINDO used in south Bali was having a negative influence on Kata Kolok in Bengkala, with deaf villagers exchanging some local signs for others with different iconic referents that are used more widely in Bali. Wahyu gave the example of the Kata Kolok sign COFFEE (*#deaftravel*, 01:15:57),[30] which has changed from an index finger pointing at the hair growing at the forehead (Figure 8.13a), a reference to the color of the coffee being like the color of the villagers' hair, to an index finger stirring a held cup (Figure 8.13b). Similarly, Wahyu commented that he sometimes felt that he was slowly forgetting his BISINDO because he spends so much time with tourists, working 14-hour days.

Erin did not observe the villagers themselves talk about language contamination or change; instead, this seemed to be more of a concern for tourists and sign language researchers who worked in Bengkala. This appears to be a common pattern in the Global South: It is often outsiders who express concern about sign language endangerment, which then inspires them to study sign languages (Braithwaite, 2020; Webster & Safar, 2020). In previous research, Annelies had observed the same phenomenon in Adamorobe, a deaf village in Ghana: Outsiders such as tourists and researchers were projecting their ideologies onto the villagers about the need to use their own sign language and to preserve it (Kusters, 2015).

ASL is also often seen as out of place in situations where no national sign language is dominant. In the Frontrunners program, where IS was used, ASL was a hot topic of debate. As explained earlier in the chapter, over the course of the program, Frontrunners expanded their repertoires; a key example of this process was certain students learning to produce versions of IS using no or less ASL. Whereas some of the other Frontrunners had had previous exposure to IS through, for

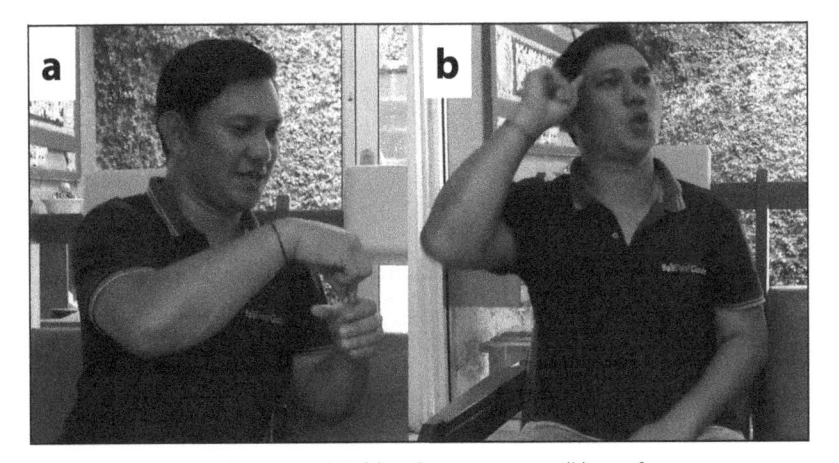

Figure 8.13. Wahyu comparing the Kata Kolok (a) and more common (b) sign for COFFEE.

---

30. https://vimeo.com/588352737#t=1h15m57s

example, European camps, others—such as Majdi, from Jordan, and Hyemi, from South Korea—had been more exposed to ASL than to "European" IS before they arrived at Frontrunners, and they were alerted by fellow students to their use of ASL signs for everyday concepts such as "day" or "have." Majdi struggled to keep ASL out of his signing:

> I have to be aware to just use IS and to avoid ASL. My signing is a mix of IS and ASL. I feel that I am using ASL a lot here. I use IS as well, but it depends—more IS or less, it fluctuates. If people give me feedback, I will remember it more. If they don't tell me, I use less IS. (*This Is IS*: Episode 1, 00:54:15)[31]

Some Frontrunners from Europe also struggled with identifying and avoiding ASL, but they had "home ground advantage": They were in Europe, were more experienced in communicating with other Europeans through IS, and had better knowledge of English as a bridging lingua franca. The irony is that some people from "outside Europe" (which is often used as a synonym for "Global South") are less exposed to IS and more to ASL (although this is changing because of increasing IS use on social media). However, they are also seen as people who understand ASL less (see Kusters, 2020), an assumption based on these people's perceived lack of knowledge of *English*. Knowledge of ASL and knowledge of English are often ideologically associated with each other, an ideology discussed in depth next. We observed multiple times across the subprojects that vilifying ASL use puts deaf people from the Global South in multiple disadvantaged positions. Deaf people originating in the Global South feel they have to work harder to learn to communicate in ways expected by the majority, especially when they experience racism and xenophobia; also, due to the history of ASL spread in the world (a process through which local sign languages were sidelined), they may have had more access to ASL than to IS or BSL, but are chided for using it.

Some deaf Americans have become aware of anti-United States and anti-ASL sentiments in many international contexts. In the film *This Is IS*: Episode 1, we see Hyemi learning more ASL from David, to improve her knowledge of ASL in addition to IS, but when David notices that she has started to use more ASL in her signing, he expresses concern that she cannot keep ASL and IS separate (00:59:36).[32] David felt responsible for not "contaminating" the Frontrunners program with ASL, and he wondered whether, as an American, he was the main ASL influence there.

Deaf American institutions (as well as European white people) are often seen as the hegemonic voice of the global deaf community; this is the context in which Julie, a white American deaf professor working at Gallaudet University, was situated. She attended and gave a keynote lecture at the SIGN8 conference in Brazil in 2017, where IS and Libras (Brazilian Sign Language) were used, and she was conscious of her visibility as an American and of ASL influences in her international signing. The quotation below comes from an interview following a workshop about IS organized by Annelies (excerpts can be seen in *This Is IS*: Episode 3). Some people in the workshop had uttered strongly negative statements about ASL, framing it as out of place in IS. Julie reflected:

---

31. https://vimeo.com/686852215#t=54m15s
32. https://vimeo.com/686852215#t=59m36s

I think if I stand up as an American with ASL and say something, they'll see that as me dictating to them. I don't want that. I'll just hold back. In both my talks and workshops, I'm always conscious of how I communicate and interact with people, being mindful that I'm an ASL user. I've always tried to learn signs; on nights out having a drink, or during meals and conversations, I'm learning how people talk to each other and their ways. I can see other people calibrating as well, such as signing Flemish [VGT], and they adapt to IS, and it's the same with me: I adopt that attitude from others too. [...] Anyway, there's these various views. That limits my conversation, as there's negativity emanating from people because I come from America and I come from Gallaudet, they look at me like that. I feel really self-conscious, and I just want to go away and hide. Chill out with the birds and stuff, just like being tired from mixing with lots of people and having my brain whirring all the time. I'm a really strong introvert, so I'll go off and have a rest. [...] [Later,] I felt able to come back and mix again. That's my strategy. (*This Is IS*: Episode 3, 00:44:36)[33]

Julie was conscious of representing Gallaudet as a hegemonic institution in the deaf space, and conscious of national stereotypes (see Chapter 5 on stereotyping). She emphasized that she consciously calibrated to others, but she was also conscious that her Americanness was visible in her signing. She also observed that she was a "strong introvert," which played a part in how she interacted with other people in the deaf space, and it reinforced her feeling that she had to "hold herself back." International events are intensive environments. The process of calibrating and of learning new signs in a short time span—at the same time as meeting new people and maybe even giving a presentation—can be exhausting; this is particularly true for deaf people who are introverted and/or have disabilities (other than deafness) or chronic illnesses. Unfortunately, we do not have a lot of data on how personality types, "hidden" disabilities (e.g., resulting from neurodivergence), and old age impact international deaf interactions.

Anti-ASL sentiments are not always dominant, however. At the DOOR campus in Kenya, ASL was seen as a lingua franca to bridge different sign languages. Simon, a translator from Kenya, explained:

Yes, I think ASL helps because when I see people from other countries like Ghana or Nigeria or Tanzania, I can see they understand some ASL, and when I ask where they got ASL from, it's because many American missionaries have gone to other poor countries to provide help, and they use ASL and teach that, so those people understand ASL. [...] Using a little ASL helps us understand each other, and makes communication easier. If each of us only used our own sign language like KSL and TSL (Tanzanian Sign Language), we would not be able to understand each other.

Because deaf Africans have learned ASL at school and the use of ASL-influenced sign languages is widespread in Africa, ASL was used in calibrating practices at DOOR, both with deaf people from other African countries and with American and other foreign visitors. It was clear to Annelies that people did not see KSL as being "at risk" from ASL but as a "strong sign language" in East Africa, influencing sign languages in adjoining countries; this is because it is comparatively well supported by institutions compared to the sign languages in many other African countries.

---

33. https://vimeo.com/744266936#t=44m36s

Additionally, at DOOR, translators were employed for the development of materials in the sign languages of their countries of origin, to be used *instead of* ASL resources; in so doing, they were contributing to the continuing development of their own sign languages. In this context, Paul, the director, was not worried about the influence of ASL in the same way that the deaf teacher in Indonesia had been worried about foreign sign languages; this was potentially also because the people working at DOOR were deaf language professionals rather than deaf schoolchildren or villagers who were seen as vulnerable to language influences:

> In DOOR, there are many different deaf people. When an American comes and signs ASL, we encourage them. We understand them, but if we miss something, we give them the KSL sign to use. There is not the worry that they will bring their language here because if you look at Africa, you can see that KSL is very strongly rooted. So, any sign language is welcome. (*This Is IS*: Episode 2: 00,44:44)[34]

In another context in the same country, ASL was seen as desirable because it was seen as out of place. In contrast to Annelies's findings in DOOR, many deaf refugees in Kakuma Refugee Camp thought that ASL was "better" than other sign languages, including KSL. This is not unusual in Africa; other researchers have reported similar language ideologies (e.g., Nyst, 2010). ASL was associated with the United States and, importantly, with resettlement. For example, Ken, a deaf Sudanese person from a Dinka tribe, desired resettlement in the United States, and he believed that learning ASL would enable him to continue his studies there:

> I love American signs better because if you know American signs you can go to university, but if you know Kenyan signs you cannot go to university. The life in Kakuma is hard: I stay at home, it's boring, I don't have work, UN[HCR] don't support me with money, my parents don't pay me, I'm alone at home. I'm asking UN how to get work; I'm searching for work. I want a job with signs, but it is hard. So, I ask UN, please help me, I want to go to the United States, and I want to study there in university. [...] I love American signs. I'm learning this language [ASL] and it is better for me.

It is not unusual for refugees to be concerned with learning languages that will be useful after resettlement, rather than the language of the host country they reside in (Netto et al., 2019). Ken believed that ASL was the language most pertinent to his future. This example shows how language education and formal language-learning are intimately tied to aspirations for self-improvement and for future mobility (see Chapter 10). In addition, language ideologies about the nature of ASL versus KSL are in play here. Ken considered ASL to be a richer language and much more extensive than KSL, with better resources and therefore easier to learn. ASL is also associated with English more than KSL is, even though English mouthings and fingerspelling are used in both languages. Margaret, a deaf Sudanese woman, had a good knowledge of English and found ASL easier to understand because "it follows English":

> I understand well. I understand faster. In Kenya [signing], the communication is short, I don't understand well [...] English sentences are easy, I learned it at school. I understand well. English sentences are longer. [...] America is better than Kenya.

---

34. https://vimeo.com/728777656#t=44m44s

Margaret said that the sentences in "American signs" are longer because they follow English and that she preferred it for this reason. Examples such as this show that people have different understandings of what "ASL" means (see also Kusters, 2020). In Kakuma Refugee Camp, and indeed in large parts of Africa, what people call "ASL" would be called "Signing Exact English" (SEE) by others. In a key example, Amandine observed a deaf teacher, John, writing "Where is the teacher?" on the blackboard (see Figure 8.14) and then signing each word in this sentence. Deaf people in the United States would probably call his language use SEE because the signs were produced in English word order and followed English grammar; conversely, the sign order attributed to KSL (TEACHER WHERE?) would be considered "correct ASL." Many deaf people in Kakuma Refugee Camp, however, believed that (what they consider to be) "ASL" (i.e., SEE) is the signed equivalent of writing and speaking (formal) English, and they ascribed a lot of value to it. KSL was understood as a form of signing that has less status and complexity than the ASL/English conflation. In this example, the "sign language out of place" is thus connected to higher status, resettlement, and the English language.

Even IS, a seemingly cosmopolitan practice, can be seen as "out of place," as observed earlier in relation to our own use of IS in our workplace at a British university. Many of the DOOR participants positioned IS as something "European," from "outside," or "from WFD." When Annelies asked people whether they knew "International Sign," most of them said that they did not know it or only knew a little bit. Because Annelies was using IS herself, especially during the first 2 days, reactions to her signing were revealing of how they perceived IS. At the end of her interview with Ingrid, a consultant from Costa Rica, Annelies asked whether people at DOOR sometimes used

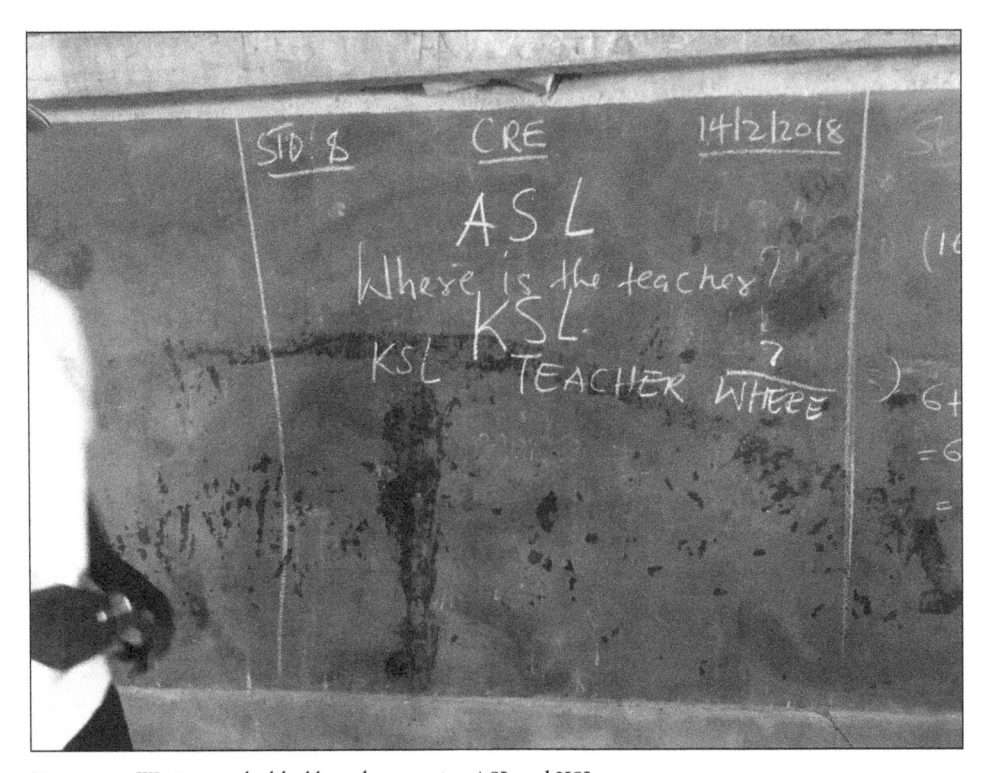

Figure 8.14. Writing on the blackboard comparing ASL and KSL.

IS. Ingrid's response was: "I've never met a person using International Sign, never. I don't know it." Annelies responded: "But I use IS." Ingrid responded: "Great! I understand you. [. . .] You asked questions, and I understood, definitely. It's easy with facial expressions and signs." This was one of many times at DOOR when Annelies got the impression that people did not recognize her signing as IS. Their expectation was that people would use "KSL mixed with own signs"; more than once, people stated that they thought Annelies was using KSL mixed with "Belgian signs."

Deaf people on the DOOR campus used many of the calibrating strategies that deaf Europeans typically call IS: using signs from different sign languages including ASL, expanding utterances by giving examples, and so on. It was the conventionalized versions of IS that were seen as non-African. Rahul mentioned that he had learned and used IS at the SIGN6 conference in India in 2013, which Annelies also had attended; the conference served as a shared point of reference (see Chapter 7). Rahul recalled:

> I met many people [at SIGN6], and there are also many videos on YouTube and the internet. Now, I see you and I recall IS—I understand you, but I am a bit weak at signing back in IS. That is because I don't meet them [people who use IS] here, I'm busy meeting with people from Burundi, Kenya, and Indians from the north and south. There are also people from Mozambique and South Sudan here, so we socialize together, eat together, and discuss things so they influence my signing. ASL is also in my signing spectrum from my previous teachers, so it's all in here. Here, I never meet with people using IS. (*This Is IS*: Episode 2, 00:33:48)[35]

At DOOR, Rahul engaged in interactions with people from a range of countries, but he did not see their signing as IS; this is likely because the signing at DOOR was not the conventionalized IS he had seen in other contexts. However, later in the same interview, Rahul also recognized that the calibrating and language mixing at DOOR *is* similar to informal interactions in IS, acknowledging that "maybe that is what International Sign is" (00:43:59).[36] In *This Is IS*: Episode 2, it becomes clear that not everyone uses "International Sign" as an overarching term to describe international deaf calibration. Instead, IS can be seen as fundamentally "out of place"—that is, not of *this* place.

In another example of IS being out of place, well-known American "super-traveler" Calvin Young explained to Erin that he had experienced criticism for using IS in the United States, especially from older deaf people. Language ideologies vary based on age and lived experiences, and Calvin observed that younger people, such as students at the deaf schools where he has given presentations about his travels, tend to be more open and interested in learning IS:

> A lot of students come up to me regarding my signing in a visual way, and copy some of what they see. They like it and then use it when socializing with their friends. That's something that IS can do!

Having IS in one's repertoire can translate into social capital; in this example, Calvin, a white hypermobile world traveler, brings IS—itself symbolic of mobility—to the schools he visits,

---

35. https://vimeo.com/728777656#t=33m48s
36. https://vimeo.com/728777656#t=43m59s

where it becomes part of the students' repertoires. From Calvin's comments, we can conclude that these students are introduced to cosmopolitanism and cosmopolitan values through their interactions with Calvin. Calvin notes that the resistance to IS is not just "an American thing," because he has experienced criticism for using IS in Australia as well. In this quotation, Calvin connects mobility with "open minds," which is a feature of cosmopolitanism:

> If they haven't gone out of their community and stay very insular without other influences, they are close-minded. [...] I've seen open-minded people be exposed to it, they find it interesting, think it's beautiful and dive in and accept it. The emphasis is on being open-minded, that is the key.

Here, IS is associated with being "open-minded," and it is therefore only marked as "out of place" by people who are perceived as being "not open to differences."

Conclusion

The study of language and languaging practices as they relate to mobility requires a lens that centers deaf social practices and the spaces where they take place. Using this lens, we have shown the ways in which different types of mobility shape languaging practices on various scales. We have shown the ways that language, languaging practices, and semiotic resources move with people as they engage in mobility; these can then be embraced but also marked as "out of place." We have noted the ways in which human mobility and people's life trajectories are reflected in their semiotic repertoires. During mobility, people also expand their repertoires—that is, they learn languages as they go along. Language learning is linked to social and linguistic capital and aspirations toward a better life, material success, and self-development. For mobile deaf people, learning IS or a new national sign language, or improving fluency in languages such as BSL or English, can be linked to the ability to capitalize on new opportunities, both social and material. Such opportunities and resources are distributed unevenly among deaf people who engage in mobility.

A core practice of deaf cosmopolitanism is calibration—the flexible and strategic use of, and rapid switching between, languages and modalities. Calibration is not limited to international deaf interactions, but it is something that deaf people bring from their everyday lives, which typically involve communicating with deaf and hearing people in a wide variety of ways (Crasborn & Hiddinga, 2015; Hodge & Goswell, 2021). Calibration is often seen as the core of IS. Conventionalized IS is a product of calibration, in which some signs have become consolidated. IS is treated as a bounded or established language in some contexts—for example, when it is expected that ASL should be kept out of it, or when IS is seen as a "European" form of communication. Calibration may be seen as central to IS, but international calibration per se may not be seen as IS.

We have shown that deaf people frequently engage in learning single signs in their international encounters. Some also aspire to learn other sign languages more fully. This is partially associated with the expectations of the contexts they are in or move through. In some contexts, it is entirely appropriate to learn only a few signs of (an)other sign language(s), especially when comparing signs—a practice we observed in all settings of our research. Signs compared and discussed can then function as sign names, as souvenirs, as anchors for future visitors, and as parts of group lexica. Although drawing comparisons between signs can be seen as a core manifestation of deaf cosmopolitanism, this does not mean that comparisons are always harmless: They can be the result of wonderment, but can also be experienced as discriminatory and even racist.

In some contexts, bounded sign language learning is expected or needed, and not just the learning of single signs. For example, many deaf people who move abroad learn other sign languages more fully. However, this expectation is found mostly in the context of migrations; migrants (including refugees) are expected to learn the language(s) of the country in which they arrive. Migrants learn new sign languages often with the assistance of a buddy, partner, or teacher who introduces them to the language. However, people are not always interested in becoming, or are able to become, fluent in the (sign) language that is most widely used in the place where they are. We showed that this is linked to individuals' responsibilities and aspirations in life, which translate into priorities.

Drawing comparisons between migrants' and nonmigrants' skills in the host country's sign language can be shaped by xenophobia. Migrants may be shamed by others for using foreign or accented signing or mouthing, or for drawing on a lingua franca (ASL or IS) to get by in the new country. They may be expected to use "correct," "pure," "appropriate," or "natural" signing. Furthermore, comparing the signing of deaf people who use (a) dominant sign language(s) and who have been to school and the signing of deaf people from other backgrounds may lead to the latter being labeled as having "no language," as shown in the discussion of attitudes toward "village signs." There is a tendency to downplay the linguistic status of the signing used in some countries or as used by some people, and migration adds an extra layer to this—especially in situations where the migrating deaf person has fled a war and/or has had no access to formal education in their country of origin.

In many cases, participants in the research project explained key moments of their lives in relation to languages and language practices—not only sign languages, but also English. In nonmigration contexts, familiarity with English may be seen as useful, but having a limited level of English may suffice. Conversely, many deaf migrants (including refugees) saw English as crucial to advancement. Yet, deaf migrants to London often find themselves facing systemic barriers to learning English (and, indeed, BSL), such as the need to pass (sometimes inaccessible) English proficiency tests to join courses or to be considered for jobs, as well as oversubscribed courses and waiting lists.

As we have noted, mobile deaf people may have internalized broad semiotic repertoires, but their repertoires do not always "fit" as they move from locale to locale (Blommaert & Dong, 2020; Busch, 2017). When a person's languages do not "fit," they are likely to also feel that *they* do not fit or belong, exacerbated by oppression linked to xenophobia, racism, and ableism (the latter of which is insufficiently covered in this research). Privilege can attenuate such effects. Hypermobile deaf travelers getting negative responses to their signing are in a different position from migrants who are made to feel unwelcome. (Post)colonial histories of language spread and language imperialism complicate these narratives. In particular, ASL is seen as "of America" and linked to mobilities to and from the United States; however, it is also seen as "being everywhere" and, therefore, "out of place," a threat, a useful resource, an aspiration, or several of these at once.

Languaging and language learning also happened during the research itself. The research team learned new signs and parts of sign languages, such as BISINDO and KSL, along the way. We learned how our language use was seen in the country or countries we had migrated to ourselves, and in our research settings. We noted how others copied signs from us, and we witnessed participants' language learning processes more fully (e.g., in courses) and supported them sometimes in their learning.

We have also noted, in varying degrees of depth, how the following factors can have an impact on interaction, communication, and languaging: race and ethnicity, gender, class, nationality, experience of language deprivation, being a new signer, being from the Global North versus the Global South, being disabled, or being introverted. The ways different identities or positions intersect in specific contexts shapes people's calibration strategies and language learning in these contexts; however, there are myriad possible combinations of factors that make it difficult, or impossible, to pinpoint which factors may matter more or be more prominent in each situation. For example, in many of the situations described in this chapter, it was not possible to separate racism from xenophobia and audism; drawing sharp distinctions between different motivators of discrimination is, to some extent, impossible because these motivations are often hidden and combined.

To return to the theme of deaf cosmopolitanism, this chapter has shown how calibration, linguistic border crossing, and a tendency toward curiosity about other people's signs are central to the concept. Because signing deaf people are often experienced in various ways of calibration, they often learn and consume new sign languages quickly. Language differences lead to comparisons, and differences are "overcome" with the help of multimodal languaging skills. Deaf cosmopolitanism, however, does not mean automatic acceptance of the language practices of others, as found in the examples involving language shaming or the use of a lingua franca such as ASL or IS in the "wrong" place. Also, the examples show that, underneath the ideology that deaf people are exceptionally well equipped to engage in cosmopolitan calibration, there are always people who (are expected to) work harder to communicate.

9

Spaces of Belonging

Sanchayeeta Iyer, Annelies Kusters, Erin Moriarty, Amandine le Maire, and Steven Emery

"Where do I belong?" is an often-asked question in the context of international mobility. Belonging is about feeling at home in places, spaces, and/or groups of people. In this chapter, we explore how deaf people on the move look for spaces where they belong. Because we are concerned with the exploration of spaces of belonging through mobility, we do not examine belonging within preexisting or natal family groups; we do, however, include "new families" in our scope. We show that in spaces of belonging, deaf people typically share interests and/or one or more other social locations. Our analysis of belonging is not limited to deaf spaces, as our participants explored various spaces of belonging, including those where they were the only deaf person among hearing people.

Yuval-Davis (2006) distinguishes between three analytical levels for the study of belonging: (1) social locations, (2) identifications and emotional attachment, and (3) political and ethical values. The first level of analysis, "social location," refers to people's positionality along mutually constituting axes of difference (gender, class, race and ethnicity, sexuality, ability, and so on). The second level, "identifications and emotional attachment," are narratives of belonging within specific groups and of what it means to be a member of a grouping; these narratives express "emotional investments and desire for attachments" (Yuval-Davis, 2006, p. 202), and they tend to come to the fore when the teller feels threatened or insecure about their position within the group. Yuval-Davis warns that (1) social location should not be equated with, conflated with, or reduced to (2) identifications. One can, for example, be a deaf lesbian but not feel at home in deaf lesbian spaces (see Lenka's story, p. 269), or be a deaf Sierra Leonean and not socialize with other deaf Sierra Leoneans (see Samba's story). Separating social location and identifications helps to "investigate what brings certain people under certain conditions to identify or not with particular identity groupings" (Yuval-Davis, 2006, p. 268). We show several examples of this in the chapter.

The third level of analysis is *political and ethical values*, which are attitudes and ideologies about the production and maintenance of boundaries of identities and groups—that is, who is "us" and who is "them." In other words, ethical and political values are about inclusion or exclusion in groups (whether nations, cultures, or other communities). Yuval-Davis calls this "the politics of belonging." The politics of belonging also involves discourse on what it takes to belong, on the nature of boundaries (which can be permeable and changeable), and on contestations of these boundaries (Yuval-Davis, 2006). Summarized, "the politics of belonging are comprised of specific political projects aimed at constructing belonging in particular ways to particular collectivities that are, at the same time, themselves being constructed by these projects in very specific ways" (Yuval-Davis, 2010, p. 266).

In the context of this book, belonging is thus not only about feelings of "(not) fitting in" but also about how others define who belongs and how. We are interested in how boundaries of collectivities are being demarcated both implicitly (making people feel "out of place") and explicitly (statements as to who belongs in the space and how or why). When someone feels that they do not belong in certain spaces, they can experience a drive to participate in or to produce alternative spaces of inclusion because distinctive groups are formed on the basis of shared, common aspects of oneself, such as nationality, language, residence status, belief, and so on. In this process, deaf people can adapt or rewrite their collective narratives around their specific ways of being (i.e., their identifications).

The terms that are most often used to talk about belonging within deaf epistemologies—both within Deaf Studies and within community discourse—are "deaf identity," "deaf culture," and "deaf community." In this chapter, we build on works that have used these framings, but we also frame "belonging" more broadly. This allows us to bring together findings collected in a range of very different contexts, and to bring out experiences that have been obscured in other Deaf Studies accounts.

Many studies have reflected on what it means to be "culturally" deaf and to be part of a collectivist culture (i.e., "the deaf community") (Ladd, 2003; Padden & Humphries, 1988). Deaf individuals' intersecting social locations (e.g., migration status, race and ethnicity, nationality, disability) mean that it is possible for them to be placed on the fringe or periphery—that is, "outside"—of what has often been described as "the deaf community," contrasting with the notion of deaf universalism (see Chapter 1). Deaf Studies has been criticized for marginalizing the voices of disabled deaf people, LGBTQIA+ deaf people, and deaf people of color from the all-encompassing term "deaf" (Dunn & Anderson, 2020; Moges, 2017; Ruiz-Williams et al., 2015). The notion of community also falls short when it is used in the singular way ("*the* deaf community"). The (singular) term "community" does not suit many of the stories in this chapter because journeys into spaces of belonging are multiple and complicated. However, we do use the term "deaf community" here and there in the chapter because our participants use it. The concept of deaf community is still pervasive in deaf epistemologies when talking about belonging, perhaps even more so than the concept of "deaf culture." People use "deaf community" in narratives about key aspects of who they are (i.e., those relating to being part of a linguistic minority signing community and that reference shared histories and/or cultures), and they use this lens as part of their worldview.

Importantly, however, we do not treat the terms "deaf community" and "sense of belonging" as synonyms, as some other scholars have done (e.g., Conama, 2022). Rather, we focus on our participants' search for spaces *where* they can belong without treating membership in communities as a prerequisite for belonging somewhere. Similarly, Breivik (2005) has engaged in case studies of internationally mobile deaf Norwegians who went to events such as the Deaflympics or who went to study abroad and looked for spaces where they could belong (both abroad and upon their return to Norway). Transnational spaces of belonging, both in Norway and abroad, were crucial for these Norwegians because the deaf community in Norway is known to be very small (Breivik, 2005, p. 43). Deaf people who feel they do not belong or that they are not part of their local deaf community may find that their sense of belonging is facilitated in global/international deaf networks (see Chapter 7).

Another term that is often used in Deaf Studies discourse on belonging is "deaf identity." "Belonging" is often treated as a synonym for "identity," for example, in relation to ethnic identity and national citizenship (Anthias, 2008; Antonsich, 2010). Also, "identity" is often used as a term that does not need a definition (Jones & Krzyżanowski, 2008). Anthias (2008) explains the difference between belonging and identity as follows:

> Identity involves individual and collective narratives of self and other, presentation and labelling, myths of origin and myths of destiny with associated strategies and identifications. Belonging on the other hand is more about experiences of being part of the social fabric and the ways in which social bonds and ties are manifested in practices, experiences and emotions of inclusion. (p. 8)

Thus, while identity and belonging are overlapping concepts (and belonging, in Yuval-Davis' opinion, also includes identifications), their emphasis differs. Key to deaf identity-focused approaches is the study of who deaf people think they are (individually and collectively), and who or what they identify with (see Leigh, 2009; Leigh & O'Brien, 2020). Yuval-Davis sees identity politics as a "specific type of project of the politics of belonging" (2010, p. 266). She notes that "identity politics tend to elevate specific location categories of belonging" (p. 266). An example of this is the phenomenon of essentializing "deaf-first" narratives, in which "deaf identities" are seen as the privileged social category under which all other distinctions are located. Many minoritized deaf people lack access to their heritage culture and languages, and/or to knowledge about their other identifications (e.g., LGBTQIA+), which further contributes to the discursive foregrounding of their being deaf.

Scholars have questioned or challenged the narratives that assume that deaf people have a universalistic, unitary sense of being deaf, around which other identities coalesce. They have often done so by studying salience hierarchies of identities, taking an "X-first" approach—that is, "placing identities, forms of power, and modes of redress in competition, but also in a pecking order" (May, 2015, p. 166). For example, James and Woll (2004) have asked whether "black deaf" or "deaf black" better suits the identities of black deaf people in the United Kingdom. Participants who identified as "black deaf" participated in black hearing spaces, and racism from other deaf people made it difficult for them to identify as "deaf black." Others identified as "deaf black" because they felt their needs as a deaf person were dominant and that communication through sign language was central to them. Others resisted ordering their identities in this way. In the same vein, Ahmad et al. (2002) asked participants—South Asian people in the United Kingdom—to place their identities in order of importance, using cards they had prepared for the purpose (e.g., Deaf, British Sign Language [BSL]-user, Asian, Pakistani, Indian, British, Muslim, Man, Young, Disabled). Foster and Kinuthia (2003) interviewed their participants about which elements of identity were more central to their experience; responses included "deaf first, then deaf Asian, then deaf Asian with low vision" (p. 287) and "being Black, then a woman, then my hearing impairment" (p. 280). The order in which identities were placed in salience hierarchies was often associated with the characteristics for which the participants felt most discriminated against, and with their experiences of white deaf people failing to recognize cultural and religious sensitivities.

Some researchers have pointed out that identifications are situation dependent. Foster and Kinuthia (2003) found that particular characteristics may become more pronounced than others when a person is situated in certain environments over time: For example, a politicized deaf identity may be dominant on a campus where deaf students reside, but some deaf students may experience increased levels of racism, ableism, or other forms of discrimination there compared to other spaces (see also James & Woll, 2004; Ruiz-Williams et al., 2015). In much of the recent Deaf Studies literature, it is recognized that deaf identities are ambiguous, various, plural, complex, and shifting (Leigh & O'Brien, 2020), and scholars have pointed out that identities are always situational, contextual, and often tied up with feelings of not fitting in or being discriminated against. We found an ethnography of "belonging" to be a suitable approach for the MobileDeaf project because the focus is on inclusion and exclusion in various spaces. Conversely, "identities" are still often treated as nested categories within individuals and studied in research activities such as interviews, rather than grounded in ethnography.

The framework of intersectionality has also challenged—even usurped—the "identities" trope. Since the term "intersectionality" was coined by Crenshaw (1989; see Chapter 1), it has been the subject of much academic discussion. Crenshaw was part of a wider black feminist movement, which itself drew on earlier historical sources (see Collins & Bilge, 2016). Although identity was a strong feature of this politics, there was an emphasis on how it called out the nature of power. Key to the debates were discussions on how to liberate people from oppression. The concept has since been expanded from its original emphasis on race, class, and gender to include other forms of oppression (e.g., those based on disability and sexuality), all of which are experienced through multiple intersecting social locations. Despite the breadth of its current application, it is important to acknowledge the labor and knowledge production of the women of color in the United States who instigated and contributed to the initial intersectionality discourse (Nash, 2019).

The use of intersectionality as a theoretical concept and analytical tool in Deaf Studies is quite a recent phenomenon, and a central focus of this work is on identity formation, perpetuating Deaf Studies' focus on identity (Emery & Iyer, 2022). The authors of these identity-focused intersectional studies reflect the general trend of challenging Deaf Studies' universalizing narratives, and a rich stream of scholarship has emerged to address the intersections between, for example, deaf and LGBTQIA+; deaf and Asian ethnic minority; black and deaf; black, deaf, and queer; black, deaf, and feminist; deaf and Latinx; and deaf and woman (for references, see Emery & Iyer, 2022; for a recent overview of the literature, see Dunn & Anderson, 2020, and Miller & Clark, 2020). Some of these studies reflect the finding that minoritized deaf people may (also) show a strong sense of identification and solidarity with hearing people from the same minority groups. Studies focusing on the intersectional experiences of, for example, deafdisabled, deafblind, and transgender deaf people remain limited in number.

The previously mentioned studies on identity, although exploring intersections, typically do not address international deaf mobility. In Chapter 4, we noted that studies of deaf ethnic minorities typically do not mention migration, even though some black people in the United Kingdom, for example, are also migrants or had parents who were migrants. Often, international mobility features only peripherally, although there are a few notable exceptions (e.g., Martens, 2020). Additionally, most studies of intersectionality (and not just in Deaf Studies) also limit their analysis to one particular country—what Patil (2013) calls "domestic intersectionality"—and do not center (international) mobility. This approach does not reflect the lives of the many people who are mobile both within countries and across national borders. For example, social locations that are privileged in one geographical location may be marginalized elsewhere (Mahler et al., 2015). Also, mobility can itself trigger new journeys in search of spaces of belonging. Migrants are often embedded in transnational networks and relations that include ties to the country they have left (Anthias, 2008; Anthias et al., 2013; Brickell & Datta, 2011; Greiner & Sakdapolrak, 2013). When deaf people mobilize to a new place, they may be drawn toward people with whom they share a country of origin, culture, spoken/written language, or religion. In the spaces of belonging that they traverse, relations with other people are uneven and are laced with power differences and inequalities, which often result in tensions and even conflicts. The analysis of belonging needs to reflect this fluidity.

Intersectional approaches to the study of belonging thus need to be multiscalar; that is, they must take into account various scales, such as local, national, regional, and global (Mahler et al., 2015). The focus on scale is in line with the translocality framework, which "disengages the experience of locality and belonging from being situated in a particular neighborhood or homeland and instead locates it in the mobile bodies and multiplicity of spaces of immigrant lives" (Low, 2017, p. 181). Translocality is a useful framework that looks at simultaneous belonging within the multiple spaces in which people are situated or with which they identify (Anthias et al., 2013). Antonsich (2010, p. 645) uses the term "place belongingness," meaning "belonging as a personal, intimate, feeling of being 'at home' in a place." "Home" is a symbolic space of familiarity, comfort, security, and emotional attachment (Antonsich, 2010; Yuval-Davis, 2011), which is not necessarily tied to one or more fixed place(s). Mobile people, such as migrants, can build, strengthen, and deepen ties to multiple homes over time, and these homes can be mobile themselves (Ralph & Staeheli, 2011). In doing so, they are homing, which is a process of becoming, an endeavor to feel at home (Boccagni, 2022).

Place belongingness and homing can also be conceptualized on multiple scales (e.g., a flat or house, a neighborhood, a national community, a global community) within which deaf people may be interconnected via networks (see Chapter 7). Place belongingness for deaf people is often related to mobility outside of one's area of residence: Deaf people visit deaf clubs, the houses of deaf friends, and deaf gatherings elsewhere in the area, the country, and even abroad (as we show using maps in Chapters 3, 4, and 7). Therefore, the study of deaf people's place belongingness must go beyond national territorial frameworks (Breivik et al., 2002), hence our engagement with translocality and intersectionality when examining mobile deaf people's spaces of belonging.

In this chapter, by drawing on observations and interviews from selected case studies across our four subprojects, we demonstrate the various ways in which deaf people navigate, maintain, and contest their sense of belonging across different contexts and on different scales. Our purpose is to focus on people's movements between groups. We consider "groups" in a looser and more flexible way than the community concept allows; for example, our analysis includes tour groups and other temporary groupings. We focus on how deaf people participate in specific spaces and institutions, and how particular spaces give rise to specific experiences of privilege and/or oppression and marginalization. By doing this, we tie into the tradition of deaf geographies, exploring a variety of deaf spaces and how they emerge within specific places (see Chapter 1). In some of the cases we discuss in the next section, we show how affiliations and feelings of belonging can *shift* across contexts according to "where one stands" (i.e., one's standpoint or position). We show how various intersections became visible to us in these contexts. Our use of "to us" in the previous sentence acknowledges that our own positionalities shaped the intersections we witnessed or experienced or that were narrated to us by participants (see Chapter 2). Language competence is perceived as one of the most important gatekeeper devices in spaces of belonging; this is covered in Chapter 8, where some of the same participants' experiences feature.

The chapter is divided into two sections. In the first section, we focus on migrants who find spaces to belong in the place to which they have migrated, in this case, London and Kakuma Refugee Camp. In the second section, we focus on spaces of belonging that emerge in the context of travel for tourism, conferences, and sports events.

Finding Spaces to Belong After Migration

In this section, we focus on deaf migrants, including refugees, who have moved at various stages of their lives (e.g., as a child with their parents, as a student, or as a newlywed). They have connected with people from their home countries and/or from the same ethnic groups, but they have also interacted on a frequent basis with people who are not from their country—that is, in multinational, multiethnic spaces, or in groups with shared interests or ways of being. Some of these are spaces in which they are the only migrant.

In London, there are multiple communities or groups of deaf people. For example, there is a deaf rainbow/LGBTQIA+ community, a deaf European migrant community, and a deaf student community. Migrants may "sample" various groups in search of spaces to belong. Here, we give two examples of locations where Sanchayeeta and Steve did participant observation, which show how deaf people were included or excluded from various deaf spaces. As we discussed in Chapters 4 and 7, deaf Londoners often meet at "deaf pub" gatherings; Sanchayeeta and Steve conducted participant observation at the Shakespeare's Head pub on several of its fortnightly deaf social gatherings in 2018. The pub is situated in central London, with good public transport links (i.e., within walking distance of London Underground and national railway stations); it is also near City Lit college, which is popular among deaf migrants and British deaf people alike, because it offers affordable, often subsidized, courses with sign language accessibility. The Shakespeare's Head pub is thus a highly suitable location for a regular deaf gathering. The pub itself is open to the public—at least, to those of an appropriate age, due to the supply of alcohol. On deaf pub evenings, the pub usually employs two security guards outside the entrance to verify people's age before granting them admittance. However, this is not to say that there were no under-18s at the deaf event: It is possible for younger patrons to enter the pub during the day (in many English pubs, children are permitted on-site to eat until 9 p.m.) and discreetly remain inside after the security guards have taken up their post.

Upon arrival at the large pub, one can spot the deaf space spreading out within the otherwise hearing public space by the moving arms and hands of diverse deaf people. Indeed, several different groups tend to meet within this larger deaf space, with some people moving in and out of different groups to greet their friends or acquaintances, while others stay with the same group the whole evening. Sanchayeeta and Steve observed that deaf migrants tended to gravitate toward deaf people who shared one or more social locations with them, such as being of the same nationality, sharing a language, having attended the same deaf school, being gay, and/or having the same religious background. Some participants stated that by doing so, they were able to feel "at home" within the larger deaf space. International deaf people—that is, visitors and newly arrived residents from different parts of the world—tended to use a variety of languages: International Sign (IS); their national sign language with others who knew it; and BSL. One Indian deaf migrant narrated that she was able to feel "free to be herself" using Indian Sign Language (ISL) with another Indian migrant. A group of deaf people from Nepal switched repeatedly between BSL and Nepalese Sign Language (NSL) because some were not familiar with BSL—including the wife of a Nepalese man who was temporarily residing in London as a postgraduate student. Nepalese deaf people were exchanging stories about living in London, about people and places they knew back home, and about their plans for the future. This regular social gathering is thus one of the deaf spaces where deaf migrants and deaf international visitors can make new friends, actualize their networks (see Chapter 7), and seek signposts to help them access certain information, advice, and resources (see Chapter 4). These acts thus help them to find, produce, and/or maintain a sense of belonging.

There are deaf Londoners who avoid attending deaf events such as the gathering in the Shakespeare's Head pub. In Sanchayeeta's experience of living and researching in the city, she has observed how deaf British people (usually white) tend to rank deaf social gatherings and deaf events based on social and class-based hierarchies. The Shakespeare's Head pub event is viewed as a site where "grassroots deaf" (see Ladd, 2003) people gather; international deaf people were thus present among crowds of grassroots British deaf people. Sanchayeeta has observed that many white, middle-class, British deaf people consider this space (i.e., this pub, and the deaf people attending it) to be a low-hierarchy social gathering, and they said that they avoid going there for various reasons (e.g., "there, usually something happens like a fight"). This draws a parallel to Ladd's (2003) findings about middle-class deaf people's attitudes toward working-class deaf people. Some British (typically white) deaf people prefer to attend social gatherings that exclude certain groups, such as youths ("troublemakers") and unemployed people, and that create spaces for a limited public of "professional deaf people." Some deaf people from certain religious backgrounds (e.g., observant Muslims, Buddhists) may prefer to avoid deaf events in places where alcohol is served. Class, professionality, religion, and age thus contribute to the production of spaces of belonging, and to the inclusion and exclusion of migrants. Migrants who have arrived relatively recently can find that it takes a while to identify spaces where they can belong, and this can necessitate active networking (see Chapters 4 and 7). The challenge of finding suitable public places to produce or maintain spaces of belonging is illustrated below.

Sanchayeeta and Steve did participant observation at a deaf Muslim organization, Al Isharah, based at the East London Mosque and London Muslim Centre. Al Isharah offers basic Quran classes for deaf adults, delivered in BSL. On average, each class contained 10 people between ages 20 and 60, and the classes were made up of various nationalities including Algerian, Pakistani, and Somali, as well as British. After the class, some of the students would socialize in nearby food places before they dispersed back to their homes in different parts of London. On one occasion, Steve and Sanchayeeta were in a food place opposite the mosque, having ordered drinks while they waited for the students to come in after their afternoon class. When three Muslim deaf women and one man arrived, the person behind the counter approached the man and told him via gestures that he could not enter the venue without making a purchase. It transpired that the proprietor was annoyed that the deaf group had been coming in and using the small venue as a meeting place without buying anything. Three of the group left; one woman stayed to buy a pie from the shop. This was not an isolated incident: We observed that the deaf students were keen to socialize with each other, but there were limited places around the mosque where they could do so without the need to spend money. Another time, Steve and Sanchayeeta accompanied a small group of deaf Muslim women to an ice cream parlor, which was also situated not far from the mosque. A few of the women were complaining among themselves about a Somali woman (who was out of sight of the conversation at the time) who typically relied on them to contribute food and drinks to her. They did not want to do so this time. The Somali woman had come to the

United Kingdom in the late 2000s after divorcing her husband, and the others found her signing difficult to understand. The group waited until the Somali woman returned to the table before going to purchase food and drink, so as to avoid paying for her. However, when they returned with their goods, the Somali woman did not have anything to eat or drink, and one of the women ended up getting her something after all.

From these observations, we conclude that the politics of belonging in public spaces is shaped by economic as well as social capital. In this example, having sufficient money and the willingness to spend it, or having someone willing to make purchases on their behalf, is an underlying factor influencing whether the students have the opportunity to interact with their deaf Muslim classmates outside of class time. It thus influences *where* they can belong. A high proportion of deaf people from ethnic minorities in London, including migrants, are not employed and receive benefits. Being in this position can restrict their ability to participate in social spaces where access is dependent on making a purchase. Place-belongingness is therefore harder to establish in proximity to the mosque than at, for example, the Shakespeare's Head pub gatherings. Here, deaf time and space are preplanned, and even though money does have to be spent to some extent, the pub is a large enough venue that individuals can get away more easily without buying drinks. However, because alcohol is consumed during the pub gathering, the space may be less comfortable for people who do not drink alcohol.

We now shift from a focus on place-nodes, in the form of public venues, to a focus on individuals (i.e., person-nodes) who try to find spaces of belonging within the larger landscape of London deaf spaces. Sana, a deaf Indian Muslim woman, met her deaf British Indian Muslim husband, Shafiq, through shared network connections, and their relationship developed online (see Chapter 7). Once in London, Shafiq acted as Sana's main guide to British deaf communities in London, taking her to deaf pub gatherings, to a caravan event outside of the city, and to various deaf clubs. The people he introduced her to were mostly grassroots deaf groups, made up of a mix of white deaf people and deaf people from ethnic minorities. Sana found their mannerisms, attitudes, and ways of life to be different from what she was used to, and she was taken aback to find that many deaf people in London made heavy use of English mouthings and wore hearing aid devices. Her expectations had also been shaped by her education: While taking an ISL course, she had learned about deafhood and deaf epistemology and ontology, and initially expected deaf people in the United Kingdom to be "strong deaf," with a strong sense of deafhood, as she had witnessed in both the United States and India. The mismatches between her expectations and reality colored her interactions with deaf people in her early years.

At British deaf community events, Shafiq told Sana not to question a person's actions or behavior, and to leave them alone if they did something that she found inappropriate. However, she continued to find it difficult to build new relationships:

> People would say "hi" to me. I would reply—they would ask how I was, and I would say "fine." That would be the end of the conversation as they went to speak to somebody else, so my exchanges were very short. People didn't talk to me at length. They would ask me how I was, how my job was going, perhaps congratulate me on coming over from India, and that's it. I resigned myself to taking a back seat, whereas my husband knew his friends really well and they would have long conversations in BSL while I watched from the sidelines, all the while taking in the language. (*Finding Spaces to Belong*, 00:45:40)[1]

---

1. https://vimeo.com/854367099#t=00h45m40s

Sana's account shows how difficult it can be to build relationships even in spaces where one wants to belong. Initially, she found it challenging to build rapport with deaf people through these brief and superficial conversations. Her lack of confidence in BSL played a part in this; although she would observe Shafiq's conversations with others, she would wait until they got home to ask for clarification of things she had not understood. Later, she learned that she could interrupt a conversation and that the signer would clarify meanings for her—a phenomenon that she recognized from her home country and attributed to the shared deaf behavior she valued: "[It is] same with [deaf people in] India! [That's] deafhood!" (See Chapter 8 for a contrasting story regarding asking for repetitions.)

Belonging was also a slow process for Aisha, one of Sanchayeeta's newlywed participants. It took her 2 years of effort to build relationships with deaf and hearing people in London through BSL and English classes (see Chapter 8), and through her employment as a carer for elderly and vulnerable deaf people. The changes in her sense of self are shown in the self-portraits she produced for Sanchayeeta (see Figure 9.1) and were also noticeable in her interviews. During her first 2 years in London, she was interviewed several times by Sanchayeeta, who noticed that Aisha gradually reduced her Indian gestures, including the Indian "head wobble." Belonging in the United Kingdom for Aisha thus meant acquiring a different body language and different ways of communicating, going far beyond acquiring a new sign language.

As with Sana and Aisha, other migrants have felt varying degrees of belonging in different deaf spaces across the city, and they have experienced difficulties finding spaces where they could belong and in which they were made to feel welcome. Fareed, a deaf Middle Eastern man, came to London in the 2000s during a period of political instability in his home country. He met his Indian wife, Shahina, via a shared friend from the Philippines (see Chapter 7); she joined him in

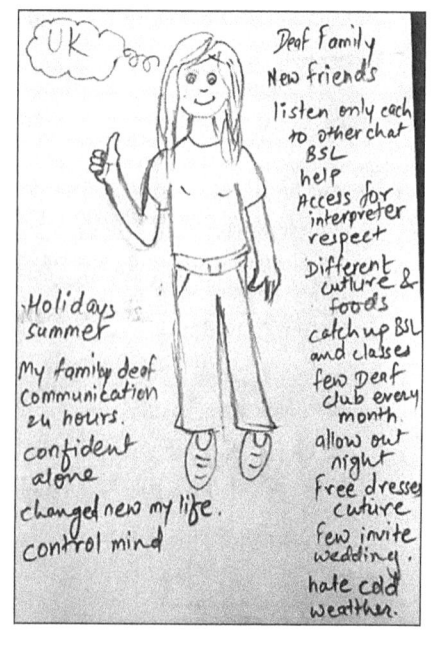

Figure 9.1. Aisha's self-portraits: reflections on how her sense of self shifted through moving from India to the United Kingdom.

London in the 2010s. In an interview with Steve, it transpired that their respective early experiences of encountering British deaf people in the city had differed considerably:

Steve: [to Fareed] Have you found deaf people to be supportive and accepting? Do you feel you "fit in"?
Fareed: Well, I went to lots of deaf nightclub gatherings and pub gatherings and met deaf people, and when I introduced myself, they always asked me where I'm from. When I [told them], they always asked why I moved here and what did I move here for. I said, well, my uncle lives here, and I moved here to learn and study English. We usually moved on with the conversation then, but they did ask every single time, and again and again, why I moved here.
Steve: They just kept questioning you?
Fareed: Yeah—they always asked the same questions about why I moved here. Some people did tell me to move back, to get out. [...] I was usually seeing them at nighttime when that happened. They didn't want foreigners here—they wanted to preserve their British culture and people—it's "theirs."
Shahina: That's so different to my experience—all British people are lovely with me.
Fareed: Oh, it's only at the pub. And it isn't so much now, just at the start.
Shahina: Oh, but still, even at the start when I moved here my experience was positive, British people were lovely. It's the opposite to your experience of being seen as a foreigner and asked to get out!

There are many layers to this narrative: Gender, class, ethnicity, and the timing of arrival in the United Kingdom emerge as factors that affect the experiences of new arrivals. This husband and wife arrived in the United Kingdom in different decades (the late 2000s and the early 2010s, respectively) and thus in different sociopolitical contexts. In the 2000s, societal attitudes toward new arrivals from the Middle East were generally hostile (Wintour, 2017); 2003 saw the invasion of Iraq, and in 2005 the London bombings took place (often referred to as 7/7), in which four coordinated suicide attacks were carried out by Islamist terrorists on the London transport system. Because many people in the United Kingdom associated "Arabs" with extremist Islamism and gender segregation, and because his home country is a member of the Arab League, Fareed seems to have run afoul of these prejudices. Shahina, on the other hand, is Indian, and attitudes toward "Indians" were generally less hostile at the time. Additionally, although Shahina is Muslim like Fareed, she does not wear a hijab or other clothing that distinguish her as such; consequently, she was likely assumed to be Hindu or Sikh. (In Britain, distinctions between different groups of Indians—itself a generalizing term often used to encompass people from various South Asian countries—are often made along religious lines, with Muslims assumed to be Pakistani.) Shahina also has a different social status and education level than her husband, which may also have positively disposed the British people she met toward her. In comparison, Fareed has less access to wealth, and he has limited English skills. He also took more initiative in interacting with British deaf people in the city and was well-known in ethnic minority groups in London. The man's proactive socializing, combined with his social locations within the spaces he visited (e.g., nightclubs), had exposed him to xenophobia and anti-Arab and Islamophobic microaggressions. By being asked what he was doing in the United Kingdom, he was made to feel that he did not belong; this is an example of boundary creation through the politics of belonging. Fareed also explained that he experienced a change over time and that he got negative responses mainly in the beginning. As we saw in Aisha's story, developing a sense of belonging can be a long process.

Although Aisha has *reduced* her "Indianness" while in the United Kingdom, other migrants have foregrounded aspects of their identities that they did not place strong emphasis on before migrating. A notable example is some migrants emphasizing, or even "discovering," their deaf identity following migration; see Rosa and Francesca's narratives of "becoming deaf" (in Chapter 4). Another key example is sexuality, of which Luis and Lenka are illustrative. In *Finding Spaces to Belong*, Luis, a young Guatemalan man in his early 20s, describes coming to the United Kingdom via Portugal, having grown up living between these two countries (00:21:58).[2] He chose to move to London to progress his education to degree level because accessibility and support for disabled students in the United Kingdom are better than in Guatemala and Portugal. At the time of the first interview (2019), Luis stated that he had planned his stay in London to be temporary, intending to have a rich social experience while getting on with his studies. During his first year of living in the city, he had interacted with two gay men from France and Germany and had learned more about their lived experiences in these countries. In Guatemala and Portugal, both predominant Catholic countries, the quality of social life within queer communities is low, and they are not very visible. Luis came to the conclusion that equality, rights, support, and social life for queer people in London are better than in these four other countries. Based on this information, he decided to stay in the city long-term. For Luis, being in London allowed him to freely explore his gay self. This social location was not at the forefront of his mind when he was planning his migration to the city; however, through his socialization with deaf gay men in the city, it became central in his thinking about his future life. In the following quotation, he explains that he sees queer deaf spaces as spaces to which he has a strong bond, based on his dual identification as queer and deaf. He noted that the wider deaf community is slow regarding the uptake of new terminology and perspectives in relation to sexual identities, especially in comparison with hearing people. He told Sanchayeeta that he consequently found it easier and more comfortable to be among the queer deaf community than the wider community:

> On the one hand you have the wider deaf community, the deaf world, and on the other hand smaller groups, such as gay and lesbian. My sign for that community is "queer" [RAINBOW]. In these subgroups, you have closer bonds with one another which you don't see in the larger deaf community. The larger community can actually be oppressive to these smaller groups [. . .], which is one of the reasons why social bonds in those smaller groups form very quickly. [. . .] The wider deaf community finds it hard to learn and understand all the different terminology for different [queer] identities, and the community is often not open-minded—they lag behind in terms of attitude changes. So, when you compare this to the wider hearing community who have taken on board these new concepts quickly, the deaf community often [. . .] suffers from gaps in information. [. . .] I have found it better with my fellow queer deaf [people] because we share much more in terms of experience and identity, so we have a dual connection. Our deafness and our membership of the queer community unites us. Of course, I am able and happy to get on with people across the full spectrum; it's more about whether the wider deaf community is accepting of me or not. I, myself, am very flexible and just want to get on with my life. (*Finding Spaces to Belong*, 00:27:27)[3]

---

2. https://vimeo.com/854367099#t=0h21m58s
3. https://vimeo.com/854367099#t=00h27m27s

Luis clearly distinguished between "social location" and "identification" here, as well as alluding to the "politics of belonging" (see Yuval-Davis, 2006). In terms of his social location, he explained that he is a gay man, but that his identification with queer people as a collective came to the forefront in London, where he found belonging in queer spaces (not exclusively *deaf* queer spaces). This experience of identification came to influence his perspective regarding his future. He flagged the politics of belonging within the wider national setting (London was identified as a "better" place to live for disabled students and queer people alike because of the "rights" and "support" available) and also within the wider deaf community, stating that he felt he belonged less in deaf spaces where people are "not accepting" of his sexuality. Although Luis talked about having a dual social location (queer and deaf), he also often gathered with people who had more than these two social locations in common with him—for example, people who were not only deaf and queer, but also male, and part of an ethnic minority, and/or a migrant. For example, he socialized at the Shakespeare's Head deaf event with mostly European gay men of different ethnic backgrounds.

Similar to Luis, Lenka N. also talked about belonging in relation to sexual orientation in the film *Finding Spaces to Belong* (00:01:19).[4] A deaf Czech woman of "Gypsy" (her term) heritage through her deaf mother, Lenka moved to England to gain work and life experiences because there were limited academic and employment opportunities for deaf people in her country of origin (see Chapter 8 for other parts of Lenka N.'s story). Like Luis, she did not arrive with the expectation that she would eventually make the United Kingdom her permanent home. After living and working in the United Kingdom for a few years, she began to question her sexuality and her desire for companionship when she entered her 30s. At that point, she was introduced to a deaf Czech man from the same region she was from, and they also share the same (Czech) signed and spoken languages. These factors played a part in the growth of their close friendship, and Lenka considered him as her "brother." He introduced her to his circle of deaf gay friends. Lenka felt "at home" among them: She had found a space where she could relax and be herself, and thus "belong." She had not yet interacted with deaf lesbians in the city because she was not comfortable entering spaces that she felt were, in her words, like a "meat market"; for example, she had attended a mainstream lesbian club and bar in which women were checking each other out, and she felt "on display." When she met her first female partner (a South African hearing woman), she became connected to a small group of hearing lesbian friends, made up of migrants of different ethnicities and nationalities. While she was with her South African partner, Lenka called this group her "core friends."

In contrast, Lenka found that deaf lesbian groups tended to question her participation in the space and that they treated her like a guest because she had a different background from many deaf lesbians, being a deaf migrant who also fluidly switched between signing and speaking. She did not find that she experienced the same ambivalence with the hearing group of friends. However, as Lenka moved into a different chapter of her life and as her relationship with this partner came to an end, she found herself increasingly distanced from this "core group," preferring to participate in a deaf (wider community) space where she could sign with anyone and take a break from lipreading. She is now in a relationship with a British deaf woman. Certain elements of Lenka's "homing" narrative, such as the years that she felt "at home" in hearing spaces with other queer people, show that her spaces of belonging ("identifications") have aligned with different social locations during different periods of her life. For Lenka, spaces of belonging were mainly with smaller groups of friends, which have shifted throughout the various stages of her life.

---

4. https://vimeo.com/854367099#t=1m19s

The previous stories have included examples of migrants connecting with people from their countries of origin as part of their journey to find spaces in which they can belong. Lenka's new Czech "brother" introduced her to the gay people who became her good friends, and Nepali people gravitated toward the Shakespeare's Head to catch up with each other. In the next paragraphs, we explore this theme further. We look at belonging on a translocal scale, by looking at deaf people's simultaneous affiliations across national borders—within the host country, within the country of origin, and within groups of deaf and hearing migrants originating from the same country.

Another story featured in *Finding Spaces to Belong* is that of Samba. Originally from Sierra Leone in West Africa, he was brought to London as a teenager after his father's marriage to a British resident. On her advice, Samba was brought to the United Kingdom to obtain quality secondary schooling. He went to a deaf school in London. When Samba was young, he socialized within a crowd of young deaf men, most of whom were first- or second-generation migrants attending the same school and football (soccer) club. However, he started to question this circle of friends as a space of belonging because they were involved in "bad boy" activities he described as "very un-Christian." He had also been threatened with a knife by a white man who was part of this crowd. Samba described his involvement with the group:

> Before, I thought that by being with [this crowd of young men], with bad boy behavior, smoking spliffs and all that, I thought it was a form of integration. It was integration in a way, but did the group have a good reputation or profile? No, they had a bad reputation, and I came to realize I didn't want to be associated with them. I didn't want to go down that path of life. I removed myself from them. It was really hard to leave them actually, but [...] I have Christian faith and that was important to me.

There is ongoing discourse, rooted in colonialism, in the U.K. news media and social policy that portrays young black men "on the street" as pathological, deviant, underachieving, unemployed, and responsible for inner-city crimes (Gunter, 2010). Samba's narrative shows the influence of this discourse: He described in the interview how he was perceived by society based on his appearance ("a bad boy") and by his association with the "bad profile" group conducting illicit activities (smoking cannabis) in public spaces—that is, fitting the racist stereotype of a young black inner-city man. He found an alternative "home" within a church close to where he lived, in which there were Christians of various backgrounds (including those from Iran, the United States, India, and elsewhere) and where he could access biblical knowledge via BSL interpreters. There were also classes provided in BSL to explain biblical texts in more depth, and a BSL Bible discussion group attended by deaf people born in the United Kingdom as well as deaf migrants. By breaking away from his former associations and aligning himself with the people at the church, Samba experienced a shift in how society perceived him, having found what would be perceived by many British people as an "appropriate" way of integrating into the mainstream. He even obtained part-time work as a caretaker at the church.

Samba presented his Christian faith as the core of his being, and he experienced place-belongingness alongside spiritual fulfillment at the church due to it being both a multicultural and multilingual Christian space:

> I am deaf, and black, but none of that matters in church [...] [T]hat doesn't mean I have to abandon my culture; I still keep that. It is an integral part of me, but the Christian faith [...] has taught me humility, given me a sense of calm and belonging. I have been able to integrate with people from

different nationalities, as well as British, and take on BSL as a rich and living language. This hasn't depleted my ASL; I have a richness of language in both signed languages.

Samba's sense of belonging was based on the access and shared values he found there. He asserted that his deafness and skin color did not matter at the church; by this, he did not mean that they were erased, but that at the church, deaf and hearing people of different nationalities and ethnicities had opportunities to come together. He was also enabled to improve his BSL skills, as well as to preserve his ASL by using it with deaf people from abroad.

The church was also attended by hearing people from the Sierra Leonean community in London. The church is located in the same borough where Samba lives, an area where Sierra Leonean people reside and socialize, and where they can go to Sierra Leonean spaces such as shops, cafés, and restaurants. Samba took Sanchayeeta and Jorn (who was filming) to a Sierra Leonean food place that was a less than 10-minute bus journey from the church (*Finding Spaces to Belong,* 00:17:34).[5] The people eating and working there were from the local Sierra Leonean community; they welcomed Samba, who gestured and used spoken English as he greeted them and interacted with the person behind the counter, but the conversations were short and superficial. As Jorn set up his video camera equipment, Samba ordered himself a meal and drinks, and a specific drink he wanted Sanchayeeta to try, and then took a seat. Samba had been expecting his father to be there, but he was not, and there was little interaction between him and the other customers. The film shows him eating his meal in silence while the other patrons and staff have a conversation, with the TV in the background displaying a program from Sierra Leone. Samba mentioned that he would sometimes bring his deaf friends (who were not from Sierra Leone) to this place, at which he was able to enjoy the Sierra Leonean ambiance and food while also having conversations in BSL. During a panel on migration organized by Sanchayeeta and Steve, Samba explained:

> My deafness is the reason I face barriers in my family, not race. However, then when you are in the deaf community, race may be more prominent. [. . .] It's about being deaf but more about being black. So, in a different context, you're experiencing different types of oppression and have to come up with different strategies and resolutions about how you're going to answer to those.

Samba found it hard to have deep interactions with Sierra Leonean people due to language barriers, yet he experienced racism in deaf spaces; this confirms the findings of James and Woll (2004), Ahmad et al. (2002), and others researching the racialized and ethnicized politics of belonging. He contrasted his belongingness in BSL-dominant spaces in the church and the café with the barriers experienced by hearing people from his country who also resided in London, and he also differentiated himself from other deaf people from Sierra Leone in London: "Other deaf people from Sierra Leone may not be Christian and would really struggle to feel they belong." Even though Samba is aware of other deaf people from Sierra Leone living in and around London, he does not socialize with them.

Despite not socializing with many deaf Sierra Leoneans in London, Samba had a strong sense of duty to help deaf people *in Africa*. He has been involved with African deaf charities that are based in London, such as Aurora Deaf Aid Africa. Sierra Leone remains in the forefront of his mind: He

---

5. https://vimeo.com/854367099#t=0h17m34s

returned to visit the country of his birth in 2003, has kept in touch with friends there, and dreams of going back to share resources and empower the deaf community there by running an organization with deaf development at the center of its work. In this way, Samba's aspirations were oriented toward deaf people in his home country and, more widely, in Africa. The diasporic connection with country and continent of origin was another value Samba shared with the people at his church, which was mostly attended by migrants or the children or grandchildren of migrants. The congregation frequently talked about development "at home" (i.e., in their countries of origin), and giving back to home countries was considered a central value. In relation to this connection to the "home country" and continent, Samba explained that he could maintain what he called his British and African identities (he used Africa and Sierra Leone interchangeably) through having dual passports. In this respect, Samba aligned belonging with national citizenship as well. A British passport has enabled him to have the right to live and use public resources in the United Kingdom while maintaining his African identity, although he also felt that gaining British citizenship had been at the cost of "weakening" his Sierra Leonean nationality. His acquired British citizenship is a formal indication that he belongs in the United Kingdom, where he has lived for the majority of his life; less officially, he saw his participation in the church as a form of integration into British society.

For Samba, Africa and Sierra Leone are present in London not only in the form of other (hearing) Sierra Leoneans living in the borough and the cultural markers they provide (including the availability of familiar food and drink), but also in the form of discourse about the homeland and in his own future aspirations. By belonging to a multicultural church, he experiences a sameness of values and an acknowledgment of his connection to both his home country and his deafness. Samba's story is an example of how migrants are not merely embedded in and shaping the locale in which they are situated, but also in translocal connections with people, places, and resources across the globe at the same time. The stories of the Indian women Sanchayeeta interviewed, all of whom had migrated upon marriage, reveal several layers of complexity as to how these women have experienced translocal belonging. Using the lens of translocality, Sanchayeeta uncovered how her participants have maintained (or created new) connections abroad, both back in India (see Chapter 10) and in other countries where they had visited or lived, but also with other Indian female marriage migrants to the United Kingdom and with British Indian or British Asian people.

Some of the women Sachayeeta interviewed would also interact with each other in their homes. Even though they were not necessarily close friends, they had several social locations in common, and some of them had known each other in Mumbai. Over the course of her data collection, Sanchayeeta noted that Rita went to Aisha's home to teach her to cook a new recipe, Meera invited Seema and her husband to her in-laws' house, Meera and Rita visited each other's homes in the same part of London, and Shahina hosted a birthday party at her home to which Meera, Seema, Aisha, Rita, and Sanchayeeta herself were invited. The latter example shows how the researcher can become part of the networks and events under study (see Chapters 2 and 7). Aisha was also drawn to meet *other* "Indian women" (used as a generalizing label) who were not recent migrants. She longed for a space where she could share experiences, struggles, advice, and resources. However, Aisha learned that although she and British Indian deaf people might share a similar skin color and heritage connection to "the motherland," some British Indian people seemed to identify as more British than Indian:

> We were the same in that we were Asian, but they had a lot of British culture; their skin looked the same as mine, but they weren't interested in what was going on in India. They were more drawn to

British culture, whereas my identity and culture is different. They have grown up more bicultural than me, but are dismissive of our home country.

Aisha had learned that the British Indian deaf people were different from the deaf people with whom she was used to interacting in India. She found that they were not particularly interested in their connection with India, and she noted that the British Asian deaf people in London had grown up exposed to Western ways of life, where, for example, marriage is not considered compulsory. The women noted other differences between themselves and British Asians/British Indians. When discussing their search for spaces of belonging, they often talked about "ethnic minorities" in London (a term that comprises both migrants and nonmigrants), and about British Asian or British Indian people in particular. For example, Shahina found it preferable to socialize with deaf people who shared a similar conversational and educational "level" as she does:

The deaf people I first met [in London] before I got married were able to communicate with me on the same level, but after I got married, the people my husband introduced me to were on a lower level [...] They didn't have education, no degree, they claimed benefits, they moved in with families, and they went to college but didn't complete their studies. They loved to be in receipt of benefits. I was shocked to learn that.

Shahina later clarified that she included people from Eastern Europe, Pakistan, Bangladesh, and so on, in this description. It was not only Shahina who found it hard to relate to other "ethnic minorities" in London: Some of the other women interviewed by Sanchayeeta saw deaf people from certain sectors of ethnic groups as being difficult to connect with due to a different ("lower") level of conversation, reflecting a lower educational status. They had not expected this because they had thought the education system in the United Kingdom was better for deaf people than in India.

The women thus viewed themselves as having better education and/or employment in India than many of the people they met in London. They also felt that they had a different mentality about employment. Like Shahina, Meera was taken aback by the discourse surrounding benefits. She said: "They think I go out and am partying all the time" (i.e., that she had no work to do) and that she was "on benefits." She felt people in the British Asian community had no idea how hard she had worked, and she resented their assumption that she claimed benefits and was unemployed. The neoliberal-capitalist economic system in India, and the absence of benefits for deaf people in that country, has contributed to the construction of a mentality of self-sufficiency (Friedner, 2015); for this reason, some of the participants who had recently migrated from India resented how they were being viewed, and judged, by the British Asian community. Two of them also experienced that older British Indians in the United Kingdom expected them to be deferential by using honorifics (e.g., "aunty" and "uncle"), and they noted a contrast with how they had interacted with older Indian people in the United States. They were thus positioning themselves within the Indian diaspora, comparing the characteristics and attitudes of "Indians" in India, in the United Kingdom, and in the United States, while also aligning themselves with their fellow Indian marriage migrants and with Sanchayeeta, who is British Indian herself.

These examples show how deaf newcomers in London may "try out" various spaces of belonging over the years, seeking out deaf people with other shared social locations and/or shared interests. The "trying out" element applies to establishing whether the deaf newcomer feels able to connect with the other people there, but it also applies to establishing whether they feel comfortable within the places in which these spaces of belonging are produced. We identified the obligation to spend money or to be around alcohol as factors that could deter people from socializing in certain spaces. In the sections that follow, we show that there are parallels, but also contrasts, between London and Kakuma Refugee Camp as places in which spaces of belonging are sought after migration.

As we saw in Chapter 3, Kakuma Refugee Camp in Kenya houses people from various countries, ethnic groups, and clans, with different languages and religious backgrounds. Violent conflicts frequently take place between and within the various refugee ethnic groups and communities, and these are often exacerbated by the politics of intratribal and national conflicts taking place in their respective home countries (Jansen, 2011). These conflicts have also influenced the organization of life in the camp, with the camps' zones of habitation having been divided by the UN High Commissioner for Refugees along ethnic and national lines. For example, the Southern Sudanese refugees are not all housed in the same area of the camp but are separated into three main groups—the Dinka, the Nuer, and the Equatorians—due to the geographical, linguistic, and ethnic distinctions among them. These habitation divisions are intended to help avoid ethnically based factional fighting (Newhouse, 2012).

Historical differences in cultural and religious practices have been propagated in conflicts between ethnic groups, but also between people of different nationalities. As an example, attacks outside of the camp by the Somalia-based Islamic terrorist group al-Shabaab typically target Christians; this creates and stokes tension between Somali and (majority Christian) South Sudanese refugees inside the camp. As a consequence, Somali people are often portrayed in a negative way by South Sudanese people, being associated with fear and suspicion (Stoddard & Marshall, 2015). This negative stereotyping goes both ways, with Somalis also negatively characterizing South Sudanese people. The general culture of fear and distrust can be seen in the many stories about spies and government agents from various countries circulating in the camp, with refugees from Ethiopia, Uganda, Rwanda, and South Sudan often discussing rumors of government or military personnel being secretly present among them (Jansen, 2011). The fact that the home countries' divisions have been transplanted into the camp is a clear example of translocality, and, as the camp contains large groups of people from the same countries and tribes, a "South Sudanese politics of belonging" (for example) applies not only in South Sudan but also within the camp.

It is thus common for groups, clans, and communities within the camp to fight each other and to talk negatively about those of other nationalities (Jansen, 2011). Deaf refugees often spoke to Amandine about their differences and disagreements with people of other ethnicities and/or from other countries, adding negative portrayals of these people as "bad" (see Chapter 3). For example, several deaf refugees from Somalia would describe hearing South Sudanese people to Amandine as having bad manners, or as being thieves, bullies, or worse; there is an interesting parallel here with the stories collected in London, described previously, in which people described others as "not being clever" or "not being educated"—an othering mechanism in the politics of belonging.

It is notable that the Somali refugees Amandine spoke to generally specified that they were talking about *hearing* South Sudanese people; similarly, deaf people in the camp often told Amandine that they did not have hearing friends from other ethnicities or countries, and they portrayed these people negatively. However, when Amandine asked her participants about friendships between *deaf* refugees of different nationalities and ethnicities, they would often say that they could tolerate being friends with deaf people of different nationalities. However, these border-crossing friendships between deaf people were constructed as "out of place" within hearing-dominant gatherings organized along national or ethnic lines. For example, Ken, who is Dinka (an ethnic group native to South Sudan), asked his Somali friend Halimo to come and watch him dance at a Christian South Sudanese cultural event held every Saturday in Kakuma 1. Halimo refused to attend, explaining that it would be too difficult for her to travel to that place. However, Amandine had observed that Halimo was normally willing to go to any deaf event or any deaf gathering, and she would make the effort to attend events that were farther away than Ken's dance event. It is possible that the distance was used as an excuse; Amandine suspects that Halimo may have (also) refused because she is a different ethnicity, nationality, and religion from Ken and the other (hearing) people who would be attending. In contrast, Atem, who was from the same ethnic group as Ken (i.e., Dinka), was willing to accompany him. In other words, it appears that the refugees were conscious of the politics of belonging along multiple lines, and deaf-hearing divisions had an impact on which social locations formed the basis of spaces of belonging.

Whereas national and ethnic border-crossing appeared to be less common in hearing gatherings in the camp, Amandine regularly participated in deaf gatherings where there was a mix of different ethnicities, tribes, nationalities, and religions. During an interview with Ken, he discussed these intertribe interactions:

> Tribes from Somalia are different [from me], but I want Somali friends to come visit me at my house and we can communicate and share stories until we are tired, and it is good for me. I ask Halimo, my friend, [to come to my house], it is good. Deaf refugees from Somalia, Sudan, Congo, Burundi are happy together.

Homes were often discussed as a core meeting place in addition to the public spaces in the camp. They functioned as places where people could exercise autonomy in terms of whom they spent time with. When considering the places where Ken would meet people, it is notable that he would usually meet with deaf refugees from other countries, tribes, and ethnicities *outside* of his home—at adult learning classes, for example, or at church. However, although he would more often host fellow South Sudanese deaf people in his home, he was also happy to host Halimo, who is Somali. In his own home, Ken was able to create a space of belonging with Halimo. Similarly, Halimo's home and shop functioned as an important place for small deaf gatherings to occur (see Chapter 3).

Gatherings in homes took place between friends, but although friendships did exist between ethnic groups and nationalities, it is worth noting that the deaf inhabitants of the camp were mostly married to, or in a relationship with, someone of the *same* ethnicity or nationality as them. When couples married, they would move in with each other (the wife usually joining the husband's household) and continue living in clusters with people from the same ethnic or national group. Homes were thus primarily spaces of ethnic sameness for deaf as well as hearing people, despite the examples given previously of ethnic and national borders being crossed within the space of the home.

In the previous quotation, Ken talks about differences between *nationalities*, and less about tribal, ethnic, or religious differences. This was a common pattern in the conversations and interviews refugees had with Amandine, possibly due to Amandine's line of questioning (i.e., about *international* interactions), and possibly due to their expectation that, as a newcomer, Amandine would have limited knowledge of the various divisions between tribes and ethnic groups within particular countries. The limited duration of Amandine's fieldwork in Kakuma Refugee Camp prevented her from doing a more fine-grained analysis of the divisions between its inhabitants.

In deaf people's narratives of belonging, a distinction was often made between deaf people living *inside* the camp and those living *outside* the camp. In Kakuma Refugee Camp, deaf refugees are physically located in Kenya, but their interactions with other deaf people mostly involve other deaf refugees (i.e., originally from *outside* Kenya), rather than deaf Kenyans. There were exceptions to this: Some deaf refugees had studied in Kenyan high schools outside of the camp (see Chapter 10), whereas some deaf Kenyans from nearby villages had studied as day pupils in the camp's schools. Additionally, Anthony was a deaf Kenyan teacher working in one of the schools in the camp; he was also friends with some of the leading figures among the deaf refugees (such as Atem and Halimo). Amandine became aware of several other friendships and relationships between Kenyan deaf people and non-Kenyan deaf people. For example, she encountered a Turkana deaf woman from a village near the camp who was in a relationship with a deaf Sudanese refugee. They met through a hairdressing course provided by the Saint Clare of Assisi training institute in Kakuma town, just outside of the camp (see Chapter 3). She explained that although marriages between refugees and Kenyan citizens are not allowed, they were living together in Kakuma 1 and were hiding their relationship from the authorities in the camp. In other words, mobility can be triggered by marriage or relationships, although there are constraints placed on this.

To summarize the previous few paragraphs, deaf people in Kakuma Refugee Camp did mix across ethnicities, religions, and nationalities to varying degrees, but more so in some places (e.g., on courses in Kakuma Town) than in others (e.g., in their homes). There are, of course, individual differences between deaf people as to how much "border crossing" they do in their socializing. Some people preferred to mostly interact with people from the same ethnicity, country, tribe, and/or religion: Abdi, a deaf Somali Muslim, spent his leisure time teaching deaf children subjects such as mathematics and English in the after-school programs run by the camp's mosques. Additionally, as we see in Chapter 10, some refugees expressed longing to return to their homelands versus resettlement elsewhere, reinforcing the relationship between spaces of belonging (both real and imagined) and personal identifications based on place, ethnicity, and other markers.

There were also deaf spaces where an apparent overpresence of a particular nationality was experienced. Amandine observed an example of this one day when she was writing up her field notes in the offices of the Lutheran World Federation (LWF), the organization managing the deaf units in the camp's schools. While there, she observed Halimo and a young deaf woman from Somalia visiting the manager of LWF in the same office. During the meeting, the Somali woman was too shy to talk with the manager, and Halimo asked on her behalf that she be moved from Nassibunda School to Fashoda School because she had moved from Kakuma 3 to Kakuma 1 and Fashoda was now more conveniently located. She was allowed to move schools. However, a few days later, the Somali woman came to the office again, by herself this time, to ask to quit Fashoda School because she did not enjoy it due to the high presence of South Sudanese deaf people. This example shows the discomfort that some of the deaf refugees felt when surrounded by deaf people from a different ethnic group or country.

Amandine also encountered examples of even more stark divisions, and even abuse, between deaf people of different backgrounds. National, ethnic, and religious divisions are infused with colorism, a form of discrimination based on the belief that lighter skin is best; the discursive history of colorism partially overlaps with that of racism (Dixon & Telles, 2017). Colorism in Africa is influenced by various geopolitical factors, and it has historically been a deep-rooted issue within, and between, Sudan and Somalia. Within Sudan, fair-skinned "Arabs," who identified themselves as such rather than as African (McDaniel et al., 2021; Monteiro & Ford, 2016), have tended to occupy senior positions of power, whereas black Africans experience discrimination and marginalization. This racial inequality has a long history in both Sudan and Somalia. There are lighter-skinned and darker-skinned people within each country, but the contrasts are also marked *between* countries. Black Sudanese people are seen as "more black" than black Somalis, and Somali people tend in general to be lighter-skinned than Sudanese people. A deaf Sudanese woman, Ayen, explained her experience of colorism at the deaf unit she attended at Nassibunda School in Kakuma 3:

Amandine: You have friends from Somalia and Sudan, both are the same?

Ayen: Yes. It is the same for me. In Tarach School, I have friends from Somalia. But in Nassibunda, Somali people don't like Sudan people. Why? [wonderingly] [...] In Tarach School in Kakuma 1, Somalis and Sudanese are friends, so it is possible. But in Nassibunda school, Somalis don't want to be friends with Sudanese people. They don't like the color of my skin and my face. Why? They blame [abuse] me because of the color of my skin. Why do they blame the color? No, God alone can do it.

Amandine: Why do they blame [abuse] you?

Ayen: I am the one, all blame [abuse] me.

Amandine: Why?

Ayen: Because of the color of my skin which is black. B-L-A-C-K. They don't like it.

In this excerpt, the young woman explained that her experience of colorism was of being "blamed" (using an ASL-concordant sign; see Figure 9.2) by Somali deaf students in her deaf unit in Nassibunda, due to her comparatively darker skin tone. She did not clarify what the "blaming" or abuse entailed. Ayen had moved to Nassibunda School when her household moved to Kakuma 4, following the destruction of their home in Kakuma 1 by extreme weather. Kakuma 1 is more

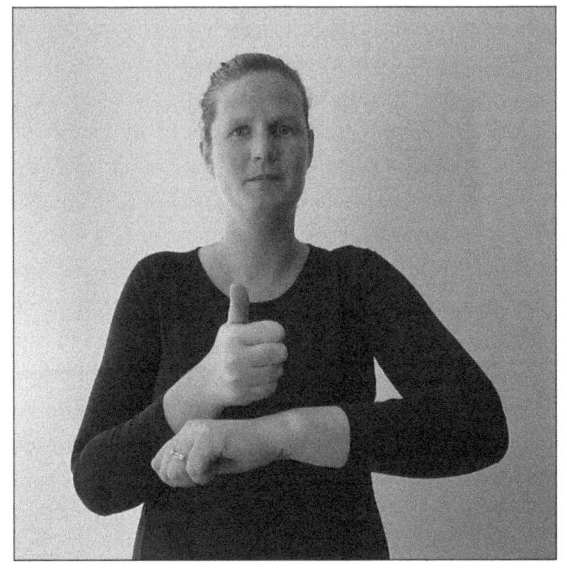

Figure 9.2. The sign used by Ayen for "blame."

diverse than Kakuma 2, 3, and 4 in terms of the ethnicities, nationalities, and religions of its inhabitants because it was established earlier; as a result, the deaf unit in Kakuma 1's Tarach School had a mix of deaf students from Somalia, Sudan, and other countries. In contrast, Ayen was the only student from Sudan in the deaf unit in Kakuma 4's Nassibunda School. In both her story and that of the Somali woman at the LWF office, Nassibunda School can be understood as a place of belonging for Somali deaf people but not for Sudanese deaf people.

In summary, in Kakuma Refugee Camp, we find divisions based on skin color, deaf-hearing, ethnicity, religion, and nationality; we also find that deaf people experience competing demands when navigating spaces of belonging, at times downplaying their involvement with hearing people and tending to overemphasize deaf–deaf connections despite there being incidents of colorism and other forms of discrimination between deaf people. There are situations and places where deaf people's different social locations come to the fore more starkly, either because of spaces being organized along ethnic or religious lines (such as cultural events and domestic residences in particular areas of the camp) or because of the dominant presence of deaf people from a particular nationality (such as in certain schools). These divisions are examples of translocality: Despite the deaf people in Kakuma Refugee Camp having fled Somalia and Sudan, their experiences in the camp mirror both the internal politics of their countries of origin and the political tensions between these countries. While they were based in Kenya, and using KSL (see Chapter 8), their experiences of belonging were thus also very much related to their homelands.

Producing Spaces to Belong When Traveling

In the previous sections, we examined how deaf people who have migrated at some point in their life (whether recently, as in the case of Aisha and Luis, or longer ago, like Lenka, Samba, and most of the refugees in Kakuma Refugee Camp) have explored various spaces of belonging over time. We now move to a set of examples in relation to another type of mobility—that is, when traveling to a country for a short period of time, such as on a touristic trip and/or to sporting events. We explore how these travelers find or create spaces of belonging in more transient contexts, and often based on brief encounters; however, lasting connections are also made, as we will show.

Erin's findings from her research on tourism in Bali show that many tourists have expectations of belonging in deaf spaces, and/or with other deaf people, in the country they are visiting. Being part of a tour led by a deaf guide, in a group of fellow deaf tourists, and visiting deaf institutions and key sites can all be understood as localized experiences of belonging to an imagined global deaf community while also exploring a specific, different culture; similarly, social media hashtags like #DeafTravel and #DeafWorld can be used during or before travel as a way of creating and participating in virtual, cosmopolitan deaf spaces of belonging (see Chapter 6). Cosmopolitanism is characterized by an openness and respect toward, and a tolerance and enjoyment of, difference (i.e., different cultures and languages) located within a *global* sense of belonging (Salazar, 2015).

As an example of a cosmopolitan deaf sense of belonging, when Erin interviewed a group of young white tourists (two women and a man) from France, one of the women said, "I don't feel like being alone. I go to places where there are deaf people. I travel to places where there are other deaf people so as not to feel alone." The other woman followed up on this comment, saying:

> I think it could be because, when I meet a deaf person, and I am deaf, we are the same, we sign—we have that in common. Two cultures meet and learn from each other. If I meet hearing people it's alright, but deaf with other deaf people it is nicer.

These people thus established spaces of belonging through the shared experience of using sign language. The French women did, however, make a distinction between their respective French and Indonesian "cultures," and they repeated several times throughout the interview that they felt "lucky" due to their French nationality and privilege in terms of material resources and legal rights, and "pity" for many deaf people in the Global South (see Chapters 6 and 10 for more on this theme). Their cosmopolitan sense of belonging was thus not based on the assumption of a universal deaf culture but, rather, on signing. The commonality of being signing deaf people is what creates the sense of belonging across different national cultures (as explored in Chapter 8).

As has been mentioned, deaf tourists often make visits to "deaf villages" in search of idealized deaf spaces, where families and community members are presumed to have no communication barriers and are thus considered inspiring (Kusters, 2010). A further impetus to visit is the aspiration to belong in a space that is far away but somehow also familiar. Tourists who visit deaf villages tend to have the expectation of being able to easily interact within the community; however, the reality is often different (see Kusters, 2015, for similar examples in Adamorobe, a deaf village in Ghana). As we saw in Chapter 6, James, a white deaf man from Australia, experienced visiting Bengkala as "an anticlimax" and felt "deflated" not to find a deaf utopia with signing in all domains (see *#deaftravel*, 01:11:52).[6] Nathalie, a white deaf woman from the Netherlands, was similarly disappointed by her experience in the village (*#deaftravel*, 01:01:27),[7] having envisioned the village as a place full of "strong deaf people." "Strong deaf people" is a common term in deaf epistemologies to refer to having a conscious and politicized deaf identity and actively participating in deaf cultural institutions. After Nathalie's group visited Bengkala, she realized that the deaf village was not an exceptional place, because hearing people were in charge there just as in other places. Nathalie did experience a feeling of DEAF-SAME, but that was not enough to establish a sense of belonging. She wanted, and expected, to belong in this "signing village" but instead felt uncomfortable and out of place.

Nathalie's group included a man of Indonesian descent whose Indonesian-born parents had moved to the Netherlands. In Bengkala, he was perceived as SAME, based on his appearance. The deaf villagers that the tourist group interacted with told him that he was "like them" because of how he looked, with a particular focus on the shape of his nose (nose shape, rather than skin color, being the more common marker of ethnic identity in Bali; indeed, the sign used for "white people" can be glossed as POINTY-NOSE) (*#deaftravel*, 01:10:00).[8] During this conversation, the man said that he felt as if Indonesia was "home." As a member of the Indonesian diaspora, he had a translocal sense of belonging in Indonesia based on his appearance and familial connections. Another aspect of (perceived) belonging based on race and ethnicity is the status afforded to tourists of East Asian descent, who can "blend in" on the surface when they travel through Indonesia. During her fieldwork, Erin spent seven days accompanying a couple who were traveling through Indonesia on their honeymoon. Sheila, an American woman of East Asian descent, was traveling with her husband, a deaf man from Italy, and she explained in an interview with Erin that because of her appearance, she had a different experience in Bali than her white husband. For example, she was often charged the "local" price for admission to various tourist sites, whereas the white people in her group were asked to pay the significantly higher "foreigner" price. People's

---

6. https://vimeo.com/588352737#t=1h11m52s
7. https://vimeo.com/588352737#t=1h1m27s
8. https://vimeo.com/588352737#t=1h10m00s

backgrounds and appearances can thus affect how they are treated by the people who live and work in the places they visit. These are examples of the politics of belonging, whereby people decide who are "insiders" and who are "outsiders" based on their perceived race or ethnicity. The politics of belonging are thus always at work, even in the case of brief encounters and short-term or one-time participation in spaces, including visits to tourist sites and the deaf village.

In line with the example of Lenka calling a fellow Czech person her "brother," there were many examples of tourists trying to make or label meaningful connections with deaf people abroad by using kinship terminology. For example, Erin met Sven, a white deaf tourist from Europe, who sponsors a girl in Bengkala and continues to support the family by sending money for renovations to their compound, paying school fees for the girl (whom he refers to as his "daughter"), and supporting other family members. Sven considers this family as his own extended family, and he considers Bengkala to be a second home. Sven initially visited Bengkala as a tourist after learning about it during a sign language conference and reading about it online. As Sven kept visiting the village, over time he transitioned from being perceived as a tourist to being a "visiting family member." He has established belonging in Bengkala by taking on the role of a provider—a gendered, supportive role that establishes his claim of belonging through his sponsorship of the family. The family often describes him as "son" or as a "father."

In another example of sponsorship and an associated sense of familial obligation, James, the Australian man mentioned previously, was a sponsor for a deaf boy, paying for his school fees to attend the deaf school in Denpasar. James first visited Bali years before he started sponsoring the boy; he came first in 2015 as part of an Australian deaf yoga retreat in Ubud, a well-known center for spiritual and yoga tourists. In an interview, James described his immediate sense of place-belongingness in Bali, which contrasts somewhat with his later experience in the deaf village:

> I never thought that I would come to Bali, it wasn't on my list. But in 2015, a group of deaf Australians who were into yoga had a retreat in Ubud. At that time, I was interested in yoga. I was more interested in yoga than in Bali. I didn't expect it, but from the moment I arrived in the airport here and the [exit] doors opened, I was in love. I didn't know what happened to me, I absolutely loved it. I had never felt connected to any other countries, but I feel that connection here. I was hooked. (*#deaftravel*, 00:27:34)[9]

James described his affective entanglement with Bali in romantic terms, as being "hooked" and "in love" with it. He returned to Bali several times and built friendships with members of the deaf organization, Bali Deaf Community, and began a romantic relationship. Through these friendships, he became a sponsor for the previously mentioned boy, the nephew of his Indonesian friends. James framed this specific relationship as a familial relationship, referring to the deaf boy as his "nephew"—an example of kinship terminology being used as a way of establishing belonging, and eliding dynamics of inequality in terms of access to social and material capital. This is, therefore, another example of translocality: These tourists have instilled a country abroad with a sense of home, making it "their" country as well.

---

9. https://vimeo.com/588352737#t=27m34s

James' commitment to supporting the Bali Deaf Community also included volunteering his time to teach at the school for deaf children in Denpasar. James spent a few days observing other teachers and learning BISINDO, and then he led theater and literature lessons as a way of "giving" to Bali. James explained, "I am not a wealthy man, but I have skills and experience as a teacher in Australia. This is a way that I can contribute to the Balinese deaf community." James engaged in fundraising for Balinese deaf people during the pandemic (see Chapter 10). After travel became possible again, James returned to Indonesia to see his deaf Indonesian boyfriend and continues to participate in translocal affective networks, supporting his boyfriend's tailoring business by advertising his products on Facebook.

In the previous sections, we focused on how tourists establish belonging with "locals" in the countries they visit. We now move to belonging within groups of tourists while continuing to focus on the theme of "family." In Chapter 8, we discussed how a German deaf tourist called a fellow German her "child" because she was teaching her how to communicate in IS and ASL. In another example, Erin joined a small tour group led by deaf Indonesian guide Wahyu, comprising Biff and Laura, a white deaf couple from Australia, and Magan, a deaf man from India. After she approached the group and introduced herself, Biff introduced himself and Magan, saying of Magan: "He is like my son." They had met in a Facebook group focused on sign languages and transnational deaf connections about 4 years prior and had since met in person three or four times, maintaining communication online. The description of their relationship as father-son reflects the power dynamics in the relationship: Magan, the "son," is of a different economic class and South Asian, whereas Biff, the "father," is white and comparatively wealthy. The couple had paid for Magan's travel expenses for his trip to Bali and explained that they were "teaching" him how to travel and experience other cultures. The couple said that they did not have children, so they invested in deaf people from countries in the Global South, "teaching" them about deaf identity and the appropriate terminology to use (such as the rejection of the word "dumb"). Other examples included Biff teaching Magan how to make change in foreign currency. When Erin, Magan, and the couple were in a café, she noticed that Magan had taken Biff's wallet and gone to pay for the drinks. Noticing her watching, Biff told her: "I am teaching him how to figure out the money." This illustrates that in situations of unequal power dynamics and access to resources, some deaf tourists frame their relations with people from other backgrounds as relations of kinship as well as of patronage. This dynamic is not always one-way, however; the group explained to Erin that when out for dinner the night before at an Indian restaurant, Magan had done all of the ordering for them, guiding them through the menu and choosing them delicious food that they both enjoyed.

Another example of establishing belonging within a group was an instance of humor during the Travass tour, based on shared understandings of the deaf ecosystem. While the group sat waiting for lunch to arrive following a visit to a site, the discussion turned to perceptions of deaf people who are on government benefits and who travel instead of working. Two of the group members, one from Germany and the other from the United States, were vocal about their perceptions that some deaf people take advantage of the welfare system. During this discussion, a tour member from London made a joke: "What does DEAF mean? It means Deaf Expect All Free!" (see *#deaftravel*, 01:38:04).[10] The shared laughter was a form of bonding among the group, who were all different nationalities but could relate to in-group humor about the foibles of deaf

---

10. https://vimeo.com/588352737#t=1h38m04s

people. Travel to a different place forces the traveler to shift their attention away from the familiar and to engage with difference in some form; the group had done this by traveling to Indonesia, yet they also bonded over shared deaf experiences and community knowledge from their countries of origin. Many deaf tourists seek out sameness by connecting with other deaf people, and this is experienced as DEAF-SAME—but also as different (Moriarty Harrelson, 2015), a notion that nuances the ideal of a deaf universalism exhibited by so many deaf tourists (see Friedner and Kusters' [2015a] edited volume on this topic).

We now move on to two examples of discrimination within tour groups. The deaf tour groups observed by Erin in Bali were generally small international deaf spaces, consisting of several people who had gathered in the context of leisure. The Travass group was composed of white deaf tourists on a tour together in Indonesia, and also Kareer, a Muslim man from London. His narrative shows tensions between his personal positionality and the collective of the group of deaf tourists. Several of the white tourists jokingly marked Kareer as "other" based on the color of his skin, teasing him about his "tan." Erin asked Kareer in an interview how he felt about these jokes; Kareer chose not to acknowledge the implications of comments about his skin color, saying that they were just joking and that he did not believe in marking his difference. He downplayed the other group members' behavior:

> We know there are countless issues happening in the world related to racism, sexism, and many others. I am trying to make fun of that because I do not want this negativity all the time. I am trying to make things more positive. The topic of being black is not important to me—it doesn't make you different or apart from others—we don't need it. [...] I am trying to be a force for change—getting rid of those labels and promoting diversity. [...] Really, I am open-minded and never bother talking about that issue. When I say open-minded, I mean we never speak specifically about that topic. [...] I instead choose to care and show interest about where a person is coming from, or other details about who they are. [...] I grew up in London and there is a strong amount of diversity. It is multicultural, including public figures—it's a melting pot of people from all across the world. [...] Being raised in that environment has helped me to travel more easily. I am open-minded to meeting people from any kind of background, race, religion, it doesn't matter to me. I grew up open-minded. That helped me—I am not a sensitive person, if someone teases me, or makes fun of me, I don't become angry or aggressive. It is a reflection of that person.[11]

This "politics of belonging" narrative suggests that despite having been singled out as "other" by the group, Kareer placed more importance on positioning himself within the bounds of the hegemonic group of travelers, seemingly focusing on what they shared as a group—that is, deafness and membership in a sign linguistic minority. He maintained his involvement within the tour group's deaf space of belonging by downplaying comments or "jokes" about his race. These sorts of comments have frequently been framed as part of a deaf way of being; it is a common stereotype that deaf people tend to be blunt, descriptive, and direct when joking and making comments (Mindess, 2006). Kareer's way of dealing with this was to have a thick skin and to be open-minded himself, with open-mindedness implying a tolerance for racist jokes. It can be difficult to call out humor as racism, or even to decide when a joke is racist, because playful

---

11. Note that this interview was undertaken in 2018, 2 years before the Black Lives Matter movement gained momentum in the United Kingdom.

subversiveness can be a marker of the genre (see the previous DEAF joke example, and also Chapter 8). It is important to note, too, that Erin's positionality as a white woman and Jorn's as a white man (he was filming the interview) are likely to have shaped how Kareer discussed racism, because black and brown people are often reluctant to talk candidly about racism with white people (Eddo-Lodge, 2017). Kareer explained that ignoring jokes is a strategy that gives him a sense of agency in ensuring his and others' continued enjoyment, because the group enacts belonging via jocular behavior and not by discussing differences. However, it puts the burden on him to remain positive and cheerful. Kareer also noted that he is from London and that this has shaped his positionality; in this and other narratives shared in this chapter, we see that affiliations to London can be complicated and that embracing multiculturalism (as in Samba's example) can be a strategy for belonging.

Another example of this strategy concerns Heena and Harish, a newlywed couple from India who had traveled to Bali for their honeymoon and joined a deaf tour, led by Indonesian deaf tour guide Wahyu and in which a few Italian deaf people also took part. They were made uncomfortable by the comments that another person in the group made regarding migration to Italy. The group visited Tirta Empul, a water temple in Bali that is popular with tourists; as they were waiting for Wahyu at the entrance, a banana vendor approached Heena and an Italian, Roberto. As they interacted with the vendor, who was being a little pushy in trying to sell them bananas, Roberto commented on "pushy" vendors in Italy, which segued into a monologue about "floods" of migrants into Italy, whom he defined as "Muslims," "Africans," and so on. Roberto signed, "... [they] need to airlift them back." Heena, who is a Muslim from India, subtly challenged Roberto, saying with a smirk: "Airlift them back? Really?" Roberto did not seem to understand that his xenophobia was making her and other observers uncomfortable, and he continued with his monologue while Heena looked at him and laughed awkwardly. This is an example showing a painful and difficult situation being strategically defused using humor, or through treating potentially objectionable statements as though they were intended to be humorous. Erin observed this conversation unfold while Jorn was filming it (*#deaftravel*, 01:26:26);[12] in a later interview, she asked Heena how she felt about it. Heena rolled her eyes, shrugged, and said, "I knew what he meant. I know. With people like that, you can't argue. Just ignore it."

Heena and Harish did not purposely seek out other deaf tourists on their trip to Bali, but because they took a tour with Wahyu, they met other deaf people through him. Not everyone that Erin interviewed and interacted with had sought out other deaf people when they traveled, but there were many examples of people experiencing deaf–deaf belonging and making claims to familial connections, as well as the discrimination that Heena experienced. Harish explained that he did not see a reason for seeking out other deaf people; even though they did meet other deaf people during the tour, Harish said that it seemed presumptuous to assume that every deaf person would want to interact with other deaf people while on holiday. He said: "So what? So what if you are deaf? Go on and do your thing." Some deaf people also seek out hearing people during tours. A member of the Travass deaf tour group, Ronja, a white woman from Germany who was a new signer and wore a cochlear implant, ran into a group of hearing Germans in the Monkey Forest, and she abandoned the deaf group to go speak in German with them. Later, Ronja said that "it felt so good to speak in German." Ronja's example of feeling pleasure and comfort in speaking German meant she enjoyed briefly participating in a German space of belonging in Bali. This is a

---

12. https://vimeo.com/588352737#t=1h26m26s

further example of another facet of translocality, that of being at home within a language environment, and with people from one's home country, while abroad.

We now move to a different context: that of the XVIII World Federation of the Deaf (WFD) Congress in Paris in 2019. Within the larger global space of deaf belonging that is the congress, there are subspaces with (invisible) boundaries determining who is included and who is not, based on the group(s) that constitutes the majority in those spaces. In Chapters 5 and 7, we gave examples of subgatherings during the WFD congress on the basis of nation, region (e.g., East Africa), and other axes of belonging. The congress constitutes a confluence of networks in a large "deafened" space, and during international events such as this, people often (re)connect with others with whom they are already networked, thus creating smaller or bigger spaces of belonging. The examples from the WFD event discussed below focus on deaf people with additional disabilities. At the WFD congress, Annelies observed more disabled people using wheelchairs, walkers, or crutches and more deafblind people (with or without guides or interpreters) than in the other transnational settings in which she did fieldwork. Next, we discuss two different accounts of deafblind persons' respective experiences of tension within the WFD global space of belonging, as related to their being deafblind, their physical mobility, and their race.

Often, presentations at deaf conferences are not properly accessible to deafblind people due to inadequate lighting, not being able to see the signing clearly (e.g., because of the signer's clothing or their position), and the ways PowerPoint presentations are created (e.g., dark lettering on light backgrounds rather than the other way around). In areas where people socialize, such as pubs and restaurants, dim lightning often makes it difficult for deafblind people to use residual sight. Deafblind people communicate in a variety of ways, including using their residual sight in a smaller signing space, hands-on signing (touching the hand of the person who is signing and following their movements), and Protactile signing (signing rooted in touch, on the interlocutor's body). Protactile signing originated in the United States (Edwards, 2014) but is less common elsewhere. Korian, a black deafblind man from the United States, prefers to use Protactile signing; his experience was that in the international space of the WFD congress, he needed to educate people on how to communicate in this way:

> The communication [here at WFD] was varied because some know PT [Protactile] well, and others don't. People that I have met have different experiences with deafblind individuals than mine. I showed them the way I sign and that they should not discriminate against me. They didn't know what PT meant. When I meet with a person, I like to feel their body—their head, for example. I touch it like this. That is their body and I want to know it. Some people were surprised that I can feel vibes. I can't see how a person feels, but I can feel it on my hand. I feel their posture. When I communicate with them, we touch each other, which is comfortable. Some people aren't comfortable and that is fine with me. I am not really anxious about that.

Korian emphasized that being black makes it harder for him to educate people on PT because it means touching other people's bodies, much more so than is the case with hands-on signing:

> I am black, which makes it even harder. The history of black people coming to the United States was as slaves. [...] When I was born, [my family] told me to be careful, especially with touching people. I became blind later in life, so I understood what my family meant. I heard that some people think I am fake. They think I am fake because I am black, and deafblind. That I play being like that. It becomes

a discussion. I don't mind, what is important is that I advocate and educate people about the importance of tactile things for deafblind people, and that my skin color doesn't matter.

Korian is aware that he is perceived differently from white deafblind people in the United States, and he appears to attribute his experience of his deafblindness being disbelieved to white people not having seen or met black deafblind people before. Like Kareer, Korian emphasized that skin color should not matter in international deaf encounters, stating that people should focus on him as a deafblind person; however, he also acknowledged that people have been prejudiced against him because of his skin color and that he has experienced barriers because of this. In this global space, he has attempted to direct attention away from his race and toward his deafblindness through his attempts to educate people about how to communicate with deafblind people by using hands-on and Protactile signing. This further confirms the pattern we observed of deaf black and brown people diverting attention away from their race or ethnicity; we assume that this is probably particularly acute when they talk to white deaf people (in this case, Annelies).

In the conference hall where poster presentations and exhibitions were organized at the WFD congress, Annelies observed a few deafblind people using Protactile signing in a circle of four while seated. One of these people was Tashi, who uses a crutch for walking; they require to be seated to use both hands to communicate for longer conversations. As a result, they told Annelies, they sometimes feel that they struggle to belong in deafblind spaces:

> One thing is deaf space, another thing is deafblind space. Yesterday there was a deafblind presenter explaining about the identity, diversity, and so on. It made me think of deafblind crip. There is a challenge in deafblind space—where does a deafblind person stand when they need tactile communication? That is causing a barrier. I can stand, yes, but tactile communication needs two hands. PT is good for giving information with two hands, but I have to hold my crutch with one hand. I can then only sign with one hand. Deafblind people ask me to use both hands, but I can't, I have to explain to them that I use crutches. I can't stand for a long time, so I ask people to sit down with me. Even in deafblind space, I face barriers. I am thinking about how deafblind people are communicating around here. If you know a deafblind crip person here, please connect me with them.

In this example of "identifications," Tashi identified as "deafblind crip" and not just as "deafblind"; they felt that this impacts on their belonging in deafblind spaces and expressed a longing for fellow deafblind crip people. Tashi said that while they do feel they belong in deafblind transnational space because of Protactile communication, they also face barriers due to their other disability because the majority of other deafblind people can communicate when standing up. For Tashi, the availability of sitting space, and the willingness of interlocutors to sit, is important to enable communication. Access to this space of belonging is therefore not only related to the material space, but it is also affected by how people use the space and respond with their bodies.

The next examples focus on the Deaflympics, and they further show how different perceptions of disability inform a politics of belonging. The Deaflympics were organized very early in the history of international multisport events: They were launched in 1924, between the launch of the Olympic Games in 1896 and the Paralympics in 1960. The Deaflympics have often been described as a participation-level event that is also a social gathering (Harrison, 2014). The combination of socialization and sports means that this "[i]nternational Deaf sport competition actively promotes the old ideal of the Olympics—the brotherhood of man through sports" (Stewart, 1991, p. 7). There have often been debates over the need to organize the Deaflympics separately from the Paralympics (Ammons & Eickman, 2011), with one frequently used argument being that deafness is not a disability—perpetuated, for example, by Jerald Jordan, president of the Comité International des Sports des Sourds (CISS, now the International Committee of Sports for the Deaf [ICSD]) from 1971 until 1995. His opinion was that including deaf athletes into the Paralympics would mean enforced integration into a hearing and speaking environment: "The Deaf athlete views the disabled athlete as being a hearing person first and disabled second" (Jordan, in Ammons & Eickman, 2011, p. 1150). The argument continues that deaf people should be considered able-bodied in sports because deaf people do not by default have mobility-related disabilities and gather together primarily based on their being signers (Stewart, 1991). This is an ableist argument that ignores the reality that deaf people may have multiple disabilities and that deafness can be constructed as a disability in itself. It also neglects the fact that deafness is very much "measured" in the context of the Deaflympics: Participants need to provide audiograms in order to compete in the Deaflympics, demonstrating that it is not sign language use but being physically deaf that lends one access.

In the global space of the Deaflympics, belonging and not belonging are thus made very explicit in rules focused on hearing status. In many international deaf events and networks (e.g., the WFD congress), there is an implicit expectation that those present are deaf (this also encompasses hard of hearing and deafened people) and/or that they are signers. In these contexts, if a person says, "I'm deaf," they are typically taken at face value, and there is no requirement to specify "how deaf" they are according to external metrics. In the Deaflympics, IS is used as lingua franca between athletes, coaches, and so on, indicating an implicit expectation that many or most people in the space are signers. This expectation, however, is trumped by the 55 decibel (dB) rule: If you have 55dB hearing loss, you are eligible to participate in the Deaflympics, regardless of whether or not you are a signer. In advance of the international championships, audiograms are checked, and there are selective hearing tests during the Deaflympics too, which are seen as equally important as (or even more important than) doping tests. The 55dB rule did not exist in the early years of the Deaflympics; when it was founded in 1924, the event was called the International Silent Games, with participation open to deaf signers. Following a number of incidents where hearing athletes were caught speaking, and consequently discovered to be hearing, the 55dB rule was implemented in 1979. The rule is considered essential for ensuring a level playing field among deaf people by excluding hearing people; neither is the use of hearing aids permitted during the competition (Harrison, 2014; Stewart, 1991; see Breivik et al., 2002, for descriptions of an incident involving a player using a hearing aid).

Over the years, there have been many discussions about whether 55dB is the "right" number of decibel loss for participation in the Deaflympics or whether the threshold should be higher. People who are moderately hard of hearing can generally access mainstream (top) sports training better than profoundly deaf people because they can communicate directly with hearing trainers and co-players. This has an impact on the level of competition and raises the chances of those with more residual hearing. People who hear more are less likely to know how to sign, however. In deaf team sports, an increasing number of sports players are nonsigners. With a higher decibel threshold (e.g., 75dB), there may be a higher proportion of deaf signers participating; however, an increasing number of profoundly deaf people do not sign either, given the spread of cochlear implants and mainstreaming. Furthermore, a higher decibel threshold may result in fewer people attending overall, making the event unsustainable. These are some of the arguments raised in relation to revising the rule.

The presence of nonsigning oral athletes has been a theme of discussion in deaf sports since their inception, and it features centrally in the Deaflympics' politics of belonging. The perceived problem with the presence of nonsigners is the impact on the general atmosphere and language ecology of the events. Nonsigners are likely to speak only with others from their own country's delegation, for example, especially if there are interpreters available to facilitate communication with sign language users. Where there is a critical mass of people who use speech with each other, the space can divide along oral/signing lines, undermining the "brotherhood" ideal. Pavel, the captain of the Russian chess team, commented during the 19th Winter Deaflympics in 2019:

> What's important for me is the gatherings and the camaraderie in sign language. When the environment becomes more oral, then signers like myself can only communicate superficially, so we seek out and revert to communicating only with other signers. One of the great things about these events is that it feels like there are no barriers because everybody can sign, so if we lose that aspect, it would be concerning.

Athletes who communicate only in spoken language are less inclined, or less able, to communicate internationally. For example, the Russian ice hockey coach, Valery, said about communication between the ice hockey teams:

> If people can't sign, how is that going to work? Back in 1991 when the American team came, we could connect with each other, everyone signing away. It was the same with the Canadian team. Today, neither team has any sign language and we're strangers to each other. It's bizarre. The Finnish team have been good, as has the team from Kazakhstan. It's just not possible to communicate with the teams from America and Canada. The only interaction we get is when we shake hands before or after the games. There is no other exchange or friendly conversation at all.

At the 2019 Winter Deaflympics, certain countries were seen as "more oral" than others because they brought "oral" sports teams, such as the American and Canadian ice hockey teams, in contrast to the Finnish and Russian teams where communication happened in sign language. Marty, the Canadian ice hockey team manager, pointed out that it created a split between signers and nonsigners: "When you see deaf people signing [IS] with each other, it's the same all over. When the hard of hearing join in, then it's different, we're two separate groups." Note that nonsigners are here dubbed "hard of hearing"; this is often the case, even though there are, of course, hard of hearing signers and deaf nonsigners.

In her study of the politics of belonging at the Deaflympics, Annelies asked her interviewees at the 2019 Winter Deaflympics whether they thought athletes should be required to sign. Several interviewees said that it is the "audiograms that decide" and that it is "the sports that matters and not the signing," but they also admitted that they would like it if the use of signing was somehow stimulated or even enforced. Being exposed to signing for weeks on end can be a transformational experience for deaf and hard of hearing nonsigners, and Isabelle Malaurie from France, a leading figure in the European Deaf Sports Organisation, said that it was crucial to include them:

> We need to help and support them, bring them into the fold, to teach and encourage them to sign. Not marginalize them, but welcome them. There are some, however, who prefer to speak, and you have to respect that. For us the most important thing is sport! And whether you sign or speak doesn't

matter. We're here for the sports. [...] They are oral and don't know sign language, but it shouldn't matter. We should all be working together as a collective. [...] They ["oral" deaf people] may be uncertain at first, but we must work actively to make them feel that they are one of us. It was that way in the past, but I think now unfortunately we've formed cliques. There is nothing wrong with being oral, they are not our opposition, and we need to respect them. My thinking is we need to keep inviting them into our team. Then they will see that we can all communicate, and that's important.

The quotation above clearly shows the tension between respecting the communicative diversity of deaf people (including the decision of some people not to sign) and the desire for an idealized, cosmopolitan, fully signing environment. Isabelle talked about the Deaflympics being a global deaf space where all should feel they belong, including deaf and hard of hearing nonsigners, and the importance of welcoming these nonsigners to the fold; this evokes cosmopolitanism in a way that includes a diversity of deaf people. At the same time, her comments held the implicit hope that the nonsigners may "convert" to signing (see Bechter, 2008). Isabelle felt that there is a need to encourage people to sign because they are in an international context where signing is the norm. She was aware that deaf sports events are important places for identity building and for exposing deaf and hard of hearing people to signing (see also Stewart, 1991). Other interviewees emphasized that exposure to signing should be increased at the national level to start with because hard of hearing, nonsigning athletes are less likely to be signers by the time they reach the Deaflympics if they have exclusively trained and competed with hearing players prior to this. Even when people do not use or learn IS at the Deaflympics, they may be exposed to the national sign language used in their team (assuming it contains enough signers) because the majority of deaf athletes spend most of their time with their national team or delegation during the Deaflympics competition.

For reasons of communication dynamics, competitive advantage, and so forth, there were a number of seemingly longstanding debates about whether deaf sports should be split into signers and nonsigners. Some people were in favor of fragmentation between a deaf and hard of hearing group, following the model of the Paralympics where there are many categories in each sport corresponding to categories of disability. This is a major difference between the Deaflympics and the Paralympics; currently in Deaflympics, everyone (e.g., deafblind, deafdisabled, hard of hearing, signing, nonsigning) competes against each other, leading to inequalities. (Note: Annelies observed more deafblind and deafdisabled people in chess competitions than in other sports.) Another type of fragmentation proposed was to distinguish between signing sports and deaf sports; however, Pavel observed that "signing sports" would probably become flooded with hearing interpreting students who want to practice their signing.

In summary, the politics of belonging in the deaf sports world is firmly influenced by the question of "what comes first" in terms of belonging—being physically deaf or hard of hearing, or being a signer? The debates around belonging in, and the priorities of, deaf transnational space are complicated by the overlapping and partially competing purposes of the Deaflympics: that is, as an occasion for deaf people to socialize *and* as an occasion for deaf people to compete.

This brings us to a second issue in terms of belonging as it relates to hearing status. Notably, there are not only tensions regarding the presence of hard of hearing people who are considered to be "like hearing people," but also regarding actual hearing people. As the standards of the Deaflympics have been raised, this development has been accompanied by an increase in the number of hearing coaches and trainers. One of the consequences of the professionalization of deaf sports is the reduction in deaf leadership, which is also related to the way in which deaf sports are funded (i.e., that more funding is available when standards are high; see Chapter 10 for more on this). There are varying perspectives on deaf versus hearing leadership in deaf sports. Some deaf athletes that Annelies spoke to were happy to work with hearing trainers, especially as there was a dearth of qualified deaf trainers. Although some hearing coaches did know the national sign language of the team they were coaching, they typically did not know IS. Other hearing coaches did not know how to sign at all, and they would communicate with their athletes and others via speech and/or through sign language interpreters.

Notably, the technical directors (TDs)—those who oversee and lead all competitions in one sport, such as alpine skiing or snowboarding, and are the supreme authority in each sports competition—were *always* deaf. This meant that, in the organizational hierarchies, the hearing coaches were "sandwiched" between the deaf athletes and the deaf technical directors. In TD meetings, two representatives of each country must be present (of whom the coach is typically one); the guidelines state that where possible, one of these must be a deaf sign language user. Hearing coaches may not address the audience directly, but they must address the audience via a deaf representative from their country. Annelies asked one of the TDs (who chose to remain anonymous) why this was the case:

> Well, it's in our rules. This is the Deaflympics, *deaf* is in the name. It's a deaf way of working, and we don't cater to hearing people. [...] If a hearing person were to come to the front, they'd have to be interpreted via two interpreters in turn, and that way you almost never get 100% of the message. With a deaf person signing, it's 100% clear. [...] The hearing people should stay seated in the audience and give deaf people their space, this is the D-E-E-E-A-F-F-F-lympics after all [signed in an expanded, emphatic, almost angry way].

The involvement of hearing trainers and coaches is thus associated with additional interpreting chains—that is, between visiting countries' national sign languages, the host country's national sign language, the host country's national spoken language, and IS. Interestingly, in the TD meetings, hearing people were positioned as nonsigners and deaf people as signers, even though a large number of the athletes did not sign; however, the deaf people representing the teams in these meetings were usually signers. The previously mentioned deaf TD regularly got frustrated when leading these meetings—for example, when hearing officials from Italy spoke over them—and with people who signed and talked over each other. The TD would lose control over the communication, having to sign STOP STOP frequently. The addition of hearing people who did not know IS and/or who did not engage in effective turn-taking, in combination with the audience not following the TD's admonitions, led to a very complicated communication dynamic.

There were thus continuous debates throughout the event about *who* belongs: deaf, hearing, hard of hearing, signing, nonsigning, familiar with IS, unfamiliar with IS, and so on. There were spaces of belonging for deaf IS signers, such as the ICSD congress and the TD meetings, and also spaces where "oral" deaf people "officially" belonged (i.e., they had the "right" to be there), such as the sports competitions. However, there were still tensions between signers and nonsigners in these latter contexts where nonsigners were in the majority, because their speaking affected the cosmopolitan communicative atmosphere. This shows how the politics of belonging encompasses much more than simply deciding who is in and who is out and making these distinctions part of the event's regulations (e.g., through the 55dB rule). Debates continue regarding who belongs "more" than others, irrespective of whether people are "officially" allowed in a space.

Conclusion

Deaf people on the move navigate and maintain their sense of belonging, and their experiences of feeling at home, alongside feelings of being marginalized and excluded from certain spaces. Deaf people who move to a new country may "sample" various spaces before they find those that suit them, seeking out people with shared backgrounds or experiences, including class, ethnicity, sexual orientation, religion, and/or shared interests. They may shift between different spaces of belonging (such as clubs or groups of friends) at different life stages.

When people are mobile to a new country, they may socialize with deaf locals of that country. Examples covered in this chapter include going to nightclubs, going to local deaf pub evenings, having a local partner, volunteering in a deaf school, and visiting a deaf village. Although mobile deaf people are often the only international deaf person among deaf locals, we have also given examples of mobile deaf people taking part in *multinational* spaces, regardless of the type of mobility. These spaces include gatherings with other deaf migrants or other deaf refugees, going to a deaf pub evening, participating in a deaf tour group, and attending a conference. In the latter cases, people may not interact a lot—or even at all—with deaf locals (see Chapter 5). Belonging as an internationally mobile deaf person can depend strongly on the "feel" of the place—specifically, is everyone welcome there and, if not, who is not? Whereas deaf migrants in London may be openly asked what they are doing in the United Kingdom, it is expected that there will be representatives of various nationalities at the WFD congress and the Deaflympics, and there is a communal history of interacting with deaf people from different parts of the world and of experiencing using various sign languages. These play a part of a sense of belonging and membership in an imagined cosmopolitan deaf community.

For brief, transient encounters, shared deafness can be the sole trigger for interaction, but for more meaningful or longer, actively maintained connections, deaf people often produce spaces of belonging based on more than just shared deafness. We have shown that some queer deaf people and deafblind people connect with each other based on shared ways of communicating and/or shared experiences of being minoritized (i.e., being deaf and queer, or being deaf and blind). However, being deaf and queer, for example, does not mean that spaces of belonging are automatically produced (or attended) based on this shared social location, and sometimes minority positions "clash" or are hierarchized in certain ways. When deafblindness (for example) intersects with being black and/or other disabilities, this can lead to complicated dynamics within international deaf spaces as people experience how relations within the space are unequal, being infused by specific politics of belonging. Identifying as a queer deafblind crip or as a black deafblind person, for example, does not automatically lead to participating in spaces constructed along these specific intersections (see Moges, 2017, about the rarity of black deaf queer spaces).

Deaf people who are part of a larger diaspora sometimes have multilayered journeys of belonging as they explore their (dual) nationality. The Indian women in Sanchayeeta's study explained that they had related in various ways to deaf and hearing Indians in India, to other deaf Indian female migrants (some of whom they had already known in India), to deaf British Indian citizens (including Sanchayeeta), and to deaf Indians in the United States. "Being Indian" was often generalized in the stories collected by Sanchayeeta to cover a range of religious and ethnic backgrounds; the term was diasporic and could be applied to those located in different places in the world, taking on different meanings in relation to the length of the person's (or their parents') stay in that country (e.g., whether they were a recent migrant or British Indian). We saw the same multiple situatedness of nationality in Kakuma Refugee Camp: Deaf refugees also belonged to more substantive groups of people originating from the same countries, tribes, and ethnic groups. Colorism and national stereotypes contributed to tensions between certain deaf refugees.

People who are minoritized in the context of international mobility may engage in producing salience hierarchies of identifications, and they may place a politics of belonging at the forefront of their experience of various spaces of belonging. For example, they may prioritize talking with deaf people who are "on the same level" or interacting with people of the same religion. We noted that constructing "salience hierarchies" appears to happen most often when people are discriminated against, abused, or subject to prejudice based on colorism, Islamophobia, xenophobia, racism, or ableism. For example, we have shown how some deaf people in Kakuma Refugee Camp foreground being deaf over national differences, and how deaf people may deemphasize the salience of their race or ethnicity, instead foregrounding other characteristics as being more significant in international deaf space—for example, being deafblind or being open-minded. The example of the Deaflympics, with its 55dB rule and its meeting policies, effectively illustrates the debates on salience hierarchies— that is, whether someone considers themselves to be "deaf first" or "a signer first," both in the context of the Deaflympics itself and in the Deaflympics versus Paralympics debates. The deaf people we encountered engaged in a politics of belonging by stating clearly where they belonged and how they saw themselves and others as belonging there (or not) as well. The burden to take the initiative to "fit in" or "adapt" to the majority (and so belong) often lies with deaf minoritized people, and sometimes such statements of belonging were not accepted by others.

Linking with the theme of cosmopolitanism running through the book (see Chapter 1), we note that a "politics of belonging" that centralizes the production and maintenance of boundaries seems to be at odds with the notion of cosmopolitanism as *challenging* boundaries—that is, as a utopian "boundariless politics of belonging" (Yuval-Davis, 2011, p. 147). People may travel or migrate to a new place where they encounter deaf people who embody different cultures and languages; they may hope that DEAF-SAME gives them automatic access to various spaces of belonging. However, they may then experience disappointment or run against boundaries set within these spaces, which may place them in a marginalized position on the basis of their intersected social locations. Being "open-minded" is often seen as central to cosmopolitanism and is often emphasized in deaf spaces; we showed this in Chapter 8 and in this chapter, with the example of Isabelle welcoming nonsigners. Being able to say that one is open-minded is, however, also related to privilege: It is "easier" for privileged people with power to perform open-mindedness or to signal a cosmopolitan attitude (see also Chapter 8). When minoritized people say they are open-minded, it may be at their own expense, inducing them to downplay markers of their minoritization (see Chapter 10 for an example of downplaying gender). Posing as a cosmopolitan can, in that respect, be interpreted as a burden.

The politics of belonging not only covers who is included and excluded, but also how people define their experience of belonging. A core concept that has often come up in our study—especially when we were looking for examples of belonging—is typically expressed in terms of "family" and "home." Both metaphors take different shapes throughout the data. The "family" metaphor is not unusual for global spaces such as the Deaflympics and the WFD congress, which serve as spaces in which one can belong within a transnational deaf community, corresponding to the ideal of a global deaf space of belonging—which is sometimes explicitly called "family" (Breivik et al., 2002, p. 29). However, "family" is also used in different ways, as shown with the example of Lenka's "brother," but mostly in the tourism examples: the Australian couple who went on holiday with their Indian deaf "son," and the various examples of foreigners fostering newly declared "family members" in Bali. Tourists will "fall in love" with specific places or countries and, from there, establish ties of belonging as they invest in the local community, perhaps by becoming a sponsor for a child or family. Thus, even in contexts where spaces of belonging can be initially short term and fleeting (typical of touristic encounters), people look for deeper and more meaningful connections, and they consolidate spaces of belonging by using kinship terminology in translocal ways.

Connected strongly to the "family" metaphor is the "home" metaphor. The concept of home in the nonmetaphorical sense—that is, a person's residence—is often fraught. In Kakuma Refugee Camp, homes are spaces where people can and do receive people from other countries and ethnic groups, although the location of residences was also organized along national or ethnic lines. Home is also connected with *homing*: the creation of new homes after migration, especially when deciding to settle down; with having a "second home" in a cherished country abroad; and/or with feeling at home in certain groups. Finally, it is also connected with "the homeland," which often means the country of origin from which mobile deaf people have traveled, sometimes decades earlier. Although refugees had fled war in their country of origin and many hoped for resettlement in a third country, in other examples there was also a yearning to return to "the homeland," either temporarily or permanently (also see Chapter 10). This was found with Samba: He chose to live in an area of London with many Sierra Leonean people and to attend a multicultural church in the area, which further fed his yearning to do something for his "home country." For many mobile deaf people, "home" is thus located in various places across the world, and it may also be associated with deaf spaces of belonging in these countries, as in the case of some (volun)tourists in Bali. The "family" and "home" metaphors bring forward the translocal nature of international deaf spaces of belonging, demonstrating the multiple associations and attachments that deaf people have and maintain—even when they are back in their country of origin.

The short-term deaf mobilities studied in this project were sometimes undertaken for, or led to, the establishment of mostly deaf spaces (see Breivik et al., 2002). In the Deaflympics, hearing people's position is contested, even if they sign; in a deaf village, some visitors (such as Nathalie) struggle with the fact that hearing people are still in charge. Some people "become deaf" upon migration, as they shift into sign language use (see Chapter 4). However, in keeping with the translocality lens, we also showed how deaf people may share identifications with hearing people from the same nation, or how they may participate in "deaf pockets" within larger hearing minoritized and/or multicultural spaces.

Our focus on belonging emerged by using an intersectional lens when analyzing our data on international mobilities: We focused on where people go, and with whom they associate, when participating in or producing spaces of belonging. In this process, they were on the receiving end of, and actively participating in, a politics of belonging. Our use of "belonging" as the overarching concept to tie together these various stories has brought out aspects of the stories for which terms such as "identity" or "community" would not be optimally suitable. The examples of "family" and the various meanings of "home" demonstrate this; additionally, the community framework would be unlikely to bring out the variety of spaces that were navigated by, for example, the Indian people Sanchayeeta interviewed, and how they felt about various "types" of British/Indian deaf people. Who is included in, and excluded from, various spaces is very much about who "belongs," about who is "us" and who is "them," whether the politics of belonging is put down in hard rules (such as the 55dB rule) or in implicit expectations. The focus on belonging within the study of mobilities has also brought out different types of belonging that people "go and look for" or long to belong in. People moving to a new country may be in search of spaces of belonging on a regular and deeper basis, while people who visit a country for a shorter period may expect to encounter transient and temporary spaces of belonging in the first instance.

10

Times of Immobility

Amandine le Maire, Annelies Kusters, Sanchayeeta Iyer, Erin Moriarty, and Steven Emery

The main focii of Mobility Studies is on movement and mobility. In Sheller and Urry's "new mobilities paradigm" (2006a), *immobility* is often overlooked, sidelined, or seen as the polar opposite of mobility. Whereas mobility has often been associated with gaining social, linguistic, and/or economic capital, immobility has been associated with restrictions, lack of aspirations, and deficiencies in capital (Carling, 2002; Sheller & Urry, 2006a). In a bid to direct focus to experiences of immobility, Bélanger and Silvey (2020) suggest that a new turn is needed, an "immobility turn" that "pays primary attention to the constraints, regulations, and limits simultaneously placed on migration, everyday mobility, and border-crossings at multiple scales" (p. 3425).

In our research, we have documented examples of deaf people of different backgrounds who aspire to move on and through different scales (e.g., local, national, and international), experiencing a lack of access to resources such as money, languages, food, and information. Regulations at national borders make it very easy for some people, and very difficult for others, to be mobile (Sheller, 2021; Toomey, 2022).

Forms of systemic oppression can prevent international mobilities, most notably institutionalized racism and xenophobia. People may also have responsibilities and care duties that prevent them from being internationally mobile. Deafblind people, deaf users of mobility aids, and neurodivergent deaf people may be confronted with disabling environments (both material and social) when traveling. In this chapter, we look at how the MobileDeaf project's deaf participants experience these various political, social, and material barriers to mobility, both in the form of large-scale international mobility (e.g., transatlantic travel to a conference) and micromobilities within the wider context of international mobility (e.g., moving through the conference venue).

International mobility is not only characterized by movements across space, but it also has specific temporal aspects; *temporality* is equally important in relation to immobility. In this chapter, we focus on how people, individually or collectively, understand and experience time in the context of (im)mobility and migration. For example, immigration policies and visa regimes operate as instruments of discipline, which often require certain types of migrants to wait for a very long time (Cwerner, 2001). Several of our participants were waiting for visas or the right to remain in the United Kingdom, and deaf people in Kakuma Refugee Camp can wait for years to be resettled. Some people wait for months for a tourist visa or are prevented from traveling to conferences due to visa complications, whereas others can travel visa-free. Thus, the border is "a timing device" (Sheller, 2021, p. 79), and not only a spatial one.

A key aspect of temporality in relation to mobility, especially in relation to conflict-induced displacement, transit, and forced migration, is *uncertainty*: "imperfect knowledge" and "the unpredictability of the future" (Horst & Grabska, 2015, p. 4). Imperfect knowledge is the lack of (often vital) information that will better enable survival, and it causes great levels of uncertainty in situations of instability. The unpredictability of the future is related to the fear of the unknown. In addition to experiencing uncertainty, migrants often express feelings of boredom and frustration due to immobility experienced during their journey, as well as their unfulfilled dreams about social or spatial mobility (El-Shaarawi, 2015). A relationship of power and domination exists between the people who wait and the people who make them wait. People who wait learn that they must follow the requirements of the structures in which the waiting is embedded to be able to receive what they need (Auyero, 2011).

Although institutions can and do exert power over people who are waiting, this does not mean that the people are passive or without agency in all areas of their lives. Those who are waiting can be active and productive in various contexts, including in their social time, while caregiving, during networking, and through political action (Ibanez Tirado, 2019). For example, during the time they are waiting to leave Kakuma Refugee Camp, deaf refugees often learn new languages and new skills and socialize with each other; furthermore, during the lockdowns in response to the coronavirus pandemic, they used the time "stuck at home" to (re)connect with family and (new) friends in other countries. This shows that "waiting is a complex dialectical process involving both a sense of empty, idle, suspended time and a kind of emotionally and cognitively demanding, active, productive time, particularly as people draw upon their own social capital and the resources available in their local setting" (Rotter, 2016, p. 86).

In a bid to describe people's attempts to be internationally mobile, it is vital to also look at the forms of capital they employ in their everyday mobilities, which can be expanded or mobilized for international mobility. Although considering capital and motility is key to the study of mobilities, it is also important to not lose sight of people's *aspirations* to be mobile or to stay put. Even though immobility is often associated with constraints, immobility may have positive as well as ambiguous valuations. People may be immobile voluntarily. Based on the work of Carling and Schewel (2018) and Salazar (2021a), we distinguish between the following:

- Voluntary mobility (e.g., moving to a new country)
- Involuntary mobility (e.g., fleeing a country, often because of war)
- Involuntary immobility (e.g., being stuck in a refugee camp, failure to migrate)
- Voluntary (or acquiescent) immobility (e.g., deciding to stay in the refugee camp, changing plans after failed attempts to move abroad)

These classifications help to center aspirations within the study of (im)mobility. However, it also obscures the fact that voluntary mobility may cover hypermobility (the mobility of "those who are allowed, and encouraged to, travel for work or leisure") as well as compelled mobility: The compelled mobile are "compelled, by design of the global economy, to move for work," such as laborers leaving a country with a weak economy (Toomey, 2022, p. 1). The compelled mobile are also restricted by further visa regulations. Similarly, voluntary immobility is not always under compulsion or underresourced; for some, it may be a privilege that allows individuals to be rooted and stable.

Thus, the questions that have to be considered are "Who moves and who doesn't; who has to move and who doesn't; when and where; and who gets to choose when and how?" (Cresswell, 2021, p. 8).

In asking these questions, we link the experience of (im)mobility to a person's aspirations (motivation for mobility), as well as to their motility (potential for mobility, including their various forms of capital). These have complex relations to various forms of privilege. For example, when people felt immobile because of having to stay at home during the coronavirus pandemic, it made a difference in terms of comfort and space whether this home was a mansion or a tiny studio. However, if the person in the mansion was confined to bed, disabled by long COVID, they might be less mobile than the person in the tiny studio. The mass confinement and mass disablement of the pandemic have brought these various types of immobility to light, because immobility was suddenly the "'good' default thing to do as a responsible citizen," and more people than ever had cause to reflect on what it means to be voluntarily or involuntarily immobile (Salazar, 2021a, p. 14). During the lockdowns, immobility (in terms of staying home) did not only restrict people—with a severe impact on mental health—but was *also* a privilege: The well-off could stay in their homes and rely on the mobility of others who had to expose themselves to the virus (e.g., to deliver food to shops and houses, to transport key workers) (Salazar, 2021a).

While focusing on aspirations and motility, and on different types of (in)voluntary (im)mobilities, we see that waiting practices and immobility happen on different spatial and temporal scales. For example, deaf tour guides and drivers in Bali spend a lot of time waiting for their clients to get through customs at the airport and to take multiple photos at tourist sites, angling for just the right "Instagrammable" photos. People wait in long queues to collect food in Kakuma Refugee Camp. Female deaf athletes wait for years after childbirth to engage in international competitions again. The emotional resonance of these various forms of immobility differs considerably, so we do not consider them to be comparable; rather, we use these examples to highlight the different temporalities of immobility. We also show how people contrast the immobility of certain people in these settings with the mobilities of others, and/or how they contrast current immobility with previous mobility in their own lives. Some experiences of immobility are exacerbated for deaf people because of their relative scatteredness and isolation from other deaf people (see Chapter 1).

This chapter is organized by spatial scale. We first focus on the experience of immobility on a local level: deaf people who feel stuck in the home or in a refugee camp after having migrated internationally. We then move to the crossing of national borders and the barriers to this and, finally, having crossed borders, to obtaining resettlement or residence permits. These two sections mostly focus on the experience of immobility in relation to migration; the final section focuses on immobility to, and during, transnational events and tourism. Within each of the sections, we talk about the everyday experience of immobility, as well as feelings of immobility when referring to longer time periods (pasts and futures). Thus, we talk about a variety of temporal scales within a structure arranged by spatial scales. Additionally, in each section, we show how (im)mobility on a local scale is connected to (im)mobility on other scales. Because we gathered most of our data prepandemic and focused on in-person interactions (see Chapter 2), we touch only briefly on virtual mobility.

(Im)mobility on the Local Level

This section focuses on people who move to a new country and then experience strongly felt tensions between mobility and immobility within that country. In common with the other Mobile-Deaf research locations, Kakuma Refugee Camp is a setting of international deaf encounters because deaf people living in the camp interact with others from different countries and with deaf people from the host country (in this case, Kenya). However, a big difference between this and the other settings was that after having fled their country (i.e., having been internationally mobile), the deaf refugees in Kakuma Refugee Camp became trapped. Many of them are unable to return to their homeland due to safety issues. They cannot settle permanently outside of the camp because the host state does not want refugees to remain indefinitely in their territory. Some deaf refugees who had been at the camp for many years have been resettled in the United States, Canada, or the United Kingdom, for which they were selected by the UN High Commissioner for Refugees (UNHCR); however, most deaf refugees do not get the opportunity to move to another country. This describes the situation of protracted (long-term) displacement where none of the three durable solutions (i.e., return to country of origin, integration into host country, or resettlement abroad) are working (UNHCR, 2022).

Most of the deaf refugees interviewed by Amandine had been living in Kakuma Refugee Camp or other refugee camps for quite a few years, some of them for decades. Halimo, the deaf woman from Somalia, often told Amandine that she had an overriding feeling of immobility, of waiting, and of being stuck in camps:

> I went to a refugee camp called Ifo [one of three refugee camps in Dadaab Refugee Complex], I came [there] in 1992, and was stuck there from 1992. I have been stuck here [in Kakuma Refugee Camp] for long years. I have been stuck as a refugee for a long time here. [There are] a lot of problems in refugee camps, a lot of problems for a long time.

Halimo described the camp as not only a place that is difficult to leave, but also a place where it is difficult to stay because of the living conditions. The unpredictability of what will happen in the future was strongly felt, alongside feelings of unsafety due to the violence that occurs in the camp.

Alongside the refugees' sense of immobility and limbo while waiting, there continued to be a lot of mobility *within* Kakuma Refugee Camp and even outside the camp. Even though the Kenyan government does not recognize refugees as Kenyan citizens, refugees have the freedom to move outside and around the camp because there is no fence around it. This shows how immobilities "encompass forms of intensive and relevant movements that are lost when we are too focused on what is not moving" (Salazar, 2021a, p. 8). Mobility is not restricted by the formal boundaries of the camp for those with access to economic capital, whether through their families or by way of employment. Some deaf refugees in the camp work for nongovernmental organizations (NGOs), in the schools as teachers, or in the food distribution centers and are thus able to earn a wage, accumulate their economic capital, and invest in physical mobility. However, refugees rarely have the necessary resources, such as money or a motorized vehicle, to be able to move smoothly through and outside the camp. As described in Chapter 3, Kakuma Refugee Camp is a huge, sprawling camp of 13.62 square kilometers (UN-Habitat, 2021), and thus ideally it requires some means of motorized transport to navigate. Walking inside and outside the camp is challenging due to the hot weather, the dryness of the desert, and the lack of shade; on wet days, people have to walk through thick mud. Successfully traversing the camp on foot thus requires a considerable amount of physical capital.

The extremes of weather and distance affect mobility within the camp, which in turn affects the frequency of deaf meeting spaces. When Amandine asked deaf refugees about the feasibility of big community gatherings, events, or sporting activities, she was told that distance, journey time, terrain, and weather conditions make these gatherings very difficult. One large event happened during Amandine's fieldwork, which was cited as a rare exception. The Starkey Hearing Foundation, an American nonprofit organization, visited Kakuma Refugee Camp to distribute free hearing aids (le Maire, 2020). This event, described later in this chapter, gathered approximately 50–60 deaf people from different parts of the camp, in contrast to the smaller deaf spaces Amandine observed in various places.

The smaller deaf spaces provided evidence of various deaf mobilities inside the camp. Deaf mobility within the camp included movement into deaf educational spaces and to the homes of other deaf refugees. Some deaf people would walk for several hours to meet other deaf people, and some of them would leave the camp and go even farther to the adjoining village to attend courses or church services where Kenyan Sign Language (KSL) interpreters were present (see Chapter 3). The examples of deaf mobility within the refugee camp in the conditions described demonstrate the physical labor involved in building social networks, and the physical and emotional labor in maintaining them. Additionally, the distances covered suggest that deaf refugees were actively seeking, and committed to taking advantage of, opportunities to engage with others and expand their knowledge and skills, however labor intensive the process was. These examples illustrate the value of social and cultural capital to deaf refugees and the effort required to build them.

Not only could deaf refugees move outside the camp to some degree, but some could also go elsewhere in Kenya, and even abroad. For example, Atem had moved to Kakuma Refugee Camp from South Sudan, but he later returned to his home country and stayed there for extended periods before returning to the camp:

> I stayed here in 2002 until eighth grade, and then, when I finished the eighth grade, I waited for high school but there was no place for me, so I decided to go back to [South] Sudan in 2006. I stayed in Sudan and waited in Sudan. I stayed at my family's place. I called some of my friends to come, and then I went back here to Kakuma and I could go to high school and I graduated from high school in 2016.

Atem had hoped to move from an in-camp primary school to a Kenyan deaf high school outside of the camp; when that proved impossible, he instead spent time with his sick mother in South Sudan, and he stayed there for 4 years. After returning to Kenya in 2012, he was then able to begin his studies at Kedowa High School in Kericho, using a scholarship provided by UNHCR.

As exemplified by Atem's story, refugees may move between the camp and their country of origin, and also within Kenya (see Figure 10.1 for a map showing some of the journeys outside the camp made by deaf refugees). The deaf units in some of the primary schools offer the opportunity to graduate with a primary education diploma, but in order to continue with their secondary studies, deaf refugees must move to a deaf boarding school in Kenya, where they come into contact with deaf Kenyans. Atem had met his girlfriend, a deaf Kenyan citizen, while at the deaf high school; after graduating, they continued a long-distance relationship with each other, Atem having returned to live at Kakuma Refugee Camp while the girlfriend remained living outside the camp. Many deaf refugees thus leave Kakuma Refugee Camp to develop their cultural, social, and linguistic capital, but upon graduating high school, most of them return to Kakuma Refugee Camp. Some of them may go on to become deaf teachers, using their linguistic capital acquired at high schools in Kenya; others may become cooks, continue their studies in adult learning education, or simply continue to wait for a positive response to their resettlement application. When

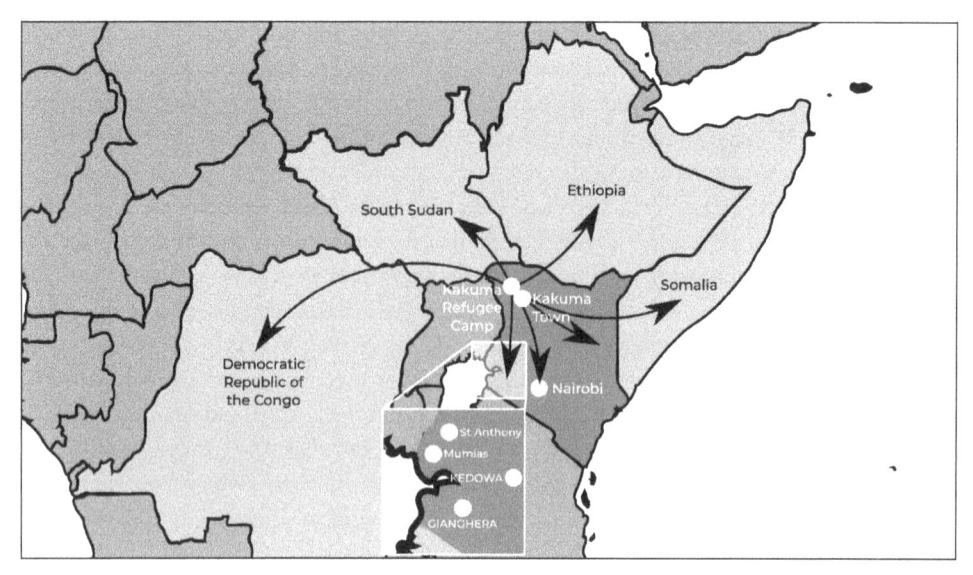

Figure 10.1. Deaf mobilities between the camp and other locations in Kenya and abroad.

Amandine interviewed him, Atem expressed a strong desire to return to South Sudan once it was safe to do so and once he had the economic capital to make the journey:

> Maybe later, maybe when the elections are finished, I would like to go back to South Sudan to see if there are still problems there, but if there are still problems, I'll stay here in Kakuma. If there is no problem, I can go back to Sudan.

A person's motivations for staying in the camp can be complex: There may be several factors impacting the decision to stay or leave, showing that motility (the potential or capacity to be mobile; see Chapter 1) does not necessarily correspond to actual mobility. Many stay and wait in the hope that the situation improves in their home countries. For some deaf refugees, the presence of education through KSL or the prospect of employment as teachers in the deaf units provides an additional motivation to stay in the camp—or even to move *into* the camp. To illustrate this point, John is one of the deaf teachers in Fashoda Primary School whose salary was being paid by the Lutheran World Federation (LWF). Unfortunately, due to budget constraints, he was informed that his work in the school would have to be terminated. When Amandine visited him in his house, he explained that if he was unable to continue his teaching job, he would have no other option but to leave with his family and return to his country of origin, South Sudan. However, a few weeks later, the LWF decided to continue to provide the wage for his teaching job, and he decided to stay longer in Kakuma Refugee Camp. Economic and/or cultural capital are important factors to be considered when exploring why deaf refugees remain at the camp or why some move out of the camp. This latter point is explored later in the chapter.

The sections above show that mobility and immobility are experienced simultaneously and on different spatial scales. Many people feel stuck in the camp because they cannot easily move out, but they are also mobile inside and outside of the camp, sometimes for long periods. Similarly, the experience of waiting can happen on different spatial *and* temporal scales. While waiting for resettlement, refugees must also wait for hours in queues to receive subsistence, to get assistance from the UNHCR Protection Delivery Unit, to register a birth, to receive necessary care in hospitals, and so on. For subsistence, they have to go to the Food Distribution Center nearest to their habitation in the first week of the month, bringing their food distribution card (issued by UNHCR once they are recognized as a refugee), which gives them permission to enter the center and to receive their ration.

Amandine visited a Food Distribution Center in Kakuma 1 (one of the four sectors of the camp) with Atem. Outside the center, a massive crowd was waiting in the hot sun. Some of them had been waiting since the morning: refugees have no way of knowing the time that the gates will be opened because this depends solely on the decision of the authorities on the day. This example illustrates another way that people in power control the refugees' waiting time. Atem did not join the crowd near the gate; instead, he waited until some police officers had arrived to prevent violence between people who were fighting to enter. There was no clear queue, and people could not know whether they would be able to pass through the gate that day or whether they would have to try again another day. People thus experience confusion and uncertainty in the process of obtaining subsistence.

Passing through the gate was only the start of several stages of waiting in queues (see Figure 10.2, a map drawn by Amandine showing the various waiting places). After entering the gate, people had to sit in a place surrounded by barbed wire and wait for the soldiers to tell them whether they could go on. When the guards first shouted that the gates were open, the people who were waiting ran very fast, fighting to be in the queue to arrive at the identification office, where the identification

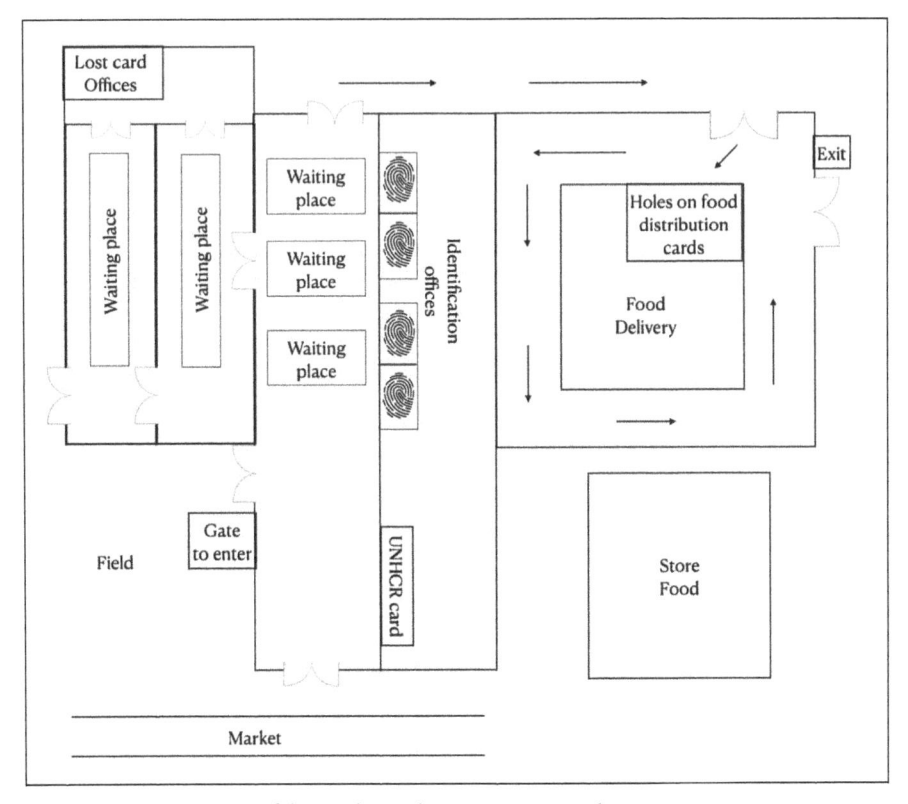

Figure 10.2. Approximate map of the Food Distribution Center in Kakuma 1.

number on their card would be checked and their fingerprints put through an identification machine. When the identification process was complete, refugees would go outside to be in line for entry to the food delivery place (see Figure 10.3). Here, their distribution card would be perforated. This was the work of a number of refugees, including Ken, a deaf Sudanese man who had been living in the camp for about 28 years. After this, refugees would finally arrive in another queue, at the front of which they could collect items such as ugali, sorghum, wheat, oil, yellow peas, and soap.

The crowd obtaining food was chaotic and violent; refugees fought to be able to enter the gate, and some of them spat at the guards who were behind the gate. Refugees ran between each location, and some of them were violent to their peers. While in the queue, Atem explained to Amandine that he was afraid of the person waiting next to him because he was violent. He told her that due to the violence, it is mostly men who collect the food, and Amandine noticed that there were very few women in the queues. She also noticed that some hearing refugees complained at and insulted Ken when they gave their food distribution card to him, upset at having waited so long (up to half an hour) to have the card perforated, and they were apparently frustrated at communicating with him through gestures. As a refugee working in the distribution center, Ken was vulnerable to their aggression; meanwhile, the offices of the overseeing NGO were protected from the violence by barbed wire fences. This indicated a clear separation of power between the officials (who were safe) and the refugees employed by the NGOs (who were not). The waiting places were areas of compliance—a space in which one must just wait instead of attempting to negotiate with authorities (Auyero, 2011). There was nothing that refugees could do about the endless queues. Throughout this process, they were expected to be patient (Auyero, 2011).

Figure 10.3. The distribution center in Kakuma 1, where Ken was working.

The example of the visit to the distribution center illustrates that contained within the long-term act of waiting for resettlement abroad (about which, more below) is the requirement for people in refugee camps to *actively wait* in order to satisfy the most basic, daily needs of their own and their families' bodies—often in violent queues and for hours, even a full day. Communication from officials tends to be minimal, and waiting for subsistence can thus be paired with severe bodily discomfort, communication problems, and violence. These experiences are likely to be exacerbated for deaf people: Deaf refugees faced additional uncertainties at the distribution center compared to their hearing counterparts due to the absence of vital information during the process, as well as greater communication difficulties with officials.

The visit to the Food Distribution Center was a regular occurrence for people in Kakuma Refugee Camp. By contrast, the visit of the Starkey Hearing Foundation was a one-off and deaf-specific event, and it is an example of how immobility and humanitarianism, or "charity," are entwined. The aim of the foundation's visit was to provide deaf refugees with free hearing aids. The foundation's media coverage of this event (see Figure 10.4) highlighted the perceived need for its mission, emphasizing the lack of hearing aid support previously offered to refugees in Kakuma Refugee Camp. The event was set up in collaboration with the LWF and took place in an LWF primary school, in which hearing aids were distributed over the course of a day. The recreational area of the school was filled with a number of large white tents, with services offered such as information about hearing aids, the checking of people's ears by nurses, the checking of people's basic level of audition, and the distribution of reused ear molds and reused hearing aids (Figure 10.5). The Starkey Hearing Foundation event was controversial in nature. On the

Figure 10.4. The Starkey Hearing Foundation filming the event at Kakuma Refugee Camp.

Figure 10.5. The distribution of used earmolds by the Starkey Hearing Foundation.

one hand, some deaf refugees do wish to be able to hear, and the Starkey Hearing Foundation believes that it can offer this through providing hearing aids, which are often presented as a quick fix. However, the reality was that many of those at the Kakuma Refugee Camp event received an uncomfortable, poorly adjusted device with which they could hear only a little or not at all. Some wore these hearing aids for only a day before discarding them because without access to long-term audiology follow-up care—and to an ongoing supply of batteries—what little benefit (if any) the deaf refugees gained from these devices could not be sustained. In this example, the immobility and poverty of some (i.e., the deaf refugees) triggers the mobility of others (i.e., representatives of the Starkey Foundation). However, despite publishing emotive media footage and seeking help from Hollywood's A-list in order to "help the helpless," the foundation's approach and execution demonstrated a stark lack of understanding as to the reality of the lives of deaf refugees as well as refugees in general.

We now move to the other setting in which we studied international migration: London. Although the settings and circumstances are very different from Kakuma Refugee Camp, there is a common theme: People can suddenly experience a keen sense of immobility in the new host country. Some new migrants feel they are suddenly restricted based on their sex, class, deafness, and new responsibilities; the coronavirus pandemic added a further, acute restriction. Next, we give examples from Sanchayeeta's research with five Indian women who moved to London to join their new spouse, each of whom she interviewed multiple times (see Chapter 2).

Moving to a new country can be associated with, or co-occur with, a sudden loss of freedom, including new restrictions associated with becoming a wife. Meera experienced this new restriction when she moved from India to marry. She was no stranger to other forms of restriction, however; public life in India is male dominated, and moral policing of women's movements is common, both by families and by husbands monitoring and controlling female bodies to ensure that they conform to the Indian core value of "respectability" (Phadke et al., 2011). Whereas men hang out in pubs, loiter on the streets, and are generally visible, there are far fewer spaces where girls, women, and transgender people can do so. Meera is from an affluent background, and her (hearing) family had relocated within India so that she could attend a good deaf school, demonstrating the role of economic capital and motility in ensuring access to education. However, while Meera was attending the school, she was not allowed to go anywhere outside its domain, except on school trips—another example of how motility does not necessarily translate into mobility. Outside of school, Meera's mobility was restricted by her family. She was not allowed to travel without them, leaving her feeling trapped. The one exception was that she was permitted to travel around and outside India with a theater group that she had joined when she was 13, even visiting the United States with them when she was 24. Her late teens and early 20s thus featured increased national and international mobility. However, when she moved into her husband's family home in the United Kingdom, she felt as trapped as she had with her own family:

> [W]hen [I got] here, I felt I was trapped, just like I was with my family back in India. My husband went out regularly to party, etc. My in-laws were out as well. I was trapped at home bringing up our children, I had no time for going out. I only went to work, then back home, and all over again. I worked hard to pass my driving test, my citizenship, I had to do these all by myself, with no help. I was sick when I did the driving lessons. I felt everyone, friends treated me like [...] a servant. [...] I felt [...] depressed.

Meera's British Indian deaf husband had the privilege to go out and socialize with deaf people; meanwhile, Meera was positioned in a gendered role wherein she was responsible for the household chores and childcare while simultaneously having to "integrate" within British society by passing particular milestones (e.g., obtaining a driving license). As explained in Chapter 8, her accumulated responsibilities affected her ability to acquire British Sign Language (BSL). Patriarchal culture and values shaped the division of labor in her in-laws' household. However,

Meera observed that her two elder, hearing sisters-in-law were not active with household work and that she alone bore that burden. She analyzed the reasons in an interview:

> [My] husband and I, we argued. [My] mother-in-law intervened, and he went [to a party]. I had to quit my work because they were complaining. What we were arguing about was [that] they have two older sons, their wives don't help, they never cook. Why did they expect me to cook for them? They thought that, because I am from India, they can tease and oppress an Indian? No, we are equal [...] We argued, I stood my ground. The elder wife, I told her to get up and help with cleaning up dishes. I stood my ground and became more assertive, [I said] if they abused me, I would call the police, if they continue to abuse me, I can do that. They backed off; they can't treat me like that. They thought deaf [people] are dumb; they thought, because I'm from India, they could use Indian women [...] British Indians are different, [but] Indian women they oppress. Why? Because we are weak? No. I roll up my sleeves to send a message to deaf Indian [women] that they must be strong and equal to the deaf people here.

Over time, middle-class Indian women such as Meera have increasingly expressed the desire to work outside the home and to be treated as equal to their male counterparts in a relationship (Twamley, 2012). However, some British Indian men and their families, including Meera's husband, tend to view a woman from India as a bearer and maintainer of traditional gendered values and beliefs (Charsley et al., 2016); thus, they burdened her with the household work, especially after she had had children. Meera's mother-in-law had the expectation that she could now "retire" from her domestic duty because it could be passed on to Meera. Meera came to realize the position she was in, and she challenged her in-laws for exploiting her. However, by emphasizing that the three women should share the burden for the household, she also did not challenge the assumption that only females are burdened with chores; this, she viewed as an (Indian) "cultural" expectation.

The fact that some of Sanchayeeta's Indian participants did not have the freedom to have social contacts outside of their homes, whereas their husbands had the privilege of socializing with deaf people, is an example of gender-disaggregated immobility between men and women (Adeel & Yeh, 2018). Gendered roles were not the only cause of the local immobility experienced by Meera: She flagged her ethnicity as an Indian-born person and her deafness as additional factors in her treatment by the family.

Meera's experience of being kept at home as a child and then again as a married woman (after a brief period of increased mobility as a youth) was echoed by several other Indian participants. Shahina, a highly mobile woman from a wealthy family in India who now lives between the United Kingdom and Dubai, had experienced many attempts to enclose her, and rebelled against them. She studied in America and experienced differences in her level of freedom between India and the United States:

> When I grew up, I was a strong rebel. Like the time when my grandmother told me that I am not allowed to go out, I ignored her. My aunt said the same thing, I ignored her too. They complained to my father, and I told my mother that I didn't want them to control me. She told them to leave me alone. When I got back from America, I knew I didn't need anyone to accompany me. I told my parents that I didn't want a bodyguard to accompany me. They said OK and removed him; I was happy. Once when I visited [family], my relatives lived in a residential enclosure. I wanted to go outside and my grandmother said, "Don't go out!" She was so worried, and I was annoyed. We had an argument.

I was like that after I got back. They were angry many times because I wanted to be independent. I don't want people to control me. [...] My grandmother said I used to be sweet and now, she blamed America. That America is bad! [laughs] I just ignored her.

When Shahina returned from the United States to visit her family in India, she experienced a shift in her spatial freedom as her family tried to render her immobile locally. Her parents had visited her in America and had witnessed deaf people's ability to be independent, which may have shaped their decision to support her against her female relatives. There also is a class angle here: Shahina's parents were able to travel due to the family's wealth. Looking at this example over a longer temporal scale (i.e., taking a life course perspective) shows that, as in Meera's example, there were periods of increased freedom in strong contrast to other periods—that is, experiences of immobility when motility and actual mobility were in conflict. Meera and Shahina felt trapped at home, which was felt to be "safer" and/or was the site of chores that they were required to do for their family. Meera felt trapped as a new wife in the United Kingdom, whereas Shahina experienced the opposite: Being internationally mobile, she experienced freedom abroad, then attempts to restrict her freedom within her home country.

Sanchayeeta's data collection started during the pandemic in 2019; one impact of pandemic lockdowns was a gendered recalibration of the domestic space to accommodate the range of its new uses, for example, the relocation of workplaces into the home (McIntyre et al., 2022). During three periods of lockdown in 2020–2021, Sanchayeeta's participants had different experiences of navigating the lockdown restrictions, ranging from the forced mobility associated with working as a key worker (and thus exposure to the COVID-19 virus) to having to homeschool children in isolation. Shahina, who had been hypermobile between India, Dubai, the United States, and other countries before the pandemic, suddenly found her mobility restricted once again. Another participant, Seema, had just moved to London from India; plans to move away from her family-in-law fell through due to the pandemic. Instead, she and her husband were stuck in her mother-in-law's house with a newborn baby and limited space.

Being locked down in a house with her hearing British Indian mother-in-law affected Seema's mental well-being. Seema felt watched by her mother-in-law, who frequently checked up on whether she was doing the chores. Because Seema felt she was constantly under surveillance, she felt tense around the house, and this put her off doing chores such as cooking. She lacked the freedom to do what she liked, including drinking alcohol. Seema often retired to her bedroom between 8 and 9 p.m. and stayed there in order to avoid her mother-in-law and to have a private space with her baby daughter. She walked around her neighborhood either in the mornings or afternoons to have space away from her mother-in-law. Seema was emotional as she told this to Sanchayeeta. She did not feel that the house was her home. She missed Sindhi dishes (her regional food), and she missed her family badly. Despite her homesickness, she was not able to fly to India to visit her family, nor was she able to have her family over. For people like Seema who had migrated just before the pandemic and who experienced the pandemic during significant life changes (a new husband, a new baby, a new mother-in-law), the sudden stuckness-at-home—in combination with homesickness—could feel overwhelming. The pandemic also affected her sense of connection with the city she lived in and with her deaf networks in London. Instead, her ongoing connections with her sister in California and her parents back in India provided her with emotional support during the pandemic.

The pandemic thus impacted these women's feelings of immobility. Aisha's story illustrates how her process of building up social capital in London was prolonged in the temporal sense. When she lived in Mumbai, Aisha was not allowed by her mother to travel outside of Mumbai to socialize with deaf people, but she was allowed to travel within the city. She is a sociable person and loved to visit people in their homes and to attend festivals and events with her friends. However, when she moved to London, she had limited opportunities to develop relationships within its deaf community or to maintain her existing relationships with other deaf female Indian migrants (see Chapter 9). She also observed that deaf people in London tended to arrange in advance to meet outside their homes, whereas she was used to socializing with deaf people in their homes without the need to plan. She found herself isolated at home, especially when her husband was working long hours, and she expressed feelings of stuckness:

> I would like to be involved in the British [deaf] community [...] I am actively learning BSL, but certain people are too busy to meet me because of their family obligations. I realized since I got married, I have been busy too, and I noticed these women are burdened with household duties [like me]; we Asian women [experience] the same. Some white people aren't aware of this. I don't mind meeting some [of them] but COVID [has restricted us from meeting up]. In 5 or 10 years' time, I may be happily involved in the community, but at the moment I'm still new. I still have a strong attachment [with my friends] back in India. It is still a strong part of me. I have only been here for 2 years.

There are multiple layers to Aisha's narrative. The coronavirus restrictions were a central theme. Even though the pandemic was restrictive for the majority of people, it led to a surge in localism in the sense of engaging in (or resurrecting) relationships with neighbors (Cresswell, 2021); this was not necessarily the case for deaf people, for whom there were often additional barriers. Deaf people typically need to travel greater distances to meet other deaf people. In Chapter 4, we showed that deaf spaces are dispersed across London and that few of these spaces consist only of local people. Mobile deaf lives are not local lives. The pandemic thus delayed Aisha's chance to develop relationships with deaf people, specifically the other people in her English and BSL courses. Like Meera, Aisha felt household obligations restricted her time for socializing with deaf people, and especially with Indian women—she was particularly keen to interact with this demographic, but all had limited time to socialize due to the domestic expectations placed on them. She experienced the different mobility of Asian deaf women in the United Kingdom, contrasting them with white deaf women.

Aisha was living with her deaf in-laws at the time; hence, she had access to BSL and was not cut off from social interactions within the home. However, she craved the wider socialization that she was used to in India, and she could not invite people over to her in-laws' home. Aisha thus wished to be mobile herself outside the home and for other people to be mobile in her direction (i.e., to visit her at home), and she keenly felt the double effect of immobility when neither was possible. She had been working hard to increase her linguistic capital in the 2 years since she had moved to London (see Chapter 8), but the pandemic slowed down the process of expanding her social capital within the city. Being immobile during the pandemic not only prolonged the time needed for "integration" as a migrant, but it also prolonged her sense of having strong ties to India. Because the pandemic was a global event, her friends in India also spent more time online and, as she was restricted to the home, she was still able (or even more able) to build up or maintain social and cultural capital through the internet, such as via various WhatsApp groups in which she could remotely keep up with topics related to deaf people, her own learning and professional development, as well as her use of Indian Sign Language (ISL). This challenges the oppositional nature of mobility and immobility, and it shows that "being immobile can be affirming and empowering" (Wang, 2022, p. 1), as well as a translocal experience (see Chapter 9).

Other interviewees described the positive aspects of being immobile. Rita had a positive experience during the "stay-at-home" period:

> During the lockdown I jumped for joy, I was so happy to stay at home! I was excited to think what we would do at home with the family. I was so happy. I went shopping to buy food, went with a mask on. I didn't go out socially. I was thinking what we would do at home. [...] Cleaned up the house, threw away unwanted things. Got new things. [Pauses] I was so happy for a year. One year of the lockdown! So happy! When the BBC News announced that shops, etc., will open in May, I was miserable returning to work. [...] Looking back, the time of the lockdown was lovely and at a slow pace, [there were] nice long hours. When returning to work, time goes by rather too quickly, when [you're] busy.

Of the five women interviewed by Sanchayeeta, Rita had been living in the United Kingdom longest; she moved to London about 20 years ago after marrying her British Indian deaf husband in India. She had thus been long settled before the pandemic started, and she had more control over her life in the United Kingdom than when she was in India. Rita did not have strong relationships with people outside her family circle, and this period of "acquiescent immobility" at home with her family brought her joy. The slow pace of time during the lockdown gave her respite from her everyday life, which she felt was going by too fast, and permitted quality time with her husband and children as well as with her in-laws.

Rita was involved in a Hare Krishna group through her husband, and the religion was embedded in their everyday lifestyle and practices. They had been actively involved in this group (consisting of a mix of deaf and hearing people) and had traveled to various places in the United Kingdom to participate in religious activities. During the pandemic, Rita became more involved with deaf Hare Krishnas in India through collaborating on moral stories. In this way, she not only engaged in translocal connections but also expanded her ISL skills, as she had not had the opportunity to socialize with Indian deaf people growing up because she attended a school with no other deaf students. This is another example of how, for Indian deaf migrants, the pandemic led to strong connections, and even new connections and skills development with people back in India.

National Borders and Bureaucracy

Having discussed experiences of immobility in a new country and how these experiences co-occur with (local or virtual) (im)mobilities, we now move to the experience of immobility on the national level. Returning to Kakuma Refugee Camp, we focus on some of the barriers to crossing national borders. Resettlement is unlikely for most refugees in the camp, who are immobile while waiting for a positive response from UNHCR; however, Amandine learned from deaf refugees still in the camp of 10–20 others who had been resettled in different countries. Deaf refugees in the camp thus have concrete examples of resettlement, which instill hope in them.

Chris, a participant in the London migration subproject, was one of those resettled, showing the unexpected connections between our seemingly disparate fieldwork locations. Chris had fled the Burundian civil war in 1996, arriving first in Kenya's capital, Nairobi, and detained there while his passport, visa, and papers were checked. The Kenyan government had wanted to send him home, but after he explained the reasons for his escape from Burundi, they sent him to Kakuma Refugee Camp. During his time in the camp, Chris formed a community with deaf people from different countries in Africa, such as Sudan, Ethiopia, Democratic Republic of the Congo, and Rwanda; together, they used ASL. Growing up in Burundi, he had attended a deaf school and learned ASL there. Chris engaged in discussions with UNHCR about the possibility of setting up a deaf unit in a school; this was the unit created in MPC1 (see Chapter 3). He communicated with hearing people by writing in English, which was frustrating for him because he was more fluent in French than in English. In Kakuma Refugee Camp, his everyday life was relentlessly the same, and there were no opportunities for him to work; because of this, he wanted to go to the United Kingdom. After 5 years of living in Kenya, Chris was successful in his application to UNHCR, and he arrived in the United Kingdom in 2000. He initially struggled with language barriers because he had to learn a new sign language, BSL, which he learned at City Lit (as described in Chapter 8). At the time of the interview, Chris worked as a social worker with deaf people.

Back in Kakuma Refugee Camp, some of Amandine's interviewees believed that the reason deaf refugees like Chris were selected for resettlement was that they were more intelligent and talented than others. They believed that growing their cultural and linguistic capital—for example, by learning ASL and English—could help them be selected for resettlement (see Chapter 8). Ken believed that unmarried deaf people would have more chance of being selected by UNHCR, an assumption that could be based on seeing other single deaf people being selected. For Halimo, building up social and economic capital within the camp was associated with her hope to be resettled (see Chapter 3).

Deaf refugees had many questions relating to resettlement, and they sought information from other deaf and hearing refugees, governmental representatives, and NGO workers about the various criteria that need to be met in order to be selected by UNHCR. Refugees are selected according to their situation of need, in terms of risk and insecurity (their need for physical safety, such as in the case of torture or gender-based violence), medical reasons, injuries and disabilities, and not having another solution available for repatriation, local integration, or family reunification (Jansen, 2011). Through his discussions with international and Kenyan researchers and refugees, Jansen (2008) discovered that corruption is present in every aspect of the resettlement process. There are thus systemic issues that individuals have to overcome in order to be resettled. "Active" refugees who are working for UNHCR or who have a good social or professional network with people working for UNHCR could have a greater chance of obtaining resettlement (Jansen, 2008). This shows the value of social capital in the process of resettlement.

There was a lot of misinformation about resettlement and UNHCR's selection process. For example, deaf refugees did not know whether it is based on random selection or on criteria connected to a refugee's vulnerability, language abilities, cultural background, nationality, or family configuration, or as the result of networking with UNHCR workers. In Kakuma Refugee Camp, deaf refugees, especially women, would often go to the Protection Delivery Unit (PDU) in the hope of being resettled by UNHCR. Amandine visited this place multiple times. Halimo, the deaf Somali woman, asked Amandine to come with her and two of her friends. The place was full of people, many of them waiting in front of a gate with barbed wire fences; these kinds of waiting situations in the camp were not restricted to the Food Distribution Center. Both of these spaces were gendered: Women spent more time waiting at the PDU than men, in contrast to the male-dominated Food Distribution Center. Figure 10.6 shows

Figure 10.6. Deaf and hearing refugees sitting waiting together near the UNHCR Protection Delivery Unit.

deaf refugees from Sudan or Somalia in colorful clothes sitting on the ground in front of the PDU and forming a circle to chat together. Amandine took the picture from inside the PDU because she was allowed by the guards to enter alone; this was due to her privilege as a white person. In addition, Amandine found that if she asked the guards, she was also permitted to bring deaf refugees inside the PDU with her. This example shows how white privilege impacts on the duration of waiting, both for the white person themselves and for the nonwhite people associated with them; Amandine's whiteness gave her differential treatment and, by extension, determined who else did not have to wait.

After passing through the gate, Halimo and her friends could wait on wooden benches under a corrugated iron roof for protection against heavy rain or the heat of the sun (see Figure 10.7). After waiting for hours, they were finally let into another place with a bench, where they waited to enter the room in which they could meet with the officers of the PDU. During the hours of waiting, and particularly outside the PDU where there were fewer hearing people in close proximity, deaf people would discuss matters regarding resettlement procedures and various UNHCR regulations and exchange gossip about people living in the camp: illnesses, births, fights between different ethnic groups. In this space, deaf people built and maintained social capital; thus, in this context, waiting was "doubly relational" because people created or mobilized a set of relations or networks to help them tolerate boring and tiring hours spent waiting and to share information with others (Auyero, 2011). Some hearing women would join the circle if they recognized some of the deaf people, and they would converse with them through gestures and mouthing in the ethnic languages that particular deaf refugees were familiar with.

Figure 10.7. The waiting place in the UNHCR Protection Delivery Unit with chicken wire fencing.

For many refugees, the purpose of the PDU was unclear and confusing. Deaf refugees would go there to report violence or other problems occurring in their homes or with family and neighbors. They would complain in the hope of improving their life circumstances in the camp, and in the hope that UNHCR would believe that they were in danger and urgently in need of resettlement. In the process of reporting issues, deaf refugees would describe their traumatic life stories and their issues with living in the camp, including situations in which they were being oppressed by hearing refugees, or complaints about their food or shelter. All this was with the aim of proving to UNHCR that they were eligible to be resettled or should be a priority compared to other refugees. As Amandine noted the confusion about the purpose of the PDU, she asked the guards in the waiting places to explain, using written English. The guards clarified that the aim of the PDU is *not* to select people for resettlement in different countries but instead to protect the inhabitants of the camp. The misunderstandings and misinformation about which offices in the camp are there to provide information and services in relation to achieving international mobility (in the form of resettlement) create barriers for refugees in the camp—especially for deaf refugees, who also experience linguistic barriers to accessing this vital information.

Some deaf refugees asked Amandine to accompany them to the PDU because they wanted her to facilitate communication with the UNHCR officials. During those meetings, Amandine supported communication by noting in English what deaf refugees signed to her. This was not an easy or quick process. For example, when accompanying Halimo, Amandine often had to interrupt her to ensure accuracy because Halimo had the tendency to go off on a tangent. Managing this was arduous at times, and it made the process complex. Amandine was rather uncomfortable in this role because there were concepts with which she was not familiar or even aware, and the bureaucratic language and its meanings were hard to get across to the deaf refugees. Amandine also faced problems in translating for other deaf refugees because they did not always engage with the questions being asked, and they would instead reply with a narrative that detailed their hardships and problems. However, for some deaf refugees, Amandine's translation helped them to better understand the processes and to therefore communicate better with the UNHCR officials.

Some deaf refugees had very good English literacy skills and did not need Amandine's presence for translation purposes; however, they too kept asking Amandine to accompany them. The reason for this was probably to leverage her white privilege and/or because they still believed that Amandine had an official relationship with UNHCR, noting that she could easily circumvent long queues and be the first person to enter the office. Kenyan officials were cooperative and appeared to take the refugees' concerns seriously during meetings in which Amandine was present; communication between the deaf refugees and the officials was thus made easier by her presence, even though Amandine is deaf and sometimes struggled with written English herself because French is her first written language. Some deaf refugees preferred a member of their family to speak for them, at which point Amandine left the room; this demonstrates that deaf refugees used Amandine's white privilege strategically, for example, to bypass queues and not necessarily to overcome communication issues.

In the case of deaf people wishing to be resettled in locations abroad, deaf refugees perceived themselves to have several strategies: staying single, learning ASL and English (see Chapter 8), frequenting the PDU, exercising patience while waiting, trying to get information from other deaf refugees, and making use of the linguistic knowledge and positionalities of other people. Regarding the lack of clarity about where to get services and information and the search for solutions for accessing information and communicating, there are similarities with the bureaucratic process that many deaf migrants face when they arrive in the United Kingdom. Most deaf migrants have to navigate this process in a new language environment; those in London move across numerous fields dominated by spoken and written English, including their place of work, their place of education, medical institutions, social services, their community or neighborhood, and their local deaf center and/or deaf community gatherings. Signing deaf migrants are immediately disadvantaged in fields where there is no sign language (interpreting) provision, especially when they have little or no knowledge of English.

Fareed's story gives an example of the bureaucratic and language barriers faced by a lot of migrants to London. Fareed faced confusion in navigating the visa process in the United Kingdom. He is originally from Lebanon and planned to move from there to the United States with his father, brother, and uncle using a U.S. visa. Before traveling to the United States, his father and uncle had been advised by an Arabic lawyer to get a fake paper stating that they were from Iraq instead of Lebanon, with which they would be able to apply for refugee status. Although they were not fleeing war, they were looking for a better life, and they believed the lawyer's advice that this would make their mobility more straightforward. As a result, they paid him $500 in U.S. dollars to "ensure" that they would get refugee status. They had their tickets ready to fly to the United States, but they had to fly into London en route; there, they became stuck due to problems with their papers. Fareed explained in an interview with Steve how he had felt in this situation, finding himself suddenly stuck in the United Kingdom:

> This left us in a terrible situation. We didn't have any information and didn't know where to turn or who to turn to for help. As deaf people, we [my brother and I] had problems accessing any advice, we were very disheartened and struggled to find anyone or anywhere to help us. We didn't know anyone either.

Fareed was confused throughout the process of interacting with the U.K. authorities because he had initially planned to go to the United States and felt himself to be stuck in the United Kingdom. Ultimately, he had to stay there, and he tried to find a network of people to help him settle in the country with his family, initially by asking around in a pub where deaf people gathered (see Chapter 7).[1]

Other deaf migrants had more successful support mechanisms in place when obtaining a visa. When Aisha agreed to marry her future husband who lived in the United Kingdom (and whom she had gotten to know online), he was able to fill out the paperwork for her. She had to wait for a long time before obtaining her visa, never knowing when she would get it:

> How long did it take? About 6 months, so when that was done, my future husband contacted me and told me to go to the visa office in Mumbai for an interview. I went and I answered their questions. Then I had to wait for a while until my visa was validated. While we were waiting, it was very difficult to make any wedding plans, as we couldn't be sure what the outcome would be.

During the waiting process, Aisha could not make any wedding preparations and did not even know when she should give her notice at work. She had told her boss about her intention to move, but she did not want to tell colleagues she was moving until she knew for sure; this placed her in professional and social limbo. The process of obtaining a visa can involve a long period of waiting, sometimes a very lonely one; international mobility here is preceded by a keen sense of time being stretched out.

The process of getting a residence permit has become more complicated for some deaf people since the decision of the United Kingdom to exit the European Union (i.e., Brexit). Deaf people who need BSL (or other sign language) access to understand the nuances of Brexit can feel confused and excluded. A scheme for settlement has been introduced for EU citizens who live and work in the United Kingdom, granting them the same access to work, study, benefits, and public services as British citizens. To find out more about the settlement scheme and to meet deaf EU citizens in the United Kingdom, Steve and Sanchayeeta did participant observation at a 2019 event for disabled and deaf people from EU countries, titled "Brexit and You," at which BSL interpreters were provided.

During the question-and-answer sessions, deaf attendees came to the front and signed their questions, which were wide-ranging—some about how Brexit would impact motility, and others about access to information: "What happens if my application for pre-settled status fails?"; "Can

---

1. There are a lot of gaps in Fareed's story. It is not clear how he managed to obtain support and get residence. This is perhaps due to Fareed being uncertain about how much to share with Steve because Fareed had traveled into the United Kingdom undocumented.

I still go on holiday in European countries, and do I need to pay for visas?" (asked by British passport holders); "Can my friends from a particular European country come and settle in the United Kingdom?"; "Where do I go to get help with communication if I don't understand how to use the smartphone app [for EU citizens to apply for settled status]?" Although the information given was repetitive and concise, questions continued to be asked about the application process, which showed that some deaf people had not fully understood the information provided. Steve and Sanchayeeta noted that the panel did not take into account the needs of deaf people attending help centers for support with their application—where there is a high likelihood that the staff would be unable to sign and would have inadequate deaf awareness training. Even in centers with support provided in BSL, not all deaf migrants are fluent in BSL; this makes the implementation of individual applications challenging because the applicants are without any support. There was much apprehension among deaf people about conducting the application process independently, given cuts to support services. The lack of support when navigating both bureaucracy and language barriers led to feelings of (impending) immobility and stuckness—and of uncertainty, because vital information was missing. Deaf people therefore often turned to deaf networks to gather information (see Chapter 7).

Barriers to obtaining a visa also often occur in relation to events organized internationally. Deaf people who are willing to travel to other countries for international events may experience late cancellations due to visa issues. During her fieldwork, Annelies observed event organizers announcing that people who had been invited and who had received funding were unable to be there. For example, at the Congress of the International Deaf Chess Federation in Manchester in July 2018, a number of delegates from Pakistan, Mongolia, and elsewhere had to cancel their congress attendance at the last minute because they were not able to secure a visa due to the strong border regulations of the United Kingdom. At the World Association of Sign Language Interpreters (WASLI) conference opening in Paris, then-President Debra Russell announced that two people who had gotten a bursary to attend had not successfully received visas. At the Clin d'Oeil festival in France, its founder David De Keyzer said in an interview that certain areas of the world (e.g., Africa) were underrepresented there for many reasons: lack of funding, but also visa problems, because financial support from the festival is not sufficient to secure a visa. A married Indian couple working in the United States had wanted to attend the same festival but, whereas the husband had traveled to France direct from the United States with no issues with the visa procedure, his wife had first traveled to India to visit her family, and her visa application from India was rejected. Annelies learned about several other Indians who had wanted to attend the Clin d'Oeil festival but had gotten their visas rejected. At the opening of Clin d'Oeil 2019, it was announced that the next edition of Clin d'Oeil would take place in the United States, and the following one again in France, alternating every year. Some Brazilian participants were worried about securing visas if the festival took place in the United States, believing that getting a U.S. tourist visa would be more difficult than getting a tourist visa for France.

In short, even if attendees receive funding or have the economic capital to self-fund their participation in international events, and even if they have the necessary social and linguistic capital to navigate the application processes, they can experience barriers due to border regulations. Wahyu, the "Bali Deaf Guide," was invited to Australia by his clients, but it turned out to be a very challenging process for him to enter Australia as opposed to his Australian clients' ability to travel to Bali. One of Wahyu's Australian sponsors had to write several letters to the authorities asserting that he would be financially responsible for Wahyu and that Wahyu had the support of several people in Australia. It took several months for Wahyu's visa to be approved, whereas most tourists who visit Bali can apply and be approved for a visa upon arrival in Indonesia. Citizenship and country of residence can thus be deciding factors in rendering people internationally immobile or in causing them to be stuck waiting for a long time before they can go abroad. In other cases, deaf people want to stay in the country they are in (e.g., become a citizen), but they experience barriers. This further leads to imbalances of representation during global events, where deaf people from already underrepresented areas are excluded from attending (and, indeed, experience other barriers while attending, as explained in Chapter 9).

(Im)mobility on/Access to the International Scale

The previous section ended with a focus on temporary international gatherings, noting that bureaucratic processes can limit deaf people's access to these even when they have access to the necessary economic capital. Access to economic capital in the form of funding was often discussed in these fields, especially in relation to sports. Access to funding sometimes operates on the national or local scale, such as national deaf associations sending out staff members or universities giving out travel bursaries. Generally, more funding is needed to participate as an athlete in the Deaflympics than to attend the Deaf Academics Conference, for example, due to the longer stay abroad (typically 5–6 weeks), resulting in higher accommodation costs and possibly unpaid leave from work. The need for sports equipment, and other costs such as support staff, also raise the level of funding required to participate.

The Deaflympics was called the World Games for the Deaf until 2001, the name change being one of the International Committee of Sports for the Deaf's (ICSD) strategies for securing more funding from national governments. By signaling in its name that the Deaflympics was related to the International Olympic Committee (IOC), and thus the wider Olympic movement, the hope was that deaf sports would be better funded. In some countries, this was successful. Pavel, the captain of the Russian chess team, gave the following narrative during the 19th Winter Deaflympics in 2019, where Annelies did fieldwork:

> Now it's good, but that wasn't the case in previous years. This was because the label of "Olympics" was not yet attached to our games. Our government [in Russia] was highly focused on funding Olympic achievement, but because we weren't part of the official movement, funding was very limited. A big step toward gaining that was us dovetailing into the movement and becoming the Deaflympics, and from that point forward you could see an exponential increase in support, so we were delighted to become part of the Olympics movement. Not only has it made a difference in the financial aspect, there is also the philosophy of the movement and the positivity and momentum that we can build on for future years. All that from being part of the Olympics.

Being in the Deaflympics helps to secure funding. Philip Gardner (Technical Director of Chess for ICSD) stated that at the 2018 International Chess Olympiad (an event independent of the Deaflympics), many participants were self-funding and only few had received financial support, whereas at the 2019 Winter Deaflympics, the number of chess players who had gotten support was higher, as well as the number of players (140 in total).

Nevertheless, in a lot of countries (e.g., the United Kingdom; see Harrison, 2014), government funding for international disability sport goes entirely to the Paralympics. It is often easier to get support if you are proven to be a successful athlete who has already won a medal at an international competition, making it harder for young athletes with unproven success to start doing elite sports on an internationally competitive level. A memorandum of understanding (MOU) was drawn up in 2004 between the International Paralympics Committee (IPC) and ICSD, recognizing both as separate organizations with separate target groups; this has helped national deaf sports associations in some countries to put pressure on their governments to release more funding for the Deaflympics separately from the Paralympics. Several countries have struggled with this because deaf sports do not reach the standard of the Paralympics and are less well known by funders and governments. For some top deaf athletes, participating in the Olympics (rather than the Deaflympics) is more feasible in terms of obtaining funding; however, the level of the competition is much higher and deaf people often feel left out in terms of communication (Harrison, 2014).

Russia was often cited as a great example of support. Russian deaf sports is well funded, and when a Russian deaf person wins a medal, they receive a large sum of money, leading to a degree of financial security. However, in many countries, deaf sports associations do not know how to use the MOU to negotiate with their governments, or they have not been successful in doing so. At the 23rd Summer Deaflympics in 2017, the Ukrainians and Russians were awarded many medals, which shows disparity between countries in relation to funding and representation. Pavel narrated stories of hearing and hard of hearing people in Russia faking or manipulating their audiograms to ensure that their hearing loss was recorded as being just over 55dB in order to pass the threshold of eligibility to the Deaflympics. Privileged forms of deaf mobility are thus attractive enough for people to fake deafness or to exaggerate their hearing loss (see also Kusters, 2017a). At the end of the 2010s, deaf Ukrainians and Russians in the sports world were seen as privileged in terms of having their professional mobilities funded; at the time of writing in 2022, the reverse is true, with many Ukrainians experiencing acute suffering and forced migration, and international sanctions placing some restrictions on Russians' mobilities.

The struggle for funding has led to a push for the professionalization of deaf sports. This has meant the privileging of athletes with mild hearing loss, and the involvement of more hearing people on the level of coaching and training (see Chapter 9). The professionalization of sports, and its relationship to the availability of funding, causes difficulties for some deaf sports professionals. Marijo, an elderly man from Croatia, described this situation when interviewed at the curling competition at the 2019 Winter Deaflympics:

> In the past, deaf people coached in whatever way they saw fit, without regulation. But that's not allowed now. At the national level, if you have no training and no qualification, then you cannot coach. It's a hard-and-fast rule. In Croatia, I used to coach the deaf team, but now I am not allowed. You have to be qualified.

In this case, international deaf mobility turns into international hearing mobility to deaf international events, and it renders some deaf sports professionals less mobile *as* professionals. Also, where governments do not provide support, or where fundraising is not successful, deaf and hard of hearing individuals are often self-funding or are funded by their families. This has led to complaints in India, for example, that it is not necessarily the best deaf athletes who compete in the Deaflympics, but those with the wealthiest families. This shows the influence of class and economic capital on deaf professional mobility.

During the 2019 Winter Deaflympics, the impact of gender on international deaf mobility was often discussed. Because sports competitions are gender segregated, gendered differences were especially visible. Deaf sports are strongly male dominated (Clark & Mesch, 2016), and female athletes are less mobile in the international sports world compared to men for several reasons, including the necessary length of the stay abroad. The Deaflympics themselves last 10 days, but they are preceded by sometimes several weeks of stay at the location for training. It is often difficult for parents to arrange to be away from home for so long, an issue that disproportionately affects mothers. Furthermore, in team sports, the team members attending the Deaflympics are often recruited from different parts of a country, making international mobility in the sports contingent on earlier local and national mobility for training and preparation. It is often particularly difficult for women to commit to frequent training away from home in other parts of the country if they have care duties, especially following childbirth. This situation differs starkly between countries. Margareth Hartvedt, head of the national deaf sport organization in Norway, explained that Norwegian women experience fewer barriers to participation in international elite sports than those in many other countries around the world. Even so, she had taken a 15-year break during the period that she had three children.

It tends to be harder to create a new women's team compared to a new men's team. Women's ice hockey has faced difficulties meeting the Deaflympics inclusion requirement of six teams from a minimum of two regional confederations (such as Europe and Africa), due to there sometimes only being teams from Europe. As a result of this, only a men's ice hockey competition took place in the 2019 Winter Deaflympics. In ice hockey, 15 players are needed; in comparison, only five players are needed in curling, making it easier to meet the requirement. There were several female curling teams at the Winter Deaflympics. The number of participants in a team sport is also problematic for the sport of chess, in which teams of four players are expected from each country; for some countries, this is not possible. If the regulations allowed for a reduced number of players per team, it is likely that we would see a growth of chess among female sportspeople, and thus an increase in international mobility for women. In other words, regulations impose structural barriers to mobility on already underrepresented people.

The underrepresentation of women in sports not only applies to the athletes themselves but also (and even more so) at the level of national and international sports leadership. It is challenging to get enough women on international deaf sports boards, such as the ICSD board; not many women apply. At the ICSD congress in 2019, a young female Swedish delegate proposed a quota for women on sports boards: Every country would have a female delegate and a male delegate, and at least two members of the board were to be women. Her proposal was received with reserve, and it was voted down. When the location for the next (24th) Summer Deaflympics was discussed at the same congress, two Brazilian women presented a bid. One of the men on the ICSD board sneered, "See, we do have some women here after all!" and did not recognize the problem as structural (see *This Is IS*: Episode 6). Where women have been leaders in sports for a long time, this has often been due to the strategy of downplaying their gender and focusing on their deafness instead. Isabelle Malaurie, from France, a leading figure in the European Deaf Sports Organisation, said:

> You're right, there are very few women at the congress, and we need to change that. In my day, we had a few strong women. We weren't many, but we were strong. The reason we were so strong is we weren't focused on our identities as women, but rather on the work. We were selfless in our determination and in our work for sport. I was one of them. I didn't concentrate on my gender, but rather on being deaf. That's what drove us. Today, as women, we see the stark gender imbalance and the need to encourage more women to get involved. [...] Clubs may say it's impossible and they can't find any women, but this is no excuse. They

should persevere in their efforts to reach out to women and girls and not just drop the issue. [...] It was never about gender to me, it was about helping deaf people through sport, and that's what gave me the drive to work hard. When men oppressed me I stood up to them as an equal and I gained their respect. I had to continue working so sometimes I would have to reprimand them, they would apologize, maybe there would be a bit of an argument, but afterward I always gained their respect. We had to be on equal footing to move forward. So, yes, you needed to be strong, and that's how I've made it this far. I was never intimidated by the power or number of men, I forged ahead by my own power.

In these male-dominated spaces of sports leadership, Isabelle downplays being a woman and foregrounds being deaf. This is reminiscent of our discussion of other deaf minoritized or marginalized people taking up this strategy by downplaying racial differences and letting racist microaggressions pass (see Chapter 9).

Gender discrepancies were also evident at DOOR International in Kenya, the translation center where Annelies did research. Here, most deaf Bible translators are men, as shown in the campus cafeteria in Episode 2 of *This Is IS*.[2] Paul, the director of DOOR, explained that women had worked at DOOR in the past but that there were "problems with women." He claimed that women "worked slowly," that men were attracted to DOOR in search of wives, and that there was a higher turnover of staff because women were more likely to leave after a short period of work (e.g., for marriage). Ingrid, from Costa Rica, who worked at DOOR as a consultant to the deaf translators, experienced a stark contrast between working in her own country and the DOOR workplace in terms of gender-related cultural attitudes. In this strongly international workplace, including all-male teams from South Sudan and Mozambique, women were rendered internationally immobile. Clarice was the only female translator from Africa who was working on campus at the time, and as she was Kenyan herself, she had thus not had to move internationally (although she had visited the DOOR campus in India).

The lack of international mobility for women was also raised in Erin's research on tourism, especially in relation to women traveling alone internationally. In an interview with Erin, a white deaf woman from the United States, Kate, shared that she has had to choose countries carefully when traveling alone:

Men can travel anywhere, [but] when women travel alone they need to consider their safety more. When I decided to move to Africa for my internship, I chose to go to Malawi because it was one of the few countries that was safe for women to travel alone. Even though there were some awkward moments, overall I felt safe.

Similarly, another white deaf woman from the United States, Tonya, noticed that social media was overwhelmingly full of male travelers with no children and no responsibilities. She was looking to network with women who had shared similar experiences as solo deaf female travelers:

I think a lot of women feel overwhelmed and they don't speak up. They are taught not to be selfish, and they sacrifice everything for their kids and everyone else except for themselves. That is why I specifically searched for them, but I found nothing. My [Facebook] group started with only 10 women, and really only two of them have actually joined solo traveling, and those two don't have children.

---

2. https://vimeo.com/728777656#t=0h25m15s

Because she found hardly any deaf women motivated to travel solo, she finally decided to open her Facebook group to everyone, changing the focus from solo female travelers to "solo deaf travelers" and, in so doing, reached a total of 1,000 members. This example reveals the challenges that deaf women overcome in order to travel alone compared to men: For reasons including time commitments to family and a lack of confidence due to safety concerns, women's mobility is curtailed. This further relates to the difficulty of finding role models and creating peer networks (see Chapter 7), as evidenced by the popularity of the "solo deaf traveler" Facebook page as opposed to the group set up specifically for deaf women who travel alone.

Embodied positionalities and corporeal identities, such as gender and disability, all shape individual (im)mobilities in international settings. People who present as cisgender or transgender women, or as feminine, are vulnerable to gender-based violence in certain contexts, and they often have to take this into consideration as they move around (or not). For example, Erin did not go out alone in Bali after 9 p.m. and avoided being alone in a hotel room if the door and locks did not seem secure; many of her participants who identified or presented as women made similar decisions.

People may experience other types of barriers when moving through settings they visit abroad, due to their embodied positionalities. Steffen, a deaf wheelchair user from Germany, emphasized the importance of tenacity, confidence, and assertiveness to get through infrastructural barriers, or barriers created by people:

> One time, I was told that it was impossible to go to Africa as a wheelchair user. I didn't care and flew there anyway. When I showed up, people were disturbed, not knowing what to do because there wasn't a lift to get off the plane for disabled people in Nigeria. I waited patiently. Seeing me made them think. Four men carried me down. The next time I flew there, they found a way to bring me down. You can see that changes happen. I didn't give up, I went there. They told me it was impossible, so I waited until something became possible. They were panicky, trying to think of something, while I only put a smile on my face and waited. They came up with something. Before my arrival they were making excuses, but when they saw me [arrive] from Germany, they had to come up with something.

Waiting and patience, in combination with agency, can thus be a conscious strategy to enable international deaf mobility; however, we also must acknowledge that Steffen's positionality as a white man from Germany most certainly had an impact on how he was perceived and received by the people at the airport. Additionally, not everyone is equipped for tenacity in situations where they experience barriers to mobility, especially when overexhausted or overstimulated. Many deaf people with disabilities are simply not mobile internationally because of the range of potential social, physical, and psychological barriers. Steffen pointed out that many deaf wheelchair users are discouraged by their families to being internationally mobile. Having been elected to the WFD board at the XVIII World Federation of the Deaf Congress in 2019, he hoped to inspire them.

Deaf people in wheelchairs who are internationally mobile and do make it to events may experience multiple instances of sudden stuckness on a daily basis. This includes material barriers, such as a lack of ramps. Wheelchair users attending an event can face barriers on their journeys to, and also within, the building(s) where the event is situated, negotiating public transport, streets, pubs and restaurants where deaf people gather, and accommodation venues. Steffen explained his experience during the WFD congress:

> The streets here in Paris are OK for a wheelchair user, but I was not able to enter the metro. Accessibility is a problem here. Buses and pedestrian streets are good. I want everything to be accessible. Pubs where deaf people go aren't accessible—there are stairs or other barriers. That is disappointing.

For Steffen, he had been able to reach Paris itself and come to the conference venue, but certain places remained inaccessible for him, rendering him immobile in relation to the social side gatherings that many people consider central to the experience of the event (Chapter 7).

A person's racialized presentation also has an impact on the spaces in which they are mobile and how these spaces are experienced. Brian, a black deaf tourist from the United States who was traveling in Bali, told Erin about his experiences traveling in different countries:

> Mostly all is good, it's very safe. When I went to Japan, they were staring at me because they had never seen a black person. They asked if they could touch my skin, which I was OK with. I didn't feel angered by it, it was innocent. They took photos with me. When I travel, I don't worry. Sometimes—such as in Colombia—I arrive at places and there are other people of color. I didn't read it in a travel book or anything, but there [they] are—the same as me. I don't worry. But, in America it is different. I worry there. If I travel by car to Mississippi, I am afraid. I don't know if I can expect to be threatened with a gun because of my skin color. There are a few places like that. I don't feel like that in other countries when I travel.

Brian interpreted people's fascination with his skin color in places where there are not a lot of black people as an example of curiosity and wonderment. It is notable that Brian felt comfortable traveling in many other countries, but he did not feel the same way while traveling in his own country due to the militarized racism there. This example shows that people can feel freer to move around in another country than their own, and it is reminiscent of Shahina's account, contrasting being free to move around abroad with her family's attempts to keep her at home.

In a further exploration of his intersectional standpoints, Brian explained to Erin that although he has the social and economic capital to travel extensively, other black people in the United States have told him that they do not have the same capital to travel:

> Last year I traveled to Vietnam, Cambodia, Thailand, Malaysia, and Singapore. When I came back home, I went to the NBDA (the National Black Deaf Association) conference. Friends and people I met there asked how the traveling was, since they had seen it on Facebook and Instagram—they wanted to know how I traveled. I explained how I used online tools. One of my friends asked if I knew why everyone was looking at me—it is because black people never travel. For example, the deaf traveler Joel Barish is a white person, the owner of Seek the World is a white person. There are other white people too. Our community is not represented [online]. I am traveling and they see it is possible and that is why they ask questions [...] Some suggested I should give lectures and explain about my travels and how it works. (#deaftravel, 01:31:08)[3]

---

3. https://vimeo.com/588352737#t=1h31m08s

Brian flagged issues of representation and social capital related to mobility, with the rarity of black deaf influencers from the United States leading to his feeling of responsibility to be a role model and share information with other black Americans who are interested in travel. His agency online is reminiscent of the story of the woman who wanted to network online with other female deaf solo travelers. Online networks are crucial for people, especially minoritized people, who wish to be mobile and access information.

Having been confronted with the international immobility of other black deaf people from his country, Brian attempted to support their mobility. Deaf people who are mobile internationally are also often confronted with the international immobility of deaf people in the countries they visit. When Erin did fieldwork in Yogyakarta, she went to see Borobudur Temple with two participants; there, she was surprised to be mobbed by smiling young Indonesian students asking for photographs. Erin felt like a celebrity and obliged them by posing for a succession of photos, mostly with young women in colorful hijabs. Later, she mentioned this experience to Gio, one of the deaf guides in Bali, and Gio explained that many young Indonesians do not have the means to travel, so they "travel" by meeting foreigners and gain (an appearance of) social capital by approaching foreigners.

A similar situation arose with a woman that the Travass deaf tour group met by accident when they visited an Indonesian restaurant in Lombok, an island off Bali. When the group arrived, they started giving Gio their orders so he could communicate them to the cook, who turned out to be deaf herself. In the film *#deaftravel: Deaf Tourism in Bali*, Gio and the woman are filmed talking for a bit. She explained to Gio that she had not been able to go to school in Bali because she needed to stay and work to support her parents (see *#deaftravel*, 01:42:00).[4] Later, she asked for a group photo, like the Indonesian students in Yogyakarta. In the film, a marked contrast in deaf motility is seen within Bali.

Whereas the deaf woman in Lombok had not even been able to leave her island for an education, Indonesian deaf tour guide Wahyu was hypermobile within Bali because of driving tourists around in his own car. Through his work with deaf tourists, Wahyu has learned about the tourists' home countries and sign languages; in that sense, his mobility through the island (with tourists) enabled him to expand his social and linguistic capital, and his cosmopolitanism. He has gained an understanding of where different people come from, as well as their cultural norms (which he could then comment on in interactions), without physically going to these other countries: The world has come to him (see Chapters 6 and 8). In a similar way, some deaf people travel to beach resorts from their village or from Denpasar, the capital of Bali, as the guests of tourists. James Kerwin, a tourist from Australia who goes to Bali regularly, treated two of his Balinese deaf friends by inviting them to join him at a resort in northeast Bali, about an hour and half away from Denpasar. They explained that they could not afford the gas for the motorcycle, which surprised James; he then helped to cover the cost so that they could enjoy the beach as well. Here, deaf Balinese people experience the benefits of social capital in the form of relationships with international tourists, which then translates into forms of economic capital.

Some deaf people in Bali thus "travel" *through meeting (and photographing) tourists* and by *traveling with tourists*: They participate in other people's international mobilities to and through their country. In Bengkala, the "deaf village," the deaf households that have received the most

---

4. https://vimeo.com/588352737#t=1h42m00s

tourists have many photos of tourists and researchers (predominantly white) on their walls as a demonstration of their social capital (see *#deaftravel*, 01:11:38).[5] These deaf Indonesian people may not themselves travel much (or at all) outside of their island or, on a smaller scale, outside of their village; in this sense, they experience immobility on the national or international scale. In an example of the inseparability of mobility and immobility, Wahyu has been more mobile on the island than many other Balinese deaf people, but through his daily interactions with tourists, he has strongly experienced his role as a *local* guide who passes on *local* knowledge (see Chapter 6). Additionally, by facilitating international tourists' local mobility, he has been confronted on a daily basis with his own position as someone who is not as internationally mobile as his customers. Wahyu does not have the resources or the necessary paperwork to travel freely on an international scale, as is shown by his experience of travel from Bali to Australia—this was not as effortless an experience as that of Australians traveling to Bali. This example shows how people's "mobility at one scale can coexist with their immobility at another" (Salazar, 2021a, p. 15).

The interrelation between immobilities on different scales becomes clear when we examine recent global events and their impact at the local level. A key example is the coronavirus pandemic and its resulting immobilizations. The pandemic and associated travel restrictions led to a sudden shift from overtourism to nontourism (Gössling et al., 2021), and this had a profound impact on Bali's economy. All tourism stopped: Most (96%) of the hotels were temporarily closed, along with many restaurants and shops, leading to mass layoffs in all sectors. The closing scenes of *#deaftravel*, in editorial production in 2020 and 2021, show empty beaches, empty streets, and a stillness in Bali.

The layoffs impacted Balinese people's ability to secure basic needs, such as food. As a result of this, Erin received many WhatsApp messages from both deaf and hearing people in Bali asking for financial assistance. She twice sent money to the hearing family that she had lived with in Bali, and she also supported efforts by Australian deaf tourists to distribute food to Balinese deaf people. During the pandemic, James established two GoFundMe campaigns to organize and pay for emergency food runs for deaf people in Bali, the first of which raised almost $5,000 in Australian dollars. James told Erin during a WhatsApp conversation that "it is a lot of work on me keeping tabs and maintaining the campaign and it actually costs me personally financially to pay back transfer fees so it is a huge job but done with love for Bali." As Bali closed down to tourism, many of the deaf Balinese participants in Erin's project moved back to their home villages, some on other islands, in a form of reverse mobility as economic opportunities diminished. Tragically, one of Erin's key participants passed away, in part due to the economic impact of the pandemic restricting his access to necessary health care. Other participants suffered economically and professionally: Wahyu, for example, did not work for over a year. However, now that Bali is open to tourists again, there is a sense of cautious optimism.

Conclusion

Mobility and immobility are scalar, and they are experienced temporally. There are diverse experiences of (im)mobilities in relation to financial, social, and/or bodily resources at each scale. Black deaf people, deaf women, and/or deafdisabled people experience site-specific immobilities and feelings of discomfort depending on the material, social, and political contexts and safety

---

5. https://vimeo.com/588352737#t=01h11m38s

considerations of the places they visit. The same goes for deaf people in Kakuma Refugee Camp waiting in lines to obtain food. On a larger scale and time frame, deaf refugees feel stuck in the camp, deaf migrants feel stuck in limbo during long visa procedures, and deaf female migrants and athletes may feel stuck at home with household and childcare responsibilities. "Stuckness," then, is a central experience resulting from enforced immobility. Feelings of stuckness shape people's temporal perspectives when considering their life trajectories. They may draw stark comparisons with their sense of stuckness in the present and their more mobile pasts and (hopes for) more mobile futures. In this chapter, our data show that immobility can be associated with particular *stages of life* (e.g., being a child, being newly married, having a baby, having childcare responsibilities). It also can be associated with *being deaf* and the scatteredness of deaf communities (wanting to expand local deaf networks but being unable to). But immobility can also be moment- and event-specific—for example, being stuck at home due to having missed out on a visa.

Access to various forms of social, cultural, and economic capital shapes experiences of (im)mobility, and (im)mobilities are also impacted by structural inequalities embedded within government policies (e.g., funding criteria, immigration procedures, visa regulations) and the policies of organizations (e.g., gender quotas on boards). In many instances, people can feel (and are) powerless against structural barriers. Yet, the experience of immobility can also translate into *agency*; people may actively go in search of information, call out abuse, or compel others to figure out how to make a space more accessible for them. When stuck or waiting, people are faced with domination from the authorities that make them wait or render them "stuck" by bureaucracy, yet the waiting period can itself be spent building up economic, social, and cultural capital. Additionally, people who experience others' stuckness and immobility may be motivated to *facilitate* their mobility. Other people may be motivated to facilitate other deaf people's mobility abroad by supporting them financially, by engaging in fundraising and (sometimes ill-conceived) charity projects, by networking online with them, and by positioning themselves as role models for deaf mobility.

Mobilities lead to international deaf encounters even for those who are *not internationally mobile themselves*. Deaf people with more localized mobility "travel" through meeting deaf people who visit their countries or villages. This illustrates that deaf cosmopolitanism is not necessarily related to international travel, formal education, and/or social class. Deaf cosmopolitanism is, above all, an openness to difference, and the ability to engage in calibration in languaging and sociality (see Chapter 8). The examples here show that when deaf people who are hypermobile come into contact with deaf people who are less mobile, it does not automatically follow that the former have a "more cosmopolitan" attitude.

Mobility and immobility are *entangled* because people experience both (multiscalar and multitemporal) mobility and immobility at the same time. For instance, being a resident of a refugee camp does not necessarily mean being "stuck" within the camp, because people are often able to leave and travel outside of the camp; rather, the stuckness is felt in relation to a person's life trajectory and long-term opportunities. In their everyday lives, deaf refugees are mobile within the camp as they go about their daily routines, but these daily mobilities also involve waiting: waiting for food to be distributed (a short-term impact), but also waiting for access to information about residence permits, visas, and so on, that they believe will affect their long-term mobility. The time spent by people waiting is thus experienced on different time scales. In a different example, Wahyu is hypermobile within Bali, but his mobility is constrained by national borders and visa regulations. This is how temporality, scale, and mobility are entwined: A person can be very mobile and yet immobile at the same time.

Furthermore, one person's immobility only exists *in contrast* to other people's mobilities. People notice how others around them are more (or less) mobile than they are: Refugees in Kakuma Refugee Camp remember others who have been resettled elsewhere; wives who have emigrated from India observe that their husbands move freely in the city while they remain at home; tour guides, quintessential deaf cosmopolitans, meet and befriend deaf people from all over the world while staying put in their country; conference attendees are reminded of those who are "not here" because of visa problems, or they learn about side events they cannot access. People's mobilities are also facilitated by other people's immobilities: Local hosts in a Balinese village must remain immobile to welcome tourists, while the tour guide facilitates other people's mobilities by capitalizing on their own positionality as a local. For some, the freedom to move *relies* on the constraints of others (Toomey, 2022).

In sum, the distinction between mobility and immobility is relative (Salazar, 2021a). The examples have demonstrated the temporal dimension of (im)mobility: It can be experienced for extended time periods, in the moment, and in contrasting time periods within a person's life trajectory (i.e., in terms of their past life, present life, and future aspirations). People are never entirely immobile or "stuck" in absolute terms, but they experience both mobility and immobility at the same time to various degrees. Immobility is experienced when comparing it to moments of greater mobility or to people who have greater mobility, whatever the scale and time frame. Immobility may even be valued or aspired to. The data we collected and analyzed illustrate that deaf international (im)mobility is dialectical, meaning that *two opposing things are true at once*.

Conclusion

The Deaf Mobility Shift

Annelies Kusters

In the wide-ranging mosaic of deaf international mobilities, we, the MobileDeaf project researchers, have studied deaf experiences in countries both familiar and unfamiliar to us. We have examined vibrant deaf spaces and networks that deaf people produce, inhabit, and navigate across local, national, and international scales. We have analyzed the parallel dynamics of mobility and immobility, recognizing the complexity of deaf people's experiences that range from hypermobile journeys to the nuanced aspects of being "stuck." It is now time to reflect on the profound implications of this project.

Deaf mobilities, translocality, and cosmopolitanism are not mere theoretical constructs. They are phenomena that pulse with life, resonating in real places and contexts, shaping the lives of deaf people, and not only forming but also maintaining, transforming, and continually reshaping deaf networks. Exploring these phenomena, the chapters of this book have revealed the various ambitions underlying international connections, the opportunities that flexible language use brings, the multifaceted spaces of belonging, and the complex interplay between mobility and immobility.

Herein lies a deeper recognition: The study of deaf mobilities is both a mirror and a window. It mirrors the aspirations, struggles, and triumphs of deaf people, reflecting complex patterns of connections, identity, and exchange. At the same time, it opens a window into the broader human condition of mobility, providing insights into the ways we connect, move, and find our place in the world.

Next, we reflect on several key aspects of our study: the lessons learned from treating deaf cosmopolitanism as a challenge; the conceptual tools, or "coffer," that guided our inquiry; the implications of deafening Mobility Studies; the essential teamwork that enabled the success of this project; and the current and anticipated societal impact of the MobileDeaf project.

On Deaf Cosmopolitanism as a Challenge

The pursuit of deaf cosmopolitanism invites us into a meaningful conversation about identity, community, privilege, and connection in a world evermore intertwined. As we have explored throughout the preceding chapters, the study of deaf mobilities both illuminates and challenges our understanding of what it means to belong in, to engage with, to understand, and to navigate a landscape rich in diversity but fraught with disparities.

The allure of deaf cosmopolitanism is compelling, sketching a vision where deaf individuals rise above national borders, forging a collective identity that unites them as global citizens. This imagined unity is made possible by the unique linguistic features inherent in signed languages, allowing deaf signers to cross international boundaries and connect with one another fluidly. However, this book has delved into the complicated and ambivalent nature of deaf cosmopolitanism, showing that it is not simple or straightforward. Instead, it reveals itself to be a challenging pursuit that is shaped and conditioned by various socioeconomic, political, and cultural elements. Key among these are language knowledges and both existing and emerging connections, which serve as pivotal factors in paving the way for engagement with this global perspective.

Deaf cosmopolitanism represents an intentional endeavor that both relies on and produces particular opportunities and affordances. However, while easy exposure to diverse nations can foster a cosmopolitan mindset, the assumption that political stability and economic prosperity are essential prerequisites has been questioned and complicated by the realities of migration, refugees' experiences, and travel restrictions. These factors underscore that the attainment of deaf cosmopolitanism is neither automatic nor uniformly accessible, but rather a nuanced process that must be actively, collaboratively, and thoughtfully pursued.

Examining the practices that underpin deaf cosmopolitanism, we discovered a multifaceted landscape filled with a rich array of engagements, arrangements, and interactions. From international travel to hosting others, searching for advice, exchanging souvenirs, sharing stories, adapting to new language environments, and supporting local deaf businesses, these practices weave a complex matrix of connections.

Deaf cosmopolitanism is a journey that requires specific dispositions such as open-mindedness, empathy, and curiosity. These traits are vital for cultivating a cosmopolitan worldview, guiding people as they navigate diverse countries, cultures, and languages. Engaging with global media, participating in metalinguistic and intercultural discussions, and adjusting to various new environments play essential roles in deaf cosmopolitanism, although they also contain limitations and invite criticisms. This dynamic reveals that deaf cosmopolitanism is not static but is a complex aspiration filled with contradictions. It challenges us to recognize that cosmopolitanism can be a path to enlightenment and growth in one context, while in another, or even for the same individual in different situations, it may be a path forged by necessity and struggle. This nuanced perspective invites us to engage, question, and reflect, and it emphasizes the multidimensional experiences and motivations that shape an individual's relationship with a cosmopolitan mindset.

On Our Conceptual Coffer

The trajectory of the MobileDeaf project from inception to completion has been a journey marked by theoretical discovery and innovation. In ethnographic projects, it is customary to start with broad theoretical orientations, refining them after data analysis. The project team soon realized that our initial main concepts, translanguaging and intersectionality, were too broad for the insights sought. Through continuous collaboration, research, and reflection, the team's conceptual approach became more refined and specific, giving way to a nuanced exploration of the dynamics and varied experiences of deaf mobilities. The evolution of this project brought about a harmonious interplay between various disciplines, including Cultural Studies, Anthropology, Geography, and International Development.

More specifically, throughout this study, we assembled a toolkit of concepts, such as "networks," "translocality," "belonging," "calibration," and "immobility," providing us with the necessary lenses to comprehend the complex dynamics at play in the challenge that is deaf cosmopolitanism. This toolkit emerged organically from our engagement with the data, as we combined our reading with our scrutiny of the empirical evidence. These concepts were invaluable in capturing the complexities and nuances that shaped the processes we studied, helping us navigate the diverse landscapes of deaf mobilities with clarity and depth. By transcending disciplinary boundaries, the project unearthed unique insights into the subject, not only engaging with the original research questions but also expanding the horizons of Deaf Studies itself.

Looking for networks that transcended traditional confines like deaf clubs and schools, we illuminated the experiences of deaf individuals as they navigate an expansive world of interconnections and convergences. Our explorations captured deaf networks as webs flowing across international and local boundaries. They pulsate with the convergence of people and ideas that is core to cosmopolitanism. These dynamic and reactive organisms require nurturing and may crumble under neglect and power differences, revealing both the resilience and fluidity of deaf communities and connections amid change.

In our examination of translocality, we paid attention to the intertwining of real places with enduring or fleeting connections. In the practice of cosmopolitanism, even temporary locales gain international significance as they host international deaf spaces, and through the lens of translocality, individual experiences become part of collective memories, connecting different locations and people circulating within them.

Language has been a fascinating area of exploration in deaf mobilities. It moves with people, who expand their repertoires on the go. Comparisons of single signs in international encounters become markers of connection, although they may also breed othering, misunderstanding, or discrimination. Calibration, as a practice of adapting and aligning with others, is at once inclusive and discerning, delicate, and sometimes fraught with tensions. We gleaned insights into the spectrum of language practices among deaf communities—a testament to their resilience and adaptability in the face of linguistic barriers.

Within a range of contexts, we have witnessed the use of languages that are seen as "local," "national," and "global"; we have emphasized in particular the use of global but adaptive lingua franca, such as International Sign, American Sign Language, and English. Our exploration has included attention to the patterns of language learning and usage across various contexts, particularly amid the complexities of migration. In the diverse scenarios found within our subprojects, expectations and attitudes hold the potential to foster xenophobia or discriminatory labeling, offering insights into the multifaceted dynamics of language and power. The experiences of mobile deaf people have laid bare enduring patterns of language imperialism, while the echoes of (post)colonial histories continue to shape contemporary interactions.

Within this mosaic of observations, the challenge of deaf cosmopolitanism remains a unifying theme. Calibration serves as the quintessential embodiment of this challenge and underscores the interplay of curiosity, shaming, and the cognitive and emotional workload involved in communication.

Mobile deaf people's search for spaces to belong encompasses a complex assemblage of culture, identity, and shared spaces; from pubs to homes to the Deaflympics, from shared deafness to intersecting identities, there is a translocal quest for connection that transcends mere geography. It is both a quest and a negotiation, marked by transient encounters and deeper bonds. Whether identifying with hearing compatriots or finding deaf pockets within multicultural spaces, deaf people's paths to belonging are polymorphous and interwoven with issues of colorism, racism, ableism, xenophobia, and more. These paths illuminate the varied meanings of "home" and "family," demonstrating how notions of "identity" and "community" may fall short in capturing the full spectrum of deaf experiences.

Finally, the interplay between mobility and immobility adds a layer of complexity that enriches our understanding. Deaf individuals' experiences are situated on a continuum where mobility and immobility are intertwined, contingent on myriad factors such as life stages, financial resources, and external policies. The means by which deaf people accumulate social, cultural, linguistic, and economic capital are pervasively influenced by societal structures and policies; the capital we access and develop not only impacts our mobility but may also be expanded through these movements.

Immobility, far from being a mere constraint, may translate into agency, inspiration, and a window into others' cosmopolitan attitudes. It is a relative condition, where people's mobilities and immobilities facilitate and reflect one another. A person can be both expansive and confined, navigating the fluctuations of life with agility, agency, and insight. Immobility as experience recognizes boundaries without being bound by them.

Our conceptual coffer has made it possible to produce invaluable insights and to paint a vivid portrait of the variable shapes and effects of deaf mobilities. By engaging with diverse concepts and uncovering a realm of new data and insights, this exploration has not only expanded Deaf Studies but has also extended its impact to the broader field of Mobility Studies.

On Deafening Mobility Studies

In the web of human connectivity, deaf mobilities occupy an extraordinary nexus, intertwining layers of complexity that redefine a broader understanding of space, language, belonging, and (im)mobility. Studying deaf mobilities is more than studying deaf people's movements from one place to another; it is an exploration of life's constraints and possibilities. As we continue to explore this field of study, its nuances and intricacies reveal new paths for understanding not only deaf connectivity but human interaction at large.

Deafening Mobility Studies is not simply an act of incorporating Deaf Studies into Mobility Studies; in essence, it is a reevaluation of how we perceive and analyze mobility. The process of "deafening" Mobility Studies is evocative of transformative movements such as queering and cripping, which challenge norms and unveil new avenues for exploration and comprehension. Beyond just a theoretical perspective, deafening Mobility Studies stands as a potent catalyst for change. It enriches the field of Mobility Studies with complexity, nuance, and depth, reframing our understanding of what mobility signifies.

Deaf individuals, navigating through diverse and often inaccessible environments, cultivate a unique form of connection, community, and mobility. Therefore, deafening is a transgressive force, capable of reshaping multiple fields by "muting" their inherent reliance on spoken languages. In essence, deafening Mobility Studies elevates the discourse by interweaving visual language perspectives as well as the study of spoken languages in both their written and spoken forms. By unraveling deaf signers' unique ability to connect across diverse linguistic landscapes, deafening Mobility Studies adds rich dimensions to our understanding of global interconnectedness.

However, the intention of deafening Mobility Studies is not only to expose normativity and undermine the supremacy of spoken languages in the field, but also to direct attention toward the specificities of the intertwining of disability and language. Concepts like the "small world" theory of deaf social networks and the worldwide notion of "DEAF-SAME" as connecting deaf individuals across different spaces and geographies have relevance to mobility. These concepts reflect the central role of mobility in the deaf experience of being scattered but (sooner or later) connected through attending deaf schools, seeking out deaf network nodes, and/or international travel.

Through our particular focus on the interconnectedness of calibration and cosmopolitanism, deaf(ened) Mobility Studies illuminates associations between multimodality, networking, disability, and belonging. Rather than elevating deaf interactions, we recognize both their specificity and their universality. The experiences of deaf individuals raise essential questions about language and embodiment in Mobility Studies.

On Deaf Research Teamwork

Expanding Deaf Studies and deafening Mobility Studies required concerted teamwork. This project stands as an exemplar of the transformative power of collaboration, illustrating how diverse perspectives enrich not only the specific field of study but also foster interdisciplinary connections. This is evident not only in our utilization of a variety of conceptual frameworks, and in the fresh insights contributed to Mobility Studies, but also within the project's intuitive methodological approaches.

Our aspiration to foreground or pioneer certain methodological practices within Deaf Studies marked a significant advancement, enhancing the field substantially. Our team leveraged ethnographic, autoethnographic, visual, and filmmaking techniques, challenging the traditional reliance on confined methods such as interviews and surveys. This shift allowed for more nuanced and deep exploration of the multifaceted realities of deaf communities, spaces, and networks.

Our methodological approach also contributed to fostering greater collective self-determination and inclusivity in academia by empowering deaf researchers to explore methodological approaches that are best suited for themselves and their participants. The synthesis of theoretical and practical shifts signifies a milestone, paving the way for future interdisciplinary efforts.

The mentoring within our all-deaf team amplified the project's success. Mentorship was multidirectional and encompassed personal development, research skills, intellectual challenge, and collegial nurturing. We recognize the uniqueness and privilege of this experience, and we are actively invested in supporting other deaf scholars to have similar experiences. Our approach to this has included hosting research methods workshops, offering hands-on exploration of various methodologies, and contributing to "deaf academic space" in general. The sense of community and empowerment cultivated within this environment has created ripple effects, influencing deaf academic exploration worldwide and nurturing creativity and intellectual curiosity.

Our contributions to deaf academic space attest to the MobileDeaf project's lasting impact and the transformative potential of mentorship, teamwork, and innovation. From inception to completion, the project illuminated the dialectical nature of deafened Mobility Studies by also incorporating and expanding our own experiences as deaf mobile people in both academic and personal contexts. The result is a rich account of perspectives woven together through our collaboration, underscoring the uniqueness of this endeavor and pointing toward a promising future for intuitive and collaborative research.

On Impact

Coming to the end of the MobileDeaf project, our intention to shift toward a greater focus on impact has been a meaningful evolution in our approach. Recognized forms of impact resulting from research include the application of research in policy making, shifts in attitudes, changes in community self-definition, utilization in teaching and training, and advisory services. However, the European Research Council Starting Grant that funded the MobileDeaf project emphasizes scientific and theoretical innovation, and it did not initially require societal impact to be built into the design of the project. This has posed challenges given the expectations of our audiences.

The call for actionable outcomes for research projects concerning deaf people has long resonated within deaf communities, which are often overresearched but seldom engaged with the findings. A prevailing ideology within deaf communities is that every research project should lead to change and empowerment. Many researchers have felt compelled to contribute to the deaf communities they have researched, be it through improving access, advocacy, translation, fundraising, development work, or documenting endangered sign languages. Unsurprisingly, questions regarding the impact of our work have arisen, both within the MobileDeaf team and from colleagues and onlookers.

These inquiries have fueled reflective and impassioned discussions within our team, particularly concerning our positionalities. The delicate balance of accessing deaf perspectives while avoiding the pitfalls of historical exploitation has been a continuous challenge. Our ongoing dialogues have sharpened our understanding of privilege, leading us to question language use and power dynamics within our work. As we conclude the project, we strive to bring our research to various audiences in diverse formats.

The MobileDeaf project exemplifies that impactful applications can be planned during later stages without violating ethical norms. Our work serves to highlight the importance of thoughtful planning and sustainable development, avoiding hasty attempts to "help" that may inadvertently cause harm. We have made strides toward impact through disseminating the MobileDeaf films and through blogs and publications; these have prompted considerable discussion and have influenced thinking, teaching, and advocacy. Collaborations, advisory roles, and our research findings have been leveraged by various bodies.

As our project reaches its conclusion, we recognize additional opportunities for utilizing our research, including creating resources for educators and advocates to enhance international deaf communication. Our purpose is for the MobileDeaf project's legacy to linger through its influence on thought, policy, education, and the enduring dialogue it has fostered within deaf communities.

In conclusion, we carry forward the lessons, reflections, and aspirations that have shaped the MobileDeaf project, trusting that they will continue to inspire, guide, challenge, and ripple through the field of Deaf Studies and beyond. The results of our collective inquiry, the complexities it has wrestled with, and the tangible transformations it has fostered stand as a tribute to the very essence of meaningful scholarship within Deaf Studies.

References

Acharya, M. N. (2016). Cosmopolitanism. In N. B. Salazar & K. Jayaram (Eds.), *Keywords of mobility: Critical engagements* (pp. 33–54). Berghahn Books.

Adam, R., Aro, M., Druetta, J. C., Dunne, S., & Af Klintberg, J. (2014). Deaf interpreters: An introduction. In R. Adam, C. Stone, S. D. Collins, & M. Metzger (Eds.), *Deaf interpreters at work: International insights* (pp. 1–18). Gallaudet University Press.

Adam, R., & Braithwaite, B. (2022). Geographies and circulations: Sign language contact at the peripheries. *Journal of Sociolinguistics, 26*(1), 99–104. https://doi.org/10.1111/josl.12521

Addley, E. (2012, February 18). Deaf woman tells court she was raped, beaten and treated as slave for 10 years. *The Guardian*. https://www.theguardian.com/uk/2012/feb/13/deaf-woman-slavery-sexual-abuse

Adeel, M., & Yeh, A. G. (2018). Gendered immobility: Influence of social roles and local context on mobility decisions in Pakistan. *Transportation Planning and Technology, 41*(6), 660–678. https://doi.org/10.1080/03081060.2018.1488932

Adey, P. (2006). If mobility is everything, then it is nothing: Towards a relational politics of (im)mobilities. *Mobilities, 1*(1), 75–94. https://doi.org/10.1080/17450100500489080

Agboola, I. O. (2014, Spring). Andrew Jackson Foster: The man, the vision, and the 30-year uphill climb. *Deaf Studies Digital Journal, 4*.

Ahmad, W. I. U., Atkin, K., & Jones, L. (2002). Being deaf and being other things: Young Asian people negotiating identities. *Social Science & Medicine, 55*(10), 1757–1769. https://doi.org/10.1016/s0277-9536(01)00308-2

Ahmad, W. I. U., Darr, A., Jones, L., & Nisar, G. (1998). *Deafness and ethnicity: Services, policy and politics*. Policy Press.

Aina, G. (2015). Andrew Foster touches eternity: From Nigeria to Fiji. In M. Friedner & A. Kusters (Eds.), *It's a small world: International deaf spaces and encounters* (pp. 127–139). Gallaudet University Press.

Akamatsu, C. T., & Cole, E. (2000). Meeting the psychoeducational needs of deaf immigrant and refugee children. *Canadian Journal of School Psychology, 15*(2), 1–18. https://doi.org/10.1177/082957350001500201

Al-Fityani, K., & Padden, C. (2009). *Sign language geography in the Arab world*. Sign Language Research Lab, University of Haifa. http://sandlersignlab.haifa.ac.il/pdf/geography.pdf

Aldersson, R. (2023). Deaf adult learners and their teacher: Knowledge construction and meaning-making through the lens of translanguaging and semiotic repertoires. *DELTA: Documentação de Estudos em Lingüística Teórica e Aplicada, 39*(1), 1–29. https://doi.org/10.1590/1678-460x202359756

Allen, C., Arshad, I., & Ögtem Young, Ö. (2013). *"Maybe we are hated": The experience and impact of anti-Muslim hate on British Muslim women*. University of Birmingham (TANDIS: Tolerance and Non-Discrimination Information System). http://hdl.handle.net/20.500.12389/21719

Amit, V. (2015). Circumscribed cosmopolitanism: Travel aspirations and experiences. *Identities: Global Studies in Culture and Power, 22*(5), 551–568. https://doi.org/10.1080/1070289X.2014.975709

Ammons, D., & Eickman, J. (2011). Deaflympics and the Paralympics: Eradicating misconceptions. *Sport in Society, 14*(9), 1149–1164. https://doi.org/10.1080/17430437.2011.614772

Amoako, S. F. (2019). Sixty years of deaf education in Ghana (1957–2017). *Journal of Communication Disorders, Deaf Studies and Hearing Aids, 7*(1). https://www.longdom.org/open-access/sixty-years-of-deaf-education-in-ghana-19572017.pdf

Anderson, B., & Blinder, S. (2019, July 10). *Who counts as a migrant? Definitions and their consequences*. The Migration Observatory, University of Oxford. https://migrationobservatory.ox.ac.uk/resources/briefings/who-counts-as-a-migrant-definitions-and-their-consequences/

Anderson, G. B., & Bowe, F. G. (1972). Racism within the deaf community. *American Annals of the Deaf, 117*(6), 617–619.

Anitha, S., & Pearson, R. (2013). *Striking women*. University of Lincoln. https://www.striking-women.org

Anthias, F. (2008). Thinking through the lens of translocational positionality: An intersectionality frame for understanding identity and belonging. *Translocations: Migration and Social Change, 4*(1), 5–20.

Anthias, F. (2012). Transnational mobilities, migration research and intersectionality: Towards a translocational frame. *Nordic Journal of Migration Research, 2*(2), 102–110. https://www.doi.org/10.2478/v10202-011-0032-y

Anthias, F., Kontos, M., & Morokvasic-Müller, M. (Eds.). (2013). *Paradoxes of integration: Female migrants in Europe*. Springer.

Antonsich, M. (2010). Searching for belonging: An analytical framework. *Geography Compass, 4*(6), 644–659. https://doi.org/10.1111/j.1749-8198.2009.00317.x

Appiah, K. A. (2006). *Cosmopolitanism: Ethics in a world of strangers*. Penguin.

Ataman, O., & Karar, E. (2017). Deaf and hearing interpreters with and without experience with Deaf refugees. In S. Pratt & T. Whistance (Eds.), *"It's all Greek to me": Versatility in the sign language interpreting profession. Proceedings of the 24th EFSLI conference, Athens, Greece, 10th–11th September 2016* (pp. 23–34). European Forum for Sign Language Interpreters (EFSLI).

Atkin, K., Ahmad, W. I. U., & Jones, L. (2002). Young South Asian deaf people and their families: Negotiating relationships and identities. *Sociology of Health & Illness, 24*(1), 21–45. https://www.doi.org/10.1111/1467-9566.00002

Atkinson, P., & Hammersley, M. (2005). *Ethnography: Principles in practice* (3rd ed.). Routledge.

Auyero, J. (2011). Patients of the state: An ethnographic account of poor people's waiting. *Latin American Research Review, 46*(1), 5–29. https://www.doi.org/10.1353/lar.2011.0014

Bagga-Gupta, S. (2000). Visual language environments: Exploring everyday life and literacies in Swedish deaf bilingual schools. *Visual Anthropology Review, 15*(2), 95–120. https://doi.org/10.1525/var.2000.15.2.95

Bahan, B. (2008). Upon the formation of a visual variety of the human race. In H.-D. L. Bauman (Ed.), *Open your eyes: Deaf Studies talking* (pp. 83–99). University of Minnesota Press.

Baker, K., & Coulter, A. (2009). Terrorism and tourism: The vulnerability of beach vendors' livelihoods in Bali. *Journal of Sustainable Tourism, 15*(3), 249–266. https://doi.org/10.2167/jost643.0

Balachandra, S. K., Carroll, J. K., Fogarty, C. T., & Finigan, E. G. (2009). Family-centered maternity care for deaf refugees: The patient-centered medical home in action. *Families, Systems, & Health, 27*(4), 362–367. https://doi.org/10.1037/a0018214

Baptista, J. A. (2012). The virtuous tourist: Consumption, development, and nongovernmental governance in a Mozambican village. *American Anthropologist, 114*(4), 639–651. https://www.jstor.org/stable/23322554

Barish, J. (2020). *Deaf refugees at Kutupanlong Refugee Camp* [Film]. https://www.joelbarish.com/videos/nb-asia/nb-bangladesh/deaf-refugees-at-kutupanlong-refugee-camp/

Barish, J. (2021). *About Joel West Barish*. http://www.joelbarish.com/about/

Barnes, L., & Atherton, M. (2015). 'What's the sign for "Catch 22"?': Barriers to professional formation for deaf teachers of British Sign Language in the Further Education sector. *Journal of Further and Higher Education, 39*(3), 417–434. https://doi.org/10.1080/0309877x.2013.869564

Barpaga, R. (Director). (2014). *Double discrimination* [Film]. Neath Productions for BSLBT. BSL Zone. https://www.bslzone.co.uk/watch/zoom-focus-2014-double-discrimination

Bauman, H. (2014). DeafSpace: An architecture toward a more livable and sustainable world. In H.-D. L. Bauman & J. J. Murray (Eds.), *Deaf gain: Raising the stakes for human diversity* (pp. 375–401). University of Minnesota Press.

Bauman, H.-D. L., & Murray, J. J. (Eds.). (2014). *Deaf gain: Raising the stakes for human diversity*. University of Minnesota Press.

Bauman, Z. (1996). From pilgrim to tourist—or a short history of identity. In S. Hall & P. du Gay (Eds.), *Questions of cultural identity* (pp. 18–36). Sage Publications.

Baynton, D. C. (2006). The undesirability of admitting deaf mutes: US immigration policy and deaf immigrants, 1882–1924. *Sign Language Studies, 6*(4), 391–415. https://doi.org/10.1353/SLS.2006.0022

Bechter, F. (2008). The deaf convert culture and its lessons for deaf theory. In H-D. L. Bauman (Ed.), *Open your eyes: Deaf Studies talking* (pp. 60–79). University of Minnesota Press.

Bélanger, D., & Silvey, R. (2020). An im/mobility turn: Power geometries of care and migration. *Journal of Ethnic and Migration Studies, 46*(16), 3423–3440. https://doi.org/10.1080/1369183X.2019.1592396

Betts, A., Omata, N., & Sterck, O. (2020). Self-reliance and social networks: Explaining refugees' reluctance to relocate from Kakuma to Kalobeyei. *Journal of Refugee Studies, 33*(1), 62–85. https://www.doi.org/10.1093/jrs/fez084

Bissell, D. (2009). Moving with others: The sociality of the railway journey. In P. Vannini (Ed.), *The cultures of alternative mobilities: The routes less travelled* (pp. 55–70). Farnham & Burlington.

Black Deaf UK. (2020). https://www.blackdeaf.co.uk/

Blommaert, J., Collins, J., & Slembrouck, S. (2005). Spaces of multilingualism. *Language & Communication, 25*(3), 197–216. https://doi.org/10.1016/j.langcom.2005.05.002

Blommaert, J., & Dong, J. (2020). *Ethnographic fieldwork: A beginner's guide* (2nd ed.). Multilingual Matters.

Bloodworth, A. (2018, March 15). *What is LGBTQ+? What does the plus stand for and is anyone left out?* Pink News. https://www.pinknews.co.uk/2018/03/15/what-is-lgbtq-what-does-the-plus-stand-for-and-is-anyone-left-out/

Boccagni, P. (2022). Homing: A category for research on space appropriation and "home-oriented" mobilities. *Mobilities, 17*(4), 585–601. https://doi.org/10.1080/17450101.2022.2046977

Boellstorff, T. (2005). *The gay archipelago: Sexuality and nation in Indonesia*. Princeton University Press.

Boland, A. S., Wilson, A. T., & Winiarczyk, R. (2015). Deaf international development practitioners and researchers working effectively in deaf communities. In M. Friedner & A. Kusters (Eds.), *It's a small world: International deaf spaces and encounters* (pp. 239–248). Gallaudet University Press.

Bonnett, A. (2022). *Multiracism: Rethinking racism in global context*. Polity Press.

Bourdieu, P. (1978). Sport and social class. *Social Science Information, 17*, 819–840.

Bourdieu, P. (1986). The forms of capital. In J. Richardson (Ed.), *Handbook of theory and research for the sociology of education* (pp. 241–258). Greenwood.

Bourdieu, P. (1992). *The logic of practice*. Stanford University Press.

Bourdieu, P., & Wacquant, L. J. (1992). *An invitation to reflexive sociology*. Polity Press.

Braithwaite, B. (2020). Ideologies of linguistic research on small sign languages in the global South: A Caribbean perspective. *Language & Communication, 74*, 182–194. https://doi.org/10.1016/j.langcom.2020.06.009

Branson, J. E., Miller, D. B., & Marsaja, I. G. (1996). Everyone here speaks sign language, too: A deaf village in Bali, Indonesia. In C. Lucas (Ed.), *Multicultural aspects of sociolinguistics in deaf communities* (pp. 39–57). Gallaudet University Press.

Branson, J. E., Miller, D. B., & Marsaja, I. G. (1999). Sign languages as a natural part of the linguistic mosaic: The impact of Deaf people on discourse forms in North Bali, Indonesia. In E. Winston (Ed.), *Storytelling and conversation: Discourse in Deaf communities* (pp. 109–148). Gallaudet University Press.

Breivik, J. K. (2002). Deaflympics and the social role of Deaf sports. In J.-K. Breivik, H. Haualand, & P. K. Solvang (Eds.), *Rome—A temporary Deaf city! Deaflympics 2001* (pp. 39–59). Stein Rokkan Center for Social Studies, Bergen University Research Foundation.

Breivik, J.-K. (2005). *Deaf identities in the making: Local lives, transnational connections*. Gallaudet University Press.

Breivik, J.-K., Haualand, H., & Solvang, P. K. (2002). *Rome—A temporary Deaf city! Deaflympics 2001*. Stein Rokkan Center for Social Studies, Bergen University Research Foundation.

Brickell, K., & Datta, A. (2011). Introduction: Translocal geographies. In K. Brickell & A. Datta (Eds.), *Translocal geographies: Spaces, places, connections* (pp. 3–22). Routledge.

Brubaker, R. (2010). Migration, membership, and the modern nation-state: Internal and external dimensions of the politics of belonging. *The Journal of Interdisciplinary History*, *41*(1), 61–78. https://www.doi.org/10.1162/jinh.2010.41.1.61

Brubaker, R., & Cooper, F. (2000). Beyond "identity." *Theory and Society*, *29*(1), 1–47. https://doi.org/10.1023/A:1007068714468

Brumann, C. (1999). Writing for culture: Why a successful concept should not be discarded. *Current Anthropology*, *40*(Special Issue), S1–S27. https://doi.org/10.1086/200058

Bruner, E. M. (2005). *Culture on tour: Ethnographies of travel*. University of Chicago Press.

Bryman, A. (2012). *Social research methods* (4th ed.). Oxford University Press.

Busch, B. (2012). The linguistic repertoire revisited. *Applied Linguistics*, *33*(5), 503–523. https://www.doi.org/10.1093/applin/ams056

Busch, B. (2017). Expanding the notion of the linguistic repertoire: On the concept of *Spracherleben*—The lived experience of language. *Applied Linguistics*, *38*(3), 340–358. https://www.doi.org/10.1093/APPLIN/AMV030

Byun, K. (2020). Community profile of an international group of sign language users: Linguistic and social aspects. In U. Zeshan & J. Webster (Eds.), *Sign multilingualism* (pp. 283–292). De Gruyter.

Byun, K. S., de Vos, C., Bradford, A., Zeshan, U., & Levinson, S. C. (2017). First encounters: Repair sequences in cross-signing. *Topics in Cognitive Science*, *10*(2), 314–334. https://doi.org/10.1111/tops.12303

Canagarajah, S. (2021a). Rethinking mobility and language: From the Global South. *The Modern Language Journal*, *105*(2), 569–608. https://doi.org/10.1111/modl.12726

Canagarajah, S. (2021b). Materialising semiotic repertoires: Challenges in the interactional analysis of multilingual communication. *International Journal of Multilingualism*, *18*(2), 206–225. https://doi.org/10.1080/14790718.2021.1877293

Carling, J. R. (2002). Migration in the age of involuntary immobility: Theoretical reflections and Cape Verdean experiences. *Journal of Ethnic and Migration Studies*, *28*(1), 5–42. https://doi.org/10.1080/13691830120103912

Carling, J., & Schewel, K. (2018). Revisiting aspiration and ability in international migration. *Journal of Ethnic and Migration Studies*, *44*(6), 945–963. https://doi.org/10.1080/1369183x.2017.1384146

Carter, B., & Brook, P. (2021). Clases, proceso de trabajo y explotación. In M. Atzeni, R. Elber, C. Marticorena, J. Montero, & J. Soul (Eds.), *Clase, proceso de trabajo y reproducción social: Ampliando las perspectivas de los estudios laborales* (pp. 40–69). Centro de Estudios e Investigaciones Laborales (CEIL-CONICET).

Charsley, K., Bolognani, M., Spencer, S., Ersanilli, E., & Jayaweera, H. (2016). *Marriage migration and integration*. University of Bristol. https://www.bristol.ac.uk/ethnicity/projects/mmi/

Cho, S., Crenshaw, K. W., & McCall, L. (2013). Toward a field of intersectionality studies: Theory, applications, and praxis. *Signs: Journal of Women in Culture and Society*, *38*(4), 785–810. https://doi.org/10.1086/669608

Chua, M., De Meulder, M., Geer, L., Henner, J., Hou, L., Kubus, O., O'Brien, D., & Robinson, O. (2022). 1001 small victories: Deaf academics and imposter syndrome. In M. Addison, M. Breeze, & Y. Taylor (Eds.),

The Palgrave handbook of imposter syndrome in higher education (pp. 481–496). Palgrave Macmillan. https://doi.org/10.1007/978-3-030-86570-2_29

Clark, B., & Mesch, J. (2016). A global perspective on disparity of gender and disability for deaf female athletes. *Sport in Society, 21*(1), 64–75. https://doi.org/10.1080/17430437.2016.1225808

Cleall, E. (2015). Deaf connections and conversations: Deafness and education in and beyond the British Empire, ca. 1800–1900. *Journal of Colonialism and Colonial History, 16*(1). https://doi.org/10.1353/cch.2015.0006

Collins, P. H., & Bilge, S. (2016). *Intersectionality* (1st ed.). Polity Press.

Conama, J. B. (2022). How to sign on and stay there: Snapshot of the feeling of belonging within the Irish deaf community. *Irish Journal of Sociology, 30*(3), 264–285. https://doi.org/10.1177/07916035221118025

Congress. (1900). *Congrès International pour l'Etude des Questions d'Assistance et d'Education des Sourds-Muets. Section des Sourds-Muets. Compte rendu des débats et relations diverses.* Imprimerie d'Ouvriers Sourds-Muets.

Cooper, A. C. (2015). Signed language sovereignties in Việt Nam: Deaf community responses to ASL-based tourism. In M. Friedner & A. Kusters (Eds.), *It's a small world: International deaf spaces and encounters* (pp. 95–111). Gallaudet University Press.

Cooper, A. C. (2017). *Deaf to the marrow: Deaf social organizing and active citizenship in Viet Nam.* Gallaudet University Press.

Cottret, B. (2009). *The Huguenots in England: Immigration and settlement c.1550–1700.* Cambridge University Press.

Crasborn, O., & Hiddinga, A. (2015). The paradox of International Sign: The importance of deaf–hearing encounters for deaf–deaf communication across sign language borders. In A. Kusters & M. Friedner (Eds.), *It's a small world: International deaf space and encounters* (pp. 59–69). Gallaudet University Press.

Crawley, H., Düvell, F., Jones, K., McMahon, S., & Sigona, N. (2018). *Unravelling Europe's "migration crisis": Journeys over land and sea.* Bristol University Press. https://doi.org/10.2307/j.ctt1xp3vrk

Crenshaw, K. (1989). Demarginalizing the intersection of race and sex: A Black feminist critique of antidiscrimination doctrine, feminist theory and antiracist politics. *University of Chicago Legal Forum, 1*(8). https://chicagounbound.uchicago.edu/uclf/vol1989/iss1/8

Cresswell, T. (2010). Towards a politics of mobility. *Environment and Planning D: Society and Space, 28*(1), 17–31. https://doi.org/10.1068/d11407

Cresswell, T. (2021). Valuing mobility in a post COVID-19 world. *Mobilities, 16*(1), 51–65. https://doi.org/10.1080/17450101.2020.1863550

Cwerner, S. B. (2001). The times of migration. *Journal of Ethnic and Migration Studies, 27*(1), 7–36. https://doi.org/10.1080/13691830125283

Day, L., & Sutton-Spence, R. (2010). British sign name customs. *Sign Language Studies, 11*(1), 22–54. https://www.doi.org/10.1353/sls.2010.0005

De Clerck, G. A. M. (2007). Meeting global deaf peers, visiting ideal deaf places: Deaf ways of education leading to empowerment, an exploratory case study. *American Annals of the Deaf, 152*(1): 5–19. https://doi.org/10.1353/aad.2007.0009

De Clerck, G. A. M., & Lutalo-Kiingi, S. (2018). Ethical and methodological responses to risks in fieldwork with deaf Ugandans. *Contemporary Social Science, 13*(3–4), 372–385. https://doi.org/10.1080/21582041.2017.1347273

De Clerck, G. A. M., & Paul, P. V. (2016). *Sign language, sustainable development, and equal opportunities.* Gallaudet University Press.

De Meulder, M. (2015). Sign language recognition: Tensions between specificity and universalism in international deaf discourses. In A. Kusters & M. Friedner (Eds.), *It's a small world: International deaf space and encounters* (pp. 160–172). Gallaudet University Press.

De Meulder, M. (2019). "So, why do you sign?" Deaf and hearing new signers, their motivation, and revitalisation policies for sign languages. *Applied Linguistics Review, 10*(4), 705–724. https://doi.org/10.1515/applirev-2017-0100

De Meulder, M., & Murray, J. J. (2021). The illusion of choice in inclusive education. *International Journal of Inclusive Education*, 1–15. https://doi.org/10.1080/13603116.2021.1956607

de Vos, C. (2012). *Spatiality in Kata Kolok: How a village sign language inscribes its signing space* [Doctoral dissertation, Radboud University]. Radboud Repository. http://hdl.handle.net/2066/99153

de Vos, C. (2016). Sampling shared sign languages. *Sign Language Studies, 16*(2), 204–226. http://www.jstor.org/stable/26191027

del Pilar Kaladeen, M. (2018a). *Hidden histories: Indenture to Windrush*. British Library (Windrush Stories). https://www.bl.uk/windrush/articles/indenture-to-windrush

del Pilar Kaladeen, M. (2018b). Windrushed. *Wasafiri, 33*(2), 22–25. https://doi.org/10.1080/02690055.2018.1431099

Delanty, G., Wodak, R., & Jones, P. (Eds.). (2008). *Identity, belonging and migration*. Liverpool University Press.

Devine, J. A. (2017). Colonizing space and commodifying place: Tourism's violent geographies. *Journal of Sustainable Tourism, 25*(5), 634–650. https://doi.org/10.1080/09669582.2016.1226849

Dikyuva, H., Escobedo Delgado, C. E., Panda, S., & Zeshan, U. (2012). Working with village sign language communities: Deaf fieldwork researchers in professional dialogue. In U. Zeshan & C. de Vos (Eds.), *Sign languages in village communities: Anthropological and linguistic insights* (pp. 313–344). De Gruyter Mouton.

Dixon, A. R., & Telles, E. E. (2017). Skin color and colorism: Global research, concepts, and measurement. *Annual Review of Sociology, 43*(1), 405–424. https://doi.org/10.1146/annurev-soc-060116-053315

Dovchin, S. (2020). The psychological damages of linguistic racism and international students in Australia. *International Journal of Bilingual Education and Bilingualism, 23*(7), 804–818. https://doi.org/10.1080/13670050.2020.1759504

Duggan, N., & Holmström, I. (2022). 'They have no language': Exploring language ideologies in adult education for deaf migrants. *Apples – Journal of Applied Language Studies, 16*(2), 147–165. https://doi.org/10.47862/apples.111809

Dunn, L. M., & Anderson, G. B. (2020). Examining the intersectionality of deaf identity, race/ethnicity, and diversity through a Black deaf lens. In I. W. Leigh & C. A. O'Brien (Eds.), *Deaf identities: Exploring new frontiers* (pp. 279–304). Oxford University Press.

Eddo-Lodge, R. (2017). *Why I'm no longer talking to white people about race*. Bloomsbury Circus.

Edwards, T. (2014). From compensation to integration: Effects of the pro-tactile movement on the sublexical structure of Tactile American Sign Language. *Journal of Pragmatics, 69*, 22–41. https://doi.org/10.1016/j.pragma.2014.05.005

Edwards, T. (2018). Re-channeling language: The mutual restructuring of language and infrastructure among DeafBlind people at Gallaudet University. *Journal of Linguistic Anthropology, 28*(3), 273–292. https://doi.org/10.1111/jola.12199

Eggers, D. (2006). *What is the what: The autobiography of Valentino Achak Deng*. Hamish Hamilton.

Ehrkamp, P., & Leitner, H. (2006). Rethinking immigration and citizenship: New spaces of migrant transnationalism and belonging. *Environment and Planning A: Economy and Space, 38*(9), 1591–1597. https://doi.org/10.1068/a38349

El-Shaarawi, N. (2015). Living an uncertain future: Temporality, uncertainty, and well-being among Iraqi refugees in Egypt. *Social Analysis, 59*(1), 38–56. https://www.doi.org/10.3167/sa.2015.590103

Elder, B. C. (2015). Stories from the margins: Refugees with disabilities rebuilding lives. *Societies Without Borders, 10*(1), Article 2. https://scholarlycommons.law.case.edu/swb/vol10/iss1/2

Ellington, D. (Director). (2014). *Lost community* [Film]. BSL Zone. https://www.bslzone.co.uk/watch/lost-community

Ellington, D. (Director). (2016). *Lost spaces* [Film]. BSL Zone. https://www.bslzone.co.uk/watch/lost-spaces

Elliott, A., & Urry, J. (2010). *Mobile lives*. Routledge.

Elmi, A. A., & Barise, A. (2006). The Somali conflict: Root causes, obstacles, and peace-building strategies. *African Security Review, 15*(1), 32–54. https://doi.org/10.1080/10246029.2006.9627386

Emerson, R. M., Fretz, R. I., & Shaw, L. L. (2011). *Writing ethnographic fieldnotes* (2nd ed.). University of Chicago Press.

Emery, S. D. (2008). *The mental health needs of Deaf Black minority ethnic people* [Research report]. Heriot-Watt University and Deaf Connections Glasgow.

Emery, S. D. (2015). A Deaf diaspora? Imagining communities across and beyond nations. In A. Kusters & M. Friedner (Eds.), *It's a small world: International deaf space and encounters* (pp. 187–198). Gallaudet University Press.

Emery, S. D., & Iyer, S. (2022). Deaf migration through an intersectionality lens. *Disability & Society, 37*(1), 89–110. https://doi.org/10.1080/09687599.2021.1916890

Endelman, T. M. (2002). *The Jews of Britain, 1656 to 2000*. University of California Press.

Escobedo Delgado, C. E. (2012). Chican Sign Language: A sociolinguistic sketch. In U. Zeshan & C. de Vos (Eds.), *Sign languages in village communities: Anthropological and linguistic insights* (pp. 377–380). De Gruyter Mouton & Ishara Press.

Fagertun, A. (2017). Waves of dispossession: The conversion of land and labor in Bali's recent history. *Social Analysis, 61*(3), 108–125. https://www.doi.org/10.3167/sa.2017.610307

Falk, J. H., Ballantyne, R., Packer, J., & Benckendorff, P. (2012). Travel and learning: A neglected tourism research area. *Annals of Tourism Research, 39*(2), 908–927. https://doi.org/10.1016/j.annals.2011.11.016

Featherstone, D., Phillips, R., & Waters, J. (2007). Introduction: Spatialities of transnational networks. *Global Networks, 7*(4), 383–391. https://www.doi.org/10.1111/j.1471-0374.2007.00175.x

Feldman, J. (2017). Key figure of mobility: The pilgrim. *Social Anthropology, 25*(1), 69–82. https://doi.org/10.1111/1469-8676.12378

Fernández-Reino, M. (2020, January 20). *Migrants and discrimination in the UK* [Migration Observatory briefing, COMPAS]. University of Oxford. https://migrationobservatory.ox.ac.uk/wp-content/uploads/2020/01/Briefing-Migrants-and-Discrimination-in-the-UK.pdf

Fians, G. (2021a). Building community through hospitality: Indirect obligations to reciprocate in a transnational speech community. *Ethnography* (online). https://doi.org/10.1177/14661381211039451

Fians, G. (2021b). *Esperanto revolutionaries and geeks: Language politics, digital media and the making of an international community*. Springer International Publishing. https://doi.org/10.1007/978-3-030-84230-7

Fishbeck, C. R. (2018). *Working with immigrant and refugee deaf students: Strategies and decision-making processes of interpreters* [Master's dissertation, SOPHIA, St. Catherine University]. St. Catherine University repository. https://sophia.stkate.edu/maisce/4

Foster, S., & Kinuthia, W. (2003). Deaf persons of Asian American, Hispanic American, and African American backgrounds: A study of intraindividual diversity and identity. *Journal of Deaf Studies and Deaf Education, 8*(3), 271–290. https://doi.org/10.1093/deafed/eng015

Friedman, T. B., Probst, F. J., Wilcox, E. R., Hinnant, J. T., Liang, Y., Wang, A., Barber, T. D., Lalwani, A. K., Anderson, D. W., Arhya, I. N., & Camper, S. A. (2000). The myosin-15 molecular motor is necessary for hearing in humans and mice: A review of DFNB3 and shaker 2. In C. I. Berlin & B. J. B. Keats (Eds.), *Genetics and hearing loss* (pp. 31–45). Singular Publishing Group.

Friedner, M. (2015). *Valuing deaf worlds in urban India*. Rutgers University Press.

Friedner, M., & Kusters, A. (2014). On the possibilities and limits of "DEAF DEAF SAME": Tourism and empowerment camps in Adamorobe (Ghana), Bangalore and Mumbai (India). *Disability Studies Quarterly, 34*(3), 1–22. https://doi.org/10.18061/dsq.v34i3.4246

Friedner, M., & Kusters, A. (Eds.). (2015a). *It's a small world: International deaf spaces and encounters*. Gallaudet University Press.

Friedner, M., & Kusters, A. (2015b). Afterword: It's a small world? In M. Friedner & A. Kusters (Eds.), *It's a small world: International deaf spaces and encounters* (pp. 287–288). Gallaudet University Press.

Friedner, M., & Kusters, A. (2020). Deaf anthropology. *Annual Review of Anthropology, 39*, 31–47. https://doi.org/10.1146/annurev-anthro-010220-034545

Fryer, P. (1984). *Staying power: The history of Black people in Britain*. Pluto Press.

Gaillard, H. (2002). *Gaillard in Deaf America: A portrait of the deaf community, 1917* (R. M. Buchanan, Ed.; W. Sayer, Trans.). Gallaudet University Press. (Original work 1917)

Gal, S. (2016). Scale-making: Comparison and perspective as ideological projects. In E. Summerson Carr & M. Lempert (Eds.), *Scale: Discourse and dimensions of social life* (pp. 91–111). University of California Press.

Gannon, J. (2011). *World Federation of the Deaf: A history*. National Association of the Deaf.

Garcia, O., & Li, W. (2014). *Translanguaging: Language, bilingualism and education*. Palgrave Pivot.

Gibb, R., Tremlett, A., & Iglesias J. D. (2020). Introduction. In R. Gibb, A. Tremlett, & J. D. Iglesias (Eds.), *Learning and using languages in ethnographic research* (n.p.). Multilingual Matters.

Glaser, B., & Strauss, A. (1967). *The discovery of grounded theory: Strategies for qualitative research*. Sociology Press.

Glatzer, B. (2002). The Pashtun tribal system. *Concept of Tribal Society, 5*, 265–282.

Glick Schiller, N., & Fouron, G. E. (1999). Terrains of blood and nation: Haitian transnational social fields. *Ethnic and Racial Studies, 22*(2), 340–366. https://doi.org/10.1080/014198799329512

Glick Schiller, N., Darieva, T., & Gruner-Domic, S. (2011). Defining cosmopolitan sociability in a transnational age: An introduction. *Ethnic and Racial Studies, 34*(3), 399–418. https://doi.org/10.1080/01419870.2011.533781

Glickman, N., & Hall, W. (2019). *Language deprivation and deaf mental health*. Routledge.

Goodfellow, M. (2019). *Hostile environment: How immigrants became scapegoats*. Verso.

Gössling, S., Scott, D., & Hall, C. M. (2021). Pandemics, tourism and global change: A rapid assessment of COVID-19. *Journal of Sustainable Tourism, 29*(1), 1–20. https://doi.org/10.1080/09669582.2020.1758708

Götz, N., & Holmén, J. (2018). Mental maps: geographical and historical perspectives. *Journal of Cultural Geography, 35*(2), 157–161. https://doi.org/10.1080/08873631.2018.1426953

Granovetter, M. S. (1983). The strength of weak ties: A network theory revisited. *Sociological Theory, 1*, 201–233. https://www.doi.org/10.2307/202051

Green, E. M. (2014). Building the tower of Babel: International Sign, linguistic commensuration, and moral orientation. *Language in Society, 43*(4), 445–465. https://doi.org/10.1017/S0047404514000396

Green, E. M. (2015). One language, or maybe two: Direct communication, understanding, and informal interpreting in international deaf encounters. In M. Friedner & A. Kusters (Eds.), *It's a small world: International deaf spaces and encounters* (pp. 70–82). Gallaudet University Press.

Green, E. M. (2022). The eye and the other: Language and ethics in deaf Nepal. *American Anthropologist, 124*(1), 21–38. https://doi.org/10.1111/aman.13709

Greiner, C. (2011). Migration, translocal networks and socio-economic stratification in Namibia. *Africa, 81*(4), 606–627. https://doi.org/10.1017/s0001972011000477

Greiner, C., & Sakdapolrak, P. (2013). Translocality: concepts, applications and emerging research perspectives. *Geography Compass, 7*(5), 373–384. https://doi.org/10.1111/gec3.12048

Grenfell, M. (Ed.). (2012). *Pierre Bourdieu: Key concepts* (2nd ed.). Routledge.

Gulliver, M. (2015). The emergence of international deaf spaces in France from Desloges 1779 to the Paris Congress of 1900. In M. Friedner & A. Kusters (Eds.), *It's a small world: International deaf spaces and encounters* (pp. 3–14). Gallaudet University Press.

Gulliver, M., & Fekete, E. (2017). Themed section: Deaf geographies—An emerging field. *Journal of Cultural Geography, 34*(2), 121–130. https://www.doi.org/10.1080/08873631.2017.1305539

Gulliver, M., & Kitzel, M. B. (2016). Deaf geography, an introduction. In G. Gertz & P. Boudreault (Eds.), *The Deaf Studies encyclopedia* (pp. 451–453). SAGE Reference.

Gunter, A. (2010). *Growing up bad? Black youth, "road" culture and badness in an East London neighbourhood*. Tufnell Press.

Hannam, K., Sheller, M., & Urry, J. (2006). Editorial: Mobilities, immobilities and moorings. *Mobilities*, *1*(1), 1–22. https://doi.org/10.1080/17450100500489189

Hannerz, U. (2004). Cosmopolitanism. In D. Nugent & J. Vincent (Eds.), *A companion to the anthropology of politics* (pp. 69–85). John Wiley & Sons.

Harrison, S. R. (2014). *Same spirit, different team: The politicization of the Deaflympics*. Action Deafness Books.

Harvey, D. (1991). *The condition of postmodernity: An enquiry into the origins of cultural change*. Wiley-Blackwell.

Hauland, H. (2002). The two-week village: A deaf ritual. In J.-K. Breivik, H. Hauland, & P. K. Solvang (Eds.), *Rome—A temporary Deaf city! Deaflympics 2001* (pp. 19–32). Stein Rokkan Center for Social Studies, Bergen University Research Foundation.

Hauland, H. (2007). The two-week village: The significance of sacred occasions for the deaf community. In B. Ingstad, & S. R. Whyte (Eds.), *Disability in local and global worlds* (pp. 33–55). University of California Press.

Hauland, H., Solvang, P., & Breivik, B. (2015). Deaf transnational gatherings at the turn of the twenty-first century and some afterthoughts. In M. Friedner & A. Kusters (Eds.), *It's a small world: International deaf spaces and encounters* (pp. 47–57). Gallaudet University Press.

Hauland, H., Kusters, A., & Friedner, M. (2016). Transnationalism. In G. Gertz & P. Boudreault (Eds.), *The SAGE Deaf Studies encyclopedia* (pp. 980–982). Sage Publications Ltd.

Heap, M. (2003). *Crossing social boundaries and dispersing social identity: Tracing deaf networks from Cape Town* [Doctoral dissertation, Stellenbosch University]. SUNScholar Research Repository. https://scholar.sun.ac.za/handle/10019.1/53339

Heap, M. (2006). Sign-deaf spaces: The Deaf in Cape Town creating community crossing boundaries constructing identity. *Anthropology Southern Africa*, *29*(1–2), 35–44. https://doi.org/10.1080/23323256.2006.11499929

Hecht, J. (2005). *The journey of the Lost Boys: A story of courage, faith, and sheer determination to survive by a group of young boys called "The Lost Boys of Sudan."* Allswell Press.

Heller, M. (2003). Globalization, the new economy, and the commodification of language and identity. *Journal of Sociolinguistics*, *7*(4), 473–492. https://doi.org/10.1111/j.1467-9841.2003.00238.x

Heller, M., Pujolar, J., & Duchêne, A. (2014). Linguistic commodification in tourism. *Journal of Sociolinguistics*, *18*(4), 539–566. https://doi.org/10.1111/josl.12082

Henley & Partners. (2022). *The Henley Passport Index*. https://www.henleyglobal.com/passport-index

Henner, J., & Robinson, O. E. (2023). Unsettling languages, unruly bodyminds: Imaging a crip linguistics. *Journal of Critical Study of Communication and Disability*, *1*(1). https://doi.org/10.48516/jcscd_2023vol1iss1.4

Hilzensauer, M., & Skant, A. (2008). SignOn! English for deaf sign language users on the internet. In C. J. Kellett Bidoli & E. Ochse (Eds.) *English in international deaf communication* (pp. 155–177). Peter Lang.

Hinnant, J. T. (2000). Adaptation to deafness in a Balinese community. In I. Berlin & B. J. B. Keats (Eds.), *Genetics and hearing loss* (pp. 111–123). Singular Publishing Group.

Hodge, G., & Goswell, D. (2021). Deaf signing diversity and signed language translations. *Applied Linguistics Review 14*(5), 1045–1083. https://doi.org/10.1515/applirev-2020-0034

Hoffmann-Dilloway, E. (2016). *Signing and belonging in Nepal*. Gallaudet University Press.

Hoffmann-Dilloway, E. (2021). Shadows and mirrors: Spatial and ideological perspectives on sign language competency. *Journal of Linguistic Anthropology*, *31*(3), 320–334. https://doi.org/10.1111/jola.12344

Holliday, A. (2010). Complexity in cultural identity. *Language and Intercultural Communication*, *10*(2), 165–177. https://doi.org/10.1080/14708470903267384

Holmström, I. (2019). *Döva nyanländas språkliga situation – en förstudie*. Stockholm University. diva2: 1296045

Holmström, B., & Sivunen, N. (2022). Diverse challenges for deaf migrants when navigating in Nordic countries, In C. Stone, R. Adam, R. Müller de Quadros, & C. Rathmann (Eds.), *The Routledge handbook of sign language translation and interpreting* (pp. 25–40). Routledge.

Holmström, I., Schönström, K., & Duggan, N. (2021, June 1–3). *Crossing borders through language learning: The case of deaf adult migrants in Sweden* [Conference presentation]. Language Education for Social Justice Summer School and Conference in Applied Language Studies, Jyväskylä, Finland. diva2: 1589790

Horst, C. (2006). *Buufis* amongst Somalis in Dadaab: The transnational and historical logics behind resettlement dreams. *Journal of Refugee Studies, 19*(2), 143–157. https://doi.org/10.1093/jrs/fej017

Horst, C., & Grabska, K. (2015). Introduction: Flight and exile—Uncertainty in the context of conflict-inducted displacement. *Social Analysis, 59*(1), 1–18. https://doi.org/10.3167/sa.2015.590101

Hou, L. Y.-S. (2017). Negotiating language practices and language ideologies in fieldwork: A reflexive meta-documentation. In A. Kusters, M. De Meulder, & D. O'Brien (Eds.), *Innovations in Deaf Studies: The role of deaf scholars* (pp. 339–360). Oxford University Press.

Hou, L. Y.-S. (2020). Who signs? Language ideologies about deaf and hearing child signers in one family in Mexico. *Sign Language Studies, 20*(4), 664–690. https://www.doi.org/10.1353/sls.2020.0023

Hou, L. Y.-S., & Kusters, A. (2020). Sign languages. In K. Tusting (Ed.), *The Routledge handbook of linguistic ethnography* (p. 340–355). Routledge.

Hou, L., & Ali, K. (2024). Critically examining inclusion and parity for deaf Global South researchers of colour in the field of sign language linguistics. In A. C. Hudley, C. Mallinson, & M. Bucholtz (Eds.), *Inclusion in linguistics and decolonizing linguistics.* Oxford University Press.

Howe, L. (2006). *The changing world of Bali: Religion, society and tourism.* Routledge.

Høyer Leivestad, H. (2016). Motility. In N. B. Salazar & K. Jayaram (Eds.), *Keywords of mobility: Critical engagements* (Vol. 1, n.p.). Berghahn Books.

Humphries, T., Kushalnagar, P., Mathur, G., Napoli, D. J., Padden, C., Rathmann, C., & Smith, S. R. (2012). Language acquisition for deaf children: Reducing the harms of zero tolerance to the use of alternative approaches. *Harm Reduction Journal, 9*(1), 16. https://doi.org/10.1186/1477-7517-9-16

Hussein, A. (2005). The Indian diaspora in Britain: Political interventionism and diaspora activism. *Asian Affairs: An American Review, 32*(3), 189–208. https://doi.org/10.3200/AAFS.32.3.189-208

Hyndman, J. (1999). A post-cold war geography of forced migration in Kenya and Somalia. *The Professional Geographer, 51*(1), 104–114. https://doi.org/10.1111/0033-0124.00150

Ibanez Tirado, D. (2019). "We sit and wait": Migration, mobility and temporality in Guliston, southern Tajikistan. *Current Sociology, 67*(2), 315–333. https://doi.org/10.1177/0011392118792923

Ilkbasaran, D. (2015). Social media practices of deaf youth in Turkey: Emerging mobilities and language choice. In A. Kusters & M. Friedner (Eds.), *It's a small world: International deaf space and encounters* (pp. 112–124). Gallaudet University Press.

Irvine, J. T., & Gal, S. (2000). Language ideology and linguistic differentiation polities, and identities. In P. V. Kroskrity (Ed.), *Linguistic anthropology: A reader* (pp. 402–434). Research Press.

James, M., & Woll, B. (2004). Black Deaf or Deaf Black? Being Black and Deaf in Britain. In A. Pavlenko & A. Blackledge (Eds.), *Negotiation of identities in multilingual contexts* (pp. 125–160). Multilingual Matters.

Jamieson, K., Discepoli, M., & Leith, E. (2021). The Deaf Heritage Collective: Collaboration with critical intent. *Journal of Ethnology and Folkloristics, 15*(1), 1–26. https://doi.org/10.2478/jef-2021-0002

Jansen, B. (2011). *The accidental city: Violence, economy and humanitarianism in Kakuma Refugee Camp* [Doctoral dissertation, Wageningen University]. Semantic Scholar. Corpus ID: 142907396. https://edepot.wur.nl/167335

Jansen, B. J. (2008). Between vulnerability and assertiveness: Negotiating resettlement in Kakuma refugee camp, Kenya. *African Affairs, 107*(429), 569–587. https://doi.org/10.1093/afraf/adn044

Johnson, R. E. (1991). Sign language, culture & community in a traditional Yucatec Maya village. *Sign Language Studies, 73*, 461–474. http://www.jstor.org/stable/26204776

Jones, P., & Krzyżanowski, M. (2008). Identity, belonging and migration: Beyond constructing "others." In G. Delanty, R. Wodak, & P. Jones (Eds.), *Identity, belonging and migration* (pp. 38–53). Liverpool University Press. https://doi.org/10.5949/UPO9781846314537.003

Joy, S., Game, A., & Toshniwal, I. G. (2020). Applying Bourdieu's capital-field-habitus framework to migrant careers: Taking stock and adding a transnational perspective. *The International Journal of Human Resource Management, 31*, 2541–2564. https://doi.org/10.1080/09585192.2018.1454490

Kaufmann, V., Bergman, M. M., & Joye, D. (2004). Motility: Mobility as capital. *International Journal of Urban and Regional Research, 28*(4), 745–756. https://doi.org/10.1111/j.0309-1317.2004.00549.x

Kellett Bidoli, C. J., & Ochse, E. (Eds.). (2008). *English in international deaf communication*. Peter Lang.

Kelly, P. F., & Lusis, T. (2006). Migration and the transnational habitus: Evidence from Canada and the Philippines. *Environment and Planning A, 38*, 831–847. https://www.doi.org/10.1068/a37214

Kierans, D. (2020). *Who migrates to the UK and why?* The Migration Observatory, University of Oxford. https://migrationobservatory.ox.ac.uk/resources/briefings/who-migrates-to-the-uk-and-why/

Kisch, S. (2008). "Deaf discourse": The social construction of deafness in a Bedouin community. *Medical Anthropology, 27*(3), 283–313. https://doi.org/10.1080/01459740802222807

Kurz, C. A. N., & Cuculick, J. (2015). International deaf space in social media: The deaf experience in the United States. In M. Friedner & A. Kusters (Eds.), *It's a small world: International deaf spaces and encounters* (pp. 225–236). Gallaudet University Press.

Kusters, A. (2010). Deaf utopias? Reviewing the sociocultural literature on the world's "Martha's Vineyard situations." *Journal of Deaf Studies and Deaf Education, 15*(1), 3–16. https://doi.org/10.1093/deafed/enp026

Kusters, A. (2012). Being a deaf White anthropologist in Adamorobe: Some ethical and methodological issues. In U. Zeshan & C. de Vos (Eds.), *Sign languages in village communities: Anthropological and linguistic insights* (pp. 27–52). Ishara Press & Mouton.

Kusters, A. (2015). *Deaf space in Adamorobe: An ethnographic study in a village in Ghana*. Gallaudet University Press.

Kusters, A. (2017a). When transport becomes a destination: Deaf spaces and networks on the Mumbai suburban trains. *Journal of Cultural Geography, 34*(2), 170–193. https://doi.org/10.1080/08873631.2017.1305525

Kusters, A. (2017b). Autogestion and competing hierarchies: Deaf and other perspectives on diversity and the right to occupy space in the Mumbai surburban trains. *Social & Cultural Geography, 18*(2), 201–223. https://doi.org/10.1080/14649365.2016.1171387

Kusters, A. (2019). Boarding Mumbai trains: The mutual shaping of intersectionality and mobility. *Mobilities, 14*(6). 841–858. https://doi.org/10.1080/17450101.2019.1622850

Kusters, A. (2020). The tipping point: On the use of signs from American Sign Language in International Sign. *Language & Communication, 75*, 51–68. https://doi.org/10.1016/j.langcom.2020.06.004

Kusters, A. (2021). International Sign and American Sign Language as different types of global deaf lingua francas. *Sign Language Studies, 21*(4), 391–426. https://doi.org/10.1353/sls.2021.0005

Kusters, A. (2022). Revealing and revaluing auto-ethnography as a catalyst in translanguaging research. *Research Methods in Applied Linguistics, 1*(3), Article 100017. https://doi.org/10.1016/j.rmal.2022.100017

Kusters, A. (Forthcoming). *Regimenting International Sign*. Multilingual Matters.

Kusters, A., & De Meulder, M. (2019). Language portraits: investigating embodied multilingual and multimodal repertoires. *Forum: Qualitative Social Research, 20*(3). https://doi.org/10.17169/fqs-20.3.3239

Kusters, A., & Fenlon, J. (2021). "It is natural, really deaf signing"—Script development for fictional programs involving sign languages. *Multilingua, 41*(4). https://doi.org/10.1515/multi-2021-0008

Kusters, A., & Friedner, M. (2015). Introduction: DEAF-SAME and difference in international deaf spaces and encounters. In M. Friedner & A. Kusters (Eds.), *It's a small world: International deaf spaces and encounters* (pp. ix–xxx). Gallaudet University Press.

Kusters, A., De Meulder, M., & O'Brien, D. (Eds.). (2017a). *Innovations in Deaf Studies: The role of deaf scholars*. Oxford University Press.

Kusters, A., De Meulder, M., & O'Brien, D. (2017b). Innovations in Deaf Studies: Critically mapping the field. In A. Kusters, M. De Meulder, & D. O'Brien, (Eds.), *Innovations in Deaf Studies: The role of deaf scholars* (pp. 1–55). Oxford University Press.

Kusters, A., Green, M., Moriarty, E., & Snoddon, K. (2020). Sign language ideologies: Practices and politics. In A. Kusters, M. Green, E. Moriarty, & K. Snoddon, (Eds.), *Sign Language ideologies in practice* (pp. 3–24). De Gruyter.

Kusters, A., Sahasrabudhe, S., & Gopalakrishnan, A. (2016). *A reflexive report on filmmaking within a linguistic ethnography with deaf and hearing people in Mumbai* (MMG Working Paper, 16-04). Max Planck Institute for the Study of Religious and Ethnic Diversity. https://www.doi.org/10.13140/RG.2.2.33034.88007

Kusters, A., Spotti, M., Swanwick, R., & Tapio, E. (2017c). Beyond languages, beyond modalities: Transforming the study of semiotic repertoires. *International Journal of Multilingualism, 14*(3), 219–232. doi: 10.1080/14790718.2017.1321651

Kusters, A., Toura-Jensen, O., Verhelst, F., & Vestergaard, O. (2015). Changing the world (or not): Reflecting on interactions in the Global South during the frontrunners program. In M. Friedner & A. Kusters (Eds.), *It's a small world: International deaf spaces and encounters* (pp. 249–261). Gallaudet University Press.

Ladd, P. (2003). *Understanding Deaf culture: In search of Deafhood*. Multilingual Matters.

Ladd, P. (2015). Global Deafhood: Exploring myths and realities. In M. Friedner & A. Kusters (Eds.), *It's a small world: International deaf spaces and encounters* (pp. 274–286). Gallaudet University Press.

Larsen, J., & Urry, J. (2008). Networking in mobile societies. In J. O. Bærenholdt & B. Granås (Eds.), *Mobility and place: Enacting northern European peripheries* (pp. 89–102). Routledge.

Lefebvre, H. (1991). *The production of space* (H. Nicolson Smith, Trans.). Blackwell Publishing. (Original work published 1974)

le Maire, A. (2015). *Les sourds et leur mobilité géographique: Une approche ethnographique des familles de la region de Namur* [Unpublished master's dissertation]. Université Catholique de Louvain, Belgique.

le Maire, A. (2020, April 7). *"The gift of hearing": Hearing aids as a quick fix in Kakuma Refugee Camp*. MobileDeaf. https://mobiledeaf.org.uk/hearingaids/

Lee, J. (2012). *They have to see us: An ethnography of deaf people in Tanzania* [Doctoral dissertation, University of Colorado Boulder]. Semantic Scholar. Corpus ID: 151072069

Leeman, J., & Modan, G. (2009). Commodified language in Chinatown: A contextualized approach to linguistic landscape. *Journal of Sociolinguistics, 13*(3), 332–362. https://www.doi.org/10.1111/j.1467-9841.2009.00409.x

Leigh, I. (2009). *A lens on deaf identities*. Oxford University Press.

Leigh, I., & O'Brien, C. (Eds.). (2020). *Deaf identities: Exploring new frontiers*. Oxford University Press.

Levitt, P., & Glick Schiller, N. (2004). Conceptualizing simultaneity: A transnational social field perspective on society. *The International Migration Review, 38*(3), 1002–1039. https://doi.org/10.1111/j.1747-7379.2004.tb00222

Lew, A. A. (2018). Why travel? Travel, tourism, and global consciousness. *Tourism Geographies, 20*(4), 742–749. https://doi.org/10.1080/14616688.2018.1490343

Lewis, I. M. (2008). *Understanding Somalia and Somaliland: Culture, history, society*. Columbia University Press.

Li, W. (2011). Moment analysis and translanguaging space: Discursive construction of identities by multilingual Chinese youth in Britain. *Journal of Pragmatics, 43*(5), 1222–1235. https://doi.org/10.1016/j.pragma.2010.07.035

Lindley, A., & Hammond, L. (2014). Histories and contemporary challenges of crisis and mobility in Somalia. In A. Lindley (Ed.), *Crisis and migration* (pp. 46–72). Routledge.

Love, N. (2017). On languaging and languages. *Language Sciences, 61*, 113–147. https://doi.org/10.1016/j.langsci.2017.04.001

Low, S. (2017). *Spatializing culture: The ethnography of space and place*. Routledge.

Lubbers, M. J., Verdery, A. M., & Molina, J. L. (2018). Social networks and transnational social fields: A review of quantitative and mixed-methods approaches. *International Migration Review*, *54*(1), 177–204. https://doi.org/10.1177/0197918318812343

Luster, T., Qin, D. B., Bates, L., Johnson, D. J., & Rana, M. (2008). The lost boys of Sudan: Ambiguous loss, search for family, and reestablishing relationships with family members. *Family Relations*, *57*(4), 444–456. https://www.doi.org/10.1111/j.1741-3729.2008.00513.x

Lutz, H. (2015). Intersectionality as method. *DiGeSt: Journal of Diversity and Gender Studies*, *2*(1–2), 39–44. https://doi.org/10.11116/jdivegendstud.2.1-2.0039

Mahler, S. J., Chaudhuri, M., & Patil, V. (2015). Scaling intersectionality: Advancing feminist analysis of transnational families. *Sex Roles*, *73*(3–4), 100–112. https://doi.org/10.1007/s11199-015-0506-9

Malkki, L. (1994). Citizens of humanity: Internationalism and the imagined community of nations. *Diaspora: A Journal of Transnational Studies*, *3*(1), 41–68. https://doi.org/10.1353/dsp.1994.0013

Mansfield, B. (2005). Beyond rescaling: Reintegrating the "national" as a dimension of scalar relations. *Progress in Human Geography*, *29*(4), 458–473. https://doi.org/10.1191/0309132505ph5600

Marsaja, I. G. (2008). *Desa Kolok: A deaf village and its sign language in Bali, Indonesia*. Ishara Press.

Martens, I. (2020). "Zonder liefde kan ik niet gelukkig leven, maar migratie is niet gemakkelijk": Kwalitatief onderzoek naar de ervaringen van dove vrouwen die naar Vlaanderen verhuizen voor de liefde [Master's dissertation, University of Ghent]. Universiteitsbibliotheek Gent. https://lib.ugent.be/catalog/rug01:002835579

Massey, D. (1994). *Space, place, and gender*. University of Minnesota Press.

Maton, K. (2012). Habitus. In M. Grenfell (Ed.), *Pierre Bourdieu: Key concepts* (2nd ed.). Routledge.

Mattos, M. B. (2022). *The working class from Marx to our times: Marx, Engels, and Marxisms* (R. Freitas, Trans.). Palgrave Macmillan.

May, V. M. (2015). *Pursuing intersectionality, unsettling dominant imaginaries*. Routledge.

McAuliff, K. (2021). *Deaf refugees: A critical review of the current literature* (Working paper 1). Centre for Development and Emergency Practice, Oxford Brookes University. https://doi.org/10.24384/CENDEP.WP-01-2021

McCall, L. (2005). The complexity of intersectionality. *Signs: Journal of Women in Culture and Society*, *30*(3). https://doi.org/10.1086/426800

McDaniel, J., Shaw, A. V., & Jok, J. M. (2021). Refugees, life in host communities, and the health challenges. In S. C. Scrimshaw, S. D. Lane, R. A. Rubinstein, & J. Fisher (Eds.), *The SAGE handbook of social studies in health and medicine* (2nd ed., pp. 230–248). SAGE Publications Ltd.

McIntyre, A. P., Negra, D., & O'Leary, E. (2022). Mediated immobility and fraught domesticity: Zoom fails and interruption videos in the Covid-19 pandemic. *Feminist Media Studies*, *23*(4), 1837–1856. https://doi.org/10.1080/14680777.2021.1996425

McKee, R., & McKee, D. (2020). Globalization, hybridity, and vitality in the linguistic ideologies of New Zealand Sign Language users. *Language & Communication*, *74*, 164–181. https://doi.org/10.1016/j.langcom.2020.07.001

Merricks, P. (2015). The World Federation of the Deaf Youth Camp in Durban: An opportunity for learning, networking, and empowerment. In M. Friedner & A. Kusters (Eds.), *It's a small world: International deaf spaces and encounters* (pp. 24–33). Gallaudet University Press.

Mesch, U., & Mesch, J. (2018). *The deaf sport movement in Europe: Deaf sport without borders*. European Deaf Sports Association.

Mijić, A. (2022). (Re-)Construction of identity and belonging after forced migration: A sociology of knowledge approach. *Journal of Refugee Studies*, *35*(3), 1107–1125. https://doi.org/doi.org/10.1093/jrs/feac033

Miller, C. A., & Clark, K. A. (2020). Deaf and queer at the intersections: Deaf LGBTQ people and communities. In I. W. Leigh & C. A. O'Brien (Eds.), *Deaf identities: Exploring new frontiers* (pp. 205–335). Oxford University Press.

Mindess, A. (2006). *Reading between the signs: Intercultural communication for sign language interpreters* (3rd ed.). Nicholas Brealy.

Mirzoeff, N. (1995). *Silent poetry: Deafness, sign, and visual culture in modern France.* Princeton University Press.

Moers, P. W. (2017). From the world's trouble spots they arrive in our classrooms: Working with deaf refugees and immigrants. *Odyssey: New Directions in Deaf Education, 18*, 44–49.

Moges, R. T. (2015). Challenging sign language lineages and geographies: The case of Eritrean, Finnish, and Swedish Sign Languages. In M. Friedner & A. Kusters (Eds.), *It's a small world: International deaf spaces and encounters* (pp. 83–94). Gallaudet University Press.

Moges, R. T. (2017). Cripping Deaf Studies and Deaf Literature: Deaf queer ontologies and intersectionality. In A. Kusters, M. De Meulder, & D. O'Brien (Eds.), *Innovations in Deaf Studies: The role of deaf scholars* (pp. 215–239). Oxford University Press.

Monteiro, N. M., & Ford, D. Y. (2016). Colorism and the educational experiences of immigrants and refugees: Global and local considerations for educators. In C. Monroe (Ed.), *Race and colorism in education* (pp. 176–190). Routledge.

Moore, A. (2008). Rethinking scale as a geographical category: From analysis to practice. *Progress in Human Geography, 32*(2), 203–225. https://doi.org/10.1177/0309132507087647

Moore, M., & Panara, R. (1996). *Great Deaf Americans* (2nd ed.). Deaf Life Press.

Morgan, H. E., Gilchrist, S. K., Burichani, E. N., & Osome, J. O. (2015). Kenyan sign language. In J. Bakken Jepsen, G. De Clerck, S. Lutalo-Kiingi, & W. B. McGregor (Eds.), *Sign languages of the world: A comparative handbook* (pp. 529–552). De Gruyter.

Morgan, N., & Pritchard, A. (2005). On souvenirs and metonymy: Narratives of memory, metaphor and materiality. *Tourist Studies, 5*(1), 29–53. https://doi.org/10.1177/1468797605062714

Moriarty, E. (2020a). "Sign to me, not the children": Ideologies of language contamination at a deaf tourist site in Bali. *Language & Communication, 74*, 195–203. https://doi.org/10.1016/j.langcom.2020.06.002

Moriarty, E. (2020b). Filmmaking in a linguistic ethnography of deaf tourist encounters. *Sign Language Studies, 20*(4), 572–594.

Moriarty, E. (in press). The aesthetics of access: Filmmaking in a Balinese "village of the deaf." In M.-C. Dietrich & A. Lawrence (Eds.), *Empirical art: Filmmaking for fieldwork in practice.* Manchester University Press.

Moriarty, E., & Kusters, A. (2021). Deaf cosmopolitanism: Calibrating as a moral process. *International Journal of Multilingualism, 18*(2), 285–302. https://doi.org/10.1080/14790718.2021.1889561

Moriarty Harrelson, E. (2015). SAME-SAME but different: Tourism and the deaf global circuit in Cambodia. In M. Friedner & A. Kusters (Eds.), *It's a small world: International deaf spaces and encounters* (pp. 199–211). Gallaudet University Press.

Moriarty Harrelson, E. (2017a). *Regimes of mobilities: Deaf development, NGOs and deaf tourism in Cambodia* [Doctoral dissertation, American University]. AUDRA: http://hdl.handle.net/1961/auislandora:68916

Moriarty Harrelson, E. (2017b). Deaf people with "no language": Mobility and flexible accumulation in languaging practices of deaf people in Cambodia. *Applied Linguistics Review, 10*(1), 55–72. https://doi.org/10.1515/applirev-2017-0081

Mottez, B. (1993). The Deaf Mute Banquet and the birth of the Deaf movement. In R. Fischer & H. Lane (Eds.), *Looking back* (pp. 143–155). Signum.

Murphy, R. (Director). (2010). *Eat pray love* [Film]. Columbia Pictures & Plan B Entertainment.

Murray, J. (2007). *"One touch of nature makes the whole world kin": The transnational lives of Deaf Americans, 1870–1924* [Doctoral dissertation, University of Iowa]. Iowa Research Online. https://iro.uiowa.edu/esploro/outputs/doctoral/One-touch-of-nature-makes-the/9983776700602771

Napier, J. (2021). *Sign language brokering in deaf-hearing families.* Palgrave-Macmillan.

Napier, J., Cameron, A., Leeson, L., Rathmann, C., Peters, C., Sheikh, H., Conama, J. B., & Moiselle, R. (2020). *Employment for deaf signers in Europe: Research findings from the Designs Project* (CDS/SLSCS Monograph No. 5). http://www.designsproject.eu/assets/eu-benchmark-report.pdf

Nash, J. C. (2019). *Black feminism reimagined: After intersectionality.* Duke University Press.

Ndurumo, M. M. (2003). Where eagles dare: The legacy of Dr. Andrew Foster. *The African Annals of the Deaf, Premier Issue.* https://view.publitas.com/african-annals-of-the-deaf/afad2003001/page/4-5

Netto, G., Hudson, M., Kamenou-Aigbekaen, N., & Sosenko, F. (2019). Dominant language acquisition in destination countries: Structure, agency and reflexivity. *Sociology, 53*(5), 843–860. https://doi.org/10.1177/0038038519826021

Newhouse, L. (2012). *South Sudan oyee! A political economy of refugee return migration to Chukudum, South Sudan* [Doctoral dissertation, University of Washington]. Research Works Archive, http://hdl.handle.net/1773/22623

Newhouse, L. (2015). More than mere survival: violence, humanitarian governance, and practical material politics in a Kenyan refugee camp. *Environment and Planning A: Economy and Space, 47*(11), 2292–2307. https://doi.org/10.1068/a140106p

Nieminen, R. (1990). *Voyage to the island.* Gallaudet University Press.

Nilsson, A.-L. (2020). From Gestuno interpreting to International Sign interpreting: Improved accessibility? *Journal of Interpretation, 28*(2), Article 6. https://digitalcommons.unf.edu/joi/vol28/iss2/6

Nowicka, M. (2015). *Bourdieu's theory of practice in the study of cultural encounters and transnational transfers in migration* (Working Papers WP 15-01). Max Planck Institute for the Study of Religious and Ethnic Diversity. https://www.mmg.mpg.de/61298/wp-15-01

Nowicka, M., & Rovisco, M. (2009). Making sense of cosmopolitanism. In M. Nowicka & M. Rovisco (Eds.), *Cosmopolitanism in practice* (pp. 1–18). Routledge.

Nyst, V. (2010). Sign languages in West Africa. In D. Brentari (Ed.), *Sign languages: A Cambridge language survey* (pp. 405–432). Cambridge University Press.

Nyst, V., Sylla, K., & Magassouba, M. (2012). Deaf signers in Douentza, a rural area in Mali. In U. Zeshan & C. de Vos (Eds.), *Sign languages in village communities: Anthropological and linguistic insights* (pp. 251–276). De Gruyter Mouton & Ishara Press.

O'Brien, D. (2005). *What's the sign for pint? An investigation into the validity of two different models to describe Bristol's current Deaf pub culture* [Master's dissertation, University of Bristol]. Deaf Geographies. https://deafgeographies.files.wordpress.com/2011/09/obrien-2005.pdf

O'Brien, D. (2020). Mapping deaf academic spaces. *Higher Education, 80*(4), 739–755. https://doi.org/10.1007/s10734-020-00512-7

O'Brien, D. (2021a). Theorising the deaf body: Using Lefebvre and Bourdieu to understand deaf spatial experience. *Cultural Geographies, 28*(4), 645–660. https://doi.org/10.1177/14744740211003632

O'Brien, D. (2021b). Bourdieu, plurilingualism and sign languages in the UK. In K. Snoddon & J. Weber (Eds.), *Critical perspectives on plurilingualism in deaf education* (pp. 60–80). Multilingual Matters.

O'Brien, D., & Emery, S. D. (2014). The role of the intellectual in Minority Group Studies: Reflections on Deaf Studies in social and political contexts. *Qualitative Inquiry, 20*(1), 27–36. https://doi.org/10.1177/1077800413508533

O'Brien, D., Stead, L., & Nourse, N. (2019). Bristol Deaf memories: Archives, nostalgia and the loss of community space in the deaf community in Bristol. *Social and Cultural Geography, 20*(7), 899–917. https://doi.org/10.1080/14649365.2017.1392591

Office for National Statistics (ONS). (2022, November 2). *International migration, England and Wales: Census 2021* (Statistical bulletin). www.ons.gov.uk/peoplepopulationandcommunity/populationandmigration/internationalmigration/bulletins/internationalmigrationenglandandwales/census2021

Ohta, I. (2005). Coexisting with cultural "others": Social relationships between the Turkana and the refugees at Kakuma, northwest Kenya. *Senri Ethnological Studies, 69*, 227–239. https://jambo.africa.kyoto-u.ac.jp/member/thesis/Ohta2005_2.pdf

Oktar, T. (2019). *Inclusion of multilingual deaf children and youth in London: Perspectives from hearing mothers from Black and minority ethnic backgrounds and ethnographic observations from two mainstream schools with deaf resource bases* [Doctoral dissertation, Brunel University]. BURA. http://bura.brunel.ac.uk/handle/2438/20877

Olsen, E. T. (2018). Deaf and refugee: A different situation. *Border Crossing*, *8*(1), 237–254. https://doi.org/10.33182/bc.v8i1.737

Olsen, E. T. (2019). Cooperation as a coping mechanism when interpreting between deaf refugees and hearing professionals. *International Journal of Interpreter Education*, *11*(2), Article 4. https://tigerprints.clemson.edu/ijie/vol11/iss2/4

Oostendorp, M. (2021). Raced repertoires: The linguistic repertoire as multi-semiotic and racialized. *Applied Linguistics*, *43*(1), 65–87. https://doi.org/10.1093/applin/amab018

Oteng, F. S. (1988). *Give them a name!* Kumasi Catholic Press.

Padden, C., & Humphries, T. (1988). *Deaf in America: Voices from a culture.* Harvard University Press.

Padden, C., & Humphries, T. (2005). *Inside Deaf Culture.* Harvard University Press.

Palfreyman, N. (2019). *Variation in Indonesian Sign Language: A typological and sociolinguistic analysis.* De Gruyter Mouton.

Palfreyman, N., & Schembri, A. (2022). Lumping and splitting: Sign language delineation and ideologies of linguistic differentiation. *Journal of Sociolinguistics*, *26*(1), 105–112. https://doi.org/10.1111/josl.12524

Parks, E. S. (2014). Constructing national and international deaf identity: Perceived use of American Sign Language. In D. Watt & C. Llamas (Eds.), *Language, borders and identity* (pp. 206–217). Edinburgh University Press.

Parr, S., Bashir, N., & Robinson, D. (2010, April). *An evaluation of the deaf third-country nationals integration project: A report to the United Kingdom border agency.* Centre for Regional and Economic Research, Sheffield Hallam University (CRESR). https://www.shu.ac.uk/centre-regional-economic-social-research/publications/an-evaluation-of-the-deaf-third-country-nationals-integration-project

Parsons, F. (2005). I dared! In B. Cyrus, E. Katz, C. Cheyney, & F. Parsons (Eds.), *Deaf women's lives: Three self-portraits* (pp. 189–304). Gallaudet University Press.

Parsons, F. M., & Chitwood, D. L. (1988). *I didn't hear the dragon roar.* Gallaudet University Press.

Patel, B., & Kelley, N. (2006). *The social care needs of refugees and asylum seekers.* SCIE Race Equality discussion paper no. 2. https://hscbusiness.hscni.net/pdf/SCIE-_Social_care_needs_of_refugees_and_asylum_seekers_Aug_2006_pdf.pdf

Patil, V. (2013). From patriarchy to intersectionality: A transnational feminist assessment of how far we've really come. *Signs*, *38*, 847–867. https://doi.org/10.1086/669560

Pennycook, A. (2010). *Language as a local practice.* Routledge.

Perniss, P., & Zeshan, U. (2008). Possessive and existential constructions in Kata Kolok. In U. Zeshan & P. M. Perniss (Eds.), *Possessive and existential constructions in sign languages* (pp. 125–150). Ishara Press.

Phadke, S., Khan, S., & Ranade, S. (2011). *Why loiter? Women and risk on Mumbai streets.* Penguin Books.

Picard, M. (1996). *Bali: Cultural tourism and touristic culture.* Archipelago Press.

Pickel-Chevalier, S., & Budarma, K. (2016). Towards sustainable tourism in Bali: A Western paradigm in the face of Balinese cultural uniqueness. *Mondes du tourisme, Hors-série*, 1–32. https://doi.org/10.4000/tourisme.1187

Pierce, C. (1970). Offensive mechanisms. In C. Pierce & F. B. Barbour (Eds.), *The Black Seventies: An extending horizon book* (pp. 265–282). Porter Sargent Publisher.

Pietikäinen, S., & Kelly-Holmes, H. (2011). The local political economy of languages in a Sámi tourism destination: Authenticity and mobility in the labelling of souvenirs. *Journal of Sociolinguistics*, *15*(3), 323–346. https://doi.org/10.1111/j.1467-9841.2011.00489.x

Piller, I. (2015). Language ideologies. In K. Tracy, T. Sandel and C. Ilie (Eds.), *The international encyclopedia of language and social interaction*, 1–10. https://doi.org/10.1002/9781118611463.wbielsi140

Piller, I. (2017, August 28–30). *Language shaming: Enacting linguistic subordination* [Invited plenary]. International Conference on Minority Languages and Summer School of Applied Language Studies, Jyväskylä & Närpes, Finland.

Porst, L., & Sakdapolrak, P. (2017). How scale matters in translocality: Uses and potentials of scale in translocal research. *Erdkunde*, *71*(2), 111–126. https://doi.org/10.3112/erdkunde.2017.02.02

Pratiwi, K. R. I., Saleh, C., & Sentanu, I. G. E. P. S. (2019). Policy implementation of tour guides license in maintaining the quality of tourism in Bali province. *Journal of Indonesian Tourism and Development Studies*, *7*(3), 175–183. https://www.doi.org/10.21776/ub.jitode.2019.007.03.06

Prawiro-Atmodjo, P., Elsendoorn, B., Reedijk, H., & Maas, M. (2020). *Educating DHH migrant children*. Royal Kentalis. https://www.kentalis.com/media/1019

Quinn, N. (2013). Participatory action research with asylum seekers and refugees experiencing stigma and discrimination: The experience from Scotland. *Disability & Society*, *29*(1), 58–70. https://doi.org/10.1080/09687599.2013.769863

Ralph, D., & Staeheli, L. A. (2011). Home and migration: Mobilities, belongings and identities. *Geography Compass*, *5*(7), 517–530. https://doi.org/10.1111/j.1749-8198.2011.00434.x

Rathmann, C., & De Quadros, R. M. (2022). *International sign language: Sociolinguistic aspects*. Editora Arara Azul.

Reed-Danahay, D. (2019). *Bourdieu and social space: Mobilities, trajectories, emplacements* (Vol. 6). Berghahn Books.

Reimers, R. R. (2011). *Influences of personal culture on the writing of a deaf refugee high school student from Somalia* [Unpublished doctoral dissertation]. Walden University.

Richardson, M. (2019). *Playing bilingual: Interweaving deaf and hearing cultural practices to achieve equality of participation in theatrical performance processes* [Doctoral dissertation, Heriot-Watt University]. ROS Thesis Repository. http://hdl.handle.net/10399/4295

Rijckaert, J. (2012). Op weg naar erkenning van Deaf Cinema? In G. De Clerck & R. Pinxten (Eds.), *Gebarentaal zegt alles: Bijdragen rond diversiteit en gebarentaal vanuit emancipatorisch perspectief*. Acco.

Roberts, K., & Harris, J. (2002). *Disabled people in refugee and asylum-seeking communities in Britain*. Joseph Rowntree Foundation. https://www.jrf.org.uk/report/disabled-people-refugee-and-asylum-seeking-communities-britain

Robertson, S. (2019). Migrant, interrupted: The temporalities of "staggered" migration from Asia to Australia. *Current Sociology*, *67*(2), 169–185. https://doi.org/10.1177/0011392118792920

Robertson, S. (2021). *Temporality in mobile lives: Contemporary Asia–Australia migration and everyday time*. Policy Press.

Robertson, S., & Roberts, R. (Eds.). (2022). *Rethinking privilege and social mobility in middle-class migration: Migrants "in-between."* Routledge.

Robinson, O. (2016). In pursuit of citizenship: Campaigns against peddling in Deaf America, 1880s–1950s. In B. H. Greenwald & J. J. Murray (Eds.), *In our own hands: Essays in deaf history, 1780–1970* (pp. 127–148). Gallaudet University Press.

Roiha, A., & Iikkanen, P. (2022). The salience of a prior relationship between researcher and participants: Reflecting on acquaintance interviews. *Research Methods in Applied Linguistics*, *1*(1), Article 100003. https://doi.org/10.1016/j.rmal.2021.100003

Rotter, R. (2016). Waiting in the asylum determination process: Just an empty interlude? *Time & Society*, *25*(1), 80–101. https://doi.org/10.1177/0961463X15613654

Roudometof, V. (2005). Transnationalism, cosmopolitanism and glocalization. *Current Sociology*, *53*(1), 113–135. https://doi.org/10.1177/0011392105048291

Ruiz-Williams, E., Burke M., Chong, V. J., & Chainarong, N. (2015). My deaf is not your deaf: Realizing intersectional realities at Gallaudet University. In M. Friedner & A. Kusters (Eds.), *It's a small world: International deaf spaces and encounters* (pp. 262–273). Gallaudet University Press.

Runnels, J. (2017). Dr. Andrew Foster: A literature review. *American Annals of the Deaf*, *162*(3), 243–252. https://doi.org/10.1353/aad.2017.0023

Runnels, J. B. (2020). *Dr. Andrew Foster's contributions to deaf education in Africa, the Ghana years (1957–1965)* [Doctoral dissertation, University of North Dakota]. ProQuest Dissertations Publishing.

https://www.proquest.com/dissertations-theses/dr-andrew-foster-s-contributions-deaf-education/docview/2480291707/se-2

Rymes, B. (2020). *How we talk about language: Exploring citizen sociolinguistics*. Cambridge University Press.

Rzepnikowska, A. (2019). Racism and xenophobia experienced by Polish migrants in the UK before and after Brexit vote. *Journal of Ethnic and Migration Studies, 45*(1), 61–77. http://doi.org/10.1080/1369183X.2018.1451308

Salazar, N. B. (2010). *Envisioning Eden: Mobilizing imaginaries in tourism and beyond*. Berghahn Books.

Salazar, N. B. (2012). Tourism imaginaries: A conceptual approach. *Annals of Tourism Research, 39*(2), 863–882. https://www.doi.org/10.1016/j.annals.2011.10.004

Salazar, N. B. (2015). Becoming cosmopolitan through traveling? Some anthropological reflections. *English Language and Literature, 61*(1), 51–67.

Salazar, N. B. (2016). Keywords of mobility: What's in a name? In N. B. Salazar & K. Jayaram (Eds.), *Keywords of mobility: Critical engagements* (pp. 1–12). Berghahn Books.

Salazar, N. B. (2017). Key figures of mobility: An introduction. *Social Anthropology, 25*(1), 5–12. https://doi.org/10.1111/1469-8676.12393

Salazar, N. B. (2021a). Immobility: The relational and experiential qualities of an ambiguous concept. *Transfers, 11*(3), 3–21. https://doi.org/10.3167/TRANS.2021.110302

Salazar, N. B. (2021b). Post-national belongings, cosmopolitan becomings and mediating mobilities. *Journal of Sociology, 57*(1) 165–176. https://doi.org/10.1177/1440783320987639

Salazar, N. B., & Graburn, N. H. (Eds.). (2014). *Tourism imaginaries: Anthropological approaches*. Berghahn Books.

Salazar, N. B., & Jayaram, K. (Eds.). (2016). *Keywords of mobility: Critical engagements*. Berghahn Books.

Samuels, E. (2017). Six ways of looking at Crip Time. *Disability Studies Quarterly, 37*(3), Article 3. https://doi.org/10.18061/dsq.v37i3.5824

Sarwar, N. (2012). Post-independence South Sudan. *Strategic Studies, 32*(2/3), 172–182. https://www.jstor.org/stable/48529366

Saved By The Sign [@savedbythesign]. (2022, July 3). *A VERY important Public Service Announcement..... Cos y'all be doing too much...* [Round Pushpin.] *Location:* @festivalclindoeil [Clapper Board.] @lydiagratis [Camera] *Videographer:* @kaleab [Video attached] [Tweet]. Twitter. https://twitter.com/SavedByTheSign/status/1543500357736824832

Saved By The Sign [@savedbythesign] & Belcher, R. [@romelbelcher]. (2022, July 19). *Candid Conversations* [Potted Plant.] *Reflecting on Clin D'Oeil & other community spaces. What does taking up space look like for you?* [Video]. Instagram. https://www.instagram.com/tv/CgLP7tOonu1/?igshid=MDJmNzVkMjY=

Schapendonk, J. (2015). What if networks move? Dynamic social networking in the context of African migration to Europe. *Population, Space and Place, 21*(8), 809–819. https://doi.org/10.1002/psp.1860

Schmitt, P. (2015). A global stage: Sign language artistic production and festivals in international contexts. In M. Friedner & A. Kusters (Eds.), *It's a small world: International deaf spaces and encounters* (pp. 15–23). Gallaudet University Press.

Schwager, W., & Zeshan, U. (2008). Word classes in sign languages: Criteria and classifications. *Studies in Language, 32*, 509–545. https://www.doi.org/10.1075/SL.32.3.03SCH

Seek the World. (2016, February 8). *American Sign Language vs. New Zealand Sign Language: Words* [Video]. YouTube. https://www.youtube.com/watch?v=6u9udAw6AfE

Sheller, M. (2021). *Advanced introduction to mobilities*. Edward Elgar Publishing.

Sheller, M., & Urry, J. (2006a). The new mobilities paradigm. *Environment and Planning A, 38*, 207–226. http://doi.org/10.1068/a37268

Sheller, M., & Urry, J. (2006b). Introduction: Mobile cities, urban mobilities. In M. Sheller & J. Urry (Eds.), *Mobile technologies of the city* (pp. 1–18). Routledge.

Shohamy, E., & Gorter, D. (2008). *Linguistic landscape: Expanding the scenery*. Routledge.

Simoni, V. (2015). Intimacy and belonging in Cuban tourism and migration. *The Cambridge Journal of Anthropology*, *33*(2). https://doi.org/10.3167/ca.2015.330204

Singleton, J. L., Jones, G., & Hanumantha, S. (2014). Toward ethical research practice with deaf participants. *Journal of Empirical Research on Human Research Ethics*, *9*(3), 59–66. https://doi.org/10.1177/1556264614540589

Sivunen, N. (2019). An ethnographic study of deaf refugees seeking asylum in Finland. *Societies*, *9*(1), Article 2. https://doi.org/10.3390/soc9010002

Sivunen, N., & Tapio, E. (2020). "Do you understand (me)?" Negotiating mutual understanding by using gaze and environmentally coupled gestures between two deaf signing participants. *Applied Linguistics Review*, *13*(6), 983–1004. https://doi.org/10.1515/applirev-2019-0065

Social Scientists Against the Hostile Environment (SSAHE). (2020). *Migration, racism and the hostile environment: Making the case for the social sciences*. https://acssmigration.wordpress.com/report/

Solvang, P. K., & Haualand, H. (2014). Accessibility and diversity: Deaf space in action. *Scandinavian Journal of Disability Research*, *16*(1), 1–13. https://doi.org/10.1080/15017419.2012.761158

Sommer Lindsay, M. (2022). *Deaf business owners' experiences of and strategies in navigating an audist normative structured labour market in Denmark* [Doctoral dissertation, Heriot-Watt University]. Signs Database. https://signs.hw.ac.uk/wp-content/uploads/PhD2022.pdf

Stein, M. S. S. (2015). Implementing the Convention on the Rights of Persons with Disabilities: Supporting the deaf community in Chile through legal expertise. In M. Friedner & A. Kusters (Eds.), *It's a small world: International deaf spaces and encounters* (pp. 173–184). Gallaudet University Press.

Stewart, D. A. (1991). *Deaf sport: The impact of sports within the Deaf community*. Gallaudet University Press.

Stoddard, E., & Marshall, K. (2015, November 15). *Refugees in Kenya: Roles of faith*. World Faiths Development Dialogue. Berkley Center for Religion, Peace & World Affairs, Georgetown University. https://berkleycenter.georgetown.edu/publications/refugees-in-kenya-roles-of-faith

Straaijer, R. (2016). Attitudes to prescriptivism: An introduction. *Journal of Multilingual and Multicultural Development*, *37*(3), 233–242. https://doi.org/10.1080/01434632.2015.1068782

Such, E., & Salway, S. (2017). *Modern slavery and public health*. GOV.UK. https://www.gov.uk/government/publications/modern-slavery-and-public-health/modern-slavery-and-public-health#definition-of-modern-slavery

Sue, D. W., Capodilupo, C. M., Torino, G. C., Bucceri, J. M., Holder, A. M., Nadal, K. L., & Esquilin, M. (2007). Racial microaggressions in everyday life: Implications for clinical practice. *The American Psychologist*, *62*(4), 271–286. https://doi.org/10.1037/0003-066X.62.4.271

Summerson Carr, E., & Lempert, M. (Eds.). (2016). *Scale: Discourse and dimensions of social life*. University of California Press.

Swinbourne, C. (Director). (2018a). *Found at the Deaf Club* [film]. Eyewitness Media and Wellington Films production for BSLBT. BSL Zone. https://www.bslzone.co.uk/watch/found-deaf-club

Swinbourne, C. (Director). (2018b). *Found in the UK* [film]. Juggle Productions for BSLBT. BSL Zone. https://www.bslzone.co.uk/watch/found-uk

Tapio, E. (2019). The patterned ways of interlinking linguistic and multimodal elements in visually oriented communities. *Deafness & Education International*, *21*(2–3), 133–150. https://doi.org/10.1080/14643154.2018.1561781

Thimm, V., & Chaudhuri, M. (2021). Migration as mobility? An intersectional approach. *Applied Mobilities*, *6*(3), 273–288. https://doi.org/10.1080/23800127.2019.1573780

Thurlow, C., & Jaworski, A. (2011). Tourism discourse: Languages and banal globalization. *Applied Linguistics Review*, *2*, 285–312. https://doi.org/10.1515/9783110239331.285

Toomey, N. (2022). The nexus of (im)mobilities: Hyper, compelled, and forced mobile subjects. *Mobilities*, *17*(2), 269–284. https://doi.org/10.1080/17450101.2021.2000840

Towner, J. (1985). The Grand Tour: A key phase in the history of tourism. *Annals of Tourism Research*, *12*(3), 297–333. https://doi.org/10.1016/0160-7383(85)90002-7

Travass Life. (2022). *Our story*. https://travass.life/

Twamley, K. (2012). Gender relations among Indian couples in the UK and India: Ideals of equality and realities of inequality. *Sociological Research Online*, *17*(4), 103–113. https://doi.org/10.5153/sro.2756

Tyler, I. E. (2018). Deportation nation: Theresa May's hostile environment. *Journal for the Study of British Cultures*, *25*(1). https://eprints.lancs.ac.uk/id/eprint/125439

U.K. Social Mobility Commission. (2021). *Shaping a society that gives everyone a fair chance*. https://social-mobility.independent-commission.uk/

UN-Habitat. (2021, June). *Kakuma & Kalobeyei spatial profile*. https://unhabitat.org/kakuma-and-kalobeyei-spatial-profile

United Nations High Commissioner for Refugees (UNHCR). (2017a, March). *Kenya: Kakuma operational update, highlights*. www.unhcr.org/ke/wp-content/uploads/sites/2/2017/04/201704012_Kakuma-Operational-Update-16th-31st-March-share-2-1.pdf

United Nations High Commissioner for Refugees (UNHCR). (2017b). *Kakuma camp—map*. Operational Data Portal, Refugee Situations. https://data.unhcr.org/en/documents/details/58199

United Nations High Commissioner for Refugees (UNHCR). (2022). *Global trends: Forced displacement in 2020*. Global Trends Reports. https://www.unhcr.org/statistics/unhcrstats/60b638e37/global-trends-forced-displacement-2020.html

Urry, J. (2000). *Sociology beyond societies*. Routledge.

Urry, J., & Larsen, J. (2011). *The tourist gaze 3.0*. SAGE Publications Ltd.

U.S. Embassy Jakarta. (2016, January 5). *U.S.-Indonesia Deaf Youth Leadership Exchange Participants Come to Jakarta*. https://id.usembassy.gov/u-s-indonesia-deaf-youth-leadership-exchange-participants-come-to-jakarta/

Van Cleve, J. V., & Crouch, B. A. (1989). *A place of their own: Creating the deaf community in America*. Gallaudet University Press.

Vargas-Silva, C., & Rienzo, C. (2022, August). *Migrants in the UK: An overview*. The Migration Observatory, University of Oxford. https://migrationobservatory.ox.ac.uk/resources/briefings/migrants-in-the-uk-an-overview/

Vasishta, M. (2011). *Deaf in DC: A memoir*. Gallaudet University Press.

Vertovec, S. (2003). Migration and other modes of transnationalism: Towards conceptual cross-fertilization. *International Migration Review*, *37*(3), 641–665. https://doi.org/10.1111/j.1747-7379.2003.tb00153.x

Vertovec, S. (2007). Super-diversity and its implications. *Ethnic and Racial Studies*, *30*(6), 1024–1054. https://doi.org/10.1080/01419870701599465

Vertovec, S. (2013). *Transnationalism*. Routledge.

Vertovec, S. (2015). Rooms without walls. In S. Vertovec (Ed.), *Diversities old and new: Migration and socio-spatial patterns in New York, Singapore and Johannesburg* (pp. 193–223). Palgrave Macmillan.

Vertovec, S., & Cohen, R. (Eds.). (2002). Introduction: Conceiving cosmopolitanism. In S. Vertovec and R. Cohen (Eds.), *Conceiving cosmopolitanism: Theory, context and practice* (pp. 1–22). Oxford University Press.

Vickers, A. (1989). *Bali: A paradise created*. Periplus.

Wang, A., Liang, Y., Fridell, R. A., Probst, F. J., Wilcox, E. R., Touchman, J. W., Morton, C. C., Morell, R. J., Noben-Trauth, K., Camper, S. A., & Friedman, T. B. (1998). Association of unconventional myosin MYO15 mutations with human nonsyndromic deafness DFNB3. *Science*, *280*(5368), 1447–1451. http://doi.org/10.1126/science.280.5368.1447

Wang, B. (2022). Immobility infrastructures: Taking online courses and staying put amongst Chinese international students during the COVID-19. *Journal of Ethnic and Migration Studies*, *48*(11), 1–19. https://doi.org/10.1080/1369183X.2022.2029376

Wang, Q., Andrews, J., Liu, H. T., & Liu, C. J. (2016). Case studies of multilingual/multicultural Asian deaf adults: Strategies for success. *American Annals of the Deaf*, *161*(1), 67–68. https://doi.org/10.1353/aad.2016.0012

Ward, K., Amas, N., & Lagnado, J. (2008, November). *Supporting disabled refugees and asylum seekers: Opportunities for new approaches*. Refugee Support, Metropolitan Support Trust. https://www.yumpu.com/en/document/view/24504829/supporting-disabled-refugees-and-asylum-seekers-metropolitan

Watts, D. J. (1999). Networks, dynamics and the small-world phenomenon. *American Journal of Sociology*, *105*(2), 493–527. https://doi.org/10.1086/210318

Wearing, S., & McGehee, N. G. (2013). Volunteer tourism: A review. *Tourism Management*, *38*, 120–130. https://doi.org/10.1016/j.tourman.2013.03.002

Webster, J., & Safar, J. (2020). Ideologies behind the scoring of factors to rate sign language vitality. *Language & Communication*, *74*, 113–129. https://doi.org/10.1016/j.langcom.2020.06.003

Webster, J., & Zeshan, U. (Eds.). (2021). *READ WRITE EASY: Research, practice and innovation in deaf multiliteracies* (Vol. 1). Ishara Press.

Wessendorf, S. (2014). *Commonplace diversity: Social relations in a super-diverse context*. Palgrave Macmillan.

Willoughby, L. J. V. (2015). Deaf children and youth from refugee backgrounds: Pressing issues and possible solutions. In M. Crock (Ed.), *Creating new futures: Settling children and youth from refugee backgrounds* (pp. 197–212). Federation Press.

Wimmer, A., & Glick Schiller, N. (2002). Methodological nationalism and beyond: Nation-state building, migration and the social sciences. *Global Networks*, *2*(4), 301–334. https://doi.org/10.1111/1471-0374.00043

Winata, S., Arhya, I. N., Moeljopawiro, S., Hinnant, J. T., Liang, Y., Friedman, T. B., & Asher, J. H., Jr. (1995). Congenital non-syndromal autosomal recessive deafness in Bengkala, an isolated Balinese village. *Journal of Medical Genetics*, *32*(5), 336–343. https://doi.org/10.1136/jmg.32.5.336

Wintour, P. (2017, September 25). Survey reveals scale of hostility towards Arabs in Britain. *The Guardian*. https://www.theguardian.com/uk-news/2017/sep/25/survey-reveals-scale-of-hostility-towards-arabs-in-britain

Wittel, A. (2001). Toward a network sociality. *Theory, Culture and Society*, *18*(6), 51–76. https://doi.org/10.1177/026327601018006003

Woodford, D. E. (2006, June 19–24). *The beginning and growth of a new language—Somali Sign Language* [Conference paper]. International Conference on Languages and Education in Africa, Oslo University, Norway.

Woolfe, T., Beedie, I., & Cormier, K. (2023). *UCL Deaf Migrants Project Report* (UCL Grand Challenges of Cultural Understanding and Justice & Equality Fund). Deafness, Language and Cognition (DCAL), London.

Wulff, H. (2002). Yo-yo fieldwork: Mobility and time in a multi-local study of dance in Ireland. *Anthropological Journal on European Cultures*, *11*, 117–136. https://www.jstor.org/stable/43234897

Young, A., & Temple, B. (2014). *Approaches to social research: The case of deaf studies*. Oxford University Press.

Youngs, M. (2010). *Real people, real needs: Deaf education in Dadaab refugee camp in Kenya* [Master's dissertation, University of Toronto]. TSpace. https://tspace.library.utoronto.ca/bitstream/1807/25685/3/Youngs_Megan_201011_MA_thesis.pdf

Yuval-Davis, N. (2006). Belonging and the politics of belonging. *Patterns of Prejudice*, *40*(3), 197–214. https://doi.org/10.1080/00313220600769331

Yuval-Davis, N. (2010). Theorizing identity: Beyond the "us" and "them" dichotomy. *Patterns of Prejudice*, *44*(3), 261–280. https://doi.org/10.1080/0031322X.2010.489736

Yuval-Davis, N. (2011). *The politics of belonging: Intersectional contestations*. SAGE Publications Ltd.

Zeshan, U. (2015). "Making meaning": Communication between sign language users without a shared language. *Cognitive Linguistics*, *26*(2), 211–260. https://doi.org/10.1515/cog-2015-0011

Zeshan, U., & de Vos, C. (Eds.). (2012). *Sign languages in village communities: Anthropological and linguistic insights*. De Gruyter Mouton & Ishara Press.

Zeshan, U., & Panda, S. (2019). Two languages at hand: Code-switching in bilingual deaf signers. In U. Zeshan & J. Webster (Eds.), *Sign multilingualism* (pp. 81–126). De Gruyter Mouton.

Zeshan, U., & Webster, J. (Eds.). (2020). *Sign multilingualism*. De Gruyter Mouton.

Zetter, R. (1991). Labelling refugees: Forming and transforming a bureaucratic identity. *Journal of Refugee Studies*, *4*(1), 39–62. https://doi.org/10.1093/jrs/4.1.39

Index

Figures and tables are indicated by f and t following the page number.

ableism, 256, 286, 291, 326
accented signing, 240–41, 256
Access to Work, United Kingdom, 116
Acharya, M. N., 8
Adamorobe, Ghana, 15, 80, 178, 249
Adedeji, Matthew, 183
agency, social and cultural capital, 116
AGREE (Catalan), 231, 231f
Ahmad, W. I. U., 260, 271
Akamatsu, C. T., 68
Al-Fityani, K., 205n6
Ali, K., 8
Al Isharah, 264
All-German Deaf-Mute Congresses, 143
American/Indonesian Deaf Youth Leadership Exchange, 179
American Sign Language (ASL)
    avoiding, deaf professional mobility and, 249–51
    cosmopolitanism and, 10–11
    influence in IS, 224
    influence in KSL, 225–26
    popularity of, 98, 215
    as threat to local or national sign languages, 215, 248–49, 251–53, 253f, 256
    used in Global South, 225–26, 250–52
Anderson, Glenn B., 112
Anthias, F., 260
Antonsich, M., 262
Appiah, K. A., 13, 19
asylum procedures, 69–70
Ataman, O., 70
ATTITUDE (International Sign), 230, 231f
audism, 11, 26, 32, 257
autoethnography, 59

Balachandra, S. K., 70
Balaguera, Johanna, 130
Bali, deaf tourism in, 149–73. *See also* Bengkala, Indonesia; BISINDO
    belonging, finding spaces of, 278–84
    COVID-19 pandemic and, 321
    deaf networks and nodes used for, 192
    deaf schools, visiting, 153, 172, 190
    deaf tour guides for, 159–67, 162f, 165f
    finding research participants for, 37–38
    global deaf circuit and, 154–57
    interviews for, 55–56
    language learning and, 215
    overview, 157–59
    participant observation and, 44–45
Bali Deaf Community, 166, 190, 280–81
Bangladesh, Kutupanlong Refugee Camp in, 153
Barish, Joel, 37, 136, 153
Barpaga, Rinkoo, 37, 50, 112–13, 116
barriers to mobility. *See* immobility
Bauman, H., 5
Beckton Deaf Club, London, 108, 188
Bélanger, D., 293
belonging, spaces of, 258–92. *See also* deaf networks and nodes; deaf spaces
    deaf culture, community, and identity, 259–60
    deaf migrants in London and, 100, 111, 263–74, 266f
    deaf professional mobility and, 284–89
    deaf refugees and, 274–77, 277f
    deaf studies on, 259–61
    deaf tourism and, 150, 278–84
    intersectionality and, 259, 261–62, 291, 326
    national sign language use and, 235
Bengkala, Indonesia. *See also* Kata Kolok
    belonging, finding spaces of, 279–80
    benefits of tourism, 197, 280
    as deaf node, 178, 194–95
    deaf tourism in, 45, 167–72, 169f, 190, 279
    immobility of locals encountering deaf tourists, 320–21
    interviews of deaf people in, 55–56
    language use and calibrating of deaf tourists, 216, 217f
    network capital of residents, 180
    out-of-place languages in, 249
Bible translations. *See* DOOR International, Nairobi
Birley, Dawn Jani, 49, 131
Birthing a Genre: Deaf Ethnographic Film, 27

BISINDO
  alphabet differences in, 234–35, 234f
  ASL as threat to, 249, 249f
  calibrating and, 216, 217f, 222–23
  International Sign compared, 222
  other sign languages as threat to, 249, 249f
  sharing signs in, 230, 231f
Black Deaf UK, 113, 116
Black Lives Matter (BLM) movement, 112–13, 115
Blank Canvas Voyage website, 153–54
blind people. *See* deafblind people
Blommaert, J., 43
Bourdieu's theory of practice. *See also* capital; fields in theory of practice; habitus in theory of practice
  deaf migrants and, 92, 107, 117
  deaf refugees and, 67–68, 74, 76–90
  overview, 19–20
Breivik, J. K., 7, 121, 155, 259
Brick, Kelby, 153
Bristol Deaf Club, United Kingdom, 186
British Deaf Association, 120
British Deaf News, 186
British Sign Language (BSL), 98–99, 107, 212, 236–40, 246, 248–49, 264
British Sign Language Broadcasting Trust (BSLBT), 185
Bruner, Edward, 149
Busch, B., 213

Cahyadi, Wahyu
  Bengkala tours, 171–72
  calibrating sign languages, 163, 216, 217f, 223, 226, 228, 229–30, 244
  as deaf node, 159, 164, 195
  English language skills, 244
  foreign contamination of local sign languages and, 249, 249f
  MobileDeaf project and, 37–38, 44–45
  mobility and immobility of, 313–14, 320–21
  participant observation and, 44–45
  photographs, 162f, 217f, 249f
  services as tour guide, 159–67, 190
calibrating. *See* language learning and calibrating
CALIBRATING, 212–13, 213f
Cambodia, deaf tourism in, 150–52, 155–56, 166
Canadian Deaf Sports Association, 120
Canagarajah, S., 13
capital
  in Bourdieu's theory of practice, 19
  cultural. *See* cultural capital
  of deaf migrants in London, 92, 97, 117
  economic. *See* economic capital
  immobility and restriction of, 293, 327
  linguistic. *See* linguistic capital
  network. *See* network capital
  physical. *See* physical capital
  of refugees at Kakuma Refugee Camp, 68
  social. *See* social capital
Carling, J. R., 294
Carmichael, Ian, 40
chaining, 222–23, 228, 236
Chaudhuri, M., 7, 23
Chicago Congress (1893), 18
Cho, S., 22
Chomsky, Noam, 104
City Literary Institute, Holborn, London
  BSL classes at, 107, 188, 246
  as deaf node, 187–88
  as deaf space, 108
  English language classes at, 246
  as field in theory of practice, 98
  MobileDeaf project and, 36–37
Clin d'Oeil, Reims, France
  "deafening" of space around, 204, 207
  as deaf node, 205–6
  economic and network capital, 197
  global deaf circuit and, 202–3
  interviews conducted at, 56
  MobileDeaf project and, 39–40
  national clustering at, 133
  participant observation at, 50
  visa issues for attendees, 313
CLSLR (Cross-Linguistic Sign Language Research) conference, Nijmegen (2007), 168
cochlear implants, 18, 286
codemixing, 227
COFFEE (BISINDO and Kata Kolok), 249, 249f
Cole, E., 68
colonialism, 5, 6, 180, 215, 242, 326
comparisons
  calibrating and learning languages, 255–56
  deaf refugees and, 85
  deaf tourism and, 152–53, 172
  essentialisms and stereotypes at international events, 135–38
  in international deaf spaces, 139
  overview, 17–19
  of signs in national sign languages, 139, 228–29
confidentiality, 57
Congress of the International Deaf Chess Federation, Manchester (2018), 313
consent, formal and informal, 40–42
Cooper, A. C., 151–52, 166
cosmopolitanism, 149–50, 278. *See also* deaf cosmopolitanism
Couchsurfing (social networking service), 192, 194
COUNTRY (International Sign), 122, 122f

COVID-19 pandemic, 198, 294–95, 305–7, 321
Crawley, H., 94
Crenshaw, K., 21, 261
crip linguistics, 242
crip time, 60–61
Cross-Linguistic Sign Language Research (CLSLR) conference, Nijmegen (2007), 168
cultural capital
    in Bourdieu's theory of practice, 19
    of deaf migrants in London, 103, 107, 108, 116
    of deaf refugees, 68, 75–76, 81, 86–87, 90, 298, 308
    deaf tourism and, 149–50, 172–73
    immobility and, 322
culture
    calibrating and, 224–25
    deaf culture. *See* deaf culture
    disrespectful signs and, 234–35, 234*f*
    lack of access for deaf people, 260
    refugee camps, conflicts in, 274
    tourism issues and, 235
    translations of interviews to written languages and, 57
curiosity, 234, 257, 319, 325–26

Dadaab Refugee Complex, Kenya, 71, 72–75
Deaf Academics Conferences (DACs), 39, 132, 143, 145, 202
Deaf Alliance, 168
deafblind people
    belonging, finding spaces of, 221, 284–85, 290
    communication modes for, 221
    deaf migrants, 203
    deaf professional mobility and, 284–85
    deaf refugees, 82–83
deaf cafés, 99, 108, 154, 187
deaf camps. *See* deaf professional mobility
deaf capital, 20, 153. *See also* deaf ecosystem
Deaf Chess Olympiad, Manchester (2018), 9, 39–40, 123–25
deaf clubs
    closures of, 186–87, 210
    as deaf nodes, 184–88
    racism in, 185
deaf community, 177, 259. *See also* belonging, spaces of; deaf networks and nodes
deaf cosmopolitanism
    belonging, finding spaces of, 278–79, 288, 291
    challenges of, 324–25
    deaf professional mobility and, 121
    deaf tourism and, 151, 153, 157, 172–73
    hospitality and hosting deaf people, 194
    intersectionality and, 21

language calibrating and, 213, 221–22, 225, 254–55, 257
linguistic shame and humor, 234–35
Mobility Studies and, 8–13
scaling and comparing, 19
sign language use and, 10–11, 194*n*5, 288
deaf culture
    belonging and. *See* belonging, spaces of
    deaf clubs and, 186
    deaf schools and, 110
    in deaf villages, 170
    right way to be deaf and, 18, 139, 215, 240
deaf ecosystem
    belonging and, 281–83
    deaf hosting and, 195
    deaf tourism and, 155, 159–60, 166, 172
    defined, 153
deaf ethnography, 25–63
    analysis and writing, 58–61, 59*f*
    consent, formal and informal, 40–42
    intersectional lens and, 21–23
    interviewing, 52–57
    labels in writing, 61–62
    networks and locations, 35–40
    participant observation, 42–51
    team composition and biographies, 28–35
    translations, 57–58
Deaf Extra Linguistic Knowledge (DELK), 70
deaf gain, 11, 159
deafhood, 11, 265–66
deaf identity. *See also* intersectionality
    belonging vs., 259–62, 326
    deaf cosmopolitanism and, 291
    deaf migrants in London and, 98–99, 268
    deaf schools and clubs, 185
    deaf tourism and, 279
    labels in writing, 61–62
    nationality and deaf professional mobility, 125, 132, 147
deaf interpreters, 69–70
deaf leaders, 138–42, 142*f*
Deaflympics
    belonging, finding spaces of, 285–86
    as deaf node, 202–3
    events in common and networking, 202
    funding for, 314–15
    gender differences at, 316–17
    hearing people at, 205–6, 286, 288–89, 315
    national identity and, 121, 147
    regulations for participation, 123, 286
    sign names for, 180–81, 180*f*
    Summer Deaflympics (Australia 2005), 183
    Summer Deaflympics (Italy 2001), 121, 180–81

Summer Deaflympics (Turkey 2017), 315
Winter. *See* Winter Deaflympics
deaf marriage migration
    belonging, finding spaces of, 265–66, 266*f*, 272–73, 290
    class and, 107
    deaf spaces and, 116
    defined, 91
    employment and, 102, 106–7, 247, 304
    immobility and mobility experiences of, 303–8
    learning new sign language and, 238–39
    motivations for, 97
    networks and nodes leading to, 190–92
    power dynamics and, 99–100
"deaf meme" video template, 227
deaf migrants in London, 91–117. *See also* deaf marriage migration
    analysis and writing of data on, 57–58
    belonging, finding spaces of, 100, 111, 263–78, 266*f*, 277*f*, 292
    deaf spaces and nodes, 107–15, 109*f*, 186–90
    discrimination and, 110–15
    employment and, 101–7, 105*t*, 247, 273, 304
    English language skills and, 245–48
    finding research participants, 35–37
    history of migration to United Kingdom, 92–93
    immigration and visa policies, 311–13
    immobility and mobility experiences of, 303–7
    informed consent procedures for, 42
    interviews of, 52–54
    language learning experiences of, 215–16, 236–41, 256
    literature review on deaf migration studies, 93–95
    networks and nodes used by, 94–95, 107, 190–92
    participant observation and, 47–49
    pathways of, 95–101
    translations of interviews to written languages, 57
deaf migrants in Sweden, 69, 90
Deaf Migration London (webinar event), 100–101
Deaf Migration Studies, 93–95
Deaf Mobilities Across International Borders. *See* MobileDeaf project
Deaf Mobility Studies, 3–24. *See also* MobileDeaf project
    Bourdieu's theory of practice and, 19–20
    comparisons and, 17–19
    deaf cosmopolitanism and, 8–13
    deaf spaces and, 14–15
    intersectional lens and, 21–23
    scale and, 15–16
    transdisciplinary nature of, 14
    translocality and, 16–17, 16*f*

deaf networks and nodes, 177–211. *See also* belonging, spaces of
    cosmopolitanism and, 12
    of deaf migrants in United Kingdom, 94–95, 107, 190–92
    for deaf professional mobility, 183, 193–95, 198–209, 199–200*f*
    for deaf refugees, 70, 77–81, 78*f*, 177, 179, 197–98
    for deaf tourism, 184–85, 190, 192–97, 196*f*
    events as, 198–209, 199–200*f*
    identity formation and, 185
    individuals as, 190–98, 196*f*
    institutional deaf spaces, 14–15, 184–90
    morality and giving back, 184
    overview, 177–79, 178*f*
    personal illustrations of, 181–84, 182*f*
    shared mental maps and new signs, 180–81, 181*f*
    translocality of, 181
Deaf Night Out event, Washington, D.C., 203
Deaf Rave, London, 108
deaf refugees in Kakuma Refugee Camp, Kenya, 67–90
    arrival at refugee camp, 72–76, 73*f*
    belonging, finding spaces of, 274–77, 277*f*, 290–92
    capital, forms of, 86–89, 88*f*
    deaf education of, 75–76, 78–81, 86–87, 185, 276–78, 297–98
    deaf nodes and, 70, 77–81, 78*f*, 177, 179, 197–98
    Deaf Refugee Studies and, 68–71
    employment of, 79, 296–97
    events leading to creation of camp, 71–72
    finding research participants, 38–39
    Food Distribution Center and, 299–300, 299–300*f*
    immobility and mobility experiences of, 293–94, 295–303, 298–302*f*
    informed consent procedures for, 41–42
    interviews of, 54–55
    knowledge and socialization process, 81–86, 85*f*
    language learning and calibrating of, 215–17, 218*f*, 225–26, 241–42, 252–54
    overview, 76–77, 77*f*
    participant observation, 45–46
    Protection Delivery Unit, 308–11, 309–10*f*
    resettlement of, 307–11
    translations of interviews to written languages, 301
Deaf Refugee Studies, 68–71
deaf researchers, 26–28
deaf rights, 139, 144, 152–53
DEAF-SAME concept
    belonging, finding spaces of, 291
    comparing and, 18–19

deaf tourism and, 155, 279, 282
defined, 12
economic capital and, 198
institutionalization of deaf expectations,
    18–19
Mobility Studies and, 327
sign comparisons and, 228–29
deaf schools
    closures of, 210
    deaf culture and, 110
    deaf migrants moving for, 96, 270
    as deaf nodes, 78, 172
    for deaf refugees, 78–79, 84, 90, 225,
        241–42, 298
    deaf sports in, 123
    deaf tourism and, 59, 153, 154, 171–72, 184–85,
        190, 249
    established in Africa, 182–83, 226
    established in Fiji, 183
    racism at, 112
    volunteering at, 281
deaf sociality, 80, 153, 156, 186, 221, 235. *See also*
    deaf spaces
deaf spaces. *See also* belonging, spaces of; deaf
    networks and nodes
    accessing, 11, 27
    "deafening" of space around international
        events, 143, 203–4, 207
    deaf tourism and, 151, 154, 156
    discrimination in, 110–15
    employment opportunities in, 103
    empowerment and, 15, 153
    finding research participants and, 35–40
    in Kakuma Refugee Camp, 77–81, 78f, 87–89,
        88f, 297
    in London, 99–100, 107–15, 109f, 116, 186–87
    loss of, 186–87, 210–11
    mapping involvement in, 107–10, 109f
    national comparisons in, 139
    overview, 14–15
    religious, 80, 100, 270–72, 292
    social capital and, 187
    social media and, 15, 107–8, 110, 278
The Deaf Sport Movement in Europe
    (Mesch & Mesch), 120
deaf sports events. *See* deaf professional mobility;
    specific events
Deaf Studies. *See also* Deaf Mobility Studies;
    MobileDeaf project
    class in, 103–7
    collaborations and interdisciplinary
        connections for, 328
    deaf community lens and, 179
    deaf cosmopolitanism and, 9, 11

on deaf migrants in United Kingdom, 93–95
deaf networks and nodes, 209–10
Deaf Refugee Studies, 68–71
deaf researchers and, 26–28
deaf space and, 14
ethnography in, 25–27
on identity and belonging, 259–61
on racism and discrimination, 111–12, 117
single-axis thinking in, 22
deaf tourism, 149–73. *See also* deaf villages
    ASL contaminating local sign languages and,
        248–49
    in Bali, overview, 157–59
    belonging, finding spaces of, 150, 278–84, 291–92
    deaf networks and nodes for, 184–85, 190,
        192–97, 196f
    deaf schools, visiting, 59, 153, 154, 172, 184–85,
        190, 249
    deaf tour guides, 159–67, 162f, 165f
    deaf village of Bengkala, 167–72, 169f. *See also*
        Bengkala, Indonesia
    economic capital channeled through, 197
    English language skills and, 244
    exchanging signs and, 227–29, 234
    finding research participants for, 37–38
    gender differences in, 317–18
    global deaf circuit and, 154–57
    interviews for, 55–56
    language learning and calibrating, 215, 216,
        217f, 221–23
    language shaming and, 234–35, 234f
    participant observation and, 44–45
    to "see how they live," 59, 151–53, 172–73,
        190, 194
    souvenir signs from, 229–30
    visa and border policies, 313–14
#deaftravel: Deaf Tourism in Bali (film), 55, 221,
    222, 228, 320
DeafUKSocials Facebook page, 110
deaf utopias, 170–72
deaf villages. *See also* Bengkala, Indonesia
    Adamorobe, Ghana, 15, 178, 249
    belonging, finding spaces of, 279–80
    Clin d'Oeil compared to, 207
    as deaf nodes, 178, 197
    global deaf circuit and, 154
    to "see how they live" as motivation for
        visiting, 59
deaf with disabilities. *See also* deafblind people
    crip linguistics, 242
    crip time, 60–61
    Deaflympics and, 286
    immobility and, 293, 318–19
    Kakuma Refugee Camp and, 82–83

De Clerck, G. A. M., 138–39
De Keyzer, David, 313
Delanty, G., 114
DELK (Deaf Extra Linguistic Knowledge), 70
Denmark. *See* Frontrunners course, Denmark
Desloges, Pierre, 8
De Vos, C., 168
de Weerdt, Danny, 200–201
DISAGREE (Catalan), 231, 231*f*
discrimination. *See also* racism; xenophobia
    ableism, 256, 286, 291
    audism, 11, 26, 32, 257
    class and, 105–6
    colorism among refugees, 276–78, 277*f*
    by deaf people toward deaf people, 240
    in deaf spaces, 110–15
    deaf tourism and, 282–86
    education testing and, 247–48
    homophobia and, 144–45
    Islamophobia and, 114–15, 145, 267
    job interviews and, 102
    language shaming and, 233–35, 240
    language use and, 326
    salience hierarchies resulting from, 260, 291
Dong, J., 43
DOOR International, Nairobi
    analysis and writing of data, 58*f*
    calibrating and, 226–27
    as deaf node, 208
    essentialisms and stereotypes at, 138
    gender-related cultural attitudes at, 317
    language learning and calibrating at, 251–54, 253*f*
    MobileDeaf project and, 39–40
    national sign languages at, 145
    participant observation at, 49–50
    returning home with new resources from, 141–42, 142*f*
Double Discrimination (film), 37, 50, 112–13
Draper, Amos, 8–9, 10, 12
Duggan, N., 242

economic capital
    belonging and, 264–65
    in Bourdieu's theory of practice, 19
    deaf knowledges and histories, 181
    of deaf migrants in London, 103–4
    deaf networks and nodes as channels for, 197–98
    deaf professional mobility and, 314–15
    of deaf refugees at Kakuma Refugee Camp, 68, 87, 90, 296, 298
    deaf tourism and, 319
    immobility and, 322

education. *See also* deaf schools
    communication quality and, 273
    of deaf migrants in London, 96, 103, 110
    for deaf refugees, 75–76, 78–81, 86–87, 90, 185, 225, 241, 276–78, 297–98
    English proficiency necessary for, 247–48
    language learning and calibrating, 225
    learning new sign language, 235–43
    mainstreaming deaf students, 96, 186, 286
    Sweden, deaf migrants to, 69
888 Club, London, 112–13, 189
Ellington, David, 186
Elliott, A., 179
Emery, Steven, 25, 30–31, 91, 177, 212, 258, 293
emotional attachment and belonging, 258, 262
empathy, 149, 325
employment
    deaf migrants in London and, 101–7, 105*t*, 247, 273, 304
    deaf networks and nodes for, 185
    of deaf refugees at Kakuma Refugee Camp, 79, 296–97
    of deaf tourists, morality and, 151
    English language skills and, 247
    interpreters provided for, 116
    marriage migration and, 102, 107, 247, 304
    unemployment and government benefits, 111, 151, 265, 273, 281–82
empowerment
    deaf professional mobility and, 139
    deaf refugees and, 79
    deaf researchers and, 328
    deaf spaces and, 15, 153
    deaf tourism and, 12, 156
    immobility and, 307
    international mobility and, 12
Enfield Deaf Club, 188
English language
    ASL and, 250, 252–53
    learning, 243–48, 256
    Signing Exact English, 225, 253
Esperanto, 121, 135, 194, 194*n*5
Essentialism, 61–62, 135–38, 142
ethics
    deaf tourism and, 151, 195
    informal and formal research consent and, 40–41
    labeling in writing and, 62
    language practices and, 222
    politics and ethics of belonging, 258
ethnographic interviews, 52
ethnography, 25. *See also* deaf ethnography
European Deaf Sports Organisation, 120–21
European Research Council, 3
European Union of the Deaf Youth (EUDY), 123, 201

Fians, G., 121, 135
field notes, 43
fields in theory of practice
    capital and, 20
    of deaf migrants in London, 92, 95, 97–98, 117
    defined, 19
Fiji, deaf schools in, 183
Finding Spaces to Belong (film), 37, 42, 53–54, 241, 268–70
fingerspelling
    alphabet differences and, 98, 222–23, 234, 234*f*, 238
    as bridge between languages, 220, 226–27, 244
    chaining for understanding, 222–23
    English language learning and, 246
    language learning and calibrating, 216–18, 217–19*f*, 220, 223
    mouthing words vs., 221
    used in International Sign, 213
FINISHED (Libras), 231, 231*f*
Finland, deaf asylum seekers in, 69–70, 90
FLAG (International Sign), 122, 122*f*
forced migration. *See* deaf refugees in Kakuma Refugee Camp, Kenya
Foster, Andrew J., 181–84
Foster, S., 260
Found at the Deaf Club (film), 185
Found in the UK (film), 99
Friedner, M., 8, 11, 136, 139, 156
Frontrunners course, Denmark
    age restrictions for, 123
    ASL, English, and IS use in, 244–45, 249–50
    deaf networks and nodes through, 193
    essentialisms and stereotypes at, 137–38
    exchange program to Ghana, 157
    interviews conducted at, 56
    language learning and calibrating at, 217–18, 219*f*, 223–25, 230–34, 231*f*, 239
    MobileDeaf project and, 39–40
    national representation at, 124, 125
    national sign languages at, 145
    networking leading to participation in, 202
    returning home with new resources from, 140–41
Fryer, P., 92

Gaillard, Henri, 155
Gallaudet University, 15, 117, 157, 178–79, 182, 192
Gardner, Philip, 314
gender. *See also* deaf marriage migration
    cosmopolitanism and, 10
    deaf professional mobility and, 120, 317
    deaf refugees and split habitus, 82

deaf researchers and participant observation, 45, 47, 50
deaf spaces, discrimination in, 110–11
deaf sporting events and mobility, 123, 316–17
deaf tourism and, 318–19
immobility and, 303–4
Islamophobia and, 114–15
national identities at international events and, 119–20
gesturing, 90, 203, 223, 242
Ghana
    Adamorobe, "deaf village" in, 15, 80, 178, 249
    deaf schools in, 182–83
    student exchange experiences in, 157
Giansanti, Terry, 156
Glasgow Deaf Club, United Kingdom, 186
Glick Schiller, N., 8, 9, 121
global deaf circuit, 150–51, 154–57, 159–60, 172, 179, 195. *See also* Deaf networks and nodes; Deaf spaces
globalization, 93, 154
Google Translate, 244
Graburn, N. H., 152
Great Big Story, 168
Grounded Theory (Glaser & Strauss), 58

habitus in theory of practice
    of deaf migrants in London, 92, 95, 97, 117
    Deaf Mobility Studies and, 20
    of deaf refugees, 81–86, 85*f*, 90
    defined, 19
Handicap International, 38
hands-on signing, 203, 221, 284–85
Hands On Tours (HOT), 155–56
Hartvedt, Margareth, 316
Harvey, David, 104, 180
Haualand, H., 6, 18, 26, 121
HEARING (Europe and Asia), 233, 233*f*
hearing people at deaf international events, 133, 205–6, 286, 288–89, 315
Henner, J., 242
Holmström, I., 69, 90, 94, 242
home, belonging and, 262
home signs. *See* village signs
homophobia, 144–45
hospitality for deaf tourists, 151, 193–95
Hou, L. Y.-S., 8
humor and jokes
    to defuse harmful comments, 283
    to establish belonging, 281–82
    linguistic, 233
    racism and, 282–83
    sign names and, 229
Humphries, T., 186

ICSD (International Committee of Sports for the Deaf) congress, 121, 129–30, 129–30f, 208, 289, 314, 316
identity. *See* deaf identity; intersectionality
IDENTITY (Finnish sign), 230, 231f
immigration and visa policies, 5, 93, 106, 293–94, 311–13
immobility, 293–323
 of deaf marriage migrants in London, 303–8
 of deaf refugees in Kakuma Refugee Camp, 293–94, 295–303, 298–302f
 financing deaf professional mobility, 314–15
 gender and deaf professional mobility, 316–17
 gender and deaf tourism, 317–18
 language deprivation and, 12
 of locals encountering deaf tourists, 320–21
 Mobility Studies and, 4–5
 national borders and bureaucracy, 307–14, 309–10f
 in relation to others' mobility, 323, 327
 visa and immigration policies, 5, 93, 106, 293–94, 311–13
imperfect knowledge, 294
inclusion
 belonging vs. identity, 261
 calibration and, 326
 deaf migration and, 264
 deaf professional mobility and, 129, 132, 145
 English use and, 243–44
 ethical and political values, 258–59
Indigenous signs. *See* village signs
Indonesia. *See* Bali, Deaf tourism in; Bengkala, Indonesia; Yogyakarta, Indonesia
informed consent, 40–42
institutional deaf spaces, 14–15, 184–90
Institut National de Jeunes Sourds de Paris, 154
International Committee of Sports for the Deaf (ICSD) congress, 121, 129–30, 129–30f, 208, 289, 314, 316
International Congress of the Deaf, Paris (1889), 9, 199
international events. *See* deaf professional mobility; *specific events*
International Sign (IS)
 calibrating and, 213, 226–27, 255
 deaf cosmopolitanism and, 10–11, 221–22
 deaf professional mobility and requirements for use, 123–24, 134, 145–47, 223–25, 244, 249–51
 national clustering at international events, 133
 politics of, 57
 as primarily European, 222–23, 225, 250, 253–54
 privilege and, 202
 translanguaging and, 213

internet use, 15, 193, 221. *See also* social media
interpreters
 deaf migrants to United Kingdom and access to, 94, 96–97, 102, 116, 240
 deaf people as, 69–70
 for deaf refugees, 69–70, 86, 90
 for national groups at international events, 133–34, 134f
 sign language brokering, 221, 225
intersectionality
 class and, 104
 conflicts among identity groups, 204
 cosmopolitanism and, 13
 deaf ethnography and, 21–23, 26
 deaf identity and belonging vs., 259, 261–62, 291, 326
 defined, 22–23
Islamophobia, 114–15, 145, 189, 267, 283, 291
isolation of deaf people, 111, 295
Italy, deaf tourism in, 155–56
It's a Small World (Friedner & Kusters), 8, 12
Iyer, Sanchayeeta, 25, 31–32, 91, 177, 212, 258, 293

James, M., 111, 260, 271
Jansen, B. J., 308
Jayaram, K., 14
Jewish Deaf Association (U.K.), 108, 187
job applications and interviews, 102–3
Johnson, R. E., 168
jokes. *See* humor and jokes
Jokinen, Markku, 201
Jordan, Jerald, 286

Karar, E., 70
Kata Kolok
 calibrating and, 216, 217f
 deaf tourism and, 167–68, 170–72
 other sign languages as threat to, 171–72, 249, 249f
 sharing signs in, 230, 231f
Kaufmann, V., 20
Kelly, P. F., 20
Kenya. *See* Deaf refugees in Kakuma Refugee Camp; DOOR International
Kenyan Sign Language (KSL)
 ASL as threat to, 251–53, 253f
 ASL influence on, 225–26
 calibrating in, 216–17, 218f, 225–26
 interpreters, 86
 popularity in Kakuma Refugee Camp, 71
 teaching in deaf schools, 84, 90, 225, 241–42, 298
Keywords of Mobility (Salazar & Jayaram), 14
Kinuthia, W., 260

Kiranmala, Adelia, 38, 163–64
Kisch, S., 168
knowledge exchange hubs, 108
Kold, Thomas, 205
Kusters, Annelies, 3, 8–11, 25, 28–29, 80, 89, 118, 136, 139, 157, 177, 187, 212, 221, 258, 293, 324
Kutupanlong Refugee Camp, Bangladesh, 153

labor migration. *See* deaf migrants in London
Ladd, P., 104, 264
language deprivation
    deaf migrants in london and, 95–96
    deaf refugees and, 68–70, 241–43, 256
    immobility and, 12
    stigma and trauma of, 216
language ideologies, 214–16, 222–23, 248–49
language learning and calibrating, 212–57
    deaf migrants in London and, 215–16, 218–19, 220*f*
    deaf professional mobility and, 213–14, 217–18, 219*f*, 223–25
    deaf refugees and, 215–17, 218*f*, 225–26
    deaf tourism and, 163, 215, 216, 217*f*, 221–23
    English, learning and using, 243–48
    examples, 216–27, 217–20*f*
    exchanging and bestowing signs, 227–35, 228*f*, 231–34*f*, 326
    language ideologies and, 214–16, 222–23, 248–49
    of MobileDeaf researchers, 11, 44–46
    morality and, 214–15
    national sign language, 235–43
    out-of-place languages, 248–55, 249*f*, 253*f*, 326
    semiotic resources, 214, 221, 222, 223
    translanguaging, 212–13
    xenophobia and, 248
language shaming, 233–35, 239–40, 248, 256
language trajectories, 214
languaging. *See* language learning and calibrating
Larsen, J., 149
Lee, J., 77
Leeman, J., 229
Lefebvre, H., 119
LGBTQIA+ people
    Bali tourism and, 159
    Deaf Studies and, 259, 261
    international events and local laws of host nations, 144–45
    Kakuma Refugee Camp and, 82
    in London, deaf groups for, 99
    migration to London and identity development, 268–69
Libras (Brazilian Sign Language), 146–47, 232, 232*f*, 250

The Limping Chicken (blog), 186
linguistic capital
    Bourdieu's theory of practice and, 19
    deaf migrants in London and, 98–99, 101, 107
    deaf professional mobility and, 225
    of deaf refugees, 68, 75–76, 79, 81, 84, 90, 308
    immobility and, 306
    privilege and, 225, 237
linguistic habitus, 84
linguistic humor, 233–34
London. *See* deaf migrants in London
Lost Community (film), 186
Lost Spaces (film), 186
Lusis, T., 20
Lutheran World Federation (LWF), 38–39, 301

Maire, Amandine le, 25, 29–30, 67, 177, 212, 258, 293
Malaurie, Isabelle, 287–88, 316–17
Malkki, L., 136
Mansfield, B., 147
Mansilla, Giovanni, 38, 45, 163–66, 171–72, 190
marriage migration. *See* deaf marriage migration
May, V. M., 21–23
McAuliff, K., 94
mental maps, shared, 180, 185, 202
Merricks, P., 133
Mesch, Urban, 128–29
microaggressions, 114, 207
migration. *See* deaf migrants in London; deaf refugees in Kakuma Refugee Camp
minorities. *See also* deaf with disabilities; gender; race and ethnicity
    deaf-first identity narratives and, 260
    finding research participants, 56
    intersectional experiences of, 261
    labels in writing, 61–62
MobileDeaf project (*Deaf Mobilities Across International Borders*)
    concepts focused on, 325–27
    deaf cosmopolitanism and, 8–13
    deaf ethnography use in, 25–63. *See also* deaf ethnography
    impact resulting from, 328–29
    intersectional lens of, 21–23
    overview, 3
    power dynamics in, 4–5, 329
    sign languages used in, 215, 236–37, 256
    subprojects of, 3–4, 4*f*
    teamwork benefits of, 328
    transdisciplinary approach of, 14–20
    types of mobility recognized by, 5–8
Mobility Studies, 4–8, 20, 327–28. *See also* Deaf Mobility Studies

Modan, G., 229
morality. *See also* ethics
    deaf tourism and, 151–53, 156, 162, 166
    language ideologies and, 214–15, 222
    networks, motivation for using, 184
    tourism issues and, 235
Moriarty, Erin, 9–10, 25, 32–33, 149, 169*f*, 177, 212, 221, 258, 293
motility inequality, 5
mouthing words
    accented, 240, 256
    chaining for understanding, 222–23
    English language knowledge for, 244
    fingerspelling vs., 221
    International Sign and, 10, 213
    translanguaging and, 212
Mulder project, Sweden, 69
Multilingual Situation of Deaf Refugees, Sweden, 69
Murangira, Ambrose, 193–94
Murray, J., 8, 12, 18, 119–20, 143, 184–85
mutual support networks, 153

national essentialisms, 135–38
national sign languages. *See also specific sign languages*
    comparisons of signs, 139, 228–29
    cosmopolitanism and, 10–11
    deaf migrants learning, 235–43
    deaf professional mobility and, 122, 122*f*, 133–35, 134*f*, 145–48, 236–37
    deaf refugees learning, 241–43
    nationalism and, 121–22
    village sign languages and, 171
national stereotypes, 136–37, 224, 251, 274
natural signing, 240, 256
network capital. *See also* deaf networks and nodes
    of deaf migrants, 189
    defined, 20, 179
    economic capital and, 197–98
    privilege and, 185, 195
    social media and, 179, 184, 191, 193–94, 204
networking capacity, 179
neurodivergence, 238, 251
Nigeria
    deaf schools in, 183
    national stereotypes of, 138
nonsigning deaf people, 286–89
Norway
    deaf community in, 259
    gender and deaf sports participation, 316
    interpreters in, 70

O'Brien, D., 15, 84
Off the Grid (voluntourism), 156–57
Olsen, E. T., 70
openmindedness, 282–83, 325
oralism, 120, 153
otherness, 152, 156
out-of-place languages, 248–55, 249*f*, 253*f*, 326

Padden, C., 186, 205*n*6
Palfreyman, N., 222
Pan–Arab Sign Language, 205, 205*n*6
Paralympics, 285–86, 288, 314–15
Paris World Fair (1900), 9
Parr, S., 95
Parsons, Frances, 155
participatory mapping, 77–78, 78*f*
Patil, V., 22, 261
Pennycook, A., 215
people with disabilities. *See* deaf with disabilities
Physical capital, 68, 80–84, 89
Pierce, C., 114
place belongingness, 262, 265, 270, 280. *See also* belonging, spaces of
place-nodes. *See* deaf networks and nodes
power dynamics. *See also* white privilege and power
    capital in theory of practice, 19
    deaf marriage migrants and, 99–100
    deaf migrants in London, 100–107, 105*t*
    deaf nodes, economic capital channeled through, 198
    deaf refugees and, 299–301, 299–300*f*
    deaf tourism and, 281
    immigration and visa policies, 294
    institutionalization of deaf expectations, 18–19
    interpreters and, 86
    intersectionality and, 22
    language shaming and, 233–35
    in MobileDeaf project, 4–5, 329
    mobility and, 4
    study abroad and foreign exchange programs, 157
privilege. *See also* deaf tourism; white privilege and power
    cosmopolitanism and, 10, 291
    deaf professional mobility and, 201, 315
    global deaf elite and, 26
    immobility and, 5
    linguistic capital and, 225, 237
    mobility and, 4, 305
    morality and giving back, 184
    network capital and, 185, 195–97
    out-of-place languages and, 256

of researchers, 36
sign language brokering and, 221
voluntary immobility and, 294–95
professional mobility. *See* deaf professional mobility
protactile signing, 203, 221, 284–85
PROUD (Arabic and Italian), 231, 231*f*

race and ethnicity. *See also* intersectionality; minorities
cosmopolitanism and, 10, 13
deafness transcending, 83–84
deaf professional mobility and, 285
of deaf researchers, 34, 46–48, 50
deaf tourism and, 150, 319–20
history of migration to United Kingdom, 92
migrant experience and, 37
mobility types and, 5
national identity and, 61, 119–20, 132
racism. *See also* white privilege and power
belonging, finding spaces of, 260, 282–85, 291
colorism among refugees, 276–78, 277*f*
deafblind people and, 284–85
in deaf clubs, 185
deaf migrants in London and, 96–97, 110–15, 270–71
deaf professional mobility and, 194, 207, 208, 250, 256
deaf tourism and, 319
historical, mobility barriers and, 182
humor and jokes on, 282–83
institutionalized, immobility and, 293
language shaming and, 233–35
language use and, 257, 326
in United Kingdom, 93
Racism Within the Deaf Community (Anderson & Bowe), 112
Redbridge Deaf Cafe, London, 108, 188
refugees. *See* deaf refugees in Kakuma Refugee Camp, Kenya
Reimers, R. R., 70
religious deaf spaces, 80, 100, 270–72, 292
repetition as calibration strategy, 224
right way to be deaf, 18, 139, 215, 240
Robinson, O. E., 104, 242
ROME (sign for Summer Deaflympics in Italy), 180, 181*f*
Rome Congress (1911), 143
Russell, Debra, 313

Saint John's Deaf Club, United Kingdom, 108, 187
Salazar, N. B., 14, 152, 173, 294
Sambo, Ezekiel, 183

Saved By The Sign, 207
scale and scaling
comparisons and, 18–19
deaf networks and nodes, 210
deaf professional mobility and, 118–19, 135, 138
intersectional approaches to study of belonging, 262
of intersectionality, 23
overview, 15–16
production process of, 119–21
scale shifts and deaf tourism, 194
translocality and, 17, 196
Schapendonk, J., 179
Schewel, K., 294
Schmitt, P., 199
schools. *See* deaf schools; education
SEE (Signing Exact English), 225, 253
See Hear (BBC), 186
semiotic resources
appropriate spaces for, 248
calibrating strategies, 214, 221–25
deaf cosmopolitanism and, 235
deaf refugees and, 225–26
mobility and language learning, 255
pooling among deaf people, 230–32, 231*f*
service learning, 157
sexual orientation. *See* LGBTQIA+ people
Shakespeare's Head pub, London, 108, 189, 239, 263–64
Shaming. *See* Language shaming
shared signing communities, 167, 171–72
Sheller, M., 5, 293
SIGN6 conference, India (2013), 143–44, 254
SIGN8 conference, Florianopolis (2018)
isolation of international attendees at, 143
MobileDeaf project and, 39–40
national clustering at, 133
national sign language use at, 146–47
participant observation at, 49
sign language requirements for presenters at, 123
SignHealth, 101
Signing Exact English (SEE), 225, 253
sign language use. *See also* fingerspelling; interpreters; national sign languages; *specific sign languages*
accented signing, 240–41, 256
belonging, finding spaces of, 278–79
brokering, 221, 225
chaining for understanding, 222–23, 228, 236
deaf migrants in London and, 98–99
deaf refugees and, 84–86, 85*f*
deaf tourism and, 152, 155, 159, 166
hands-on signing, 284–85

at international events, 133–35, 134f, 145–47, 213–14, 286–88
language learning and calibrating, 212–57. *See also* language learning and calibrating
language shaming and humor, 233–35, 240, 248, 256
local preservation of, 248–49
national, comparisons of signs in, 139, 228–29
natural signing, 240, 256
new signs for collective experiences and memories, 180–81, 181f
right way to be deaf and, 18, 139, 215, 240
in shared signing communities, 167, 171–72
souvenir signs, 180–81, 181f, 229–30
translanguaging and, 212–13, 237
translations of interviews to written languages, 57–58
sign names
for people, 125, 229, 255
for places, 180–81, 181f
Silvey, R., 293
single-axis thinking, 21–23
Sivunen, N., 69, 90, 94
slavery, modern-day, 100–101
Slug and Lettuce pub gathering, London, 98, 188
"small world" phenomenon, 180, 327
smartphones to facilitate understanding, 221
social capital
belonging and, 264–65
in Bourdieu's theory of practice, 19, 74
deaf knowledges and histories, 181
of deaf migrants in London, 108, 116
deaf networks and nodes, 179
of deaf refugees, 68, 74, 79, 83, 84, 86–90, 308–9
deaf spaces and, 187
deaf tourism and, 150, 320
immobility and, 306, 322
International Sign and, 254–55
sharing new signs and, 230–32, 231f
sign language brokering and, 221, 225
social locations, 22–23, 258–61, 263, 268–69, 278
social media
deaf ecosystem and, 153
"deaf meme" video template, 227
deaf tourism and, 150, 153–54, 161, 318
exchanging signs through, 227
finding deaf spaces through, 107–8, 110
finding research participants through, 38, 40, 55
International Sign, 11
network capital through, 179, 184, 191, 193–94, 204
racism and, 114
virtual deaf spaces and, 15, 278

social values and expectations, 151, 235, 258
Somali refugees, 72. *See also* deaf refugees in Kakuma Refugee Camp, Kenya
Sommer Lindsay, M., 20, 104
souvenir signs, 180–81, 181f, 229–30
SOZIAL (International Sign), 200–201, 200f
spaces of belonging. *See* belonging, spaces of
SPORTS (International Sign), 200–201
sports events. *See* deaf professional mobility; *specific events*
Starbucks, London, 108
Starkey Hearing Foundation, 81, 90, 297, 301–3, 301–2f
status and language calibration, 226, 253
Stein, M. S. S., 132
stereotypes
of deaf people, 281–82
deaf professional mobility and, 135–38, 147
national, 136–38, 224, 251, 274
racism and, 270
study abroad programs, 157
Sudanese refugees, 71–72. *See also* deaf refugees in Kakuma Refugee Camp, Kenya
Sue, D. W., 114
Summer Deaflympics
Australia (2005), 183
Italy (2001), 121, 180–81
Turkey (2017), 315
Sweden, deaf migrants to, 69, 90
systemic oppression, 18–19, 293

Tetteh-Ocloo, Seth, 183
Thimm, V., 7, 23
THIRUVANANTHAPURAM, 180–81, 181f
This Is IS (film), 122, 125, 137, 145–46, 201–2, 227–31, 250–51
time–space compression, 180, 211
tokenism, 135, 147
Toomey, N., 5, 6
tourism. *See* Bali, deaf tourism in; deaf tourism
tourist imaginaries, 152, 154, 167–72, 178. *See also* deaf villages
translanguaging, 212–13, 237
translocality. *See also* deaf networks and nodes
belonging, finding spaces of, 261–62, 270–72
deaf tourism and, 150–51, 154, 157, 196, 284
overview, 16–17, 16f
transnationalism, 9, 121–22, 199–200. *See also* deaf cosmopolitanism; deaf professional mobility

UK Deaf Britannia Facebook group, 114
undocumented immigrants, 93, 106
United Kingdom. *See* deaf marriage migration; deaf migrants in London

United Nations High Commissioner for Refugees (UNHCR), 46–47, 67. *See also* deaf refugees in Kakuma Refugee Camp, Kenya
Universal Congress of Esperanto, 121, 135
universalism, 10
University of Bristol's Center for Deaf Studies, 186
Urry, J., 149, 179, 293

Valle, Marlene, 153
video-recording observations, 27
Vietnam, deaf tourism in, 151–52, 166
village signs
    devaluing of, 216
    of refugees at Kakuma Refugee Camp, 46, 81, 84, 85*f*, 225–26
    as sign language, 242–43, 256
visa and immigration policies, 5, 93, 106, 293–94, 311–13
voluntourism, 156–57
vulnerable deaf migrants, 100–101

Ward, K., 94
WASLI (World Association of Sign Language Interpreters) conference, Paris (2019), 39, 125, 313
"We are Deaf" (video clip), 136
welfare benefits, 111, 151, 265, 273, 281–82
WFD. *See entries at* World Federation of the Deaf Congress
WhatsApp, 204, 218, 220, 220*f*, 306–7
white privilege and power. *See also* racism
    in deaf communities, 115–16, 185, 250
    deaf migrants and spaces of belonging, 264
    in deaf professional mobility, 119–20, 132, 201, 205, 207–8
    deaf refugees, differential treatment from, 309, 311
    in Deaf Studies, 117
    deaf tourism and, 150, 158–59, 279–81, 319
    deaf transnationalism, history of, 199
    language learning and calibrating, 225
    new racism and, 114
    racial jokes and, 282–83
    stereotypes and, 138
Willoughby, L. J. V., 69
Wimmer, A., 121
Winter Deaflympics (Italy 2019)
    calibrating and adapting sign languages, 221
    communication modes at, 287–88
    "deafening" of space around, 203
    as deaf node, 202
    financial support of participants, 314
    hearing people at, 206
    interviews conducted at, 56
    MobileDeaf project and, 39
    national representation at, 123, 125–31, 126–28*f*
    national stereotypes at, 136–37
    participant observation at, 49–50
Wirth, Roberto, 156
Woll, B., 111, 260, 271
World Association of Sign Language Interpreters (WASLI) conference, Paris (2019), 39, 125, 313
World Congress of the Deaf, Colorado (1910), 143
World Deaf Games, Rome (2021), 6
World Federation of the Deaf (WFD) Congress, Paris (2019)
    belonging, finding spaces of, 284–85
    "deafening" of space around, 203
    as deaf node, 203
    deaf with disabilities and barriers for, 318–19
    interpreters at, 133–35, 134*f*
    MobileDeaf project and, 39
    national clustering at, 133–34
    national representation at, 129–32, 130*f*
    national sign languages at, 145–46
    networking at, 208
    participant observation at, 49–50
    regulations for participation in, 123, 134–35
    satellite events at, 204–5
    scale production and, 119–20
World Federation of the Deaf (WFD) Congress, South Korea (2023), 145
World Federation of the Deaf Youth (WFDY) camp, Durban (2011), 133, 139–40
World Federation of the Deaf Youth Section (WFDYS), 123, 201
World's Fair, Chicago (1893), 120

xenophobia
    belonging, finding spaces of, 291
    deaf migrants in London and, 110–15, 189, 267
    deaf professional mobility and, 250
    deaf tourism and, 283
    institutionalized, immobility and, 293
    Islamophobia, 114–15, 145, 189, 267, 283, 291
    language use and, 248, 256–57, 326

Yanto, Ferdy, 234–35
Yogyakarta, Indonesia, 45, 179, 195, 196*f*, 320
Young, Calvin, 37, 153, 164
Youngs, Megan, 68, 71, 73
YouTube, 11
Yuval-Davis, N., 22, 258